An Introduction to

the Structural Econometrics

of Auction Data

An Introduction to
the Structural Econometrics
of Auction Data

HARRY J. PAARSCH

HAN HONG

with contributions by

M. RYAN HALEY

The MIT Press
Cambridge, Massachusetts
London, England

GAUSS is a trademark of Aptech Systems Inc., Mathematica is a registered trademark of Wolfram Research Inc., and MATLAB is a registered trademark of The Mathworks, Inc.

MIT Press books may be purchased at special quantity discounts for business or sales promotional use. For information, please send email to `special_sales@mitpress.mit.edu` or write to Special Sales Department, The MIT Press, 55 Hayward Street, Cambridge, MA 02142.

This book was set in Computer Modern by Harry J. Paarsch using TEX as well as macros developed by Robert Picard.

Printed and bound in the United States.

Library of Congress Cataloging-in-Publication Data

Paarsch, Harry J.
 An introduction to the structural econometrics of auction data / Harry J. Paarsch, Han Hong ; with contributions by M. Ryan Haley.
  p. cm.
 Includes bibliographic references.
 ISBN 0-262-16235-0 (alk. paper)
 1. Auctions—Econometric models. I. Hong, Han. II. Haley, M. Ryan. III. Title.
HF5476.P33 2006
381′.17015195—dc22   2005054432

10 9 8 7 6 5 4 3 2 1

HARRY J. PAARSCH is Professor of Economics and Robert Jensen Research Fellow in the Henry B. Tippie College of Business at the University of Iowa where he has taught since 1996. He has also held appointments at the University of British Columbia and the University of Western Ontario and has been a visiting professor at Aarhus Universitet, Universitat Autònoma de Barcelona, Helsingin yliopisto, the University of New South Wales, and Stanford University. Professor Paarsch was the Arch W. Shaw National Fellow at the Hoover Institution as well as a visiting scholar at the Institut d'Economie Industrielle and the Instituto de Análisis Económico (CSIS). Professor Paarsch received a B.A. (Honours), First Class, in economics from Queen's University in 1980 as well as a M.S. in statistics in 1983 and a Ph.D. in economics with a minor in statistics in 1987, both from Stanford University. His primary research interests are in applied econometrics, particularly forestry economics. In fact, his interest in auctions grew out of his policy work concerning British Columbia forestry. He has published journal articles in both applied and theoretical econometrics as well as labor economics and personnel economics.

HAN HONG is Professor of Economics at Duke University where he has taught since 2003. Prior to that he was an assistant professor in the economics department at Princeton University as well as a visiting research fellow at the Université Catholique de Louvain. Professor Han received a B.A. in economics from Sun Yat-sen (Zhongshan) University in 1993 as well as a M.S. in statistics in 1996 and a Ph.D. in economics in 1998, both from Stanford University. His primary research interests are in theoretical econometrics, but he has also published journal articles in economic theory as well industrial organization.

M. RYAN HALEY is Assistant Professor of Economics at the University of Wisconsin–Oshkosh where he has taught since 2003. Professor Haley received a B.A. in economics, mathematics, and applied statistics from the University of St. Thomas in 1996 as well as a M.A. in economics in 2000, a M.S. in mathematics in 2002, and a Ph.D. in economics in 2003, all from the University of Iowa. His primary research interests are in agricultural, financial, and forestry economics. He has published journal articles in applied econometrics as well as labor and personnel economics.

To our families

Table of Contents

Preface

$\mathcal{A}$UCTIONS INTEREST economists for a number of reasons, on several levels. First, while the role of the fictional Walrasian auctioneer in the *tâtonnement* process of equilibrium-price determination is recognized as important, the mechanics of how such prices obtain are typically left vague. Prices are very important to economists because, under certain conditions, they represent the opportunity cost of goods and, thus, can aid both consumers and producers in making decisions. Because auction models can often provide simple analytic formulae describing the mechanics of price formation, such models have provided useful insights into what such prices represent.

Second, theoretical models of auctions are one of the major success stories in the application of game-theoretic methods, in particular John C. Harsanyi's (1967/68) *Noncooperative Games of Incomplete Information.* In fact, Harsanyi, along with John F. Nash, Jr. and Reinhard Selten, won the 1994 Nobel Prize in economics for their research in game theory. Auction theory delivers very specific predictions concerning how purposeful bidders should behave in equilibrium and how a seller might use this information to construct optimal selling mechanisms. Thus, from a purely scientific perspective, empirical estimation of auction models appears particularly fruitful.

Third, from a practical perspective, using auction theory to understand what happens in the real world is particularly relevant because many commodities and goods are bought and sold at auction. These include antiques, art, cotton, fish, flowers, furs, houses, land, livestock, oil, securities, timber, and, of course, the ever-important Beanie Babies on eBay.

This book is concerned with the empirical analysis of field data from auctions. For us, it is the culmination of nearly two decades of field research in which we have personally attended or studied in detail the following: bankruptcy and liquidation auctions in Clinton, British Columbia, Canada as well as Iowa City, Iowa; confiscated Oriental carpet sales held by Revenue Canada in Vancouver, Canada; fish auctions near Kiel, Germany, in Tokyo, Japan, in Grenå, Denmark, in Arenys de

Mar, Spain, in Alacante, Spain, and in Sydney, Australia; standing timber and tree-planting procurement auctions in the Prince George region of British Columbia, Canada; timber-export permit sales in the Krasnoyarsk region of Siberia, Russia; milk quotas in Toronto, Canada; highway-repair contracts in New Jersey; cattle in Kalona, Iowa; flowers in Aalsmeer, Holland and Aarhus, Denmark; used-car auctions in Mount Vernon, Iowa; furs in Copenhagen, Denmark; PCS spectrum auctions in the United States; real estate in Sydney, Australia; and Receiver General cash-management auctions conducted by the Bank of Canada in Ottawa, Canada.

1 Focus of the Book

Auction theory, when viewed as an application of Harsanyi's theory concerning noncooperative games of incomplete information, is a well-developed subfield of economic theory. Vijay Krishna (2002) claims that the *EconLit* CD lists over one thousand papers with *auction* in their title, over half of them theoretical. The complementary portion of these papers is presumably applied, with many of the papers being empirical ones.

In this book, we provide an introduction to the econometrics concerning auctions. But, like Krisha's treatment of auction theory, which is presented in his elegant text *Auction Theory*, we too have been selective. In particular, we have considered only some of the recent developments in what we refer to as the *structural econometrics of auction data* (SEAD). We have limited ourselves to what many economists refer to as the *structural-econometric approach* (SEA) for two reasons. First, we believe that the SEA is an internally-consistent one in the sense that the economic-theoretic model is mapped virtually seamlessly to the econometric specification; this is not true for another contending approach to the empirical analysis of auction data, often referred to by economists as the *reduced-form approach*. Second, we also believe that some of the most exciting applications of theoretical econometric research in the past decade have been in the SEAD.

Because the literature associated with the SEAD is somewhat large and growing, we have constrained ourselves to a subset of this literature concerned with economic models of agents who live in an environment sometimes referred to by theorists as the *independent private-values paradigm* (IPVP); we shall discuss this paradigm in detail below.

We have selected the IPVP for pedagogical reasons: first, models within the IPVP are relatively easy to investigate with a minimum of mathematics. Second, many of the important empirical techniques can be illustrated within this informational environment in a straightforward way. Of course, one problem with a strategy involving omission is that some researchers are going to feel slighted—they should not. Our decision was not personal, but pedagogical.

We have also written this book in a particular style. Specifically, we have explicitly chosen not to judge the relative merits of the various approaches, even though in some cases we have strong opinions. Instead, we have provided the reader with a variety of different empirical exercises. By solving these exercises, a diligent learner will be able to form her or his own opinion concerning the merits as well as the difficulties of the various approaches.

2 Who Should Read This Book?

This book will be of primary interest to graduate students in industrial organization because auctions represent explicit examples involving the economics of strategic behavior under asymmetric information. Auctions are just one example of this; Reiss and Wolak (2005) document the structural econometric analysis of others. Of course, professional economists in industrial organization will also find the book of interest. However, because auctions are used to sell agricultural commodities as well as natural resources in most developed and some developing countries, we think graduate students in such fields as agriculture and forestry will also find this book useful. In fact, based on anecdotal evidence from our refereeing for journals in agricultural and forestry economics, we believe that students in these fields will be increasingly more interested in the use of market mechanisms such as auctions. Because of a recent interest in payment systems in monetary economics (and their relationship to such fiscal institutions as treasury-bill auctions) as well as the interest in market microstructure in finance, graduate students and professional economists in these fields may find the book of use too. We also believe that graduate students of microeconometrics will find a good portion of this book relevant to their research.

We believe this book fills an important gap in the literature. We can think of over two dozen researchers who are actively working on problems concerned solely with the SEAD. Most of the papers are written in different notations; often, no attempt is made to relate these papers to one another. Also, the economic theory motivating these papers, while well developed, is often implicitly assumed by the authors. Thus, integrating and understanding this literature is difficult for both students and professionals. By developing one of the existing theoretical models in a common notation and then mapping it into econometric specifications that can be implemented in practice, we believe the following material will be a useful resource. By reviewing many of the major contributions, within a consistent framework, we hope to provide readers with enough information to evaluate the relative merits of different strategies and, thus, to make informed choices on how to proceed in research. Consequently, we hope this book will make it easier for both students and professionals to enter this exciting field.

3 Material We Intend to Presume

The minimum amount of economics that a reader will need is a good course in microeconomic theory at the level of Hal Varian's (1999) *Intermediate Microeconomics: A Modern Approach* as well as familiarity with some notions from game theory at the level of that covered in Robert Gibbon's (1992) *Game Theory for Applied Economists*. Of course, we presume knowledge of differential and integral calculus as well as linear algebra. We also presume that the reader has had courses in probability, statistics, and econometrics at the level of the text *Econometric Theory and Methods* by Russell Davidson and James G. MacKinnon (2004). Beyond that, we develop enough auction theory at the level of the 1987 survey paper by R. Preston McAfee and John McMillan in the *Journal of Economic Literature*.

   We presume no background in numerical analysis, although anyone serious about using the SEA in her or his research should probably own and read avidly Kenneth L. Judd's (1998) *Numerical Methods in Economics*. Nevertheless, because one of our goals is to provide a serious learner with the tools necessary to implement an empirical analysis of data from an actual auction, we have devoted considerable space to describing how the various methods are implemented on a computer.

   Implementing the methods described in this book on a computer will typically require using either a programming language (such as C or FORTRAN), with or without the aid of a scientific subroutine library, or a high-level programming environment (such as GAUSS or MATLAB). We have chosen to use MATLAB to implement the solutions to those practice problems that involve computation because we believe that it represents a reasonable compromise between speed of computation and elegance in presentation; MATLAB is also easy to learn. Moreover, many scholars around the world have written books describing how to harness MATLAB's features in a variety of different fields, so supporting documentation is readily available. When we tested this book in the classroom, our students found one such useful text to be Hanselman and Littlefield (2005), but as MATLAB evolves others will surely appear.

Many graduate students in industrial organization will be familiar with or will have read Vijay Krishna's *Auction Theory*. We believe our book complements that text. However, our book is not as comprehensive as Krishna's because the structural econometrics of auctions is not as mature a literature as the literature concerning auction theory. The modern theoretical literature on auctions is well over four decades old, while the structural-econometric literature concerning auctions is less than two decades old, with the first published papers only appearing about fifteen years ago. In addition, because ours is an introduction, we have made an explicit pedagogical decision to restrict ourselves to a particular theoretical paradigm, and to work out quite extensively implications within that paradigm. While this limits the applicability of our results, we believe that a motivated learner will be able to understand, to appreciate, and to extend the existing literature.

4 What a Learner Will Know

Having read this book, we hope that a student or a professional will be able to analyze data from an actual auction and then to derive policy conclusions from this research. As mentioned above, one aim is to provide both students and professionals with the practical tools to structure their research. To this end, our book is accompanied by a CD on which sample data sets reside. At the end of each chapter, we have also provided practice problems in the form of mathematical questions or empirical exercises that one of us (Paarsch) has used previously when teaching courses on auctions. Solutions to the mathematical questions are provided at the end of the book, while examples of the MATLAB code which implement solutions to the empirical exercises are contained on the CD that accompanies the book. By working through the empirical exercises, a motivated learner will be able to evaluate the relative merits of the different empirical strategies presented in this book.

5 Notation

In this book, we have sought to adopt a logically-consistent notation, but as in virtually all attempts to create languages that have such a property, we have not been totally successful. Because the main focus in auction theory is asymmetric information, which economic theorists have chosen to represent as random variables, the bulk of our notation centers around a consistent way to describe random variables. Typically, we denote random variables by uppercase roman letters; for example, V,

W, X, Y, and Z. Realizations of random variables are then denoted by lowercase roman letters; for example, v is a realization of V.

Two lowercase Greek letters, β and σ, are used to denote equilibrium bid functions, while the lowercase Greek letter κ is used to denote a kernel-density function. The lowercase script Greek letter φ is used to denote a function and, sometimes, the lowercase Greek letter λ is either a Lagrange multiplier or a function. Typically, however, lowercase Greek letters are used to denote parameters. Uppercase Greek letters are then used to denote the spaces in which the corresponding lowercase Greek letters live; e.g., $\theta \in \Theta$.

The calligraphic letter $\mathcal{N}$ is special and used to denote the number of potential bidders at an auction, while the calligraphic letters $\mathcal{C}$, $\mathcal{E}$, and $\mathcal{V}$ denote the characteristic function as well as the expectation and variance operators, respectively; the calligraphic letter $\mathcal{L}$ denotes the logarithm of the likelihood function. Boldfaced versions of the calligraphic letters $\boldsymbol{\mathcal{E}}$, $\boldsymbol{\mathcal{N}}$, and $\boldsymbol{\mathcal{W}}$ are used to denote the distribution of exponential, normal, and Weibull random variables, respectively. Thus, $\boldsymbol{\mathcal{E}}(\lambda)$ is an exponential random variable with hazard rate λ, $\boldsymbol{\mathcal{N}}(\mu, 1)$ is a normal random variable with mean μ and variance one, while $\boldsymbol{\mathcal{W}}(\lambda, \gamma)$ is a Weibull random variable with parameters λ and γ. Under this notation, $\boldsymbol{\mathcal{W}}(\lambda, 1)$ corresponds to an exponential random variable $\boldsymbol{\mathcal{E}}(\lambda)$.

Vectors are denoted by boldfaced letters. Thus, the (1×3) vector of realized random variables (v_1, v_2, v_3) is denoted by the boldfaced, lowercase, math italic letter $\boldsymbol{v}$. The superscript $\top$ denotes the transpose operator, and an $(n \times 1)$ vector of constants $(c_1, c_2, \ldots, c_n)^{\top}$ is denoted by the boldfaced, lowercase roman letter $\mathbf{c}$. Uppercase, boldfaced, math italic letters, like $\boldsymbol{V}$, denote vectors of random variables, while matrices of constants are typically denoted by uppercase, boldfaced, roman letters. Thus, $\mathbf{H}$ would be a matrix, while $\boldsymbol{H}$ would be a vector of random variables. While boldfaced, lowercase Greek letters typically denote vectors of parameters, with boldfaced, uppercase, Greek letters denoting the spaces in which those parameters live (hence $\boldsymbol{\theta} \in \boldsymbol{\Theta}$), the notable exceptions are, of course, $\boldsymbol{\beta}$ and $\boldsymbol{\sigma}$, which denote vectors of equilibrium-bid functions. Uppercase, boldfaced, but not math font, Greek letters, such as $\boldsymbol{\Sigma}$, denote matrices of parameters; e.g., a variance-covariance matrix of constants. Because we use the boldfaced number 1 to denote an indicator function of an event (e.g., $\mathbf{1}(\mathsf{A})$ equals one when the event A occur and zero otherwise), we use the boldfaced, lowercase Greek letter $\boldsymbol{\iota}_K$ to denote a $(K \times 1)$ vector of ones where, in general, the trailing subscript denotes the dimension of the vector. The matrix $\mathbf{I}_n$ denotes the $(n \times n)$ identity matrix, while $\mathbf{i}$ denotes the imaginary number $\sqrt{-1}$.

Whenever possible the uppercase letter F is used to denote a cumulative distribution function, while the lowercase letter f is used to denote a probability density function. On some occasions, we denote the survivor function by S and the hazard-rate function by h. The uppercase subscript following F, f, S, and h then indicates the corresponding random variable. Hence, $F_V(v)$ denotes the cumulative distribution function of the random variable V, while $f_W(w)$ denotes the probability density function of the random variable W, $S_X(x)$ denotes the survivor function of the random variable X, and $h_Y(y)$ denotes the hazard-rate function of the random variable Y. We denote the joint cumulative distribution of two random variables X and Y by $F_{XY}(x, y)$ and its corresponding joint probability density function by $f_{XY}(x, y)$. The conditional cumulative distribution and probability density functions of Y given X are denoted $F_{Y|X}(y|x)$ and $f_{Y|X}(y|x)$, respectively.

The i subscript is invariably used to index (potential or actual) bidders and typically goes from 1 to $\mathcal{N}$ or n, depending on the situation. Thus, an independent and identically distributed sample of size $\mathcal{N}$ from $F_V(v)$ might be denoted by $\{V_i\}_{i=1}^{\mathcal{N}}$. The j subscript is used to index different distributions and typically goes $j = 1, \ldots, J$. Thus, if there are J different distributions from which valuations can be drawn, these will be typically denoted $\{F_j(v)\}_{j=1}^{J}$. These might be collected in the $(J \times 1)$ vector $\boldsymbol{F}$. When transformations of the V_is from the distribution F_j result in additional cumulative distribution and probability density functions, we typically use G_j and g_j next, and then H_j and h_j. Sometimes, however, H_k doubles as a Hermite polynomial of order k, while h doubles as the hazard-rate function, and triples as a bandwidth parameter in nonparametric estimation. In these cases, the trailing subscript should make clear our intent.

In estimation problems, the subscript t indexes different observations, different auctions, and typically goes from $t = 1, \ldots, T$. The superscript "0" typically denotes the truth or population value, while a " $\hat{\ }$ " atop a letter, particularly an F, an f, or a lowercase Greek letter, typically denotes an estimator (or estimate). Thus, for example, $\hat{F}_V(v)$ would represent an estimator (or estimate) of the true cumulative distribution function $F_V^0(v)$ at the point v, while $\hat{\theta}$ would denote an estimator (or estimate) of the true parameter value θ^0. Also, $\hat{\gamma}$ would denote an estimator (or estimate) of the vector of true parameter values γ^0.

Note, under our conventions, because an estimator is a random variable, it should be an uppercase letter, while an estimate (a realization of the random variable) should be a lowercase letter. But we do not adopt this extension for the obvious reason: we can't. Also, when more than one estimator (estimate) exists, we distinguish among alternatives by first using " $\tilde{\ }$ ", then " $\bar{\ }$ ", with the symbol " $\breve{\ }$ " being used rarely.

The k subscript is used to index observed covariate or other heterogeneity and typically goes $k = 1, \ldots, K$. An exception, however, would be for auction t, where the vector of covariates, when a constant is included, z_t would be conformable to an unknown parameter vector $(\gamma_0, \gamma_1, \ldots, \gamma_{K-1})^\top$.

We have adopted a numbering convention for chapters, sections, and subsections as well as for assumptions, corollaries, lemmata, theorems, and equations within chapters. Thus, with regard to parts of the book, the first number refers to the chapter, the second number to the section, and the third number to the subsection. Hence, **2.4.3** would mean subsection 3 of section 4 of chapter 2, while **A.2.3** would mean section 3 of appendix 2. As a visual aid, we have made chapter headings in seventeen-point font, section headings in twelve-point font, and subsection headings in ten-point font. For assumptions, corollaries, lemmata, and theorems, the following **Assumption 4.3.1:** conveys the first assumption made in section 3 of chapter 4. Tables are numbered sequentially throughout a chapter—Table 1.1 denotes the first table in chapter 1. We have also numbered equations sequentially throughout each chapter, so (3.10) marks the tenth numbered equation in chapter 3, while (A.2.1) marks the first numbered equation in the second appendix.

6 Comments and Suggestions

While several pairs of eyes have proofread the camera-ready copy of this book, we recognize that some typographical errors will remain; we apologize to the reader for these. We shall appreciate reports via e-mail of the typographical errors so that they may be eliminated in future printings. Also, although we hope that no errors exist in this book, we are realistic. Thus, we shall also appreciate reports of any errors too. In addition, readers are encouraged to send us e-mail should they have questions or comments concerning any part of the book. We shall endeavor to answer the questions as quickly as we can. As people move around a lot, perhaps the easiest way to find a current e-mail address for any one of us is to Google his name.

The sample MATLAB code contained on the CD that accompanies this book was developed to be accessible to beginning- and intermediate-level users of MATLAB. In addition to any written solutions provided at the end of the book, we have also included comments in the code which make clear the coding steps. While coding, we sought clarity rather than elegance, sometimes at the expense of efficiency and parsimony. While we have endeavored to check this code very carefully, we realize that errors often creep into computer programs. We regret any errors that may exist in the code. No warranty is provided with this code, nor is any implied. We do, however, welcome comments via e-mail from users of the code. If you have found an error, then documenting the conditions under which this error occurs will be most helpful. In fact, the better the documentation, the more likely we shall be able to find a solution.

7 Acknowledgments

Many people have helped us write this book. Initially, perhaps our greatest overall intellectual debts are to our teachers: Takeshi Amemiya, Thomas E. MaCurdy, Paul R. Milgrom, and Robert B. Wilson. But our most recent intellectual debts are to our "auction" coauthors: Bjarne Brendstrup, Victor Chernozhukov, Stephen G. Donald, Philip A. Haile, Jacques Robert, and Matthew Shum. Each has taught us a great deal. In fact, we are certain they will see their direct influence in the pages that follow. We are also grateful to them for their comradeship as well as for the patience they have shown when our efforts to complete this book distracted us from our research with them.

M. Ryan Haley provided us with the kind of assistance that one encounters only once in a career, if at all. In addition to providing extensive comments and suggestions on the text of the book, Ryan also helped us develop sample solutions to the mathematical questions at the end of some of the chapters and a primer on MATLAB as well as a complete suite of MATLAB programs, which implement solutions to the empirical exercises listed at the end of the first five chapters of the book. We are forever in his debt.

We are also grateful to Kenneth A. Fyie, Srihari Govindan, Timothy P. Hubbard, Ayça Kaya, Clinton J. Levitt, Tong Li, and Denis Nekipelov who provided useful suggestions on the manuscript, particularly in reporting pesky typographical errors. Clint and Tim also double-checked the solutions to the mathematical questions and empirical exercises as well as helped to create the name and subject indexes to the book. Anyone who has written a book knows what a thankless task that is; we are grateful to them for doing such a good job.

A number of anonymous referees vetted some early parts of the book at the various stages of their development. We are grateful to them for the generous gift of their time and for their persistent prodding. Because we did not follow all of their advice, they cannot be held responsible for any remaining errors of omission or commission.

During the winter of 2003, Paarsch developed early versions of the material in this book for graduate courses taught in the Danish Graduate Programme in Economics at Aarhus Universitet and in the International Doctorate in Economic Analysis program at the Universitat Autònoma de Barcelona. He is grateful to the students in these programs for their early input, particularly Bjarne Brendstrup, Róbert Veszteg, and Helmuts Azacis.

In the spring of 2004, Whitney K. Newey tested a draft of the manuscript in the classroom using the Ph.D. students of 14.387, Topics in Applied Econometrics, at MIT as subjects; we are grateful to him. In the spring term of 2005, the Ph.D. students in 06E:299, Contemporary Topics in Economics, at the University of Iowa worked through the entire book as well as the mathematical questions and empirical exercises, while in the spring quarter of 2005 the Ph.D. students in 312000, Empirical Analysis III, at the University of Chicago, taught by Hong, worked through some of the mathematical questions and empirical exercises; we are in their debt too. In the summer of 2005, just before we sent this book to press, Paarsch used parts of the first four chapters to teach a course in the Finnish Doctoral Programme in Economics at Helsingin yliopisto; we are grateful to the students there for their indulgence.

Paarsch is also grateful to his coauthors Bjarne Brendstrup, Stephen G. Donald, and Jacques Robert as well as the *Journal of Applied Econometrics*, the *Journal of Econometrics*, and the journal *Econometric Theory* for giving permission to borrow liberally from published work. Thus, some material in this book derives from the following papers:

> Paarsch, Harry J., "Deciding between the Common and Private Value Paradigms in Empirical Models of Auctions," *Journal of Econometrics*, 51 (1992), 191–215.

> Paarsch, Harry, J., "Deriving an Estimate of the Optimal Reserve Price: An Application to British Columbian Timber Sales," *Journal of Econometrics*, 78 (1997), 333–357.

> Donald Stephen G. and Harry J. Paarsch, "Superconsistent Estimation and Inference in Structural Econometric Models Using Extreme Order Statistics," *Journal of Econometrics*, 109 (2002), 305–340.

> Brendstrup, Bjarne and Harry J. Paarsch, "Identification and Estimation in Sequential, Asymmetric, English Auctions," *Journal of Econometrics*, (forthcoming).

and is reprinted with the permission of Elsevier Publishing. Also, some material in this book derives from the following paper:

> Donald, Stephen G. and Harry J. Paarsch, "Identification, Estimation, and Testing in Parametric Empirical Models of Auctions within the Independent Private Values Paradigm," *Econometric Theory*, 12 (1996), 517–567.

and is reprinted with the permission of Cambridge University Press.

Acknowledgments

Finally, some material in this book derives from the following paper:

> Donald, Stephen G., Harry J. Paarsch, and Jacques Robert, "An Empirical Model of the Multi-Unit, Sequential, Clock Auction," *Journal of Applied Econometrics*, (forthcoming).

and is reprinted with the permission of John Wiley and Sons Publishers.

Just before we began to put our manuscript together, we benefitted from several instructive conversations with A. Colin Cameron, James G. MacKinnon, and Martin Osborne on how to produce a book. James and Martin were particularly helpful with some of the subtle mechanics of typesetting a book in TeX, as was Robert Picard, who created a number of useful macros, which proved essential in creating the table of contents as well as the name and subject indexes. Martin also provided us with the names and e-mail addresses of publishers, which ultimately helped us find a home for this book.

At The MIT Press, Elizabeth Murry was particularly efficient in putting together an attractive set of terms for us as well as guiding our project through the production process, while Yasuyo Iguchi provided helpful stylistic advice at a critical point in producing the TeX macros, Krista Magnuson provided helpful stylistic suggestions concerning the camera-ready copy, and Jean Wilcox designed an interesting cover. We thank them all for their expertise and professionalism.

Last, but not least, we thank our families for their love and support.

HARRY J. PAARSCH

Iowa City, Iowa
October 2005

HAN HONG

Durham, North Carolina
October 2005

Chapter 1

Introduction

$\mathcal{C}$ONSIDER A seller of an object who faces $\mathcal{N}$ potential buyers. The seller may have some notion concerning the object's value to himself, but little or no information concerning how much any one of the potential buyers values the object. How should the seller choose to sell the object? A variety of different selling mechanisms exists. One commonly used mechanism involves announcing a take-it-or-leave-it price and then selling the object to the first person who accepts that price. Another might involve the seller's engaging in pair-wise negotiations with individual potential buyers, either simultaneously or sequentially. Yet a third way is to sell the object at auction.

Auctions are ubiquitous in market economies; they are also ancient, their durability suggesting that auctions serve an important allocational role. Over the past forty-five years, economic theorists have made considerable progress in understanding the factors influencing prices realized from goods sold at auction. For example, they have found that the seller's expected revenue depends on the auction format employed as well as the amount of competition, the information available to potential buyers, and the attitudes of bidders toward risk.

But what does holding an auction entail? The description of an *auction format* typically involves outlining the rules governing how the potential buyers must behave during the selling process; to wit, how bids must be tendered, who wins the auction, what the winner pays, and so forth. We shall introduce a number of different auction formats later in this book. Most importantly, however, the seller must commit to abide by the rules under a particular auction format.

Perhaps the most important feature defining environments in which auctions are used involves the existence of an asymmetry of information between the seller and the potential buyers. Typically, the seller knows little or nothing concerning the valuations of potential buyers. Moreover, these potential buyers have no incentive to tell the seller anything about their valuations. The role of the auction format is to get the potential

1

buyers to reveal to the seller information concerning their valuations of the object.

But how do the valuations of potential buyers obtain? The way in which potential buyers form their valuations remains an open question in economics. In fact, in auction theory, researchers are unusually vague concerning what generates the demand structure, unlike in standard demand theory where considerable care is taken to specify the structure of preferences. Suffice it to say that, in auction theory, when economic theorists come to modeling this asymmetry in information as well as the heterogeneity in valuations across agents, they use random variables. Often, it is assumed that each potential bidder demands at most one unit of the object in question. In the simplest model, the marginal utility of this one unit, for each potential bidder, is assumed an independent and identically distributed realization of a continuous random variable V which has a differentiable cumulative distribution function $F_V(v)$ and probability density function $f_V(v)$ equal to $dF_V(v)/dv$. By and large, the budget constraint as well as issues of substitution are ignored.

1.1 An Example

For example, in the most common paradigm of an auction, referred to in the preface as the independent private-values paradigm (IPVP), each of $\mathcal{N}$ potential bidders gets an independent and identically distributed draw $\{v_i\}_{i=1}^{\mathcal{N}}$ from $F_V(v)$. If one orders these $\mathcal{N}$ valuations

$$v_{(1:\mathcal{N})} \geq v_{(2:\mathcal{N})} \geq \cdots \geq v_{(\mathcal{N}:\mathcal{N})}$$

and then plots the highest valuation first, for which aggregate demand at that price is one, and then the second-highest valuation next, for which aggregate demand at that price is two, and so forth, one obtains the step function of aggregate demand, which is depicted in figure 1.1 for $\mathcal{N}$ equal five.

One way to interpret $F_V(v)$ is as follows: First, define the *survivor function*

$$\Pr(V > v) = S_V(v) = [1 - F_V(v)] = [1 - \Pr(V \leq v)]$$

which is the proportion of the population having demand when the price is v. Plotting the price p on the ordinate, as economists are wont to do, and $\mathcal{N}S_V(p)$ on the abscissa, one has an *expected-demand curve* as is depicted in figure 1.2. Each potential bidder, of which there are $\mathcal{N}$, is assumed to demand at most one unit, so aggregate demand is at most $\mathcal{N}$ when p is zero.

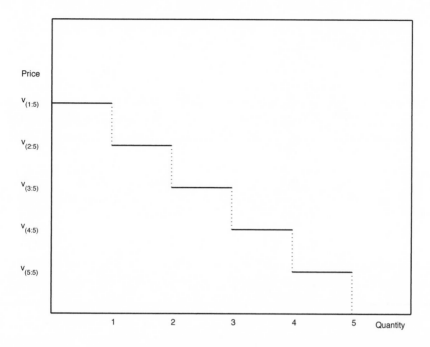

Figure 1.1
Aggregate Demand Step-Function

Now, the ordered marginal utilities of the $\mathcal{N}$ potential bidders are $\{v_{(i:\mathcal{N})}\}_{i=1}^{\mathcal{N}}$. From these one can create the sample analogue of $S_V(v)$, the empirical survivor function $\hat{S}_V(v)$; e.g., using the Kaplan–Meier product-limit estimator. We have depicted an estimate of expected demand, based on the estimated survivor function, generated from a sample of size $\mathcal{N}$ equal five, along with the population expected-demand function when $\mathcal{N}$ is five, in figure 1.3.

The idea of empirical work involving auction data is to estimate the expected-demand function $\mathcal{N}S_V(p)$ using the bids of the n participants at the auction. What makes this endeavor sometimes difficult, but invariably interesting, is that the n participants are often a subset of the potential bidders. Sample selection, in the Heckman sense, often exists. Also, depending on the auction format, bidders do not always reveal their true marginal utility.

In fact, one way to view auction theory is as demand analysis with a small number of consumers. But, unlike in standard demand analysis, where one typically assumes that the prices faced by an individual consumer are fixed, in auction theory one must take into account that the format and the rules of the auction, the primitive information giving

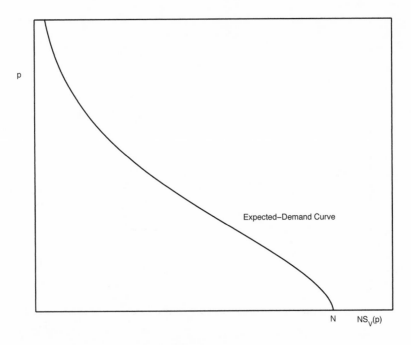

Expected–Demand Curve

p

N $NS_V(p)$

Figure 1.2
Expected-Demand Curve

rise to heterogeneity in beliefs concerning valuations, the preferences of potential bidders, the strategic behavior of the participants as well as the notion of equilibrium will *all* have an effect on the traded price, the winning bid. Thus, in the language of the econometrician, prices are *endogenous*. How can a researcher learn about the preferences of agents using either the bids submitted at auctions or just the winning bids?

The SEA uses the twin hypotheses of optimizing behavior and market equilibrium (henceforth optimization and equilibrium) to identify $F_V(v)$, the distribution of valuations.[1]

This is important. For, prior to applications of the SEA, many believed that it was impractical to implement mechanism-design theory to calculate the optimal selling mechanism because the optimal selling mechanism depended on quantities typically unobserved by the designer; viz., $F_V(v)$. Moreover, the actions (equilibrium strategies) of the agents, their bids $\{s_i\}_{i=1}^n$, while positively related to the valuations, were not always fully revealing; e.g., specifically, in the case of first-price, sealed-

---

[1] Typically, one assumes that potential bidders maximize the expected profit or the expected utility of profit from winning the auction and then uses either dominance or Bayes–Nash as an equilibrium concept.

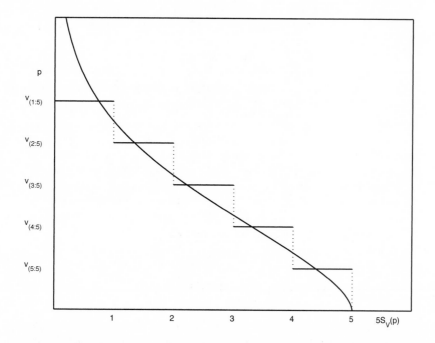

Figure 1.3
Empirical and Population Expected-Demand Curves

bid and oral, descending-price auctions. Thus, some believed that no way existed to estimate this distribution of latent types $F_V(v)$.

Now, one can typically estimate consistently the cumulative distribution function of observed actions (strategies) $F_S(s)$ using well-known empirical methods. Note, too, that in auction theory the strategy S is often a continuous and differentiable function σ of V. For example, at first-price, sealed-bid auctions the Bayes–Nash, equilibrium-bid function is

$$\sigma(V) = v - \frac{\int_0^v F_V(u)^{\mathcal{N}-1} \, du}{F_V(v)^{\mathcal{N}-1}}. \tag{1.1}$$

In general, when

$$S = \sigma(V) \quad \sigma'(V) > 0,$$

as is the case of (1.1),

$$V = \sigma^{-1}(S)$$

and

$$f_S(s) = \frac{f_V[\sigma^{-1}(s)]}{\sigma'[\sigma^{-1}(s)]}.$$

Thus, under suitable regularity conditions, which are usually met in theoretical models of auctions, one can construct an estimator $\hat{F}_S(s)$ of $F_S^0(s)$ where the superscript "0" denotes the true population value. Moreover, as the sample size increases, the estimator $\hat{F}_S(s)$ converges in probability to $F_S^0(s)$. Also, from $\hat{F}_S(s)$ one can usually construct a consistent estimator $\hat{f}_S(s)$ of $f_S^0(s)$ and subsequently, $\hat{F}_V(v)$, a consistent estimator of $F_V^0(v)$. Thus, the SEAD is an econometric *identification strategy*.

One can quite rightfully ask why, given the detailed research existing in standard demand theory, would one use such a blunt instrument to investigate demand? In the SEAD, strategic behavior is the most important consideration. Reverse engineering in the face of deception by market participants is the goal. Thus, all other considerations, typically deemed important in standard demand theory, have been shunted to the side in order that the main focus not be lost.

1.2 Some Intriguing Problems

One of the most intriguing problems faced by researchers who investigate data from auctions using the SEA is that different auction formats typically generate different kinds of information, so one omnibus empirical procedure to analyze these data cannot be proposed. One can, however, propose a general strategy; in this book, we describe several of many recent contributions to this general strategy.

To see how different auction formats generate different amounts of information, consider first the most informative auction format, the second-price, sealed-bid auction. At second-price, sealed-bid auctions within the IPVP, as will be shown below, each of the $\mathcal{N}$ bidders reveals his valuation truthfully. Thus, in the absence of a minimum bid price, the empirical distribution of bids $\{b_i\}_{i=1}^{\mathcal{N}}$ can be used to estimate the cumulative distribution of valuations. To wit, construct $\hat{F}_V(v)$, an estimate of $F_V^0(v)$, using the empirical distribution function

$$\hat{F}_V(v) = \frac{1}{\mathcal{N}} \sum_{i=1}^{\mathcal{N}} \mathbf{1}(b_i \leq v)$$

where $\mathbf{1}(\mathsf{A})$ denotes the indicator function of the event A. The identifying assumption in this case is that bidders tell the truth, bid their actual valuations

$$B_i = \beta(V_i) = V_i.$$

6

Of course, the properties of $\hat{F}_V(v)$ can be improved by kernel-smoothing; in other words, using the estimator

$$\tilde{F}_V(v) = \frac{1}{\mathcal{N}} \sum_{i=1}^{\mathcal{N}} K\left(\frac{b_i - v}{h_F}\right)$$

where h_F is often referred to as the *bandwidth parameter*, while the function $K(\cdot)$, which is often referred to as the *cumulative kernel function*, has the following properties:

$$\lim_{y \to -\infty} K(y) = 0$$
$$\lim_{y \to \infty} K(y) = 1$$
$$K(y) \geq 0 \quad -\infty < y < \infty.$$

Unfortunately, the standard asymptotics are typically undertaken as $\mathcal{N}$ goes to ∞ and this does not happen at an auction. What to do?

Typically, to get more data, researchers combine data from auctions of objects that are not exactly alike. Thus, the independent and identically distributed assumption commonly made in empirical work may not apply. In some cases, the objects for sale may differ in observable ways that can be summarized for auction t by an observed vector of covariates z_t. If one is willing to adopt a single-index model, then one can write

$$V_{it} = \mu(z_t^\top \gamma) + U_{it}$$

where

$$\mathcal{E}(U_{it} | z_t) = 0,$$

and use the methods discussed in Horowitz (1998). Of more concern than the dearth of data concerning identical objects is the fact that second-price, sealed-bid auctions are rarely, if ever, used.

The most commonly used auction format and, under certain assumptions to be outlined below, also the next most informative format, from the perspective of an econometrician, is the oral, ascending-price auction. As we shall see below, at oral, ascending-price auctions within the IPVP, assuming the *clock model* of Milgrom and Weber (1982), each nonwinning bidder reveals his valuation truthfully, while all one knows about the winner is that his valuation is above the second-highest valuation. It is in this last sense that data from oral, ascending-price auctions are not as informative as second-price, sealed-bid auctions. Now, under clock model assumptions, the cumulative distribution function $F_W(w)$

of the winning price W is the cumulative distribution function of the second-highest valuation $V_{(2:\mathcal{N})}$ which is defined by

$$F_W(w) = \mathcal{N}(\mathcal{N}-1) \int_0^{F_V(w)} u^{\mathcal{N}-2}(1-u) \; du.$$

In the absence of a minimum bid price, when the number of potential bidders $\mathcal{N}$ is fixed and known, the empirical distribution of winning bids $\{w_t\}_{t=1}^T$ for a sample of T auctions, can be used to estimate the cumulative distribution of valuations by solving the following equation:

$$\hat{F}_W(v) = \frac{1}{T} \sum_{t=1}^T \mathbf{1}(w_t \leq v)$$

$$= \mathcal{N}(\mathcal{N}-1) \int_0^{\hat{F}_V(v)} u^{\mathcal{N}-2}(1-u) \; du$$

at each point v. In this case, the identifying assumptions are that bidders tell the truth

$$B_i = \beta(V_i) = V_i$$

and that the winning price is the second order statistic of valuations

$$W_t = \beta[V_{(2:\mathcal{N}),t}] = V_{(2:\mathcal{N}),t}.$$

Of course, kernel-smoothing methods can improve the small-sample behavior of the estimator. Also, kernel-smoothing methods are needed to provide estimates of the optimal selling mechanism, which takes the form of an optimal minimum bid price ρ^* solving the following equation:

$$\rho^* = v_0 + \frac{[1 - F_V(\rho^*)]}{f_V(\rho^*)}$$

where v_0 is the seller's valuation of the object for sale.

Another intriguing problem arises when a binding minimum bid price exists because, in that circumstance, not all of the $\mathcal{N}$ potential bidders may participate at the auction. For example, when the minimum bid price is r, the number of *participating* bidders N is a random variable defined by

$$N = \sum_{i=1}^{\mathcal{N}} \mathbf{1}(V_i \geq r).$$

Because each of the random variables $\{\mathbf{1}(V_i \geq r)\}_{i=1}^{\mathcal{N}}$ is an independent and identically distributed Bernoulli random variable, their sum, the random variable N, is distributed binomially with two parameters, $\mathcal{N}$

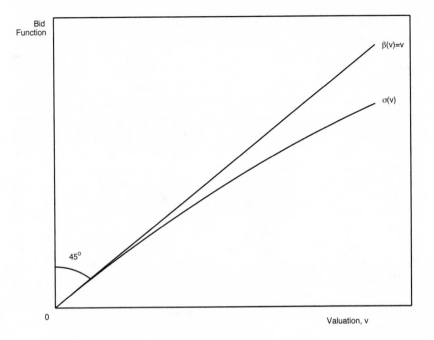

Figure 1.4
Graphs of Bid Functions:
First-Price and Second-Price, Sealed-Bid Auctions

and $[1 - F_V(r)]$. Moreover, the bids submitted at auction represent a *truncated* sample: only those potential bidders having valuations greater than r appear in the sample.

One feature that makes oral, ascending-price and second-price, sealed-bid auctions particularly tractable, at least numerically, is that the bid function in each case is a trivial function of the valuation. This is not the case at either first-price, sealed-bid or oral, descending-price auctions. At these auctions, within the symmetric IPVP and assuming risk-neutral potential bidders, the Bayes–Nash, equilibrium-bid function is

$$\sigma(v) = v - \frac{\int_0^v F_V(u)^{\mathcal{N}-1}\, du}{F_V(v)^{\mathcal{N}-1}}.$$

The first thing to notice about this strategy function is that it is monotonic, having positive slope less than one when v exceeds zero. What this means is that bidders with higher valuations bid more, but they bid systematically less than their true value. Moreover, the higher a potential bidder's valuation, the larger is the extent of this deception. Thus, the winner of either a first-price, sealed-bid or an oral, descending-price

9

sealed-bid auction, the potential bidder with the highest valuation, will be the most deceptive: for a set of potential bidders, the winning bid will be the furthest from the actual valuation. We depict an example of this equilibrium-bid function at first-price, sealed-bid auctions in figure 1.4. In this figure, the 45°-line, denoted $\beta(v)$, depicts the equilibrium-bid function at the second-price, sealed-bid auction, while the curve that is everywhere below it (except at zero where they are equal), denoted $\sigma(v)$, depicts the equilibrium-bid function at the first-price, sealed-bid auction. Notice how a small change in the rules of the auction has an important impact on the behavior of the bidders at the auction.

The least informative format is the oral, descending-price auction. At these auctions, the researcher only gets to observe an action of the winner. A major portion of the potential bidders, $[(\mathcal{N}-1)/\mathcal{N}]$ to be exact, reveals no information. It is, in fact, somewhat surprising that one can make any statements concerning the cumulative distribution function $F_V(v)$ by just observing the winning bids from a sample of these auctions, particularly if a binding minimum bid price exists because the number of participants is then endogenous, but such is the power of the twin identifying hypotheses, optimization and equilibrium.

1.3 Plan of Book

In this book, we present an introduction to modern econometric techniques that are used in conjunction with the SEA to interpret field data from auctions. We do not consider the application of structural econometric methods to experimental data because, in those cases, the researcher typically knows $F_V^0(v)$ as he or she has selected it to generate the data for the subjects of the experiments. However, the methods we describe below can be used to test particular hypotheses using data from experiments. Thus, our book should be of interest to experimental workers who study auctions.

In chapter 2, we present an overview of single-object auction theory assuming auctions can be modeled as noncooperative games of incomplete information. We begin by describing the four most commonly studied auction formats and then some additional rules. Subsequently, we describe three models of information structures. Because the preferences of bidders are closely related to the structure of information, we discuss them next, but separately, to highlight the importance of risk aversion in formulating the decision problem faced by potential bidders under two of the auction formats. Ultimately, we derive the equilibrium-bid functions under the four auction formats, for risk-neutral and risk-averse bidders, without and with binding minimum bid prices. We then discuss the revenue equivalence proposition and characterize the optimal auction. We also show how risk aversion affects expected revenues under the four auction formats and outline Myerson's (1981) method for constructing optimal auctions. At the end of the chapter, we present a brief description of the winner's curse, perhaps the most well-known phenomenon in auction theory, showing why it is irrelevant for the models considered below.

While Krishna (2002) has provided an elegant and complete treatment of the material presented in chapter 2, we use this chapter to develop a notation, to introduce well-known results, and to outline the material necessary to formulate the major questions of interest.

In chapter 3, we then investigate the econometrics of oral, ascending-price and second-price, sealed-bid auctions. Even though it is rarely used, we begin with the second-price, sealed-bid auction because this format allows us to develop the basic intuition of the SEA within a nonparametric framework. Subsequently, we introduce covariates and then discuss single-index models and semiparametric estimation methods. The implications of a binding minimum bid price are discussed next. Endogenous participation, induced by a binding reserve price, highlights the limitations of nonparametric methods, so we introduce parametric methods.

Having developed most of the important econometric results concerning second-price auctions within the symmetric IPVP, we then present an extended policy application by Paarsch (1997), who estimated the optimal selling mechanism for timber in the province of British Columbia, Canada.

The fact that most oral, ascending-price auctions have either known bid increments or random, bidder-induced jumps in the price leads us naturally to an analysis of incomplete data and inference following the work of Haile and Tamer (2003).

In the final section of the chapter, we introduce asymmetric bidders, outlining a proof of nonparametric identification based on Meilijson (1981) and used by Brendstrup and Paarsch (forthcoming). The model as well as the methods of identification and estimation introduced in this section will prove useful in the specification of multi-unit auctions described in chapter 5.

In chapter 4, we investigate the econometrics of first-price, sealed-bid and oral, descending-price auctions. Following Paarsch (1989, 1992), we first derive the data-generating processes of the equilibrium-bid function as well as the winning bid. We then use the work of Guerre, Perrigne, and Vuong (2000) to demonstrate nonparametric identification. In the following section, we describe four different estimation strategies: First, we describe the nonparametric estimation methods of Guerre et al.

Subsequently, in an effort to deal effectively with observed covariate heterogeneity, we introduce parametric models, specifically discussing the method of maximum likelihood of Donald and Paarsch (1993, 1996) and then the method of simulated nonlinear least-squares of Laffont, Ossard, and Vuong (1995). Finally, we address some criticisms of the maximum-likelihood approach, examining the work of Donald and Paarsch (2002).

We then introduce a binding reserve price. In these cases, as noted by Brendstrup and Paarsch (2003), the extensive-form games at first-price, sealed-bid and oral, descending-price auctions are different because the number of participants is typically observed at oral, descending-price auctions, but realistically assumed unknown at first-price, sealed-bid auctions.

In most structural-econometric analyses of auction data, researchers have typically assumed that the potential bidders are risk neutral with respect to winning the auction. At oral, ascending-price and second-price, sealed-bid auctions, such an assumption is irrelevant because the dominant-strategy, equilibrium-bid function remains unchanged under these formats when potential bidders are risk averse. For example, at second-price, sealed-bid auctions, risk-averse bidders continue to bid their valuations when they exceed the minimum bid price. On the other hand, at first-price, sealed-bid and oral, descending-price auctions the attitudes of potential bidders toward risk matter. Thus, in the next section of chapter 4, we describe the effects of symmetric, von Neumann–Morgenstern preferences on the structural-econometric analysis, first using parametric methods, as in Donald and Paarsch (1996), and then using semiparametric methods, following Campo, Guerre, Perrigne, and Vuong (2000).

All of the surveyed research concerning first-price, sealed-bid and oral, ascending-price auctions has been within the symmetric IPVP. We go on to examine the effects of stochastic private-values, following the research of Lu (2004), who used the theoretical work of Éso and White (2004). We also consider asymmetric bidders, those whose valuations are drawn from different distributions, especially in the presence of a binding reserve price, examining Brendstrup and Paarsch (2003), who have extended the results of Guerre et al. We then consider the work of Krasnokutskaya (2004), who investigated the effects of unobserved heterogeneity within the IPVP.

To illustrate a policy experiment, we examine the research of Brendstrup and Paarsch (forthcoming) in which the performance of the oral, ascending-price vis-a-vis the oral, descending-price auction is compared when potential bidders are asymmetric. Under these conditions, Maskin and Riley (2000) have demonstrated that inefficient allocations can obtain at oral, descending-price auctions, while at oral ascending-price auctions efficient allocations always obtain, at least within the IPVP. Moreover, the revenue equivalence proposition breaks down. Using data from fish auctions in Grenå, Denmark, Brendstrup and Paarsch estimated the incidence and economic importance of inefficiencies at oral, descending-price auctions and then compared the expected revenues of the two auction formats.

Finally, we consider a model of fixed costs to bidding and endogenous auction participation, examining Li's (2005) application of a simulated, generalized method-of-moments estimator within a parametric specification.

We devote chapter 5 to an investigation of multi-unit auctions. During the past four decades, economic theorists have systematically investigated simple theoretical models of behavior at auctions in which only one object is sold to buyers demanding at most one object each. In reality, however, many auctions involve the sale of multiple units of the same object to buyers who may demand several units. Recent research concerning multi-unit auction models suggests that such institutions introduce a host of additional economic issues typically absent in the analysis of single-object auction models.

We begin the chapter by first making the distinction between multi-object and multi-unit auctions and then introducing Weber's (1983) classification of multi-unit auctions. Subsequently, we introduce models of singleton demand and then describe two models of multi-unit demand, nonrandom and random demand. For completed research, we then describe identification and estimation strategies. Because multi-unit demand and supply models are topics of current research, our discussion in this chapter is incomplete.

In our last chapter, chapter 6, we discuss briefly directions for future research. We first describe some research that is currently either under revision or under way, and then speculate on a few fruitful directions in which researchers might go. Finally, we summarize the book, briefly.

We have written a number of technical appendixes to this book. We encourage the reader to master the material in them *before* attempting the next four chapters of the book. In these appendixes are included a review of some basic probability theory concerning distributions of transformations of random variables and, particularly, order statistics. We have also presented a brief review of first-order asymptotic methods as well as simulation methods and the bootstrap; the application of these methods to the evaluation of different estimation strategies is also described. The implementation of different estimation strategies is motivated by descriptions of some elementary tools from numerical analysis. Because using numerical methods requires their implementation in some sort of programming environment, our final appendix is a primer concerning MATLAB.

In an effort to provide readers with instruments to gauge their understanding of this material, at the end of this chapter, we have presented several practice problems. Other practice problems, which build on the material covered in the problems at the end of this chapter, are included at the end of each of the next four chapters. A reader who has successfully completed these practice problems will be able to analyze data from an actual auction and then derive policy conclusions from this research. We hope that readers will make this effort and thus enter the exciting field of SEAD.

1.4 Practice Problems

The problems at the end of this chapter are designed to give you some practice with the basics of probability theory as well as statistical estimation and inference that are presumed in the remainder of the book. By implementing the estimation strategies in the programming language MATLAB (or any other programming language for that matter), you will also gain some practice in the elementary numerical methods needed later in the book.

1. Consider a discrete random variable N having probability mass function

$$f_N(n; \theta^0) = \frac{-(\theta^0)^n}{n \log (1 - \theta^0)} \qquad n = 1, 2, \ldots, \ 0 < \theta^0 < 1$$

which is often referred to as the *logarithmic series* distribution for reasons that will become clear later in the problem.

a) Prove that

$$\sum_{n=1}^{\infty} f_N(n; \theta^0) = 1.$$

(Hint: consider the Maclaurin-series expansion of $\log (1 + x)$ and substitute in $x = -\theta^0$.)

b) Find the expected value of N, $\mathcal{E}(N)$. (Hint: $\sum_{n=1}^{\infty} \rho^n = \frac{\rho}{1-\rho}$.)

c) Find the variance of N, $\mathcal{V}(N)$. (Hint: remember that the derivative of a sum is the sum of the derivatives of each of the sum's parts.)

d) Define the method-of-moments estimator $\hat{\theta}_{\mathrm{MM}}$ of θ^0.

N	1	2	3	4	5	6	7	8	9+
Frequency	700	205	50	26	10	6	1	1	1

Table 1.1
Observed Frequency Distribution of N

e) Show that the condition that defines $\hat{\theta}_{MM}$ has a unique solution. (Hint: draw a graph.)

f) Set up the recursion you would use in order to employ Newton's method to solve for $\hat{\theta}_{MM}$.

g) Define the maximum-likelihood estimator $\hat{\theta}_{ML}$ of θ^0.

h) Demonstrate that $\hat{\theta}_{MM}$ and $\hat{\theta}_{ML}$ are consistent estimators of θ^0.

i) Find an approximation to the variance of $\hat{\theta}_{MM}$ and $\hat{\theta}_{ML}$.

j) Characterize the asymptotic distribution of $\hat{\theta}_{MM}$ and $\hat{\theta}_{ML}$ and explain your reasoning.

After considerable effort, a researcher has obtained a random sample of one thousand measurements on N. These data are summarized in Table 1.1.

k) Write a MATLAB program to implement Newton's method and then calculate the maximum-likelihood estimate of θ^0 using the above data.

l) At size 0.05, test the following hypothesis:

$$H_0 : \theta^0 = 0.50$$

$$H_1 : \theta^0 \neq 0.50.$$

m) At size 0.10, test the following hypothesis:

$$H_0 : \log \theta^0 = -0.70$$

$$H_1 : \log \theta^0 \neq -0.70.$$

n) At size 0.05, ignoring the fact that $\hat{\theta}_{ML}$ is estimated and that no observed counts exist above nine, use Fisher's χ^2, *goodness-of-fit* test to decide whether the empirical frequency is consistent with the logarithmic series distribution.

15

2. Consider a random sample $\{V_t\}_{t=1}^T$ from the log-normal distribution, having probability density function

$$f_V(v; \theta_1^0, \theta_2^0) = \frac{1}{v}\frac{1}{\sqrt{2\pi\theta_2^0}}\exp\left[\frac{-(\log v - \theta_1^0)^2}{2\theta_2^0}\right]$$

$$v > 0, \ \theta_2^0 > 0, \ \text{and} -\infty < \theta_1^0 < \infty.$$

Note that the kth raw moment of V is

$$\mathcal{E}(V^k) = \exp\left(k\theta_1^0 + \frac{k^2}{2}\theta_2^0\right) \quad k = 1, 2, \dots.$$

   a) Write down the likelihood function, the logarithm of the likelihood function, and the score vector for this sample. Solve for the maximum-likelihood estimators $\hat{\theta}_1^{\text{ML}}$ and $\hat{\theta}_2^{\text{ML}}$ of θ_1^0 and θ_2^0.
   b) Calculate the expectations of $\hat{\theta}_1^{\text{ML}}$ and $\hat{\theta}_2^{\text{ML}}$. Are the MLEs unbiased estimators? Calculate the variance and the small-sample, exact distribution of $\hat{\theta}_1^{\text{ML}}$.
   c) Derive the method-of-moments estimators $\hat{\theta}_1^{\text{MM}}$ and $\hat{\theta}_2^{\text{MM}}$. Are MMEs unbiased estimators of θ_1^0 and θ_2^0? Explain your answer.
   d) Prove that the MMEs are consistent estimators of θ_1^0 and θ_2^0.
   e) For simplicity, assume that θ_2^0 is known to equal one. Using the delta method, find the asymptotic distribution of $\hat{\theta}_1^{\text{MM}}$. Compare the asymptotic variance of this estimator with the exact variance of the MLE. Which estimator is more efficient? Why?

3. Suppose that, in the model of practice problem 1, θ^0 depends on a $(K \times 1)$ vector of covariates $\mathbf{z}$. Assume further that the unknown $\theta(\mathbf{z})$ can be modeled as a logistic function, so

$$\theta(\mathbf{z}) = \frac{\exp(\mathbf{z}^\top\boldsymbol{\gamma})}{[1 + \exp(\mathbf{z}^\top\boldsymbol{\gamma})]}$$

where the vector of unknown parameters $\boldsymbol{\gamma}$, or $(\gamma_0, \gamma_1, \dots, \gamma_{K-1})^\top$, is conformable to $\mathbf{z}^\top$.

   a) For a sample $\{(\mathbf{z}_t, n_t)\}_{t=1}^T$, write down the likelihood function, the logarithm of the likelihood function $\mathcal{L}(\boldsymbol{\gamma})$, the score vector $\mathbf{g}(\boldsymbol{\gamma})$, and the Hessian matrix $\mathbf{H}(\boldsymbol{\gamma})$
   b) Set up the recursion you would need in order to solve for the maximum-likelihood estimate $\hat{\boldsymbol{\gamma}}$.

c) In the file `logser.dat`, which is located on the CD accompanying this book, you will find five columns of numbers. In the first is recorded an identification number, which ranges from 1 to 1000, while in the second is recorded the dependent variable n_t. In the next three are recorded the covariates $z_{1,t}$, $z_{2,t}$, and $z_{3,t}$. The entire file has $1,000$ rows, so $1,000$ observations. Write a MATLAB program to calculate the maximum-likelihood estimate of γ when a constant is present in $z^\top \gamma$.

d) Using the likelihood-ratio test, decide whether the following hypothesis can be rejected at size 0.05:

$$\text{H}_0 : \gamma_1^0 = \gamma_2^0 = \gamma_3^0 = 0$$

$$\text{H}_1 : \text{not H}_0.$$

4. To get some practice implementing the bootstrap, complete the following:

a) In MATLAB, generate 1,000 samples of size twenty-five for normal pseudo-random variables having mean zero and variance one. For each sample, calculate the sample median and then simulate the nonparametric bootstrap standard error of the sample median using 100 bootstrap samples. Using this information, gauge the accuracy of the asymptotic formula for the variance of the sample median, which is

$$\frac{\pi \sigma^2}{2T}$$

where σ^2 is the variance (one in this case), T is the sample size (twenty-five in this case), and π can be approximated by 3.14159.

b) In MATLAB, generate 1,000 samples of size twenty-five for uniform pseudo-random numbers. Using the property that cumulative distribution function of a continuous random variable is distributed uniformly on the interval $[0,1]$, generate pseudo-random variables from the exponential distribution having hazard rate one. Using the bootstrap with 100 samples, evaluate the asymptotic formula for the standard error of the sample lower quartile $\hat{\xi}$ as an estimator of the population lower quartile ξ^0 when the asymptotic distribution of the lower quartile is

$$\sqrt{T}(\hat{\xi} - \xi^0) \xrightarrow{\text{d}} \mathcal{N}\left[0, \frac{3}{16T f_V^0 \left(\xi^0\right)^2}\right]$$

17

where $f_V^0(\cdot)$ is the true exponential probability density function.

5. Consider the following function

$$f_V^0(v) = \exp\left[v - v^2 - \sqrt{v} + \sin(v)\right] \quad v \in [0, 3].$$

a) Plot this function in MATLAB.

In MATLAB, evaluate the above function at each point from 0 to 3 for a constant step-size 0.1; store the thirty-one ordered pairs.

b) On the interval $[0, 3]$, estimate the generalized Chebyshev polynomial approximations of the function $f_V^0(v)$ for orders one, four, and seven using MATLAB. Graph these three polynomials superimposing them on a graph of the true function $f_V^0(v)$. Do the approximations improve as the order of the approximating polynomial increases?

c) Using the thirty-one ordered pairs of numbers from part a) above, estimate, by the method of least squares, the appropriate coefficients for a polynomial of order one, four, and seven and then plot these functions along with the true function $f_V^0(v)$.

6. In a variety of circumstances in econometrics, researchers often need to evaluate an integral of the following form:

$$\Gamma(a, b) = \int_a^b f(u) \, du.$$

In some circumstances $\Gamma(a, b)$ will have a closed-form solution that can be calculated in a straightforward fashion. For example, suppose that

$$f(u) = \exp(-u) \quad u > 0.$$

In this case,

$$\Gamma(a, b) = [1 - \exp(-b)] - [1 - \exp(-a)] = [\exp(-a) - \exp(-b)].$$

In many cases, $\Gamma(a, b)$ does not have a closed-form solution. In these cases, quadrature methods are often used to calculate $\Gamma(a, b)$. Quadrature involves dividing the interval $[a, b]$ up into subintervals, evaluating the area under $f(u)$ for each subinterval, and then adding up the areas to find $\Gamma(a, b)$. In higher dimensions (more than three) quadrature rules can become numerically unreliable and difficult to implement with any precision. In such cases, researchers often use Monte Carlo methods to simulate the integral $\Gamma(a, b)$. Monte Carlo simulation involves sampling from a known distribution on the interval $[a, b]$, for example the uniform, and then taking the average of $f(u)$ evaluated at each random draw. As the number of simulation draws K goes to infinity, this estimator converges to the truth.

In this problem, you will use simple trapezoidal quadrature as well as Monte Carlo methods to evaluate

$$\Gamma(0, 1) = \int_0^1 \exp(-u) \, du$$

which you know equals $[1 - \exp(-1)]$ or 0.6321.

a) Approximate $\Gamma(0, 1)$ by the area of a trapezoid defined by the points $(0, 0)$, $(0, 1)$, $(1, 0)$, and $(1, \exp(-1))$, then calculate the error associated with using this rule.

b) Now divide the interval $[0, 1]$ up into ten subintervals of the same width. Calculate the area for each trapezoid, and then the estimated area for $\Gamma(0, 1)$. What is the estimation error now?

c) Derive a formula for the estimation error as a function of the points a and b as well as the number of subintervals on $[a, b]$, assuming that the trapezoid rule is used and that the function $f(u)$ equals $\exp(-u)$.

d) Now consider making independent and identically distributed draws concerning uniform random variable U on the interval $[0, 1]$. Calculate the expected value of $\exp(-U)$ on the interval $[0, 1]$. Calculate the variance of $\exp(-U)$ on the interval $[0, 1]$.

e) Provide a simulation estimator $G_K(0, 1)$ of the integral $\Gamma(0, 1)$ where K is the number of simulation draws. Find its asymptotic distribution.

f) How large must K be before the root mean-squared error of $G_K(0, 1)$ equals the error in part a)?

Chapter 2

Overview of Auction Theory

$\mathcal{I}$N THIS chapter, we present an overview of single-object auction theory when viewed through the lens of Harsanyi's theory of noncooperative games of incomplete information. We begin by describing the four most commonly studied auction formats and then some additional rules. Subsequently, we describe three models of information structures. Because the preferences of bidders are closely related to the structure of information, we discuss them next, but separately, to highlight the importance of risk aversion in formulating the decision problem faced by potential bidders under two of the auction formats. Ultimately, we derive the equilibrium-bid functions under the four auction formats, for risk-neutral as well as risk-averse bidders, with and without binding minimum bid prices.

We then discuss the revenue equivalence proposition, which was first demonstrated in by Vickrey (1961) using an example with uniformly-distributed valuations, and later proven under general conditions by Riley and Samuelson (1981). Subsequently, we present a derivation of the optimal selling mechanism based on the analysis of Riley and Samuelson. We also show how risk aversion affects expected revenues under the four different formats and outline Myerson's (1981) method for constructing optimal auctions under bidder asymmetries. At the end of the chapter, we present a brief description of the winner's curse, perhaps the most well-known phenomenon in auction theory, showing why it is irrelevant for the models considered here.

While Krishna (2002) has provided an elegant and complete treatment of the material contained in this chapter, we use the chapter to develop a notation, to introduce well-known results, and to outline some of the major questions of interest. At the end of the chapter, we also include some practice problems designed to give the reader experience in manipulating some of the most commonly used theoretical models of auctions.

2.1 Auction Formats and Rules

Four auction formats have been typically studied by economic theorists. In order of real-world frequency, they are the oral, ascending-price; the first-price, sealed-bid; the oral, descending-price; and the second-price, sealed-bid formats. In this section, we describe each. We also describe some additional rules that often apply at auctions.

2.1.1 Oral, Ascending-Price (English) Format

The most frequently used format is the oral, ascending-price auction. The format of this auction accords with the notion most laypeople have of an auction. In particular, the auctioneer begins the bidding at some low price, and then urges the bidders to raise the price. When no member of the audience is willing to raise the price further, the auctioneer has some device to signal the close of the auction (for example, shouting "going once, going twice, sold to the man in the yellow shirt") and the auction ends. In fact, the word *auction* is believed to derive from the Latin verb *augere*, which means *to raise*. For reasons that do not appear well-documented, oral, ascending-price auctions are often referred to as *English auctions*, at least by economic theorists.

2.1.2 First-Price, Sealed-Bid Format

The next most frequently used auction is the first-price, sealed-bid auction, often referred to as *sealed-bid tenders*. According to Cassady (1967), some laypeople do not even consider this format to be an auction, but economic theorists do. At first-price, sealed-bid auctions, each participant submits a bid in a sealed envelope and then, at some prespecified time, all of the envelopes are opened, more or less simultaneously, with the participant who tendered the highest bid winning the auction and paying what he bid. Sealed-bid auctions probably account for the bulk of transactions by value. The reason why sealed-bid auctions account for such a large fraction of the value of transactions is that procurement is often undertaken using *low-price, sealed-bid tenders*. Economic theorists consider procurement at sealed-bid tenders to be an auction format too, something that also surprises some lay people.

2.1.3 Oral, Descending-Price (Dutch) Format

The third most-frequently-used format is the oral, descending-price auction, which is often referred to as the *Dutch auction*. It is unclear how

22

this latter name came to be used; most laypeople are unaware of the name Dutch auction. It is quite possible that the name derives from the way flowers are sold at auction in Aalsmeer near Amsterdam in The Netherlands, but this is simply conjecture on our part.

In any case, at Dutch auctions, the price is set initially very high and then allowed to drop continuously. In Aalsmeer, the price is determined by the relative position of lights on a clockface where the lights illuminate clockwise in descent relatively quickly. Each potential bidder has an electronic device with a button; when the button is depressed, the clock stops and that particular bidder wins the object at the price currently listed on the clock. Most Dutch auctions have these mechanical features too, although the devices used to implement them vary. In addition to flowers, Dutch auctions are frequently used to sell fish; for example, in Australia, Denmark, France, and Spain.

2.1.4 Second-Price, Sealed-Bid (Vickrey) Format

The last format we shall discuss is the second-price, sealed-bid auction. At second-price, sealed-bid auctions (like at first-price, sealed-bid auctions) each participant submits a bid in a sealed envelope. Again, at some prespecified time, all of the envelopes are opened, with the participant who tendered the highest bid winning the auction. However, the price the winner pays is what his nearest opponent bid. If one thinks of the winner's bid as the first order statistic of bids, then his nearest opponent's bid is the second order statistic of bids. Hence, the name *second-price, sealed-bid auctions*. This auction format is also often referred to as the *Vickrey auction* in honor of William Vickrey, the 1996 Nobel laureate who first analyzed the format in his 1961 classic *Journal of Finance* paper.

The Vickrey auction is a bit of a theoretical curiosity: economic theorists discuss this format frequently, but it is rarely seen in practice. David Lucking-Reiley (2000) reports that stamps are essentially sold at Vickrey auctions. In fact, he claims that this practice goes back to the late nineteenth century, well before Vickrey's birth. According to Lucking-Reiley, stamp auctions are conducted initially using the oral, ascending-price (English) format but, for those who cannot attend the auction, bids submitted by mail are accepted. After the English-auction part of a stamp sale has determined a winner, the sealed envelopes are opened. If the highest among the sealed tender exceeds the highest of the English-auction bids, then that mail-in bidder wins the stamp and pays what his nearest opponent bid. Obviously, this last part of the stamp auction is a second-price, sealed-bid (Vickrey) auction.

Few other sightings of Vickrey auctions have been reported. In fact, Rothkopf, Teisberg, and Kahn (1990) have presented a detailed analysis of why Vickrey auctions, however desirable theoretically, are seldom observed in the field. This format is often studied because it is easy to illustrate certain properties (such as efficiency); also, under certain condition, with this format, the winning bid can be interpreted as the opportunity cost of the good for sale. Such an interpretation is obviously attractive to economists. It also seems likely that in the future second-price, sealed-bid auctions will still be called Vickrey auctions, despite the fact that Vickrey may not have invented them; Vickrey is surely honored as much for his insightful and elegant theoretical analysis of second-price, sealed-bid auctions as for the invention of the format itself.

2.1.5 Additional Rules

Other, additional rules often apply at auctions. For example, a minimum price that must be bid, often referred to as the *reserve price*, may be imposed. The reserve price can be either publicly announced or remain secret until a winner is declared. Even when the reserve price is secret, the winner may have to engage in subsequent negotiation with the seller; this often happens at used-car auctions.

Also, a minimum amount needed to raise a bid, often referred to as the *bid increment*, will typically exist; bid increments can be large or small. In fact, bid increments may change during the course of the auction. For example, at some fur auctions, the bid increment may start out at, say, $0.10 per unit, but then increase to, say, $0.25 when the price per unit exceeds some prespecified bound.

Depending on what is being sold, the bidding variable may be a lump-sum or, in the case of multi-unit auctions, a price for each unit purchased. At some auctions, the bidding variable is the fraction of the price that the winner gets when he resells the object. In such cases, the bidding variable is often referred to as the *royalty rate*.

Because auctions are used widely to buy and to sell goods and services, a plethora of other rules also exists, but many of these rules are often so specific to a particular environment that they do not really warrant extensive discussion. Ralph Cassady, Jr., in his classic book *Auctions and Auctioneering*, described a variety of unusual auction rules, beyond what we have just discussed.

Many important rules, beyond those concerning format, apply when there are multiple units of the same good or when there are many objects for sale. Typically, a distinction is made between multi-unit and multi-object auctions. At multi-unit auctions, the objects are assumed identical, so it matters not which unit a bidder wins but rather the aggregate number of units he wins, while at multi-object auctions the objects are assumed different, so a bidder is concerned about which specific object(s) he wins. An example of a multi-object auction would be the sale of an apple, an orange, and a pear, while an example of an multi-unit auction would involve the sale of three identical oranges. Because we initially investigate single-object auctions, and because multi-unit and multi-object auctions will be investigated later, we delay discussing additional rules until then.

2.2 Information Structure

While the formats and the rules of the auction are important in determining the extensive form of the game of incomplete information, the information structure is no less important. Who knows what and when, and how that information affects the payoffs of the potential bidders—the players of the game—is central to strategic behavior in the game.

2.2.1 Independent Private-Values Paradigm

A good portion of theoretical and econometric research concerning auctions has been undertaken within the independent private-values paradigm. In fact, in this book, for pedagogical reasons, we shall only study methods within this paradigm. Within the IPVP, auctions play an important allocational role, something we shall elaborate on later in detail. Within the other important competing informational paradigm, the common-value paradigm (CVP), which will be discussed briefly below, it is the distribution of information that is important.

Within the IPVP, each of the $\mathcal{N}$ potential bidders gets an independent and identically distributed draw from the distribution $F_V(v)$. As was mentioned in the introduction, a transformation of $F_V(v)$, the survivor function $S_V(v)$ which equals $[1 - F_V(v)]$, can be thought of as the proportion of the population that would demand the object were the price v charged. If there are $\mathcal{N}$ potential bidders, then the expected-demand curve is just $\mathcal{N}S_V(v)$. Note that, within this paradigm, prior to drawing their valuations, each potential bidder is the same. Economic theorists often refer to the potential bidders under this assumption as *symmetric*, at least *ex ante*. We shall only use this qualifier when we are trying to distinguish between this case and another, the *asymmetric* case, to be discussed later.

25

2.2.2 Common-Value Paradigm

The second most commonly investigated theoretical paradigm in auction theory is the common-value paradigm. This paradigm is often explained in terms of a real-world example, oil exploration. The anecdote typically told is the following: A number of different oil-exploration firms have seismic information concerning the likelihood of finding oil on a particular tract. Conditional on having found oil, however, the value of this oil is the same to all potential bidders. Bidders differ in their estimates of oil incidence, whether oil is there, as well as oil volume, how much oil is there, conditional on having found some.

Bidding environments in which the value of the object is the same to all potential bidders, having this *common-value* feature, are referred to as the CVP. Within the CVP, the sole explanation for heterogeneity in bids across auction participants is differences in opinions concerning the object's true value. In the oil example, the physical properties of the oil and its market value are unchanged by these opinions. Clearly, the CVP is quite different from the IPVP.

When economic theorists model within the CVP, each potential bidder is typically assumed to get a draw from an estimator X which, with some loss of generality, is assumed to be an unbiased estimator of the true value v, so

$$\mathcal{E}(X|v) = \int_{-\infty}^{\infty} x f_{X|V}(x|v) \ dx = v.$$

While potential bidders do not know v, they are assumed to have knowledge of V's distribution in the form of a *prior* probability density function $f_V(v)$ which is common knowledge among the potential bidders. Given an estimate x, which is a realization of X, a potential bidder is assumed to use Bayes' rule to find the *posterior* probability density function of V according to

$$f_{V|X}(v|x) = \frac{f_{XV}(x,v)}{f_X(x)} = \frac{f_{X|V}(x|v)f_V(v)}{f_X(x)} = \frac{f_{X|V}(x|v)f_V(v)}{\int_{-\infty}^{\infty} f_{X|V}(x|v)f_V(v) \ dv}.$$

Under these assumptions, at least two problems remain to be solved: First, how should potential bidders use the information in the posterior density function to form a bid? And, second, what is the equilibrium bidding strategy?

Note that, within the CVP paradigm, the auction really plays no important allocational role because each potential bidder has the same post-sale value. Thus, for example, in the case of oil, one could allocate the tract efficiently using an $\mathcal{N}$-sided fair die. One way to think of the object for sale is as a pie. The auction is simply one way to decide how the pie is divided between the buyer and the seller.

At the time the CVP was being developed, economic theorists, such as Robert B. Wilson, were extremely interested in knowing whether the distribution of information could have real effects in an economy. They also wanted to know whether, in environments where each agent possessed a little information, a market mechanism, like an auction, could aggregate all of this information. Wilson (1977) demonstrated that, as the number of bidders got large, the winning bid at a first-price, sealed-bid auction within the CVP converged almost surely to the true value. This is a very striking result. Later researchers, such as Pesendorfer and Swinkels (1997, 2000) as well as Hong and Shum (2004) have extended Wilson's research in richer bidding environments, treating auction formats as if they were statistical estimators of the unknown true value v and then comparing the asymptotic behavior of different formats.

2.2.3 Affiliated-Values Paradigm

Obviously, the CVP and the IPVP represent the polar extremes of information in auction models: The real world lies somewhere between the CVP and the IPVP. Milgrom and Weber (1982) constructed a more general informational paradigm, the affiliated-values paradigm (AVP), which has as special cases the CVP and IPVP. While the AVP is an exceptionally rich paradigm within which to conduct theoretical investigations, as Laffont and Vuong (1996) have demonstrated, models within this paradigm are often unidentified in the econometric sense. Thus, however attractive this paradigm may be theoretically, it is sometimes difficult to do empirical work within this paradigm. Athey and Haile (2002, 2005) have documented, in considerable detail, identification of models within this paradigm as well as others, too; they have also studied how additional information can be used to obtain identification. The interested reader is referred to their papers.

2.2.4 Asymmetries

Potential bidders at auctions within the IPVP typically have different valuations, different realizations of the random variable V, so obviously, ex post, they are asymmetric with respect to the intensities they demand the object for sale. When economists say auctions have *asymmetric bidders*, they typically mean that, *ex ante*, potential bidders get their draws from different distributions, different urns so to speak. To make

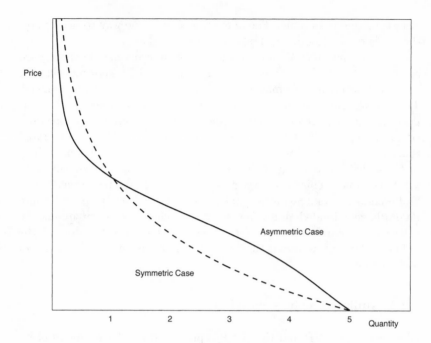

Figure 2.1
Aggregate Expected-Demand:
Symmetric and Asymmetric Cases

this formal, let us consider the IPVP where each potential bidder gets an independent draw, but now assume that bidder i draws his valuation from distribution $F_j(v)$ where $j = 1, \ldots J$. We shall introduce the function $\texttt{type}(i)$ which maps bidder i's identity into a particular class j of bidder. We shall collect the $\mathcal{N}$ cumulative distribution functions $[F_{\texttt{type}(1)}(v), F_{\texttt{type}(2)}(v), \ldots, F_{\texttt{type}(\mathcal{N})}(v)]^\top$ in the $\mathcal{N}$-vector $\boldsymbol{F}$.

Asymmetries will mean that the *aggregate* expected-demand curve of $\mathcal{N}$ bidders can have quite different shapes. Consider the dotted curve in figure 2.1, which represents the expected-demand function for $\mathcal{N}$ equal five symmetric bidders having valuations drawn from the same exponential distribution. On the other hand, the solid curve represents the expected-demand function for $\mathcal{N}$ of five asymmetric bidders where two are from the same exponential distribution, while three are from the same Weibull distribution. The symmetric IPVP can be thought of as a stochastic model of a representative agent, while the asymmetric IPVP can be thought of as a stochastic, multi-agent model.

2.3 Bidder Preferences

In the bulk of theoretical work concerning auctions, economic theorists have typically assumed that the potential bidders are risk-neutral with respect to winning the object for sale. For most of this book, we shall maintain the assumption of risk-neutral potential bidders too. Thus, within the IPVP, when a potential bidder has valuation v and chooses strategy s, the payoff to participating at the auction is

$$U = (v - s)\mathbf{1}(\text{strategy } s \text{ wins the auction}).$$

Risk neutrality is a strong assumption concerning preferences. In an effort to relax this assumption, economic theorists have investigated a richer preference structure known as *von Neumann–Morgenstern preferences*. Two parametric classes of von Neumann–Morgenstern preference functions have been typically applied. The first class of preferences exhibits *constant absolute risk aversion* (CARA). For a constant parameter α, these preferences take the form

$$U(Y) = 1 - \exp(-\alpha Y) \quad \alpha \geq 0$$

for some random prospect Y. Under CARA preferences, the Arrow–Pratt measure of absolute risk aversion is

$$-\frac{U''(Y)}{U'(Y)} = \alpha,$$

so the parameter α has a convenient interpretation. Under CARA preferences, the outcome of Y can occur anywhere on the real line. Unfortunately, CARA preferences do not easily nest the risk-neutral case via a parameter restriction.

Preferences of a second class take the following form:

$$U(Y) = \eta Y^{1/\eta} \quad Y \geq 0, \ \eta \geq 1$$

for some random prospect Y. These preferences are often referred to as *HARA preferences* because the the Arrow–Pratt measure of absolute risk aversion

$$-\frac{U''(Y)}{U'(Y)} = \frac{(\eta - 1)}{\eta Y}$$

is an hyperbola; in orther words, hyperbolic absolute risk aversion. HARA preferences are particularly useful in empirical models of auctions because when η equals one these preferences are linear, so the agents are risk neutral. Thus, HARA preferences nest risk neutrality by a simple parameter restriction. When η exceeds one, preferences are concave in Y, so agents are risk averse with respect to the prospect Y. HARA preferences are sometimes said to exhibit *constant relative risk aversion* because the Arrow–Pratt measure of relative risk aversion

$$-\frac{YU''(Y)}{U'(Y)} = \frac{(\eta - 1)}{\eta}$$

is a constant.

2.4 Purposeful Bidding and Game Equilibrium

Having specified the formats and the rules of the auction, the primitive information structure, and the preferences of potential bidders, we are now in a position to characterize the decision problem faced by a representative, purposeful bidder as well as to define an equilibrium to the game. Because Vickrey auction games are very easy to understand and to solve, we begin with them. Subsequently, because under certain assumptions English auctions are essentially identical to Vickrey auctions, we solve for the equilibrium under this format next. Finally, we solve for the equilibrium at Dutch and first-price, sealed-bid auctions.

2.4.1 Vickrey Auctions

We initially assume that no reserve price is imposed and that the potential bidders are risk-neutral. Under these assumptions, within the IPVP, the dominant-strategy, equilibrium-bid function at a Vickrey auction for bidder i who has valuation V_i is of the following form:

$$B_i = \beta(V_i) = V_i. \tag{2.1}$$

In words, it is a dominant strategy for the bidder to tell the truth, to reveal what the object is really worth to him. This result sometimes surprises lay people, but it is relatively straightforward to convince them that this really is the optimal equilibrium strategy. To see this, assume initially that a potential bidder were to bid less than his valuation. Given such a choice, the potential bidder would risk losing the object to another who bid higher than him, but who had a lower valuation. Moreover, bidding higher has no cost to bidder i because the bid of his nearest opponent determines the winning price, so bidding below V_i could not be optimal.

Of course, bidding more than V_i would increase the chance of winning, but potential bidder i would then risk paying more than the object is worth to him. This would happen were the bidder with the highest valuation to bid below potential bidder i. Since we have ruled out bids both above and below V_i, the only remaining possibility is to bid V_i. Because we have constructed this argument for a representative bidder i and because all potential bidders are *ex ante* symmetric, having valuations draws which are from the same distribution, equation (2.1) constitutes the symmetric, dominant-strategy, equilibrium-bid function at Vickrey auctions.

Obviously, the bidder with the highest valuation $V_{(1:\mathcal{N})}$ will win a Vickrey auction, but he will pay what his nearest opponent, the bidder having valuation $V_{(2:\mathcal{N})}$, was willing to pay. Hence, the winning bid W is the second order statistic from a sample of size $\mathcal{N}$.

2.4.2 English Auctions

While constructing the dominant-strategy equilibrium at the Vickrey auction is simple and the argument elegant, it is often difficult to convince a layperson that, within the IPVP, equation (2.1) constitutes the equilibrium at an English auction, at least for nonwinners. Many of the difficulties arise because reality gets in the way. A variety of different rules exists at oral, ascending-price auctions. At some auctions, the bidding behavior of participants is essentially secret or difficult to observe. At others, discrete bid increments are imposed. Milgrom and Weber (1982) constructed a theoretical model of an English auction often referred to as the *clock model*. This model is both simple and elegant. Moreover, when employed appropriately, it implies that equation (2.1) applies for all nonwinners at English auctions.

The mechanics of the Milgrom–Weber clock model are as follows: First, the clock is set initially at some minimum (reserve) price; in the absence of a reserve price let this be zero. Subsequently, the price is allowed to rise continuously. As the price rises, a bidder must decide whether to continue or to exit. When described in this fashion, it becomes clear what a potential bidder i, who is a nonwinner of the auction, should do: continue in the auction until the price reaches his valuation V_i. Thus, for nonwinners, equation (2.1) constitutes the equilibrium bidding strategy. When all but one of the bidders have dropped out, according to the Milgrom–Weber clock model, the auction ends.

What does this imply about the winning bid? For $\mathcal{N}$ potential bidders, having ordered valuations

$$V_{(\mathcal{N}:\mathcal{N})} < V_{(\mathcal{N}-1:\mathcal{N})} < \ldots < V_{(3:\mathcal{N})} < V_{(2:\mathcal{N})} < V_{(1:\mathcal{N})}$$

we know that the bidder having valuation $V_{(\mathcal{N}:\mathcal{N})}$ will drop out first, followed by the bidder having valuation $V_{(\mathcal{N}-1:\mathcal{N})}$. This will continue with the bidder having $V_{(3:\mathcal{N})}$ dropping out second to last and the bidder having $V_{(2:\mathcal{N})}$ dropping out last. Thus, when all but one of the bidders have dropped out, the remaining bidder is the winner and the price he pays is the last bid his last opponent was willing to pay, the second order statistic $V_{(2:\mathcal{N})}$. It is for this reason that English auctions are sometimes referred to as *second-price auctions*, at least by economists.

2.4.3 Dutch and First-Price, Sealed-Bid Auctions

How should a risk-neutral potential bidder behave at either a Dutch or a first-price, sealed-bid auction? Initially, assume that the seller imposes no reserve price. Now, the ith bidder has a valuation v_i for the object, which is known to him, but not to the $(\mathcal{N}-1)$ other potential bidders. Heterogeneity across bidders in valuations obtains from independent and identically distributed draws of the random variable V, which has cumulative distribution function $F_V(v)$ and which, for technical and practical reasons, is assumed to have support on the interval $[\underline{v}, \overline{v}]$ as well as a continuous probability density function $f_V(v)$ equal $dF_V(v)/dv$. The number of potential bidders $\mathcal{N}$ as well as the cumulative distribution function $F_V(v)$ are assumed common knowledge.

Under the above conditions, Dutch auctions and first-price, sealed-bid auctions are strategically equivalent. To see this, consider the decision problem faced by a bidder at a Dutch auction. At Dutch auctions, the price starts high and then falls continuously until someone stops it. Depending on the bidder's valuation for the object, he must decide at what point to stop the auction by signaling his willingness to pay the existing price. This situation is strategically identical to that faced by a bidder at a first-price, sealed-bid auction who must decide how high to bid for the object.

Since, before valuations are drawn, all potential bidders are symmetric, without loss of generality, we focus on the representative behavior of potential bidder 1 who has valuation v_1. Under risk neutrality, the expected profit to potential bidder 1 when s_1 is tendered is

$$(v_1 - s_1)\Pr(\text{win}|s_1).$$

But what is $\Pr(\text{win}|s_1)$? Well, bidder 1 wins when all of his opponents bid less than him, so

$$\Pr(\text{win}|s_1) = \Pr[(S_2 \leq s_1) \cap \ldots \cap (S_{\mathcal{N}} \leq s_1)].$$

Since bidders are independent, this can be written as

$$\text{Pr(win}|s_1) = \prod_{i=2}^{\mathcal{N}} \text{Pr}(S_i \leq s_1).$$

To analyze this case, we shall focus on symmetric, Bayes–Nash equilibria. To construct an equilibrium, suppose that the $(\mathcal{N} - 1)$ opponents of bidder 1 are using a common bidding rule $\hat{\sigma}(V)$, which is increasing and differentiable in V. The probability of bidder 1 winning with strategy s_1 equals the probability that every other opponent bids lower because each has a lower valuation

$$F_V\big[\hat{\sigma}^{-1}(s_1)\big]^{(\mathcal{N}-1)}.$$

Here, $\hat{\sigma}^{-1}(s_1)$ denotes the inverse of the bid function. Given that bidder 1's valuation v_1 is determined before the bidding, his choice of strategy s_1 has only two effects on his expected profit

$$(v_1 - s_1)F_V\big[\hat{\sigma}^{-1}(s_1)\big]^{(\mathcal{N}-1)}.$$

The higher is s_1, the higher is $F_V\big[\hat{\sigma}^{-1}(s_1)\big]^{(\mathcal{N}-1)}$, which is bidder 1's probability of winning the auction, but the lower is the payoff following a win $(v_1 - s_1)$. Maximizing behavior implies that the optimal bidding strategy solves the following necessary first-order condition:

$$-F_V\big[\hat{\sigma}^{-1}(s_1)\big]^{(\mathcal{N}-1)} +$$
$$(v_1 - s_1)(\mathcal{N} - 1)F_V\big[\hat{\sigma}^{-1}(s_1)\big]^{(\mathcal{N}-2)} f_V\big[\hat{\sigma}^{-1}(s_1)\big]\frac{d\hat{\sigma}^{-1}(s_1)}{ds_1} = 0. \qquad (2.2)$$

Symmetry among potential bidders implies

$$s_1 = \hat{\sigma}(v_1). \qquad (2.3)$$

Substituting equation (2.3) into equation (2.2) and recalling that, by monotonicity, $[d\hat{\sigma}^{-1}(s_1)/ds_1]$ equals $[1/\hat{\sigma}'(v_1)]$, and requiring equation (2.2) to hold for all feasible values of v_1, yields the following differential equation for $\hat{\sigma}$:

$$\hat{\sigma}'(v) + \frac{(\mathcal{N} - 1)f_V(v)}{F_V(v)}\hat{\sigma}(v) = \frac{(\mathcal{N} - 1)v f_V(v)}{F_V(v)}. \qquad (2.4)$$

Now, equation (2.4) is among the few differential equations that have closed-form solutions. Following Boyce and DiPrima (1977) and using a notation that will be familiar to students of calculus, we note that when differential equations are of the following form:

$$y' + p(x)y = q(x)$$

there exists a function $\mu(x)$ such that

$$\mu(x)[y' + p(x)y] = [\mu(x)y]'$$

$$= \mu(x)y' + \mu'(x)y.$$

Thus,

$$\mu(x)p(x)y = \mu'(x)y.$$

When μ is positive, as it will be in the auction case,

$$\frac{\mu'(x)}{\mu(x)} = p(x),$$

so

$$\log[\mu(x)] = \int^x p(u) \, du,$$

whence

$$\mu(x) = \exp\left[\int^x p(u) \, du\right].$$

Therefore,

$$\mu(x)y = \int^x \mu(u)q(u) \, du + c$$

for some constant c, or

$$y = \frac{1}{\mu}\left[\int^x \mu(u)q(u) \, du + c\right]$$

where c is chosen to satisfy a boundary condition $y(x_0)$ equals y_0.

Solving equation (2.4) when, in the absence of a reserve price, we impose the boundary condition $\sigma(\underline{v})$ equals $\underline{v}$, yields the unique solution

$$\sigma(v) = v - \frac{\int_{\underline{v}}^v F_V(u)^{(\mathcal{N}-1)} \, du}{F_V(v)^{(\mathcal{N}-1)}}. \tag{2.5}$$

Note that $\sigma(v)$ depends on v and $\mathcal{N}$ as well as $F_V(\cdot)$. The winner at Dutch and first-price, sealed-bid auctions will be the bidder with the highest valuation $v_{(1:\mathcal{N})}$, but what is the relationship between the opportunity cost $v_{(2:\mathcal{N})}$, its value in its next best use, and the winning price $\sigma[v_{(1:\mathcal{N})}]$? Under the conditions assumed here, we can provide an answer and do so below. Note, however, that the agent submits a bid that is less than his valuation; he is deceptive.

As mentioned earlier, unlike at English and Vickrey auctions, where it remains a dominant strategy to bids one's valuation, at Dutch and first-price, sealed-bid auctions the attitudes of potential bidders toward the risk of losing the auction matter. Typically, it is difficult to construct models in which risk aversion of the von Neumann–Morgenstern kind can be incorporated and which have closed-form solutions. However, if one constrains oneself to HARA preferences

$$U(Y) = \eta Y^{1/\eta} \quad \eta \geq 1, \ Y \geq 0,$$

then the Bayes–Nash, equilibrium-bid function is

$$\sigma(v; \eta, \mathcal{N}) = v - \frac{\int_{\underline{v}}^{v} F_V(u)^{\eta(\mathcal{N}-1)} \, du}{F_V(v)^{\eta(\mathcal{N}-1)}}. \tag{2.6}$$

In fact, demonstrating that equation (2.6) constitutes a Bayes–Nash equilibrium to the auction game is left as a practice problem. Note that under symmetric HARA preferences bidders behave as if they were competing against more opponents than in the risk-neutral case.

2.5 A Binding Reserve Price

As was mentioned earlier in the chapter, most auctions have a minimum price that must be bid, a reserve price. How does the presence of a binding reserve price r change optimal equilibrium bidding? At Vickrey auctions, the equilibrium-bid function is now

$$B_i = \beta(V_i) = V_i \quad \text{if} \quad r \leq V_i,$$

while at English auctions, the equilibrium-bid function for nonwinners is the same. In words, participants at Vickrey and English auctions will bid no more than their valuation. When the reserve price exceeds the valuations of potential bidders, we assume that they then do not attend the auction, that they do not participate. When a binding reserve price exists, the number of participants at an auction, which we shall denote by N, and the number of potential bidders $\mathcal{N}$ can differ.

What is the relationship between N and $\mathcal{N}$? To investigate this, introduce the following Bernoulli random variable for potential bidder i:

$$I_i = \begin{cases} 1 & \text{if } V_i \geq r, \\ 0 & \text{otherwise}; \end{cases}$$

35

where $\Pr(I_i = 1)$ equals $\Pr(V_i \geq r)$ or $[1 - F_V(r)]$. Now, the number of participants, the sum of the Bernoulli sequence $\{I_i\}_{i=1}^{\mathcal{N}}$,

$$N = \sum_{i=1}^{\mathcal{N}} I_i$$

has a binomial distribution, with parameters $\mathcal{N}$ and $[1 - F_V(r)]$, so its probability mass function is

$$f_N(n) = \binom{\mathcal{N}}{n} F_V(r)^{\mathcal{N}-n} [1 - F_V(r)]^n \quad n = 0, 1, \ldots, \mathcal{N}.$$

In the presence of a binding reserve price, an econometrician would say that the number of participants is *endogenous*; the importance of the endogeneity will depend on both r and $\mathcal{N}$ as well as the shape of $F_V(v)$. Note, however, that at English auctions, one can reasonably assume participants know the number of opponents they face. Moreover, in the presence of a binding reserve price, it is quite possible that only one potential bidder will actually attend the auction. In this circumstance, the solo participant would obviously not bid against himself, so his optimal strategy, under the clock model, would be to drop out immediately and to win the object at the reserve price. Thus, behavior at English auctions depends on observed competition.

A binding reserve price has no effect on the decision problem solved by potential bidders at first-price, sealed-bid auctions since it is reasonable to assume that these potential bidders are unaware of the actual number of bidders, the number of participants. Thus, in this situation, a binding reserve price only changes the boundary condition for the solution to (2.4), so instead of having the boundary condition $\sigma(\underline{v})$ equal $\underline{v}$, one now has $\sigma(r)$ equal r. The equilibrium-bid function is then

$$\sigma(v) = v - \frac{\int_r^v F_V(u)^{\mathcal{N}-1} \, du}{F_V(v)^{\mathcal{N}-1}} \quad r \leq v.$$

Note that, in addition to depending on v and $\mathcal{N}$ as well as $F_V(\cdot)$, $\sigma(v)$ now also depends on r.

It is important to note that, when the number of participants is endogenous, Dutch and first-price, sealed-bid auctions are no longer strategically equivalent because, like at English auctions, the participants at Dutch auction can surely observe the number of opponents they face. Obviously, if a participant shows up at a Dutch auction and the room is empty, then he will behave differently from when he faces one (or more) other participants.

It might also seem plausible that a binding reserve price will change the decision problem solved by bidders attending a Dutch auction because the shape of the right tail of the valuation distribution $F_V(v)$ above r could be important. To see that this, in fact, is not true within the IPVP, define

$$G_V(v) = \frac{F_V(v)}{[1 - F_V(r)]} \quad r \leq v.$$

When n is the realized number of participants at a Dutch auction, substitute $G_V(v)$ and $g_V(v)$ into an equilibrium first-order condition similar to equation (2.4) above. The Bayes–Nash, equilibrium-bid function under risk neutrality is then

$$
\begin{aligned}
\sigma(v) &= v - \frac{\int_r^v G_V(u)^{n-1}\, du}{G_V(v)^{n-1}} \\
&= v - \frac{\int_r^v \left\{ \frac{F_V(u)}{[1-F_V(r)]} \right\}^{n-1} du}{\left\{ \frac{F_V(v)}{[1-F_V(r)]} \right\}^{n-1}} \\
&= v - \frac{\int_r^v F_V(u)^{n-1}\, du}{F_V(v)^{n-1}} \quad r \leq v.
\end{aligned}
$$

Note, this bid function is similar in structure to that at a first-price, sealed-bid auction, except that n replaces $\mathcal{N}$.

2.6 Expected Revenues and Optimal Auctions

Having derived the dominant-strategy and Bayes–Nash equilibrium-bid functions for the four common auction formats, assuming risk-neutral as well as risk-averse potential bidders, with and without a reserve price, it is of considerable interest to know which format garners the most revenue for the seller. Because the valuations of the bidders are random variables, one can only answer this question in expectation, but to many laypeople the answer is a surprise. Another question of some interest concerns the optimal structure of an auction. In this section, we discuss each of these in turn.

2.6.1 Revenue Equivalence Proposition

Within the IPVP assuming risk-neutral potential bidders, the four common auction formats all generate the same average revenue for the seller. This result, which is known as the *revenue equivalence proposition* (REP), was first demonstrated by Vickrey (1961) in an example with values drawn from the uniform distribution. In addition to the REP, one can also show that the allocations which obtain under each of the four common formats are *efficient*: the potential bidder with the highest valuation wins the object at auction. Of course, the presence of a binding reserve price means that the object could go unsold, which could imply an inefficient allocation.

The general proof of the REP is due to Riley and Samuelson (1981). Within the symmetric IPVP, where potential risk-neutral bidders participate at auctions when their valuations exceed the reserve price, Riley and Samuelson showed that all auction formats at which the highest bidder wins the auction yield the same expected revenue to the seller. Moreover, the equilibrium-bid functions within this environment are strictly increasing, symmetric functions. Riley and Samuelson also showed that the expected revenue at all auctions with these properties must equal

$$\mathcal{N} \int_r^{\bar{v}} \left[u f_V \left(u \right) + F_V \left(u \right) - 1 \right] F_V \left(u \right)^{\mathcal{N}-1} \, du. \tag{2.7}$$

One can derive this result in a very intuitive way. Given the symmetry assumption (viz., that before the valuations are drawn each potential bidder is the same), one can simplify notation, without any loss of generality, by focusing on the behavior of bidder 1. Given a bid strategy $\mathsf{bid}\left(\cdot\right)$, choosing a bid is equivalent to choosing a level of the private value x to report. Formally, this is the *revelation principle*.[1] Intuitively, the auctioneer can calculate the bid function $\mathsf{bid}\left(\cdot\right)$ and calculate a bid for bidder 1 when he reports his private value to be x. The expected gain to bidder 1 can be written as

$$\Pi\left(x, v_1\right) = v_1 \times \Pr\left(\mathsf{winning}\right) - \mathsf{Expected\ Payment}.$$

Under the risk-neutrality assumption, one can separate the probability of winning from the expected payment because the utility to bidder 1 is linear in the monetary payoffs. Note that the payment by bidder 1 can be a general function of the bids submitted by all bidders. Suppose

---

[1] Myerson (1991, p. 260) explained the revelation principle in Bayesian equilibrium as follows:

> There is no loss in generality in assuming that players communicate with each other through a mediator who first asks each player to reveal all of his private information and who then reveals to each player only the minimum information needed to guide his action, in such a way that no player has any incentive to lie or disobey.

all bidders other than bidder 1 follow the bidding strategy bid $(\cdot)$, and bidder 1 decides to report x, which means he tenders bid (x), then the payment Payment$(\cdots)$ by bidder 1 will be a function of x as well as $(v_2, \ldots, v_{\mathcal{N}})$; viz.,

$$\text{Payment}\left[\text{bid}\left(x\right), \text{bid}\left(v_2\right), \ldots, \text{bid}\left(v_{\mathcal{N}}\right)\right].$$

However, bidder 1 does not know $(v_2, \ldots, v_{\mathcal{N}})$, so he must take the expectation over them using the joint cumulative distribution function of $(V_2, \ldots, V_{\mathcal{N}})$. Bidder 1's expected payment is then

$$P\left(x\right) = \mathcal{E}\left\{\text{Payment}\left[\text{bid}\left(x\right), \text{bid}\left(V_2\right), \ldots, \text{bid}\left(V_{\mathcal{N}}\right)\right]\right\}.$$

Bidder 1 wins if and only if bid (x) exceeds bid (v_j) for all j other than 1; i.e., provided x exceeds v_j. Therefore, the probability of winning when bidder 1 reports his value to be x is

$$\Pr\left(v_j < x, j \neq 1\right) = F_V\left(x\right)^{\mathcal{N}-1},$$

so bidder 1's expected profit is

$$\Pi\left(x, v_1\right) = v_1 F_V\left(x\right)^{\mathcal{N}-1} - P\left(x\right).$$

Under truth-telling, the first-order condition for bidder 1's expected-profit maximization problem is

$$\frac{\partial \Pi\left(x^*, v_1\right)}{\partial x} = v_1\left(\mathcal{N}-1\right) F_V\left(x^*\right)^{\mathcal{N}-2} f_V\left(x^*\right) - P'\left(x^*\right) = 0,$$

only when x^* equals v_1. In words, it is optimal in equilibrium for bidder 1 to report his true valuation v_1, whence

$$P'\left(v_1\right) = v_1\left(\mathcal{N}-1\right) F_V\left(v_1\right)^{\mathcal{N}-2} f_V\left(v_1\right).$$

Since a bidder having a valuation equal to the reserve price r should expect to pay

$$P\left(r\right) = r F_V\left(r\right)^{\mathcal{N}-1},$$

from bidder 1's perspective, the expected payment is then

$$P\left(v_1\right) = r F_V(r)^{\mathcal{N}-1} + \int_r^{v_1} P'(u) \, du$$

$$= r F_V(r)^{\mathcal{N}-1} + \int_r^{v_1} u \, dF_V(u)^{\mathcal{N}-1}$$

$$= v_1 F_V\left(v_1\right) - \int_r^{v_1} F_V(u)^{\mathcal{N}-1} \, du.$$

What bidder 1 expects to pay is what the seller expects to receive. Since there are $\mathcal{N}$ bidders, the expected revenue to the seller is $\mathcal{N}$ times the expectation of this amount

$$\mathcal{N} \int_r^{\bar{v}} P(u) \, dF_V(u)$$
$$= \mathcal{N} \int_r^{\bar{v}} \left[u F_V(u)^{\mathcal{N}-1} - \int_r^u F_V(v)^{\mathcal{N}-1} \, dv \right] \, dF_V(u).$$

Integration by parts yields equation (2.7) above.

Note that in establishing the expected payments only direct mechanisms have been considered. Hence, the result does not depend on the actual auction format and, therefore, proves revenue equivalence.

What is the interpretation of the winning bid? Assuming the reserve price r is zero, Krishna (2002) has given a simplified proof that one can interpret the winning bid in terms of the good's opportunity cost. Let

$$Z = \max_{j \neq 1} (V_j)$$

where

$$F_Z(z) = F_V(z)^{\mathcal{N}-1}.$$

In words, Z is the maximum of the private values for bidder 1's competitors, and $F_Z(z)$ is its cumulative distribution function. We shall also use $f_Z(z)$ to denote its corresponding probability density function. With this notation, bidder 1's expected profit can be written as

$$\Pi(x, v_1) = v_1 F_Z(x) - P(x).$$

The optimality condition for bidder 1 is then

$$\frac{\partial \Pi(x^*, v_1)}{\partial x} = v_1 f_Z(x^*) - P'(x^*) = 0$$

when x^* equals v_1. Hence,

$$P'(z) = f_Z(z) z,$$

for all z greater than zero and

$$P(v_1) = \int_0^{v_1} z f_Z(z) \, dz = \mathcal{E}(Z|Z < v_1) F_Z(v_1).$$

The expected payment of a bidder is the seller's expected revenue from this bidder. Because there are $\mathcal{N}$ bidders, the seller's expected revenue is then

$$\mathcal{N} \int_0^{\bar{v}} P(u) \, dF_V(u) = \mathcal{N} \int_0^{\bar{v}} \mathcal{E}(Z|Z < u) F_Z(u) \, du.$$

40

One can verify that this expression is equivalent to

$$\mathcal{E}\left[V_{(2:\mathcal{N})}\right],$$

the expected value of the second order statistic of valuations from a sample of size $\mathcal{N}$. Within this model, this is simply the expected value of the opportunity cost of the object at auction. It is the expected value of the object in its next best use. Thus, the expected revenue at these auctions is simply the expected opportunity cost.

2.6.2 Optimal Reserve Price

Some have interpreted the REP to imply that a risk-neutral seller should be indifferent among the four common formats. Of course, what a seller would really like to know is whether he can improve on the four common formats. To wit, what is the structure of the optimal selling mechanism?

Since all increasing bid functions that allocate the object to the participant with the highest bid yield the same expected revenue, the only remaining variable that a seller can manipulate is the reserve price. What is the optimal reserve price ρ^*? Note that the utility to the seller is the sum of the expected revenue and the expected utility of retaining the object for sale. The total utility for the seller is

$$v_0 F_V\left(r\right)^{\mathcal{N}} + \mathcal{N}\int_r^{\bar{v}}\left[uf_V\left(u\right) + F_V\left(u\right) - 1\right]F_V\left(u\right)^{\mathcal{N}-1}\,du.$$

Differentiating this with respect to the reserve price r gives the following first-order condition that should hold when r equals ρ^*:

$$\mathcal{N}v_0 F_V\left(r\right)^{\mathcal{N}-1}f_V\left(r\right) - \mathcal{N}\left[rf_V\left(r\right) + F_V\left(r\right) - 1\right]F_V\left(r\right)^{\mathcal{N}-1} = 0.$$

Factoring out the common terms $\mathcal{N}$, $F_V\left(r\right)^{\mathcal{N}-1}$, this becomes

$$v_0 f_V\left(r\right) - rf_V\left(r\right) - F_V\left(r\right) + 1 = 0.$$

Therefore, within the symmetric IPVP, the optimal selling mechanism requires that the optimally-chosen reserve price ρ^* solves the following equation:

$$\rho^* = v_0 + \frac{\left[1 - F_V(\rho^*)\right]}{f_V(\rho^*)} \tag{2.8}$$

where v_0 is the seller's valuation of the object at auction.[2]

---

[2] For those readers familiar with duration analysis, the term

$$\frac{\left[1 - F_V(\rho^*)\right]}{f_V(\rho^*)} = \frac{S_V(\rho^*)}{f_V(\rho^*)} = \frac{1}{h_V(\rho^*)},$$

is the inverse of the hazard-rate function $h_V(v)$ evaluated at ρ^*.

2.6.3 Expected Revenues under Risk Aversion

The REP does not hold when potential bidders are risk averse. In fact, under risk aversion, Riley and Samuelson (1981) have shown that the expected revenues at Dutch and first-price, sealed-bid auctions exceed those at English and Vickrey auctions. In the following, we shall demonstrate this result using $\hat{\sigma}(\cdot)$ to denote the bid function at Dutch and first-price, sealed-bid auctions with risk-neutral potential bidders and $\tilde{\sigma}(\cdot)$ to denote the bid function when potential bidders are risk averse.

Given a von Neumann–Morgenstern utility function $U(\cdot)$, the decision problem faced by bidder 1 under risk aversion is to report an x to maximize

$$U\left[v_1 - \tilde{\sigma}(x)\right] F_V(x)^{\mathcal{N}-1}.$$

The necessary first-order condition corresponding to this decision problem is

$$-U'\left[v_1 - \tilde{\sigma}(x^*)\right]\tilde{\sigma}'(x^*) F_V(x^*)^{\mathcal{N}-1} +$$

$$U\left[v_1 - \tilde{\sigma}(x^*)\right](\mathcal{N}-1)F_V(x^*)^{\mathcal{N}-2} f_V(x^*) = 0.$$

Equilibrium behavior requires that x^* equal v_1. This can then be written as

$$\tilde{\sigma}'(v_1) = \frac{U\left[v_1 - \tilde{\sigma}(v_1)\right]}{U'\left[v - \tilde{\sigma}(v_1)\right]} \frac{(\mathcal{N}-1)f_V(v_1)}{F_V(v_1)}.$$

With risk neutrality, where $U(Y)$ equals Y and $U'(Y)$ is one, the corresponding first-order condition for the bid function is:

$$\hat{\sigma}'(v_1) = \left[v_1 - \hat{\sigma}(v_1)\right]\frac{(\mathcal{N}-1)f_V(v_1)}{F_V(v_1)}.$$

When $U(\cdot)$ is strictly concave, because $U(0)$ can be normalized to zero without loss of generality, it is clear that, for Y exceeding zero,

$$\frac{U(Y)}{U'(Y)} > Y.$$

Now, when $\tilde{\sigma}(v_1)$ weakly exceeds $\hat{\sigma}(v_1)$ for some v_1, we have the following:

$$\tilde{\sigma}'(v_1) \geq \left[v_1 - \hat{\sigma}(v_1)\right]\frac{(\mathcal{N}-1)f_V(v_1)}{F_V(v_1)} = \hat{\sigma}'(v_1).$$

This implies that $\tilde{\sigma}(v_1')$ weakly exceeds $\hat{\sigma}(v_1')$ for all v_1' which weakly exceed v_1. Now, at the boundary where $\underline{v}$ is assumed to be zero, $\hat{\sigma}(0)$ and $\tilde{\sigma}(0)$ both equal zero, so it follows that

$$\tilde{\sigma}(v_1) \geq \hat{\sigma}(v_1)$$

for all positive v_1. In words, at Dutch and first-price, sealed-bid auctions, participants bid more aggressively when they are risk-averse than when they are risk-neutral. Since the expected revenues are identical at both first-price and second-price auctions under risk neutrality, when bidders are risk averse, expected revenues will be higher at first-price auctions than at second-price auctions.

2.6.4 Optimal Auctions

Myerson (1981) constructed the optimal selling mechanism under a more general set of assumptions than Riley and Samuelson (1981); he also showed that the four common auction formats are optimal for the seller in regular cases when a set of *virtual evaluation functions* are strictly increasing in the private types.

Myerson assumed that each of the $i = 1, \ldots, \mathcal{N}$ potential bidders has private information in the form of a type T_i, where the types are assumed independent of one another. Denote the probability density function of T_i by

$$f_i(t_i) \quad t_i \in [\underline{t}_i, \bar{t}_i].$$

Let $\boldsymbol{S} = \times_{i=1}^{\mathcal{N}} [\underline{t}_i, \bar{t}_i]$ denote the set of strategies for all bidders and $\boldsymbol{S}_{-i}$ denote the set of strategies for all bidders except i. Now, we denote the joint probability density functions of all types and all types excluding bidder i by

$$f_{\boldsymbol{T}}(\boldsymbol{t}) = \prod_{i=1}^{\mathcal{N}} f_i(t_i), \quad \text{and} \quad f_{-i}(\boldsymbol{t}_{-i}) = \prod_{j \neq i} f_j(t_j).$$

Denote the seller's type by t_0. Given all of the type information, Myerson assumed that the valuation of bidder i takes the following form:

$$v_i(\boldsymbol{t}) = t_i + \sum_{j \neq i} e_j(t_j),$$

where $e_i(t_i)$ for $i = 1, \ldots, \mathcal{N}$ is a set of *revision-effect functions*. The revision effects of any bidder on all other bidders and the seller are identical. Therefore, the valuations of bidders are correlated, but the information they possess concerning their own private types is independent of one another. This may seem an odd assumption because, if the valuations of bidders are correlated, then their signals, or private types, might reasonably be correlated. Myerson assumed that the seller's valuation, as a function of all bidder types as well as his own t_0, is of the following form:

$$v_0(t_0, \boldsymbol{t}) = t_0 + \sum_{i=1}^{\mathcal{N}} e_i(t_i).$$

A selling mechanism is a pair of outcome-function vectors $(\boldsymbol{p}, \boldsymbol{s})$ where $\boldsymbol{p}: \boldsymbol{\mathcal{S}} \to \boldsymbol{R}^{\mathcal{N}}$ and $\boldsymbol{s}: \boldsymbol{\mathcal{S}} \to \boldsymbol{R}^{\mathcal{N}}$. $p_i(\boldsymbol{t})$ is the probability that bidder i wins the object, while $s_i(\boldsymbol{t})$ is the payment by bidder i to the seller. The seller as well as all of the bidders are assumed risk neutral and only direct-revelation mechanisms are considered.[3]

The seller seeks to maximize his expected payoff

$$U_0(\boldsymbol{p}, \boldsymbol{s}) = \int_{\boldsymbol{\mathcal{S}}} \left\{ v_0(t_0, \boldsymbol{t}) \left[1 - \sum_{i=1}^{\mathcal{N}} p_i(\boldsymbol{t}) \right] + \sum_{i=1}^{\mathcal{N}} s_i(\boldsymbol{t}) \right\} f_{\boldsymbol{T}}(\boldsymbol{t}) \ d\boldsymbol{t}.$$

The expected payoff of bidder i, when he reports the truth, is

$$U_i(\boldsymbol{p}, \boldsymbol{s}, t_i) = \int_{\boldsymbol{\mathcal{S}}_{-i}} [v_i(\boldsymbol{t}) p_i(\boldsymbol{t}) - s_i(\boldsymbol{t})] f_{-i}(\boldsymbol{t}_{-i}) \ d\boldsymbol{t}_{-i}.$$

The seller seeks to maximize $U_0(\boldsymbol{p}, \boldsymbol{s})$ subject to two constraints: First, a participation constraint, a bidder must want to bid; and, second, an incentive-compatibility (or truth-telling) constraint, a bidder must want to reveal his type.

The participation constraint requires that, for all t_i,

$$U_i(\boldsymbol{p}, \boldsymbol{s}, t_i) \geq 0.$$

As we shall see, $U_i(\boldsymbol{p}, \boldsymbol{s}, t_i)$ is increasing in t_i, so this is equivalent to requiring that for all i

$$U_i(\boldsymbol{p}, \boldsymbol{s}, \underline{t}_i) \geq 0.$$

Incentive-compatibility, truth-telling, requires that, for all x_i not equal to t_i,

$$U_i(\boldsymbol{p}, \boldsymbol{s}, t_i) \geq \int_{\boldsymbol{\mathcal{S}}_{-i}} [v_i(\boldsymbol{t}) p_i(\boldsymbol{t}_{-i}, x_i) - s_i(\boldsymbol{t}_{-i}, x_i)] f_{-i}(\boldsymbol{t}_{-i}) \ d\boldsymbol{t}_{-i}.$$

Note that this condition involves a continuum of inequality constraints, one for each $x_i \in [\underline{t}_i, \bar{t}_i]$. One can deal with this using the so-called *first-order approach*. For this purpose, define

$$\bar{U}_i(\boldsymbol{p}, \boldsymbol{s}, t_i, x_i) =$$

$$\int_{\boldsymbol{\mathcal{S}}_{-i}} [v_i(\boldsymbol{t}) p_i(\boldsymbol{t}_{-i}, x_i) - s_i(\boldsymbol{t}_{-i}, x_i)] f_{-i}(\boldsymbol{t}_{-i}) \ d\boldsymbol{t}_{-i} =$$

$$\int_{\boldsymbol{\mathcal{S}}_{-i}} [v_i(\boldsymbol{t}_{-i}, t_i) p_i(\boldsymbol{t}_{-i}, x_i) - s_i(\boldsymbol{t}_{-i}, x_i)] f_{-i}(\boldsymbol{t}_{-i}) \ d\boldsymbol{t}_{-i}.$$

---

[3] Direct-revelation mechanisms are ones where the seller asks bidders to reveal their types truthfully. Under the revelation principle, one can consider direct-revelation mechanisms without loss of generality.

This is the payoff that i receives if he is of type t_i and reports type x_i. Clearly, when x_i equals t_i, this expression is going to yield the payoff for i under an incentive-compatible mechanism; i.e.,

$$U_i\left(\boldsymbol{p}, \boldsymbol{s}, t_i\right) = \bar{U}_i\left(\boldsymbol{p}, \boldsymbol{s}, t_i, t_i\right).$$

Incentive-compatibility requires that $\bar{U}\left(\boldsymbol{p}, \boldsymbol{s}, t_i, x_i\right)$ as a function of x_i be maximized where x_i equals t_i.

Applying the envelope theorem, we have

$$\frac{d}{dt_i} U_i\left(\boldsymbol{p}, \boldsymbol{s}, t_i\right) = \left.\frac{\partial}{\partial t_i} \bar{U}_i\left(\boldsymbol{p}, \boldsymbol{s}, t_i, x_i\right)\right|_{x_i = t_i}$$

$$= \int_{\boldsymbol{\mathcal{S}}_{-i}} p_i\left(\boldsymbol{t}\right) f_{-i}\left(\boldsymbol{t}_{-i}\right) \, d\boldsymbol{t}_{-i} \equiv Q_i\left(\boldsymbol{p}, t_i\right).$$

Now, we can write the payoff of i in an incentive-compatible mechanism as follows:

$$U_i\left(\boldsymbol{p}, \boldsymbol{s}, t_i\right) = U_i\left(\boldsymbol{p}, \boldsymbol{s}, \underline{t}_i\right) + \int_{\underline{t}_i}^{t_i} Q_i\left(\boldsymbol{p}, x_i\right) \, dx_i.$$

In the expression above, $U_i(\boldsymbol{p}, \boldsymbol{s}, \underline{t}_i)$ represents the expected payoff of the lowest-type of bidder i that is possible, while $Q_i(\boldsymbol{p}, t_i)$ represents the *marginal information rent* that needs to be paid to the higher types to induce them to reveal their types. We can rewrite the seller's payoff as follows:

$$U_0\left(\boldsymbol{p}, \boldsymbol{s}\right) = \int_{\boldsymbol{\mathcal{S}}} v_0\left(t_0, \boldsymbol{t}\right) f_{\boldsymbol{T}}\left(\boldsymbol{t}\right) \, d\boldsymbol{t} +$$

$$\sum_{i=1}^{\mathcal{N}} \int_{\boldsymbol{\mathcal{S}}} p_i\left(\boldsymbol{t}\right) \left[v_i\left(\boldsymbol{t}\right) - v_0\left(t_0, \boldsymbol{t}\right)\right] f_{\boldsymbol{T}}\left(\boldsymbol{t}\right) \, d\boldsymbol{t} +$$

$$\sum_{i=1}^{\mathcal{N}} \int_{\boldsymbol{\mathcal{S}}} \left[s_i\left(\boldsymbol{t}\right) - p_i\left(\boldsymbol{t}\right) v_i\left(\boldsymbol{t}\right)\right] f_{\boldsymbol{T}}\left(\boldsymbol{t}\right) \, d\boldsymbol{t}.$$

Note that the last term is the negative of the sum of expected payoffs for all bidders and can be written as

$$-\sum_{i=1}^{\mathcal{N}} \int_{\underline{t}_i}^{\bar{t}_i} U_i\left(\boldsymbol{p}, \boldsymbol{s}, t_i\right) f_i\left(t_i\right) \, dt_i =$$

$$-\sum_{i=1}^{\mathcal{N}} \int_{\underline{t}_i}^{\bar{t}_i} \left[U_i\left(\boldsymbol{p}, \boldsymbol{s}, \underline{t}_i\right) + \int_{\underline{t}_i}^{t_i} Q_i\left(\boldsymbol{p}, x_i\right) \, dx_i\right] f_i\left(t_i\right) \, dt_i.$$

Rewriting the above and performing integration by parts yields

$$= -\sum_{i=1}^{\mathcal{N}} U_i\left(\boldsymbol{p},\boldsymbol{s},\underline{t_i}\right) - \int_{\underline{t_i}}^{\bar{t_i}} \int_{\underline{t_i}}^{t_i} Q_i\left(\boldsymbol{p},x_i\right)\ dx_i\ f_i\left(t_i\right)\ dt_i$$

$$= \sum_{i=1}^{\mathcal{N}} \left\{ -U_i\left(\boldsymbol{p},\boldsymbol{s},\underline{t_i}\right) - \int_{\underline{t_i}}^{\bar{t_i}} \left[1 - F_i\left(t_i\right)\right] Q_i\left(\boldsymbol{p},t_i\right)\ dt_i \right\}$$

$$= \sum_{i=1}^{\mathcal{N}} \left\{ -U_i\left(\boldsymbol{p},x,\underline{t_i}\right) - \int_{\boldsymbol{S}} \frac{\left[1 - F_i\left(t_i\right)\right]}{f_i\left(t_i\right)} p_i\left(\boldsymbol{t}\right) f_{\boldsymbol{T}}\left(\boldsymbol{t}\right)\ d\boldsymbol{t} \right\}.$$

Note too that
$$v_i\left(\boldsymbol{t}\right) - v_0\left(t_0,\boldsymbol{t}\right) = t_i - t_0 - e_i\left(t_i\right).$$

Therefore, the seller's expected payoff can be written as follows:

$$U_0\left(\boldsymbol{p},\boldsymbol{s}\right) = \int_{\boldsymbol{S}} v_0\left(t_0,\boldsymbol{t}\right) f_{\boldsymbol{T}}\left(\boldsymbol{t}\right)\ d\boldsymbol{t} +$$

$$\sum_{i=1}^{\mathcal{N}} \int_{\boldsymbol{S}} \left\{ t_i - t_0 - e_i\left(t_i\right) - \frac{\left[1 - F_i\left(t_i\right)\right]}{f_i\left(t_i\right)} \right\} p_i\left(\boldsymbol{t}\right) f_{\boldsymbol{T}}\left(\boldsymbol{t}\right)\ d\boldsymbol{t}$$

$$-\sum_{i=1}^{\mathcal{N}} U_i\left(\boldsymbol{p},\boldsymbol{s},\underline{t_i}\right).$$

Clearly, given any $\boldsymbol{p}$, the optimal choice of $\boldsymbol{s}$ for the seller requires

$$\sum_{i=1}^{\mathcal{N}} U_i\left(\boldsymbol{p},\boldsymbol{s},\underline{t_i}\right) = 0,$$

for all i. To wit, the lowest type of bidder i possible should receive zero rent. Moreover, this can be achieved by the choice of $s(\cdot)$. To see this, note that

$$U_i\left(\boldsymbol{p},\boldsymbol{s},\underline{t_i}\right) = U_i\left(\boldsymbol{p},\boldsymbol{s},t_i\right) - \int_{\underline{t_i}}^{t_i} Q_i\left(\boldsymbol{p},x_i\right)\ dx_i$$

$$= \int_{\boldsymbol{S}_{-i}} p_i\left(\boldsymbol{t}\right) v_i\left(\boldsymbol{t}\right) f_{-i}\left(\boldsymbol{t}_{-i}\right)\ d\boldsymbol{t}_{-i} -$$

$$\int_{\boldsymbol{S}_{-i}} \left\{ \left[\int_{\underline{t_i}}^{t_i} p_i\left(\boldsymbol{t}_{-i},x_i\right)\ dx_i \right] - s_i\left(\boldsymbol{t}\right) \right\} f_{-i}\left(\boldsymbol{t}_{-i}\right)\ d\boldsymbol{t}_{-i}.$$

Therefore, given $\boldsymbol{p}$, $\boldsymbol{s}$ can be chosen by

$$s_i\left(\boldsymbol{t}\right) = p_i\left(\boldsymbol{t}\right) v_i\left(\boldsymbol{t}\right) - \int_{\underline{t_i}}^{t_i} p_i\left(\boldsymbol{t}_{-i},x_i\right)\ dx_i,$$

so that $U_i\left(\boldsymbol{p}, \boldsymbol{s}, \underline{t_i}\right)$ equals zero for all i, the seller's optimal choice of $\boldsymbol{p}$ then reduces to choosing $\boldsymbol{p}$ to maximize

$$\int_{\mathcal{S}} \sum_{i=1}^{\mathcal{N}} \left\{ t_i - t_0 - e_i\left(t_i\right) - \frac{\left[1 - F_i\left(t_i\right)\right]}{f_i\left(t_i\right)} \right\} p_i\left(\boldsymbol{t}\right) f_{\boldsymbol{T}}\left(\boldsymbol{t}\right) \; d\boldsymbol{t}.$$

Myerson defined the *regular case* to be when

$$t_i - t_0 - e_i\left(t_i\right) - \frac{\left[1 - F_i\left(t_i\right)\right]}{f_i\left(t_i\right)}$$

is an increasing function of t_i. In the regular case, the optimal auction is one where the seller allocates the object for sale to the bidder with the highest value of this function when it exceeds zero; otherwise the seller keeps the object. For example, if the revision effects $\{e_i\left(t_i\right)\}_{i=1}^{\mathcal{N}}$ are all zero, then a modified second-price auction will implement the optimal selling mechanism. At this modified second-price auction, the seller announces a reserve price ρ^* such that

$$\rho^* - t_0 - \frac{\left[1 - F_i\left(\rho^*\right)\right]}{f_i\left(\rho^*\right)} = 0,$$

and keeps the object if the highest bid is less than this reserve price. The similarity of the above condition to equation (2.8) is obvious, particularly when the ith player's type T_i is interpreted as his valuation V_i.

2.7 Winner's Curse

Perhaps one of the most well-known phenomena in auction theory is the *winner's curse*. It is important to understand, however, that the winner's curse cannot obtain at auctions within the IPVP, but is a potential problem within the CVP. We devote some space here to explaining why.

Recall the anecdote we used to motivate the CVP in an earlier section of this chapter. Each potential bidder used an unbiased estimator to value an oil lease that was sold at a first-price, sealed-bid auction. In a famous paper, Capen, Clapp, and Campbell (1971) suggested that the winner of a first-price, sealed-bid auction of an oil lease was cursed in the sense that the bidder with the most optimistic estimate of the lease's valuation bid the most and won the auction: the expectation of highest draw concerning an unbiased estimator is an overestimate of the true mean. Thus, if potential bidders only used their estimates in formulating their bids, the winner would, on average, pay more for the object than it was worth.

To many laypeople, this argument sounds quite compelling. However, rational purposeful bidders in equilibrium will behave quite differently from the naïve statistical decision makers described above. In fact, Wilson (1977) pointed out that rational potential bidders would anticipate the possibility of the winner's curse in their calculations and this would be reflected in equilibrium bids. Wilson went on to solve the decision problem faced by a representative bidder, assuming Bayes–Nash equilibrium, and to show that, as the number of bidders got large, the winning bid converged almost surely to the true value of the object.

Intuitively, the less information the winner has, the more cursed he is. In the extreme, if the potential winner has no private information regarding the value of the object that is not already known by the other bidders, then he should not expect any positive profit. His best strategy is not to participate at the auction. This result was formalized by Milgrom and Weber (1982).

A simple example about firm takeovers is provided by Thaler (1988) to illustrate the extent of the winner's curse. In this example, an acquiring firm $\mathcal{A}$ contemplates a bid to take over a target firm $\mathcal{T}$. Now, firm $\mathcal{A}$ is assumed only to know that firm $\mathcal{T}$'s value is uniformly distributed between 0 and 100. Firm $\mathcal{A}$ is also assumed to know that it is more efficient than company $\mathcal{T}$ and that it can increase company $\mathcal{T}$'s value by fifty percent.

In a classroom experiment, most MBA students in a business school suggested that firm $\mathcal{A}$ should bid between 50 and 75 to gain positive profit. These students reasoned that the average value of firm $\mathcal{T}$ was 50, so firm $\mathcal{A}$ could make it fifty percent higher. However, this does not take into account firm $\mathcal{T}$'s strategic behavior: Suppose firm $\mathcal{A}$ offers a bid to firm $\mathcal{T}$. Now, firm $\mathcal{T}$ will only accept this bid if its value is below bid. Conditioning on winning the takeover, the average value of firm $\mathcal{T}$ is only (bid/2). Therefore, the average value to firm $\mathcal{A}$ is $[\text{bid}/2\,(1+0.5)]$, which is $\frac{3}{4}$bid and is less than bid. Therefore, firm $\mathcal{A}$ will always lose money. The optimal strategy for firm $\mathcal{A}$ is simply not to bid at all.

2.8 Practice Problems

The problems at the end of this chapter are designed to give you practice in completing standard calculations used in the construction of equilibria at auctions within the IPVP. Knowing how to construct the equilibrium-bid functions is central to specifying the data-generating processes of observed bids. Thus, solving these problems is particularly important to your understanding of later topics in this book. We urge you to persevere.

Practice Problems

1. Within the IPVP, assume $\mathcal{N}$ potential bidders and no reserve price as well as
$$F_V(v) = \frac{v}{\theta} \quad \forall \, v \in [0, \theta]$$
so
$$f_V(v) = \frac{1}{\theta} \quad \forall \, v \in [0, \theta].$$

   a) Find $\sigma(v)$, the Bayes–Nash, equilibrium-bid function at a first-price, sealed-bid auction.
   b) Find the probability density function of Y equal $V_{(2:\mathcal{N})}$.
   c) Find the cumulative distribution function of Y.
   d) Find the mean of Y.
   e) Find the variance of Y.
   f) Find the cumulative distribution function of Z equal $V_{(1:\mathcal{N})}$.
   g) Find the probability density function of Z.
   h) Find the mean of Z.
   i) Find the variance of Z.
   j) Find the probability density function of the winning bid W at a first-price sealed-bid auction where W equals $\sigma[V_{(1:\mathcal{N})}]$.
   k) Find the mean of W.
   l) Find the variance of W.
   m) Which mechanism would a risk-averse seller prefer? Why?

2. Within the IPVP environment of practice problem 1, assume a positive reserve price r which is less than θ.

   a) Find $\sigma(v)$, the Bayes–Nash, equilibrium-bid function at a first-price, sealed-bid auction.
   b) Find the probability mass function of the number of participants N at both English and first-price, sealed-bid auctions.
   c) Find the optimal reserve price ρ^*.

3. Within the IPVP environment of practice problem 1, assume that each potential bidder has a von Neumann–Morgenstern utility function
$$U(Y; \eta) = \eta Y^{1/\eta} \quad \eta \geq 1.$$

   a) Find $\beta(v)$, the dominant-strategy equilibrium-bid function at an English auction.

49

b) Find $\sigma(v)$, the Bayes–Nash, equilibrium-bid function at a first-price, sealed-bid auction.

c) Find the probability density function of the winning bid W at a first-price sealed-bid auction where W equals $\sigma[V_{(1:\mathcal{N})}]$.

d) Find the mean of W.

e) Find the variance of W.

f) Which mechanism would a risk-neutral seller prefer? Why?

4. Consider a government that seeks to perform a task at the lowest cost. It requests sealed-bid tenders from a group of $\mathcal{N}$ potential suppliers and, assuming that no reserve price is imposed, uses as the selection rule that the lowest bidder will win the auction. Suppose that the cost of performing the service for any one bidder C is an independent and identically distributed draw from a distribution $F_C(c)$ which is common knowledge to all potential bidders, and that potential suppliers behave noncooperatively. Assume, initially, that potential bidders are risk neutral with regard to winning the right to perform the task for the government.

a) Calculate the symmetric, Bayes–Nash, equilibrium-bid function for a representative bidder at the auction. In the course of this calculation be sure to highlight where you have used the assumptions of independence, symmetry, and Bayes–Nash behavior.

b) Assuming that the distribution of unobserved heterogeneity is from the exponential family having cumulative distribution function
$$F_C(c; \lambda) = [1 - \exp(-\lambda c)] \quad \lambda > 0,$$
λ a parameter, calculate the equilibrium-bid function.

c) Assuming that the distribution of unobserved heterogeneity is from the Pareto family having cumulative distribution function
$$F_C(c; \theta_0, \theta_1) = 1 - \left(\frac{\theta_0}{c}\right)^{\theta_1} \quad \theta_0 > 0,\ \theta_1 > 1,$$
θ_0 and θ_1 parameters, calculate the equilibrium-bid function.

d) Assuming that the distribution of unobserved heterogeneity is from the Weibull family having cumulative distribution function
$$F_C(c; \theta_2, \theta_3) = \left[1 - \exp\left(-\theta_2 c^{\theta_3}\right)\right] \quad \theta_2 > 0,\ \theta_3 > 0,$$

θ_2 and θ_3 parameters, calculate the equilibrium-bid function.

e) Evaluate the equilibrium-bid function at the lower bound of support for the distribution of costs. Noting that the integral of the survivor function $S_C(c)$, which equals $[1 - F_C(c)]$, is the expected value of C, when that expectation exists, provide an interpretation for the lower bound on the equilibrium bid function.

f) Assuming that agents are risk averse, having preferences that exhibit hyperbolic absolute risk aversion, so the von Neumann–Morgenstern utility function is

$$U(Y;\eta) = \eta Y^{1/\eta} \quad \eta \geq 1,$$

derive the equilibrium-bid function in general, and then specifically for each of exponential, Pareto, and Weibull distributed unobserved heterogeneity.

g) Explain how potential bidders would use trapezoidal quadrature to solve for the equilibrium-bid function in the case of Weibull unobserved heterogeneity.

h) Suppose that instead of being the bidder, who knows his cost, you work for the government, and it only observes a bid. Assuming that the government knows the family of the cost distribution and its parameters and assuming rational behavior on the part of all potential bidders, explain how you would use Newton's method to solve for the cost consistent with the bid.

i) Derive the distribution of bids when costs are exponential.

j) Derive the distribution of bids when costs are Pareto.

k) Derive the distribution of bids when costs are Weibull.

l) Derive the distribution of the winning bid when costs are exponential.

m) Derive the distribution of the winning bid when costs are Pareto.

n) Derive the distribution of the winning bid when costs are Weibull.

5. Consider an all-pay auction of an indivisible object where $\mathcal{N}$ bidders submit sealed bids simultaneously. At an all-pay auction, each bidder pays what he has bid, but only the highest bidder wins the object. Assume that the bidders' valuations are independent draws from the uniform distribution on the interval $[0, 1]$ and that bidders are risk neutral.

a) Write down the expected payoff function of a representative bidder.

b) Characterize the necessary, first-order condition for optimal bidding.

c) Find the symmetric, Bayes–Nash equilibrium bidding strategy.

d) How does the seller's revenue in this auction compare to that of a first-price, sealed-bid auction?

Chapter 3

Vickrey and English Auctions

$\mathcal{B}$ECAUSE THE dominant-strategy, equilibrium-bid functions at English and Vickrey auctions within the symmetric IPVP are very simple, especially in the absence of a reserve price, we begin our investigation of the SEAD by analyzing these formats first. As mentioned in chapter 1, however, data from Vickrey auctions are more informative than those from English auctions. Thus, even though the Vickrey format is rarely used, we begin our work by analyzing it. The spirit of this work is similar to that undertaken in theoretical analyses of auctions. In that research, the Vickrey format is investigated as a benchmark to contrast equilibrium behavior at auctions held under other formats.

Subsequently, we introduce covariates and then discuss semiparametric estimation within a single-index model. The implications of a binding minimum bid price are discussed next. Endogenous participation, induced by a binding reserve price, highlights the limitations of nonparametric methods, so we introduce parametric methods.

Having developed most of the important econometric ideas concerning second-price auctions within the symmetric IPVP, we then present an extended policy application by Paarsch (1997) who estimated the optimal selling mechanism for timber in the province of British Columbia, Canada. This application is particularly noteworthy since the conclusions of the study appear to have influenced public policy.

The fact that most English auctions have either known bid increments or random, bidder-induced jumps in the price leads us naturally to an analysis of incomplete data and inference following the work of Haile and Tamer (2003).

In the final section of the chapter, we introduce asymmetric bidders, outlining a proof of nonparametric identification based on Meilijson (1981) and used by Brendstrup and Paarsch (forthcoming). The model as well as the methods of identification and estimation introduced in this section will prove useful in the specification of multi-unit auctions described in chapter 5.

3.1 Nonparametric Identification and Estimation

Initially, we assume that no reserve price exists. Under the IPVP assumptions, the dominant-strategy, equilibrium-bid function at Vickrey auctions is

$$B_i = \beta(V_i) = V_i \quad i = 1, \ldots, \mathcal{N}.$$

Thus, the probability density function of observed bids is related to that of valuations by

$$f_B^0(b) = f_V^0(v),$$

so

$$F_V^0(v) = F_B^0(v)$$

where the superscripts "0" denote the true population values. To wit, the distribution of bids identifies the distribution of valuations. This result must seem trivial.

One should note, however, that even if only the winning bid were observed at a Vickrey auction, $F_V^0(v)$ would be nonparametrically identified. To see this, note that the winning bid satisfies

$$W = V_{(2:\mathcal{N})},$$

so

$$\begin{aligned} F_W^0(w) &= \mathcal{N}(\mathcal{N}-1) \int_0^{F_V^0(w)} u^{\mathcal{N}-2}(1-u) \, du \\ &= \varphi[F_V^0(w)|\mathcal{N}] \end{aligned}$$

where $\varphi(\cdot|\mathcal{N})$ is a known, strictly monotonic function. Thus, $F_V^0(v)$ is identified from the distribution of observed winning bids $F_W^0(w)$, when $\mathcal{N}$ is known.

What about estimation within the above framework? Consider a sample of T independent auctions of an identical object with identical number of bidders $\mathcal{N}$. Index the auctions by $t = 1, \ldots, T$. A natural way to estimate $F_V^0(v)$ would be to substitute the sample analogue for the population quantity, so one estimator of $F_V^0(v)$ is defined by

$$\hat{F}_V(v) = \frac{1}{T\mathcal{N}} \sum_{t=1}^{T} \sum_{i=1}^{\mathcal{N}} \mathbf{1}(B_{it} \leq v).$$

When $\mathcal{N}$ does not vary across auctions, another estimator is defined by

$$\hat{F}_W(v) = \frac{1}{T} \sum_{t=1}^{T} \mathbf{1}(W_t \leq v) = \mathcal{N}(\mathcal{N}-1) \int_0^{\hat{F}_V(v)} u^{\mathcal{N}-2}(1-u) \, du$$

or

$$\hat{F}_V(v) = \varphi^{-1}[\hat{F}_W(v)|\mathcal{N}].$$

Now, under standard regularity conditions, which are satisfied in this theoretical model of an auction, the asymptotic analysis of $\hat{F}_W(v)$ is well understood. In particular,

$$\sqrt{T}[\hat{F}_W(v) - F_W^0(v)] \xrightarrow{\text{d}} \mathcal{N}\left\{0, \mathcal{V}_W\left[F_V^0(v); \mathcal{N}\right]\right\}$$

where
$$\begin{aligned}\mathcal{V}_W\left[F_V^0(v); \mathcal{N}\right] &= F_W^0(v)\left[1 - F_W^0(v)\right]\\ &= \varphi[F_V^0(v)|\mathcal{N}]\left\{1 - \varphi[F_V^0(v)|\mathcal{N}]\right\}.\end{aligned}$$

Thus, one can apply the delta method to demonstrate that the pointwise distribution of the estimator $\hat{F}_V(v)$ has the following properties:

$$\sqrt{T}[\hat{F}_V(v) - F_V^0(v)] \xrightarrow{\text{d}} \mathcal{N}\left\{0, \mathcal{V}_V\left[F_V^0(v); \mathcal{N}\right]\right\}$$

where
$$\begin{aligned}\mathcal{V}_V\left[F_V^0(v); \mathcal{N}\right] &= \frac{\varphi[F_V^0(v)|\mathcal{N}]\left\{1 - \varphi[F_V^0(v)|\mathcal{N}]\right\}}{\left\{\varphi'\left[F_V^0(v)\right]\right\}^2}\\ &= \frac{\varphi[F_V^0(v)|\mathcal{N}]\left\{1 - \varphi[F_V^0(v)|\mathcal{N}]\right\}}{\mathcal{N}^2\left(\mathcal{N}-1\right)^2 F_V^0(v)^2\left[1 - F_V^0(v)\right]^2}.\end{aligned}$$

3.2 Covariates

In many situations, while the seller may know little concerning how much any potential bidder values the object, each potential bidder, roughly speaking, knows the value of an object to himself. Such an asymmetry of information often implies that pair-wise negotiation concerning the terms of sale for the object can yield an inefficient outcome. This is known as the *Myerson–Satterthwaite* theorem; see Myerson and Satterthwaite (1983). In auction models, within the IPVP, it is assumed that each potential bidder knows what he is willing to pay, but the seller knows none of these valuations. Under these conditions, the seller uses an auction to induce the bidder with the highest valuation to bid the most and, thus, to win the object. The institution of an auction is quite different from the other major way of selling things, *posted prices*. Under posted prices, the seller simply announces a take-it-or-leave-it price. Posted prices are frequently used to sell commonly used commodities, such as groceries; auctions are often used for one-of-a-kind objects, such as art.

Because real-world auctions are over-represented by sales of one-of-a-kind objects, one major problem faced by an empirical researcher is that getting a sample of *identical* objects to analyze is often difficult. Even if the objects are identical, their location or the time of year when they are sold potentially make them different; controlling for this heterogeneity can be difficult.

Now, in some circumstances, researchers can control for factors that make the objects at auction different. For example, Z_1 might denote a covariate for the year, while Z_2 could denote a covariate for the month, and so forth. Collect these quantified factors in a $(K \times 1)$ vector $\boldsymbol{Z}$, so the probability density function of V conditional on a particular $\boldsymbol{Z}$, denoted $\boldsymbol{z}$, then becomes

$$f^0_{V|\boldsymbol{Z}}(v|\boldsymbol{z}).$$

If the outcomes of $\boldsymbol{Z}$ are discrete and the number of combinations finite, then for a particular combination of the $\boldsymbol{z}$s one can use the nonparametric methods described in the previous section to define an estimator of $F^0_{V|\boldsymbol{Z}}(v|\boldsymbol{z})$; e.g.,

$$\hat{F}_{W|\boldsymbol{Z}}(v|\boldsymbol{z}) = \mathcal{N}(\mathcal{N}-1) \int_0^{\hat{F}_{V|Z}(v|z)} u^{\mathcal{N}-2}(1-u)\ du.$$

A practical problem exists with this approach: often, the number of combinations of $\boldsymbol{Z}$s is prohibitively large. Also, if $\boldsymbol{Z}$ contains continuous covariates, then the proposed nonparametric approach based on a discrete $\boldsymbol{Z}$ is infeasible. While it is possible to use kernel-smoothing methods to combine nearby values of $\boldsymbol{z}$ to form nonparametric estimates, these methods suffer from the *curse of dimensionality* when the dimension of $\boldsymbol{Z}$ is large. What to do?

3.3 Single-Index Models: Semiparametric Estimation

To get around this problem, researchers have sought *dimension-reducing* techniques. A variety of methods exists, but in this section we shall investigate one of the most commonly used, *semiparametric, single-index* methods. While many estimators exist for single-index models, we shall discuss the pioneering methods of Powell, Stock, and Stoker (1989) using conditional-mean functions; we shall also discuss the maximum rank-correlation estimator of Han (1987) and Sherman (1993). Once the principle is understood, other variants of these methods can be devised; see Horowitz (1998) for more on semiparametric econometrics.

In a single-index model, it is a maintained assumption that the conditional distribution of V depends on the covariates z only through an index $z^\top \gamma^0$ where γ^0 is a vector of unknown parameters that is conformable to $z^\top$. In other words, under the single-index assumption

$$F_{V|Z}^0 (v|z) = F_{V|Z} (v|z^\top \gamma^0).$$

This implies that

$$F_{W|Z}^0 (w|z) = F_{W|Z} (w|z^\top \gamma^0).$$

Estimation of $F_{W|Z}^0 (w|z)$ can be done in two steps: In the first, the unknown parameter vector γ^0 is estimated using a semiparametric procedure. Having estimated γ^0, the second step involves estimating the distribution of W conditional on the single-index $z^\top \hat{\gamma}$, nonparametrically. The estimator $\hat{F}_{W|Z} (w|z)$ can then be transformed into $\hat{F}_{V|Z} (v|z)$ and the delta method can then be used to find its asymptotic distribution.

An implication of the single-index assumption is that the conditional mean of W given Z is only a function of the index $z^\top \gamma^0$.[1] Thus,

$$\mathcal{E} (W|z) = \mu (z^\top \gamma^0)$$

for some unknown function $\mu (\cdot)$. Since $\mu (\cdot)$ is unknown, γ^0 can only be identified up to some location and scale normalizations. Typically, to obtain identification, γ^0 is assumed not to include the coefficient for a constant term. In addition, γ^0 is often assumed either to lie on the unit simplex or its first element is normalized to one. Other normalizations are, however, possible. The particular normalization used is unimportant when the goal is to use the single-index assumption as a dimension-reducing device to estimate the distribution of V conditional on Z.

3.3.1 Density-Weighted Derivative Estimator

The density-weighted derivative estimator of Powell et al. makes use of the fact that, under the single-index assumption,

$$\mathcal{E} \left[\frac{\partial}{\partial Z} \mathcal{E} (W|Z) f_Z (Z) \right] = \mathcal{E} \left[\frac{\partial}{\partial Z} \mu (Z^\top \gamma^0) f_Z (Z) \right]$$

$$= \mathcal{E} \left[\mu' (Z^\top \gamma^0) f_Z (Z) \right] \gamma^0.$$

---

[1] In fact, the single-index assumption guarantees that the conditional mean of any function of W, such as other conditional moments, or any conditional quantiles, such as the median of W, depends on Z only through the single-index $Z^\top \gamma^0$. In empirical work within the IPVP, the mean is a natural moment to consider because of the REP.

In words, the weighted average of slopes of the mean function are proportional to the γ^0 vector. Since we can estimate any normalization of γ^0, we can estimate the density-weighted derivative; viz.,

$$\mathcal{E}\left[\frac{\partial}{\partial \mathbf{Z}}\mathcal{E}\left(W|\mathbf{Z}\right) f_{\mathbf{Z}}\left(\mathbf{Z}\right)\right]$$

and use it as an estimator $\hat{\gamma}$ of γ^0.

Powell et al. simplified the estimation procedure further by noting that the integrals

$$\mathcal{E}\left[\frac{\partial}{\partial \mathbf{Z}}\mathcal{E}\left(W|\mathbf{Z}\right) f_{\mathbf{Z}}\left(\mathbf{Z}\right)\right] = \int f_{\mathbf{Z}}\left(\mathbf{Z}\right)^2 \, d\mathcal{E}\left(W|\mathbf{Z}\right)$$

$$= -\int \mathcal{E}\left(W|\mathbf{Z}\right) \, df_{\mathbf{Z}}\left(\mathbf{Z}\right)^2$$

$$= -2\int \mathcal{E}\left(W|\mathbf{Z}\right) f_{\mathbf{Z}}'\left(\mathbf{Z}\right) f_{\mathbf{Z}}\left(\mathbf{Z}\right) \, d\mathbf{Z}$$

$$= -2\mathcal{E}\left[W f_{\mathbf{Z}}'\left(\mathbf{Z}\right)\right].$$

The sample analogue

$$-2\frac{1}{T}\sum_{t=1}^{T} w_t f_{\mathbf{Z}}'\left(z_t\right)$$

is a potential estimate of this quantity, provided the probability density function $f_{\mathbf{Z}}\left(z\right)$ is known. In practice, however, $f_{\mathbf{Z}}\left(z\right)$ is unknown, but it can be estimated by a kernel-smoothed density:

$$\hat{f}_{\mathbf{Z}}\left(z\right) = \frac{1}{T}\sum_{t=1}^{T}\frac{1}{h_g^K}\kappa_K\left(\frac{\mathbf{Z}_t - z}{h_g}\right)$$

where K is the dimension of $\mathbf{Z}_t$, h_g is a sequence of bandwidth parameters which goes to zero, and Th_g goes to infinity as T increases without bound. The function $\kappa_K\left(\cdot\right)$ is a K-dimensional kernel-smoothing function. A natural estimate of $f_{\mathbf{Z}}'\left(z\right)$ is the derivative of $\hat{f}_{\mathbf{Z}}\left(z\right)$, which is

$$\hat{f}_{\mathbf{Z}}'\left(z\right) = \frac{1}{T}\sum_{t=1}^{T}\frac{1}{h_g^K}\frac{\partial}{\partial \mathbf{Z}}\kappa_K\left(\frac{\mathbf{Z}_t - z}{h_g}\right).$$

Hence, the density-weighted derivative estimator of γ^0 is given by

$$\hat{\gamma} = -2\frac{1}{T^2}\sum_{t=1}^{T}\sum_{s=1}^{T}W_t\frac{1}{h_g^K}\frac{\partial}{\partial \mathbf{Z}}\kappa_K\left(\frac{\mathbf{Z}_t - z_s}{h_g}\right).$$

As noted before, W_t can be replaced by any function of W_t. Like many semiparametric estimators, $\hat{\gamma}$ takes the form of a U-statistic. While each $f_Z(z)$ can only be estimated at a slow nonparametric rate that depends on the dimension of Z and on the smoothness of $f_Z(z)$, averaging over Z_t significantly reduces the curse of dimensionality and speeds up the rate of convergence. In particular, using the theory of U-statistics, Powell et al. showed that $\hat{\gamma}$ is $\sqrt{T}$ consistent and asymptotically normally distributed. Once $\hat{\gamma}$ has been calculated, $F^0_{W|Z}(w|z)$ can be estimated using the usual one-dimensional, kernel-smoothing techniques; viz.,

$$\hat{F}_{W|Z}(w|z) = \frac{\frac{1}{T}\sum_{t=1}^{T} \mathbf{1}(W_t \le w) \frac{1}{h_g} \kappa\left(\frac{Z_t^\top \hat{\gamma} - z^\top \hat{\gamma}}{h_g}\right)}{\frac{1}{T}\sum_{t=1}^{T} \frac{1}{h_g} \kappa\left(\frac{Z_t^\top \hat{\gamma} - z^\top \hat{\gamma}}{h_g}\right)}.$$

The curse of dimensionality is not severe here because $\kappa(\cdot)$ is only a one-dimensional kernel function. From $\hat{F}_{W|Z}(w|z)$, one can then construct an estimator of $F^0_{V|Z}(v|z)$ according to

$$\hat{F}_{W|Z}(v|z) = \mathcal{N}(\mathcal{N}-1) \int_0^{\hat{F}_{V|Z}(v|z)} u^{\mathcal{N}-2}(1-u)\, du.$$

3.3.2 Maximum Rank-Correlation Estimator

An alternative approach to estimating single-index models involves the notion of rank-correlation; see, for example, Han (1987) as well as Sherman (1993). These methods are based on a slightly stronger single-index assumption; viz.,

$$W = \mu\left(z^\top \gamma^0 + U\right) \tag{3.1}$$

where $\mu(\cdot)$ is an unknown function that is strictly increasing in the index $z^\top \gamma^0 + U$. Location and scale normalizations are obviously necessary to identify the parameters γ, but these methods also allow one to estimate a transformation of W. For example, note that equation (3.1) can be rewritten as

$$\tau(W) = z^\top \gamma^0 + U$$

where $\tau(\cdot)$ is an unknown, strictly-increasing function of W. Typically, U is assumed independent of Z. Under these assumptions, consider two values of Z, z_1 and z_2. Under the monotonicity and independence assumptions, when

$$z_1^\top \gamma^0 > z_2^\top \gamma^0,$$

it is more likely that W_1 will be greater than W_2, so the probability that W_1 is larger than W_2 should be greater than one half. The maximum rank-correlation estimator is defined by the following optimization problem:

$$\max_{<\boldsymbol{\gamma}>} \frac{1}{T(T-1)} \sum_{t=1}^{T} \sum_{s=1, s \neq t}^{T} \left[\mathbf{1}\left(W_t > W_s\right) - \frac{1}{2} \right] \mathbf{1}\left(z_t^\top \boldsymbol{\gamma} > z_s^\top \boldsymbol{\gamma}\right).$$

The above objective function is a U-statistic of order two for any given $\boldsymbol{\gamma}$. To see why this estimator is consistent, consider its population limit

$$Q\left(\boldsymbol{\gamma}\right) = \mathcal{E}\left\{ \left[\mathbf{1}\left(W_t > W_s\right) - \frac{1}{2} \right] \mathbf{1}\left(\boldsymbol{Z}_t^\top \boldsymbol{\gamma} > \boldsymbol{Z}_s^\top \boldsymbol{\gamma}\right) \right\}$$

which can be written as

$$Q\left(\boldsymbol{\gamma}\right) = \mathcal{E}_{\boldsymbol{Z}_t, \boldsymbol{Z}_s}\left\{ \left[\Pr\left(W_t > W_s | \boldsymbol{Z}_t, \boldsymbol{Z}_s\right) - \frac{1}{2} \right] \mathbf{1}\left(\boldsymbol{Z}_t^\top \boldsymbol{\gamma} > \boldsymbol{Z}_s^\top \boldsymbol{\gamma}\right) \right\}.$$

Clearly, to maximize this limit objective function, we would like the indicator function

$$\mathbf{1}\left(z_t^\top \boldsymbol{\gamma} > z_s^\top \boldsymbol{\gamma}\right)$$

to take on the value one whenever

$$\left[\Pr\left(W_t > W_s | z_t, z_s\right) - \frac{1}{2} \right] > 0.$$

But this happens, if and only if,

$$z_t^\top \boldsymbol{\gamma}^0 > z_s^\top \boldsymbol{\gamma}^0.$$

In other words, the set of $\boldsymbol{\gamma}$s that will maximize the limit objective function is the set of $\boldsymbol{\gamma}$s where

$$z_t^\top \boldsymbol{\gamma} > z_s^\top \boldsymbol{\gamma}$$

if and only if

$$z_t^\top \boldsymbol{\gamma}^0 > z_s^\top \boldsymbol{\gamma}^0.$$

The true parameter $\boldsymbol{\gamma}^0$ clearly satisfies this condition and belongs to the set of $\boldsymbol{\gamma}$s that maximizes the limit objective function.

The next question is whether $\boldsymbol{\gamma}^0$ is point identified; i.e., does $\boldsymbol{\gamma}^0$ uniquely maximize the limit objective function. A sufficient condition for point identification is that, for any $\boldsymbol{\gamma}$ not equal to $\boldsymbol{\gamma}^0$, there exist sets of $\boldsymbol{Z}_t$ and $\boldsymbol{Z}_s$ with positive probabilities, such that $\boldsymbol{Z}_t^\top \boldsymbol{\gamma}^0$ is larger than

$Z_s^\top \gamma^0$, but $Z_t^\top \gamma$ is smaller than $Z_s^\top \gamma$ on these sets. We denote two sets by $\mathcal{A}_t$ and $\mathcal{A}_s$. Two assumptions that ensure this condition are:

1) the support of the distribution of Z is not contained in any proper linear space;

2) there exists at least one component z_h, $h \in [1, \dim(Z)]$ with $\gamma_h^0 \neq 0$ and with a distribution that has everywhere positive Lebesgue density conditional on $Z_{-h} = (z_1, z_{h-1}, z_{h+1}, \ldots)^\top$, almost surely in Z_{-h}.

Under either of these assumptions, it is clear that

$$\left[Q\left(\gamma^0\right) - Q\left(\gamma\right)\right] \geq$$

$$\mathcal{E}_{Z_t, Z_s} \left\{ \mathbf{1}\left(Z_t \in \mathcal{A}_t\right) \mathbf{1}\left(Z_s \in \mathcal{A}_s\right) \mathbf{1}\left(Z_t^\top \gamma^0 > Z_s^\top \gamma^0\right) \right.$$

$$\left. \left[\Pr\left(W_t > W_s | Z_t, Z_s\right) - \frac{1}{2} \right] \right\}.$$

Therefore, $Q\left(\gamma^0\right)$ is larger than $Q\left(\gamma\right)$ for any γ not equal to γ^0, and the rank estimator will be consistent under suitable assumptions that guarantee uniform convergence of the finite sample objective function to the limit objective function. As the asymptotic distribution of rank estimators was developed completely by Sherman (1993), we shall not repeat it here.

3.4 Reserve Prices and Parametric Estimation

Many auctions have minimum prices that must be bid, reserve prices. Typically, reserve prices are public information, often announced when the auctions are advertised, but sometimes they are secret. Economists often model secret reserve prices as random variables. The reason for this is that the decision problem faced by bidders is modeled more easily under such an assumption than it would were some other assumption made. In the remainder of this section, however, we shall assume that reserve prices are fixed and known to all potential bidders.

As was demonstrated in chapter 2, the presence of a binding reserve price r makes participation at the auction endogenous. Thus, for a random sample of $\mathcal{N}$ valuations $\{V_1, \ldots, V_\mathcal{N}\}$ from the distribution $F_V^0(v)$ where

$$I_i = \begin{cases} 1 & \text{if } V_i \geq r, \\ 0 & \text{otherwise;} \end{cases}$$

the total number of participants at an auction having reserve price r is

$$N = \sum_{i=1}^{\mathcal{N}} I_i,$$

which is distributed binomially having parameters $[1 - F_V^0(r)]$ and $\mathcal{N}$ as well as probability mass function

$$f_N(n) = \binom{\mathcal{N}}{n} F_V^0(r)^{\mathcal{N}-n}[1 - F_V^0(r)]^n \quad n = 0, 1, \ldots, \mathcal{N}.$$

The most important empirical implication of endogenous participation at English and Vickrey auctions is that the distribution of bids represents a truncated distribution of valuations: only those potential bidders who had valuations exceeding the reserve price participated at the auction. Thus, *sample selection*, in the Heckman sense, exists, which then means that trying to estimate the unconditional distribution $F_V^0(v)$ using only the truncated distribution $F_{V|V \geq r}^0(v|V \geq r)$ is impossible without additional structure.

While it may be clear that the number of participants at both English and Vickrey auctions is endogenous, what may not be obvious is that the properties of the probability density and cumulative distribution functions $f_W^0(w)$ and $F_W^0(w)$ are quite different too.

To illustrate this point, note that, at Vickrey auctions, a potential bidder will use the following bid function:

$$B_i = \beta(V_i) = V_i \quad r \leq V_i$$

regardless of the number of participants N. If a potential bidder at a Vickrey auction is the solo bidder, then according to Vickrey's rules that solo bidder will win the object for sale and pay the reserve price. At an English auction, under the clock model and within the IPVP, a participant's behavior will depend on whether he faces an opponent. Thus, when N is two or more, the English auction proceeds as before, but if N equals one, then the solo participant drops out at the reserve price. Of course, when no one attends, the object goes unsold under either format.

Thus, the probability density function of the winning bid at English and Vickrey auctions has three parts: W equals zero, when the object goes unsold; W equals the reserve price, when only one potential bidder shows up; and W equals the second-highest valuation, when more than one potential bidder attends. Hence, the winning bid W is a mixed discrete-continuous random variable of the sort discussed in Maddala

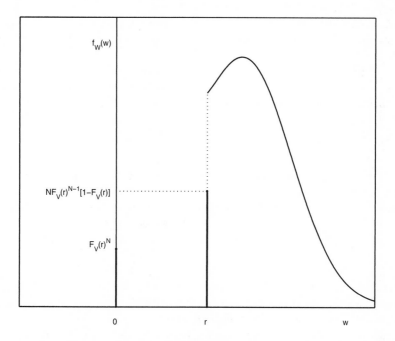

Figure 3.1
Mixed Discrete-Continuous Density of Winning Bid

(1983) or Amemiya (1985); the sample would be referred to as *censored* by Amemiya because observations are recorded, but the true values are not. A graph of such a probability density function is presented in figure 3.1.

In words, one can explain this graph as follows: the object goes unsold when no one has a valuation above the reserve price; with independence, this is simply the product of the $\mathcal{N}$ cumulative distribution functions evaluated at the reserve price. Hence, the spike at W equals zero. When the object is sold at the reserve price, only one potential bidder has a valuation above the reserve price while $(\mathcal{N}-1)$ have valuations below it. In a random sample of $\mathcal{N}$ draws, one can get the combination of one above r and $(\mathcal{N}-1)$ below r, $\mathcal{N}$ different ways. Hence, the spike at the reserve price r. Of course, under the clock model, when N is two or more, the probability density function of W is simply the density of the second order statistic of valuations. Hence, the continuous part of the probability density function.

Now, identification of $F_V^0(v)$ from $F_W^0(w)$ remains unaffected by the discrete-continuous nature of the probability density function of $f_W^0(w)$ for values of w above r. However, when $f_W^0(w)$ is neither differentiable nor even continuous, standard application of nonparametric methods to estimate $F_W^0(w)$, without additional assumptions concerning the process determining the reserve price r, is difficult. What to do?

In this section, we advocate putting additional structure on $F_V^0(v)$ by assuming that it comes from a family of parametric distributions, which can be characterized up to some unknown $(p \times 1)$ parameter vector $\boldsymbol{\theta}$. Thus,

$$F_V^0(v) = F_V(v; \boldsymbol{\theta}^0)$$

where the "0" on $\boldsymbol{\theta}^0$ denotes the true value of $\boldsymbol{\theta}$.

Some researchers object to such an assumption; they are unwilling to impose additional structure, and remain content just to make statements concerning the valuation distribution above the reserve price. They claim that to do otherwise would be to assume structure which cannot be tested. This is true. However, without knowing the distribution of valuations over the entire range of valuations, it can be impossible to calculate the optimal reserve price. When confronted with this reality, some researchers have argued that the optimal reserve price will surely be above the existing, observed reserve price, so knowing only the conditional distribution of V when it is above r is not a problem. Absent prior information, however, it is unclear to us that the optimal reserve price must be above the observed reserve price. To assume that it is seems, to us at least, very similar to assuming that $F_V^0(v)$ comes from a family of distributions.

When $F_V^0(v)$ is assumed to come from a family of parametric distributions, calculating the components of this density is relatively straightforward. Note that the probability of the object's going unsold is simply $f_N(0)$ or

$$\Pr(W = 0) = F_V(r; \boldsymbol{\theta})^{\mathcal{N}}.$$

When the object is sold at the reserve price, only one potential bidder has a valuation above the reserve price while $(\mathcal{N} - 1)$ have valuations below it. The probability of W's equaling r is simply $f_N(1)$, so

$$\Pr(W = r) = \mathcal{N} F_V(r; \boldsymbol{\theta})^{\mathcal{N}-1}[1 - F_V(r; \boldsymbol{\theta})].$$

Of course, under the clock model, when N is two or more, the probability density function of W, for W greater than r, is simply

$$f_{W,N}(w, n > 2; \boldsymbol{\theta}) = \mathcal{N}(\mathcal{N} - 1) F_V(w; \boldsymbol{\theta})^{\mathcal{N}-2}[1 - F_V(w; \boldsymbol{\theta})] f_V(w; \boldsymbol{\theta}).$$

Introducing the indicator variables

$$D_0 = \begin{cases} 1 & \text{if } N = 0, \\ 0 & \text{otherwise;} \end{cases}$$

and

$$D_1 = \begin{cases} 1 & \text{if } N = 1, \\ 0 & \text{otherwise}; \end{cases}$$

the probability density function of the winning bid at English and Vickrey auctions in the presence of a binding reserve price is

$$f_W(w; \boldsymbol{\theta}, \mathcal{N}) =$$

$$\left\{ [F_V(r; \boldsymbol{\theta})]^{\mathcal{N}} \right\}^{D_0}$$

$$\left\{ \mathcal{N} [F_V(r; \boldsymbol{\theta})]^{\mathcal{N}-1} [1 - F_V(r; \boldsymbol{\theta})] \right\}^{D_1} \tag{3.2}$$

$$\left\{ \mathcal{N}(\mathcal{N} - 1) [F_V(w; \boldsymbol{\theta})]^{\mathcal{N}-2} [1 - F_V(w; \boldsymbol{\theta})] f_V(w; \boldsymbol{\theta}) \right\}^{1-D_0-D_1}.$$

Of course, in a sample that contains information concerning objects that *sold* at auction, one would need to condition on N being greater than zero; such a sample would be referred to as *truncated* by Amemiya (1985) because only some of the observations, those that sold, are recorded. Thus, in this circumstance, the probability density function would be

$$f_{W|N}(w|n > 0; \boldsymbol{\theta}, \mathcal{N}) =$$

$$\left\{ \frac{\mathcal{N} F_V(r; \boldsymbol{\theta})^{\mathcal{N}-1} [1 - F_V(r; \boldsymbol{\theta})]}{1 - F_V(r; \boldsymbol{\theta})^{\mathcal{N}}} \right\}^{D_1} \tag{3.3}$$

$$\left\{ \frac{\mathcal{N}(\mathcal{N} - 1) F_V(w; \boldsymbol{\theta})^{\mathcal{N}-2} [1 - F_V(w; \boldsymbol{\theta})] f_V(w; \boldsymbol{\theta})}{1 - F_V(r; \boldsymbol{\theta})^{\mathcal{N}}} \right\}^{1-D_1}.$$

Depending on the sampling scheme, given a sample of T observations concerning the winning bids and the number of potential bidders $\{(w_t, \mathcal{N}_t)\}_{t=1}^{T}$, one can use either equation (3.2) or equation (3.3) to create the logarithm of the likelihood function for the sample, and then use the method of maximum likelihood to calculate an estimate of $\boldsymbol{\theta}^0$.

Demonstrating the parameter consistency of the MLE $\hat{\boldsymbol{\theta}}$ and deriving its asymptotic distribution are quite standard, so we omit them; the mechanics are described in appendix A.6.2.

3.5 Policy Application

The literature concerned with mechanism design has sometimes been criticized as lacking practical value because the optimal selling mechanism depends on random variables whose distributions are typically unknown to the designer. In the past, because the distributions of valuations have been unknown, calculating the optimal reserve price for a real-world auction has appeared impossible.

Riley and Samuelson (1981) have shown that within the IPVP the selling mechanism which maximizes the seller's expected gain is a selling mechanism where a reserve price ρ is chosen optimally. This ρ is different from the seller's valuation v_0. In fact, as was shown above, Riley and Samuelson have calculated that the optimal reserve price ρ^* satisfies

$$\rho^* = v_0 + \frac{[1 - F_V(\rho^*)]}{f_V(\rho^*)}.$$

Thus, for example, when V is distributed uniformly on the interval $[0, 1]$, ρ^* solves

$$\rho^* = v_0 + \frac{1 - \rho^*}{1} \qquad \text{or} \qquad \rho^* = \frac{v_0 + 1}{2}.$$

If v_0 equals zero, then ρ^* equals one half, and if v_0 equals the expectation of V, $\mathcal{E}(V)$, which is one half, then ρ^* equals three quarters. Clearly, to calculate ρ^* requires information concerning $F_V(v)$, the distribution of valuations.

At auctions within the IPVP, the equilibrium bidding strategies of potential bidders are increasing functions of their valuations. For example, at the English auctions considered in this chapter, the dominant-strategy, equilibrium-bid function for bidders who lose the auction is to bid their valuations. Thus, in principle, it is possible to estimate the underlying probability law of valuations using the empirical distribution of bids from a cross-section of auctions.

In a policy application, Paarsch (1997) used information from the distribution of bids tendered at English auctions of timber in the province of British Columbia, Canada to uncover the distribution of valuations. An attractive feature of using data from English auctions, when viewed through the lens of the Milgrom–Weber clock model, is that, for those who bid, their tenders map out the valuation distribution.

At least four potential problems exist with such an approach. First, the winning bid does not reveal complete information concerning the winner's true valuation. Second, in the presence of a reserve price, the empirical distribution of observed bids represents a truncated sample of data: only those potential bidders whose valuations exceed the reserve price will choose to bid. Third, as in all empirical studies of auctions, the joint distribution of bidding and nonparticipation depends on the number of potential bidders $\mathcal{N}$, but finding a credible measure of potential competition is often difficult, and when it can be done, the specific proxy is often inaccurate. Finally, at many auctions the objects for sale are not exactly identical: covariate heterogeneity is important.

Paarsch (1997) developed an empirical framework that allowed him to estimate the probability law of valuations using the empirical distribution of bids from a truncated and potentially incomplete sample of data in the absence of a measure of potential competition and with considerable observed covariate heterogeneity. He implemented his approach to derive an estimate of the optimal reserve price for auctions of timber in British Columbia using information from a sample of timber sales held by the British Columbia Ministry of Forests between 1984 and 1987. This exercise was of considerable practical value because the IPVP appeared to capture well the important aspects of timber sales in British Columbia. Moreover, understanding how to obtain the most from the sale of province-owned (Crown) timber is an extremely important task in British Columbia because about ninety percent of all timber is owned by the Crown. In addition, forest products have historically accounted for over twenty percent of the province's manufactured output and almost ten percent of the entire provincial product; British Columbia has historically accounted for about twenty-five percent of North American lumber production.

3.5.1 Some Institutional Background

In British Columbia, the Forest Act of 1979 permitted small businesses to acquire the right to harvest timber on Crown land. The Minister of Forests sets aside a portion of each year's allowable cut to sell to eligible loggers and sawmillers through a series of public auctions held under the Small Business Forest Enterprise Program (SBFEP). Although both English and first-price, sealed-bid auctions have been used to sell the right to harvest timber on Crown land, Paarsch focused solely on English auctions. At the time, the type of bidding admitted at English auctions was quite simple. Essentially, the Minister of Forests assigned a minimum price per cubic meter of timber harvested, or *scaled*. This minimum price, which was often referred to as the *upset rate*, varied across species and depended on past lumber prices. The upset rate was known in advance to all potential bidders. Bidders could then verbally tender an additional amount per cubic meter of timber harvested, called the *bonus bid*. Bonus bids were uniform across species. Although the auction rules in British Columbia varied slightly across Forest Districts, bidders were typically required to tender increments of no less than $0.01 per cubic meter of timber harvested.[2] The total amount bid was called

---

2   Thus, the assumption of the Milgrom–Weber clock model was not strictly met in the data used by Paarsch. Because bidders were required to increase bids by at least $0.01 per cubic meter of timber, or in increments of $100 for a sale involving 10,000 cubic meters of timber, the average volume in Paarsch's data, the key identifying condition of the clock model was not met, so the continuous-price feature of the clock model is only approximately true for the

the *stumpage rate*, and it varied across species as it was the sum of the species-specific upset rate and the uniform bonus bid.

Each potential bidder had considerable information concerning the timber for sale. For example, from the timber cruise report and other supporting documents he could obtain detailed information concerning the location of the timber, the surrounding terrain, and access to the timber by roads.[3] Typically, timber sold under the SBFEP was in areas having well-developed road networks, so road construction costs were usually negligible. A statistically unbiased estimate of the volume of standing timber by species and grade (known as the *cruised volume*) was also available from the Ministry of Forests. Errors might exist in the cruised-volume estimates, but potential bidders could and did inspect sales themselves. In any case, there is no reason to believe that any one potential bidder had more information than the others concerning the volume or quality of timber for sale.

For 129 sales of timber at English auction, Paarsch observed the district, year, and month in which the sale was held; the volume of timber by species; the upset rate by species; the distance to the nearest timber processing facility; the number of actual bidders; and the final recorded bonus bids for each of the bidders. From other sources, he also derived measures for the price of logs — timber that has been felled, limbed, and bucked.

3.5.2 Bidding of Timber in British Columbia

Paarsch modeled the timber sales as noncooperative games of incomplete information at which a single seller (the Minister of Forests) disposed of one object, a stand of timber, to $\mathcal{N}$ potential bidders (loggers). Thus, Paarsch ignored all of the potential dynamic elements of the problem, and treated it as a *one-shot* game. The ith player was assumed to know his valuation v_i, but not those of his opponents. Heterogeneity in valuations was modeled as a continuous random variable V having cumulative distribution function $F_V(v)$ and probability density function $f_V(v)$. The valuations of players were assumed to be independent draws from $F_V(v)$. Together, Paarsch's assumptions constituted the symmetric IPVP.

---

data-generating process. Also, discrete jumps in bids are also possible, and these can cause the maximum valuations of some participants to be skipped, so these participants may not appear in the data. In the next section of this chapter, we shall discuss how Haile and Tamer (2003) have investigated these issues. Suffice it to say here that Paarsch ignored these issues in his work.

[3] The timber cruise report is a document prepared for the Ministry of Forests in which the timber for sale is described.

The strategies available to the loggers were their bids. The Minister of Forests was assumed to have valuation v_0; he was also assumed to impose a known minimum price r that must be bid. As mentioned above, bidding at English auctions was modeled using the clock model. Under this model, the winner is the player with the highest valuation, and he pays the second-highest valuation.[4] Formally, for nonwinning loggers with at least one opponent, the dominant bidding strategy was

$$\beta(V) = V \quad r \leq V.$$

Notice that risk aversion with respect to winning the auction does not affect the equilibrium bidding strategy: Any utility function that is increasing in the net return will yield the same strategy. Note, too, that this strategy does not depend on $\mathcal{N}$.

The only behavioral assumptions of the model are that potential bidders bid independently and that losers tell the truth. By focusing on English auctions, Paarsch avoided the stronger common-knowledge-of-F_V assumption needed to solve for the equilibrium-bid function at first-price, sealed-bid auctions. Of course, this strength derives from the IPVP assumption. Within other paradigms (e.g., the CVP or the AVP), he would have needed to employ the common-knowledge-of-F_V assumption to solve the game.

3.5.3 Defense of IPVP Assumption

Anecdotal evidence suggests that English auctions are typically used in environments where little information useful to all of the bidders concerning the value of the object is revealed in the course of the auction. Sales of oil and gas leases, for example, are not undertaken using English auctions because the proprietary information of any particular bidder concerning the probability of discovering oil (and thus the value of the lease) would be revealed in the course of bidding. That English auctions are used to sell timber lends support to the IPVP assumption.

In the case of British Columbian timber sales, Paarsch argued that several other factors suggested that the IPVP is a good approximation to the environment within which loggers bid for timber. For example, log prices were generally fixed to loggers either by contract or by list prices at sawmills. Moreover, during the period considered in this analysis (1984 to 1987) considerable price stability existed, so any asymmetries in expectations concerning future prices were unlikely important. Thus,

---

[4] Note that if all save one logger dropped out at r, then the winner paid r, while if all dropped out the timber went unsold.

Paarsch assumed also that log prices were fixed and the same to all
potential bidders. Also, because each potential bidder knew a considerable amount about the timber to be sold, any asymmetries of information concerning the volume and quality of timber were assumed away
by Paarsch. Note, too, that because the payment scheme used by the
Ministry of Forests involves payment for the volume of timber removed
from the forest (also known as *scaled volume*), harvesters were perfectly
insured by the government against any errors in the timber-cruise estimates. Therefore, Paarsch conjectured that a natural explanation for
differences in bidding behavior were differences in harvesting costs; he
assumed that these were individual-specific effects. Paarsch assumed
that for a given sale, these cost differences were random and independent across potential bidders as well as being identically distributed.

3.5.4 Mapping Observables into Bids

To develop an empirically tractable model of bidding for timber within
the environment, Paarsch assumed that only one stand of timber was to
be auctioned, and on that stand at most J different species of timber
existed. Letting p_j denote the price of species j (measured in dollars per
cubic meter) and q_j denote the volume of species j (measured in cubic
meters of timber), he assumed next that a logger's valuation of a sale v
depended on total revenues $\sum_{j=1}^{J} p_j q_j$ and total harvesting costs. Total
harvesting costs were assumed to depend on the total volume of timber
felled, but not to vary with the species composition. That is, holding
stem diameters and stem densities constant, it cost the same to fell
Douglas fir timber as Sitka spruce timber. In addition, such harvesting
costs were also assumed to depend on the distance to the nearest timber
processing facility (sawmill). Transportation costs were assumed to
depend only on the total volume, and not on the species composition. As
with felling, the argument here was that different species of timber did
not have different transportation costs because they involved essentially
the same amount of effort when being transported to a sawmill. Letting
q denote the total volume of timber to be harvested (where q equals
$\sum_{j=1}^{J} q_j$) and d denote the distance in kilometers to the nearest timber
processing facility, total harvesting costs were denoted $C(q,d)$. Because
Paarsch assumed that timber prices were known perfectly and were the
same to all potential bidders, for any particular logger, the value of a
timber sale V was then

$$V = \sum_{j=1}^{J} p_j q_j - C(q,d).$$

Introducing the weights $\{\ell_j\}_{j=1}^{J}$ where ℓ_j equals (q_j/q), Paarsch wrote V as

$$V = \left(\sum_{j=1}^{J} p_j \ell_j - A \right) q$$

where A equals $[C(q,d)/q]$ which denotes average harvesting costs for the sale. Paarsch assumed that variation in average harvesting costs across bidders could be modeled as a continuous random variable A having cumulative distribution function $F_A(a)$ and probability density function $f_A(a)$.[5]

Conditional on d, $\{p_j\}_{j=1}^{J}$, and $\{q_j\}_{j=1}^{J}$ bidding depended on how expensive it was for loggers to harvest. In the case of British Columbian timber sales, loggers had to bid a non-negative bonus b above the species-specific upset rates $\{u_j\}_{j=1}^{J}$ set by the Minister of Forests. Hence, the species-specific stumpage rates $\{s_j\}_{j=1}^{J}$ tendered to the Crown had to satisfy

$$s_j = u_j + b \geq u_j \quad j = 1, \ldots, J.$$

What made the bidding problem simple in the case of British Columbian timber sales was the fact that the bonus bid b had to be the same across all species, so only one decision existed, the choice of b.

In general, the ith losing participant at an English auction bid up to the point where zero profit obtained:

$$\sum_{j=1}^{J}(p_j - A_i - s_{ji})q_j = \sum_{j=1}^{J}(p_j - A_i - u_j - b_i)q_j = 0. \quad (3.4)$$

Dividing both sides of (3.4) by q implies that the bonus bid B_i is a function β of the average harvesting cost A_i for participant i

$$B_i = \beta(A_i) = \sum_{j=1}^{J}(p_j - u_j)\ell_j - A_i = \hat{a} - A_i$$

where $\hat{a}$ equals $\sum_{j=1}^{J}(p_j - u_j)\ell_j$ and was known to all potential bidders. An English auction ended when the bidder with the lowest average harvesting costs (the highest valuation) bid just over the final offer of

---

[5] Note that $f_V(v)$ is related to $f_A(a)$ by

$$f_V(v) = f_A(a) \left| \frac{da}{dv} \right| = \frac{f_A\left(\sum_{j=1}^{J} p_j \ell_j - \frac{v}{q} \right)}{q}.$$

his opponent who had the second-lowest average harvesting costs (the second-highest valuation). Letting $\{A_{(i:\mathcal{N})}\}_{i=1}^{\mathcal{N}}$ denote the $\mathcal{N}$ average harvesting costs indexed in ascending order, the winning bonus bid W was

$$W = \beta[A_{(2:\mathcal{N})}] = \hat{a} - A_{(2:\mathcal{N})}.$$

Of course, when a bidder faced no opponents his winning bonus bid was zero.

The bonus-bidding rule defined above is a monotonically decreasing function of A over a relevant region: A bidder continues either until he wins or zero profit obtains. The lower a bidder's a (the higher his v), the longer he remains at the auction. Because the bonus-bidding rule is a function of a random variable, it too is a random variable and its distribution is related to $F_A(a)$ and, therefore, $F_V(v)$.

3.5.5 Deriving the Empirical Specification

Central to the empirical specification of Paarsch's study was the joint density of bidding and nonparticipation. To derive this, Paarsch initially ignored the reserve price and admitted nonpositive bids. For an ordered sample of average costs $\{A_{(i:\mathcal{N})}\}_{i=1}^{\mathcal{N}}$, he noted that the joint density of bids, where $B_{(i:\mathcal{N})}$ equals $\left[\hat{a} - A_{(i:\mathcal{N})}\right]$, is

$$f_{\boldsymbol{B}_{(\mathcal{N})}}\left[b_{(1:\mathcal{N})}, b_{(2:\mathcal{N})}, \ldots, b_{(\mathcal{N}:\mathcal{N})}\right] = \mathcal{N}! \prod_{i=1}^{\mathcal{N}} f_A\left[a_{(i:\mathcal{N})}\right]$$

$$= \mathcal{N}! \prod_{i=1}^{\mathcal{N}} f_A\left[\hat{a} - b_{(i:\mathcal{N})}\right]$$

where $\boldsymbol{B}_{(\mathcal{N})}$ denoted the $\mathcal{N}$-vector of ordered bids. Introducing a reserve price and admitting the fact that any observed bid must be greater than or equal to zero and less than $\hat{a}$ required that this density be manipulated further. Three different regimes exist: they include more than one bidder, one bidder, and no bidders.

In the first, the number of actual bidders N has realization n, which is two or greater. In this case, the winning bid $B_{(1:\mathcal{N})}$ (or W) equals $\left[\hat{a} - A_{(2:\mathcal{N})}\right]$ with $A_{(2:\mathcal{N})}$ being less than $\hat{a}$. Integrating out the nonpositive bids and admitting that $A_{(1:\mathcal{N})}$ is less than $(\hat{a} - w)$ involves

$$\mathcal{N}! \int_{\hat{a}}^{\infty} f_A \left[a_{(\mathcal{N}-n+1:\mathcal{N})} \right]$$

$$\int_{a_{(\mathcal{N}-n+1:\mathcal{N})}}^{\infty} f_A \left[a_{(\mathcal{N}-n+2:\mathcal{N})} \right] \cdots \int_{a_{(\mathcal{N}-1:\mathcal{N})}}^{\infty} f_A \left[a_{(\mathcal{N}:\mathcal{N})} \right]$$

$$\prod_{i=2}^{n} f_A \left[a_{(i:\mathcal{N})} \right] \int_{0}^{a_{(2:\mathcal{N})}} f_A \left[a_{(1:\mathcal{N})} \right] \, da_{(1:\mathcal{N})} \, da_{(\mathcal{N}:\mathcal{N})} \cdots$$

$$da_{(\mathcal{N}-n+2:\mathcal{N})} da_{(\mathcal{N}-n+1:\mathcal{N})}.$$

This yields the following joint density of bidding and nonparticipation:

$$\frac{\mathcal{N}!}{(\mathcal{N}-n)!} [1 - F_A(\hat{a})]^{(\mathcal{N}-n)} \prod_{i=2}^{n} f_A \left[a_{(i:\mathcal{N})} \right] F_A \left[a_{(2:\mathcal{N})} \right] =$$

$$\binom{\mathcal{N}}{n} [1 - F_A(\hat{a})]^{(\mathcal{N}-n)} n! \prod_{i=2}^{n} f_A \left[\hat{a} - b_{(i:\mathcal{N})} \right] F_A(\hat{a} - w). \tag{3.5}$$

As mentioned above, when only one bidder shows up at the auction, the dominant strategy for that logger is to submit the minimum acceptable bid, a bonus bid of zero. In this case, $(\mathcal{N} - 1)$ bidders have costs greater than $\hat{a}$, and one has costs less than $\hat{a}$. The binomial probability of such an event is

$$\mathcal{N}[1 - F_A(\hat{a})]^{\mathcal{N}-1} F_A(\hat{a}). \tag{3.6}$$

The probability of no one bidding, when all costs are greater than $\hat{a}$, is

$$[1 - F_A(\hat{a})]^{\mathcal{N}}. \tag{3.7}$$

Collecting (3.5) and (3.6) as well as (3.7) Paarsch wrote the contribution to the likelihood function of observed bids and nonparticipants as

$$\left\{ [1 - F_A(\hat{a})]^{\mathcal{N}} \right\}^{D_0} \left\{ \mathcal{N}[1 - F_A(\hat{a})]^{\mathcal{N}-1} F_A(\hat{a}) \right\}^{D_1}$$

$$\left\{ \binom{\mathcal{N}}{n} [1 - F_A(\hat{a})]^{(\mathcal{N}-n)} n! \prod_{i=2}^{n} f_A \left[\hat{a} - b_{(i:\mathcal{N})} \right] F_A(\hat{a} - w) \right\}^{(1-D_0-D_1)} \tag{3.8}$$

where

$$D_0 = \begin{cases} 1 & \text{if } N = 0, \\ 0 & \text{otherwise;} \end{cases}$$

and

$$D_1 = \begin{cases} 1 & \text{if } N = 1, \\ 0 & \text{otherwise.} \end{cases}$$

Accurate and reliable measures of $\mathcal{N}$ are notoriously difficult to obtain. Even under the best of conditions, measurement error in $\mathcal{N}$ is still possible. This can result in mismeasuring the number of nonparticipants $(\mathcal{N} - n)$ in the term $[1 - F_A(\hat{a})]^{(\mathcal{N}-n)}$. Thus, Paarsch chose to focus on the conditional (truncated) distribution of costs because in such a specification $(\mathcal{N} - n)$ would be absent.

To see this, consider the joint distribution of the number of actual bidders N and the ordered average costs for those bidders

$$f_{\boldsymbol{A}_{(N)}, N}\left[a_{(1:\mathcal{N})}, a_{(2:\mathcal{N})}, \ldots, a_{(n:\mathcal{N})}, n\right] =$$

$$\binom{\mathcal{N}}{n}[1 - F_A(\hat{a})]^{(\mathcal{N}-n)} n! \prod_{i=1}^{n} f_A\left[a_{(i:\mathcal{N})}\right].$$

This probability density function can be factored as follows:

$$f_{\boldsymbol{A}_{(N)}|N}\left[a_{(1:\mathcal{N})}, a_{(2:\mathcal{N})}, \ldots, a_{(n:\mathcal{N})}|n\right] f_N(n) =$$

$$n! \prod_{i=1}^{n} \frac{f_A\left[a_{(i:\mathcal{N})}\right]}{F_A(\hat{a})} \binom{\mathcal{N}}{n}[1 - F_A(\hat{a})]^{(\mathcal{N}-n)} F_A(\hat{a})^n$$

where

$$f_N(n) = \binom{\mathcal{N}}{n}[1 - F_A(\hat{a})]^{(\mathcal{N}-n)} F_A(\hat{a})^n$$

is the binomial probability mass function for the number of actual bidders N. This implies that the probability density function of the average costs for bidders, conditional on the number of actual bidders N being n, is

$$f_{\boldsymbol{A}_{(N)}|N}\left[a_{(1:\mathcal{N})}, a_{(2:\mathcal{N})}, \ldots, a_{(n:\mathcal{N})}|n\right] = n! \prod_{i=1}^{n} \frac{f_A\left[a_{(i:\mathcal{N})}\right]}{F_A(\hat{a})}.$$

Recognizing that the winning bidder does not fully reveal his costs yields the following conditional probability density function for observed bids:

$$n! \prod_{i=2}^{n} \frac{f_A\left[\hat{a} - b_{(i:\mathcal{N})}\right]}{F_A(\hat{a})} \frac{F_A(\hat{a} - w)}{F_A(\hat{a})}. \tag{3.9}$$

Estimates derived from a specification defined by equation (3.9) will be less efficient than those derived from an equation like (3.8) but will be robust to errors in $\mathcal{N}$. Because the specification based on equation (3.9) is conditional on realized actual competition, n can be treated as as constant. Moreover, as the research of Andersen (1970) and Vuong (1983) has shown within parametric specifications, the conditional maximum-likelihood estimator of parameters in specification (3.9) is consistent and distributed normally, asymptotically. Within the IPVP, specification (3.9) is quite robust. For it avoids the Bayes–Nash assumption, is unaffected by the attitudes of bidders toward risk, and does not require information concerning $\mathcal{N}$.

3.5.6 Implementing the Empirical Specification

To estimate the optimal reserve price, one must recover information concerning the latent unobserved variable A. A natural way to proceed in recovering an estimate of A's distribution $F_A(a)$ would be to examine the empirical distribution of bonus bids and then to map back to the distribution of A. For example, as was shown earlier in this chapter, in the absence of covariates and reserve prices and given a large enough sample, one could perform this exercise nonparametrically. However, the presence of a reserve price complicates matters because parts of the valuation distribution are unobserved. Because it is potentially necessary to have the entire valuation distribution in order to calculate the optimal reserve price, an alternative method to nonparametric estimation must be sought. Paarsch chose to estimate $F_A(a)$ using parametric methods. Implicit in any parametric assumption concerning $F_A(a)$ is an assumption concerning how a differential equation in A behaves locally. Paarsch assumed that this local behavior could be extended into regions he could not observe in order to get estimates of $F_A(a)$, and consequently of $F_V(v)$. Parametric models also provided Paarsch a parsimonious framework within which to introduce observed heterogeneity across sales into the empirical specifications. Empirical work in auctions is plagued by small samples; Paarsch's sample of 129 observations was simply not rich enough to support nonparametric methods.

In Paarsch's case, at least four types of observed heterogeneity appeared important. First, upset rates varied across timber sales. Second, log prices varied across species, so bidding could vary systematically across sales with different species compositions. Third, the volume of timber varied across sales, which could affect average harvesting costs. Fourth, the distance to the nearest timber processing facility varied from sale to sale.

In order to write down an exact specification for the empirical model of an English auction considered above, Paarsch needed to describe precisely how these covariates affected harvesting costs and bonus bidding. He also needed to choose a family for $F_A(a)$. Paarsch assumed that $f_A(a)$ came from a particular family of distributions, the Weibull, which can be characterized up to some unknown parameter vector $\boldsymbol{\theta}$

$$f_A(a) = f(a; \boldsymbol{\theta}).$$

Thus, the parameter vector $\boldsymbol{\theta}$ will embed itself in (3.9). For his sample of $t = 1, \ldots, 129$ sales, Paarsch denoted the upset rates and timber prices for species j at sale t by u_{jt} and p_{jt} respectively, yielding

$$\hat{a}_t = \sum_{j=1}^{J} (p_{jt} - u_{jt}) \ell_{jt}$$

where ℓ_{jt} equal (q_{jt}/q_t) was the weight for species j at sale t. Paarsch also assumed that the *ex ante* total harvesting cost function $C(d,q)$ depended on d and q in the following way:

$$C(d,q) = \gamma_0 + \gamma_{q1}q + \gamma_{q2}q^2 + \gamma_{q3}q^3 + \gamma_{dq}dq.$$

Thus, felling costs were cubic in q, but transportation costs were linear in the product of volume and to distance to the nearest mill. Cubic felling costs admitted an optimal volume for sales. Separability between felling and transportation costs was reasonable because these two activities are distinct. Proportionality of transportation costs was reasonable within this environment because the timber was relatively close to timber processing facilities and many firms existed to transport the logs. Average harvesting costs for the tth sale a_t then depended on d_t and q_t according to

$$a_t = \gamma_{q1} + \gamma_{q2}q_t + \gamma_{q3}q_t^2 + \gamma_0 q_t^{-1} + \gamma_{dq}d_t. \tag{3.10}$$

Paarsch considered a number of ways of introducing randomness into equation (3.10) above, but we do not discuss them here. Suffice it to say that Paarsch estimated the parameters of $f_A(a;\boldsymbol{\theta})$ using the method of conditional maximum likelihood.

3.5.7 Estimates of the Optimal Reserve Price

Paarsch's preferred empirical specification was one in which γ_{q1} followed the Weibull law. Using this estimated specification in conjunction with the sample covariates, Paarsch calculated auction-specific estimates of the optimal reserve price assuming different values for v_0, the seller's valuation of the timber. When v_0 was assumed equal to zero, a little over forty percent of the estimated optimal reserve prices were within two standard errors of the actual total upset price. The sample mean of the estimated optimal reserve prices was \$92,281.13, but the sample average of the total upset price $(\sum_{j=1}^{J} u_j q_j)$ was \$26,891.18, suggesting that the Minister of Forests was too lenient in the setting of the reserve price for timber.

Because there was considerable heterogeneity with respect to the volume of timber to be harvested, Paarsch presented the empirical distribution of the optimal reserve prices divided by the sample volume for each sale. The upset rate sample average was \$2.39 per cubic meter, while the average optimal reserve price per cubic meter was \$8.59.

Paarsch also assumed that the sample total upset price was, in fact, the optimal reserve price. In this case, the average seller's valuation over the sample covariates was $-\$89,948.16$; the median seller's valuation over the sample covariates, on the other hand, was $-\$62,792.45$. Only one of the revealed seller's valuation estimates was positive.

From this research, Paarsch concluded that the reserve prices set by the Minister of Forests were too low. It is also interesting to note that, in April 1994, after the release of Paarsch's working paper, which was published as Paarsch (1997), the Ministry of Forests almost doubled the stumpage rates it charged firms, suggesting that Paarsch's findings had real-world policy relevance.

3.6 Incomplete Data

Haile and Tamer (2003) have pointed out that observed behavior at English auctions is often at variance with the behavior assumed by economic theorists. For example, in the work discussed in a previous section, we employed the Milgrom–Weber clock model of behavior at English auctions as an identifying assumption to relate the observed, winning bid W to the unobserved, latent valuation $V_{(2:\mathcal{N})}$. Haile and Tamer have noted that at many English auctions the seller forces the bidders to increase their bids in discrete increments, and that sometimes these increments are large. Moreover, even when bid increments are small, some bidders choose to increase their bids by more than one increment, sometimes by many, a phenomenon often referred to as *jump bidding*.

Within the IPVP, the presence of discrete bid increments can result in inefficient allocations, but as the bid increment gets very small, the likelihood of these inefficiencies vanishes. At many real-world auctions, bid increments arise because of the smallest denomination of the currency. For example, in the United States, the smallest denomination of the currency is the cent, so at many auctions this is a natural bid increment. At some auctions, however, when the selling price is quite large, the increment is stated in percentage points of the existing price; e.g., one percent. In such situations, bid increments can be quite large; e.g., thousands of dollars.

The presence of jump bidding is troubling from both a theoretical and an empirical perspective. First, why would a rational bidder choose to do this? Part of the answer could derive from the simple fact that the IPVP is an approximation to reality and the environments in which jump bidding occur do not fall within the IPVP. However, if one constrains oneself to the IPVP, then only a few plausible explanations exist. One such explanation is that time has value, and bidders have some knowledge concerning the valuations of their opponents and the opportunity cost of their own time. Jump bidding is then a solution to a decision problem faced by a bidder who tradesoff paying more than he might need to with the opportunity cost of his time. Of course, modeling such behavior in equilibrium is another matter; Avery (1998) has presented one approach.

In this section, we shall maintain the assumptions of the symmetric IPVP, and pursue another line of investigation suggested by Haile and Tamer (2003). In particular, Haile and Tamer investigated the relationship between observed bidding and unobserved valuations when jump bids are admitted. As one might expect, when the identifying link between the observed, winning bid and the unobserved, latent valuation is severed, getting an exact relationship is impossible. Haile and Tamer accepted this fact and sought to bound the distribution of valuations $F_V^0(v)$. By applying the path-breaking research of Horowitz and Manski (1995), who investigated the general problem of identification and estimation in the presence of contaminated and corrupted data, to the case of jump bidding at English auctions, Haile and Tamer provided a fruitful extension of the models discussed earlier. For those readers who think in terms of regression models, the research of Haile and Tamer has obvious links to regression models in which the outcome variable is recorded in intervals; such cases were studied extensively by Manski and Tamer (2002).

Haile and Tamer proposed that, instead of getting exact estimates of $F_V^0(v)$ by imposing an untestable identifying assumption, one should attempt to bound $F_V^0(v)$ using less restrictive, but intuitively reasonable, assumptions. In addition to the assumptions that make up the symmetric IPVP, Haile and Tamer made two additional assumptions:

Assumption 3.5.1: Bidders do not bid more than they are willing to pay.

and

Assumption 3.5.2: Bidders do not allow an opponent to win at a price they are willing to beat.

As Haile and Tamer noted, the motivation for Assumption 3.5.1 is clear: no bidder should pay more than his valuation. Assumption 3.5.2 simply adjusts the Milgrom–Weber clock model for discrete bids. Moreover, both these assumptions hold in dominant-strategy equilibrium of the models discussed previously in this chapter, so the model of Haile and Tamer nests the models we have already discussed.

As in our previous work, we begin by considering auctions at which no reserve price is imposed, but at which discrete bid increments as well as jump bidding exist. We first show how Haile and Tamer bounded

$F_V^0(v)$ from above. Under the conditions above, Assumption 3.5.1 tells us that

$$b_i \leq v_i \quad \forall\, i = 1, \ldots, \mathcal{N}.$$

Letting $G_B^0(b)$ denote the true population $\Pr(B \leq b)$, Haile and Tamer have

$$G_B^0(v) \geq F_V^0(v) \quad \forall\, v.$$

In words, the distribution $G_B^0(v)$ dominates the distribution $F_V^0(v)$ in the first-order sense. Now, $B_{(i:\mathcal{N})}$ must also be less than or equal to $V_{(i:\mathcal{N})}$, so

$$G_{(i:\mathcal{N})}^0(v) \geq F_{(i:\mathcal{N})}^0(v) \quad \forall\, i,\, v.$$

From our technical appendix, we know that

$$F_{(i:\mathcal{N})}^0(v) = \frac{\mathcal{N}!}{(\mathcal{N}-i)!(i-1)!} \int_0^{F_V^0(v)} u^{\mathcal{N}-i}(1-u)^{i-1}\, du$$

which is a known, strictly-positive transformation, so we know there exists a function $\varphi^{-1}(\cdot)$ such that

$$F_V^0(v) = \varphi^{-1}[F_{(i:\mathcal{N})}^0(v); i, \mathcal{N}].$$

Thus,

$$F_V^0(v) \leq F_U^0(v) \equiv \min_{i \in \{1,\ldots,\mathcal{N}\}} \varphi^{-1}[G_{(i:\mathcal{N})}^0(v); i, \mathcal{N}].$$

In words, the cumulative distribution of valuations is bounded from above by the lower envelope of the transformed bid distributions.

To derive a lower bound on $F_V^0(v)$, Haile and Tamer made use of bid increment information. Let Δ denote the bid increment. From Assumption 3.5.2, we know that when the winning bid W (also $B_{(1:\mathcal{N})}$) goes unchallenged

$$V_i \leq U_i \equiv \begin{cases} \bar{v} & \text{when } B_i = W; \\ W + \Delta & \text{when } B_i < W; \end{cases} \quad \forall\, i.$$

Letting $H_U^0(\cdot)$ denote the cumulative distribution function of U_i, Haile and Tamer noted that $F_V^0(v)$ dominates $H_U^0(v)$ in the first-order sense. Note, however, that

$$V_{(2:\mathcal{N})} < W + \Delta$$

which implies

$$V_{(j:\mathcal{N})} < W + \Delta \quad \forall\, j > 2.$$

In words, the second-highest valuation $V_{(2:\mathcal{N})}$ is bounded from above by the winning bid W plus the bid increment. Were this not true, some bidder with the second-highest valuation would have countered the standing bid and raised it.

Now, letting $G^0_{W+\Delta}(v)$ denote the distribution of $(W+\Delta)$, we know that

$$F^0_{(2:\mathcal{N})}(v) = \mathcal{N}(\mathcal{N}-1) \int_0^{F^0_V(v)} u^{\mathcal{N}-2}(1-u)\, du > G^0_{W+\Delta}(v) \quad \forall\, v.$$

Applying the $\varphi^{-1}(\cdot)$ transformation introduced above, Haile and Tamer proved that

$$F^0_V(v) \geq F^0_L(v) \equiv \varphi^{-1}[G^0_{W+\Delta}(v); 2, \mathcal{N}].$$

Haile and Tamer noted that when Δ is zero, $F^0_L(v)$ and $F^0_U(v)$ are identical, so this model collapses to the Milgrom–Weber clock model. Haile and Tamer also noted that the following must be true:

$$F^0_L(v) \leq F^0_U(v) \quad \forall\, v.$$

Violations of this set of inequalities suggest that the symmetric IPVP does not apply.

A natural way in which to implement the Haile and Tamer framework is to replace the population quantities with sample analogues. Thus, for an independent and identically distributed sample of T observations indexed by $t = 1, \ldots, T$, estimate $G^0_{(i:\mathcal{N})}(v)$ by

$$\hat{G}_{(i:\mathcal{N})}(v) = \frac{1}{T} \sum_{t=1}^{T} \mathbf{1}[B_{(i:\mathcal{N}),t} \leq v]$$

and $G^0_{W+\Delta}(v)$ by

$$\hat{G}_{W+\Delta}(v) = \frac{1}{T} \sum_{t=1}^{T} \mathbf{1}(W_t + \Delta_t \leq v)$$

whence Haile and Tamer proposed consistent estimators of $F^0_L(v)$ and $F^0_U(v)$ according to

$$\hat{F}_U(v) = \min_{i \in \{1,\ldots,\mathcal{N}\}} \varphi^{-1}[\hat{G}_{(i:\mathcal{N})}(v); i, \mathcal{N}]$$

and

$$\hat{F}_L(v) = \varphi^{-1}[\hat{G}_{W+\Delta}(v); 2, \mathcal{N}].$$

The proofs of consistency follow directly from the continuous mapping theorem. Deriving the asymptotic distribution is much more involved.

Essentially, because the "min($\cdot$)" function is not differentiable, a delta-method type of analysis is ruled out. One alternative proposed by Haile and Tamer is to use Efron's (1982) bootstrap; see section A.5.3 of the appendix for a description of how to implement the bootstrap on a computer and Horowitz (2001) for applications in econometrics.

The other problem is that, because of sampling variability, no guarantee exists that $\hat{F}_U(v)$ will be larger than $\hat{F}_L(v)$. Therefore, Haile and Tamer suggested smoothing the "min($\cdot$)" function and choosing the smoothing parameter so that $\hat{F}_L(v)$ is less than $\hat{F}_U(v)$.

3.7 Incomplete Inference

When data are incomplete in the sense discussed in the previous section, the decision problem faced by the seller when devising the optimal-selling mechanism is fundamentally different. Demonstrating this difference is made easy through an example. To begin, imagine that the Milgrom–Weber clock model applies at an English auction. For simplicity, assume that no reserve price exists. Under these conditions, the following defines $\hat{F}_V(v)$, the nonparametric MLE of $F_V^0(v)$:

$$\hat{F}_W(v) = \mathcal{N}(\mathcal{N} - 1) \int_0^{\hat{F}_V(v)} u^{\mathcal{N}-2}(1 - u) \, du.$$

If $\hat{F}_W(w)$ is smoothed in an appropriate way, then so too will be $\hat{F}_V(v)$. From statistics, we know that the MLE of a function of a parameter is the function evaluated at the MLE of the parameter. Thus, the MLE of the optimal reserve price ρ^*, which is the optimal selling mechanism within the IPVP, is

$$\hat{\rho}^* = v_0 + \frac{[1 - \hat{F}_V(\hat{\rho}^*)]}{\hat{f}_V(\hat{\rho}^*)}.$$

Suppose now, instead of the Milgrom–Weber clock model, the model of Haile and Tamer (2003) from the previous section applies. Now, because the optimal reserve price is a function of both the cumulative distribution and the probability density functions in a nonlinear way, a bound on the optimal reserve price cannot be found simply by substituting $\hat{F}_L(v)$ and $\hat{F}_U(v)$ in lieu of $F_V^0(v)$. In fact, Haile and Tamer showed that bounding the optimal selling mechansim requires additional work. While noting these differences may seem like technical minutiae, it may have important policy implications, and should be considered when evaluating the policy application presented in a previous section of this chapter.

To bound the optimal reserve price in the framework above, Haile and Tamer first noted that the above definition for $\hat{\rho}^*$ is actually the solution to the following optimization problem:

$$\hat{\rho}^* = \operatorname*{argmax}_{\rho} \ \pi\left(\rho\right)$$

where

$$\pi\left(\rho\right) = \left(\rho - v_0\right)\left[1 - \hat{F}_V\left(\rho\right)\right].$$

To ensure that this optimization problem is well-defined, Haile and Tamer assumed that $\pi\left(\rho\right)$ is strictly pseudo-concave in ρ.

To begin, assume no reserve price exists. Haile and Tamer obtained bounds on $\hat{\rho}^*$ using the estimators $\hat{F}_L\left(v\right)$ and $\hat{F}_U\left(v\right)$. In particular, Haile and Tamer defined

$$\pi_U\left(\rho\right) = \left(\rho - v_0\right)\left[1 - \hat{F}_U\left(\rho\right)\right]$$

and

$$\pi_L\left(\rho\right) = \left(\rho - v_0\right)\left[1 - \hat{F}_L\left(\rho\right)\right].$$

Note that, by construction,

$$\hat{F}_L\left(v\right) \leq \hat{F}_V\left(v\right) \leq \hat{F}_U\left(v\right),$$

so, for every ρ,

$$\pi_U\left(\rho\right) \leq \pi\left(\rho\right) \leq \pi_L\left(\rho\right).$$

Intuitively, the bounds on the cumulative distribution function $\hat{F}_V\left(v\right)$ translate into bounds on the function that $\hat{\rho}^*$ is defined to maximize. Haile and Tamer then showed that such bounds on the function to be maximized can be translated into the value of the argument that actually maximizes the function.

To find bounds on $\hat{\rho}^*$, define

$$\hat{\rho}_U^* = \operatorname*{argmax}_{\rho} \ \pi_U\left(\rho\right)$$

and construct the upper and lower bounds in the following way:

$$\hat{\rho}_L = \sup\{\rho < \hat{\rho}_U^* : \pi_L\left(\rho\right) \leq \pi_U\left(\hat{\rho}_U^*\right)\},$$

and

$$\hat{\rho}_U = \inf\{\rho > \hat{\rho}_U^* : \pi_L\left(\rho\right) \leq \pi_U\left(\hat{\rho}_U^*\right)\}.$$

Haile and Tamer then showed that $\hat{\rho}^*$ satisfies

$$\hat{\rho}_L \leq \hat{\rho}^* \leq \hat{\rho}_U.$$

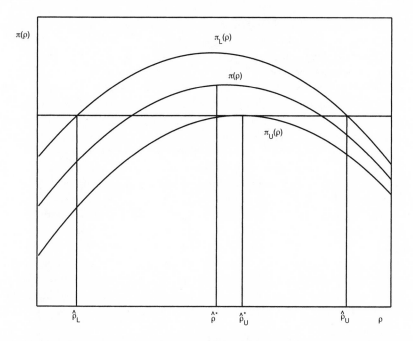

Figure 3.2
Bounds on the Optimal Reserve Price

In words, these bounds are constructed in the following way: first, calculate $\hat{\rho}_U^*$, the maximum of the lower-envelope function $\pi_U(\rho)$ in figure 3.2. Now, draw a horizontal line at this maximum, which intersects the upper-envelope function at a lower point $\hat{\rho}_L$ and a higher point $\hat{\rho}_U$. The true $\hat{\rho}^*$ that maximizes the function in the middle is bounded by these two points.

Formally, consider, for example, the relationship between $\hat{\rho}^*$ and $\hat{\rho}_L$. By the construction of $\hat{\rho}_L$,

$$\pi\left(\hat{\rho}_L\right) \leq \pi_L\left(\hat{\rho}_L\right) \leq \pi_U\left(\hat{\rho}_U^*\right) \leq \pi\left(\hat{\rho}_U^*\right).$$

Now, the concavity of $\pi\left(\cdot\right)$ implies that

$$\pi\left(\hat{\rho}_L\right) \leq \pi\left(\hat{\rho}_U^*\right),$$

so

$$\hat{\rho}_L \leq \hat{\rho}^*.$$

The relationship between $\hat{\rho}^*$ and $\hat{\rho}_U$ can be proven by a similar argument.

3.8 Asymmetric Bidders

In this section, we describe how asymmetries in bidders at single-object English auctions have been addressed following the work of Brendstrup and Paarsch (forthcoming). Brendstrup and Paarsch considered an English auction of a single object assuming that each of the $\mathcal{N}(\geq 2)$ potential bidders is from one of J different *classes* where J is less than or equal to $\mathcal{N}$. A potential bidder of class j draws his valuation independently from the cumulative distribution function $F_j(v)$ having corresponding probability density function $f_j(v)$. The F_js are assumed to have common support on the interval $[0, \infty)$. For simplicity, assume no reserve price.

Brendstrup and Paarsch used the Milgrom–Weber clock model of an English auction to structure the data. Specifically, the clock is assumed to be set initially at zero and then proceeds to rise continuously. As the price rises, bidders signal their exit from the auction. Thus, Brendstrup and Paarsch ignored the criticisms of Haile and Tamer (2003). When all but one of the bidders have dropped out, the remaining bidder is the winner and the price he pays is the last bid his last opponent was willing to pay.

At English auctions within the IPVP, it is a dominant strategy for nonwinners to bid up to their true valuation. Hence, the winner will be the bidder with the highest valuation and the winning bid will be the second-highest valuation. From appendix A.2 concerning order statistics, we know that the probability density function of the second-highest order statistic of $\mathcal{N}$ independent draws, each from a different *type* of distribution, has the following form:

$$f_{(2:\mathcal{N})}(y|\boldsymbol{F}) = \frac{1}{(\mathcal{N}-2)!}\text{Perm}\begin{pmatrix} F_{\text{type}(1)}(y) & \cdots & F_{\text{type}(\mathcal{N})}(y) \\ \vdots & \ddots & \vdots \\ F_{\text{type}(1)}(y) & \cdots & F_{\text{type}(\mathcal{N})}(y) \\ f_{\text{type}(1)}(y) & \cdots & f_{\text{type}(\mathcal{N})}(y) \\ [1 - F_{\text{type}(1)}(y)] & \cdots & [1 - F_{\text{type}(\mathcal{N})}(y)] \end{pmatrix}$$

where the vector $\boldsymbol{F}$ collects the cumulative distribution functions of the J parent classes. The above matrix on the right is $(\mathcal{N} \times \mathcal{N})$ where each column represents a bidder. The first $(\mathcal{N} - 2)$ rows list the cumulative distribution functions, while the last row lists the survivor functions, the $[1 - F_{\text{type}(i)}(y)]$s, and the second-to-last row has the probability density functions of the $F_{\text{type}(i)}(y)$s. Here, $\text{type}(\cdot)$ is a function which returns a bidder's class; e.g., if bidder i is of class j, then $\text{type}(i)$ returns j, so

$F_{\text{type}(i)}(y)$ equals $F_j(y)$. The symbol "Perm" outside the matrix above denotes the permanent operator and is discussed in appendix A.2.2.

To see that the equation for $f_{(2:\mathcal{N})}(y)$ collapses to the probability density function of the second-highest order statistic when the F_js are identical, recall that the probability density function of the second-highest order statistic from $\mathcal{N}$ independent and identically distributed draws from $F_V(v)$ is

$$f_{(2:\mathcal{N})}(y) = \mathcal{N}(\mathcal{N}-1)F_V(y)^{\mathcal{N}-2}[1-F_V(y)]f_V(y).$$

For computational ease, consider the following illustrative example where $\mathcal{N}$ and J are three. By the equation above,

$$f_{(2:3)}(y|\boldsymbol{F}) = \text{Perm} \begin{pmatrix} F_1(y) & F_2(y) & F_3(y) \\ f_1(y) & f_2(y) & f_3(y) \\ [1-F_1(y)] & [1-F_2(y)] & [1-F_3(y)] \end{pmatrix}$$

$$= F_1(y)[1-F_3(y)]f_2(y) + F_1(y)[1-F_2(y)]f_3(y)+$$
$$F_2(y)[1-F_3(y)]f_1(y) + F_2(y)[1-F_1(y)]f_3(y)+$$
$$F_3(y)[1-F_2(y)]f_1(y) + F_3(y)[1-F_1(y)]f_2(y),$$

which one can show by direct substitution is

$$f_{(2:3)}(y) = 6F_V(y)[1-F_V(y)]f_V(y)$$

when $F_j(v)$ equals $F_V(v)$ for $j = 1, 2, 3$. The purpose of introducing the equation of the complete probability density function as well as the above example is to illustrate that $f_{(2:3)}(y)$, the probability density function of the winning bid at the auction, will be a mixture of the J probability density functions $\{f_j(y)\}_{j=1}^J$, where the mixing weights vary with y. The model is nonparametrically unidentified when only data on the number of potential bidders $\mathcal{N}$ and the winning bid Y are observed.

3.8.1 Nonparametric Identification

The data available to a researcher determine identification. This case is no different. Typically, at English auctions, the winning bid for each unit sold is readily available. Often, too, one can obtain transaction information (e.g., receipts of sale or tax records) from the seller concerning who won the objects sold as well as the number of potential bidders (e.g., a list of customers). Brendstrup and Paarsch assumed that the researcher can classify each of the bidders present; this may just mean that the researcher assumes each bidder is different from each of his opponents; i.e., J equals $\mathcal{N}$. Given this information and under suitable regularity conditions, one can identify and estimate the parent cumulative distribution functions $\{F_j\}_{j=1}^J$.

By assumption, the identity of the winning bidder is known, so the model falls under Theorem 2 of Athey and Haile (2002) who cite Meilijson (1981) and Prakasa Rao (1992) to claim that all of the F_js are nonparametrically identified. Brendstrup and Paarsch adapted the work of Meilijson (1981) to their application. We present this proof here because it will help the reader understand the proof in the multi-unit case, which is presented in chapter 5.

To begin, let us introduce some additional notation. Let $G^0_{(2:\mathcal{N})}(y, i)$ denote the true population cumulative distribution function of the winning bid at an auction won by bidder i and $F^0_{\mathbf{type}(i)}(y)$ denote the true population cumulative distribution function for class $\mathbf{type}(i)$. Now

$$
\begin{aligned}
G^0_{(2:\mathcal{N})}(y, i) &= \Pr[(V_i \geq V_j) \text{ and } (V_j \leq y\ j \neq i)] \\
&= [1 - F^0_{\mathbf{type}(i)}(y)] \prod_{j \neq i} F^0_{\mathbf{type}(j)}(y) + \\
&\quad \int_0^y \prod_{j \neq i} F^0_{\mathbf{type}(j)}(u)\, dF_{\mathbf{type}(i)}(u).
\end{aligned}
\tag{3.11}
$$

Differentiating with respect to y both sides of equation (3.11) above, for each i, yields:

$$
\begin{aligned}
dG^0_{(2:\mathcal{N})}(y, i) &= [1 - F^0_{\mathbf{type}(i)}(y)]\, d\left[\prod_{j \neq i} F^0_{\mathbf{type}(j)}(y)\right] - \\
&\quad \prod_{j \neq i} F^0_{\mathbf{type}(j)}(y)\, dF_{\mathbf{type}(i)}(y) + \\
&\quad \prod_{j \neq i} F^0_{\mathbf{type}(j)}(y)\, dF_{\mathbf{type}(i)}(y) \\
&= [1 - F^0_{\mathbf{type}(i)}(y)]\, d\left[\prod_{j \neq i} F^0_{\mathbf{type}(j)}(y)\right].
\end{aligned}
$$

Integrating back, one obtains

$$G^0_{(2:\mathcal{N})}(y,i) = \int_0^y [1 - F^0_{\mathsf{type}(i)}(u)] \; d \left[\prod_{j \neq i} F^0_{\mathsf{type}(j)}(u) \right].$$

Summing over i, one obtains the marginal

$$G^0_{(2:\mathcal{N})}(y) = \sum_{i=1}^{\mathcal{N}} G^0_{(2:\mathcal{N})}(y,i)$$

$$= \sum_{i=1}^{\mathcal{N}} \int_0^y [1 - F^0_{\mathsf{type}(i)}(u)] \; d \left[\prod_{j \neq i} F^0_{\mathsf{type}(j)}(u) \right].$$

From

$$dG^0_{(2:\mathcal{N})}(y,i) = [1 - F^0_{\mathsf{type}(i)}(y)] \; d \left[\prod_{j \neq i} F^0_{\mathsf{type}(j)}(y) \right],$$

one obtains for each i

$$\prod_{j \neq i} F^0_{\mathsf{type}(j)}(y) = \int_0^y [1 - F^0_{\mathsf{type}(i)}(u)]^{-1} \; dG^0_{(2:\mathcal{N})}(u,i).$$

Hence, Brendstrup and Paarsch have a system of so-called Pfaffian integral equations. Taking the natural logarithm of both sides for each i yields

$$\sum_{j \neq i} \log F^0_{\mathsf{type}(j)}(y) = \log \int_0^y [1 - F^0_{\mathsf{type}(i)}(u)]^{-1} \; dG^0_{(2:\mathcal{N})}(u,i)$$

$$= \log \int_0^y \exp \left\{ -\log[1 - F^0_{\mathsf{type}(i)}(u)] \right\} \; dG^0_{(2:\mathcal{N})}(u,i)$$

or, in matrix notation,

$$\mathbf{A} \log[\boldsymbol{F}^0_{\mathsf{type}}(y)] =$$

$$\log \left[\int_0^y \mathrm{diag} \left(\exp \left\{ -\log[\boldsymbol{\iota}_{\mathcal{N}} - \boldsymbol{F}^0_{\mathsf{type}}(u)] \right\} \; d\boldsymbol{G}^0(u)^\top \right) \right]$$

where $\boldsymbol{\iota}_{\mathcal{N}}$ is an $(\mathcal{N} \times 1)$ vector of ones and

$$\mathbf{A} = \begin{pmatrix} 0 & 1 & 1 & \ldots & 1 & 1 \\ 1 & 0 & 1 & \ldots & 1 & 1 \\ 1 & 1 & 0 & \ldots & 1 & 1 \\ & \vdots & & \ddots & & \vdots \\ 1 & 1 & 1 & \ldots & 0 & 1 \\ 1 & 1 & 1 & \ldots & 1 & 0 \end{pmatrix} = \boldsymbol{\iota}_{\mathcal{N}} \boldsymbol{\iota}_{\mathcal{N}}^\top - \mathbf{I}_{\mathcal{N}},$$

while $\boldsymbol{F}^0_{\text{type}}$ and $d\boldsymbol{G}^0$ are column vectors whose i^{th} rows equal $F^0_{\text{type}(i)}(y)$ and $dG^0_{(2:\mathcal{N})}(y,i)$. From Meilijson (1981), it is known that this system of Pfaffian integral equations, which can be written as

$$\boldsymbol{F}^0_{\text{type}}(y) = \hspace{8cm} (3.12)$$

$$\exp\left\{\mathbf{A}^{-1}\log\left[\text{diag}\left(\int_0^y \exp\left\{-\log[\boldsymbol{\iota}_{\mathcal{N}} - \boldsymbol{F}^0_{\text{type}(i)}(u)]\right\} \; d\boldsymbol{G}^0(u)^\top\right)\right]\right\}$$

has a unique solution, which leads to the following:

Theorem 3.8.1: The distributions of the valuations are identified from the winning bids and the identities of the winners.

Clearly, when J is less than $\mathcal{N}$, testable overidentifying restrictions exist.

3.8.2 Semi-Nonparametric Estimation

A natural way in which to estimate the $\{F^0_j(v)\}^J_{j=1}$ would be to replace the $G^0_{(2:\mathcal{N})}(y,i)$s with their sample analogues and then to solve for the $\hat{F}_j(v)$s consistent with equation (3.12). The arduous and sometimes delicate computations involved in solving equation (3.12) for a functional in a Banach space made Brendstrup and Paarsch adopt a computationally simple strategy to estimate the F_js, the semi-nonparametric (SNP) approach developed by Gallant and Nychka (1987).

In the SNP approach, Brendstrup and Paarsch worked off the probability density function of the winning bid as defined by equation (3.11) above. The idea is to approximate flexibly an unknown probability density function by a Laguerre polynomial; see Judd (1998) as well as appendix A.7.5. The Laguerre polynomial was chosen initially because its domain is $[0,\infty)$, which corresponds to the notion that the marginal utility of an object should be non-negative. Also, Brendstrup and Paarsch parameterized the Laguerre polynomial to guarantee that the probability density function is non-negative. When they admitted covariates, Hermite polynomials were used.

In order to apply the SNP framework, Brendstrup and Paarsch made some now standard technical assumptions. In particular, they assumed that the probability density function f_j lives in the space $\mathcal{F}_j$, which consists of densities having several properties. To describe these properties, they introduced the following notation. First, they let d denote the number of derivatives for the unknown but true probability density function f^0_j on $[0,\infty)$. Now, for some integer $d_0(> \frac{1}{2})$, for some bound $\mathcal{D}_0$, for some $\varepsilon_0 (> 0)$, and for some $\delta_0 (> \frac{1}{2})$ the space $\mathcal{F}_j$ consists of the probability density functions having the following form:

$$f_j(y) = [h_j(y)]^2 + \varepsilon \exp(-y)$$

with $||h_j||_{d+d_0,2,\mu}$ being less than $\mathcal{D}_0$ and ε being greater than ε_0 where μ equals $(1+y^2)^{\delta_0}$ and $||h||_{d+d_0,q,\mu}$ is the Sobolev norm; i.e.,

$$||h||_{d+d_0,q,\mu} = \left(\sum_{|\alpha| \leq d+d_0} |D^\alpha h(y)|^q \mu(y) \, dy \right)^{\frac{1}{q}} \quad q > 0$$

where D^α is the differential operator. The bound $\mathcal{D}_0$ imposes a restriction on the densities in $\mathcal{F}_j$ by restricting the tails of these densities from above. This restriction was needed to ensure that the space $\mathcal{F}_j$ is compact.

The term $\varepsilon \exp(-y)$ is a lower bound on the density used to avoid $\log f_j(y)$ going to $-\infty$ and $\int \log f_j(y) f_{j'}(y) \, dy$ going to $-\infty$ for any two elements f_j and $f_{j'}$ in $\mathcal{F}_j$. In practice, the restriction proved relatively unimportant.

To make the discussion described above concrete, consider the following: it is well-known that any density $f_j \in \mathcal{F}_j$ can be written in terms of an infinite-order polynomial of the form

$$f_j(y) = \left[\sum_{k=0}^{\infty} \theta_{jk} L_k(y) \right]^2 \exp(-y) + \varepsilon \exp(-y)$$

where $L_k(y)$ is the Laguerre polynomial of order k. Approximate the infinite-order polynomial above by a finite-order polynomial of the form

$$f_j^{p_T}(y) = \left[\sum_{k=0}^{p_T} \alpha_{jk} L_k(y) \right]^2 \exp(-y) + \varepsilon \exp(-y).$$

Of course, when truncating an infinite-order polynomial to obtain a finite-order one, error is introduced. However, by letting the degree of the approximation get better as the sample size increases (i.e., by letting p_T increase at a rate that is slower than the rate at which the sample size T increases), Brendstrup and Paarsch argued, at least heuristically, that the approximation should converge to the truth. Thus, for this approach to be strictly nonparametric, one needs to allow the degree of the polynomial to tend to infinity as the sample size increases to infinity.

A natural way to implement this finite-order approximation is the method of quasi-maximum-likelihood. To wit, the estimator $\{\hat{f}_{jT}\}_{j=1}^J$ is defined by

$$\{\hat{f}_{jT}\}_{j=1}^J = \underset{f_j \in \mathcal{F}_{jT}}{\mathrm{argmax}} \frac{1}{T} \sum_{t=1}^{T} \log g_{(2:\mathcal{N})}(y_t, i_t | \boldsymbol{F})$$

where

$$\mathcal{F}_{jT} = \left\{ f_{jT} \in \mathcal{F}_j : f_{jT}(y|\boldsymbol{\alpha}_j) = \left[\sum_{k=0}^{p_T} \alpha_{jk} L_k(y) \right]^2 \exp(-y) + \varepsilon \exp(-y), \right.$$

$$\left. \boldsymbol{\alpha}_j \in \boldsymbol{\Theta}_{jT} \right\}$$

and

$$\boldsymbol{\Theta}_{jT} = \left\{ \boldsymbol{\alpha}_j = (\alpha_{j0}, \dots, \alpha_{jp_T}) : \int_0^\infty f_{jT}(y|\boldsymbol{\alpha}_j)\, dy = 1 \right\}$$

and $\{p_T\}$ is a nondecreasing sequence of integers. It will often be possible to set ε to be zero without the logarithm of the likelihood function becoming ill-behaved.

Having outlined the SNP framework, introducing observed covariates can be done easily without much additional computation. Imagine that at the tth auction the draw of bidder i who is of class j can be written as

$$\tau(V_t^{ij}) = \boldsymbol{z}_t \boldsymbol{\gamma}_j + U_t^{ij}$$

where $F_j(u)$ is the cumulative distribution function of U_t^{ij} and $\boldsymbol{z}_t \boldsymbol{\gamma}_j$ represents how the location of the jth class is shifted as a result of the observed $(K \times 1)$ covariate vector $\boldsymbol{z}_t$ at auction t and the conformable unknown vector $\boldsymbol{\gamma}_j$ for each class $j = 1, \dots, J$. Here, $\tau(\cdot)$ is a monotonically increasing function which is potentially unknown. When U_t^{ij} is independent of the $\boldsymbol{z}_t$, incorporating the covariate vector $\boldsymbol{z}$ into this quasi-maximum likelihood framework simply involves optimizing with respect to $(J \times K)$ additional parameters. Brendstrup and Paarsch chose the logarithmic tranformation of V for $\tau(\cdot)$ to ensure that the marginal utility, the valuation, of the object is positive.

In the presence of observed covariates, Brendstrup and Paarsch approximated $f_j(u)$ by an infinite-order polynomial of the form:

$$f_j(u) = \left[\sum_{k=0}^\infty \omega_{jk} H_k(u) \right]^2 \exp(-u^2/2) + \varepsilon \exp(-u^2/2)$$

because the support of the distribution of the Us is potentially the entire real line. Here, $H_k(u)$ denotes an Hermite polynomial of order k. Of course, the support of the conditional distribution of the Vs is still the positive real line. In practice, Brendstrup and Paarsch truncated to get

$$f_j^{p_T}(u) = \left[\sum_{k=0}^{p_T} \delta_{jk} H_k(u) \right]^2 \exp(-u^2/2) + \varepsilon \exp(-u^2/2).$$

Brendstrup and Paarsch adapted the work of Gallant and Nychka (1987) as well as Fenton and Gallant (1996) to argue that the SNP estimation strategy is a consistent one. Of course, demonstrating consistency is just one part of the exercise; characterizing the asymptotic distribution remains. Following Eastwood and Gallant (1991), Brendstrup and Paarsch advocated characterizing the asymptotic distribution for a fixed p_T using standard first-order, asymptotic methods.

3.9 Practice Problems

The problems at the end of this chapter are designed to give you practice in estimating models of Vickrey and English auctions using parametric, semi-nonparametric, and nonparametric methods.

1. Assume that, in any period, the test score of an individual V is distributed normally with mean μ and variance σ^2. Suppose that in period t for a class of size $\mathcal{N}_t$, only the highest score Y_t is recorded. Thus, the researcher receives the sequence $\{(y_t, \mathcal{N}_t)\}_{t=1}^{T}$.

   a) Assuming that test scores are independent and identically distributed, derive the cumulative distribution function of Y_t in terms of the cumulative distribution function $\Phi(z)$ for a standard normal random variable as well as $\mathcal{N}_t$. Also, derive the probability density function of Y_t, using $\phi(z)$ to denote the probability density function for a standard normal random variable.

   b) Derive the expectation of Y_t. (Hint: note that the normal random variable V lives within the location-scale family of random variables, so V equals $\mu + \sigma Z$, which means that Y_t equals $\mu + \sigma Z_{(1:\mathcal{N}_t)}$ where the following holds: $Z_{(1:\mathcal{N}_t)} \geq Z_{(2:\mathcal{N}_t)} \geq \ldots Z_{(\mathcal{N}_t:\mathcal{N}_t)}$; i.e., the $Z_{(i:\mathcal{N}_t)}$s are order statistics concerning standard normal randoms.)

   c) Write down the logarithm of the likelihood function for a sample of size T.

   d) Write down the regression equation for Y_t conditional on $\mathcal{N}_t$.

   e) On the CD accompanying this book, find `testscor.dat`. This file has 100 lines, 100 observations. In the first column of each line is an identification number while in the second column is the dependent variable y_t, while in the third column is the covariate $\mathcal{N}_t$. Write a MATLAB program to estimate the parameters μ and σ by the method of maximum likelihood using the data in `testscor.dat`.

f) Write a MATLAB program which implements trapezoidal quadrature, for each $\mathcal{N}_t$ in your data set, and then use it to estimate $\mathcal{E}[Z_{(1:\mathcal{N}_t)}]$.

g) Using the data contained in the file `testscor.dat` as well as your estimate of $\mathcal{E}[Z_{(1:\mathcal{N}_t)}]$ from part f), use MATLAB to estimate the parameters μ and σ by the method of least squares (LS). Provide standard errors that are robust to arbitrary forms of heteroskedasticity.

2. Suppose that the logarithm of the valuation for a potential bidder $\log V$ is distributed normally with mean μ and variance σ^2. Consider a sequence of Vickrey auctions $t = 1, \ldots, T$ each having no reserve price, so all $\mathcal{N}_t$ potential bidders participate. Suppose only the winning bid W_t and $\mathcal{N}_t$ are recorded. Thus, the researcher receives the sequence $\{(w_t, \mathcal{N}_t)\}_{t=1}^T$.

a) Assuming that valuations are independent and identically distributed, derive the cumulative distribution function of winning bid W_t in terms of the cumulative distribution function $\Phi(z)$ for a standard normal random variable as well as $\mathcal{N}_t$. Also, derive the probability density function of W_t, using $\phi(z)$ to denote the probability density function for a standard normal random variable.

b) Derive the expectation of $\log W_t$. (Hint: note that the normal random variable $\log V$ lives within the location-scale family of random variables, so $\log V$ equals $\mu + \sigma Z$, which means that $\log W_t$ equals $\mu + \sigma Z_{(2:\mathcal{N}_t)}$.)

c) Write down the logarithm of the likelihood function for a sample of size T.

d) Write down the regression equation for $\log W$.

e) On the CD accompanying this book, find `vickrey.dat`. This file has 100 lines, 100 observations. In the first column of each line is an identification number while in the second column is the dependent variable w_t, while in the third column is the covariate $\mathcal{N}_t$, and in the fourth column is a covariate z_t. Using these data, estimate the parameters μ and σ by the method of maximum likelihood where $\mu(z_t)$ equals $\gamma_0 + \gamma_1 z_t$.

f) Using trapezoidal quadrature, estimate $\mathcal{E}[Z_{(2:\mathcal{N}_t)}]$ for each $\mathcal{N}_t$ in your data set.

g) Using the data contained in the file `vickrey.dat`, estimate the parameters γ_0, γ_1 and σ by the method of least squares (LS). Also report standard errors for your estimates and explain how these were calculated.

3. Consider $\mathcal{N}$ potential bidders who are vying to purchase an object at a Vickrey auction within the IPVP. At Vickrey auctions, the dominant bidding strategy is to bid ones valuation, so bidder i's bid B_i is related to his valuation V_i according to

$$B_i = \beta(V_i) = V_i \quad r \leq V_i$$

where r is the reserve price, the minimum price which must be bid. Clearly, those potential bidders for whom V_i is less than r will choose not to participate at the auction; they will not appear in data collected.

Suppose that a collection of homogeneous objects is sold individually at a sequence of T different Vickrey auctions where the same reserve price 0.50 has been imposed. Consider two different sampling schemes: under the first, at auction t, only the winning bid w_t as well as a measure of the number of potential competitors $\mathcal{N}_t$ is recorded, while under the second, at auction t, only the bids submitted $\boldsymbol{b}_t$, which equals $[b_{(1:n_t)}, b_{(2:n_t)}, \ldots, [b_{(n_t:n_t)}]^\top$ are observed.

a) Derive the logarithm of the likelihood function under the first sampling scheme where $\{(\mathcal{N}_t, w_t)\}_{t=1}^T$ are available.

b) Derive the logarithm of the likelihood function, conditional on realized competition, under the second sampling scheme where $\{(\boldsymbol{b}_t, n_t)\}_{t=1}^T$ are available.

On the CD that accompanies this text you will find the data files `win.dat` and `bids.dat`. Each file contains data concerning fifty auctions under the two sampling schemes. In the file `win.dat` four columns of numbers exist. In the first is an auction identification number, while in the second is the recorded winning bid at that auction, while in the third is the value z_t of a covariate for auction t which is thought to influence the distribution of valuations, and in the fourth column is a measure of potential competition $\mathcal{N}_t$ for auction t. In the file `bids.dat` three columns of numbers exist. In the first is an auction identification number, while in the second is the recorded bid at that auction for a participant, while in the third is the value of the covariate. Obviously, one can recover n_t, realized

competition at auction t, from a count of the bids for any auction
having the same identification number.

Assume that the distribution of heterogeneity is from the Weibull
family, so the probability density function is

$$f_V(v; \boldsymbol{\theta}) = \theta_1 \theta_2 v^{\theta_2 - 1} \exp\left(-\theta_1 v^{\theta_2}\right) \quad v \geq 0, \ \theta_1 > 0, \ \theta_2 > 0$$

where $\boldsymbol{\theta} = (\theta_1, \theta_2)^\top$.

c) Calculate the maximum-likelihood estimate of $\boldsymbol{\theta}$ based on the
empirical specification you derived in part a) under the Weibull
law.

d) Calculate the maximum-likelihood estimate of $\boldsymbol{\theta}$ based on the
empirical specification you derived in part b) under the Weibull
law.

e) In the case when all bids are observed, calculate the kernel-
smoothed estimate of $f_V^0(v)$ for valuations that are above the
reserve price. Use a graph to compare this estimate with the
maximum-likelihood estimate you calculated in part d).

f) In the case when only the winning bids are observed, calculate an estimate of $F_V^0(v)$ for valuations that are above the
reserve price. Use a graph to compare this estimate with the
maximum-likelihood estimate you calculated in part c).

g) Under the empirical specifications considered in parts c) and
d), assuming that a bidder's valuation is his type in the sense of
Myerson (1981) and that the revision-effect functions are zero,
formulate an hypothesis so that you can test whether these
auctions fall within Myerson's regular case, and then test this
hypothesis at size 0.05.

Introduce the covariate z_t into the probability density function of
V using the following functional-form assumption:

$$f_V(v; \theta_{10}, \theta_{11}, \theta_2, z_t) = \exp(\theta_{10} + \theta_{11} z_t) \theta_2 v^{\theta_2 - 1}$$

$$\exp\left[-\exp(\theta_{10} + \theta_{11} z_t) v^{\theta_2}\right].$$

Thus, $\theta_1(z_t)$ equals $\exp(\theta_{10} + \theta_{11} z_t)$.

h) Under the empirical specification considered in part c) and
given the above functional form to introduce the observed
heterogeneity, estimate the parameter vector $(\theta_{10}, \theta_{11}, \theta_2)^\top$ by

the method of maximum likelihood and then test whether θ_{11} equals zero using the likelihood-ratio test. To decide use size 0.05.

i) Under the empirical specification considered in part d) and given the above functional form to introduce the observed heterogeneity, estimate the parameter vector $(\theta_{10}, \theta_{11}, \theta_2)^\top$ by the method of maximum likelihood and then test whether θ_{11} equals zero using the likelihood-ratio test. To decide use size 0.05.

j) Using your estimates from part d) above, derive the maximum-likelihood estimate of the optimal reserve price

$$\rho^* = v_0 + \frac{[1 - F_V(\rho^*)]}{f_V(\rho^*)}$$

when v_0 is zero. Also, calculate the standard error of the estimate and conjecture what the asymptotic distribution will be for your estimates. Test whether the existing reserve price of 0.50 is optimal in light of your estimates.

k) Using your estimates from part d), derive the maximum-likelihood estimate of the optimal reserve price when v_0 is the maximum-likehood estimate of the mean of V, and test whether the existing reserve price of 0.50 is optimal in light of your estimates.

4. Consider eight potential bidders who are vying to purchase an object at an English auction within the IPVP. On the CD that accompanies this text you will find the data file **english.dat**. The file contains data concerning 100 auctions. Three columns of numbers exist. In the first is an auction identification number, while in the second is the recorded winning bid at that auction, while in the third is the recorded value of a covariate Z thought to influence the distribution of valuations.

a) Ignoring the covariate Z, initially, estimate $F_V^0(v)$ nonparametrically.

b) Now, admit the observed covariate Z and then calculate the density-weighted derivative estimator of Powell et al. (1989) to estimate $F_{V|Z}^0(v|z)$ using a single-index model.

c) Finally, assume that the valuation primitive follows the exponential law with parameter θ. Using the knowledge you developed in problems 3.2 and 3.3, compute the maximum-likelihood estimate of θ. Compare your results to the actual valuation distribution (which is given in the code appearing on the CD), the nonparametric result from part a), the single-index-model result from part b), and the empirical distribution function of the *winning* bids.

5. Consider five potential bidders who are vying to purchase an object at an English auction within the IPVP where the bid increment is $1.00. On the CD that accompanies this text you will find the data file `jump.dat`. The file contains data concerning 100 auctions; there are 500 observations. Two columns of numbers exist. In the first is an auction identification number, while in the second is the final observed bid by that bidder (in dollars) at that auction. No reserve price exists at this auction, so the price always starts at $0.00, but because the minimum bid increment is $1.00 it effectively becomes the reserve price. This manifests itself by there sometimes being fewer observed bids than potential bidders.

   a) Construct estimates of the lower and upper bounds of the distribution $F_V^0(v)$ when it exceeds the reserve price.

   b) Construct estimates of the lower and upper bounds on the optimal reserve price ρ^* if it is above the existing reserve price, assuming v_0 is two.

   c) Assuming a Weibull distribution of valuations, so

   $$F_V^0(v) = [1 - \exp(-\theta_1^0 v^{\theta_2^0})],$$

   and using data on the winning bids, calculate the maximum-likelihood estimates of the unknown parameters θ_1^0 and θ_2^0.

   d) Use the maximum-likelihood estimates θ_1^0 and θ_2^0 from part c) to calculate the maximum-likelihood estimate of the optimal reserve price ρ^*, again assuming v_0 is two. Compare this estimate with the bounds constructed in part b).

Chapter 4

First-Price, Sealed-Bid and Dutch Auctions

$\mathcal{T}$ HE ECONOMETRICS of Vickrey and English auctions are made simple by the fact that the dominant-strategy, equilibrium-bid functions are trivial functions of bidder valuations. This is not the case at either Dutch or first-price, sealed-bid auctions where the Bayes–Nash, equilibrium-bid functions are complicated, nonlinear functions of both bidder valuations and the number of bidders as well as the cumulative distribution function of valuations. This nonlinear relationship introduces a number of interesting computational and econometric issues.

In this chapter, we investigate these issues, beginning with Paarsch's (1989) derivation of the data-generating process (DGP) of all bids at first-price, sealed-bid auctions and the winning bid at Dutch and first-price, sealed-bid auctions when potential bidders are risk-neutral and face no reserve price. Subsequently, in the next section, following the research of Guerre, Perrigne, and Vuong (2000), we demonstrate non-parametric identification. We then describe four different estimation strategies, the first being the nonparametric approach of Guerre et al. In an effort to deal effectively with observed covariate heterogeneity, we then introduce parametric models, specifically discussing the method of maximum likelihood of Donald and Paarsch (1993, 1996) as well as the method of simulated nonlinear least-squares of Laffont, Ossard, and Vuong (1995). Finally, we address some criticisms of the maximum-likelihood approach, examining the extreme-order, generalized method-of-moments estimator of Donald and Paarsch (2002).

We then introduce a binding reserve price. In these cases, the extensive-form games at Dutch and first-price, sealed-bid auctions are different because the number of participants is typically observed at Dutch auctions, but realistically assumed unknown at first-price, sealed-bid auctions. In addition, the straightforward application of nonparametric methods is plagued by bias. We outline a clever strategy, due to Guerre et al., to circumvent this problem.

In most structural econometric analyses of auction data, researchers have typically assumed that the potential bidders are risk neutral with respect to winning the auction. At English and Vickrey auctions, such an assumption is irrelevant because the dominant-strategy, equilibrium-bid function remains unchanged under these formats when potential bidders are risk averse. On the other hand, at Dutch and first-price, sealed-bid auctions the attitudes of potential bidders toward risk matter, so we describe the effects of symmetric, von Neumann–Morgenstern preferences on the structural-econometric analysis, following the work of Campo, Guerre, Perrigne, and Vuong (2000). We also examine the work of Lu (2004), who has extended the work of Campo et al., by considering a richer model—stochastic private values—based on the research of Éso and White (2004).

Thus far, all of the surveyed research concerning Dutch and first-price, sealed-bid has been within the symmetric IPVP. Following Brendstrup and Paarsch (2004), we then go on to examine the effects of asymmetric bidders, those whose valuations are draws from different distributions, especially in the presence of a binding reserve price. We also investigate the research of Krasnokutskaya (2004), who considered auction-specific unobserved heterogeneity, a particular form of asymmetry across auctions.

We then consider a policy experiment undertaken by Brendstrup and Paarsch (forthcoming) in which the performance of the English vis-a-vis the Dutch auction is compared when potential bidders are asymmetric. Under these conditions, Maskin and Riley (2000) have demonstrated that English (as well as Vickrey) auctions are efficient, while Dutch (as well as first-price, sealed-bid) auctions can lead to inefficient allocations. Moreover, the revenue equivalence proposition breaks down. Using data from fish auctions in Grenå, Denmark, Brendstrup and Paarsch estimated the incidence and economic importance of inefficiencies at Dutch auctions and then compared the expected revenues of the two auction formats.

Finally, we consider the question of endogenous participation. While a number of authors have considered this issue, we describe the work of Li (2005).

4.1 Deriving the Data-Generating Process

As in the previous chapter, we shall assume initially that no reserve price exists. Paarsch (1989) pointed out that the probability density function of $\sigma(V)$ at a first-price, sealed-bid auction is complicated to calculate because σ is a nonlinear function of V. He also demonstrated that the joint density of bids S which is an $(\mathcal{N} \times 1)$ vector where S equals $(S_1, S_2, \cdots, S_{\mathcal{N}})^{\top}$ is

$$
\begin{aligned}
f_S(s) &= \prod_{i=1}^{\mathcal{N}} \left\{ \frac{f_V\left[\sigma^{-1}(s_i)\right]}{\sigma'\left[\sigma^{-1}(s_i)\right]} \right\} \\
&= \prod_{i=1}^{\mathcal{N}} \left\{ \frac{F_V\left[\sigma^{-1}(s_i)\right]^{\mathcal{N}}}{(\mathcal{N}-1) \int_{\underline{v}}^{\sigma^{-1}(s_i)} F_V(u)^{(\mathcal{N}-1)} \, du} \right\}
\end{aligned}
\tag{4.1}
$$

where it follows from equations (2.5) that

$$
\sigma'(v) = \frac{(\mathcal{N}-1) f_V(v) \int_{\underline{v}}^{v} F_V(u)^{(\mathcal{N}-1)} \, du}{F_V(v)^{\mathcal{N}}}
$$

is the Jacobian for the transformation of V to $\sigma(V)$.

The winning bid is also a function of the Vs. Thus, the probability density function of the observed winning bid at either a Dutch or a first-price, sealed-bid auction is related to $f_V(v)$. Now, the probability density function of the highest valuation for the object Z, which equals $V_{(1:\mathcal{N})}$, is

$$
f_Z(z) = \mathcal{N} F_V(z)^{\mathcal{N}-1} f_V(z),
$$

so the probability density function of the winning bid W equal $\sigma(Z)$ is

$$
f_W(w; \mathcal{N}) = \frac{f_Z\left[\sigma^{-1}(w)\right]}{\sigma'\left[\sigma^{-1}(w)\right]} = \frac{\mathcal{N} F_V\left[\sigma^{-1}(w)\right]^{2\mathcal{N}-1}}{(\mathcal{N}-1) \int_{\underline{v}}^{\sigma^{-1}(w)} F_V(u)^{\mathcal{N}-1} \, du}.
\tag{4.2}
$$

4.2 Identification and Estimation: Simplest Case

Within the IPVP, the DGP at Dutch and first-price, sealed-bid auctions is nonparametrically identified. This result, which was first proven by Guerre et al., is not only important because it leads naturally to an elegant nonparametric estimation strategy, but also because it is useful in demonstrating parameter consistency within parametric models, including the method of maximum likelihood.[1] It should be noted that nonparametric identification holds whether all of the bids are observed or just the winning bid is observed.

---

[1] The proof by Guerre et al. is not absolutely necessary in parametric models as Donald and Paarsch (1996) demonstrated identification in such cases.

In our description of estimation strategies, we first consider empirical specifications in the absence of binding reserve prices or observed covariate heterogeneity. We begin by describing the nonparametric methods proposed by Guerre et al. and then discuss the limitations of these methods, particularly when considerable observed covariate heterogeneity exists. Thus, we entertain parametric models, examining first the method of maximum likelihood, next the method of simulated nonlinear least-squares, and finally the method of extreme-order generalized method-of-moments.

4.2.1 Nonparametric Identification

To begin, consider the simplest case of a first-price, sealed-bid auction at which no reserve price exists. In this case, all the bids are observed. What a researcher would like to know is whether the population distribution of valuations $F_V^0(v)$ can be identified from the population distribution of bids $F_S^0(s)$.

As is typically done in identification proofs, one assumes that the population probability density function of the observed bids $f_S^0(s)$ is known, so $F_S^0(s)$, which equals $\int_0^s f_S^0(u)\,du$, is then known too. Now, from equation (2.4), we know that

$$\sigma'(v) = [v - \sigma(v)]\frac{(\mathcal{N}-1)f_V^0(v)}{F_V^0(v)}.$$

This then implies that the private value v and the strategy $\sigma(v)$ are related according to

$$v = \sigma(v) + \frac{F_V^0(v)}{(\mathcal{N}-1)f_V^0(v)}\sigma'(v).$$

But, in equilibrium, s equals $\sigma(v)$. In addition, using the change of variable formula, the probability density function of bid S is related to the probability density function of valuation V and the derivative of the bid function through

$$f_S^0(s) = \frac{f_V^0(v)}{\sigma'(v)}.$$

Because $\sigma(v)$ is a strictly increasing function of v, it is also clear that $F_S^0(s)$ equals $F_V^0\left[\sigma^{-1}(s)\right]$. Therefore,

$$v = s + \frac{F_S^0(s)}{(\mathcal{N}-1)f_S^0(s)}.$$

Put another way, $f_V^0(v)$ is identified from $f_S^0(s)$.

When only the winning bid W is observed, as in the case of a Dutch auction, identification also holds. In this case, let $F_W^0(w)$ denote the true cumulative distribution function of the winning bid W and $f_W^0(w)$ its probability density function. Under the symmetric IPVP assumptions,

$$F_W^0(w) = F_S^0(w)^{\mathcal{N}}.$$

Therefore,

$$F_S^0(w) = F_W^0(w)^{\frac{1}{\mathcal{N}}},$$

and

$$f_S^0(w) = \frac{1}{\mathcal{N}} F_W^0(w)^{\frac{1}{\mathcal{N}}-1} f_W^0(w).$$

Once $F_S^0(s)$ and $f_S^0(s)$ are identified, one can apply the previous arguments to identify $f_V^0(v)$. Alternatively, note that

$$\frac{F_S^0(w)}{f_S^0(w)} = \frac{\mathcal{N} F_W^0(w)}{f_W^0(w)},$$

so we can write

$$v_{(1:\mathcal{N})} = w + \frac{\mathcal{N}}{\mathcal{N}-1} \frac{F_W^0(w)}{f_W^0(w)}.$$

This suggests that we can recover the value of $V_{(1:\mathcal{N})}$ for every possible W in the population. Therefore, the distribution function of $V_{(1:\mathcal{N})}$ is identified. Because we know that this distribution function is $F_V^0(\cdot)^{\mathcal{N}}$, $F_V^0(\cdot)$ is also identified.

4.2.2 Nonparametric Estimation

Perhaps one of the most elegant identification results in the SEAD concerns Dutch and first-price, sealed-bid auctions. This result, which was derived by Guerre et al., leads naturally to a nonparametric strategy to estimate the distribution of valuations $F_V^0(v)$ within the symmetric IPVP, assuming risk-neutral potential bidders.

To begin, consider a first-price, sealed-bid auction with no reserve price. In this case, all potential bidders submit bids. Recall, from the nonparametric identification results of the previous section, that for bidder i the unobserved valuation v_i is related to the observed bid s_i for bidder i according to

$$v_i = s_i + \frac{F_S^0(s_i)}{(\mathcal{N}-1) f_S^0(s_i)}.$$

Now, the population values of $F_S^0(s)$ and $f_S^0(s)$ are unknown, but can be estimated nonparametrically from a sample of bids. For a random sample of T observations with identical number of bidders $\mathcal{N}$,

$$\left\{ \left[(S_{it})_{i=1}^{\mathcal{N}}, \mathcal{N} \right] \right\}_{t=1}^{T},$$

a consistent estimator of $F_S^0(s)$ is the sample empirical distribution function:

$$\hat{F}_S(s) = \frac{1}{T} \sum_{t=1}^{T} \frac{1}{\mathcal{N}} \sum_{i=1}^{\mathcal{N}} \mathbf{1}(S_{it} \leq s).$$

The probability density function of the observed bids, $f_S^0(s)$, on the other hand, can also be estimated nonparametrically using such methods as kernel-smoothing. Thus, one such estimator is

$$\hat{f}_S(s) = \frac{1}{T} \sum_{t=1}^{T} \frac{1}{\mathcal{N}} \sum_{i=1}^{\mathcal{N}} \frac{1}{h_g} \kappa \left(\frac{S_{it} - s}{h_g} \right)$$

where h_g is a sequence of bandwidth parameters such that h_g goes to zero and Th_g goes to infinity as T increases without bound. $\kappa(\cdot)$ is a kernel-smoothing function. Any proper probability density function can be used as a kernel-smoother. Moreover, in general, $\kappa(\cdot)$ can be a mth high-order kernel function, which satisfies the following conditions:

$$\int \kappa(u) \ du = 1, \quad \text{where} \quad \int u^{\ell} \kappa(u) \ du = 0, \ \forall \ \ell < m$$

and

$$\int |u|^m |\kappa(u)| \ du < \infty.$$

The bandwidth parameter h_g is a sequence of constants that converges to zero as T goes to ∞. Smaller values of h_g reduce the bias, but increase the variance of the nonparametric estimator $\hat{f}_S(s)$. The optimal choice of h_g must achieve a balance between variance and bias. When the bandwidth parameter is h_g, effectively, only observations that are within a neighborhood of length h_g are used in the estimation. The number of observations in this neighborhood is approximately proportional to Th_g, resulting in a variance term of the order of magnitude of $[1/(Th_g)]$. If the true probability density function is smoothly differentiable up to the ℓth order, then the bias term is typically of the order h_g^{ℓ}. The optimal bandwidth sets $[1/(Th_g)]$ approximately equal to $h_g^{2\ell}$ and is approximately $(1/T)^{\frac{1}{1+2\ell}}$. The choice of optimal bandwidth achieves an optimal convergence rate $(\log T/T)^{\frac{1}{1+2\ell}}$ where the presence of the

$\log T$ is due to the use of a Bernstein-type exponential inequality in calculating the uniform rates over a partition of the support of observed bids. This results in an optimal uniform rate of convergence of the order of $(\log T/T)^{\ell/(1+2\ell)}$.

Estimated *pseudo-values* can then be recovered from the bids via

$$\hat{V}_{it} = S_{it} + \frac{\hat{F}_S(S_{it})}{(\mathcal{N}-1)\hat{f}_S(S_{it})}.$$

Straightforward estimators of $F_V^0(v)$ and $f_V^0(v)$ can then be constructed as

$$\hat{F}_V(v) = \frac{1}{T}\sum_{t=1}^{T}\frac{1}{\mathcal{N}}\sum_{i=1}^{\mathcal{N}}\mathbf{1}\left(\hat{V}_{it} \leq v\right),$$

and

$$\hat{f}_V(v) = \frac{1}{T}\sum_{t=1}^{T}\frac{1}{\mathcal{N}}\sum_{i=1}^{\mathcal{N}}\frac{1}{h_g}\kappa\left(\frac{\hat{V}_{it}-v}{h_g}\right).$$

One problem with this application of kernel-smoothing using $\hat{V}_{it}$ is that the kernel-density estimates of $\hat{f}_S(s)$ are not uniformly consistent near the boundary of support for $F_S^0(s)$. This inconsistency at the boundary contaminates the second-stage estimation of $\hat{f}_V(v)$. To address this issue, Guerre et al. suggested trimming the boundary values of the bids when constructing the nonparametric estimates of $\hat{f}_V(v)$. Effectively, they suggested replacing $\hat{f}_V(v)$ by the following estimator:

$$\hat{f}_V(v) = \frac{1}{T}\sum_{t=1}^{T}\frac{1}{\mathcal{N}}\sum_{i=1}^{\mathcal{N}}\frac{1}{h_g}\kappa\left(\frac{\hat{V}_{it}-v}{h_g}\right)\mathbf{1}\left(S_{\min}+h_g \leq S_{it} \leq S_{\max}-h_g\right),$$

where $S_{\min}$ and $S_{\max}$ are the minimum and maximum of the observed bids.

Consider now the case where only winning bids are observed. In this case, we can estimate $F_W^0(w)$ by

$$\hat{F}_W(w) = \frac{1}{T}\sum_{t=1}^{T}\mathbf{1}\left(W_t \leq w\right)$$

and estimate $f_W^0(w)$ by

$$\hat{f}_W(w) = \frac{1}{T}\sum_{t=1}^{T}\frac{1}{h_g}\kappa\left(\frac{W_t-w}{h_g}\right).$$

The valuation of the highest bidder for each auction can then be recovered from the relation:

$$\hat{V}_{(1:\mathcal{N})t} = W_t + \frac{\mathcal{N}}{\mathcal{N}-1} \frac{\hat{F}_W(W_t)}{\hat{f}_W(W_t)}.$$

In turn, this can be used to estimate the distribution function of the highest valuation Z of the bidders:

$$\hat{F}_Z(z) = \frac{1}{T} \sum_{t=1}^{T} \mathbf{1} \left[\hat{V}_{(1:\mathcal{N})t} \leq z \right]$$

and the distribution of the valuation can then be estimated as

$$\hat{F}_V(v) = \hat{F}_Z(v)^{\frac{1}{\mathcal{N}}} = \left\{ \frac{1}{T} \sum_{t=1}^{T} \mathbf{1} \left[\hat{V}_{(1:\mathcal{N})t} \leq v \right] \right\}^{\frac{1}{\mathcal{N}}}.$$

Similarly, the probability density function of the highest valuation of the bidders Z can be estimated by

$$\hat{f}_Z(z) = \frac{1}{T} \sum_{t=1}^{T} \frac{1}{h_g} \kappa \left(\frac{z - \hat{V}_{(1:\mathcal{N})t}}{h_g} \right) \mathbf{1} \left(W_{\min} + h_g \leq W_t \leq W_{\max} - h_g \right)$$

where $W_{\min}$ and $W_{\max}$ are the minimum and maximum observed winning bids in the sample. Finally, if one is interested in estimating $f_V^0(v)$, then use

$$\hat{f}_V(v) = \frac{\hat{F}_Z(v)^{\frac{1}{\mathcal{N}}-1} \hat{f}_Z(v)}{\mathcal{N}}.$$

As was mentioned in chapter 3, one major problem faced by an empirical researcher is that getting a sample of identical objects to analyze is often difficult. In empirical work involving auctions, samples of one hundred observations would be considered large. Covariate heterogeneity is usually present. Suppose the observed covariate heterogeneity can be quantified in terms of a $(K \times 1)$ vector of covariates $\mathbf{z}$, so the probability density function of S conditional on $\mathbf{z}$ then becomes

$$f_{S|\mathbf{Z}}^0(s|\mathbf{z}).$$

When the outcomes of $\mathbf{z}$ are discrete and the number of combinations finite, then for a particular combination of the $\mathbf{z}$s one can use the nonparametric methods described in the previous section to define an estimator of $F_{V|\mathbf{Z}}^0(v|\mathbf{z})$, but often the number of combinations of $\mathbf{z}$s is prohibitively large. Nonparametric methods are difficult to implement reliably when many covariates exist, a problem that is often encountered in practice. For this reason, we focus next on parametric methods.

4.2.3 Maximum Likelihood Estimation

Having established identification nonparametrically, and proposed estimators for Dutch and first-price, sealed-bid auctions in the absence of covariates or a reserve price, we now concentrate on estimating an unknown parametric distribution of valuations. We focus on parametric models because, as was shown in chapter 3, they admit covariates in a numerically parsimonious way and they allow one to estimate the distribution of valuations over its entire range. Previously, we discussed the limitations of parametric models, so we shall not repeat them here. Suffice it to say that parametric models are an approximation to the real process. As in all empirical work, the researcher must decide where to make the approximation. We assume that when researchers constrain themselves to parametric models, they understand the approximations present in their research.

To fix ideas, we begin with the simple case where F_V^0 belongs to a parametric family of distributions that does not depend on covariates, so it can be written as

$$F_V^0(v) = F_V(v; \boldsymbol{\theta}^0)$$

where $\boldsymbol{\theta}^0$ is a $(p \times 1)$ vector of unknown parameters. We make this initial simplification to highlight the technical problem that must be solved in order to estimate the parameter vector $\boldsymbol{\theta}^0$ by the method of maximum likelihood; we shall consider covariates later.

The main technical problem is that the support of both the individual bid and the winning bid distributions depends on the parameters of interest. To see this, evaluate $\sigma(v)$ at its upper bound of support $\bar{v}$. Note that

$$\sigma(\bar{v}) = \bar{v} - \frac{\int_{\underline{v}}^{\bar{v}} F_V(u; \boldsymbol{\theta}^0)^{\mathcal{N}-1} \, du}{F_V(\bar{v}; \boldsymbol{\theta}^0)^{\mathcal{N}-1}}$$

$$= \bar{v} - \int_{\underline{v}}^{\bar{v}} F_V(u; \boldsymbol{\theta}^0)^{\mathcal{N}-1} \, du$$

$$= \bar{s}(\boldsymbol{\theta}^0; \mathcal{N})$$

since $F_V(\bar{v}; \boldsymbol{\theta}^0)$ equals one. Here, $\bar{s}(\boldsymbol{\theta}^0, \mathcal{N})$ is just the mean of the highest value from $(\mathcal{N} - 1)$ opponents. Even when $\bar{v}$ is ∞, $\bar{s}$ is finite and depends on $\boldsymbol{\theta}^0$. Thus, a standard regularity condition of maximum-likelihood estimation, typically assumed, no longer holds. Moreover, the standard way that parameter consistency is demonstrated in econometrics is unsatisfactory in this context.[2] To deal with both the Dutch and

---

[2] This was first pointed out in the job-search literature by Flinn and Heckman

the first-price, sealed-bid cases at the same time, Donald and Paarsch (1996) focused on only the winning bids, but the methods they proposed would apply were all bids used.

A simple example will illustrate the nonstandard nature of the estimation problem a researcher faces when attempting to estimate parametric structural econometric models of Dutch or first-price sealed-bid auctions. Consider a random sample of size T for a random variable W that is distributed uniformly on the interval $[0, \theta^0]$, where θ^0 is an unknown parameter which the investigator seeks to estimate. The probability density function of W is

$$\frac{\mathbf{1}(0 \leq w \leq \theta^0)}{\theta^0}$$

where $\mathbf{1}(\cdot)$ is the indicator function of the event argument. The standard approach to finding the maximum-likelihood estimator of θ^0 would involve maximizing the following logarithm of the likelihood function with respect to θ:

$$\frac{1}{T}\mathcal{L}_T(\theta; W_1, W_2, \ldots, W_T) = -\log\theta + \frac{1}{T}\sum_{t=1}^{T}\log\left[\mathbf{1}(0 \leq W_t \leq \theta)\right].$$

The standard approach to demonstrating the parameter consistency of the maximum-likelihood estimator, following Amemiya (1985), would involve showing that this function converges uniformly over some parameter set to a function that is maximized at the true value.[3]

The problem with this approach is that showing uniform convergence is difficult, unless the parameter set is restricted to be $[\theta^0, \theta^0 + \delta]$ for some positive value of δ. This is because the usual dominance condition, such as Assumption A3 of White (1982), can only be satisfied on this set, implying that the maximum is θ^0, a somewhat unsatisfactory result that obviously depends on knowledge of the true parameter value.

The approach that Donald and Paarsch used to demonstrate parameter consistency avoided this difficulty. Donald and Paarsch noted

---

(1982) and in the auction literature by Paarsch (1992), while Donald and Paarsch (1993) presented a first step toward solving the problem, and Donald and Paarsch (1996) solved it fully, for the case of discrete covariates.

[3] Note that some variant of Wald's (1949) proof or Hoadley's (1971) proof of parameter consistency could potentially be used, although as Amemiya (1985) has noted, some of Wald's conditions may be difficult to verify in practice. LeCam (1953) has also presented high-level conditions for demonstrating consistency that may be easier to verify and could provide an alternative route to demonstrating consistency.

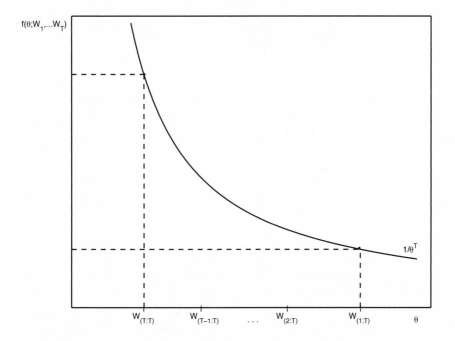

Figure 4.1
Maximum-Likelihood Estimator: Uniform Case

that an equivalent representation to maximizing the likelihood function is to solve the following constrained optimization problem:

$$\max_{\langle\theta\rangle} \frac{1}{\theta^T} \quad \text{subject to} \quad \begin{cases} W_1 \leq \theta \\ W_2 \leq \theta \\ \vdots \\ W_T \leq \theta. \end{cases}$$

This approach is also more in line with the way the estimator is calculated in practice. A further advantage to this approach is that treating the problem in this way provided Donald and Paarsch a link to the distribution theory. For, as Donald and Paarsch demonstrated, the binding constraints are an important part of the solution. For example, in the uniform example considered above, it is easy to see that the solution for the MLE involves one binding constraint. In fact, the MLE is

$$\hat{\theta} = \max(W_1, W_2, \ldots, W_T) = W_{(1:T)}.$$

Abstracting from ties in the data, $(T-1)$ of the constraints do not bind. This is depicted in figure 4.1 where $f(\theta; W_1, \ldots, W_T)$ denotes the likelihood function of the sample $(W_1, \ldots, W_T)$, without the indicator function, and equals $(1/\theta^T)$.

Note too that the conventional methods used to determine the asymptotic distribution of $\hat{\theta}$ do not apply. In particular, only the largest W_t is important in determining the distribution of $\hat{\theta}$. Donald and Paarsch presented a detailed analysis of the problems that arise in performing the asymptotic analysis under these conditions. Suffice to say here that the maximum-likelihood estimator of the unknown parameter vector θ^0 will be defined in a similar fashion.

Having outlined the major technical problem in the application of the method of maximum likelihood, we now admit covariates, the principal motivation for going to parametric approach in the first place. Assume that $F_V(v; \theta^0)$ depends on a vector of covariates Z, denoted $F_V(v; \theta^0, Z)$, which then implies that the observed bids must lie in the interval $[\underline{v}, \bar{s}(\theta^0; \mathcal{N}, Z)]$.

Optimization Problem and Parameter Consistency

Let X_t denote $(\mathcal{N}_t, Z_t)$, the vector of all covariates for observation t, and let x_t denote a particular realization of X_t. Donald and Paarsch made the following assumption concerning the data-generating process:

Assumption 4.3.1: The (W_t, X_t)s are independent as well as identically distributed, so that the probability density function of W_t given $X_t = x_t$ is given by

$$f_W(w_t; \theta, x_t)\mathbf{1}\left[0 \leq w_t \leq \bar{s}(\theta; x_t)\right]$$

where θ is an $(p \times 1)$ dimensional parameter vector of interest. Assume too that X_t can be partitioned so that $X_t = (X_{1t}, X_{2t})$ where the elements of the vector X_{1t} are discrete with finite support χ_1 and the elements of the vector X_{2t} are continuous with compact support χ_2. Let $\chi = \chi_1 \times \chi_2$, and assume that for any non-empty subset $\mathcal{A}_1$ of χ_1 and any non-empty open subset $\mathcal{A}_2$ of χ_2, $\Pr(\mathcal{A}_1 \times \mathcal{A}_2) > 0$.

Letting

$$\mathcal{L}_T(\theta) = \frac{1}{T}\sum_{t=1}^{T} \log f_W(W_t; \theta, X_t),$$

Donald and Paarsch denoted the set of feasible values of θ (that are consistent with the data in the sense described above) by

$$\Theta_T^* = \{\theta \in \bar{\Theta} \mid 0 \leq W_t \leq \bar{s}(\theta; X_t) \ \forall \ t = 1, \dots, T\}$$

where $\bar{\Theta}$ is some compact set that contains the true value of the parameter θ^0. Note that by definition $\theta^0 \in \Theta_T^*$ for all T. Now, $\hat{\theta}$, the MLE of θ^0, is defined as the solution to

$$\max_{<\theta>} \mathcal{L}_T(\theta) \quad \text{subject to} \quad \theta \in \Theta_T^*.$$

In proving the parameter consistency of the MLE, the main complication that arises is that the set Θ_T^* shrinks as the sample size increases. To prove consistency in this case, Donald and Paarsch characterized the behavior of Θ_T^* as T grows.

To do this, Donald and Paarsch made an assumption that restricts the behavior of the true probability density function near the upper bound of support. This will be useful in determining the limiting behavior of the set Θ_T^*.

Assumption 4.3.2: For any $\varepsilon > 0$,

$$\inf_{x \in \chi} \Pr[W > \bar{s}(\theta^0, x) - \varepsilon] = \delta(\varepsilon) > 0.$$

A final assumption that is used to analyze the behavior of Θ_T^* involves the nature of the $\bar{s}(\theta; x)$ function.

Assumption 4.3.3: For any $\theta \in \bar{\Theta}$, $\bar{s}(\theta; x)$ is continuous in x on χ. Moreover,

$$\underline{v} < \inf_{x \in \chi} \bar{s}(\theta^0; x) < \sup_{x \in \chi} \bar{s}(\theta^0; x) < \infty.$$

In providing conditions for consistency, Donald and Paarsch first showed that the set Θ_T^* converges to the set

$$\Theta^* = \{\theta \in \bar{\Theta} \mid \bar{s}(\theta^0; x) \leq \bar{s}(\theta; x) \ \forall \ x \in \chi\}.$$

This is the set of θs that obeys the constraints for all possible values of X and W. Notice that by construction $\Theta^* \subset \Theta_T^*$. After showing that Θ_T^* converges to Θ^*, Donald and Paarsch gave a set of conditions in terms of Θ^* that guarantee consistency. The sense in which Θ_T^* converges to Θ^* is given in the following definition.

Definition 4.3.1: $\Theta_T^* \overset{\text{a.s.}}{\longrightarrow} \Theta^*$ if $\Theta^* \subset \Theta_T^*$ and if for any $\theta \notin \Theta^*$ there is a finite value $\bar{T}$ such that $\theta \notin \Theta_T^*$ for all $T \geq \bar{T}$ with probability one.

Under these assumptions, Donald and Paarsch proved the following consistency result.

Theorem 4.3.1: Given Assumptions 4.3.1 to 4.3.3, $\Theta_T^* \overset{\text{a.s.}}{\longrightarrow} \Theta^*$.

The following result contains the general consistency result for the MLE. Notice that the result proved in Theorem 4.3.1 is one of the assumptions used to prove consistency.

Theorem 4.3.2: Given Assumptions 4.3.1 to 4.3.3, and

a) $\bar{\boldsymbol{\Theta}}$ is compact;

b) $\mathcal{L}_T(\boldsymbol{\theta}) \xrightarrow{\text{a.s.}} \mathcal{L}_\infty(\boldsymbol{\theta}) = \mathcal{E}[\log f_W(W_t; \boldsymbol{\theta}, \boldsymbol{X}_t)]$ uniformly over $\boldsymbol{\Theta}^*$;

c) $\mathcal{L}_\infty(\boldsymbol{\theta}) \geq \mathcal{L}_\infty(\boldsymbol{\theta}^0)$ and $\boldsymbol{\theta} \in \boldsymbol{\Theta}^*$ implies that $\boldsymbol{\theta} = \boldsymbol{\theta}^0$,

then $\hat{\boldsymbol{\theta}} \xrightarrow{\text{a.s.}} \boldsymbol{\theta}^0$.

Calculating the Maximum Likelihood Estimator

In order to calculate the maximum-likelihood estimator on a computer using nonlinear programming techniques as well as to determine its asymptotic distribution, Donald and Paarsch made the following two assumptions:

Assumption 4.3.4: The $\log f_W(\boldsymbol{\theta}; w, \boldsymbol{x})$ function is twice continuously differentiable in $\boldsymbol{\theta}$.

Assumption 4.3.5: The $\bar{s}(\boldsymbol{\theta}; \boldsymbol{x})$ functions are quasi-concave and twice continuously differentiable in $\boldsymbol{\theta}$.

The MLE $\hat{\boldsymbol{\theta}}$ can be computed by solving the following optimization problem:

$$\max_{\langle\boldsymbol{\theta}\rangle} \sum_{t=1}^{T} \log f_W(\boldsymbol{\theta}; W_t, \boldsymbol{X}_t) \quad \text{subject to} \quad \begin{cases} W_1 \leq \bar{s}(\boldsymbol{\theta}; \boldsymbol{X}_1) \\ W_2 \leq \bar{s}(\boldsymbol{\theta}; \boldsymbol{X}_2) \\ \quad \vdots \\ W_T \leq \bar{s}(\boldsymbol{\theta}; \boldsymbol{X}_T). \end{cases}$$

In practice, solving for the MLE will involve maximizing the following Lagrangean:

$$\mathcal{J}_T(\boldsymbol{\theta}, \boldsymbol{\lambda}) = \sum_{t=1}^{T} \{\log f_W(\boldsymbol{\theta}; W_t, \boldsymbol{X}_t) + \lambda_t [\bar{s}(\boldsymbol{\theta}; \boldsymbol{X}_t) - W_t]\}$$

with respect to the vector $\boldsymbol{\theta}$, where $\boldsymbol{\lambda}$ collects the Lagrange multipliers in a vector $(\lambda_1, \ldots, \lambda_T)^\top$. The MLE $\hat{\boldsymbol{\theta}}$ satisfies the following conditions:[4]

$$\sum_{t=1}^{T} \left[\nabla_{\boldsymbol{\theta}} \log f_W(\hat{\boldsymbol{\theta}}; W_t, \boldsymbol{X}_t) + \hat{\lambda}_t \nabla_{\boldsymbol{\theta}} \bar{s}(\hat{\boldsymbol{\theta}}; \boldsymbol{X}_t) \right] = \boldsymbol{0}_p$$

$$\hat{\lambda}_1 \left[\bar{s}(\hat{\boldsymbol{\theta}}; \boldsymbol{X}_1) - W_1 \right] = 0$$

$$\hat{\lambda}_2 \left[\bar{s}(\hat{\boldsymbol{\theta}}; \boldsymbol{X}_2) - W_2 \right] = 0$$

$$\vdots$$

$$\hat{\lambda}_T \left[\bar{s}(\hat{\boldsymbol{\theta}}; \boldsymbol{X}_T) - W_T \right] = 0.$$

At most, p of the T constraints will ever bind at one time; i.e., $(T - p)$ of the Lagrange multipliers will be zero at the optimum.

Asymptotic Distribution of the Estimator

A natural way to calculate the variance-covariance matrix of $\hat{\boldsymbol{\theta}}$ would be to consider the behavior of the Hessian matrix of the Lagrangean

$$\nabla_{\boldsymbol{\theta}\boldsymbol{\theta}} \, \mathcal{J}_T(\hat{\boldsymbol{\theta}}) = \sum_{t=1}^{T} \left[\nabla_{\boldsymbol{\theta}\boldsymbol{\theta}} \, \log f_W(\hat{\boldsymbol{\theta}}; W_t, \boldsymbol{X}_t) + \hat{\lambda}_t \nabla_{\boldsymbol{\theta}\boldsymbol{\theta}} \bar{s}(\hat{\boldsymbol{\theta}}; \boldsymbol{X}_t) \right].$$

This is useful when the solution to the optimization problem occurs along a smooth and differentiable part of the constraint set, but typically the solution obtains at the intersection of the constraints. In this case, the Hessian is ill-defined. Moreover, the properties of the perturbed optimum are determined solely by the constraints. To see this, consider the simple problem introduced in the first part of this section. There, the properties of the maximum-likelihood estimator $\hat{\boldsymbol{\theta}}$ were solely determined by the behavior of the largest W_t in a sample of size T. Here, the properties will often be determined by the solution to some set of the largest p order statistics of W_t given p different combinations of the $\boldsymbol{X}_t$s.

As may be expected from the previous discussion, the distribution theory for the estimator can be quite complicated. Because of technical difficulties that arise with T constraints when T is going to infinity, Donald and Paarsch chose to analyze the case of discrete covariates,

---

[4] Under the stated conditions, these Kuhn–Tucker conditions are necessary, but not sufficient for a global maximum. If the logarithm of the likelihood function is pseudo-concave, then it is well-known that the Kuhn–Tucker conditions are both necessary and sufficient; see Mangasarian (1969).

which implies that a finite number of constraints exist asymptotically. Hence,

Assumption 4.3.6: $\boldsymbol{X}_t$ is a discrete random vector with probability mass function $\pi(\boldsymbol{x})$, with K being the number of points that have $\pi(\boldsymbol{x}) > 0$.

Denote each possible point in the set by $\boldsymbol{x}(k)$, and let $\pi_k = \pi[\boldsymbol{x}(k)]$ for $k = 1, \ldots, K$. Despite the assumption of discrete covariates, the results are of considerable interest. Indeed, the limiting distributions of the estimators will depend on the relationship between K and p, and will only fall into the usual normal limiting family in a special case.

The advantage of having discrete covariates is that the sample optimization problem may be written as

$$\max_{<\boldsymbol{\theta}>} \sum_{k=1}^{K} \hat{\pi}_k \mathcal{L}_T \left[\boldsymbol{\theta}, \boldsymbol{x}(k)\right] \quad \text{subject to} \quad \hat{W}\left[\boldsymbol{x}(k)\right] \leq \bar{s}[\boldsymbol{\theta}; \boldsymbol{x}(k)] \quad k = 1, \ldots, K$$

where $\hat{W}\left[\boldsymbol{x}(k)\right]$ is the $\max\{W_t : \boldsymbol{x}_t = \boldsymbol{x}(k)\}$, the largest order statistic of W_t over all observations that have $\boldsymbol{X}_t$ equal to $\boldsymbol{x}(k)$, $\hat{\pi}_k$ equals (T_k/T) is the proportion of the sample with $\boldsymbol{X}_t$ equal $\boldsymbol{x}(k)$, and

$$\mathcal{L}_T\left[\boldsymbol{\theta}, \boldsymbol{x}(k)\right] = \frac{1}{T_k} \sum_{t=1}^{T} \log f_W\left[\boldsymbol{\theta}; W_t, \boldsymbol{x}(k)\right] \mathbf{1}\left[\boldsymbol{X}_t = \boldsymbol{x}(k)\right]$$

is the average of the contributions to the logarithm of the likelihood function of observations with $\boldsymbol{X}_t$ equaling $\boldsymbol{x}(k)$. The fact that the constraints involve order statistics and that some of the constraints bind at the MLE will lead to the unusual limiting distributions discussed below.

Donald and Paarsch appealed to some theorems presented in Galambos (1987) and discussed in Reiss (1989), that give the limiting distribution of order statistics and their relationship to the Weibull distribution. An heuristic discussion of these theorems is presented in section 5 of appendix 4 in this book.

Lemma 4.3.1: Suppose that the $\{W_t\}_{t=1}^{T}$ are drawn randomly from a population having probability density function $f_W(w)$ and cumulative distribution function $F_W(w)$, on $[\underline{v}, \bar{s}]$ such that for all $z > 0$ and $\bar{s} < \infty$,

$$\lim_{\tau \to \infty} \frac{1 - F_W(\bar{s} - \frac{1}{\tau z})}{1 - F_W(\bar{s} - \frac{1}{\tau})} = \frac{1}{z^\gamma}.$$

112

Then

$$\frac{1}{d_T^*}[\bar{s} - \max(W_1, \ldots, W_T)] \to \boldsymbol{\mathcal{W}}(1, \gamma)$$

where $\boldsymbol{\mathcal{W}}(1, \gamma)$ denotes a random variable that is distributed Weibull with parameters 1 and γ, and $d_T^* = \bar{s} - F_W^{-1}\left(1 - \frac{1}{T}\right)$.

When γ is one, the Weibull distribution collapses to the exponential distribution having hazard rate one, which we denote by $\boldsymbol{\mathcal{E}}(1)$. Lemma 4.3.1 provides conditions under which the limiting distribution function of the largest order statistic is

$$[1 - \exp(-z^\gamma)].$$

Note that it is only defined for positive values of z. This gives the well-known fact that extreme order statistics are biased estimators of the upper bound of the distribution, although they generally converge very quickly as shown in the previous result. Note too that the γ parameter will depend on the behavior of the probability density function near the upper bound of the support. Donald and Paarsch demonstrated that, in the auction case, the probability density function is strictly positive at the upper bound of support $\bar{s}$.

Lemma 4.3.2: Under Assumption 4.3.3, from equation (4.2) above, we have

$$\lim_{w \to \bar{s}(\boldsymbol{\theta}^0; \boldsymbol{x})} f_W(w; \boldsymbol{\theta}^0, \boldsymbol{x}) = \frac{\mathcal{N}}{(\mathcal{N} - 1) \int_{\underline{v}}^{\bar{v}} F_V(u; \boldsymbol{\theta}^0, \boldsymbol{z})^{\mathcal{N}-1} \, du} > 0.$$

This fact was important in their proof of Corollary 4.3.1, which is presented below. There, it is shown that the largest order statistic for each possible value of $\boldsymbol{X}$ consistently estimates the upper bound for each possible value of $\boldsymbol{X}$. Moreover, these order statistics are consistent at rate T. This result was useful to Donald and Paarsch when they demonstrated that the MLE depends on order statistics. In fact, in some cases, the MLE is obtained by solving for the parameters purely as functions of the order statistics. In such cases, the MLE will also be consistent at rate T. The particular limiting distribution that results will, however, depend on the number of possible values of $\boldsymbol{X}$ as well as the number of parameters.

Combining the two lemmata, Donald and Paarsch showed that the limiting distribution of the largest winning bid for each possible covariate value will be exponential with intensity parameter equal to one. In addition, a convenient form for the normalizing constant can always be found.

Corollary 4.3.1: Under Assumptions 4.3.1 to 4.3.6,

$$\frac{1}{d_T(k)} \left\{ \bar{s} \left[\boldsymbol{\theta}^0; \boldsymbol{x}(k) \right] - \hat{W} \left[\boldsymbol{x}(k) \right] \right\} \xrightarrow{\mathrm{d}} \boldsymbol{\mathcal{W}}(1,1) = \boldsymbol{\mathcal{E}}(1)$$

and

$$d_T(k) = \frac{(\mathcal{N} - 1) \left\{ \bar{v} - \bar{s} \left[\boldsymbol{\theta}^0; \boldsymbol{x}(k) \right] \right\}}{\mathcal{N} T_k} = O_p(T^{-1})$$

and

$$d_T(k) = O_p(T).$$

Letting the superscript 0 on the function denote population values, introduce the following notation

$$\mathcal{L}^0 \left[\boldsymbol{\theta}; \boldsymbol{x}(k) \right] = \mathcal{E}^0 \left\{ \log f_W \left[W; \boldsymbol{\theta}, \boldsymbol{x}(k) \right] \right\}$$

where $\mathcal{E}^0$ denotes that the expectation is taken at the true parameter values $\boldsymbol{\theta}^0$. Also, define the following population optimization problem (P_k):

$$\max_{<\boldsymbol{\theta}>} \mathcal{L}^0 \left[\boldsymbol{\theta}; \boldsymbol{x}(k) \right] \quad \text{subject to} \quad \bar{s} \left[\boldsymbol{\theta}; \boldsymbol{x}(k) \right] \leq \bar{s} \left[\boldsymbol{\theta}^0; \boldsymbol{x}(k) \right]$$

as well as the aggregate problem (P)

$$\max_{<\boldsymbol{\theta}>} \sum_{k=1}^{K} \pi_k^0 \mathcal{L}^0 \left[\boldsymbol{\theta}; \boldsymbol{x}(k) \right] \quad \text{subject to} \quad \bar{s} \left[\boldsymbol{\theta}; \boldsymbol{x}(k) \right] \leq \bar{s} \left[\boldsymbol{\theta}^0; \boldsymbol{x}(k) \right]$$
$$k = 1, \ldots, K.$$

Donald and Paarsch assumed throughout that one could interchange integration and differentiation. Because of Lemman 4.3.2, the solution to P_k is $(\boldsymbol{\theta}^0, \lambda_k^0)$ with λ_k^0 positive, so that the constraint binds. This permitted Donald and Paarsch to use the implicit function theorem to concentrate the likelihood function using the binding constraints, so that standard expansions could be used to obtain the asymptotic distribution. Consequently, when K weakly exceeds p, the MLE is determined solely by the constraints, and its distribution will depend only on the distribution of the order statistics.

Assumption 4.3.7: The matrix whose columns contain the K-vectors

$$\nabla_{\boldsymbol{\theta}} \bar{s} \left[\boldsymbol{\theta}; \boldsymbol{x}(k) \right]$$

is of full rank $\min(K, p)$ uniformly in a neighborhood of $\boldsymbol{\theta}^0$.

Donald and Paarsch analyzed three cases: K greater than p, K equal p, and K less than p. Because the latter case is a bit of a curiosity, we omit a discussion of it, focusing our explanation on the former cases.

When K equals p, all K constraints bind, so the parameter estimates are determined by the constraints, no averages are involved and the distribution is related to that of $\hat{\boldsymbol{W}}$, which is a $(K \times 1)$ vector of extreme order statistics, one for each covariate combination. The limiting distributions in this case are related to the exponential family, and the estimators will converge at rate T. This unusual result is contained in Theorem 4.3.3. To state the theorem succinctly, Donald and Paarsch first developed some notation. Note that in this case for large enough T, $\hat{\boldsymbol{\theta}}$ is the solution to

$$\hat{W}\left[\boldsymbol{x}(k)\right] = \bar{s}\left[\hat{\boldsymbol{\theta}}; \boldsymbol{x}(k)\right],$$

so

$$\hat{\boldsymbol{\theta}} = \psi(\hat{\boldsymbol{W}}, \boldsymbol{x})$$

where $\psi(\cdot)$ is a smooth function of $\hat{\boldsymbol{W}}$ near the limiting values $\bar{s}^0$. To characterize the limiting distribution, Donald and Paarsch expanded the function about $\bar{s}^0$.

Theorem 4.3.3: Under the above assumptions, when K equals p,

$$-\hat{\boldsymbol{D}}_T^{-1}\hat{\boldsymbol{J}}_T(\hat{\boldsymbol{\theta}} - \boldsymbol{\theta}^0) \xrightarrow{\mathrm{d}} [\boldsymbol{\mathcal{E}}_1(1), \ldots, \boldsymbol{\mathcal{E}}_K(1)]^\top$$

where

$$\hat{\boldsymbol{D}}_T = \mathrm{diag}\{d_T(k)\}$$

of dimension K, where $d_T(k)$ is given in Corollary 4.3.1, and

$$\hat{\boldsymbol{J}}_T = \nabla_{\boldsymbol{\theta}}\bar{s}(\hat{\boldsymbol{\theta}})$$

with $\nabla_{\boldsymbol{\theta}}\bar{s}(\boldsymbol{\theta})$ being the matrix formed by the vectors $\nabla_{\boldsymbol{\theta}}\bar{s}[\boldsymbol{\theta}, \boldsymbol{x}(k)]$ for $k = 1, \ldots, K$.

Note that the standardization in Theorem 4.3.3 is proportional to T, so that the estimators converge at the rate T, and the limiting distribution is that of a vector of independent exponential $\boldsymbol{\mathcal{E}}(1)$ random variables. This result does not imply that the estimators themselves have one-sided distributions, only that there is a linear transformation of the estimators that has a one-sided distribution.

When K exceeds p, there will generally be more than one way of determining the parameters from the constraints. Moreover, in the aggregate problem (P), the objective function may be tangent to one of the constraints. These facts make it possible for the solution to the sample problem to be such that p constraints bind, or less than p constraints bind, and this will be random from sample to sample. This introduces potential difficulties in the asymptotic analysis. To proceed, Donald and Paarsch made the following assumption, which guaranteed that for large T the solution to (P) has at least p constraints binding.

Assumption 4.3.8: In problem (P), the matrix

$$\left\{ \nabla_{\boldsymbol{\theta}} \mathcal{L}^0(\boldsymbol{\theta}), [\nabla_{\boldsymbol{\theta}} \bar{s}(\boldsymbol{\theta})]_{p-1} \right\}$$

has full rank over a neighborhood of $\boldsymbol{\theta}^0$ where

$$[\nabla_{\boldsymbol{\theta}} \bar{s}(\boldsymbol{\theta})]_{p-1}$$

is a collection of derivatives of any $(p-1)$ distinct upper bounds.

When there are K constraints and p parameters, then there will be $\binom{K}{p}$ possible combinations of constraints at which the solution may occur. Denote the set of possibilities by Ξ. Note that, by assumption, each possible combination will possess a solution. Donald and Paarsch let ℓ index each solution and let $\hat{\boldsymbol{\theta}}(\ell)$ be the solution to the ℓth set of constraints. The limiting distribution in this case is a weighted sum of the limiting distribution for each $\hat{\boldsymbol{\theta}}(\ell)$ where the weights are a complicated function of the distribution $f_V^0(v)$. Donald and Paarsch (1996) were able to characterize this distribution. Hong (1998), in his Ph.D. dissertation, as well as Chernozhukov and Hong (2004) have shown that the asymptotic distribution can be simulated by repeatedly solving a linear programming problem. Despite this, one of the major criticisms of the MLE of Donald and Paarsch is that performing inference with it is extremely difficult. For this reason, researchers have proposed at least two alternatives, which we shall survey below.

4.2.4 Simulated Nonlinear Least-Squares

While modern computation is cheap and fast, programming computers is time-consuming and expensive. Thus, one criticism of the MLE proposed by Donald and Paarsch (1996) is that it is difficult to implement on a computer. However, the main, biting criticism of the MLE is that performing inference is difficult. Laffont, Ossard, and Vuong (1995) have suggested that researchers replace the laborious calculation of definite integrals and inverse functions with simulation. In what follows, we shall assume the absence of a binding reserve price to simplify exposition, but admitting a binding reserve price involves no significant technical complications, which is one of the attractions of their approach.

Borrowing from the pioneering research of Lerman and Manski (1981) as well as Pakes and Pollard (1989) and McFadden (1989), Laffont et al. proposed the following strategy: instead of calculating the exact distribution of the winning bid according to (4.2) and then maximizing the logarithm of the likelihood function consistent with this probability density function, invoke the REP. Now, for risk-neutral bidders within the symmetric IPVP, the expected winning bid is

$$\mathcal{E}\left\{\sigma\left[V_{(1:\mathcal{N})}\right]\right\} = \mathcal{E}\left[V_{(2:\mathcal{N})}\right].$$

When $f_V^0(v)$ comes from a parametric family of distributions, which can be characterized up to some unknown parameter vector $\boldsymbol{\theta}^0$,

$$\mathcal{E}\left\{\sigma\left[V_{(1:\mathcal{N})}\right]\right\} = \mathcal{E}\left[V_{(2:\mathcal{N})}\right]$$
$$= \mathcal{N}(\mathcal{N}-1)\int_{\underline{v}}^{\bar{v}} uF_V(u;\boldsymbol{\theta}^0)^{\mathcal{N}-2}S_V(u;\boldsymbol{\theta}^0)f_V(u;\boldsymbol{\theta}^0)\,du$$
$$\equiv \mu_{(2:\mathcal{N})}(\boldsymbol{\theta}^0,\mathcal{N}).$$

For a random sample of T observations $\{(W_t,\mathcal{N}_t)\}_{t=1}^T$, one can define an estimator of $\boldsymbol{\theta}^0$ according to:

$$\hat{\boldsymbol{\theta}} = \underset{<\theta>}{\operatorname{argmin}} \sum_{t=1}^T \left[W_t - \mu_{(2:\mathcal{N}_t)}(\boldsymbol{\theta},\mathcal{N}_t)\right]^2.$$

Solving the above integral, which defines $\mu_{(2:\mathcal{N})}(\cdot)$, the regression function, is probably as difficult numerically as calculating the logarithm of the likelihood function. On the other hand, for a given value of $\boldsymbol{\theta}$, simulating the second order statistic from a sample of $\mathcal{N}_t$ draws is relatively easy. Thus, Laffont et al. proposed replacing $\mu_{(2:\mathcal{N})}(\boldsymbol{\theta},\mathcal{N})$ with an estimate. But what estimate? Laffont et al. proposed simulating the mean of a mechanism that, like the first-price, sealed-bid auction, yields an efficient allocation; they chose to use the second-price, sealed-bid (Vickrey) auction.

We first discuss what is done at each of the J simulations. Again, for notational simplicity, we omit the subscript j indicating the simulation draw and, only after having discussed what is done at each draw, do we describe the way in which the draws are combined.

For each of the $i = 1,\ldots,\mathcal{N}_t$ participants at auction t, one draws a valuation V_i from $F_V(v;\boldsymbol{\theta},\boldsymbol{z}_t)$. One then estimates the regression function above unbiasedly at a value $\boldsymbol{\theta}$ using the sample average of the simulated prices for each unit

$$\hat{\mu}^J_{(2:\mathcal{N}_t)}(\boldsymbol{\theta}, \mathcal{N}_t, \boldsymbol{z}_t) = \frac{1}{J}\sum_{j=1}^{J} W_t^j(\boldsymbol{\theta}).$$

Here, $W_t^j(\boldsymbol{\theta})$ denotes the winning price at second-price, sealed-bid auction t based on the jth set of random draws of $\mathcal{N}_t$ valuations. A straightforward implementation of W_t^j would be the second-highest valuation from $\mathcal{N}_t$ independent and identically distributed draws from the distribution $F_V(v; \boldsymbol{\theta}, \boldsymbol{z}_t)$. However, under this sort of simulation the objective function will not be differentiable. In addition, the complicated theory of empirical processes will then be needed to derive the limiting distribution of the simulated nonlinear least square (SNLS) estimator. In light of this, Laffont et al. proposed to use an *importance sampler* instead. The idea behind importance sampling is the following: Let

$$g_t(u) \equiv g(u|\boldsymbol{z}_t, \mathcal{N}_t)$$

denote a known conditional probability density function that can depend on both $\boldsymbol{z}_t$ and $\mathcal{N}_t$ and introduce

$$\boldsymbol{g}(\boldsymbol{u}) = \prod_{t=1}^{\mathcal{N}_t} g(u_t|\boldsymbol{z}_t, \mathcal{N}_t).$$

Now, the expected revenue, conditional on $\boldsymbol{z}_t$ and $\mathcal{N}_t$, can be written as

$$\mu_{(2:\mathcal{N}_t)}(\boldsymbol{\theta}; \mathcal{N}_t, \boldsymbol{z}_t)$$
$$= \int \cdots \int u_{(2:\mathcal{N}_t)} f_V(u_1; \boldsymbol{\theta}, \boldsymbol{z}_t) \cdots f_V(u_{\mathcal{N}_t}; \boldsymbol{\theta}, \boldsymbol{z}_t) \, du_1 \cdots du_{\mathcal{N}_t}$$
$$= \int \cdots \int u_{(2:\mathcal{N}_t)} \frac{f_V(u_1; \boldsymbol{\theta}, \boldsymbol{z}_t) \cdots f_V(u_{\mathcal{N}_t}; \boldsymbol{\theta}, \boldsymbol{z}_t)}{\boldsymbol{g}(\boldsymbol{u})} \boldsymbol{g}(\boldsymbol{u}) \, d\boldsymbol{u}.$$

In words, the importance-sampling simulation estimator draws J independent samples, each of size $\mathcal{N}_t$, denoted $U_1^{jt}, \ldots, U_{\mathcal{N}_t}^{jt}$, where U_i^{jt} is independently drawn from the distribution with probability density function $g_t(\cdot)$ for $j = 1, \ldots, J$. Under these assumptions,

$$W_t^j(\boldsymbol{\theta}) = U_{(2:\mathcal{N}_t)}^{jt} \frac{f_V(U_1^{jt}; \boldsymbol{\theta}, \boldsymbol{z}_t) \cdots f_V(U_{\mathcal{N}_t}^{jt}; \boldsymbol{\theta}, \boldsymbol{z}_t)}{g_t(U_1^{jt}) \cdots g_t(U_{\mathcal{N}_t}^{jt})}$$

and

$$\hat{\mu}^J_{(2:\mathcal{N}_t)}(\boldsymbol{\theta}; \mathcal{N}_t, \boldsymbol{z}_t) = \frac{1}{J}\sum_{j=1}^{J} W_t^j(\boldsymbol{\theta}).$$

For any finite J, $\hat{\mu}^J_{(2:\mathcal{N}_t)}(\boldsymbol{\theta}, \mathcal{N}_t, \boldsymbol{z}_t)$ is an unbiased simulator; viz.,

$$\mathcal{E}\left[\hat{\mu}^J_{(2:\mathcal{N}_t)}(\boldsymbol{\theta}; \mathcal{N}_t, \boldsymbol{z}_t)\right] = \mu_{(2:\mathcal{N}_t)}(\boldsymbol{\theta}; \mathcal{N}_t, \boldsymbol{z}_t).$$

Since the U_i^{jt}s are drawn randomly prior to the estimation from a distribution that does not depend on $\boldsymbol{\theta}$, for any given $\boldsymbol{\theta}$, the random variables $W_t^j(\boldsymbol{\theta})$ and, hence, $\hat{\mu}^J_{(2:\mathcal{N}_t)}(\boldsymbol{\theta}; \mathcal{N}_t, \boldsymbol{z}_t)$ are conditionally independent of W_t given $\boldsymbol{z}_t$. Now, because all the U_i^{jt}s are drawn from the importance probability density functions—the $g_t(\cdot)$s—that are independent of $\boldsymbol{\theta}$ and because $\boldsymbol{\theta}$ only appears in the $f_V(\cdot; \boldsymbol{\theta}, \boldsymbol{z}_t)$s, $W_t^j(\boldsymbol{\theta})$, the function $\hat{\mu}^J_{(2:\mathcal{N}_t)}(\boldsymbol{\theta}; \mathcal{N}_t, \boldsymbol{z}_t)$ and, hence, the objective function are all twice differentiable in $\boldsymbol{\theta}$ so long as $f_V(\cdot; \boldsymbol{\theta}, \boldsymbol{z}_t)$ is.

While $\hat{\mu}^J_{(2:\mathcal{N}_t)}(\boldsymbol{\theta}; \mathcal{N}_t, \boldsymbol{z}_t)$ is an unbiased estimator for any finite number of simulations J, the least-squares objective function itself is biased. In particular,

$$\mathcal{E}\left\{\left[W_t - \hat{\mu}^J_{(2:\mathcal{N}_t)}(\boldsymbol{\theta}, \mathcal{N}_t)\right]^2\right\} \neq \mathcal{E}\left\{\left[W_t - \mu_{(2:\mathcal{N}_t)}(\boldsymbol{\theta}, \mathcal{N}_t)\right]^2\right\}.$$

In fact, it is easy to see that the bias term equals

$$\mathcal{E}\left\{\left[W_t - \hat{\mu}^J_{(2:\mathcal{N}_t)}(\boldsymbol{\theta}, \mathcal{N}_t)\right]^2\right\} - \mathcal{E}\left\{\left[W_t - \mu_{(2:\mathcal{N}_t)}(\boldsymbol{\theta}, \mathcal{N}_t)\right]^2\right\}$$

$$= \mathcal{E}\left\{\left[\hat{\mu}^J_{(2:\mathcal{N}_t)}(\boldsymbol{\theta}, \mathcal{N}_t) - \mu_{(2:\mathcal{N}_t)}(\boldsymbol{\theta}, \mathcal{N}_t)\right]^2\right\}$$

$$= \mathcal{V}\left[\hat{\mu}^J_{(2:\mathcal{N}_t)}(\boldsymbol{\theta}, \mathcal{N}_t)\right]$$

$$= \frac{1}{J}\mathcal{V}\left[W_t^j(\boldsymbol{\theta})\right].$$

However, the bias term can be consistently estimated in any sample by

$$\Delta_{J,T}(\boldsymbol{\theta}) = \frac{1}{T}\sum_{t=1}^{T}\frac{1}{J(J-1)}\sum_{j=1}^{J}\left[W_t^j(\boldsymbol{\theta}) - \hat{\mu}^J_{(2:\mathcal{N}_t)}(\boldsymbol{\theta}, \mathcal{N}_t)\right]^2.$$

This can be verified by applying the law of large numbers and checking that

$$\frac{1}{(J-1)}\mathcal{E}\left\{\left[W_t^j(\boldsymbol{\theta}) - \hat{\mu}^J_{(2:\mathcal{N}_t)}(\boldsymbol{\theta}, \mathcal{N}_t)\right]^2\right\} = \frac{1}{J}\mathcal{V}\left[W_t^j(\boldsymbol{\theta})\right].$$

Note that such a bias-correction term could be avoided were one to use a simulated GMM approach instead of SNLS. The SNLS estimator of Laffont et al. is then defined as

$$\hat{\boldsymbol{\theta}} = \underset{<\boldsymbol{\theta}>}{\operatorname{argmin}}\ \frac{1}{T}\sum_{t=1}^{T}\left[W_t - \hat{\mu}^J_{(2:\mathcal{N}_t)}(\boldsymbol{\theta}, \mathcal{N}_t)\right]^2 - \Delta_{J,T}(\boldsymbol{\theta}).$$

Laffont et al. demonstrated that $\hat{\boldsymbol{\theta}}$ is $\sqrt{T}$ parameter consistent; they also demonstrated that the asymptotic distribution is normal, derived its asymptotic variance-covariance matrix, and provided a consistent estimator of this matrix.

4.2.5 Extreme-Order, Generalized Method-of-Moments

At either Dutch or first-price, sealed-bid auctions, the MLE is often difficult to calculate and usually has a nonstandard limiting distribution, which makes inference difficult. In particular, the MLE is often a function of extreme order statistics rather than averages, and its limiting distribution is related to the exponential distribution rather than to the normal distribution. Also, the distribution of the MLE usually depends on nuisance parameters. In this section, we describe an estimator proposed by Donald and Paarsch (2002), which they named the *extreme-order, generalized method-of-moments estimator* (EGMME).

The EGMME is typically simpler to compute than the MLE and retains some of the advantages that the MLE has over MMEs and GMMEs as well as the SNLS estimator; viz., a form of parameter superconsistency. Besides being easier to compute than the MLE, the EGMME is easier to use when testing parameter restrictions and model specification. Relative to the methods described in previous sections of this chapter, the method outlined in this section represents a compromise between the well-developed MMEs for such models and the MLE. An attractive feature of the EGMME is that much of the theory of GMM estimation carries over, but with two important differences.

First, since the results are based on the use of extreme order statistics, which will be shown to be superconsistent with exponential limiting distributions, the limiting distributions of the estimators will be related to those of exponential random variables. Thus, the trinity (Wald, Lagrange-multiplier, and distance-metric) of test statistics are quadratic forms in exponential random variables instead of being quadratic forms in normal random variables. Although these distributions generally depend on unknown, nuisance parameters, Donald and Paarsch proposed a method of simulating p-values for test statistics that only requires consistent estimates of these parameters. In general, their proposed simulation method is quite easy to implement and less computationally arduous than bootstrapping, which requires repeated estimation of the empirical specification.

Second, because the underlying extreme order statistics are superconsistent, the parameter estimators, being approximately linearly related to the order statistics, are themselves superconsistent, possessing the most desirable property of the MLE.

Donald and Paarsch considered the situation where the support of the dependent variable Y, conditional on a ℓ-dimensional covariate vector x, depends on a $(p \times 1)$ vector of unknown parameters $\boldsymbol{\theta}$. They assumed that the probability density function of the tth observation Y_t, conditional on the covariate vector x_t, is given by

$$f_Y(y; x_t, \boldsymbol{\theta}^0) \qquad \underline{v} \le y \le \bar{s}(\boldsymbol{\theta}^0; x)$$

where the true value $\boldsymbol{\theta}^0$ lives in the set $\boldsymbol{\Theta}$. Within this framework, Y could be a bid S or the winning bid W.

Donald and Paarsch made the following assumption regarding the probability density function, its support, and the distribution of the covariates x_t.

Assumption 4.3.10: $\{Y_t, x_t\}_{t=1}^T$ are a random sample having distributions with the following characteristics:

(i) x_t is an independently and identically distributed discrete random vector taking on values in $\mathcal{X}$, which contains $K < \infty$ distinct points denoted $x(k)$ for $k = 1, \ldots, K$, having probability mass function $\pi[x(k)] = \pi_k^0 = \Pr[x_t = x(k)]$ for $x(k) \in \mathcal{X}$;

(ii) $|\bar{s}[\boldsymbol{\theta}^0; x(k)]| \le \Delta < \infty$ for $k = 1, \ldots, K$;

(iii) $f_Y[y; x(k), \boldsymbol{\theta}^0]$ is a continuous function of y on $\left[\underline{v}, \bar{s}[\boldsymbol{\theta}^0; x(k)]\right]$ for $k = 1, \ldots, K$;

(iv) $f_Y[u; x(k), \boldsymbol{\theta}^0] \ge \delta > 0$ if $u \in \left[\bar{s}[\boldsymbol{\theta}^0; x(k)] - \varepsilon, \bar{s}[\boldsymbol{\theta}^0; x(k)]\right]$ for some $\varepsilon > 0$ and for $k = 1, \ldots, K$.

Now, for each k, introduce

$$\hat{Y}(k) = \max_{<t>}[Y_t : x_t = x(k)]$$

which is the largest order statistic among the Y_ts associated with the covariate $x(k)$. Also, define again

$$\hat{\pi}_k = \frac{\sum_{t=1}^T \mathbf{1}[x_t = x(k)]}{T} \equiv \frac{\hat{T}[x(k)]}{T} \equiv \frac{T_k}{T}$$

to be the proportion of the sample having covariates equal to the value $x(k)$. As above, let $\boldsymbol{\mathcal{E}}(1)$ denote a random variable with an exponential distribution having mean one.

Under Assumption 4.3.10, extreme order statistics converge quickly to the upper bound of the support of the distribution but are, in general, biased. However, the bias disappears at the same rate as the rate of convergence to the limiting exponential distribution. Consequently, the limiting distribution for the standardized extreme order statistic is not centered about zero, a feature often referred to as *asymptotic bias*.[5]

Since Donald and Paarsch based the EGMME on an analogy between the extreme order statistic and the upper bound of the distribution, this asymptotic bias will, in general, be transmitted to the parameter estimates. To address this problem, without affecting the convergence rate of the estimator, Donald and Paarsch adjusted the upper-bound function so that the extreme order statistic becomes asymptotically unbiased. To admit this, define the following adjusted upper bound:

$$\bar{s}_B[\boldsymbol{\theta}^0; \boldsymbol{x}(k), \hat{T}(k)] = \bar{s}[\boldsymbol{\theta}^0; \boldsymbol{x}(k)] - \frac{1}{\hat{T}(k)\bar{f}_Y[\boldsymbol{x}(k), \boldsymbol{\theta}^0]}$$

where $\bar{f}_Y[\boldsymbol{x}(k), \boldsymbol{\theta}^0]$ is the probability density function evaluated at the upper bound of support $\bar{s}[\boldsymbol{\theta}^0; \boldsymbol{x}(k)]$; viz.,

$$\bar{f}_Y[\boldsymbol{x}(k), \boldsymbol{\theta}^0] = f_Y\{\bar{s}[\boldsymbol{\theta}^0; \boldsymbol{x}(k)]; \boldsymbol{x}(k), \boldsymbol{\theta}^0\}$$

and that Assumptions 4.3.10 (iii) and (iv) translate directly into assumptions on $\bar{f}_Y$. Note too that the adjustment factor depends on the sample size and will remove the asymptotic bias from the extreme order statistic.

The asymptotic properties (viz., as T goes to infinity) of these statistics under Assumption 4.3.10 are summarized in the following lemma.

Lemma 4.3.3: Given Assumption 4.3.10,

   (i) $\hat{\pi}_k \xrightarrow{\text{a.s.}} \pi_k^0$;

   (ii) $\hat{Y}(k) \xrightarrow{\text{a.s.}} \bar{s}[\boldsymbol{\theta}^0; \boldsymbol{x}(k)]$;

   (iii) $\hat{T}(k)\bar{f}_Y[\boldsymbol{x}(k), \boldsymbol{\theta}^0]\{\bar{s}[\boldsymbol{\theta}^0; \boldsymbol{x}(k)] - \hat{Y}(k)\} \xrightarrow{\text{d}} \mathcal{E}(1)$;

   (iv) $T\bar{f}_Y[\boldsymbol{x}(k), \boldsymbol{\theta}^0]\{\bar{s}[\boldsymbol{\theta}^0; \boldsymbol{x}(k)] - \hat{Y}(k)\} \xrightarrow{\text{d}} \frac{\mathcal{E}(1)}{\pi_k^0}$;

   (v) $T\bar{f}_Y[\boldsymbol{x}(k), \boldsymbol{\theta}^0]\{\bar{s}_B[\boldsymbol{\theta}^0; \boldsymbol{x}(k), \hat{T}(k)] - \hat{Y}(k)\} \xrightarrow{\text{d}} \frac{[\mathcal{E}(1)-1]}{\pi_k^0}$.

Result (i) obtains because the empirical distribution of $\boldsymbol{x}_t$ is a strongly consistent estimator of the corresponding probability mass function; this follows from the strong law of large numbers and because the $\boldsymbol{x}_t$s

---

[5] The use of the term asymptotic bias is similar to that for asymptotic variance; it refers to the mean of the nondegenerate asymptotic distribution of the standardized estimator. This is consistent with the use of the term in Lehmann (1983) and Bierens (1987).

have a discrete distribution. Result (ii) shows that the extreme order statistics are strongly consistent estimators of the upper bounds of the distributions for each $\boldsymbol{x}(k)$. Results (iii) and (iv) are essentially the same; viz., the limiting distributions of the extreme order statistics are asymptotically exponential. Result (iv) indicates that because of the discreteness in the distribution of $\boldsymbol{x}_t$ the rate of convergence of these extreme order statistics is T rather than the usual $\sqrt{T}$. Because the extreme order statistics are converging at rate T, they are said to be superconsistent. Finally, result (v) shows that one can adjust the upper bound in such a way that the extreme order statistic is now asymptotically unbiased.

Lemma 4.3.3 shows that $\hat{Y}(k)$ is a strongly consistent estimator of $\bar{s}[\boldsymbol{\theta}^0; \boldsymbol{x}(k)]$, so one approach to estimation would be to choose a value for $\boldsymbol{\theta}$, say $\hat{\boldsymbol{\theta}}$, which makes the vector of functions $\bar{s}[\boldsymbol{\theta}; \boldsymbol{x}(k)]$ (for $k = 1, \ldots, K$) as close to the vector of $\hat{Y}(k)$s as possible. Provided that the only value of $\boldsymbol{\theta}$ which gives $\bar{s}[\boldsymbol{\theta}^0; \boldsymbol{x}(k)]$ is $\boldsymbol{\theta}^0$, $\hat{\boldsymbol{\theta}}$ should be close to $\boldsymbol{\theta}^0$. Because $\hat{Y}(k)$ is a biased estimator, however, Donald and Paarsch adopted a second approach, focusing on the fact that the heuristics discussed above are unaffected when $\boldsymbol{\theta}$ is chosen to make the vector of functions $\bar{s}_B[\boldsymbol{\theta}; \boldsymbol{x}(k), \hat{T}(k)]$ close to the vector of $\hat{Y}(k)$s. Under the assumptions made by Donald and Paarsch, the functions $\bar{s}_B[\boldsymbol{\theta}; \boldsymbol{x}(k), \hat{T}(k)]$ and $\bar{s}[\boldsymbol{\theta}; \boldsymbol{x}(k)]$ approach one another (almost surely) as T grows. The advantage of the second approach is the absence of asymptotic bias.

In proving the parameter consistency of the EGMME, Donald and Paarsch invoked a few identifying assumptions. To state these succinctly, introduce some additional notation. Let

$$\bar{s}(\boldsymbol{\theta}) = \left\{ \bar{s}[\boldsymbol{\theta}; \boldsymbol{x}(1)], \ldots, \bar{s}[\boldsymbol{\theta}; \boldsymbol{x}(K)] \right\}^{\top}.$$

The conditions that allow the heuristic of Donald and Paarsch to work are contained in the following assumption.

Assumption 4.3.11:

(i) $K \geq p$;

(ii) $\|\bar{s}(\boldsymbol{\theta}) - \bar{s}(\boldsymbol{\theta}^0)\|_2 = 0$ implies that $\boldsymbol{\theta} = \boldsymbol{\theta}^0$;

(iii) for each $k = 1, \ldots, K$, $\bar{s}[\boldsymbol{\theta}; \boldsymbol{x}(k)]$ is continuous in $\boldsymbol{\theta}$;

(iv) for each $k = 1, \ldots, K$, $\bar{f}[\boldsymbol{x}(k), \boldsymbol{\theta}]$ is bounded away from zero.

Assumption 4.3.11 is a fairly standard set of conditions that permits identification of $\boldsymbol{\theta}^0$ with Assumption 4.3.11 (i) and (ii) corresponding to order and rank conditions for identification that would appear in simultaneous-equations models as well as GMM and classical extremum estimation. In this case, Assumption 4.3.11 (i) requires that there be at least as many points in the support of x_t as there are parameters (and hence as many moment conditions as parameters), while Assumption 4.3.11 (ii) is a stronger condition that there be a unique value of the parameter that gives the same vector of upper-bound functions as would be obtained with the true value of the parameter. Assumption 4.3.11 (iii) is a continuity condition that is standard, while Assumption 4.3.11 (iv) allows one to show that the bias-adjusted functions converge to the upper-bound functions.

These assumptions and Lemma 4.3.3 will admit an easy derivation of parameter consistency for a wide class of estimators. In fact, Donald and Paarsch considered estimators $\hat{\boldsymbol{\theta}}$ that solve the following optimization problem:

$$\min_{<\boldsymbol{\theta} \in \Theta>} \|\hat{\boldsymbol{Y}} - \bar{\boldsymbol{s}}_B(\boldsymbol{\theta})\|$$

where $\hat{\boldsymbol{Y}}$ equals $[\hat{Y}(1), \ldots, \hat{Y}(K)]^\top$ and

$$\bar{\boldsymbol{s}}_B(\boldsymbol{\theta}) = \left\{\bar{s}_B[\boldsymbol{\theta}; \boldsymbol{x}(1), \hat{T}(1)], \ldots, \bar{s}_B[\boldsymbol{\theta}; \boldsymbol{x}(K), \hat{T}(K)]\right\}^\top.$$

In practice, however, Donald and Paarsch chose to focus on an estimator that is simpler to compute. Thus, they proposed an estimator $\hat{\boldsymbol{\theta}}(\mathbf{A}_T)$ that is defined by the solution to the following, quadratic minimization problem:

$$\min_{<\boldsymbol{\theta} \in \Theta>} [\hat{\boldsymbol{Y}} - \bar{\boldsymbol{s}}_B(\boldsymbol{\theta})]^\top \mathbf{A}_T [\hat{\boldsymbol{Y}} - \bar{\boldsymbol{s}}_B(\boldsymbol{\theta})]$$

where $\mathbf{A}_T$ is a (potentially) stochastic matrix with a positive-definite limit. The attractive feature of this subclass of estimators is that the objective function is differentiable in $\boldsymbol{\theta}$ provided that $\bar{s}_B(\cdot)$ is, so with the results in Lemma 4.3.3 and an application of the delta method one can derive simple expressions for the limiting distributions of the estimators. Because the estimators depend on the choice of the weighting matrix, Donald and Paarsch needed to consider how to choose $\mathbf{A}_T$. Nevertheless, this estimator is parameter consistent as the following theorem summarizes.

Theorem 4.3.4: Given Assumptions 4.3.10 and 4.3.11, and assuming that $\mathbf{A}_T$ is a uniformly positive-definite matrix, $\hat{\boldsymbol{\theta}}(\mathbf{A}_T) \xrightarrow{\text{a.s.}} \boldsymbol{\theta}^0$.

One interesting feature of the estimation problem is the unusual nature of the asymptotic distribution. First, as might be expected given Lemma 4.3.3, the estimators have limiting distributions that are not in the normal family. In fact, the limiting distributions of the estimators are related to the family of exponential random variables. Second, the estimators generally have convergence rates that are faster than the usual $\sqrt{T}$ rate. This property, along with the suggestions for inference, makes the estimation strategy particularly attractive in situations where T is small.

Before introducing the assumptions sufficient to derive the limiting distribution of the estimators, let us introduce some additional notation. Let

$$\mathbf{G}(\boldsymbol{\theta})^{\top} = \left\{ \nabla_{\boldsymbol{\theta}}\bar{s}[\boldsymbol{\theta}; \boldsymbol{x}(1)], \ \nabla_{\boldsymbol{\theta}}\bar{s}[\boldsymbol{\theta}; \boldsymbol{x}(2)], \ \ldots, \nabla_{\boldsymbol{\theta}}\bar{s}[\boldsymbol{\theta}; \boldsymbol{x}(K)] \right\}$$

where each of the $\nabla_{\boldsymbol{\theta}}\bar{s}[\boldsymbol{\theta}; \boldsymbol{x}(k)]$ is a $(p \times 1)$ column vector consisting of the partial derivatives of the $\bar{s}[\boldsymbol{\theta}; \boldsymbol{x}(k)]$ function. Note that

$$\nabla_{\boldsymbol{\theta}}\bar{s}_B[\boldsymbol{\theta}; \boldsymbol{x}(k)] = \nabla_{\boldsymbol{\theta}}\bar{s}[\boldsymbol{\theta}; \boldsymbol{x}(k)] - \frac{\nabla_{\boldsymbol{\theta}}\bar{f}_Y[\boldsymbol{x}(k), \boldsymbol{\theta}]}{\hat{T}(i)\bar{f}_Y[\boldsymbol{x}(k), \boldsymbol{\theta}]^2}.$$

Given the assumptions made by Donald and Paarsch, $\nabla_{\boldsymbol{\theta}}\bar{s}_B[\boldsymbol{\theta}; \boldsymbol{x}(k)]$ will be asymptotically the same as $\nabla_{\boldsymbol{\theta}}\bar{s}[\boldsymbol{\theta}; \boldsymbol{x}(k)]$. Denote $\mathbf{G}(\boldsymbol{\theta}^0)$ by $\mathbf{G}_0$ and let $\mathbf{G}_B(\boldsymbol{\theta})$ denote the $(K \times p)$ matrix whose k^{th} row is $\nabla_{\boldsymbol{\theta}}\bar{s}_B[\boldsymbol{\theta}; \boldsymbol{x}(k)]$.

Assumption 4.3.12:

  (i) $\boldsymbol{\theta}^0$ is an interior point of $\boldsymbol{\Theta}$;

  (ii) $\bar{s}(\boldsymbol{\theta})$ is continuously differentiable in a neighborhood of $\boldsymbol{\theta}^0$;

  (iii) for each $k = 1, \ldots, K$ $\bar{f}_T[\boldsymbol{x}(k), \boldsymbol{\theta}]$ is continuously differentiable in $\boldsymbol{\theta}$ with bounded derivative in a neighborhood of $\boldsymbol{\theta}^0$;

  (iv) $\mathbf{G}(\boldsymbol{\theta})$ is continuous in $\boldsymbol{\theta}$ and of full rank p in a neighborhood of $\boldsymbol{\theta}^0$;

  (v) $\mathbf{A}_T \xrightarrow{\text{a.s.}} \mathbf{A}$ where $\mathbf{A}$ is positive definite and symmetric;

  (vi) the matrix $\mathbf{G}(\boldsymbol{\theta})^{\top}\mathbf{A}\mathbf{G}(\boldsymbol{\theta})$ is nonsingular for all $\boldsymbol{\theta}$ in a neighborhood of $\boldsymbol{\theta}^0$.

The above are standard differentiability conditions similar to those used in proofs of asymptotic normality for GMMEs and extremum estimators; they are used to accomodate the usual mean-value expansions. The differences arising here are that the mean-value expansions involve extreme order statistics and the limiting distributions involve exponential random variables. In deriving the main distributional result, we introduce the notation $\boldsymbol{\mathcal{E}}_K$ to denote a $(K \times 1)$ vector of independent $\boldsymbol{\mathcal{E}}(1)$ random variables and the notation $\boldsymbol{\iota}_K$ to denote a K vector of ones. Let $\mathbf{R}$ denote a diagonal matrix whose k^{th} diagonal element is

$$r_{kk} = \pi_k^0 \bar{f}_Y[\boldsymbol{x}(k), \boldsymbol{\theta}^0].$$

Theorem 4.3.5: Given Assumptions 4.3.10 to 4.3.12 and assuming $\mathbf{A}_T \xrightarrow{\text{a.s.}} \mathbf{A}$, where $\mathbf{A}$ is positive definite,

$$T[\hat{\boldsymbol{\theta}}(\mathbf{A}_T) - \boldsymbol{\theta}^0] \xrightarrow{\text{d}} (\mathbf{G}_0^\top \mathbf{A}\mathbf{G}_0)^{-1} \mathbf{G}_0^\top \mathbf{A}\mathbf{R}^{-1}(\boldsymbol{\mathcal{E}}_K - \boldsymbol{\iota}_K).$$

Thus, the limiting distribution of the estimator is that of a linear combination of centered exponential random variables. The use of the bias-adjusted functions $\bar{s}_B[\boldsymbol{\theta}; \boldsymbol{x}(k)]$ implies that the estimators are asymptotically unbiased without affecting the variance that is given by

$$(\mathbf{G}_0^\top \mathbf{A}\mathbf{G}_0)^{-1} \mathbf{G}_0^\top \mathbf{A}\mathbf{R}^{-2}\mathbf{A}\mathbf{G}_0(\mathbf{G}_0^\top \mathbf{A}\mathbf{G}_0)^{-1}.$$

Note too that the estimator converges at rate T, so that the estimators are superconsistent. Had Donald and Paarsch used the unadjusted functions $\bar{s}[\boldsymbol{\theta}; \boldsymbol{x}(k)]$ they would have obtained an estimator that was also superconsistent and asymptotically distributed as the same linear combination of (unadjusted) exponential random variables. For that estimator, some asymptotic bias would generally exist, and this would manifest itself in poor size properties of test statistics.

Given the result in Theorem 4.3.5 and the form of the asymptotic variance, Donald and Paarsch then addressed the issue of selecting an optimal weighting matrix. Using arguments similar to those used for GMM and MD estimators, they showed that the optimal weighting matrix is a matrix whose probability limit equals $\mathbf{R}^2$, in which case the variance reduces to $(\mathbf{G}_0^\top \mathbf{R}^2 \mathbf{G}_0)^{-1}$.

In practice, Donald and Paarsch claimed that at least two possibilities exist for implementing the optimal weighting matrix. The first is to use the weighting matrix equal to $\hat{\mathbf{R}}^2$, which is a diagonal matrix whose k^{th} diagonal element equals $\hat{\pi}_k^2 f_Y[\hat{Y}(k); \boldsymbol{x}(k), \hat{\boldsymbol{\theta}}]^2$ where $\hat{\boldsymbol{\theta}}$ is some preliminary estimator of $\boldsymbol{\theta}^0$. This uses the fact that the assumptions plus Lemma 4.3.3 and Theorem 4.3.4 imply

$$\hat{\pi}_k^2 f_Y[\hat{Y}(k); \boldsymbol{x}(k), \hat{\boldsymbol{\theta}}]^2 \xrightarrow{\text{a.s.}} (\pi_k^0)^2 f_Y \left\{ \bar{s}[\boldsymbol{\theta}^0; \boldsymbol{x}(k)]; \boldsymbol{x}(k), \boldsymbol{\theta}^0 \right\}^2.$$

Similar reasoning suggests a second possibility—to use a weighting matrix that has as its kth diagonal element the term $\hat{\pi}_k^2 \bar{f}_Y \{\boldsymbol{x}(k), \hat{\boldsymbol{\theta}}\}^2$. Regardless of the procedure used, the optimally weighted estimator $\hat{\boldsymbol{\theta}}$ solves the following problem:

$$\min_{<\boldsymbol{\theta} \in \boldsymbol{\Theta}>} [\hat{\boldsymbol{Y}} - \bar{\boldsymbol{s}}_B(\boldsymbol{\theta})]^\top \hat{\mathbf{R}}^2 [\hat{\boldsymbol{Y}} - \bar{\boldsymbol{s}}_B(\boldsymbol{\theta})]$$

which has properties summarized in the following theorem.

Theorem 4.3.6: Given Assumptions 4.3.10 to 4.3.12,

(i) $\hat{\boldsymbol{\theta}} \xrightarrow{\text{a.s.}} \boldsymbol{\theta}^0$;

(ii) $T(\hat{\boldsymbol{\theta}} - \boldsymbol{\theta}^0) \xrightarrow{\text{d}} (\mathbf{G}_0^\top \mathbf{R}^2 \mathbf{G}_0)^{-1} \mathbf{G}_0^\top \mathbf{R}(\mathcal{E}_K - \boldsymbol{\iota}_K)$.

While this result provides a full characterization of the properties of the estimator $\hat{\boldsymbol{\theta}}$, it does not suggest a way of performing inference. In particular, it appears difficult to obtain a limiting distribution that does not depend on nuisance parameters. We shall discuss this matter next, but first we should like to relate this estimator to the MLE.

Donald and Paarsch gave at least two related reasons for proposing the above estimation strategy; both concern the nature of the ML estimation problem given by

$$\max_{<\boldsymbol{\theta} \in \boldsymbol{\Theta}>} \sum_{t=1}^{T} \log \left\{ f_Y(Y_t; \boldsymbol{x}_t, \boldsymbol{\theta}) \mathbf{1}[\underline{v} \le Y_t \le \bar{s}(\boldsymbol{\theta}; \boldsymbol{x}_t)] \right\}.$$

As we have seen, the above maximization problem is difficult to solve because the indicator function $\mathbf{1}(\cdot)$ inside the contribution to the logarithm of the likelihood function is undefined for values of the parameter vector when Y_t is greater than $\bar{s}(\boldsymbol{\theta}; \boldsymbol{x}_t)$. As has been demonstrated above, computational and statistical concerns suggest that the problem is better posed as the following constrained maximization problem:

$$\max_{<\boldsymbol{\theta} \in \boldsymbol{\Theta}>} \sum_{t=1}^{T} \log f_Y(Y_t; \boldsymbol{x}_t, \boldsymbol{\theta})$$
$$\text{subject to} \quad \underline{v} \le Y_t \le \bar{s}(\boldsymbol{\theta}; \boldsymbol{x}_t) \quad \text{for all} \quad t = 1, \dots, T$$

which, in the discrete case considered here, is equivalent to the following constrained maximization problem:

$$\max_{<\boldsymbol{\theta} \in \boldsymbol{\Theta}>} \sum_{t=1}^{T} \log f_Y(Y_t; \boldsymbol{x}_t, \boldsymbol{\theta})$$
$$\text{subject to} \quad \underline{v} \le \hat{Y}(k) \le \bar{s}[\boldsymbol{\theta}; \boldsymbol{x}(k)] \quad \text{for all} \quad k = 1, \dots, K.$$

Thus, the ML estimation problem is equivalent to solving a constrained maximization problem with the data-dependent constraints.

As mentioned above, when the MLE is implemented only a subset of the constraints is binding at the optimum of the likelihood function. Because of this, the MLE has a somewhat unusual asymptotic distribution under the conditions assumed by Donald and Paarsch. As shown earlier in this chapter, the distribution of the MLE is that of a vector of exponential random variables conditional on certain linear combinations of exponential random variables being smaller than these variables. In particular, the MLE has a distribution that depends on a *combination* of p of the K $\mathcal{E}(1)$ random variables. The particular combination may vary from sample to sample, and the resulting distribution is a rather complicated mixture of overlapping exponential random vectors. Except in very simple cases, such as the one-parameter exponential model considered in Paarsch (1994), it would appear that the result, while interesting, may not be helpful in terms of permitting a way of doing inference.

Also, it is not obvious in this context that bootstrapping would provide a useful inferential tool.[6] This is especially true given the potential computational difficulties generally associated with the MLE. But the EGMME approach of Donald and Paarsch provides the advantage of providing a more concrete, more generally applicable distribution that can easily be simulated.

Donald and Paarsch focused on testing a set of linear restrictions concerning the parameters of interest. In particular, they sought to test hypotheses of the following form:

$$H_0 : \ \mathbf{Q}\boldsymbol{\theta}^0 = \mathbf{r}$$

against

$$H_1 : \ \mathbf{Q}\boldsymbol{\theta}^0 \neq \mathbf{r}$$

where $\mathbf{Q}$ is a known matrix of dimension $(q \times p)$ which has full rank with q being less than or equal to p and $\mathbf{r}$ is an $(q \times 1)$ vector of known constants. Obviously, tests of a single component of $\boldsymbol{\theta}$ are a special case. Donald and Paarsch considered analogues to the Wald, Lagrange-multiplier, and distance-metric type tests, but we limit ourselves to just the Wald test here.

The form of the Wald test that Donald and Paarsch considered is

$$S_W = T^2 (\mathbf{Q}\hat{\boldsymbol{\theta}} - \mathbf{r})^\top [\mathbf{Q}(\hat{\mathbf{G}}^\top \hat{\mathbf{R}}^2 \hat{\mathbf{G}})^{-1} \mathbf{Q}^\top]^{-1} (\mathbf{Q}\hat{\boldsymbol{\theta}} - \mathbf{r})$$

where $\hat{\mathbf{G}}$ denotes $\mathbf{G}(\hat{\boldsymbol{\theta}})$. (The reader should note that Donald and Paarsch proved that each of the three test statistics has the same limiting distribution under the null hypothesis.)

---

[6] Indeed, Bickel and Freedman (1981) have shown that applying the naïve bootstrap to the MLE of the upper bound for a uniform $[0, \theta]$ distribution fails to work because of nonuniformity in convergence. They argue, however, that it may be possible to use a parametric bootstrap to obtain asymptotically valid inferences.

Theorem 4.3.7: Under Assumptions 4.3.10 to 4.3.12 and the null hypothesis, the Wald test statistic is asymptotically distributed as

$$(\boldsymbol{\mathcal{E}}_K - \boldsymbol{\iota}_K)^\top \mathbf{A}(\mathbf{A}^\top \mathbf{A})^{-1}\mathbf{A}^\top(\boldsymbol{\mathcal{E}}_K - \boldsymbol{\iota}_K)$$

where $\mathbf{A}^\top$ equals $\mathbf{Q}(\mathbf{G}_0^\top \mathbf{R}^2 \mathbf{G}_0)^{-1}\mathbf{G}_0^\top \mathbf{R}$.

As in the case of GMMEs, Donald and Paarsch also proposed using the value of the unrestricted objective function to obtain a partial specification test or a test of any overidentifying restrictions. Thus, the following "J" statistic:

$$S_J = T^2[\hat{\boldsymbol{Y}} - \bar{\boldsymbol{s}}_B(\hat{\boldsymbol{\theta}})]^\top \hat{\mathbf{R}}^2[\hat{\boldsymbol{Y}} - \bar{\boldsymbol{s}}_B(\hat{\boldsymbol{\theta}})]$$

can be used for this purpose.

Theorem 4.3.8: Under Assumptions 4.3.10 to 4.3.12 and the null hypothesis, the "J" statistic is distributed as

$$(\boldsymbol{\mathcal{E}}_K - \boldsymbol{\iota}_K)^\top[\mathbf{I} - \mathbf{R}\mathbf{G}_0(\mathbf{G}_0^\top \mathbf{R}^2 \mathbf{G}_0)^{-1}\mathbf{G}_0^\top \mathbf{R}](\boldsymbol{\mathcal{E}}_K - \boldsymbol{\iota}_K).$$

The limiting distribution of the Wald and Lagrange-multiplier as well as the minimum-distance and "J" tests depends on unknown nuisance parameters. In order to conduct tests, Donald and Paarsch needed critical values, which themselves would depend on nuisance parameters. All of the test statistics considered by Donald and Paarsch, which we denote generically below using the notation S_T, satisfied the following type of result:

$$S_T \xrightarrow{\text{d}} S = (\boldsymbol{\mathcal{E}}_K - \boldsymbol{\iota}_K)^\top \boldsymbol{\Gamma}(\boldsymbol{\mathcal{E}}_K - \boldsymbol{\iota}_K)$$

for some constant matrix $\boldsymbol{\Gamma}$, which possibly depends on the parameters, and where $\boldsymbol{\mathcal{E}}_K$ is a K vector of independent $\boldsymbol{\mathcal{E}}(1)$ random variables. A simple way of approximating this random variable involves using methods similar to, but simpler than, those used by Hansen (1996). The idea is to use an artificial random vector $\hat{\boldsymbol{\mathcal{E}}}_K$ and a strongly consistent estimate of the matrix $\boldsymbol{\Gamma}$, denoted here by $\hat{\boldsymbol{\Gamma}}(\omega)$. To recognize explicitly the dependence of $\hat{\boldsymbol{\Gamma}}$ on the particular sample (sequence) ω we denote it $\hat{\boldsymbol{\Gamma}}(\omega)$. Suppose that $\hat{\boldsymbol{\Gamma}}(\omega)$ is strongly consistent in the sense that the set of ω for which $\hat{\boldsymbol{\Gamma}}(\omega)$ converges to $\boldsymbol{\Gamma}$, say Ω, has probability one. Now, conditional on the particular sample, consider the distribution of $S_T(\omega)$, which equals $(\hat{\boldsymbol{\mathcal{E}}}_K - \boldsymbol{\iota}_K)^\top \hat{\boldsymbol{\Gamma}}(\omega)(\hat{\boldsymbol{\mathcal{E}}}_K - \boldsymbol{\iota}_K)$, conditional on ω, where $\hat{\boldsymbol{\mathcal{E}}}_K$

is independent of the sample and independent of the sample size. For a particular sample,

$$(\hat{\boldsymbol{\mathcal{E}}}_K - \boldsymbol{\iota}_K)^\top \hat{\boldsymbol{\Gamma}}(\omega)(\hat{\boldsymbol{\mathcal{E}}}_K - \boldsymbol{\iota}_K) \rightarrow (\hat{\boldsymbol{\mathcal{E}}}_K - \boldsymbol{\iota}_K)^\top \boldsymbol{\Gamma}(\hat{\boldsymbol{\mathcal{E}}}_K - \boldsymbol{\iota}_K)$$

by continuity in the argument $\hat{\boldsymbol{\Gamma}}(\omega)$ and the convergence of $\hat{\boldsymbol{\Gamma}}(\omega)$ to $\boldsymbol{\Gamma}$. Because $\Pr(\Omega)$ is one, the result obtains with probability one. Let $F_S(s)$ denote the distribution of the quantity $(\hat{\boldsymbol{\mathcal{E}}}_K - \boldsymbol{\iota}_K)^\top \boldsymbol{\Gamma}(\hat{\boldsymbol{\mathcal{E}}}_K - \boldsymbol{\iota}_K)$, which is identical to the distribution of the quantity $(\boldsymbol{\mathcal{E}}_K - \boldsymbol{\iota}_K)^\top \boldsymbol{\Gamma}(\boldsymbol{\mathcal{E}}_K - \boldsymbol{\iota}_K)$. Let the distribution of $(\hat{\boldsymbol{\mathcal{E}}}_K - \boldsymbol{\iota}_K)^\top \hat{\boldsymbol{\Gamma}}(\omega)(\hat{\boldsymbol{\mathcal{E}}}_K - \boldsymbol{\iota}_K)$, conditional on ω, be given by $\hat{F}_{S(\omega)}(s)$. Thus, conditional on ω, $\hat{F}_{S(\omega)}(s)$ converges uniformly to $F_S(s)$, because the distribution of the latter is continuous; see Prakasa Rao (1992, Proposition 1.3.15). But this occurs for nearly all possible samples implying that, with probability one,

$$\tilde{\alpha}^T = [1 - \hat{F}_{S(\omega)}(s)]$$
$$= [1 - F_S(s)] + [F_S(s) - \hat{F}_{S(\omega)}(s)]$$
$$= [1 - F_S(s)] + o(1)$$
$$\xrightarrow{\ \mathrm{d}\ } [1 - F_S(s)] = \tilde{\alpha}$$

where $\tilde{\alpha}$ is, by construction, distributed uniformly on the interval $[0, 1]$ and is the asymptotic p-value.

Calculating $\hat{F}_{S(\omega)}(\cdot)$ analytically appears difficult; instead Donald and Paarsch simulated a solution. They used the following to approximate $\tilde{\alpha}^T$:

$$\hat{\alpha}^T = \frac{1}{J} \sum_{j=1}^{J} \mathbf{1}[(\boldsymbol{\mathcal{E}}_{Kj}^* - \boldsymbol{\iota}_K)^\top \hat{\boldsymbol{\Gamma}}(\omega)(\boldsymbol{\mathcal{E}}_{Kj}^* - \boldsymbol{\iota}_K) > S^T]$$

where $\boldsymbol{\mathcal{E}}_{Kj}^*$ is the jth draw from an independent vector of pseudo-randomly generated $\boldsymbol{\mathcal{E}}(1)$ random variables. By making J sufficiently large they could accurately approximate the p-value $\tilde{\alpha}^T$. A formal size-α test could then be performed by simply rejecting the null if $\hat{\alpha}^T$ is less than some size α^0.

4.3 Binding Reserve Price

The nonparametric estimator of Guerre et al. discussed above was defined assuming the absence of a binding reserve price. As was discussed in chapter 3, when the seller announced a binding reserve price r, truncation is introduced. Potential bidders having valuations below r do not bid. Under this circumstance, at auction t, the number of participants N_t is different from the number of potential bidders $\mathcal{N}_t$. For simplicity of exposition, let us assume that $\mathcal{N}_t$ is a constant $\mathcal{N}$.

With a binding reservation price, the first-order optimality condition for bidder i continues to hold, but the boundary condition is now

$$\sigma(r) = r.$$

The cumulative distribution of the observed bids $G_S^0(s)$ for the actual number of bidders is a truncated distribution of $F_S^0(s)$ and $F_V^0(v)$. In fact, the observed bid distribution $G_S^0(s)$ corresponds to

$$G_S^0(s) = \frac{\left[F_V^0(v) - F_V^0(r)\right]}{\left[1 - F_V^0(r)\right]}$$

and the probability density function of bid s is

$$g_S^0(s) = \frac{1}{\sigma'(v)} \frac{f_V^0(v)}{\left[1 - F_V^0(r)\right]}.$$

Now, when

$$F_V^0(v) = \left[1 - F_V^0(r)\right] G_S^0(s) + F_V^0(r)$$

and

$$\frac{\sigma'(v)}{f_V^0(v)} = \frac{1}{\left[1 - F_V^0(r)\right] g_S^0(s)}$$

are substituted into the first-order condition (2.4), then

$$v = s + \frac{1}{\mathcal{N}-1} \left\{ \frac{G_S^0(s)}{g_S^0(s)} + \frac{F_V^0(r)}{\left[1 - F_V^0(r)\right] g_S^0(s)} \frac{1}{g_S^0(s)} \right\}.$$

so the unobserved valuation can be expressed in terms of the observable, truncated bid distribution and the number of potential bidders $\mathcal{N}$. In words, the truncated valuation distribution $F_V^0(v)$ is identified by the observed truncated bid distribution $G_S^0(s)$. Of course, the distribution of valuations below r cannot be identified by any observable because nothing is observed there.

Often, $\mathcal{N}$ and $F_V^0(r)$ are unknown, but they can be identified when $\mathcal{N}$ and r do not vary across auctions. If either r or $\mathcal{N}$ vary across auctions, then one cannot identify them.

As mentioned in chapters 2 and 3, under the symmetric IPVP assumptions, N_t has a binomial distribution with parameters $\mathcal{N}$ and $\left[1 - F_V^0(r)\right]$. Therefore, any estimation method that is useful for recovering the two parameters of a binomial distribution can be used. For example, a natural candidate estimator of $\mathcal{N}$ would be

$$\hat{\mathcal{N}} = \max_{t=1,\ldots,T} N_t$$

which will be exactly equal to $\mathcal{N}$ with probability one because of the discrete nature of $\mathcal{N}$. Because

$$\mathcal{E}(N_t) = \mathcal{N}\left[1 - F_V^0(r)\right]$$

and $\mathcal{E}(N_t)$ can be estimated by

$$\bar{N}_T = \frac{1}{T}\sum_{t=1}^{T} N_t,$$

$F_V^0(r)$ can be estimated by

$$\hat{F}_V(r) = 1 - \frac{\bar{N}_T}{\hat{\mathcal{N}}}.$$

Of course, it remains to provide estimators of $G_S^0(s)$ and $g_S^0(s)$.

A technical difficulty arises when trying to estimate $G_S^0(s)$ and $g_S^0(s)$ because, as Guerre et al. have shown,

$$g_S^0(s) \propto \frac{1}{\sqrt{s-r}} \qquad \text{as} \quad s \searrow r.$$

This makes

$$g_S^0(s) \to \infty \qquad \text{as} \quad s \searrow r.$$

To solve this technical difficulty, Guerre et al. have suggested the following transformation of the observed bids be used:

$$S(r) = \sqrt{S-r}.$$

Under this transformation, the observed cumulative distribution and probability density functions of bids can be rewritten as

$$G_{S(r)}^0\left[s(r)\right] = G_S^0\left[r + s(r)^2\right]$$

and

$$g_{S(r)}^0\left[s(r)\right] = 2s(r)g_S^0\left[r + s(r)^2\right].$$

Substituting these expressions into the first-order condition

$$v = s + \frac{1}{\mathcal{N}-1}\left\{\frac{G_S^0(s)}{g_S^0(s)} + \frac{F_V^0(r)}{\left[1 - F_V^0(r)\right]}\frac{1}{g_S^0(s)}\right\}$$

yields

$$v = s(r)^2 + r + \frac{2s(r)}{(\mathcal{N}-1)}\left\{\frac{G_{S(r)}^0\left[s(r)\right]}{g_{S(r)}^0\left[s(r)\right]} + \frac{F_V^0(r)}{\left[1 - F_V^0(r)\right]}\frac{1}{g_{S(r)}^0\left[s(r)\right]}\right\}.$$

Under the above transformation, the probability density function $g_{S(r)}^0[s(r)]$ is bounded on its support. Both $G_{S(r)}^0[s(r)]$ and $g_{S(r)}^0[s(r)]$ can be estimated using the empirical distribution function as well as the kernel-smoothed probability density function; i.e.,

$$\hat{G}_{S(r)}[s(r)] = \frac{1}{T}\sum_{t=1}^{T}\frac{1}{N_t}\sum_{i=1}^{N_t}\mathbf{1}\left[S_{it}(r) \leq s(r)\right]$$

and

$$\hat{g}_{S(r)}[s(r)] = \frac{1}{Th_g}\sum_{t=1}^{T}\frac{1}{N_t}\sum_{i=1}^{N_t}\kappa\left[\frac{S_{it}(r) - s(r)}{h_g}\right].$$

The unobserved valuations can then be estimated by

$$\hat{V}_{it} = S_{it}(r)^2 + r +$$

$$\frac{2S_{it}(r)}{\mathcal{N}-1}\left\{\frac{\hat{G}_{S(r)}[S_{it}(r)]}{\hat{g}_{S(r)}[S_{it}(r)]} + \frac{\hat{F}_V(r)}{\left[1 - \hat{F}_V(r)\right]}\frac{1}{\hat{g}_{S(r)}[S_{it}(r)]}\right\}.$$

The probability density function of the truncated distribution of the latent values V_{it} conditional on V_{it} exceeding r can be estimated as

$$\hat{f}_{V|V\geq r}(v|V \geq r) = \frac{1}{Th_g}\sum_{t=1}^{T}\frac{1}{N_t}\sum_{i=1}^{N_t}\kappa\left(\frac{\hat{V}_{it} - v}{h_g}\right).$$

When the valuation V exceeds the reserve price r, an estimator of $f_V^0(v)$ can then be recovered from $\hat{f}_{V|V\geq r}(v|V \geq r)$ and $\hat{F}_V(r)$; viz.,

$$\hat{f}_V(v) = \hat{f}_{V|V\geq r}(v|V \geq r)\left[1 - \hat{F}_V(r)\right].$$

Of course, the presence of covariates complicates this nonparametric analysis considerably. The presence of covariates is easily accommodated in the parametric models considered above, particularly for the ML and the SNLS estimators. To save space, in the case of the ML estimator, we incorporate a binding reserve price as well as covariates in our analysis of risk aversion in the next section. We leave it to the reader to introduce a binding reserve price as well as covariates in the case of the SNLS estimator.

4.4 Risk-Averse Bidders

In most structural-econometric analyses of auction data, researchers have typically assumed that the potential bidders are risk neutral with respect to winning the auction. At English and Vickrey auctions, such an assumption is irrelevant because the dominant-strategy, equilibrium-bid function remains unchanged under these formats when potential bidders are risk averse. On the other hand, at Dutch and first-price, sealed-bid auctions the attitudes of potential bidders toward risk matter. In this section, we describe the effects of symmetric, von Neumann–Morgenstern preferences on the structural-econometric analysis. We begin first with a parametric analysis within the HARA family of preferences; this fits easily within the framework of Donald and Paarsch (1996). Risk aversion cannot be investigated using the simulation methods of Laffont et al. (1995) because the REP is invoked to get the mean function of the winning bid. As mentioned in chapter 2, the REP breaks down in the presence of risk-averse potential bidders. Subsequently, we then investigate the semiparametric methods proposed by Campo, Guerre, Perrigne, and Vuong (2000), again within the HARA family of preferences. In a later section, we also analyze the effects of risk aversion within the stochastic independent, private-values paradigm — a model due to Ésö and White (2004).

4.4.1 Parametric Identification and Estimation

At Dutch and first-price, sealed-bid auctions, the attitudes of potential bidders to risk matters. In fact, in the absence of a reserve price, when preferences fall within the HARA family having constant relative risk aversion $[(\eta - 1)/\eta]$, the Bayes–Nash, equilibrium-bid function is

$$\sigma(v) = v - \frac{\int_{\underline{v}}^{v} F_V^0(u)^{\eta(\mathcal{N}-1)} \, du}{F_V^0(v)^{\eta(\mathcal{N}-1)}}.$$

Basically, HARA risk aversion effectively changes the number of potential bidders.

Donald and Paarsch (1996) demonstrated identification in models of Dutch and first-price, sealed-bid auctions within the IPVP and developed parametric estimation techniques. In this case, a latent structure $\left[F_V^0(\cdot), \eta^0\right]$ is said to be identified if it is the only pair of value distribution and risk-aversion parameter consistent with the true distribution of the winning bid at a Dutch auction and for all the bids at a first-price, sealed-bid auction. Donald and Paarsch (1996) demonstrated that identification holds under the assumption that $F_V^0(\cdot)$ is known to belong to a family of cumulative distribution functions supported on a known interval $[\underline{v}, \bar{v}]$ that are strictly increasing, continuously differentiable with continuous probability density function $f_V^0(v)$ such that $f_V^0(v)$ is positive on $[\underline{v}, \bar{v}]$. In the case of Donald and Paarsch, identification holds even when no variation in the number of potential bidders $\mathcal{N}$ or auction-specific covariates $\mathbf{Z}$ exists.

To understand this result, consider first the case of first-price, sealed-bid auctions at which all bids are observed. Note that the latent valuation is related to the observed bid and the distribution of the observed bid distribution via

$$v_i = s_i + \frac{1}{\eta^0 (\mathcal{N} - 1)} \frac{F_S^0 (s_i)}{f_S^0 (s_i)}.$$

Evaluating this at the upper support $\bar{v}$ yields

$$\bar{v} = \bar{s}^0 + \frac{1}{\eta^0 (\mathcal{N} - 1)} \frac{F_S^0 (\bar{s}^0)}{f_S^0 (\bar{s}^0)}.$$

Clearly, $\bar{s}^0$, $F_S^0 (\bar{s}^0)$, and $f_S^0 (\bar{s}^0)$ are all known quantities from the observed bid distribution, or from the bid distribution induced by the structure $\left[F_V^0 (\cdot), \eta^0 \right]$ according to the bid function $\sigma(v)$. Therefore, once $\bar{v}$ is specified, the above relation, which is a one-to-one function in η^0, can be used to recover the unique risk-aversion parameter η^0. Once the risk-aversion parameter η^0 is determined, the entire bid distribution can then be recovered from

$$v = s + \frac{1}{\eta^0 (\mathcal{N} - 1)} \frac{F_S^0 (s)}{f_S^0 (s)}$$

for every possible value of s in the range of the bid distribution $F_S^0 (s)$. The same result holds for Dutch auctions at which only the winning bid is observed because $F_S^0 (s)$ and $f_S^0 (s)$ can be recovered from the distribution of the winning bids. These identification results also hold for the case where the reserve price is binding. Of course, with a binding reserve price the identification of $F_V^0 (\cdot)$ is only possible on the portion of the valuation distribution above the reserve price. To see this, note that, under HARA risk aversion, the first-order condition is

$$v = s + \frac{1}{\eta(\mathcal{N} - 1)} \left\{ \frac{G_S^0 (s)}{g_S^0 (s)} + \frac{F_V^0 (r)}{[1 - F_V^0 (r)]} \frac{1}{g_S^0 (s)} \right\}.$$

Identification of $F_V^0 (\cdot)$ below the reserve price obtains by parametric extrapolation.

With a binding reserve price r, the bid function takes the form

$$\sigma(v) = v - \frac{\int_r^v F_V^0 (u)^{\eta^0 (\mathcal{N} - 1)} \, du}{F_V^0 (v)^{\eta^0 (\mathcal{N} - 1)}}$$

for v weakly exceeding r, with the boundary condition that $\sigma(r)$ equals r. Again, note that the assumption that $\bar{v}$ is known is important because then the equation between $\bar{v}$ and $\bar{s}$ can identify the risk-aversion parameter η^0 without any additional variation in $\mathcal{N}$ and $\boldsymbol{Z}$.

Estimation by the method of maximum likelihood, as developed by Donald and Paarsch (1996), minimizes the Kullback–Leibler distance between the model considered above and the observed bid distribution. In parametric models, the probability density function of the valuations depends on a finite number of parameters; i.e., $f_V(v; \boldsymbol{\theta})$. The likelihood function applies to the joint likelihood of the observed bids and the number of actual bidders. It takes different forms depending on whether the data come from a first-price, sealed-bid auction or a Dutch auction. At first-price, sealed-bid auctions, both the number of actual bidders N and the entire vector of bids submitted by actual bidders whose valuations are above the reserve price, are observed. Thus, the likelihood function, up to a constant that does not depend on the parameters, is

$$
\begin{aligned}
f(\boldsymbol{\theta}, \eta) &= \prod_{t=1}^{T} F_V(r; \boldsymbol{\theta})^{\mathcal{N}-N_t} \prod_{i=1}^{N_t} \left\{ \frac{f_V\left[\sigma^{-1}(s_{it}; \boldsymbol{\theta}, \eta)\right]}{\sigma'\left[\sigma^{-1}(s_{it}; \boldsymbol{\theta}, \eta)\right]} \right\} \\
&= \prod_{t=1}^{T} F_V(r; \boldsymbol{\theta})^{\mathcal{N}-N_t} \\
&\quad \prod_{i=1}^{N_t} \left\{ \frac{F_V\left[\sigma^{-1}(s_{it}; \boldsymbol{\theta}, \eta)\right]^{\eta(\mathcal{N}-1)+1}}{\eta(\mathcal{N}-1) \int_r^{\sigma^{-1}(s_{it}; \boldsymbol{\theta}, \eta)} F_V(u; \boldsymbol{\theta})^{\eta(\mathcal{N}-1)} \, du} \right\},
\end{aligned}
$$

where $F_V(r; \boldsymbol{\theta})$ denotes the probability of nonparticipation, and

$$
\sigma'(v; \boldsymbol{\theta}, \eta) = \frac{\eta(\mathcal{N}-1) f_V(v; \boldsymbol{\theta}) \int_r^v F_V(u; \boldsymbol{\theta})^{\eta(\mathcal{N}-1)} \, du}{F_V(v; \boldsymbol{\theta})^{\eta(\mathcal{N}-1)+1}}
$$

is the Jacobian of the transformation from V to $\sigma(V)$.

On the other hand, at a Dutch auction, either the winning bid is observed when at least one participant is present, or the object goes unsold when no participants are observed. However, when only one potential bidder is present, that solo bidder allows the price to fall until the reserve price r obtains, so the winning bid is r with some point-mass. When N exceeds one, the probability density function of the highest valuation of the object Z equal $V_{(1:\mathcal{N})}$ determines the winning bid. The probability density function of Z is

$$
f_Z(z; \boldsymbol{\theta}) = \mathcal{N} F_V(z; \boldsymbol{\theta})^{\mathcal{N}-1} f_V(z; \boldsymbol{\theta}).
$$

Therefore, the likelihood function for data from a Dutch auction, which depends on observed participation, is given by

$$
f\left(\boldsymbol{\theta}, \eta\right) = \prod_{t=1}^{T} \left\{ \frac{\mathcal{N} F_V\left[\sigma^{-1}\left(w_t; \boldsymbol{\theta}, \eta\right); \boldsymbol{\theta}\right]^{\mathcal{N} + \eta(N_t - 1)}}{\eta\left(N_t - 1\right) \int_r^{\sigma^{-1}(w_t; \boldsymbol{\theta}, \eta)} F_V\left(u; \boldsymbol{\theta}\right)^{\eta(N_t - 1)} du} \right\}^{\mathbf{1}(N_t > 1)}
$$
$$
\left\{ \mathcal{N} F_V\left(r; \boldsymbol{\theta}\right)^{\mathcal{N} - 1} \left[1 - F_V(r; \boldsymbol{\theta})\right] \right\}^{\mathbf{1}(N_t = 1)}
$$
$$
\left\{ F_V\left(r; \boldsymbol{\theta}\right)^{\mathcal{N}} \right\}^{\mathbf{1}(N_t = 0)}.
$$

For both Dutch and first-price, sealed-bid auctions, the upper bound of support of the bid function $\bar{s}$ depends on $\boldsymbol{\theta}$ as well as η. Thus, the statistical properties of the maximum-likelihood estimator will be nonstandard. These properties were discussed in detail above in our discussion of Donald and Paarsch (1996), so they will not be repeated.

4.4.2 Semiparametric Identification and Estimation

Campo, Guerre, Perrigne, and Vuong (2000) studied semiparametric identification and estimation in models of Dutch and first-price, sealed-bid auctions within the symmetric IPVP when potential bidders are risk averse. In contrast to the work of Guerre et al., where nonparametric identification was established within the symmetric IPVP when potential bidders are risk neutral, Campo et al. showed that models admitting risk aversion are, in general, unidentified. Moreover, models admitting risk aversion do not impose testable restrictions on the observed bid data either. Furthermore, Campo et al. showed that even if one were willing to impose parametric asssumptions on the utility function, the latent distribution of private values still cannot be nonparametrically identified. Identification can, however, be established if one is willing to impose parametric assumptions on both the utility function and a single quantile of the distribution $F_V^0(v)$.

Campo et al. also introduced the term *rationalizability*. Rationalizability of the observed bid distribution is an important concept, closely related to semiparametric identification. In particular, if the observed bid data are generated from a true model structure $\left[F_V^0\left(\cdot\right), \eta^0\right]$, then identifiability will imply that the observed bid distribution can be uniquely rationalized by $\left[F_V^0\left(\cdot\right), \eta^0\right]$. On the other hand, it is also possible that the observed bid distribution is not generated by any model structure $\left[F_V^0\left(\cdot\right), \eta^0\right]$, in which case the symmetric IPV auction model with HARA preferences is misspecified. Campo et al. showed that if $\bar{v}$

is left unspecified, then it is always possible to find a range of η large enough to rationalize any observed bid distribution, such that the relation between v and s for the parameter η in this range is strictly increasing. Each such η is associated with a corresponding value of $\bar{v}$. In other words, a model of a first-price, sealed-bid auction within the symmetric IPVP where bidders have HARA preferences will always ensure $\bar{v}$ is correctly specified, in fact too correctly specified.

Campo et al. assumed that $\bar{v}$ is an unknown constant to be estimated. In this case, in order to identify the two parameters, $\bar{v}$ and η, two equations are required. Therefore, at least two values of $\mathcal{N}$ or $\boldsymbol{Z}$ are required to estimate these two parameters. If more flexible parameterizations of $\bar{v}$ are used, then more variations in $\mathcal{N}$ and $\boldsymbol{Z}$ will be needed.

On the other hand, when $\bar{v}$ is specified by the researcher, it might not always be the case that the resulting relation between v and s using the nonparametric estimate of the inverse bid function is always strictly increasing over the range of s, raising an issue of possible misspecification.

Campo et al. considered the general case where the initial wealth is strictly positive, but is common among all bidders. For simplicity, we shall discuss the case where the initial wealth is zero. In general, the results are unaffected by our focus on the case of zero initial wealth.

Let the utility function, which is common to all bidders, be denoted $U(\cdot)$. Now, the expected payoff to bidder i who submits a bid $\sigma(v_i)$ is

$$U\left[v_i - \sigma(v_i)\right] \Pr\left[\sigma(v_i) \geq \sigma(v_j), \ \forall\, j \neq i\right].$$

In equilibrium, s_i equals $\sigma(v_i)$, so

$$U(v_i - s_i) \Pr\left[s_i \geq \sigma(v_j), \ \forall\, j \neq i\right].$$

Under the assumption of symmetric IPVP, expected utility is

$$U(v_i - s_i) F_V\left[\sigma^{-1}(s_i)\right]^{\mathcal{N}-1}.$$

Therefore, the necessary, first-order condition is

$$\sigma'(v_i) = (\mathcal{N} - 1)\frac{f_V(v_i)}{F_V(v_i)}\lambda(v_i - s_i)$$

where the function $\lambda(\cdot)$ is related to the utility function $U(\cdot)$ through the relation

$$\lambda(\cdot) = \frac{U(\cdot)}{U'(\cdot)}.$$

This first-order condition can be written as

$$(\mathcal{N} - 1) \frac{f_S(s_i)}{F_S(s_i)} \lambda (v_i - s_i) = 1$$

which can be used to solve for v_i as a function of s_i, so

$$v_i = s_i + \lambda^{-1} \left[\frac{1}{(\mathcal{N} - 1)} \frac{F_S(s_i)}{f_S(s_i)} \right] \equiv \sigma^{-1}(s_i; U, F_S, \mathcal{N}).$$

At this point, Campo et al. introduced and made use of the notion of rationalizability. Their use of this term is somewhat different from how some economic theorists employ the term. Paarsch and Robert (2003) have referred to rationalizability as *Bayes–Nash consistent*. In any case, to Campo et al., in order for the bid distribution to be rationalizable by a utility function $U(\cdot)$ and a distribution $F_V(v)$, the bid function must be monotonically increasing. Thus, it is natural to require

$$s_i + \lambda^{-1} \left[\frac{1}{(\mathcal{N} - 1)} \frac{F_S(s_i)}{f_S(s_i)} \right]$$

to be a strictly increasing function, which then implies

$$1 + \frac{\partial}{\partial s_i} \lambda^{-1} \left[\frac{1}{(\mathcal{N} - 1)} \frac{F_S(s_i)}{f_S(s_i)} \right] > 0.$$

In models with risk-neutral bidders, $\lambda(\cdot)$ is the identity function. Therefore, requiring

$$1 + \frac{\partial}{\partial s_i} \left[\frac{1}{(\mathcal{N} - 1)} \frac{F_S(s_i)}{f_S(s_i)} \right] > 0$$

imposes a testable restriction on the observable bid distribution $F_S(s_i)$ and $f_S(s_i)$. It is important to note that this is a test of *regularity* in the nomenclature of Myerson (1981); it is a test of the monotone-likelihood ratio property assumed to guarantee a unique bid function at the first-price, sealed-bid auction. It is not really a test of rational behavior.

On the other hand, Campo et al. have shown that, under risk aversion, for any observable bid distribution $F_S(\cdot)$ and $f_S(\cdot)$, it is always possible to find a utility function and a corresponding $\lambda(\cdot)$ such that

$$1 + \frac{\partial}{\partial s_i} \lambda^{-1} \left[\frac{1}{(\mathcal{N} - 1)} \frac{F_S(s_i)}{f_S(s_i)} \right] > 0.$$

In fact, they have shown this to be true even if the set of utility functions is constrained to the HARA family of von Neumann–Morgenstern utility functions, which have constant relative risk aversion, or the CARA family of utility functions, which have constant absolute risk aversion.

From our work above, we know that under HARA utility functions,

$$U(v) = \eta v^{1/\eta}, \eta \geq 1,$$

so

$$\lambda(v) = \eta v$$

and the relation between the observed bid and the valuation becomes

$$v_i = s_i + \frac{1}{\eta(\mathcal{N}-1)} \frac{F_S(s_i)}{f_S(s_i)} \equiv \sigma^{-1}(s_i).$$

In order for the derivative of $\sigma^{-1}(s_i)$ to be positive for all s_i,

$$1 + \frac{1}{\eta(\mathcal{N}-1)} \frac{\partial}{\partial s_i} \left[\frac{F_S(s_i)}{f_S(s_i)} \right] > 0.$$

This relation automatically holds when

$$\inf_{s_i} \frac{\partial}{\partial s_i} \left[\frac{F_S(s_i)}{f_S(s_i)} \right] > 0.$$

On the other hand, even if

$$-\infty < \inf_{s_i} \frac{\partial}{\partial s_i} \left[\frac{F_S(s_i)}{f_S(s_i)} \right] < 0,$$

it is always possible to choose η close enough to ∞ to make the second term as small, in absolute value, as possible. Therefore, the derivative is positive uniformly over s_i. In particular, it suffices to choose η such that

$$\frac{1}{\eta} < \frac{(\mathcal{N}-1)}{\left\{ -\inf_{s_i} \frac{\partial}{\partial s_i} \left[\frac{F_S(s_i)}{f_S(s_i)} \right] \right\}}.$$

Thus, the HARA family of utility functions can be used to rationalize *any* bid distribution $F_S(\cdot)$ and $f_S(\cdot)$ as long as some regularity conditions are satisfied.

Utility functions within the CARA family, on the other hand, take the form

$$U(v) = \frac{[1 - \exp(-\alpha v)]}{[1 - \exp(-\alpha)]}.$$

In this case,

$$\lambda(v) = \frac{[\exp(\alpha v) - 1]}{\alpha}$$

and

$$\lambda^{-1}(s) = \frac{\log(1+\alpha s)}{\alpha}.$$

Therefore, the inverse bidding strategy is given by

$$v_i = \sigma^{-1}(s_i) = s_i + \frac{1}{\alpha}\log\left[1 + \frac{\alpha F_S(s_i)}{(\mathcal{N}-1)f_S(s_i)}\right].$$

Differentiating this inverse bidding function, we see that, when

$$\frac{\partial \sigma^{-1}(s_i)}{\partial s_i} > 0,$$

for all s_i in the range of bids, α must be chosen so

$$\alpha > \sup_{s_i \in (\underline{s}, \bar{s}]} -\frac{f_S(s_i)}{F_S(s_i)}\left\{(\mathcal{N}-1) + \frac{\partial}{\partial s_i}\left[\frac{F_S(s_i)}{f_S(s_i)}\right]\right\}.$$

This is satisfied for an infinity of values for positive α as long as

$$\sup_{s_i \in (\underline{s}, \bar{s}]} -\frac{f_S(s_i)}{F_S(s_i)}\left\{(\mathcal{N}-1) + \frac{\partial}{\partial s_i}\left[\frac{F_S(s_i)}{f_S(s_i)}\right]\right\} < \infty.$$

As long as the right-hand side is assumed to be continuously differentiable, this will be satisfied if it can be shown that

$$\alpha > \lim_{s_i \downarrow \underline{v}} -\frac{f_S(s_i)}{F_S(s_i)}\left\{(\mathcal{N}-1) + \frac{\partial}{\partial s_i}\left[\frac{F_S(s_i)}{f_S(s_i)}\right]\right\}.$$

This is true because

$$\lim_{s_i \downarrow \underline{v}} \frac{\partial}{\partial s_i}\left[\frac{F_S(s_i)}{f_S(s_i)}\right] = 1$$

and

$$\lim_{s_i \downarrow \underline{v}} -\frac{f_S(s_i)}{F_S(s_i)}\left\{(\mathcal{N}-1) + \frac{\partial}{\partial s_i}\left[\frac{F_S(s_i)}{f_S(s_i)}\right]\right\} = -\infty.$$

Therefore, any observed bid distribution $F_S(\cdot)$ can be rationalized by an infinite number of CARA utility functions as long as α is chosen to be a large number. Given the choice of the HARA or CARA utility function, the distribution of v_i equal $\sigma^{-1}(s_i)$ can be used as the $F_V(\cdot)$ that rationalizes the observed bid data. The only testable implication of the bid data is the assumption of independent and identically distributed private values.

A natural corollary to the rationalizability result is that, within the symmetric IPVP, models of first-price, sealed-bid auctions with symmetric, risk-averse potential bidders are, in general, unidentified. This is true even when potential bidders have identical preferences from either the HARA or the CARA family of von Neumann–Morgenstern utility functions. This result obtains because any observed bid distribution function can be justified by an infinite number of risk-averse utility functions or distributions of private valuations, even with those two families of utility functions.

To achieve semiparametric identification, Campo et al. proposed making both the utility function $U(\cdot)$ and a quantile of $F_V^0(\cdot)$ a function of the parameters and the covariates. Thus,

$$U(\cdot) = U(\cdot; \boldsymbol{\theta})$$

and

$$F_V^{-1}(\tau | \boldsymbol{z}, \mathcal{N}) = F_V^{-1}(\tau | \boldsymbol{z}, \mathcal{N}; \boldsymbol{\gamma}).$$

In other words, they assumed that for some known τ, the τth quantile of the valuation distribution conditional on $\boldsymbol{z}$ and $\mathcal{N}$, $F_V(\cdot | \boldsymbol{z}, \mathcal{N})$, is a parametric function of $\boldsymbol{\gamma}$, $\boldsymbol{z}$, and $\mathcal{N}$.

The key semiparametric identification assumption that Campo et al. imposed is that the function

$$\lambda \big[F_V^{-1}(\tau | \boldsymbol{z}, \mathcal{N}; \boldsymbol{\gamma}) - F_S^{-1}(\tau | \boldsymbol{z}, \mathcal{N}); \boldsymbol{\theta} \big]$$

$$= \frac{U \big[F_V^{-1}(\tau | \boldsymbol{z}, \mathcal{N}; \boldsymbol{\gamma}) - F_S^{-1}(\tau | \boldsymbol{z}, \mathcal{N}); \boldsymbol{\theta} \big]}{U' \big[F_V^{-1}(\tau | \boldsymbol{z}, \mathcal{N}; \boldsymbol{\gamma}) - F_S^{-1}(\tau | \boldsymbol{z}, \mathcal{N}); \boldsymbol{\theta} \big]}$$

uniquely identifies the parameters $\boldsymbol{\theta}$ and $\boldsymbol{\gamma}$. This means that, for

$$(\boldsymbol{\theta}_1, \boldsymbol{\gamma}_1) \neq (\boldsymbol{\theta}_2, \boldsymbol{\gamma}_2),$$

we can find some values of $(\boldsymbol{z}, \mathcal{N})$ such that

$$\lambda \big[F_V^{-1}(\tau | \boldsymbol{z}, \mathcal{N}; \boldsymbol{\gamma}_1) - F_S^{-1}(\tau | \boldsymbol{z}, \mathcal{N}); \boldsymbol{\theta}_1 \big]$$

$$\neq \lambda \big[F_V^{-1}(\tau | \boldsymbol{z}, \mathcal{N}; \boldsymbol{\gamma}_2) - F_S^{-1}(\tau | \boldsymbol{z}, \mathcal{N}); \boldsymbol{\theta}_2 \big].$$

To see why this condition is sufficient for identification, evaluate the first-order condition:

$$(\mathcal{N} - 1) \frac{f_S(s_i)}{F_S(s_i)} \lambda (v_i - s_i) = 1$$

at the s_i equal $F_S^{-1}(\tau|z,\mathcal{N})$. Now,

$$\lambda\left[F_V^{-1}(\tau|z,\mathcal{N};\gamma) - F_S^{-1}(\tau|z,\mathcal{N});\theta\right]$$

$$=\frac{1}{\mathcal{N}-1}\frac{\tau}{f_S\left[F_S^{-1}(\tau|z,\mathcal{N})|z,\mathcal{N}\right]}.$$

Since the right-hand side of this equation can be recovered from the population of bids, or can be estimated from the sample of observed bids, for any given z and $\mathcal{N}$, the identification condition amounts to requiring that if one varies the z and $\mathcal{N}$ in the previous equation to generate a system of equations, the solution of γ and θ to this system of equations is unique, and hence can be recovered from the sample. In particular, Campo et al. verified this identification condition for both HARA and CARA utility functions when a given conditional τ^{th} quantile is specified to be a constant parameter, $F_V^{-1}(\tau|z,\mathcal{N};\gamma)$ is equivalent to γ, and when there exists $(z_1,\mathcal{N}_1)$ not equal to $(z_2,\mathcal{N}_2)$ such that

$$F_S^{-1}(\tau|z_1,\mathcal{N}_1) \neq F_S^{-1}(\tau|z_2,\mathcal{N}_2).$$

One can think of $F_S^{-1}(\tau|z,\mathcal{N})$ as the regressor. In order to identify two parameters θ and γ, one needs at least two different values.

A semiparametric, multistep estimation strategy can then be based on this identification strategy. In the first step,

$$F_S^{-1}(\tau|z,\mathcal{N}) \quad \text{and} \quad f_S\left[F_S^{-1}(\tau|z,\mathcal{N})|z,\mathcal{N}\right]$$

can be estimated, nonparametrically, from the data using a variety of different nonparametric estimation methods. In the second step, the method of least squares can be used to estimate the parameters γ and θ via

$$\left(\hat{\gamma},\hat{\theta}\right) = \operatorname*{argmin}_{\gamma,\theta} \sum_{t=1}^{T}\left\{\lambda\left[F_V^{-1}(\tau|z_t,\mathcal{N}_t;\gamma) - \hat{F}_S^{-1}(\tau|z_t,\mathcal{N}_t);\theta\right] - \frac{1}{\mathcal{N}-1}\frac{\tau}{\hat{f}_S\left[\hat{F}_S^{-1}(\tau|z_t,\mathcal{N}_t)|z_t,\mathcal{N}_t\right]}\right\}^2.$$

4.5 Stochastic Private Values

Lu (2004) has extended the framework of Campo et al. (2000) to study identification and estimation in models of first-price, sealed-bid auctions within the stochastic IPVP. The stochastic IPVP is a special case of a general model due to Éso and White (2004). Within the stochastic IPVP, each bidder is assumed to have an *ex ante* private signal about his random private value. The expected value of the ex post private value equals the signal. The ex post private value is a random variable unobserved at the time of bidding. An agent's bid is a function of his *ex ante* signal. Bidders are assumed symmetrically risk averse; they take into account the risk premium of the ex post risk when deciding on their bidding strategies.

To put additional structure on this problem, let the ex post private value of bidder i be denoted

$$\tilde{V}_i = V_i + E_i$$

where E_i is an independent and identically distributed error term that is also independent of V_j for all j. Denote the cumulative distribution function of E_i by $F_E(\cdot)$ and its probability density function by $f_E(\cdot)$. Lu normalized the mean of E_i to be zero. He also studied a symmetric auction game where initial wealth is assumed to be the same for all bidders. For simplicity, we shall describe the case where initial wealth is zero for all. Bidders are risk averse and evaluate their monetary gains according to a von Neumann–Morgenstern concave utility function $U(\cdot)$ where $U(0)$ is zero. The expected payoff to bidder i who submits a bid $\sigma(v_i)$ is

$$\Pr\left[\sigma(v_i) > \sigma(v_j), j \neq i\right] \mathcal{E}_E \left\{ U\left[v_i + E_i - \sigma(v_i)\right] \right\}$$

where the subscript E on $\mathcal{E}$ denotes that the expectation is taken over E. In equilibrium, s_i equals $\sigma(v_i)$, so the expected payoff becomes

$$\mathcal{E}_{E_i} \left\{ U(v_i + E_i - s_i) \right\} \Pr\left[s_i \geq \sigma(v_j), j \neq i \right].$$

Within the IPVP, this is

$$\mathcal{E}_{E_i} \left\{ U(v_i + E_i - s_i) \right\} F_V \left[\sigma^{-1}(s_i) \right]^{\mathcal{N}-1}.$$

The necessary, first-order condition with respect to s_i is

$$\sigma'(v_i) = (\mathcal{N} - 1) \frac{f_V(v_i)}{F_V(v_i)} \lambda(v_i - s_i)$$

or, equivalently,

$$1 = (\mathcal{N} - 1) \frac{f_S(s_i)}{F_S(s_i)} \lambda(v_i - s_i)$$

where now $\lambda\left(\cdot\right)$ is defined by

$$\lambda\left(v_i - s_i\right) = \frac{\mathcal{E}_{E_i}\left[U\left(v_i - s_i + E_i\right)\right]}{\mathcal{E}_{E_i}\left[U'\left(v_i - s_i + E_i\right)\right]}.$$

When the reservation utility of not participating in the auction is normalized to zero, the boundary condition for the bidder of the lowest type with signal $\underline{v}$ is

$$\mathcal{E}_E\left\{U\left[\underline{v} - \sigma\left(\underline{v}\right) + E\right]\right\} = 0.$$

In other words,

$$\sigma\left(\underline{v}\right) = \underline{v} - \pi$$

where π is the risk premium of the lottery E, defined by

$$\mathcal{E}_E\left[U\left(E + \pi\right)\right] = 0.$$

Lu studied identification under the CARA family of von Neumann–Morgenstern utility function $U\left(\cdot\right)$. As we noted in a previous section, a CARA utility function, up to location and scale normalizations, takes the following form:

$$U\left(v\right) = \left[1 - \exp\left(-\alpha v\right)\right].$$

In this case, we know that

$$\pi = \frac{1}{\alpha}\log\left\{\mathcal{E}\left[\exp\left(-\alpha E\right)\right]\right\}$$

and

$$\lambda\left(v\right) = \frac{\exp\left[\alpha\left(v - \pi\right)\right] - 1}{\alpha}.$$

Using this functional form for $\lambda\left(\cdot\right)$, the first-order condition can be used to invert out the private signal as a function of the observed bids:

$$\begin{aligned}
v_i &= s_i + \lambda^{-1}\left[\frac{1}{\mathcal{N} - 1}\frac{F_S\left(s_i\right)}{f_S\left(s_i\right)}\right]\\
&= s_i + \pi\left[\alpha, F_E\left(\cdot\right)\right] + \frac{1}{\alpha}\log\left[1 + \frac{\alpha}{\mathcal{N} - 1}\frac{F_S\left(s_i\right)}{f_S\left(s_i\right)}\right]\\
&= \sigma^{-1}\left[s_i; \alpha, F_S\left(\cdot\right), F_E\left(\cdot\right), \mathcal{N}\right]
\end{aligned}$$

where the dependence of the risk premium on α and $F_E\left(\cdot\right)$ is denoted by

$$\pi = \pi\left[\alpha, F_E\left(\cdot\right)\right].$$

Relative to the "deterministic" private-value model of Campo et al., in which no ex post risk exists, this equation illustrates that, for a given private signal, the bid will be smaller because of a risk premium. In other words, bidders shade their bids down further by an amount related to π.

As discussed in the previous section, Campo et al. showed that the deterministic private-value model with CARA utility is unidentified without additional quantile-based semiparametric restrictions. Because the stochastic private-value model of Lu is a generalization of Campo et al., one would expect it too to be unidentified.[7] Without additional assumptions or additional data, this is, in fact, the case.

In order to achieve identification, Lu assumed that the ex post realization of $\tilde{V}$ for the winner, denoted $\tilde{V}^w$, is available. Therefore, the joint distribution of the winning bid W and the ex post value of the winner $\tilde{V}^w$, is available to the researcher. Note that $\tilde{V}^w$ is *not* the maximum order statistic of the ex post value $\tilde{V}_i$ across all bidders. The ex post value shock to the winner is denoted ε^w and equals $[\tilde{V}^w - V_{(1:\mathcal{N})}]$. ε^w is *not* the maximum order statistic of the *ex post* value shock E_i of all bidders either. Because the Es are independently realized after the winning bid has been determined, ε_w is independently distributed of W.

Lu showed that the joint distribution of W and $\tilde{V}^w$ is sufficient to identify the primitive parameters of the model, including α, $F_E(\cdot)$, and $F_V(\cdot)$. He also proposed a semiparametric, multistep estimation procedure based on the identification argument.

The identification argument takes $F_{W,\tilde{V}^w}$ as given. Because W is a one-to-one function of $V_{(1:\mathcal{N})}$,

$$\mathcal{E}\left(\tilde{V}^w | W\right) = \mathcal{E}\left[\tilde{V}^w | V_{(1:\mathcal{N})}\right] = \mathcal{E}\left[V_{(1:\mathcal{N})} + \varepsilon_w | V_{(1:\mathcal{N})}\right] = V_{(1:\mathcal{N})}.$$

The last equality is due to the fact that ε^w is independent of $V_{(1:\mathcal{N})}$ and has mean zero. This implies that the distribution of $V_{(1:\mathcal{N})}$ can be identified as the distribution of $\mathcal{E}\left(\tilde{V}^w | W\right)$, so

$$F_{V_{(1:\mathcal{N})}}(v) = \Pr\left[\mathcal{E}\left(\tilde{V}^w | W\right) \leq v\right].$$

The private signal distribution $F_V(v)$ is then identified as

$$F_V(v) = F_{V_{(1:\mathcal{N})}}(v)^{\frac{1}{N}}.$$

Next, note that since

$$\underline{v} = \mathcal{E}\left(\tilde{V}^w | W = \underline{s}\right)$$

---

[7] In fact, the model of Campo et al. is a special case of the Lu model with the distribution of $F_E(\cdot)$ being one; i.e., degenerate point mass at zero.

and
$$\underline{s} = \underline{v} - \pi,$$

π, which equals $\pi\,[\alpha, F_E\,(\cdot)]$, can be identified as

$$\pi = \underline{v} - \underline{s} = \mathcal{E}\left(\tilde{V}^w | W = \underline{s}\right) - \underline{s}.$$

The next step is to identify α. Using the first-order condition, evaluated at W equal $\bar{s}$, we have

$$\mathcal{E}\left(\tilde{V}^w | W = \bar{s}\right) = \bar{s} + \pi + \frac{1}{\alpha}\log\left[1 + \frac{\mathcal{N}\alpha}{\mathcal{N}-1}\frac{1}{f_W\,(\bar{s})}\right].$$

Once π is known, everything in this equation is known from the population except for the parameter α. Therefore, α can be solved as the solution to this equation. Alternatively, evaluating the first-order condition at any other quantile other than the upper support will give rise to a continuum of equations to solve for α. To make use of all the quantiles together, which is important for obtaining $\sqrt{T}$ parameter-consistent and asymptotically normal estimators of π and α, Lu suggested that π and α can be identified as the unique solution to the following nonlinear, least-squares optimization problem in the population:

$$\left(\alpha^0, \pi^0\right) = \underset{\alpha, \pi}{\operatorname{argmin}} \mathcal{E}\left\{\tilde{V}^w - W - \pi - \frac{1}{\alpha}\log\left[1 + \frac{\mathcal{N}\alpha}{(\mathcal{N}-1)}\frac{F_W\,(W)}{f_W\,(W)}\right]\right\}^2.$$

This is because at the true (α, π), the first-order condition implies

$$\mathcal{E}\left(\tilde{V}^w | W\right) = V_{(1:\mathcal{N})} = W + \pi^0 + \frac{1}{\alpha^0}\log\left[1 + \frac{\mathcal{N}\alpha}{(\mathcal{N}-1)}\frac{F_W\,(W)}{f_W\,(W)}\right].$$

Finally, the distribution of ε^w is identical to the distribution of E. Therefore, the distribution of E can be identified from the distribution of

$$\varepsilon^w = \tilde{V}^w - W - \pi - \frac{1}{\alpha}\log\left[1 + \frac{\mathcal{N}\alpha}{(\mathcal{N}-1)}\frac{F_W\,(W)}{f_W\,(W)}\right].$$

Based on this identification argument, Lu proposed the following, multistep, semiparametric estimation procedure using a data set of T auctions with identical number of bidders $\mathcal{N}$. In the first step, $F_W\,(w)$ and $f_W\,(w)$ are estimated from the data using nonparametric methods such as a kernel method:

$$\hat{F}_W\,(w) = \frac{1}{T}\sum_{t=1}^{T}\mathbf{1}\,(W_t \le w) \quad \text{and} \quad \hat{f}_W\,(w) = \frac{1}{T}\sum_{t=1}^{T}\frac{1}{h_g}\kappa\left(\frac{W_t - w}{h_g}\right).$$

In the second step, a NLS estimator is used to estimate α and π. In particular,

$$(\hat{\alpha}, \hat{\pi}) = \underset{\alpha, \pi}{\text{argmin}} \sum_{t=1}^{T} \left\{ \tilde{V}_t^w - W_t - \pi - \frac{1}{\alpha} \log \left[1 + \frac{\mathcal{N}\alpha}{\mathcal{N}-1} \frac{\hat{F}_W(W_t)}{\hat{f}_W(W_t)} \right] \right\}^2.$$

In the third step, the private value distribution $F_{V_{(1:\mathcal{N})}}$ can be estimated either as the distribution of

$$\hat{V}_t^w = \frac{\frac{1}{T}\sum_{t'=1}^{T} \frac{1}{h_g} \tilde{V}_{t'}^w \kappa \left(\frac{W_{t'}-W_t}{h_g} \right)}{\frac{1}{T}\sum_{t'=1}^{T} \frac{1}{h_g} \kappa \left(\frac{W_{t'}-W_t}{h_g} \right)}$$

or as the distribution of

$$\hat{V}_t^w = W_t + \hat{\pi} + \frac{1}{\hat{\alpha}} \log \left\{ \log \left[1 + \frac{\mathcal{N}\hat{\alpha}}{\mathcal{N}-1} \frac{\hat{F}_W(W_t)}{\hat{f}_W(W_t)} \right] \right\}.$$

These two distributions can be compared to each other yielding a semi-parametric specification test of the stochastic private-value model. Using either one of the definitions for $\hat{V}_t^w$, the pseudo-*ex-post*-shocks can be estimated as

$$\hat{\varepsilon}_t^w = \tilde{V}_t^w - \hat{V}_t^w.$$

This gives rise to two estimates of the marginal distribution of ε_t^w. Another specification test for the model is a test of the independence between $\hat{\varepsilon}_t^w$ and $\hat{V}_t^w$. In other words, it is possible to test whether the joint distribution

$$\hat{F}_{\varepsilon_t^w, V_t^w}(\varepsilon, v) = \frac{1}{T}\sum_{t=1}^{T} \mathbf{1}\left(\hat{\varepsilon}_t^w \le \varepsilon, \hat{V}_t^w \le v \right)$$

is statistically close to the product of the marginal distributions:

$$\hat{F}_{\varepsilon_t^w}(\varepsilon) \hat{F}_{V_t^w}(v) = \frac{1}{T}\sum_{t=1}^{T} \mathbf{1}\left(\hat{\varepsilon}_t^w \le \varepsilon \right) \frac{1}{T}\sum_{t=1}^{T} \mathbf{1}\left(\hat{V}_t^w \le v \right).$$

4.6 Asymmetric Bidders

The assumptions of the symmetric IPVP are obviously a simplification of reality. At some auctions, potential bidders might be better modeled as independent draws from different distributions, different urns so to speak. Collusion might be modeled well under the assumption of asymmetries. For example, each potential bidder gets an independent and identically distributed draw from a distribution of valuations, but then some of the potential bidders form a collusive compact. Within the compact, some mechanism is used to choose the "winner" for the compact. Under this structure, the "valuations" of bidders in the compact are from a different distribution relative to those who are not in the compact. Asymmetries also make sense outside of collusion; e.g., bidders may be identical except for a measured location based on the spatial distance between their office and the object at auction.

Thus, in this section, we consider models within the asymmetric IPVP. In particular, we consider the sale of a single object at either Dutch or first-price, sealed-bid auction assuming that each of the $\mathcal{N}$ potential bidders is from one of J different classes where J is less than or equal to $\mathcal{N}$. To admit full generality, however, set J equal to $\mathcal{N}$; i.e., each potential bidder draws from his own, unique urn. A potential bidder of class j draws his individual-specific valuation independently from the cumulative distribution functions $F_j(v)$ having probability density function $f_j(v)$, which is strictly continuous. For technical reasons, we require that the F_js have common support $[\underline{v}, \overline{v}]$.

Initially, we assume risk neutrality and no reserve price. To begin, we solve the decision problem faced by a representative bidder at a first-price, sealed-bid auction when only two classes of bidders exist, $\mathcal{N}_1$ bidders whose valuations are from $F_1(v)$ and $\mathcal{N}_2$ bidders whose valuations are from $F_2(v)$, where $(\mathcal{N}_1 + \mathcal{N}_2)$ equals $\mathcal{N}$ and where $\mathcal{N}_1$ and $\mathcal{N}_2$ as well as $F_1(v)$ and $F_2(v)$ are common knowledge. We show the computational difficulties in this simple case. Subsequently, we move on to the general case where J equals $\mathcal{N}$.

Now, under risk neutrality, the expected payoff to a bidder of class j who has valuation v and chooses strategy s_j is

$$(v - s_j)\Pr(\text{win}|s_j) \quad j = 1, 2.$$

Suppose that all bidders of class j use a monotonically increasing strategy $\hat{\sigma}_j(v)$ for $j = 1, 2$. Under this assumption, one can put structure on the probability of winning an auction, conditional on a particular strategy s_j. In particular, for a bidder of class 1, it will be

$$\Pr(\text{win}|s_1) = F_1[\hat{\sigma}_1^{-1}(s_1)]^{\mathcal{N}_1 - 1} F_2[\hat{\sigma}_2^{-1}(s_1)]^{\mathcal{N}_2},$$

while, for a bidder of class 2, it will be

$$\Pr(\text{win}|s_2) = F_1[\hat{\sigma}_1^{-1}(s_2)]^{\mathcal{N}_1} F_2[\hat{\sigma}_2^{-1}(s_2)]^{\mathcal{N}_2 - 1}.$$

The necessary first-order conditions for expected-profit maximization are:

$$0 = -F_1[\hat{\sigma}_1^{-1}(s_1)]^{\mathcal{N}_1-1}F_2[\hat{\sigma}_2^{-1}(s_1)]^{\mathcal{N}_2}+$$

$$(v-s_1)\left\{\frac{(\mathcal{N}_1-1)F_1[\hat{\sigma}_1^{-1}(s_1)]^{\mathcal{N}_1-2}f_1[\hat{\sigma}_1^{-1}(s_1)]F_2[\hat{\sigma}_2^{-1}(s_1)]^{\mathcal{N}_2}}{\hat{\sigma}_1'}+\right.$$

$$\left.\frac{F_1[\hat{\sigma}_1^{-1}(s_1)]^{\mathcal{N}_1-1}\mathcal{N}_2F_2[\hat{\sigma}_2^{-1}(s_1)]^{\mathcal{N}_2-1}f_2[\sigma_2^{-1}(s_1)]}{\hat{\sigma}_2'}\right\}$$

and

$$0 = -F_1[\hat{\sigma}_1^{-1}(s_2)]^{\mathcal{N}_1}F_2[\hat{\sigma}_2^{-1}(s_2)]^{\mathcal{N}_2-1}+$$

$$(v-s_2)\left\{\frac{\mathcal{N}_1F_1[\hat{\sigma}_1^{-1}(s_2)]^{\mathcal{N}_1-1}f_1[\hat{\sigma}_1^{-1}(s_2)]F_2[\hat{\sigma}_2^{-1}(s_2)]^{\mathcal{N}_2-1}}{\hat{\sigma}_1'}+\right.$$

$$\left.\frac{F_1[\hat{\sigma}_1^{-1}(s_2)]^{\mathcal{N}_1}(\mathcal{N}_2-1)F_2[\hat{\sigma}_2^{-1}(s_2)]^{\mathcal{N}_2-2}f_2[\hat{\sigma}_2^{-1}(s_2)]}{\hat{\sigma}_2'}\right\}$$

where we have used the fact that

$$\frac{d\hat{\sigma}_j^{-1}(s_i)}{ds_i} = \frac{1}{\hat{\sigma}_j'[\sigma_j^{-1}(s_i)]}$$

when $\hat{\sigma}_j$ is a monotonic function.

Several different strategies exist to solve systems of differential equations. However, because the Lipschitz conditions are not satisfied for the above system of differential equations, it cannot be solved analytically.

4.6.1 First-Price, Sealed-Bid Auctions

Consider an equilibrium to the first-price, sealed-bid auction game at which a class j bidder follows the strategy σ_j that is strictly increasing and differentiable in his valuation v, having inverse function ϕ_j defined to be σ_j^{-1}. Given that, together the bidders follow the strategy vector $\boldsymbol{\sigma}$, which collects the strategies for each of the $\mathcal{N}$ potential bidders, the expected profit of bidder i when his valuation is v_i and he bids s is

$$\pi_i(v_i, s) = (v_i - s)\Pr(\text{win}|s)$$

where $\Pr(\text{win}|s)$ is his probability of winning, given bid s. Above, we showed that, in the symmetric IPVP case, calculating $\Pr(\text{win}|s)$ was straightforward. This is not the case when bidders are asymmetric because $\Pr(\text{win}|s)$ is a function of all opponents' distribution functions as well as their inverse-bid functions.

Brendstrup and Paarsch (2003) noted, however, that for bidder i who is of class j, has valuation V_i, and bid S_{ji} equal $\sigma_j(V_i)$, the probability density function of his bid is

$$g_j(s) = f_j[\phi_j(s)]\phi_j'(s).$$

Also, if bidder i has a winning bid of w, then

$$\max_{h \neq i} S_{jh} < w,$$

so the cumulative distribution function of $\max_{h \neq i} S_{jh}$ is given by

$$H_i(w|f_1, \ldots, f_{i-1}, f_{i+1}, \ldots, f_{\mathcal{N}}, \sigma_1, \ldots, \sigma_{i-1}, \sigma_{i+1}, \ldots, \sigma_{\mathcal{N}}) =$$

$$\prod_{h \neq i} G_h(w).$$

Following the work on asymmetric English auctions presented earlier, we know that

$$H_i'(w|f_1, \ldots, f_{i-1}, f_{i+1}, \ldots, f_{\mathcal{N}}, \sigma_1, \ldots, \sigma_{i-1}, \sigma_{i+1}, \ldots, \sigma_{\mathcal{N}})$$

$$= \frac{1}{(\mathcal{N}-1)!} \text{Perm} \begin{pmatrix} G_1(w) & \ldots & G_i(w) & G_{i+1}(w) & \ldots & G_{\mathcal{N}}(w) \\ \vdots & \ddots & \vdots & \vdots & \ddots & \vdots \\ G_1(w) & \ldots & G_i(w) & G_{i+1}(w) & \ldots & G_{\mathcal{N}}(w) \\ g_1(w) & \ldots & g_i(w) & g_{i+1}(w) & \ldots & g_{\mathcal{N}}(w) \end{pmatrix}.$$

Having obtained the expected profit for bidder i, given that his opponents follow strategies $\boldsymbol{\sigma}_{-1}$, Brendstrup and Paarsch then derived a necessary, first-order condition for bidder i's decision problem

$$\max_{<s>} (v_i - s)H_i(s)$$

which is

$$(v_i - s)H_i'(s) = H_i(s).$$

A first-order condition like the one above must hold for each bidder i; the solution to this system of differential equations, one for each bidder, together with the relevant boundary conditions, typically stated in terms of the reserve price r as well as the upper bound of support $\bar{v}$, constitutes an equilibrium to this first-price, sealed-bid auction game; see Maskin and Riley (2000) as well as Krishna (2002). Note that the conditions assumed by Brendstrup and Paarsch on the cumulative distribution functions allow them to invoke a theorem of Lebrun (1999) to assert that an equilibrium exists.

Nonparametric Identification

Brendstrup and Paarsch (2003) demonstrated nonparametric identification of the $\{F_j\}_{j=1}^J$. They noted that, from the first-order conditions,

$$v_i = s_i + \frac{H_i^0(s_i)}{H_i^{0'}(s_i)}. \tag{4.3}$$

Thus, again, the twin hypotheses of purposeful behavior and market equilibrium are used to identify bidder i's private value v_i as a function of *his* equilibrium bid and the distribution of the highest bid of his opponents. When it is possible to obtain the distribution of the highest bid of the opponents' bids, no reason exists to solve for the equilibrium strategies. Typically, at first-price, sealed-bid auctions all the bids of participants as well as their identities are recorded, so when a sequence of T auctions indexed by $t = 1, \ldots, T$ of an identical object are held, it is possible to estimate H_i from observed data.

Nonparametric Estimation

The basic idea of nonparametric estimation in this case derives from the simple, yet elegant and powerful, work of Guerre et al. (2000). The symmetric IPVP was discussed in section 4.2; here we describe the natural way in which Brendstrup and Paarsch (2003) have extended that work to the asymmetric IPVP. Note that, while H_i^0 and $H_i^{0'}$ are unknown, they can be estimated from the observed bids as well as bidder identities. Having estimated H_i^0 and $H_i^{0'}$, one can then use (4.3) to form an estimate of bidder i's valuation using the Guerre et al. framework.

In the first step, Brendstrup and Paarsch proposed constructing a sample of pseudoprivate-values from equation (4.3) using the nonparametric estimates of H_i^0 and $H_i^{0'}$, while in the second step, they propose using this pseudosample to estimate nonparametrically the probability density function of bidder i's latent valuation. A natural estimator of H_i^0 is then

$$\hat{H}_i(s) = \frac{1}{T}\sum_{t=1}^T \mathbf{1}\left(\max_{j\neq i} S_{jt} \leq s\right),$$

while

$$\hat{H}_i'(s) = \frac{1}{Th_g}\sum_{t=1}^T \kappa\left(\frac{s - \max_{j\neq i} S_{jt}}{h_g}\right)$$

152

where κ is a kernel function and h_g is a bandwidth parameter. Also,

$$\hat{V}_{it} = S_{it} + \frac{\hat{H}_i(S_{it})}{\hat{H}_i'(S_{it})}.$$

Brendstrup and Paarsch proposed using these pseudo-values to estimate the probability density function of latent valuations via

$$\tilde{f}_i(v) = \frac{1}{Th_g} \sum_{t=1}^{T} \kappa\left(\frac{\hat{V}_{it} - v}{h_g}\right).$$

Of course, the limitations of this estimator as described by Guerre et al. apply here too.

4.6.2 Dutch Auctions

In the absence of a reserve price, Dutch and first-price, sealed-bid auctions are strategically equivalent. Nevertheless, as was mentioned earlier, from an econometrician's perspective Dutch auctions are different from first-price, sealed-bid auctions in that only the winning bid is observed. As we have seen above, however, within the symmetric IPVP one can identify and estimate, nonparametrically, the distribution of latent valuations $F_V^0(v)$ at Dutch auctions using only data on the winning bid.

When a reserve price binds, Dutch and first-price, sealed-bid auctions are no longer strategically equivalent because actual competition is typically observed at Dutch auctions, but reasonably assumed unobserved at first-price, sealed-bid auctions. Thus, at first-price, sealed-bid auctions $\mathcal{N}$ is used in the solution to the decision problem, while at Dutch auctions n is used in the solution to the decision problem. Moreover, in the presence of asymmetries, it matters to bidders at Dutch auctions which participants showed up; i.e., the identities of the participants is used in the solution to the decision problem.

Despite the fact that asymmetries are going to complicate matters, Brendstrup and Paarsch (2003) demonstrated that the distributions of valuations, above the reserve price r, are identified from the observed winning bid at Dutch auction within the asymmetric IPVP. To understand their results, it is important to note that, on the one hand, the observed winning bid contains information concerning actual competition but, on the other hand, less information exists because only one bid is observed. The practical implications of these two facts is that the methods proposed to deal with asymmetries at first-price, sealed-bid auctions no longer apply.

In what follows, assume that the reserve price binds and that more than one potential bidder attends the auction. From the first-order condition, one knows that when bidder i wins

$$v_i = w_i + \frac{H_i^0(w_i|P)}{H_i^{0'}(w_i|P)} \qquad (4.4)$$

where w_i is the winning bid and the H_i function is now conditioned on realized competition P, the set of bidders whose valuations have weakly exceeded the reserve price r. Under these conditions, Brendstrup and Paarsch (2003) have demonstrated

Theorem 4.5.2: $F_i^0(v)$ is nonparametrically identified on $[r, \bar{v}]$ from the winning bid, the number and identities of the potential bidders, the number and identities of actual bidders, and the identity of the winner.

To see this, denote the set of participating bidders by P. Define the random variable W to be the maximum of $(B_1, \ldots, B_n)$ where n is the number of participating bidders. Let I denote the index of the winner; i.e., W equals B_j means I equals j. We observe the distribution of bids for winners, given by P. Denote the cumulative distribution function of W at an auction won by bidder i by $Q_i(w|P)$. Now, $Q_i(w|P)$ is the union of two disjoint events: B_i being the maximum among $(B_1, \ldots, B_n)$ and B_i being less than or equal to w. Thus,

$$
\begin{aligned}
Q_i(w|P) &= \Pr(W \leq w|I = i) \\
&= \int_{-\infty}^{w} \prod_{j \neq i} G_j(u|P) \, dG_i(u|P) \\
&= \int_{-\infty}^{w} \frac{\prod_{j=1}^{n} G_j(u|P)}{G_i(u|P)} \, dG_i(u|P) \\
&= \int_{-\infty}^{w} \frac{\Pr(W \leq u)}{G_i(u|P)} \, dG_i(u|P) \\
&= \int_{-\infty}^{w} \frac{\sum_{j=1}^{n} Q_j(u|P)}{G_i(u|P)} \, dG_i(u|P) \\
&= \int_{-\infty}^{w} \sum_{j=1}^{n} Q_j(u|P) \, d\log[G_i(u|P)].
\end{aligned}
$$

Therefore,

$$dQ_i(w|P) = \sum_{j=1}^{n} Q_j(w|P) \, d\log[G_i(w|P)]$$

154

or

$$G_i(w|P) = \exp\left\{ \int_{-\infty}^{w} \left[\sum_{j=1}^{n} Q_j(u|P) \right]^{-1} dQ_i(u|P) \right\}$$

$$= \left[\sum_{j=1}^{n} Q_j(w|P) \right]^{\pi_i}$$

where π_i is the probability that i wins the auction. As i was arbitrary, we have identified the distribution of bids. Now, from the distribution of bids, we can find $H_i(w|P)$ via

$$H_i(w|P) = \prod_{j \neq i} G_j(w|P)$$

and the probability density function from

$$H_i'(w|P) = \frac{d\left[\prod_{j \neq i} G_j(w|P) \right]}{dw}.$$

The idea is to use consistent estimators of $Q_j(u|P)$ and $Q_j'(u|P)$ as well as π_i to define the estimator

$$\hat{G}_i(w|P) = \left[\sum_{j=1}^{n} \hat{Q}_j(u|P) \right]^{\frac{T_i}{T}}$$

and then to form estimators of $H_i(w|P)$ and $H_i'(w|P)$ via

$$\hat{H}_i(w|P) = \prod_{j \neq i} \hat{G}_j(w|P)$$

and

$$\hat{H}_i'(w|P) = \frac{d\left[\prod_{j \neq i} \hat{G}_j(w|P) \right]}{dw}.$$

At this point, one can use the estimation strategy developed for first-price, sealed-bid auctions; i.e., form the pseudowinning-values

$$\hat{V}_{it} = W_{it} + \frac{\hat{H}_i(W_{it}|P)}{\hat{H}_i'(W_{it}|P)}.$$

These pseudo-values are from the distribution $F_i(v)$, but they are conditional on the fact that the bidder won, so are not a random sample from $F_i(v)$. One way to take account of this fact is to divide this conditional distribution by $H_i[w(v)]$. Note that by doing so one can estimate the truncated distribution of latent valuations, truncated by the reserve price:

$$F_i^*(v) = \frac{F_i(v)}{[1 - F_i(r)]}.$$

4.6.3 Unobserved Heterogeneity

Building on the work of Li, Perrigne, and Vuong (2000), Krasnokutskaya (2004) studied identification and estimation in a model of a first-
price sealed-bid auction within the asymmetric IPVP in the presence of
auction-specific unobserved heterogeneity. In her model, the value to
bidder i is the product of a common component Y that is known to all
bidders and a private component V_i that is privately observable only by
bidder i,

$$Y \times V_i.$$

The component Y is unobserved to the econometrician; one interpretation of it is unobserved heterogeneity. In her model, only two classes of
bidders exist, but Krasnokutskaya could extend the model to the case
of many classes. Without loss of generality, bidders $i = 1, \ldots, \mathcal{N}_1$ are
assumed of class 1, having cumulative distribution function $F_1(v_1)$ and
probability density function $f_1(v_1)$, while bidders $i = \mathcal{N}_1 + 1, \ldots, \mathcal{N}$ are
assumed of class 2, having cumulative distribution function $F_2(v_2)$ and
probability density function $f_2(v_2)$. Denoting $(\mathcal{N} - \mathcal{N}_1)$ by $\mathcal{N}_2$, we have,
when both Y and the V_is are assumed to be mutually independent,

$$\Pr\left(Y \leq y, V_1 \leq v_1, \ldots, V_{\mathcal{N}} \leq v_{\mathcal{N}}\right) = F_Y\left(y\right) \prod_{i=1}^{\mathcal{N}_1} F_1\left(v_i\right) \prod_{i=\mathcal{N}_1+1}^{\mathcal{N}} F_2\left(v_i\right).$$

Here, $F_Y\left(y\right)$ is the cumulative distribution function for the common
component, which is interpreted as unobserved heterogeneity.

Krasnokutskaya argued that ignoring unobserved heterogeneity can
mislead a researcher into believing that more variation in V exists than
is actually present. In figure 4.2, we present a four-panel graph. In the
top left panel is graphed a common probability density function $f_V(v)$
and four draws, the •s in the graph, from it. In the bottom left panel
is graphed the Bayes–Nash, equilibrium-bid function corresponding to
$f_V(v)$. In the top right panel is graphed two probability density functions
$f_V(v|y_1)$ and $f_V(v|y_2)$ conditional on two realizations of heterogeneity y_1
and y_2, observed by the decision makers, but not by the econometrician;
four draws, the •s exist as well. In the bottom right panel are graphed
the Bayes–Nash, equilibrium-bid functions corresponding to $f_V(v|y_1)$
and $f_V(v|y_2)$. Krasnokutskaya argued that if the data are from the
process on the right, but interpreted through the lens of the left, then
an econometrician might conclude that more variation in V exists than is
actually present: unobserved auction-specific heterogeneity will appear
as variation in V. She then went on to argue that this could have
important policy implications, particularly in procurement auctions. In

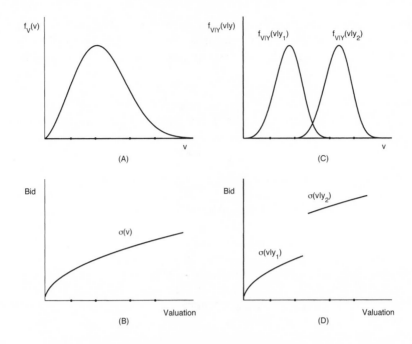

Figure 4.2
Effects of Unobserved Heterogeneity

her application, Krasnokutskaya studied procurement auctions at which the lowest bidder wins, but for consistency with our previous work, we shall reformulate the results in terms of first-price, sealed-bid auctions at which a good is for sale and at which the highest bidder wins.

To investigate the effects of unobserved heterogeneity, Krasnokutskaya used tools from deconvolution theory. When deconvoluting, a researcher, who observes the distribution of the sum of two (or more) random variables, tries to identify the marginal distributions of each of the components. Obviously, without additional structure, this is impossible to do. Typically, independence among the random variables of the sum is assumed. Also, monotonic transformations of random variables leave some deconvolution arguments unaffected. Thus, Krasnokutskaya investigated how to identify $F_Y^0(y)$ as well as $F_1^0(v_1)$ and $F_2^0(v_2)$ when only the bids of participants at auctions are observed. Her model is different from that in Li, Perrigne, and Vuong (2003) in that Y is assumed to be common knowledge. The work of Krasnokutskaya is related to that of Li et al. in that Li et al. backed out the valuations before deconvoluting; Krasnokutskaya proposed deconvoluting before backing out the valuations. We study Krasnokutskaya because her analysis admits models with asymmetric bidders, while Li et al. only dealt with the symmetric case. Krasnokutskaya's analysis is different from that of Li et al. in that she assumed multiplicative separability, while Li et al. assumed additive separability.

Under her assumptions, Krasnokutskaya showed that the Bayes–Nash, equilibrium-bid function takes a special functional form. In particular, for bidders of class 1, the Bayes–Nash, equilibrium-bid function is

$$S_i = Y \times \sigma_1 \left(V_i \right),$$

while for bidders of class 2, the Bayes–Nash, equilibrium-bid function is

$$S_i = Y \times \sigma_2 \left(V_i \right)$$

where $\sigma_1 \left(V_i \right)$ and $\sigma_2 \left(V_i \right)$ denote Bayes–Nash, equilibrium-bid functions for class 1 and 2 bidders in an auction where Y is one.

To see how this works, first denote $\sigma_1 \left(V_i \right)$ by S_i^1 for class 1 bidders and $\sigma_2 \left(V_i \right)$ by S_i^2 for class 2 bidders. To derive $\sigma_1 \left(\cdot \right)$ and $\sigma_2 \left(\cdot \right)$, consider the objective function of a class 1 bidder:

$$\left(v - \hat{s}^1 \right) F_1 \left[\sigma_1^{-1} \left(\hat{s}^1 \right) \right]^{\mathcal{N}_1 - 1} F_2 \left[\sigma_2^{-1} \left(\hat{s}^1 \right) \right]^{\mathcal{N}_2},$$

and for a class 2 bidder:

$$\left(v - \hat{s}^2 \right) F_1 \left[\sigma_1^{-1} \left(\hat{s}^2 \right) \right]^{\mathcal{N}_1} F_2 \left[\sigma_2^{-1} \left(\hat{s}^2 \right) \right]^{\mathcal{N}_2 - 1}.$$

Evaluating the necessary, first-order conditions for s^1 and s^2 yields the following system of differential equations:

$$\frac{1}{v - s^1} = \frac{\left(\mathcal{N}_1 - 1 \right) f_1 \left(v \right)}{F_1 \left(v \right) \sigma_1' \left(v \right)} + \frac{\mathcal{N}_2 f_2 \left[\sigma_2^{-1} \left(s^1 \right) \right]}{F_2 \left[\sigma_2^{-1} \left(s^1 \right) \right] \sigma_2' \left[\sigma_2^{-1} \left(s^1 \right) \right]}$$

and

$$\frac{1}{v - s^2} = \frac{\mathcal{N}_1 f_1 \left[\sigma_1^{-1} \left(s^2 \right) \right]}{F_1 \left[\sigma_1^{-1} \left(s^2 \right) \right] \sigma_1' \left[\sigma_1^{-1} \left(s^2 \right) \right]} + \frac{\left(\mathcal{N}_2 - 1 \right) f_2 \left(v \right)}{F_2 \left(v \right) \sigma_2' \left(v \right)}.$$

Using the monotonicity of bid functions, these can also be written as:

$$\frac{1}{v - s^1} = \frac{\left(\mathcal{N}_1 - 1 \right) g_1 \left(s^1 \right)}{G_1 \left(s^1 \right)} + \frac{\mathcal{N}_2 g_2 \left(s^1 \right)}{G_2 \left(s^1 \right)}$$

and

$$\frac{1}{v - s^2} = \frac{\mathcal{N}_1 g_1 \left(s^2 \right)}{G_1 \left(s^2 \right)} + \frac{\left(\mathcal{N}_2 - 1 \right) g_2 \left(s^2 \right)}{G_2 \left(s^2 \right)}$$

where $g_i(\cdot)$ and $G_i(\cdot)$ denote the probability density and cumulative distribution functions of S_i, respectively. Therefore, the valuations V for bidders of classes 1 and 2 can be recovered from S^1, S^2, and their joint distribution functions. In particular,

$$v^1 = s^1 + \frac{G_1^0\left(s^1\right) G_2^0\left(s^1\right)}{\left(\mathcal{N}_1 - 1\right) g_1^0\left(s^1\right) G_2^0\left(s^1\right) + \mathcal{N}_2 g_2^0\left(s^1\right) G_1^0\left(s^1\right)}$$

and

$$v^2 = s^2 + \frac{G_2^0\left(s^2\right) G_1^0\left(s^2\right)}{\left(\mathcal{N}_2 - 1\right) g_2^0\left(s^2\right) G_1^0\left(s^2\right) + \mathcal{N}_1 g_1^0\left(s^2\right) G_2^0\left(s^2\right)}.$$

In other words, the cumulative distributions of the valuations $F_1^0(\cdot)$ and $F_2^0(\cdot)$ are completely determined by the cumulative distributions of $G_1^0(\cdot)$ and $G_2^0(\cdot)$.

However, the presence of unobserved heterogeneity Y means that $G_1^0(\cdot)$ and $G_2^0(\cdot)$ are, in reality, unobservable. Instead, only the joint distribution of $(Y \times S^1)$ and $(Y \times S^2)$ is observable. Using deconvolution techniques based on a result due to Prakasa Rao (1992), Krasnokutskaya has shown that $F_Y^0(\cdot)$, $G_1^0(\cdot)$, and $G_2^0(\cdot)$ can all be identified from the joint distribution of $(Y \times S^1)$ and $(Y \times S^2)$.

Deconvolution methods work with the sum of random variables. Denote the joint characteristic function of $(\log Y + \log S^1)$ and $(\log Y + \log S^2)$ by $\mathcal{C}_{12}(\cdot, \cdot)$ where

$$\mathcal{C}_{12}\left(\tau_1, \tau_2\right) = \mathcal{E}\left\{\exp\left[\mathbf{i}\tau_1\left(\log Y + \log S^1\right) + \mathbf{i}\tau_2\left(\log Y + \log S^2\right)\right]\right\}$$

where $\mathbf{i}$ denotes the imaginary number $\sqrt{-1}$. The first step of the analysis is to recover the characteristic functions of $\log Y$, $\log S^1$, and $\log S^2$ from the knowledge of $\mathcal{C}_{12}(\tau_1, \tau_2)$. To do this, Krasnokutskaya normalized $\mathcal{E}(\log S^1)$ to be zero. Thus,

$$\mathcal{C}_1\left(0, \tau_2\right) = \mathcal{E}\left\{\left(\mathbf{i}\log Y + \mathbf{i}\log S^1\right) \exp\left[\mathbf{i}\tau_2\left(\log Y + \log S^2\right)\right]\right\}$$

$$= \mathcal{E}\left[\mathbf{i}\log Y \exp\left(\mathbf{i}\tau_2 \log Y\right)\right] \times \mathcal{E}\left[\exp\left(\mathbf{i}\tau_2 \log S^2\right)\right]$$

where the second equality follows from both the independence and the normalization assumptions. Note too that

$$\mathcal{C}\left(0, \tau_2\right) = \mathcal{E}\left[\exp\left(\mathbf{i}\tau_2 \log Y\right)\right] \times \mathcal{E}\left[\exp\left(\mathbf{i}\tau_2 \log S^2\right)\right].$$

Therefore,

$$\frac{\mathcal{C}_1\left(0, \tau_2\right)}{\mathcal{C}\left(0, \tau_2\right)} = \frac{\mathcal{E}\left[\mathbf{i}\log Y \exp\left(\mathbf{i}\tau_2 \log Y\right)\right]}{\mathcal{E}\left[\exp\left(\mathbf{i}\tau_2 \log Y\right)\right]}.$$

This can be used to recover the characteristic function of Y. Note that

$$\mathcal{C}_{\log Y}(\tau) = \mathcal{E}\left[\exp\left(\mathbf{i}\tau\log Y\right)\right]$$

and

$$\frac{d\log\mathcal{C}_{\log Y}(\tau)}{d\tau} = \frac{\mathcal{E}\left[\mathbf{i}\log Y\exp\left(\mathbf{i}\tau\log Y\right)\right]}{\mathcal{E}\left[\exp\left(\mathbf{i}\tau\log Y\right)\right]}.$$

Now, $\mathcal{C}_{\log Y}(\tau)$ can be recovered by integrating this relation together with the following boundary condition:

$$\log\mathcal{C}_{\log Y}(0) = 0$$

through the formula

$$\mathcal{C}_{\log Y}(\tau) = \exp\left[\int_0^\tau \frac{\mathcal{C}_1(0,\tau_2)w}{\mathcal{C}(0,\tau_2)}\,d\tau_2\right].$$

Once $\mathcal{C}_{\log Y}(\tau)$ is known,

$$\mathcal{C}(\tau,0) = \mathcal{C}_{\log Y}(\tau)\times\mathcal{C}_{\log S^1}(\tau)$$

and

$$\mathcal{C}(0,\tau) = \mathcal{C}_{\log Y}(\tau)\times\mathcal{C}_{\log S^2}(\tau),$$

it is straightforward to recover $\mathcal{C}_{\log S^1}(\tau)$ and $\mathcal{C}_{\log S^2}(\tau)$.

Having derived the characteristic functions of $\log Y$, $\log S^1$ and $\log S^2$, the inverse formula can be used to back out the probability density functions of $\log Y$, $\log S^1$, and $\log S^2$. By a change of variables, these then will yield the probability density functions of Y, S^1, and S^2. Finally, the probability density functions of S^1 and S^2 can be used to back out $F_1(\cdot)$ and $F_2(\cdot)$.

This identification result used only one pair of bids, one from a class 1 bidder and one from a class 2 bidder. If more than two bids are available, then additional identifying power can be added. Krasnokutskaya considered the case where the joint distribution of $(Y\times S^1)$, $(Y\times\bar{S})$, and $(Y\times S^2)$ is observable, where $\bar{S}$ is an independent copy of either S^1 or S^2. $(Y\times\bar{S})$ is a bid submitted by another bidder other than the two that submitted $(Y\times S^1)$ and $(Y\times S^2)$. This made sense in Krasnokutskaya's application as it represented the best estimate of the state's engineer, which was reported in her data. At most auctions, however, this will probably not be reported.

Now, let $\mathcal{C}_{12}(\tau_1,\tau_2)$ denote the joint characteristic function of

$$\log\left(\frac{YS^1}{Y\bar{S}}\right)$$

and

$$\log\left(\frac{YS^2}{Y\bar{S}}\right)$$

where the Y cancels out, so

$$C_{12}(\tau_1,\tau_2) = \mathcal{E}\left[\exp\left(\mathbf{i}\tau_1\log\frac{S^1}{\bar{S}} + \mathbf{i}\tau_2\log\frac{S^2}{\bar{S}}\right)\right].$$

Note now that

$$C_1(0,u_2) = \mathcal{E}\left[\mathbf{i}\log\frac{S^1}{\bar{S}}\exp\left(\mathbf{i}\tau_2\log\frac{S^2}{\bar{S}}\right)\right],$$

and

$$\frac{C_1(0,\tau_2)}{C(0,\tau_2)} = \frac{\mathcal{E}\left\{\mathbf{i}\left(-\log\bar{S}\right)\exp\left[\mathbf{i}\tau_2\left(-\log\bar{S}\right)\right]\right\}}{\mathcal{E}\left\{\exp\left[\mathbf{i}\tau_2\left(-\log\bar{S}\right)\right]\right\}}.$$

Since

$$\frac{d\log C_{-\log\bar{S}}(\tau)}{d\tau} = \frac{\mathcal{E}\left\{\mathbf{i}\left(-\log\bar{S}\right)\exp\left[\mathbf{i}\tau\left(-\log\bar{S}\right)\right]\right\}}{\mathcal{E}\left\{\exp\left[\mathbf{i}\tau\left(-\log\bar{S}\right)\right]\right\}}$$

$C_{-\log\bar{S}}(\tau)$ can be recovered by

$$C_{-\log\bar{S}}(\tau) = \exp\left[\int_0^u \frac{C_1(0,\tau_2)}{C(0,\tau_2)}\,d\tau_2\right].$$

Subsequently,

$$C_{\log S^1}(\tau) = \frac{C(\tau,0)}{C_{-\log\bar{S}}(\tau)}$$

and

$$C_{\log S^2}(\tau) = \frac{C(0,\tau)}{C_{-\log\bar{S}}(\tau)}.$$

$C_{\log S^1}(\tau)$ and $C_{\log S^2}(\tau)$ should be close to $C_{\log S^1}(\tau)$ and $C_{\log S^2}(\tau)$ if the model is correctly specified. This provides a testable implication of her model.

Krasnokutskaya also showed that her identification results can be extended to models with both additive and multiplicative unobserved heterogeneities; e.g., where a valuation is given by $(Y_1 + Y_2 V^j)$, for $j = 1,2$, with both Y_1 and Y_2 being common knowledge among the bidders. Multistep deconvolution is used in this case.

The estimation procedure proposed by Krasnokutskaya follows the identification arguments closely and is performed in multiple steps. In the first step, the joint characteristic function of $\log(YS^1)$ and $\log(YS^2)$ is estimated from their empirical analogues:

$$\hat{\mathcal{C}}(\tau_1, \tau_2) =$$

$$\frac{1}{T\mathcal{N}_1\mathcal{N}_2} \sum_{t=1}^{T} \sum_{i_1=1}^{\mathcal{N}_1} \sum_{i_2=\mathcal{N}_1+1}^{\mathcal{N}} \exp\left[\mathbf{i}\tau_1 \log\left(Y_{i_1,t}S_{i_1,t}^1\right) + \mathbf{i}\tau_2 \log\left(Y_{i_2,t}S_{i_2,t}^2\right)\right].$$

In the second step, the characteristic functions of the logarithm of the individual components and the common component are estimated by

$$\hat{\mathcal{C}}_{\log Y}(\tau) = \exp\left[\int_0^\tau \frac{\hat{\mathcal{C}}_1(0, \tau_2)}{\hat{\mathcal{C}}(0, \tau_2)}\, d\tau_2\right]$$

and

$$\hat{\mathcal{C}}_{\log S^1}(\tau) = \frac{\hat{\mathcal{C}}(\tau, 0)}{\hat{\mathcal{C}}_{\log Y}(\tau, 0)}$$

and

$$\hat{\mathcal{C}}_{\log S^2}(\tau) = \frac{\hat{\mathcal{C}}(0, \tau)}{\hat{\mathcal{C}}_{\log Y}(0, \tau)}.$$

In the third step, the inversion formula is used to back out estimates of the probability density functions from the estimated characteristic functions:

$$\hat{f}_{\log Y}(v) = \frac{1}{2\pi} \int_{-M}^{M} \exp\left(-\mathbf{i}\tau v\right) \hat{\mathcal{C}}_{\log Y}(\tau)\, d\tau$$

and, for $j = 1, 2$,

$$\hat{f}_{\log S^j}(v) = \frac{1}{2\pi} \int_{-M}^{M} \exp\left(-\mathbf{i}\tau v\right) \hat{\mathcal{C}}_{\log S^j}(\tau)\, d\tau.$$

In the above inversion formulae, M is a large constant that is used to trim off the tails of the estimated empirical characteristic function. This trimming device is neccessary because the empirical characteristic function is not integrable over the entire real line. The constant M is related to the bandwidth parameters used in kernel-smoothing methods. In principle, the tails of the characteristic functions are related to the smoothness of the underlying density, and vice versa.

In the fourth step, the probability density functions of Y as well as S^1 and S^2 are obtained through a change of variable formula:

$$\hat{f}_Y(y) = \frac{1}{y} \hat{f}_{\log Y}(\log y)$$

and

$$\hat{g}_j\left(s\right) = \frac{1}{s}\hat{f}_{\log S^j}\left(\log s\right) \quad j = 1, 2.$$

In the fifth step, the implied probability density functions $\hat{f}_1\left(\cdot\right)$ and $\hat{f}_2\left(\cdot\right)$ are recovered from $\hat{g}_1\left(\cdot\right)$ and $\hat{g}_2\left(\cdot\right)$. Krasnokutskaya has suggested doing this by simulating from the estimated bid distribution, evaluating the corresponding pseudo-value, and then estimating the distribution of the resulting pseudo-values. This gives $\hat{f}_1\left(\cdot\right)$ and $\hat{f}_2\left(\cdot\right)$.

Finally, Krasnokutskaya normalized the mean to be one and scaled $\hat{f}_Y\left(y\right)$ correspondingly. The probability density function of the total value $(Y \times V^j)$, for $j = 1, 2$, can then be estimated as

$$\hat{f}_{Y \times V^j}\left(v\right) = \int \hat{f}_j\left(\frac{v}{y}\right)\hat{f}_Y\left(y\right)\,dy.$$

4.7 Policy Experiment

In this section, we present a policy experiment undertaken by Brendstrup and Paarsch (forthcoming) that involved comparing the performance of alternative auction formats when bidders are asymmetric. Maskin and Riley (2000) have argued that in the presence of asymmetries the REP no longer holds, so the expected revenues under Dutch and first-price, sealed-bid auctions could be higher or lower than under English auctions. Also, in the presence of asymmetries, English auctions will yield efficient allocations, while Dutch and first-price, sealed-bid auctions can yield inefficient ones. However, very little is known concerning the economic extent and importance of these inefficiencies in practice.

4.7.1 Some Institutional Background

Brendstrup and Paarsch investigated the Grenaa Fiskeauktion, which is an English auction held each weekday morning at 5:00 a.m. in Grenå, Denmark. The English-auction format is frequently used to sell fish because it is fast and thus well-suited to selling perishable products. Another commonly used format is the Dutch auction. In fact, in Denmark the bulk of fish is sold at Dutch auctions. Brendstrup and Paarsch wondered why all the other Danish fish auctions used the Dutch format, but the one in Grenå used the English format. To answer this question, they applied the empirical techniques discussed in chapter 3 to provide estimates of the primitives (i.e., the f_js) necessary to undertake a comparative institutional analysis where expected revenues under

Dutch auctions are compared with those under English auctions when a single unit of the good is supplied.

By international standards, the Grenaa Fiskeauktion is very small. The sellers are the local fishermen who ply the Kattegat and beyond. They have banded together to create the auction house. The bidders are mostly resale trade firms. One feature of this auction is that there are two major bidders and several other much smaller bidders. Therefore, it is natural to analyze the behavior of these two classes of bidders as if their valuations are draws from different distributions.

The bidders at the Grenaa Fiskeauktion can be considered agents of retail sellers who have placed orders at pre-specified prices. Brendstrup and Paarsch imagined that these retail sellers lived in spatially separated markets where, because of location, some market power existed. In these markets, the retail sellers had individual-specific marginal revenue curves. Brendstrup and Paarsch imagined that these marginal-revenue curves were the source of the variation in valuations for the bidders. In short, Brendstrup and Paarsch believed that the IPVP is a reasonable model of the market for fish in and around Grenå.

The fish supplied at the auction are graded into four main quality categories: E, A, B, and C in descending order where E is the best and C is the worst, unfit for human consumption. These *grades* are a function of fish size and freshness. Each grade has five subcategories, 1 to 5. Subsequently, the fish are packed into thirty-five kilogram units which are then sold at oral, ascending-price auctions.

While other species are sold, often irregularly, the three main species on sale in Grenå are cod (*Gadus morhua*), Greenland halibut (*Reinhardtius hippoglossoides*), and plaice (*Pleuronectes platessa*). This last species is called rødspætte in Denmark and sometimes referred to as right-eyed flounder in North America because both of its eyes are on the right-hand side of its head.

For each species and grade of fish, a reserve price exists; this is set by the Danish government in accordance with regulations determined by the European Union. The local auction is allowed to deviate from this reserve price by up to ten percent.

The particular product they chose to study is plaice, grade A3, because it was sold more or less steadily throughout the three-year period they chose to examine: 2 January 2000 to 31 December 2002.

After consulting with the auctioneer in Grenå and after examining the raw data, Brendstrup and Paarsch found that a total of seven potential bidders, two major and five minor, existed. Each of these bidders attended virtually every auction so, despite the presence of a reserve price, which typically induces endogenous participation, they believed that issues of endogenous participation could be safely ignored

Some Institutional Background

Bidder	Wins
1	110
2	94
3	35
4	14
5	27
6	11
7	10

Table 4.1
Observed Number of Wins by Bidder Identity

in this case.

In the archives at the Grenaa Fiskeauktion, for each auction indexed by t, information concerning the following variables was available:

1) winning bid y_t;
2) number of potential bidders n_t, which is seven;
3) identity of the winner.

In total, Brendstrup and Paarsch were able to gather data concerning 301 single-object auctions of plaice, grade A3.

4.7.2 Empirical Results

One of the implications of the symmetric IPVP is that, on average, bidders should win the same proportion of auctions over time. To examine this implication, Brendstrup and Paarsch calculated the number of times each bidder won. These are listed in table 4.1. Since there were 301 auctions, the expected number of times that a particular bidder would be expected to win is $(301/7)$ or 43 times. Now, using the observed number of wins and the expected number of wins by bidder i, Brendstrup and Paarsch calculated Fisher's χ^2 goodness-of-fit statistic, which is distributed $\chi^2(6)$ under the null hypothesis of the symmetric IPVP. Their calculated χ^2 statistic was 241.02, which has a p-value less than 0.0001, suggesting that their data were not from a process within the symmetric IPVP.

From table 4.1, it would appear that two classes of bidders exist: major bidders, who have identities 1 and 2, and minor bidders, who have identities 3 through 7.[8] Brendstrup and Paarsch adopted the convention

---

[8] The reader might feel that there are three classes of bidders: majors—1 and 2; middles—3 and 5; and minors—4, 6, and 7. Brendstrup and Paarsch undertook their analysis with these three classes of bidders as well. Their results were qualitatively similar.

165

that $\mathbf{type}(i)$ equal 1 denotes a minor bidder, while $\mathbf{type}(i)$ equal 2 denotes a major bidder. Thus, $G_{(2:7)}(y, 1)$ denotes the distribution of the winning bid at last-unit auctions won by minor bidders, while $G_{(2:7)}(y, 2)$ denotes the distribution of the winning bid at last-unit auctions won by major bidders.

Using the data described above and a fourth-order Laguerre polynomial for the SNP estimator, Brendstrup and Paarsch implemented the SNP estimator of chapter 3. To wit, they calculated the following:

$$\{\hat{f}_{1T}, \hat{f}_{2T}\} = \underset{f_j \in \mathcal{F}_{jT}}{\operatorname{argmax}} \; \frac{1}{T} \sum_{t=1}^{T} \log g_{(2:7)}(y_t, i_t | \boldsymbol{F})$$

where

$$\mathcal{F}_{jT} = \left\{ f_{jT} \in \mathcal{F}_j : f_{jT}(y|\boldsymbol{\alpha}_j) = \left[\sum_{k=0}^{4} \alpha_{jk} L_k(y) \right]^2 \exp(-y), \boldsymbol{\alpha}_j \in \boldsymbol{\Theta}_{jT} \right\},$$

and where

$$\boldsymbol{\Theta}_{jT} = \left\{ \boldsymbol{\alpha}_j = (\alpha_{j0}, \dots, \alpha_{j4}) : \int_0^\infty f_{jT}(y|\boldsymbol{\alpha}_j) \; dy = 1 \right\}.$$

In figure 4.3, we present graphs of the two estimated cumulative distribution functions estimated by Brendstrup and Paarsch. The main thing to note from these graphs is that these estimated cumulative distribution functions are very different.

4.7.3 Comparing Institutions

Some interesting policy experiments are possible given the empirical results of Brendstrup and Paarsch. Based on the estimates derived above, Brendstrup and Paarsch estimated the average difference in revenues as well as the relative incidence and economic importance of inefficiencies.

In section 6 of this chapter, we solved the decision problem faced by a representative bidder of each class at a single-object Dutch auction when two classes of bidders exist, n_1 (five in this case) bidders whose valuations are from $F_1(v)$ and n_2 (two in this case) bidders whose valuations are from $F_2(v)$, where $(n_1 + n_2)$ equals n (seven in this case). Expected profit $\mathcal{E}(\pi_j)$ to a bidder of class j who has valuation v and adopts strategy s_j is

$$\mathcal{E}(\pi_j) = (v - s_j) \Pr(\text{win}|s_j) \quad j = 1, 2.$$

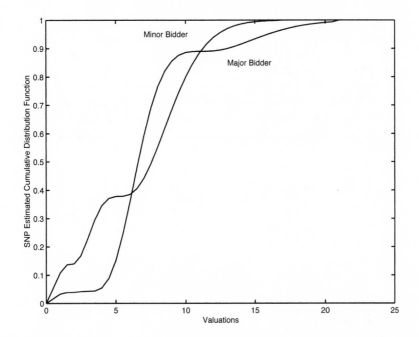

Figure 4.3
Laguerre-Polynomial Estimates of $F_j(v)$s

The necessary first-order conditions for expected-profit maximization are:

$$0 = - F_1[\sigma_1^{-1}(s_1)]^{n_1-1} F_2[\sigma_2^{-1}(s_1)]^{n_2} +$$

$$(v - s_1)\left\{ \frac{(n_1-1)F_1[\sigma_1^{-1}(s_1)]^{n_1-2} f_1[\sigma_1^{-1}(s_1)] F_2[\sigma_2^{-1}(s_1)]^{n_2}}{\sigma_1'} + \right.$$

$$\left. \frac{F_1[\sigma_1^{-1}(s_1)]^{n_1-1} n_2 F_2[\sigma_2^{-1}(s_1)]^{n_2-1} f_2[\sigma_2^{-1}(s_1)]}{\sigma_2'} \right\}$$

and

$$0 = - F_1[\sigma_1^{-1}(s_2)]^{n_1} F_2[\sigma_2^{-1}(s_2)]^{n_2-1} +$$

$$(v - s_2)\left\{ \frac{n_1 F_1[\sigma_1^{-1}(s_2)]^{n_1-1} f_1[\sigma_1^{-1}(s_2)] F_2[\sigma_2^{-1}(s_2)]^{n_2-1}}{\sigma_1'} + \right.$$

$$\left. \frac{F_1[\sigma_1^{-1}(s_2)]^{n_1} (n_2-1) F_2[\sigma_2^{-1}(s_2)]^{n_2-2} f_2[\sigma_2^{-1}(s_2)]}{\sigma_2'} \right\}.$$

A number of different strategies exists to solve systems of differential equations. However, because the Lipschitz conditions are not satisfied for the above system of differential equations, it cannot be solved analytically. Brendstrup and Paarsch followed Bajari (2001), specifically his third method which involves approximating the inverse-bid functions using a flexible functional form, such as high-order polynomials, and then finding a set of coefficients that approximately satisfy the differential equations above. Bajari assumed that for bidder i the inverse-bid function takes the form

$$\sigma_i^{-1}(s; \bar{s}, \boldsymbol{\alpha}) = \bar{s} + \sum_{k=0}^{K} \alpha_{i,k}(s - \bar{s})^k.$$

In equilibrium, bidder i's first-order condition for profit maximization can be written as

$$1 + \sum_{j \neq i} \frac{f_j\left[\sigma_j^{-1}(s)\right]\left[s - \sigma_i^{-1}(s)\right]}{F_j\left[\sigma_j^{-1}(s)\right]\left[s - \sigma_j^{-1}(s)\right]} \frac{d\sigma_j^{-1}(s)}{ds} = 0.$$

Bajari introduced

$$
\begin{aligned}
G_i(s; \bar{s}, \boldsymbol{\alpha}) &= 1 + \sum_{j \neq i} \frac{f_j\left[\sigma_j^{-1}(s; \bar{s}, \boldsymbol{\alpha})\right]\left[s - \sigma_i^{-1}(s; \bar{s}, \boldsymbol{\alpha})\right]}{F_j\left[\sigma_j^{-1}(s; \bar{s}, \boldsymbol{\alpha})\right]\left[s - \sigma_j^{-1}(s; \bar{s}, \boldsymbol{\alpha})\right]} \frac{d\sigma_j^{-1}(s; \bar{s}, \boldsymbol{\alpha})}{ds} \\
&= 0.
\end{aligned}
$$

He then evaluated the first-order condition on a grid of points, uniformly between $[\underline{v}, \bar{s}]$. Let L denote the number of points and define the ℓth point by

$$s_\ell = \bar{s} - \frac{\ell(\bar{s} - \underline{v})}{L}.$$

Bajari then introduced the nonlinear, sum-of-squared residual criterion function

$$\sum_{i=1}^{\mathcal{N}} \sum_{\ell=1}^{L} \left[G_i(s_\ell; \bar{s}, \boldsymbol{\alpha})\right]^2 + \sum_{i=1}^{\mathcal{N}} \left[\bar{s} - \sigma_i^{-1}(\bar{s}; \bar{s}, \boldsymbol{\alpha})\right]^2 + \sum_{i=1}^{\mathcal{N}} \left[\underline{v} - \sigma_i^{-1}(\underline{v}; \bar{s}, \boldsymbol{\alpha})\right]^2.$$

When this criterion function is zero, the differential equations as well as the boundary conditions are all met. Standard application of a nonlinear, least-squares optimization algorithm can be used to find $\boldsymbol{\alpha}$ as well as $\bar{s}$. Note that this objective function is highly nonlinear, having many local optima. When the starting values are close to the final estimates, this algorithm behaves well numerically. In other cases, finding suitable estimates is often trying.

To be consistent with Bajari's framework, Brendstrup and Paarsch restricted themselves to a compact interval of the real line $[6.75, 40.00]$ where virtually all of the mass is. On this interval, they approximated the true unknown inverse-bid function by a fourth-order polynomial. They chose the coefficients of this polynomial using the method of non-linear least squares.

In figure 4.4, we present the Brendstrup-Paarsch estimates of the bid functions for major and minor bidders. Note that the Bayes–Nash equilibrium bid function for minor bidders is everywhere above that for major bidders, except at the endpoints where they are constrained by theory to be the same.

To estimate the winner under either Dutch or English auctions, Brendstrup and Paarsch used simulation methods. In particular, they generated a sample of uniform $[0, 1]$ random numbers, one for each bidder, in each of $1,000$ simulation auctions; i.e., $\{U_{1k}, U_{2k}, \ldots, U_{7k}\}_{k=1}^{1000}$. For bidder i, they used the estimated inverse cumulative distribution function $\hat{F}_{\texttt{type}(i)}^{-1}(u_{ik})$ to generate an estimated valuation $\hat{v}_{ik}$. Using these estimated valuations $(\hat{v}_{1k}, \hat{v}_{2k}, \ldots, \hat{v}_{7k})$ for each simulation k, in conjunction with the estimated bid functions above, they determined the estimated winning bid at the Dutch auction $\hat{w}_k$, the identity of the winner at the Dutch auction, the winning bid at the English auction $\hat{y}_k$, the identity of the bidder with the highest valuation, and an estimate of the highest valuation

$$\hat{v}_{\mathrm{max},k} = \max(\hat{v}_{1k}, \hat{v}_{2k}, \ldots, \hat{v}_{7k}).$$

They then averaged over simulations to get the average winning bid under Dutch and English auctions, $\bar{w}$ and $\bar{y}$ respectively, as well as an estimate of inefficiency incidence—the proportion of simulations resulting in an inefficient allocation—and an estimate of the value of this inefficiency using $(\hat{v}_{\mathrm{max}} - \hat{y})$ when a misallocation obtained. In none of their experiments did an inefficient allocation obtain. For English auctions, the average winning bid was 14.94 DKK with a standard deviation of 0.39, a minimum of 10.92, and a maximum of 15.98. For Dutch auctions, the average winning bid was 12.39 DKK with a standard deviation of 0.16, a minimum of 8.92, and a maximum of 12.42. Thus, it appears that the English auction, at which an efficient allocation always obtains, also garnered more revenue than the Dutch auction. The administrators of the Grenå auction appear to have made a good choice of selling mechanism.

4.7.4 Another Way to Solve Asymmetric Auctions

An alternative way to solve this system of differential equations is a

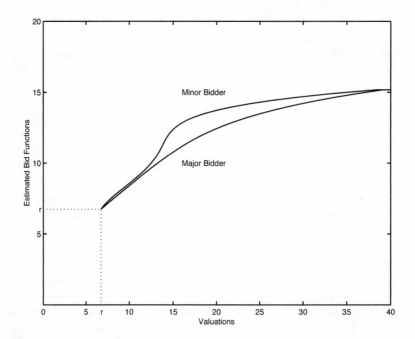

Figure 4.4
Estimated Bid Functions for Dutch Auctions

valuation-based version of Bajari's (2001) first method. In this approach, the standard assumptions concerning the bidder-specific valuation primitives apply; i.e., they are all supported on the same compact interval and are bounded away from zero on that interval. Also, as before,

$$\sigma_j^{-1}(\underline{v}) = \underline{v}$$

and

$$\sigma_j^{-1}(\bar{s}) = \bar{v}.$$

While the first condition, the left-boundary condition, is straightforward, the second, the right-boundary condition, is worthy of further explanation. This condition means that there exists some maximum equilibrium bid which bidders of all types will submit when they draw the highest possible valuation $\bar{v}$. However, this common maximum bid $\bar{s}$ is unknown to the analyst and must be determined as part of the solution process. In the vocabulary of a mathematician, this feature makes this system of differential equations a *free-boundary value problem*.

Implementing Bajari's first method involves a sequence of carefully-chosen guesses (using bisection) for $\bar{s}$ that result in a solution characterized by $[\sigma_j^{-1}(\underline{v}) - \underline{v}]$ being less than some user-specified stopping tolerance (perhaps on the order of 10^{-3}) for all bidders j. The bisection process is governed by the convergence properties of the system of differential equations that results from the current guess of $\bar{s}$. In particular, if the guess for $\bar{s}$ is too low (below the true $\bar{s}$), then the system of differential equations will be well-behaved (i.e., finite and monotone), but not necessarily consistent with the user-specific stopping tolerance for the left-boundary condition. On the other hand, if the guess for $\bar{s}$ is too high (above the true $\bar{s}$), then the system of differential equations will be ill-behaved (i.e., not finite). These two rules, taken together, allow the user to determine how to produce a new, better guess for $\bar{s}$. Following this process until the stopping tolerance obtains delivers a good approximation to $\bar{s}$ and, thus, good approximations to the inverse-bid functions as well.

From a programming perspective, it is important to note that in the programming environment MATLAB, the differential equation solvers (e.g., `ode23.m` or `ode45.m`) are designed for initial-value problems. Here, we have a free-boundary, initial-value problem that is essentially reversed; i.e., the "initial value" we are working with is actually a terminal condition. While coding, the user must find a way to adapt MATLAB to this reality. Note that this complication is absent in the procurement version originally proposed in Bajari (2001).

4.8 Endogenous Bidding Participation

In previous sections of this chapter, we have assumed that the number of bidders who intend to submit a bid at auction equals the number of potential bidders. In fact, we have used $\mathcal{N}_t$ to denote the number of potential bidders at auction t. However, at many first-price, sealed-bid auctions the number of *active* bidders is unobserved at the time of bidding, especially in the presence of entry costs; viz., a fixed cost to participating at the auction that is foregone if the auction is lost. Thus, in the presence of a binding reserve price r, only bidders whose valuations, net of the fixed entry cost, exceed r will tender a bid. Therefore, the number of actual bidders participating at auction is a random variable that is smaller than the number of active bidders. Fixed entry costs introduce additional complications because they complicate the process of endogenous bidder participation. When fixed entry costs are positive, some potential bidders might decide not to participate, regardless of the reserve price, because the expected profit from participating is less than the fixed entry cost. In such cases, the number of potential bidders can be substantially different from the number of active bidders.

Li (2005) developed an econometric model of a first-price, sealed-bid auction taking into account the distinction between the number of potential bidders and the number of active bidders by explicitly modeling participation and bidding in the presence of fixed entry costs and reserve prices. In his model, each auction t has $\mathcal{N}_t$ potential bidders, which is observed by the econometrician. Participation in the auction is costly. Each potential bidder must first decide whether to incur a positive entry cost and thus participate in the auction. If a potential bidder decides not to incur the entry cost, then he does not observe the object for sale and is assumed not to get a draw from the valuation distribution. On the other hand, if a potential bidder decides to incur the fixed entry cost and participate in the auction, then he gets an independent and identically distributed valuation draw from $F_V^0(v)$. If that valuation draw exceeds the reserve price, then he will submit a bid that is above the reserve price.

An equilibrium in this model involves potential bidders randomizing between incurring and not incurring the fixed entry cost. The probability that a potential bidder chooses to incur the entry cost q_t^* is determined by the expected profit from participating at the auction equaling the entry cost. Therefore, the number of active bidders, which we denote N_t, follows a binomial distribution with mean equal to $q_t^* \mathcal{N}_t$ and variance equal to $q_t^* (1 - q_t^*) \mathcal{N}_t$. Conditional on the realization of N_t, the (observed) number of actual bidders M_t follows another binomial distribution with mean equal to $\left[1 - F_V^0(r_t)\right] N_t$ and variance equal to $F_V^0(r_t) \left[1 - F_V^0(r_t)\right] N_t$.

Li assumed that the number of potential bidders $\mathcal{N}_t$ and the reserve price r_t in each auction are known. He noted that, since q_t^* is endogenously determined by a zero profit condition, it is, in principle, a function of the primitive underlying structure, including $\mathcal{N}_t$, r_t, and $F_V(\cdot|z_t, \boldsymbol{\theta})$. However, since estimating the distribution of the private values is of primary interest, Li proposed adopting a flexible, discrete-choice-probability functional-form for q_t^*; e.g., the logistic or normal distribution. He denoted this parametric function by q_t^* equal $q^*(z_t, r_t, \boldsymbol{\gamma})$, and the resulting probability mass function for N_t by

$$f_N(N_t | z_t, r_t, \boldsymbol{\gamma}) = \binom{\mathcal{N}_t}{N_t} q^*(z_t, r_t, \boldsymbol{\gamma})^{N_t} \left[1 - q^*(z_t, r_t, \boldsymbol{\gamma})\right]^{\mathcal{N}_t - N_t}.$$

Li proceeded by first deriving the moments of the observable bids, conditional on the active number of bidders N_t. He then averaged these conditional moment conditions over the latent distribution of N_t given the number of actual bidders M_t in order to derive observable conditional moment conditions that can be confronted by the data.

Given N_t, r_t, z_t, and the parameter $\boldsymbol{\theta}$, the mean of the actual observable bids takes the following form:

$$\mathcal{E}(S_{it} | S_{it} \geq r_t, N_t, z_t, \boldsymbol{\theta}) = \mu(N_t, z_t, r_t, \boldsymbol{\theta})$$

where, when N_t is greater than two,

$$\mu\left(N_t, \boldsymbol{z}_t, r_t, \boldsymbol{\theta}\right) = \frac{(N_t - 1)}{(N_t - 2)} \mathcal{E}\left(V_{it} | V_{it} \geq r_t, \boldsymbol{z}_t, \boldsymbol{\theta}\right) +$$

$$\frac{r_t}{(N_t - 2)} \frac{F_V\left(r_t | \boldsymbol{z}_t, \boldsymbol{\theta}\right)}{[1 - F_V\left(r_t | \boldsymbol{z}_t, \boldsymbol{\theta}\right)]} -$$

$$\frac{\bar{s}\left(N_t, \boldsymbol{z}_t, r_t, \boldsymbol{\theta}\right)}{(N_t - 2)} \frac{1}{F_V\left(r_t | \boldsymbol{z}_t, \boldsymbol{\theta}\right)}$$

where $\bar{s}\left(N_t, \boldsymbol{z}_t, r_t, \boldsymbol{\theta}\right)$ is the upper support of the distribution of the bids S_t as a function of N_t, $\boldsymbol{z}_t$, r_t, and the parameters $\boldsymbol{\theta}$.

In addition, for N_t equal one and N_t equal two,

$$\mu\left(1, \boldsymbol{z}_t, r_t, \boldsymbol{\theta}\right) = r_t,$$

and

$$\mu\left(2, \boldsymbol{z}_t, r_t, \boldsymbol{\theta}\right) = -\frac{r_t F_V\left(r_t | \boldsymbol{z}_t, \boldsymbol{\theta}\right)}{[1 - F_V\left(r_t | \boldsymbol{z}_t, \boldsymbol{\theta}\right)]} \log F_V\left(r_t | \boldsymbol{z}_t, \boldsymbol{\theta}\right)$$
$$- \mathcal{E}\left[V_{it} \log F_V\left(r_t | \boldsymbol{z}_t, \boldsymbol{\theta}\right) | V_{it} > r_t, \boldsymbol{z}_t, \boldsymbol{\theta}\right].$$

However, at most auctions, the number of active bidders N_t is typically unobserved. Only M_t, the number of actual bidders who bid above the reserve price, is available. Therefore, Li proceeded to derive the conditional mean of observed bids, given the actual number of bidders M_t, by averaging over the conditional distribution of N_t given M_t:

$$\mathcal{E}\left(S_{it} | S_{it} \geq r_t, M_t, \boldsymbol{z}_t, \boldsymbol{\theta}\right) = \sum_{N_t = M_t}^{\mathcal{N}_t} \mu\left(N_t, \boldsymbol{z}_t, r_t, \boldsymbol{\theta}\right) \Pr\left(N_t | M_t, \boldsymbol{z}_t, \boldsymbol{\theta}, \boldsymbol{\gamma}\right)$$

where the conditional distribution of the number of active bidders N_t given the number of actual bidders M_t is given by

$$\Pr\left(N_t | M_t, \boldsymbol{z}_t, \boldsymbol{\theta}, \boldsymbol{\gamma}\right) =$$

$$\sum_{N_t = M_t}^{\mathcal{N}_t} \binom{\mathcal{N}_t - M_t}{N_t - M_t} \left[\frac{F_V\left(r_t | \boldsymbol{z}_t, \boldsymbol{\theta}\right) q_t^*}{F_V\left(r_t | \boldsymbol{z}_t, \boldsymbol{\theta}\right) q_t^* + 1 - q_t^*}\right]^{N_t - M_t}$$

$$\left[\frac{1 - q_t^*}{F_V\left(r_t | \boldsymbol{z}_t, \boldsymbol{\theta}\right) q_t^* + 1 - q_t^*}\right]^{\mathcal{N}_t - N_t}.$$

While $\mathcal{E}\left(S_{it} | S_{it} \geq r_t, M_t, \boldsymbol{z}_t, \boldsymbol{\theta}\right)$ makes use of the first moment of S_{it} to generate an unconditional moment condition, Li also made use of both other conditional moment restrictions based on the number of actual observed bids. He noted first that

$$\mathcal{E}\left(M_t|N_t, \boldsymbol{z}_t, r_t, \boldsymbol{\theta}\right) \equiv \mu^{\{1\}}\left(N_t, \boldsymbol{z}_t, r_t, \boldsymbol{\theta}\right)$$
$$= N_t \left[1 - F_V\left(r_t|\boldsymbol{z}_t, \boldsymbol{\theta}\right)\right],$$

and

$$\mathcal{E}\left(M_t{}^2|N_t, \boldsymbol{z}_t, r_t, \boldsymbol{\theta}\right) \equiv \mu^{\{2\}}\left(N_t, \boldsymbol{z}_t, r_t, \boldsymbol{\theta}\right)$$
$$= N_t \left[1 - F_V\left(r_t|\boldsymbol{z}_t, \boldsymbol{\theta}\right)\right]$$
$$\left\{F_V\left(r_t|\boldsymbol{z}_t, \boldsymbol{\theta}\right) + N_t \left[1 - F_V\left(r_t|\boldsymbol{z}_t, \boldsymbol{\theta}\right)\right]\right\}.$$

These moments are then averaged using the distribution of N_t conditional on the event that M_t weakly exceeds one:

$$\mathcal{E}(M_t|M_t \geq 1, \boldsymbol{z}_t, r_t, \boldsymbol{\theta}) =$$
$$\sum_{N_t=1}^{\mathcal{N}_t} \mu^{\{1\}}\left(N_t, \boldsymbol{z}_t, r_t, \boldsymbol{\theta}\right) \Pr\left(N_t|M_t \geq 1, \boldsymbol{z}_t, r_t, \boldsymbol{\theta}\right)$$

and

$$\mathcal{E}(M_t|M_t \geq 1, \boldsymbol{z}_t, r_t, \boldsymbol{\theta}) =$$
$$\sum_{N_t=1}^{\mathcal{N}_t} \mu^{\{2\}}\left(N_t, \boldsymbol{z}_t, r_t, \boldsymbol{\theta}\right) \Pr\left(N_t|M_t \geq 1, \boldsymbol{z}_t, r_t, \boldsymbol{\theta}\right)$$

where the distribution of N_t conditional on the event that M_t is one or greater is given by:

$$\Pr\left(N_t|M_t \geq 1, \boldsymbol{z}_t, r_t, \boldsymbol{\theta}\right) = \frac{h_N\left(N_t|\boldsymbol{z}_t, r_t, \boldsymbol{\gamma}\right)}{1 - \sum_{N_t=0}^{\mathcal{N}_t} h_N\left(N_t|\boldsymbol{z}_t, r_t, \boldsymbol{\gamma}\right)\left[F_V\left(r_t|\boldsymbol{z}_t, \boldsymbol{\theta}\right)\right]^{N_t}}.$$

The denominator in the previous equation

$$1 - \sum_{N_t=0}^{\mathcal{N}_t} h_N\left(N_t|\boldsymbol{z}_t, r_t, \boldsymbol{\gamma}\right)\left[F_V\left(r_t|\boldsymbol{z}_t, \boldsymbol{\theta}\right)\right]^{N_t}$$

is the unconditional probability that M_t weakly exceeds one.

Since the discrete distribution of M_t, given M_t is one or greater, is parametric by the specification of $q^*\left(\boldsymbol{z}_t, r_t, \boldsymbol{\gamma}\right)$ and $F_V\left(\cdot|\boldsymbol{z}_t, \boldsymbol{\theta}\right)$, Li suggested that it is also possible to write down the logarithm of the likelihood function for the parameters of M_t, and use the score functions as additional moment conditions. In practice, however, Li only used the above three conditional moments for $\mathcal{E}\left(S_{it}|S_{it} \geq r_t, M_t, \mathbf{z}_t, \boldsymbol{\theta}\right)$, $\mathcal{E}\left(M_t|M_t \geq 1, \mathbf{z}_t, r_t, \boldsymbol{\theta}\right)$, and $\mathcal{E}\left[M_t^2|M_t \geq 1, \mathbf{z}_t, r_t, \boldsymbol{\theta}\right]$. Li formed a set of unconditional moment conditions from these three conditional-moment conditions. Let $\mathbf{X}_t$ denote a matrix of functions of $\mathbf{z}_t$ and r_t of column dimension three and row dimensions larger than

$$[\dim\left(\boldsymbol{\theta}\right) + \dim\left(\boldsymbol{\gamma}\right)].$$

The set of unconditional moment conditions are formed by

$$\boldsymbol{\mu}\left(S_{it}, \boldsymbol{\theta}, \boldsymbol{\gamma}\right) = \mathbf{X}_t \begin{pmatrix} \mathcal{E}\left(S_{it}|S_{it} \geq r_t, M_t, \mathbf{z}_t, \boldsymbol{\theta}\right) \\ \mathcal{E}\left(M_t|M_t \geq 1, \mathbf{z}_t, r_t, \boldsymbol{\theta}\right) \\ \mathcal{E}\left(M_t^2|M_t \geq 1, \mathbf{z}_t, r_t, \boldsymbol{\theta}\right) \end{pmatrix}.$$

This leads to the population moment condition that

$$\mathcal{E}\left[\boldsymbol{\mu}\left(S_{it}, \boldsymbol{\theta}^0, \boldsymbol{\gamma}^0\right)\right] = \mathbf{0}.$$

The population moment condition can be replaced by its sample analogue, so

$$\hat{\boldsymbol{\mu}}_T\left(\boldsymbol{\theta}, \boldsymbol{\gamma}\right) = \frac{1}{T} \sum_{t=1}^{T} \frac{1}{M_t} \sum_{i=1}^{M_t} \boldsymbol{\mu}\left(S_{it}, \boldsymbol{\theta}, \boldsymbol{\gamma}\right).$$

Li then proposed to estimate $\boldsymbol{\theta}^0$ and $\boldsymbol{\gamma}^0$ by minimizing the GMM quadratic loss function, so $\hat{\boldsymbol{\theta}}$ and $\hat{\boldsymbol{\gamma}}$ are defined by

$$\underset{\boldsymbol{\theta}, \boldsymbol{\gamma}}{\arg\min} \; \hat{\boldsymbol{\mu}}_T(\boldsymbol{\theta}, \boldsymbol{\gamma})^{\top} \mathbf{A}_T \hat{\boldsymbol{\mu}}_T(\boldsymbol{\theta}, \boldsymbol{\gamma}).$$

Li noted one problem when implementing his estimator: calculating the upper support $\bar{s}\left(N_t, \mathbf{z}_t, r_t, \boldsymbol{\theta}\right)$ is difficult. This term appears in the conditional moment $\mathcal{E}\left(S_{it}|S_{it} \geq r_t, M_t, \mathbf{z}_t\right)$ linearly through the term

$$-\frac{\bar{s}\left(N_t, \mathbf{z}_t, r_t, \boldsymbol{\theta}\right)}{(N_t - 2)} \frac{1}{F_V\left(r_t|\mathbf{z}_t, \boldsymbol{\theta}\right)}.$$

Therefore, he suggested estimating $\bar{s}\left(N_t, \mathbf{z}_t, r_t, \boldsymbol{\theta}\right)$ by simulation. Li also suggested simulating over the conditional distribution of N_t given M_t, but for simplicity we shall focus on $\bar{s}\left(N_t, \mathbf{z}_t, r_t, \boldsymbol{\theta}\right)$ instead. First, note that

$$\bar{s}\left(N_t, \mathbf{z}_t, r_t, \boldsymbol{\theta}\right) = \mathcal{E}\left\{\max\left[V_{(1:N_t-1)}, r_t\right]; \mathbf{z}_t, \boldsymbol{\theta}\right\} =$$

$$\int \cdots \int \max\left[u_{(1:N_t-1)}, r_t\right] \frac{f_V\left(u_1; \mathbf{z}_t, \boldsymbol{\theta}\right) \dots f_V\left(u_{N_t-1}; \mathbf{z}_t, \boldsymbol{\theta}\right)}{g\left(\boldsymbol{u}\right)} \boldsymbol{g}\left(\boldsymbol{u}\right) \; d\boldsymbol{u}$$

where $\boldsymbol{u}$ equals $(u_1, \ldots, u_{N_t-1})$ and

$$g(\boldsymbol{u}) = \prod_{t=1}^{\mathcal{N}_t} g\left(u_t | \boldsymbol{z}_t, \mathcal{N}_t\right).$$

Written in this manner, a natural, unbiased, simulation estimator of $\bar{s}\left(N_t, \boldsymbol{z}_t, r_t, \boldsymbol{\theta}\right)$, using importance sampling, is suggested. In particular, the importance sampler draws J independent samples, each of size $(N_t - 1)$, denoted $U_1^{jt}, \ldots, U_{N_t-1}^{jt}$, where U_i^{jt} is independently drawn from the distribution with probability density function $g_t\left(\cdot\right)$ for $j = 1, \ldots, J$. These can then be used to estimate the upper bid support by

$$\hat{\bar{s}}\left(N_t, \boldsymbol{z}_t, r_t, \boldsymbol{\theta}\right) = \frac{1}{J} \sum_{j=1}^{J} W_t^j\left(\boldsymbol{z}, \boldsymbol{\theta}\right),$$

where

$$W_t^j\left(\boldsymbol{z}, \boldsymbol{\theta}\right) = \max\left(U_{(1:N_t-1)}^{jt}, r_t\right) \frac{f_V\left(U_1^{jt}; \boldsymbol{z}, \boldsymbol{\theta}\right) \cdots f_V\left(U_{N_t-1}^{jt}; \boldsymbol{z}, \boldsymbol{\theta}\right)}{g_t\left(U_1^{jt}\right) \cdots g_t\left(U_{N_t-1}^{jt}\right)}.$$

Li then replaced the method-of-moments estimator with a simulated method-of-moments estimator in which $\bar{s}\left(N_t, \boldsymbol{z}_t, r_t, \boldsymbol{\theta}\right)$ is replaced by the simulated analogue $\hat{\bar{s}}\left(N_t, \boldsymbol{z}_t, r_t, \boldsymbol{\theta}\right)$. Since the moment conditions are linear in the simulation draws, the simulated moments are unbiased estimators of the true population moment. Therefore, the simulated method-of-moments estimator will be consistent and asymptotically normal even with a finite fixed number of simulation J for each observation. Thus, unlike the SNLS method of Laffont et al. (1995), it is unnecessary to use an estimate of the variance of the simulation error to correct for the bias in the simulated objective function.

4.9 Practice Problems

The problems at the end of this chapter are designed to give you practice in estimating models of Dutch and first-price, sealed-bid auctions using both parametric and nonparametric methods.

1. Suppose that V is distributed uniformly on the interval $[0, \theta^0]$. Consider a random sample of size T.

   a) Find $F_V(v; \theta^0)$.

b) Find $\mathcal{E}(V)$.

c) Find $\mathcal{V}(V)$.

d) Find $\mathcal{E}(M_1)$ where M_1 equals $\sum_{t=1}^{T} V_t / T$.

e) Find $\mathcal{V}(M_1)$.

f) Find $\hat{\theta}_{\mathrm{MM}}$, the method-of-moments estimator of θ^0.

g) Find the mean of $\hat{\theta}_{\mathrm{MM}}$.

h) Find the variance of $\hat{\theta}_{\mathrm{MM}}$.

i) Describe the asymptotic distribution of

$$\frac{[M_1 - \mathcal{E}(M_1)]}{\sqrt{\mathcal{V}(M_1)}}$$

and explain the reasoning behind your claim.

j) Explain why the method of maximum likelihood, as you know it, cannot be used to estimate θ^0.

Consider Z the maximum of all the V_ts; i.e.,

$$Z = \max(V_1, V_2, \ldots, V_T).$$

k) Find $F_Z(z; \theta^0)$.

l) Find $f_Z(z; \theta^0)$.

m) Find $\mathcal{E}(Z)$.

n) Find $\mathcal{V}(Z)$.

o) Find the probability limit of Z.

p) Find the asymptotic distribution of Z.

q) Explain why using a function of the maximum order statistic Z is a good estimator of θ^0; e.g.,

$$\hat{\theta}_{\mathrm{ML}} = h(Z) = \frac{(T+1)Z}{T}.$$

r) Find $\mathcal{E}(\hat{\theta}_{\mathrm{ML}})$.

s) Find $\mathcal{MSE}(\hat{\theta}_{\mathrm{ML}})$.

t) Plot

$$\mathcal{RE}(\hat{\theta}_{\mathrm{ML}}, \hat{\theta}_{\mathrm{MM}}) \equiv \frac{\mathcal{MSE}(\hat{\theta}_{\mathrm{ML}})}{\mathcal{MSE}(\hat{\theta}_{\mathrm{MM}})}$$

for various values of T.

2. Suppose that C is distributed Pareto having probability density function

$$f_C(c; \theta^0) = \frac{3(\theta^0)^3}{c^4} \qquad 0 < \theta \le c < \infty.$$

Consider a random sample of size T.

a) Find $F_C(c; \theta^0)$.

b) Find $\mathcal{E}(C)$.

c) Find $\mathcal{V}(C)$.

d) Find $\mathcal{E}(M_1)$ where M_1 equals $\sum_{t=1}^{T} C_t/T$.

e) Find $\mathcal{V}(M_1)$.

f) Find $\hat{\theta}_{\text{MM}}$, the method-of-moments estimator of θ^0.

g) Find $\mathcal{E}(\hat{\theta}_{\text{MM}})$.

h) Find $\mathcal{V}(\hat{\theta}_{\text{MM}})$.

i) Describe the asymptotic distribution of

$$\frac{(M_1 - \mathcal{E}(M_1))}{\sqrt{\mathcal{V}(M_1)}}$$

and explain the reasoning behind your claim.

j) Explain why the method of maximum likelihood, as you know it, cannot be used to estimate θ^0.

Consider X the minimum of all the C_ts; i.e.,

$$X = \min(C_1, C_2, \ldots, C_T).$$

k) Find $F_X(x; \theta^0)$.

l) Find $f_X(x; \theta^0)$.

m) Find $\mathcal{E}(X)$.

n) Find $\mathcal{V}(X)$.

o) Find the probability limit of X.

p) Find the asymptotic distribution of X.

q) Explain why using a function of the minimum order statistic X is a good estimator of θ; e.g.,

$$\hat{\theta}_{\text{ML}} = g(X) = \frac{(3T - 1)X}{3T}.$$

r) Find $\mathcal{E}(\hat{\theta}_{\text{ML}})$.

s) Find $\mathcal{MSE}(\hat{\theta}_{\mathrm{ML}})$.

t) Plot

$$\mathcal{RE}(\hat{\theta}_{\mathrm{ML}}, \hat{\theta}_{\mathrm{MM}}) \equiv \frac{\mathcal{MSE}(\hat{\theta}_{\mathrm{ML}})}{\mathcal{MSE}(\hat{\theta}_{\mathrm{MM}})}$$

for various values of T.

3. Consider a government that seeks to perform a task at the lowest cost. It requests sealed-bid tenders from a group of $\mathcal{N}$ potential suppliers and, assuming that no reserve price is imposed, uses as the selection rule that the lowest bidder will win the auction. Suppose that the cost of performing the service for any one bidder C is an independent and identically distributed draw from a distribution $F_C(c)$ which is common knowledge to all potential bidders, and that potential suppliers behave noncooperatively. Assume that potential bidders are risk neutral with regard to winning the right to perform the task for the government.

   a) Calculate the symmetric, Bayes–Nash equilibrium-bid function for a generic bidder at the auction. In the course of this calculation, be sure to highlight where you have used the assumptions of independence, symmetry, and Bayes–Nash behavior.

   b) Assuming that the distribution of unobserved heterogeneity is from the Pareto family having cumulative distribution function

   $$F_C(c; \theta_0^0, \theta_1^0) = 1 - \left(\frac{\theta_0^0}{c}\right)^{\theta_1^0} \qquad c > \theta_0^0 > 0,\ \theta_1^0 > 0$$

   where θ_0^0 and θ_1^0 are parameters, calculate the equilibrium bid function.

   c) Derive $f_W(w; \theta_0^0, \theta_1^0, \mathcal{N})$, the probability density function of the winning bid W, at an auction and characterize its support.

   Consider a sample of T auctions at which for auction t both the the number of potential competitors $\mathcal{N}_t$ and the winning bid w_t are observed.

   d) For the sample $\{(\mathcal{N}_t, w_t)\}_{t=1}^{T}$, derive the logarithm of the likelihood function and explain why the method of maximum likelihood as conventionally applied does not apply to this problem.

   e) Write down the constrained optimization problem, the solution to which defines $\hat{\boldsymbol{\theta}}$, the maximum-likelihood estimator of $\boldsymbol{\theta}^0$, which equals the vector $(\theta_0^0, \theta_1^0)^\top$. Explain how you would implement this estimator. (Hint: be as precise as you can concerning what kind of problem you are solving, and why your proposed method of solution will give the correct optimum.)

f) In the file `nlp.dat`, which is located on the CD accompanying this book, you will find four columns of numbers. In the first is an identification number, while in the second is a measure of potential competition N_t at a sequence of $t = 1, \ldots, T$ auctions where T is 144, while in the third is a measure of the winning bid w_t at each of the auctions, and in the fourth is a covariate z_t. Ignoring the covariate, initially, in (θ_0, θ_1) space, graph the constraint set.

g) Ignoring the covariate z_t, estimate the cumulative distribution function $F_C^0(c)$, nonparametrically.

h) Ignoring the covariate, solve for $\hat{\boldsymbol{\theta}}_{\mathrm{ML}}$, the maximum-likelihood estimate of $\boldsymbol{\theta}^0$. Superimpose level sets of the logarithm of the likelihood function on the constraint set characterized in part f).

i) Ignoring the covariate, solve for $\hat{\boldsymbol{\theta}}_{\mathrm{GMM}}$, the generalized method-of-moments estimate of $\boldsymbol{\theta}^0$ using the first two population moments of the winning bid.

j) Ignoring the covariate, solve for $\hat{\boldsymbol{\theta}}_{\mathrm{EGMM}}$, the extreme-order generalized method-of-moments estimate of $\boldsymbol{\theta}^0$.

k) Subsequently, introduce the covariate into θ_0 using the following transformation:

$$\theta_{0t} = \exp(\gamma_0 + \gamma_1 z_t).$$

Now, estimate by the method of maximum likelihood the parameter vector $(\gamma_0, \gamma_1, \theta_1)^\top$.

4. Consider two bidders who are vying for the right to perform a task for a government. Suppose each has an independent, private-cost draw, but each is from a different distribution. Hence, one might call this the *asymmetric, independent, private-costs paradigm*. Assume that no reserve price is imposed at this low-price, sealed-bid auction. Suppose that bidder 1's marginal cost is drawn from

$$F_1(c) = [1 - \exp(-\theta c^{1.5})],$$

while bidder 2's marginal cost is drawn from

$$F_2(c) = [1 - \exp(-\theta c^{3.5})],$$

where θ equals one and where $c \in [0.01, 2.5]$.

a) Using any of the three algorithms described in Bajari (2001), approximate the Bayes–Nash, equilibrium-bid functions and present these in a single graph.

b) Using your graph from part a), explain how inefficient procurement may obtain.

c) Simulate the incidence of inefficient procurement.

Now suppose that bidder 2's marginal cost is drawn instead from

$$F_2(c) = [1 - \exp(-\theta c^2)],$$

where, again, θ equals one and $c \in [0.01, 2.5]$. Assume that bidder 1's distribution remains unchanged.

d) In this new circumstance, approximate the equilibrium-bid functions and present these in a single graph. Are the bid functions less similar or more similar than those found in part a)?

e) Recompute the incidence of inefficient procurement. Has the amount of inefficient procurement increased or decreased, and by what amount? Based on your graphical interpretation of inefficient procurement outlined in your answer to part b), does this result make sense?

Chapter 5

Multi-Unit Auctions

$\mathcal{D}$URING THE past four decades, theoretical models of auctions at which only one object is sold to potential bidders demanding at most one object each have been studied extensively. In reality, however, many auctions involve the sale of several objects. At the outset, it is important to distinguish between multi-object auctions and multi-unit auctions. At multi-unit auctions, the objects are assumed identical, so it matters not which unit a bidder wins but rather the aggregate number of units he wins, while at multi-object auctions the objects are assumed different, so a bidder is concerned about which specific object(s) he wins. An example of a multi-object auction would be the sale of an apple, an orange, and a pear, while an example of a multi-unit auction would involve the sale of three identical oranges. In addition, economists often make a distinction between bidders who demand just one unit of the good, referred to by Milgrom (2004) as singleton-demand, and those who have multi-unit demand.

In this chapter, we shall investigate multi-unit auctions. At these auctions, several units of the same object are sold to bidders who may demand just one or several units. Understanding how such changes in the economic environment affect bidding behavior at auctions and how these behavioral changes in turn affect the process of price formation are open research questions.

Some research in the 1990s concerning multi-unit auction models suggests that such institutions provide a host of additional economic issues that are typically absent in the analysis of single-object auction models. For example, within the common-value paradigm, McAfee and Vincent (1993) have shown that the equilibrium at some multi-unit auctions can involve mixed strategies. In addition, as the theoretical work of Weber (1983); McAfee and Vincent (1993); and Laffont, Loisel, and Robert (1994) has shown, multi-unit, singleton-demand auction models can provide richer explanations of observed behavior than can be obtained in single-object-supply, singleton-demand auction models.

For example, within the affiliated private-values paradigm and assuming risk-averse single-unit buyers Laffont, Loisel, and Robert (1994) have been able to derive inverse U-shaped expected price paths across units sold.

5.1 Weber's Classification System

In auction models with single-object supply, four different formats have been studied extensively: Dutch; English; first-price, sealed-bid; and Vickrey auctions. The bidding rules under each format along with an information structure assumed by the researcher determine the extensive-form structure of the strategic auction game of incomplete information. This extensive-form structure, in conjunction with preferences of the players and a concept of equilibrium, determines the equilibrium strategies of the potential bidders at these auctions, which in turn determines the DGP. A natural next step in the research program is to investigate the structural econometrics of auction models in which several units are sold to bidders who may demand more than one unit. However, because any game-theoretic investigation of multi-unit auctions will be specific to a particular auction format, we first need to outline the three most common multi-unit formats. Fortunately, Weber (1983) has already classified multi-unit auctions for us.

5.1.1 Simultaneous-Dependent Auctions

The first format Weber described is the *simultaneous-dependent* auction. Under this format, which is typically a first-price, sealed-bid auction, bidders are required to take a single action that determines both the allocation of the units and the payments to the seller. Weekly auctions of U.S. Treasury bills are an example of this format. Under this format, the highest bidders win the available units, but two different rules are commonly used to determine traded prices. The first is under the *uniform-price* rule, which means that each bidder who wins some fraction of the allocation pays the same price. Typically, this price is the highest of the losing bids. Under the second rule, a *discriminatory-price* rule, each winner pays what he bid for the unit that he has won; these auctions are often referred to as *pay-as-bid* auctions. Wilson (1979) constructed a simple model of the simultaneous-dependent auction and solved some examples under this format, which is sometimes referred to as the *share auction*.

5.1.2 Simultaneous-Independent Auctions

A special case of the simultaneous-dependent auction, viewed as a distinct format by Weber, is the *simultaneous-independent auction*. Under this format, the sale of one unit does not depend on the outcome of other sales. Sales of mineral rights, such as oil and gas leases, are good examples of such auctions; they are typically undertaken using the first-price, sealed-bid format, with the highest bidder for any unit winning that unit, and paying his bid.

5.1.3 Sequential Auctions

The final format described by Weber is the *sequential auction*, at which one unit (or lot containing several units of the same item) is sold at a time. Art, stamps, and coins as well as cattle, fish, flowers, timber, vegetables, and wine are often sold at sequential auctions. Sequential auctions are conducted under all of the three common formats; viz., Dutch, English, and first-price, sealed-bid.

Because sequential auctions, by construction, involve the passage of time, additional rules often exist at these auctions. For example, under Dutch and English sequential auctions, the winner of the current sale in the auction often has the option to choose how many of the remaining units to take at the current price. Sometimes, too, the selling price of a previous unit is important in determining the reserve price for subsequent units. These two additional rules are often thought to motivate risk-averse bidders.

5.2 Pricing Rules

From a theoretical perspective, it must seem obvious now that the pricing rule used at an auction will determine how bidders behave. In fact, Vickrey's (1961) model is an example of how a slight change in pricing at a single-object, first-price, sealed-bid auction within the IPVP—the second-price, sealed-bid rule—changed equilibrium behavior a great deal. This is true a fortiori at multi-unit auctions.

The choice among pricing rules has been an issue of debate since at least Friedman (1959). At simultaneous dependent auctions, Friedman argued that, under the discriminatory-pricing rule, bidders shade their bids. Moreover, Vickrey (1961) demonstrated that at single-object auctions within the IPVP the extent of the shading was greatest at high valuations. Friedman argued further that, under a uniform-pricing rule,

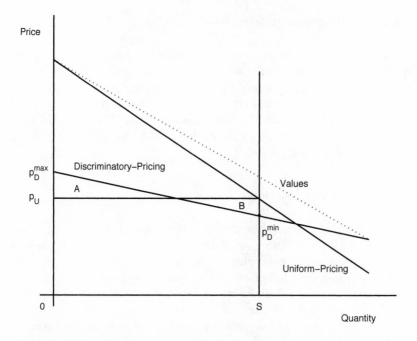

Figure 5.1
Revenues: Pay-as-Bid and Uniform-Price Auctions

because a bidder was less likely to influence the price at which he traded, he would bid closer to his valuation than at a pay-as-bid auction.

Recently, however, Ausubel and Cramton (2002) have pointed out that, even under the uniform-pricing rule, bidders have an incentive to shade their bids. However, under uniform-pricing, instead of shading relatively more at high values than at low values, bidders shade relatively more at low values than at high values. The reason why bidders shade the bids on lower-value units relatively more is that these bids are more likely to be pivotal in determing the traded price. Ausubel and Cramton (2002) referred to this behavior as *demand reduction*.

In figure 5.1, we depict a stylized example in which the ordered true values are the dotted line, and labeled as such, while bid functions under discriminatory- and uniform-pricing rules are solid lines labeled as such. The policy question is an empirical one: Is the area of the triangle labeled A greater than or less than the triangle labeled B? For the area of the trapezoid $0p_D^{max}p_D^{min}S$ is the revenue generated under discriminatory pricing, while the rectangle of dimension ($p_U \times S$) is the revenue generated under uniform pricing. In fact, this is what concerned Hortaçsu (2002a,b) in his investigation of treasury-bill auctions in Turkey.

5.2.1 Shading and Demand Reduction

The intuition behind why participants shade their bids at multi-unit, pay-as-bid auctions is virtually the same as that for single-object, pay-as-bid auctions, so we shall not repeat it here. On the other hand, the shading that occurs under uniform-pricing, often referred to as *demand reduction*, has been missed by even the most astute observers. In what follows, we devote considerable space and effort to investigating this phenomenon within the IPVP.

In multi-unit environments, the common wisdom has been that pay-as-bid and uniform-price auctions can be viewed as multi-unit extensions of first-price and second-price auctions of single objects. This has led some to believe that the uniform-price auction inherits the attractive truth-telling and efficiency properties of the Vickrey auction. It has also led some observers to infer, wrongly we might add, that the uniform-price auction ought to generate greater expected revenues to the seller than the pay-as-bid auction.

Ausubel and Cramton (2002) have shown that this reasoning is flawed. In fact, in general, the ranking between pay-as-bid and uniform-price auctions is ambiguous in terms of both allocational efficiency and expected revenue, which is consistent with our figure 5.1. Note that, under both pricing rules, Ausubel and Cramton assumed that bidders submit entire demand curves for all the units desired. Therefore, they did not consider sequential auctions at which different numbers of units are sold in lots, one after another.

Ausubel and Cramton first showed that bidders tend to shade their bids and to reduce their demand for larger quantities at uniform-price auctions. The intuition is as follows: when a bidder desires several units of the good being sold, and if the number of units desired is sufficiently large, then there is a positive probability that his bid on the later units will be pivotal in the sense that it will determine the price that the bidder will pay on all the units he wins. In such circumstances, the bidder's incentive is to bid less than his true valuation on later units in order to reduce the expected price he will pay on earlier units.

With discrete goods, this intuition suggests that the bidder will bid his true valuation on the first unit demanded, but strictly less than his true valuation on all subsequent units. With divisible goods, this intuition suggests that the demand curve a bidder submits will take on the qualitative features of a monopolist's marginal-revenue curve: at zero quantity the demand curve and the bid curve (marginal-revenue curve) intersect, but at all positive quantities, the bid curve (marginal-revenue curve) lies strictly below the true demand curve. One can see this in figure 5.1.

With discrete units, the results of Ausubel and Cramton can be illustrated relatively simply using the following two-by-two example within the IPVP: suppose two identical units of a good are sold to two bidders using a third-price auction, the uniform-price auction with two units. Suppose bidder 1 demands just one unit which has value V^1, while bidder 2 demands up to two units, each having a constant marginal value V^2. Here, and to follow in this chapter, we adopt the convention that the bidder's identity i is a superscript, while his valuation for unit j is a subscript j. Hence, in this example, V_1^2 equals V_2^2, or V^2 for short, while V_1^1 is V^1 and V_2^1 is zero.

Suppose the privately known values V^1 and V^2 are drawn independently from the uniform distribution on $[0, 1]$. Each bidder must submit two non-negative bids. The seller ranks the four bids, awards the units to the submitters of the two highest bids, with the winners paying the third-highest bid for each unit won.

As at second-price auctions for a single object, it is a weakly dominant strategy for each participant to bid his true value for the first unit. The only time a bidder's first bid determines the price is when it is the third-highest, in which case the bidder wins zero units and the price is irrelevant to the bidder. However, when the bid does not set the price, profits are maximized by making this bid compete favorably against all bids up to the bidder's true value, so that the bidder wins whenever it is profitable. Hence, the first bids of 1 and 2 are V^1 and V^2. Bidder 1 bids zero for the second unit, since his second value is zero. The only remaining question is what 2 bids for the second unit.

Clearly, bidder 2 does not want to bid more than his value for the second unit. By bidding B_2^2, which is weakly less than V^2, two outcomes exist: first, if B_2^2 is less than V^1, then bidder 2 wins one unit and pays B_2^2; second, if B_2^2 is greater than V^1, then bidder 2 wins two units and pays V^1 for each. Thus, bidder 2's expected profit $\Pi^2\left(B_2^2, V^2\right)$ from the bid B_2^2 for the second unit is

$$\Pi^2\left(B_2^2, V^2\right) = \left(V^2 - B_2^2\right)\left(1 - B_2^2\right) + \int_0^{B_2^2} 2\left(V^2 - V^1\right)\, dV^1$$
$$= V^2 - \left(1 - V^2\right) B_2^2.$$

In the above example, $\left(1 - B_2^2\right)$ is the probability that V^1 is larger than B_2^2 since V^1 is uniformly distributed between 0 and 1.

Thus, submitting a second bid B_2^2 of zero maximizes bidder 2's profit $\Pi^2\left(B_2^2, V^2\right)$ for all $V^2 \in [0, 1]$, so he optimally bids zero on the second unit, regardless of his valuation for the second unit. The behavior exhibited in this example is an extreme form of demand reduction: both bidders win a single unit and neither pays anything for his unit. The auction performs poorly in terms of both efficiency and revenue.

Pay-as-bid auctions may be more efficient than uniform-price auctions because, at pay-as-bid auctions, the incentive to shade bids need not increase in the quantity demanded: a bid on an additional unit at pay-as-bid auctions has no effect on the price paid for earlier units. Consequently, it is possible for bidders with similar marginal valuations at different quantities to shade their bids by similar amounts, which is consistent with efficiency.

Given that, for pedagogical reasons, we have chosen to avoid the CVP and AVP in this book, we shall describe a version of the Ausubel–Cramton flat-demand, share-auction model within the IPVP. But the reader should note that, in their paper, Ausubel and Cramton studied a general, affiliated, interdependent-values model in which both common-value and private-values components were present. With interdependent values, each bidder's true demand may depend on information known by others. In such an environment, it is essential that a bidder condition his bid on the information revealed by his winning a particular quantity of the good. Ausubel and Cramton assumed that winning a larger quantity of the good is "bad" news about the good's value because winning more means that others do not value the good as highly as they might. Consequently, a rational bidder shades his bid to avoid bidding above his conditional marginal value for the good, often referred to as avoiding the winner's curse. Ausubel and Cramton referred to bid shading as bidding below the bidder's conditional marginal value for the good, rather than merely the shading that arises from winner's curse avoidance.

Ausubel and Cramton considered the following model: a seller has a quantity, normalized to one, of a divisible good to sell to $\mathcal{N}$ bidders. The seller's valuation for the good is zero. Each bidder i can consume any quantity $Q^i \in [0, \lambda^i]$, where $\lambda^i \in (0, 1)$. Without loss of generality, assume $\lambda^1 \geq \lambda^2 \geq \cdots \geq \lambda^{\mathcal{N}}$. Competition for each quantity of the good exists; i.e.,

$$\lambda^2 + \lambda^3 + \cdots + \lambda^{\mathcal{N}} \geq 1. \tag{5.1}$$

Ausubel and Cramton interpreted Q^i as bidder i's share of the total quantity and λ^i as a quantity restriction.

Each bidder is assumed to observe his valuation, his type V^i, before the bids are submitted. Assume $V^i \in [0, 1]$ and let $\boldsymbol{V}$ denote $\left(V^1, \ldots, V^{\mathcal{N}}\right)$, and $\boldsymbol{V}^{-i}$ denote the elements of $\boldsymbol{V}$ excluding V^i. Types are drawn independently from $F_i(\cdot)$, which has a strictly positive probability density function $f_i(\cdot)$ on $[0, 1]$. While the cumulative distribution functions F_i for all i are commonly known to all bidders, the realization of V^i is known only to bidder i.

Bidder i has a flat marginal value $V^i \in [0, 1]$ for the good up to the capacity λ^i. A bidder i, having marginal value V^i, consuming Q^i, and paying R^i has payoff

$$\Pi^i \left(V^i, Q^i, R^i \right) = Q^i V^i - R^i \quad \text{where} \quad Q^i \in \left[0, \lambda^i \right].$$

The seller uses a mechanism referred to as a conventional auction to allocate the good. A conventional auction is one at which participants submit bids and the units are awarded to the highest bidders. The simplest formulation is for each bidder i, simultaneously and independently, to submit a demand curve of the form $q^i \left(p, V^i \right) : [0, 1] \to \left[0, \lambda^i \right]$, where his marginal value equals V^i. The demand curve expresses the quantity that bidder i is willing to purchase at a price of p. The function $q^i \left(p, V^i \right)$ is required to be left-continuous in the p dimension at the point where p equals one, and right-continuous at all $p \in [0, 1)$, and weakly decreasing. The market-clearing price p_0 is determined by the highest rejected bid:

$$p_0 = \inf \left[p \,\middle|\, \sum_{i=1}^{\mathcal{N}} q^i \left(p, V^i \right) \leq 1 \right].$$

The inverse of the demand equation with respect to p is the bid function of bidder i, which is denoted by

$$b^i \left(q, V^i \right) : \left[0, \lambda^i \right] \to [0, 1].$$

It is required to be right-continuous at the value of q that equals zero, left-continuous at all $q \in (0, \lambda^i]$, and weakly decreasing. The seller inverts each bid function to obtain a demand curve and then determines the market-clearing price as above.

Because each $q^i \left(p, V^i \right)$ is weakly decreasing and because of the structure imposed on the inverse-bid functions—see, for example, footnote 4 of Ausubel and Cramton (2002)—the requirements that $q^i(0, V^i)$ equals λ^i and $q^i(1, V^i)$ equal zero are met, so p_0 exists, is unique, and contained in $(0, 1)$. If

$$\sum_{i=1}^{\mathcal{N}} q^i(p_0, V^i) = 1,$$

then each bidder i is assigned a quantity of Q^i that equals $q^i(p_0, V^i)$. If

$$\sum_{i=1}^{\mathcal{N}} q^i(p_0, V^i) > 1,$$

then the aggregate demand curve is flat at p_0 and some bidders' demands at p_0 will need to be rationed. All that remains is to specify the pricing rule R; this is how conventional auctions differ. Ausubel and Cramton chose to study the two most common rules, the uniform-pricing rule under which each bidder i who is assigned Q^i pays the market-clearing price p_0, so

$$R^i = p_0 \times Q^i,$$

and the discriminatory-pricing rule under which each bidder i assigned Q^i pays his winning bids, so

$$R^i = \int_0^{Q^i} b^i\left(u, V^i\right)\ du.$$

The equilibrium concept used by Ausubel and Cramton is the usual one, Bayes–Nash. In this case, a Bayes–Nash equilibrium is a profile of bid functions $\{b^i(q, V^i)\}_{i=1}^{\mathcal{N}}$ for every type of every bidder which are mutual best responses. Given the bid functions, the allocated quantity Q^i for bidder i depends on the entire vector of valuations $\boldsymbol{V}$. An equilibrium outcome $Q^i\left(\boldsymbol{V}\right)$ of a conventional auction is said to be ex post efficient if the units are allocated to the bidders with the highest values; i.e.,

$$Q^i\left(\boldsymbol{V}\right) = Q^{i*}\left(\boldsymbol{V}\right) \quad i = 1, \ldots, \mathcal{N}$$

with probability one. Here, $\boldsymbol{Q}^*\left(\boldsymbol{V}\right)$ denotes $\left[Q^{1*}, \ldots, Q^{\mathcal{N}*}\right]$, an efficient assignment of the good; i.e., an assignment that maximizes

$$\sum_{i=1}^{\mathcal{N}} V^i Q^i\left(\boldsymbol{V}\right)$$

subject to the constraints

$$Q^i\left(\boldsymbol{V}\right) \in \left[0, \lambda^i\right] \quad i = 1, \ldots, \mathcal{N}$$

and

$$\sum_{i=1}^{\mathcal{N}} Q^i\left(\boldsymbol{V}\right) = 1.$$

Ausubel and Cramton (2002) first showed that uniform-price auctions are inefficient. Their first lemma states that in an ex post efficient, Bayes–Nash equilibrium of a conventional auction with flat demands (i.e., constant marginal values), all bidders must use symmetric, flat-bid functions.

Lemma 5.2.1: Consider an ex post efficient equilibrium. There exists a strictly increasing function $\phi : [0,1] \to [0,1]$ such that $b^i(q, V^i) = \phi(V^i)$ for all of the bidders $i = 1, \ldots, \mathcal{N}$ and for all quantities $q \in [0, \lambda^i]$, and for almost every type $V^i \in [0,1]$.

Proof of Lemma 5.2.1: The proof proceeds first by showing that each bidder must use a flat-bid function, and then showing these flat-bid functions must be identical for all bidders.

Ex post efficiency requires that Q^i equal λ^i if bidder i has the highest V^i and Q^i is zero if bidder i has the lowest V^i. For any two types of bidder i, i_1 and i_2, such that V^{i_1} exceeds V^{i_2}, it must be true that

$$b^i\left(\lambda^i, V^{i_1}\right) \geq b^i\left(0, V^{i_2}\right).$$

Otherwise, in the event (which can occur with positive probability) that all of the competing types of bidders $\boldsymbol{V}^{-i}$ lie strictly between V^{i_1} and V^{i_2}, V^{i_1} must win λ^i and V^{i_2} must win 0 to fulfill the efficiency requirement, which is impossible if $b^i\left(\lambda^i, V^{i_1}\right)$ is less than $b^i\left(0, V^{i_2}\right)$. Consequently,

$$b^i\left(0, V^{i_1}\right) \geq b^i\left(\lambda^i, V^{i_1}\right) \geq b^i\left(0, V^{i_2}\right) \geq b^i\left(\lambda^i, V^{i_2}\right).$$

Letting V^{i_1} approach V^{i_2}, then $b^i\left(\lambda^i, V^{i_1}\right)$ weakly exceeds $b^i\left(0, V^{i_2}\right)$, but $b^i\left(\lambda^i, V^{i_2}\right)$ is weakly less than $b^i\left(0, V^{i_2}\right)$. Therefore, $b^i\left(\lambda^i, V^{i_2}\right)$ equals $b^i\left(0, V^{i_2}\right)$. Given that $b^i\left(\cdot, V^i\right)$ is monotonically decreasing in the first argument, it has to be a constant function in the first argument, denoted $\phi^i\left(V^i\right)$. This also shows that $\phi^i\left(V^i\right)$ has to be at least weakly increasing in V^i.

Second, $\phi^i\left(V^i\right)$ equals $\phi\left(V^i\right)$; it is symmetric across i. To show this, consider the following reductio ad absurdum argument: suppose not, then for some V, $\phi^i(V)$ is less than $\phi^j(V)$, and for some V^i greater than V, which is greater than V^j, $\phi^i\left(V^i\right)$ is less than $\phi^j(V^j)$. But then, in the positive probability event, when all other competing bids lie between V^i and V^j, it is impossible to achieve the efficient outcome, which requires that i wins λ^i and j wins nothing.

Finally, $\phi\left(V^i\right)$ must be strictly increasing. Otherwise, one can find an interval $\left[V^{i_1}, V^{i_2}\right]$ such that $\phi(\cdot)$ is constant on this interval. In the positive probability event that $\boldsymbol{V}^{-i}$ lies strictly between V^{i_1} and V^{i_2}, type V^{i_1} must win only 0 and V^{i_2} must win λ^i, which is impossible if $\phi(\cdot)$ is a constant on $\left[V^{i_1}, V^{i_2}\right]$. *QED*

Using this lemma, Ausubel and Cramton demonstrated that, for bids of sufficiently small quantities, the uniform-price auctions behaves like the second-price auction of a single unit: participants optimally bid their true values. This is formalized in Theorem 1 of Ausubel and Cramton, which states the following:

Theorem 5.2.1. Suppose an ex post efficient equilibrium exists in a flat-demands environment under uniform-pricing, then every bidder i uses the symmetric flat-bid function

$$b^i \left(q, V^i \right) \equiv \phi \left(V^i \right) \equiv V^i$$

for every type $V^i \in [0, 1]$ and every quantity $q \in [0, \lambda^i]$.

Note that Lemma 5.2.1 already states that in an efficient equilibrium, each bidder i submits a flat-bid schedule $b^i \left(q, V^i \right)$, which is equal to $\phi \left(V^i \right)$ with probability one. Theorem 5.2.1 adds that $\phi \left(V^i \right)$ equals V^i. Note, too, that within the IPVP these results do not rely on any symmetry conditions.

Proof of Theorem 5.2.1: For each $i = 1, \ldots, \mathcal{N}$, define

$$J^{-i} = \operatorname*{argmax}_{I \subset \{1, \ldots, \mathcal{N}\} \setminus \{i\}} \left(\sum_{j \in I} \lambda^j \,\middle|\, \sum_{j \in I} \lambda^j < 1 \right).$$

If there are multiple sets J^{-i}, then select one arbitrarily. Also define

$$L^i = 1 - \sum_{j \in J^{-i}} \lambda^j.$$

In words, J^{-i} is the combination of bidders other than bidder i that has a combined capacity $(1 - L^i)$ that is closest to but strictly less than one, the total quantity available. By definition, L^i is greater than zero. If, in the definition of L^i, L^i exceeds λ^i, then redefine L^i equals $(1 - \lambda^i)$. In other words, L^i is effectively defined as

$$L^i = \min \left(1 - \sum_{j \in J^{-i}} \lambda^j, \lambda^i \right).$$

Consider the optimization problem facing bidder i. Given $\boldsymbol{V}^{-i}$, and given any $q \in \left(0, \lambda^i \right)$, define $\tau_q^i \left(\boldsymbol{V}^{-i} \right)$ to be the minimum value of V^i such that the efficient allocation for bidder i is at least q:

$$\tau_q^i \left(\boldsymbol{V}^{-i} \right) = \inf \{ x \in (0, 1) : Q^{i*} \left(x, \boldsymbol{V}^{-i} \right) \geq q \}.$$

$\tau_q^i \left(\boldsymbol{V}^{-i} \right)$, as a random variable, is a function of only $\boldsymbol{V}^{-i}$, and therefore is independent of V^i. Ausubel and Cramton noted that for $q \in \left(0, L^i \right)$ $\tau_q^i \left(\boldsymbol{V}^{-i} \right)$ is independent of q. They then denote this random variable, independent of q, as Y^{-i}. Its density function is denoted by $f_{-i} \left(Y^{-i} \right)$.

By Lemma 5.2.1, all bidders submit flat-bid functions $b^j \left(q, V^j \right)$ equal $\phi \left(V^j \right)$ with probability one. For bidder i, consider any quantity $q \in \left(0, L^i \right)$. Then, by the definition of L^i, we note that for any combination J of opponents of bidder i, it must be true that

$$q + \sum_{j \in J} \lambda^j \neq 1.$$

Therefore, bidder i cannot be pivotal whenever $q \in \left(0, L^i \right)$. Because bidder i is not pivotal, he does not determine the price. Therefore, the price will be determined by $\phi \left(Y^{-i} \right)$. Hence, if bidder i bids b, then the payoff to bidder i is given by

$$L^i \int_0^{\phi^{-1}(b)} \left[V^i - \phi \left(Y^{-i} \right) \right] f_{-i} \left(Y^{-i} \right) \, dY^{-i}.$$

The first-order condition for this optimization problem is given by

$$L^i \{ V^i - \phi \left[\phi^{-1} \left(b \right) \right] \} \frac{\partial \phi^{-1} \left(b \right)}{\partial b} = 0.$$

Because of Lemma 5.2.1,

$$\frac{\partial \phi^{-1} \left(b \right)}{\partial b} > 0.$$

Therefore, it must be true that the optimal b equals V^i.

Finally, we note that the bid function is constant over the entire range $\left(0, \lambda^i \right)$. Therefore, we can extend the above construction of b equal V^i from $q \in \left(0, L^i \right)$ to $\left(0, \lambda^i \right)$, and the theorem is proven.

However, Ausubel and Cramton showed in their Theorem 2 that, in bids for a sufficiently large quantity, there is, in general, a positive probability that a bidder will simultaneously influence price and win a positive quantity. This provides an incentive for the bidder to bid below his marginal valuation on larger quantities, thereby upsetting efficiency. Formally, their Theorem 2 states that in a flat-demand environment, unless all λ^is are the same λ and $(1/\lambda)$ is an integer, there does not exist an ex post efficient equilibrium of the uniform-price auction. We restate Theorem 2 as

Theorem 5.2.2: In the flat-demand environment considered above, unless λ^i equals a constant λ for all $i = 1, \ldots, \mathcal{N}$ and $(1/\lambda)$ is an integer, there does not exist an ex post efficient equilibrium of the uniform-price auction.

Proof of Theorem 5.2.2: The proof again is by reductio ad absurdum: Suppose there exists an ex post efficient equilibrium of the uniform-price auction when either λ^i equals λ and $(1/\lambda)$ is not an integer, or when λ^1 exceeds λ^j, for all $j = 2, \ldots, \mathcal{N}$. One can do this, without loss of generality, by using a particular labeling of bidder identities.

By Theorem 5.2.1, an efficient equilibrium requires that all bidders $i = 2, \ldots, \mathcal{N}$ use the bid function $b^i\left(q, V^i\right)$ equal V^i, for all quantities $q \in \left(0, \lambda^i\right)$.

Now consider bidder 1, and recall the definitions of L^1 and J^{-1} defined in the proof of Theorem 5.2.1. In the proof of Theorem 5.2.1, it was shown that it is, indeed, a best response for bidder 1 to bid

$$b^1\left(q, V^1\right) \equiv V^1$$

for any $q \in \left(0, L^1\right)$. The goal now is to construct a number $R^1 \in \left(L^1, \lambda^1\right)$ such that it is not a best response for bidder 1 to bid $b^1\left(q, V^1\right)$ equal V^1 for any $q \in \left(R^1, \lambda^1\right)$.

First, we need to show that L^1 is less than λ^1, so that it is possible to find R^1 at all. Consider the case where λ^i equals λ for all i and the case where the λ^is do not equal a constant λ for all i separately.

If λ^i equals λ for all i, then define m to be the largest integer such that $m\lambda$ is less than one, which exists because of equation (5.1) above. Now,

$$L^i = 1 - m\lambda,$$

which is strictly less than λ, since $(1/\lambda)$ is not an integer.

Consider now the second case where λ^1 is greater than $\lambda^{\mathcal{N}}$. Define

$$j' = \max\{j \,|\, j \notin J^{-1}\}.$$

Because of the competitive assumption, equation (5.1) above, it must be the case that j' weakly exceeds 2. Consider then separately the case where $\lambda^{j'}$ is less than λ^1, case I, and $\lambda^{j'}$ equal λ^1, case II.

In case I, by definition of L^1 and j', we have

$$1 - L^1 + \lambda^{j'} > 1.$$

This implies that λ^1 is greater than $\lambda^{j'}$, which weakly exceeds L^1.

In case II, since j' does not equal $\mathcal{N}$, $\mathcal{N} \in J^{-1}$. Consider the set $j' \cup J^{-1} \backslash \mathcal{N}$. By the definition of L^1,

$$1 - L^1 + \lambda^{j'} - \lambda^{\mathcal{N}} \geq 1.$$

This also implies that

$$\lambda^1 = \lambda^{j'} \geq \lambda^{\mathcal{N}} + L^1 > L^1.$$

Next, we introduce R^1. For this purpose, define

$$J' = \arg \min_{I \subset \{2,\ldots,\mathcal{N}\}} \left\{ \sum_{j \in I} \lambda^j \,\middle|\, \sum_{j \in I} \lambda^j > 1 - \lambda^1 \right\},$$

and R^1 equals $(1 - \sum_{j \in J'} \lambda^j)$.

By comparing J' to J^{-1}, which satisfies $\sum_{j \in J^{-1}} \lambda^j$ which equals $(1 - L^1)$ which is greater than $(1 - \lambda^1)$, it is clear that R^1 weakly exceeds L^1. The definition of J' above also implies that R^1 is less than λ^1.

Given $\boldsymbol{V}^{-1}$, a realization of valuations for all bidders other than bidder 1, $\tau_q^1(\boldsymbol{V}^{-1})$, $q \in (0, \lambda^1)$ is the minimium value of V^1 such that the efficient allocation for bidder 1 is at least q. According to Ausubel and Cramton, $\tau_q^1(\boldsymbol{V}^{-1})$ is a constant in q on $q \in (R^1, \lambda^1)$. Denote this by the random variable Y^{-1}. Ausubel and Cramton call this $\tau_2^1(\boldsymbol{V}^{-1})$. They also note that for some positive ϵ, which is small, $\tau_q^1(\boldsymbol{V}^{-1})$ is also a constant in $q \in (R^1 - \epsilon, R^1)$. Denote this random variable by Z^{-1}. Ausubel and Cramton call this $\tau_1^1(\boldsymbol{V}^{-1})$.

Consider an alternative bidding strategy for bidder 1 where he bids V^1 for $q \in (0, R^1)$ and bids β weakly less than V^1 for $q \in (R^1, \lambda^1)$. Here β is the choice parameter of the proposed bidding strategy.

Consider $\Pi^1(\beta)$, the expected payoff from this two-step strategy given that the other firms are bidding V^i, for all $i = 2, \ldots, \mathcal{N}$. The goal of the following analysis is to show that

$$\left. \frac{d\Pi^1(\beta)}{d\beta} \right|_{\beta = V^1} < 0,$$

so that bidder 1 can strictly improve expected payoff by bidding β less than V^1 on $q \in (R^1, \lambda^1)$. Consider three regions of the types of competing bidders when calculating $\Pi^1(\beta)$.

Region 1: $\beta > Y^{-1} = \tau_2^1(\boldsymbol{V}^{-1})$. Then bidder 1 wins quantity λ^1, and $\tau_2^1(\boldsymbol{V}^{-1})$ determines the price. The contribution from this region to $\Pi^1(\beta)$ is

$$\lambda^1 \int_0^\beta \left(V^1 - Y^{-1} \right) f_{Y^{-1}}\left(Y^{-1} \right) \, dY^{-1}.$$

Region 2: $Z^{-1} < \beta < Y^{-1}$. Then bidder 1 wins quantity R^1 and β determines the price. The contribution of this region to $\Pi^1(\beta)$ is

$$R^1 \int_0^\beta \int_\beta^1 \left(V^1 - \beta \right) f_{Y^{-1}Z^{-1}}\left(Y^{-1}, Z^{-1} \right) \, dZ^{-1} \, dY^{-1}.$$

Region 3: β is less than Z^{-1}. In this case, whenever V^1 is larger than Z^{-1}, bidder 1 wins quantity R^1 and Z^{-1} determines the price. The contribution of this region to $\Pi^1(\beta)$ is

$$R^1 \int_{\beta}^{V^1} \left(V^1 - Z^{-1}\right) f_{Z^{-1}}\left(Z^{-1}\right)\ dZ^{-1}.$$

Differentiating the sum of these contributions with respect to β and evaluating it at β equals V^1 yields

$$
\left.\frac{d\Pi^1(\beta)}{d\beta}\right|_{\beta=V^1} = -R^1 \int_0^{V^1} \int_{V^1}^1 f_{Y^{-1}Z^{-1}}\left(Y^{-1}, Z^{-1}\right)\ dZ^{-1} dY^{-1}
$$
$$
= -R^1 \Pr\left(Z^{-1} < V^1 < Y^{-1}\right),
$$

where only the second region contributes to the derivative of the expected profit function evaluated at V^1 equal β.

Since bidder 1 strictly gains by bidding β less than V^1, it cannot be an equilibrium for each bidder to bid the symmetric flat-bid function V^i. But, by theorem 5.2.1, bidding V^i is the only candidate for an ex post efficient equilibrium. This yields a contradiction.

The intuition behind Theorem 5.2.2 is that bidders have market power, even under the uniform-pricing rule. If a bidder has a positive probability of influencing price in a situation where the bidder wins a positive quantity, then that bidder has an incentive to shade his bid. Bidder i cannot be pivotal for quantities $q \in \left[0, \lambda^i\right]$, so bidder i bids his expected value on the left subinterval. However, bidder i is pivotal with positive probability for quantities $q \in \left(R^i, \lambda^i\right]$, so bidder i gains by shading his bid on the right subinterval. His marginal gain consists of the quantity at which the bidder becomes pivotal times the probability of his being pivotal.

If λ^is are the same constant λ and $(1/\lambda)$ is an integer, then the bidder only affects price when he wins nothing, so bidding his value is a best response and efficiency is achieved. However, efficiency is the exception rather than the rule.

Using these above results, Ausubel and Cramton found that the ranking between pay-as-bid and uniform-price auctions is ambiguous. Of course, a natural question to ask is; are there other pricing rules? One of the reasons that the uniform-price auction does not have the properties that Friedman conjectured it would is that the price paid by a bidder can be potentially influenced by the actions of that bidder. Can one construct a pricing rule under which a bidder's action will not affect the price he pays, as in the single-object Vickrey auction?

5.2.2 Generalized Vickrey Auction

What is the multi-unit analogue of the Vickrey auction? Well, the generalized Vickrey auction (GVA). Sometimes this mechanism is referred to as a Vickrey–Groves–Clarke mechanism in honor of Theodore Groves and Edward H. Clarke, who contributed to the analysis of this mechanism in their pioneering papers published in *Econometrica* in 1973 and *Public Choice* in 1971, respectively. Within the IPVP, a GVA will result in an efficient allocation. But how does a GVA work?

At a GVA, the M units for sale are allocated to the bidders who have the highest M reported valuations, bids, but the price that each winner pays for the unit he wins does not depend on his report (i.e., his bid for that unit), but rather on the bids of others. Before providing a general description of the algorithm, we first provide a solved example.

Consider the case where four units are for sale, and three bidders are participating at the auction; i.e., M is four and n is three. Suppose that the reported valuations by bidder 1 for the four units is V^1 equal $\{5, 4, 2, 0\}$, while for bidder 2 it is V^2 equal $\{6, 3, 1, 0\}$ and for bidder 3 it is V^3 equal $\{4.5, 2.5, 0, 0\}$. Given these reports, the aggregate-demand vector is $\{6, 5, 4.5, 4, 3, 2.5, 2, 1\}$. Thus, the four units will be allocated to bidders having reported valuations $\{6, 5, 4.5, 4\}$. The list and order of winners is $\{2, 1, 3, 1\}$. The price of the first unit sold will be V_4^{-2} or 2.5, which is the fourth-highest reported valuation, given that the reported valuations of bidder 2 have been eliminated from the aggregate-demand vector, while the price of the second unit sold will be V_4^{-1} or 2.5, and the price of the third unit will be V_4^{-3} or 3, with the price of the last unit being V_3^{-1} or 3. This last price warrants some explanation. In this case, bidder 1 wins the unit, but since he has already won a previous unit, one must use the third-highest of the remaining reported valuations in the aggregate-demand vector to price this unit.

In general, the algorithm for finding the prices paid at a GVA is the following: Let V^i denote the reported ordered valuations of bidder i and denote by V the ordered valuations of all bidders. Denote by V^{-i} the ordered valuations of all bidders, excluding bidder i. At a GVA, the M units are allocated to the bidders with the M highest reported valuations. If he wins ℓ_i units, then the price paid by bidder i for the first unit is the Mth highest reported valuation in V^{-i}, while the price paid by bidder i for the second unit is the $(M-1)^{\text{st}}$ highest reported valuation in V^{-i}, and so forth.

Because the equilibria of auction formats under some models are efficient but difficult to calculate, some researchers have proposed estimating their average behavior by simulating the GVA, which is also efficient but whose equilbrium one can easily calculate.

Value	Bidder A	Bidder B	Bidder C	Bidder D	Bidder E
Unit 1	123	75	125	85	45
Unit 2	113	5	125	65	25
Unit 3	103	3	49	7	5

Table 5.1
Ausubel's (2004) Illustrative Example of Bidder Values

5.2.3 Ausubel Auction

Recently, a new auction format has been proposed by Lawrence M. Ausubel (2004), who has noted that standard auctions generally yield inefficient outcomes. Above, we have seen that this happens within the IPVP, when asymmetries across bidder are present, but it can also happen when the valuations of bidders are dependent. Ausubel has proposed a mechanism that has the outcome features of the GVA, but is an oral, ascending-price auction, where the prices of all units rise simultaneously. The purpose of having simultaneous and observed prices is information release, which is relatively unimportant within the IPVP, but which can be very important in other informational paradigms.

Ausubel has noted that two important theoretical prescriptions from auction theory are: First, the price a bidder pays should be independent of his actions, his bids; and, second, an auction should be structured to maximize the amount of information available to each participant. Clearly, the GVA satisfies the first precept, but, because it is a sealed-bid format, the GVA does not satisfy the second. Ausubel's newly proposed auction format satisfies this second precept.

According to the rules of Ausubel's format, the auctioneer calls a price, bidders respond with quantities, and the process iterates with increasing prices until demand is no greater than supply. A bidder's payment does *not*, however, equal his final quantity times the market-clearing price, but rather, at each price, the auctioneer determines whether, for any bidder i, the aggregate demand of his rivals is less than the supply. If this obtains, then the difference is deemed *clinched* in Ausubel's vocabulary, a term borrowed from baseball. Any units clinched are awarded to bidder i at the clinching price.

Ausubel's mechanism is best illustrated by the example presented in his paper. In this example, five bidders exist—A, B, C, D, and E— while five units are for sale. In Table 5.1, we present the marginal values Ausubel chose for each bidder. In this example, no bidder wants more than three units, so the values for units four and five are zero, and are omitted from the table.

Consider now starting Ausubel's dynamic, ascending-price auction with a price p of ε greater than zero. At this price, all five bidders demand all three units, so let the price rise. As the price rises continuously, each bidder must ask whether, at the current price, he would be willing to purchase one unit at this price. Obviously, the answer to this question is yes, up to the value p equal $(3 + \varepsilon)$ at which price bidder B drops out for that unit. Aggregate demand is now down from 15 to 14, but aggregate supply is five. The price continues to rise with both E dropping his demand for unit three at $(5 + \varepsilon)$ and B dropping his demand for unit two at that price too. At price $(25 + \varepsilon)$, E drops out for unit two, and, at price $(45 + \varepsilon)$, E drops out of the auction totally. Aggregate demand at price 46 is nine, while aggregate supply is still five. Continue this process with bidder C dropping out for unit three at price $(49 + \varepsilon)$. Aggregate demand is eight, but aggregate supply is five.

Now, at a price just over 65 bidder D drops out for unit two, so each bidder demands the following number of units

Price	Bidder A	Bidder B	Bidder C	Bidder D	Bidder E
65	3	1	2	1	0

From bidder A's perspective, his four opponents demand a total of four units, while five are available. Thus, A clinches a unit at price 65. The price continues to rise, with bidder B dropping out of the auction totally at a price just over 75, so each bidder demands the following number of units

Price	Bidder A	Bidder B	Bidder C	Bidder D	Bidder E
75	3	0	2	1	0

Again, A clinches a second unit, but now at price 75. However, bidder C, too, has clinched a unit at 75, leaving only two units. The market finally clears at a price just over 85. At this price, bidders A and C both pay 85 for the last two units.

Price	Bidder A	Bidder B	Bidder C	Bidder D	Bidder E
85	3	0	2	0	0

Note that this mechanism delivers the same prices as the GVA. To wit, if A, B, C, D, and E were to tender bids (valuations) at a GVA within the IPVP, then the aggregate bid vector would be

$$\{125, 125, 123, 113, 103, 85, 75, 65, 49, 45, 25, 7, 5, 5, 3\}$$

with the identity of the winners, in order, being

$$\{C, C, A, A, A\}.$$

Thus, deleting C's bids from the aggregate bid vector would yield

$$\{123, 113, 103, 85, 75, 65, 45, 25, 7, 5, 5, 3\},$$

so C would pay 75 for the first unit, the fifth-highest bid, and 85 for the second unit, the fourth-highest bid. Deleting A's bids from the aggregate bid vector would yield

$$\{125, 125, 85, 75, 65, 49, 45, 25, 7, 5, 5, 3\}$$

so A would pay 65 for the first unit, the fifth-highest bid; 75 for the second unit, the fourth-highest bid; and 85 for the third unit, the third-highest bid.

5.3 Singleton Demand

In a multi-unit auction model, singleton demand is used by Milgrom (2004) to refer to the assumption that each potential bidder demands at most one unit of the good. The singleton-demand assumption delivers Weber's (1983) famous martingale result. To wit, at a sequence of M auctions the expected price of the $(m+1)^{\text{th}}$ unit, given unit m's price P_m is:

$$\mathcal{E}(P_{m+1}|P_m) = P_m.$$

To understand the basic intuition of why bid prices remain the same, on average, at least within the independent private-values paradigm, consider a Milgrom–Weber clock model of an English auction, where each buyer demands at most one unit and there are fewer units M for sale than there are participants n at the auction. Under these assumptions, the winning bid will be constant: Each participant will bid up to his first valuation until the $(n-M)^{\text{th}}$ participants drops out. Then the M remaining participants will withdraw simultaneously. The winning bid will correspond to the $(M+1)^{\text{th}}$-highest valuation, which we denote V_{M+1}. In the next sale, the winner, having satisfied his unit demand, withdraws from the remainder of the auction, so the bidding will stop as the price reaches the Mth next-highest valuation which is again V_{M+1}. Here, there is one fewer participant and one fewer unit for sale, so these two factors exactly offset one another.

5.4 Multi-Unit Demand

Multi-unit demand in multi-unit auction models refers to at least two different assumptions concerning the demand structure of potential bidders: *Nonrandom demand* and *random demand*.

5.4.1 Nonrandom Demand

One compelling model of nonrandom, multi-unit demand has been developed by Brendstrup (2003). Brendstrup assumed an auction at which M identical units are to be sold. He assumed that all $\mathcal{N}$ potential bidders have weakly positive marginal utility for all units of the good for sale so that, in the absence of a reserve price, each potential bidder demands each of the M units. In Brendstrup's symmetric IPVP world, each potential bidder draws his M independent valuations from the cumulative distribution function $F_V(v)$.

5.4.2 Random Demand

Paarsch and Robert (1995) were the first to propose a model of random, multi-unit demand. They considered the case of a seller who wants to sell M units of a homogeneous good. They assumed that there are $\mathcal{N}$ potential bidders who may bid for the units at auction, but that some of these $\mathcal{N}$ potential bidders may not participate at a given auction. In fact, at any given auction, the seller faces a random number of participants N, each having some private values for the lots on sale. The valuation for some participant i takes the form of a vector

$$\boldsymbol{V}^i = \{V_1^i, V_2^i, \ldots, V_{d_i}^i, 0, 0, \ldots\}$$

where V_j^i represents participants i's valuation of his j^{th} unit of the good, and d_i denotes the number of positive valuations for participant i. Thus, the number of elements in this vector represents the number of units that a bidder desires, while valuation V_j^i represents the marginal utility of the jth unit to bidder i. Paarsch and Robert assumed decreasing marginal utility, so $V_1^i \geq V_2^i \geq \cdots \geq V_{d_i}^i > 0$. They also assumed that the number of units demanded was determined according to a Poisson process having intensity parameter λ, so the number of valuations drawn by each potential bidder D has mean λ and probability mass function

$$\Pr(D = d) = \frac{\lambda^d \exp(-\lambda)}{d!} \quad d = 0, 1, \ldots. \tag{5.2}$$

When D is zero, so a bidder demands no units, Paarsch and Robert assumed that he did not attend the auction, signaling that he will not bid. Conversely, all participants present at the auction have at least one positive valuation. Consequently, the number of participants N is distributed binomially with parameters $\mathcal{N}$ and $[1 - \Pr(D = 0)]$ or $[1 - \exp(-\lambda)]$. Thus,

$$\Pr(N = n) = \binom{\mathcal{N}}{n} [1 - \exp(-\lambda)]^n \exp(-\lambda)^{\mathcal{N}-n}. \tag{5.3}$$

Paarsch and Robert also assumed that each valuation V is an independently and identically distributed draw from the cumulative distribution function $F_V(v)$. Thus, for potential buyer i, each of the d_i draws ranked in descending order represents another opportunity, the value of which is the marginal utility associated with an extra unit purchased. The valuations are ranked in descending order to reflect the fact that participants will exploit their most lucrative opportunities first. The highest valuation V_1^i corresponds to the marginal utility accruing to participant i from his first unit, while his j^{th} valuation corresponds to the marginal utility of the jth unit if purchased. The vector $\boldsymbol{V}^i$ and the number of positive valuation d_i are assumed to be the private information of participant i. Paarsch and Robert also assumed that the actual number of participants n, the cumulative distribution function $F_V(v)$, and the intensity parameter of the Poisson process λ are common knowledge.

The state of nature or realization of types can be represented by a vector of descending valuations, which ranks valuations of all n participants for all lots

$$\boldsymbol{V} = \{V_1, V_2, \ldots, V_m, \ldots, V_{\sum_{i=1}^{n} d_i}\}$$

where $V_1 \geq V_2 \geq \ldots \geq V_m \geq \ldots \geq V_{\sum_{i=1}^{n} d_i}$. This is just like the step-function of demand depicted in figure 1.1 of chapter 1. Here, following Paarsch and Robert, V_m denotes the mth highest valuation among all n participants. Under their notation, the expression $V_m = V_2^i$ means that participant i's second highest valuation is the mth highest valuation overall. Finally, let $\boldsymbol{V}_k$ equal $\{V_k^1, V_k^2, \ldots, V_k^n\}$ denote the list for all participants of their individual k^{th} valuations.

In the remaining sections of this chapter, we discuss some empirical applications of auction theory to multi-unit auctions. We begin first with the work of Donald, Paarsch, and Robert (forthcoming), who investigated sequential, multi-unit, clock auctions when potential bidders have random, multi-unit demand within the symmetric IPVP. Subsequently, we study the work Brendstrup and Paarsch (forthcoming) who investigated sequential, multi-unit, clock auctions when potential bidders have nonrandom, multi-unit demand within the asymmetric IPVP.

5.5 Sequential, Clock Auctions: Random Demand

Donald, Paarsch, and Robert (forthcoming) constructed a simple theoretical model of the multi-unit, sequential, Milgrom–Weber clock auction in which potential bidders could have multi-unit demand. Their model was developed to interpret data concerning the outcomes at 37 multi-lot, sequential, English auctions of export permits for timber held between May 1993 and May 1994 in the Krasnoyarsk Region of Russia. These auctions had two important empirical regularities: First, bidders often won more than one lot. Second, different numbers of bidders attended different auctions. In addition, only a small amount of information was recorded; e.g., the reserve price, the number of lots on sale, the number of participants at the auction, the winning bid for each lot sold, and the number of lots won by each participant at the auction.

Donald et al. assumed that the reserve price was known to everyone prior to auction. Although the participants at the auction observed the prices at which their opponents dropped out, as researchers, they assumed they did not. Thus, an asymmetry of information between the decision makers, the participants at the auction, and the researcher exists. They incorporated this reality into their model by ruling out the econometrician's ability to observe dropout prices.

Donald et al. considered a seller seeking to dispose of M units of a homogeneous good through a sequence of M Milgrom–Weber (1982) clock auctions. Specifically, the price of the unit for sale is raised continuously and bidders continuously affirm their participation in the auction by holding down a button or holding up a card. The price rises progressively and, as it does, bidders signal that they are dropping-out of the auction by releasing the button or dropping the card until only one bidder remains; the last active bidder wins the unit for sale and pays the price at which his last opponent dropped out.

Donald et al. assumed that the seller is committed to selling all M units and that the above process is repeated until all M units are sold. In order to avoid carrying around an unobserved state variable, unfulfilled demand, Donald et al. also assumed that the unfulfilled demands of participants at any auction disappear (evaporate) completely after the M units have been sold.

Milgrom and Weber (1982) analyzed the case where only one good is for sale. In this case, at every price, a bidder must ask himself whether he should drop out of or remain in the auction. Because a bidder can always drop out at the next (infinitesimal) higher price, his calculation is myopic. Nevertheless, he must answer the following simple question:

> If all other bidders were to drop out simultaneously at the current price, would I prefer to win the auction or would I prefer to drop out now?

Within the independent, private-values paradigm, a bidder's best strategy is to drop out at his valuation. On the other hand, within the affiliated-values paradigm, a bidder must calculate, at any given price, the expected value of the good on sale—given his own private information, the dropout prices of those who have already withdrawn, and assuming that all remaining bidders were to drop out simultaneously at the current price. In this case, a bidder should drop out when the current price exceeds this expected value.

When two or more identical units of a good are sold sequentially using the above auction format, where each participant may demand more than one unit, the strategic analysis becomes complex. Donald et al. computed a symmetric, perfect-Bayesian equilibrium of such a game. At any auction, they assumed a known number of risk-neutral potential bidders $\mathcal{N}$ who may bid for the M units for sale. They denoted by $\boldsymbol{V}^i$ the vector of ordered valuations $(V_1^i, V_2^i, \ldots, V_M^i)$ for potential bidder i where V_m^i represents bidder i's valuation for the mth unit of the good. Hence, for all i, decreasing marginal utility obtains

$$V_1^i \geq V_2^i \geq \ldots \geq V_M^i.$$

5.5.1 Two-Bidder, Two-Unit Example

Donald et al. illustrated the intuition behind their analysis by considering the case of just two bidders, i and j, who are competing for two identical units that are sold sequentially using a Milgrom–Weber clock auction. Each bidder has private information. For example, for bidder i, it takes the form of the valuation pair (V_1^i, V_2^i). They used backward induction to help them construct their argument. Consider first behavior involving the last unit sold: each bidder will drop out only when the price reaches his valuation for the unit on sale. If i has won the first unit, then he will bid up to V_2^i, his value of having a second unit, and pay V_1^j if he wins. Otherwise, when j wins the first sale, i will bid up to V_1^i and pay V_2^j in order to win. Bidder j will win both units when V_2^j is greater than V_1^i, while bidder i will win both units when V_1^j is less than V_2^i.

Now, at a two-unit auction, when the first unit is for sale, a bidder can wait until the second sale to purchase a unit, so as the price rises that bidder must ask himself the following question:

> If all other active bidders were to drop out simultaneously at the current price, would I prefer to win the current sale at the current price and then try to win a second unit in the next sale, or would I prefer to forgo the opportunity to buy two units and wait for the next sale in order to try to win my first unit?

A bidder must compare the value of winning the first unit at price p plus the expected gain from participating in the second sale having won the first with the expected gain from participating in the second sale having lost the first. Let $b_j(V_1^j, V_2^j)$ denote j's bidding function in the first sale. When the current price is p, bidder i should stay in the auction if

$$\left(V_1^i - p\right) + \mathcal{E}[\max(0, V_2^i - V_1^j) | p = b_j(V_1^j, V_2^j)] \geq$$
$$\mathcal{E}[\max(0, V_1^i - V_2^j) | p = b_j(V_1^j, V_2^j)].$$

Calculating the expected values in the expression above is the difficult part of solving this decision problem because the information contained in the dropout prices depends on the bidding strategies of others and a bidder's strategy depends on the information contained in the dropout prices. Not surprisingly, many equilibria can exist to this two-stage game.[1] However, under the assumption of symmetry, the calculation is simplified. Bidder i should calculate his dropout price p^i assuming active bidder j has the same one; i.e., assuming V_1^j equals V_1^i. Under this assumption, because V_1^j equals V_1^i, which is greater than or equal to V_2^i, bidder i cannot expect to win profitably a second unit if he wins the first sale, while, because V_1^i equals V_1^j, which is weakly less than V_2^j, he could expect to win the next sale if some other active bidder j wins the first sale. Hence,

$$V_1^i - p^i = V_1^i - \mathcal{E}(V_2^j | V_1^j = V_1^i)$$
$$p^i = \mathcal{E}(V_2^j | V_1^j = V_1^i) \leq V_1^i.$$

Bidder i's dropout price is the expected price he will need to pay in order to win the next sale, were he to lose the current sale, assuming V_1^j equals V_1^i. Note that the actual bidding function will depend on the distribution of V_2^j, winner j's second-highest valuation, given V_1^j equals V_1^i.[2] But as long as the assumed distributions are symmetric across bidders, the bidding function will be symmetric (as assumed) and the above will constitute a symmetric, perfect-Bayesian equilibrium.

---

[1] In fact, in his paper on two-stage sequential auctions with multi-unit demand, which builds on the work of Black and de Meza (1992), Katzman (1999) has presented a list of these possible equilibria.

[2] Note that, as in the affiliated private-values paradigm, bids depend on information revealed by the bids of others within the current round of bidding. However, the reason for this dependence is different from that typically encountered with affiliated values. With affiliated values, the gains from winning depend on the private information of others. Here, the gains from winning depend on the willingness of others to buy. In all but the last sale, losing bidders can always win a later sale; the expected price they will need to pay in order to win this later sale will depend on the willingness of others to pay.

5.5.2 Two-Bidder, Three-Unit Example

The above logic can be extended to a sequence of M sales *only* when the distributions of valuations in every sale remain symmetric. In order to highlight this symmetry condition, consider a sequential, three-unit clock auction with two bidders.

Suppose that j has won the first sale, so he enters the game involving the last two sales having valuations (V_2^j, V_3^j), while i enters having valuations (V_1^i, V_2^i). Following the reasoning presented above, the bidding strategies in the second sale would be as follows: bidder i will bid up to $\mathcal{E}(V_3^j | V_2^j = V_1^i)$, while j will drop out at price $\mathcal{E}(V_2^i | V_1^i = V_2^j)$. This would constitute a symmetric equilibrium only when the distribution of V_3^j, given V_2^j, is the same as the distribution of V_2^i, given V_1^i. Hence, a necessary condition is that the distribution of valuations must remain identical across players, regardless of the number of units they have purchased in previous sales; i.e., the distribution of V_{k+1}^i, given V_k^i, must be independent of the indexes i and k.

When this symmetry condition holds, the equilibrium of the three-unit clock auction has a nice recursive structure. Donald et al. exploited this recursive structure. Recall that j will drop out of the second sale, when he has won the first one, at price $\mathcal{E}(V_2^i | V_1^i = V_2^j)$. By the symmetry condition assumed above, this equals $\mathcal{E}(V_3^j | V_2^j)$. Hence, conditional on V_1^j equaling V_1^i, the price i will need to pay in order to win the second sale when j has won the first one, is $\mathcal{E}[\mathcal{E}(V_3^j | V_2^j) | V_1^j = V_1^i]$, which equals $\mathcal{E}(V_3^j | V_1^j = V_1^i)$, so in the first sale, when the price reaches p or $\mathcal{E}(V_3^j | V_1^j = V_1^i)$, conditional on j's having dropped out at price p, i is indifferent between winning at price p and losing to j, but winning the next sale. For lower prices, i will strictly prefer the former and, for higher prices, he will strictly prefer the latter. Dropping out at price p equal $\mathcal{E}(V_3^j | V_1^j = V_1^i)$ forms i's best response when j follows the symmetric strategy. Hence, the equilibrium bidding strategy can be written as an expected value, which turns out be the expected price he would pay were he to wait until the very last round in order to purchase one extra unit.

Donald et al. demonstrated that this result generalizes to the case of $\mathcal{N}$ potential bidders and M units for sale. To guarantee this result, Donald et al. introduced a process that delivered the critical symmetry condition.

5.5.3 Demand-Generation Scheme

In order to solve the auction game, Donald et al. needed to specify the process generating the random vector of decreasing valuations for the ith

potential bidder; i.e., the demand curve $\boldsymbol{V}^i$, which for potential bidder i equals $(V_1^i, V_2^i, \ldots, V_M^i)$.

As mentioned above, they assumed that the number of valuations for participant i, denoted D_i, is random having support in $\{0, 1, 2, \ldots\}$; D_i may be higher or lower than M. In the former case, only the highest M values will matter; in the latter, some values of $\boldsymbol{V}^i$ will be zero. At any auction, they assumed that the number of valuations drawn by each potential bidder is a Poisson random variable having mean λ and probability mass function

$$\Pr(D_i = d) = \frac{\lambda^d \exp(-\lambda)}{d!} \quad d = 0, 1, 2, \ldots$$

When D_i is positive, each of the positive valuations is drawn independently and identically from some twice-differentiable cumulative distribution $F_V(\cdot)$ having support on the interval $[0, \infty)$; these valuations are then ranked in descending order. They also assumed these draws are independent across auctions. Thus, potential bidders are *ex ante* symmetric at a given auction and across auctions through time.

The above stochastic process provided Donald et al. with a useful device to generate aggregate demand because it guaranteed certain properties sufficient to solve the auction game. Note that by ranking the valuations in descending order they brought attention to the fact that participants will exploit their most lucrative opportunities first. Under these assumptions, when D_i is less than M, the valuation vector of the ith participant takes the form of a M-dimensional vector with $(M - D_i)$ zeros of padding, so

$$\boldsymbol{V}^i = (V_1^i, V_2^i, \ldots, V_{D_i}^i, 0, \ldots, 0)$$

where $V_1^i \geq V_2^i \geq \ldots \geq V_{D_i}^i \geq V_{D_i+1}^i = 0$. Note, too, that the aggregate and individual demands are independent of M, the quantity supplied.

For all j less than k and $i \in \mathbf{N}$, where $\mathbf{N}$ denotes the set of participants, the function $G(y|x)$, which denotes $\Pr(V_k^i \leq y|V_j^i = x)$, is strictly decreasing in x for all y less than x when $F_V(y)$ is positive. This reflects the fact that order statistics are correlated: if the jth-highest valuation of a bidder is high, then his k^{th}-highest valuation, where k exceeds j, is more likely to be high than low.

One of the realities when bringing theoretical models of bidding to data is that some of the $\mathcal{N}$ potential bidders do not participate at any given auction. At first-price, sealed-bid auctions non-participation does not typically introduce a problem in deriving the data-generating process of either the observed bids or the winning bid because the decision rule depends on the number of potential bidders $\mathcal{N}$, not the number of participants n. But at English auctions the number of participants n is critical to the price determination process. Having a random number of participants is one way to admit differential participation across auctions.

In the model of Donald et al., the number of participants at each auction is random. Specifically, when a potential bidder demands nothing, so D_i is zero, they assumed that he does not attend the auction, hence signaling he will not bid. Conversely, they assumed that all participants present at the auction have at least one positive valuation. Because, at any auction, the number of positive valuations drawn by each potential bidder D_i follows a Poisson process, the number of participants N (those potential bidders having D_i greater than zero) will be random and is distributed binomially with parameters $\mathcal{N}$ and $[1 - \Pr(D = 0)]$ or $[1 - \exp(-\lambda)]$, so its probability mass function is that given in equation (5.3) above.

Another way to admit differential participation across auctions would have been to introduce a reserve price. However, in the auction game Donald et al. studied, the presence of a reserve price, while sufficient to guarantee differential participation, does not provide enough probabilistic structure to solve the game.

Finally, note that the distribution of types have a structure that guarantees symmetry across the game. This condition follows from the Poisson assumption concerning D_i.

5.5.4 Solving the Auction Game

Donald et al. constructed an equilibrium of the auction game induced by the sequence of M sales. They assumed that the vector $\boldsymbol{V}^i$ and the number of positive valuations D_i are the private information of participant i. The cumulative distribution function $F_V(\cdot)$, the intensity parameter of the Poisson process λ, and the number of bidders n present are assumed common knowledge.

A bidding strategy at these sales specifies a stopping rule that indicates at what price a participant should withdraw from the current sale. Such a stopping rule can be contingent on the entire history of previous sales as well as the current one; i.e., contingent on the prices at which other participants have withdrawn, previous winning bids, private information concerning the valuation attached to each unit purchased, the information shared by all participants, and so on. Hence, the strategies may be quite complex not just because they will be history dependent but because each participant may want to manipulate his actions to influence the future bidding behavior of others. Donald et al. focused on an equilibrium with a relatively simple structure. This equilibrium was a direct generalization of the two-bidder, three-unit example presented above.

Before stating the theorem, introduce some notation: let ℓ_i denote the number of units already purchased by bidder i and collect these for all n bidders in $\mathbf{L}$, $\{\ell_1, \ell_2, \ldots, \ell_n\}$. Thus, $\mathbf{L}$ summarizes the past history of winners at the auction. Whenever i has purchased ℓ_i units, his valuation of the next unit is $V_{1+\ell_i}^i$, which we shall refer as i's next-highest valuation. The next-highest valuation overall is given by $\max_j\{V_{1+\ell_j}^j\}$. A sale will be deemed efficient if its winner is the bidder with the highest next valuation overall. When all previous rounds were efficient and some bidder h has previously won a unit, then $V_{\ell_h}^h \geq \max_j\{V_{1+\ell_j}^j\}$. We denote by V_k^{-i} the kth-highest valuation among all valuations of i's opponents. In particular, when q_i denotes $\sum_{j\neq i}\ell_j$, the number of units already purchased by i's opponents, we have $V_{q_i}^{-i} \geq V_{1+q_i}^{-i}$ which equals $\max_{j\neq i}\{V_{1+\ell_j}^j\}$.

Donald et al. considered a bidding strategy for each bidder i that depends on $\mathbf{L}$ and $V_{1+\ell_i}^i$ as well as the observed bidding behavior of others in the current sale.

> **Theorem 5.5.1:** For every sale of a M-unit auction, bidder i remains active until all other bidders stop, or until the price equals or exceeds
>
> $$\mathcal{E}(V_{M-\ell_i}^{-i} | V_{1+q_i}^{-i} = V_{1+\ell_j}^j = V_{1+\ell_i}^i, \forall\, j \in \mathbf{R}; V_{1+\ell_k}^h = v^h, \forall\, h \in \mathbf{S}) =$$
>
> $$\mathcal{E}(V_{M-q_i-\ell_i}^{-i} | V_1^{-i} = V_1^j = V_{1+\ell_i}^i, \forall\, j \in \mathbf{R}; V_1^h = v^h, \forall\, h \in \mathbf{S})$$
>
> $$(5.4)$$
>
> where $\mathbf{R}$ denotes the subset of bidders still active, $\mathbf{S}$ denotes the subset of bidders that have withdrawn for the current sale, and v^h denotes the valuations for all bidders in $h \in \mathbf{S}$ that is consistent with the price at which h has withdrawn in the current sale and the equilibrium strategy.

Recall that a bidder's decision to drop out is always based on the conjecture that all currently active bidders will simultaneously drop out at the current price. As the price converges to i's equilibrium dropout price, i's conjecture will converge, under the assumption of symmetry, to the conjecture that all remaining bidders have the same next-highest valuation as his; i.e.,

$$V_{1+\ell_j}^j = V_{1+\ell_i}^i, \forall\, j \in \mathbf{R}.$$

Hence, i's conjecture will be that

$$V_{1+q_i}^{-i} = \max_{j\neq i}\{V_{1+\ell_j}^j\} = V_{1+\ell_i}^i.$$

In the last round, when only one unit remains to be sold, so $(M - \ell_i)$ equals $(1 + \sum_{j \neq i} \ell_j)$ or $(1 + q)$, Theorem 5.5.1 prescribes that bidder i drops out at $\mathcal{E}(V_{M-\ell_i}^{-i} | V_{1+q}^{-i} = V_{1+\ell_i}^i)$, which equals $V_{1+\ell_i}^i$, his next-highest valuation. Thus, the prescribed strategy indeed forms an equilibrium in the last round.[3] Note that no information from past auctions, other than the number of units won by others and left to be sold, enters the current bidding function. The basic idea is that all information obtained from previous sales is superfluous. Along the equilibrium path, the price at which inactive bidders have dropped out must be consistent with the previous play and the equilibrium. Hence, information from previous rounds is redundant. For active players, regardless of what occurred in the past, a bidder should always base his dropout decision on the conjecture that all of his opponents will drop out simultaneously at the current price. From a strategic point of view, the fact that no information from past sales enters the current bidding function is important. No one can influence future bidding by deviating—dropping-out earlier or staying longer than the equilibrium. Implicit in this solution is the property that bid manipulation designed only to signal is ignored. Along the equilibrium path, it turns out to be just the same as if he were to use all the previously available information.

Note that the value $V_{M-\ell_i}^{-i}$ corresponds to the price i would need to pay in order to get an extra unit were he to wait until the very last sale to purchase it. Theorem 5.5.1 states that bidder i should drop out at a price that equals the expected value of $V_{M-\ell_i}^{-i}$, conditional on all active bidders' dropping-out the same price and on the dropout prices of inactive bidders in the current sale.

5.5.5 Properties of the Equilibrium

The symmetric, perfect-Bayesian equilibrium has several important and interesting properties listed in the following theorem.

---

[3] When the number of bidders still active in the current sale exceeds the number of units left to be sold t, i conjectures that

$$V_{M-\ell_i}^{-i} = V_{t+q}^{-i} = V_{r+q}^{-i} = \max_{j \neq i}\{V_{1+\ell_j}^j\} = V_{1+\ell_i}^i,$$

and

$$\mathcal{E}(V_{T-\ell_i}^{-i} | V_{1+q}^{-i} = V_{1+\ell_i}^i) = V_{1+\ell_i}^i.$$

Bidder i will bid up to his next-highest valuation.

Theorem 5.5.2: Given the above structure,

(i) Bids are strictly monotonic and symmetric functions of next-highest valuations, $V_{1+\ell_i}^i$.

(ii) The allocation induced by the equilibrium is efficient; i.e., the M units are allocated to the buyers with the highest valuations.

(iii) If all other participants follow their equilibrium strategies, then in order to win a sale, participant i must pay the price

$$\mathcal{E}(V_{M-\ell_i}^{-i}|\Omega_m)$$

where Ω_m denotes the information available to participants at the end of sale m.

Note that efficiency is not an intrinsic property of the sequential auction game. The efficiency result depends on crucial assumptions Donald et al. have made. Their assumptions ensure that those who have won previous sales behave in the remaining sales like the others. Without the above assumptions, computing the equilibrium would have been extremely difficult, perhaps impossible. This is why, in most game-theoretic papers concerning sequential auctions, researchers have limited their attention to simple cases—such as two-unit, two-player examples—or to cases where bidders have singleton demand.

Note, most importantly, the expected price paid by buyer i for his $(\ell_i + 1)^{\text{th}}$ unit equals the expected value of $V_{M-\ell_i}^{-i}$, the $(M - \ell_i)^{\text{th}}$-highest valuations among all valuations of the other participants. The result in Theorem 5.5.2 (iii) is reminiscent of the dominant-strategy implementation of the efficient allocation, the generalized Vickrey auction for multi-unit demand. Consider the following mechanism: First, each participant i is asked to reveal his willingness to pay $\boldsymbol{V}^i$ equal to $\{V_1^i, V_2^i, \ldots, V_{D_i}^i, 0, \ldots, 0\}$; second, the M units are allocated to the participants with the M highest (revealed) values; and third, each winner i pays V_M^{-i} for his first unit, V_{M-1}^{-i} for his second unit, and $V_{M-\ell}^{-i}$ for his $(\ell + 1)^{\text{st}}$ unit, and so forth. One can verify that it is a dominant strategy for each participant to reveal his actual valuations and that it implements the efficient allocation.[4] Theorem 5.5.2 (iii) implies that the expected price paid by each winner in the sequential, clock auction equals the expected price he would pay in the above mechanism.

---

[4] Let V_ℓ denote the ℓth-highest value announced by some participant i. If $V_{\ell-1}$ is less than $V_{M-\ell+2}^{-i}$, then for all announced V_ℓ less than $V_{\ell-1}$, i will not receive the ℓth unit, so i cannot gain by mis-reporting V_ℓ^i. Now, suppose $V_{\ell-1}$ weakly exceeds $V_{T-\ell+2}^{-i}$, so that i receives at least $(\ell - 1)$ units. Bidder i cannot gain by overstating his ℓ^{th} value because this will not affect the prices he will pay for any of his units, and it could only make a difference if V_ℓ weakly exceeds

Hence, Donald et al. argued that they could use the dominant-strategy implementation of the efficient allocation in conjunction with simulation methods to calculate the expected winning bid for the sale of the mth unit. Note that the vector of winning bids at the sequential, clock auction need not correspond to the vector of generalized-Vickrey prices; however, on average, they are equal.

Donald et al. demonstrated that their theoretical results could be easily extended to admit a binding reserve price r which is the same for each unit on sale at a given auction. A potential bidder will participate in a sale if and only if his next highest valuation is higher than the reserve price; i.e., when $V^i_{1+\ell_i}$ weakly exceeds r. If $V^i_{1+\ell_i}$ does exceed r, then a participant should withdraw from the auction when the current price reaches:

$$\mathcal{E}[\max(r, V^{-i}_{M-\ell_i})|V^{-i}_{1+q_i} = V^j_{1+\ell_j} = V^i_{1+\ell_i}, \forall\, j \in \mathbf{R}; V^h_{1+\ell_k} = v^h, \forall\, h \in \mathbf{S}].$$

Note that $\max(r, V^{-i}_{M-\ell_i})$ corresponds to the price bidder i would need to pay were he to wait until the very last period to win an extra unit. As before, the optimal strategy is for a participant to bid up to the expected value of that price given the dropping prices of inactive bidders and under the conjecture that active bidders simultaneously drop out.

Note, too, that a potential bidder will not participate at the auction when none of his valuations exceeds the reserve price r; the probability of this event is then $(1 - \exp\{-\lambda[1 - F(r)]\})$. The number of valuations above r now follows a Poisson process with mean $\lambda[1 - F(r)]$. The probability mass function of N is then given by

$$\Pr(N = n) = \binom{\mathcal{N}}{n}(1 - \exp\{-\lambda[1 - F(r)]\})^n \exp\{-\lambda[1 - F(r)]\}^{\mathcal{N}-n}.$$

5.5.6 Estimating the Model

Because the equilibrium of their model is difficult–some might say impossible–to calculate, Donald et al. proposed to estimate its average behavior by simulating another auction format, the GVA, which is also efficient, so the expected price will be the same, but whose equilibrium we can easily calculate. As we have seen in chapter 4, in single-object auctions, such a strategy was first proposed by Laffont, Ossard, and

---

$V^{-i}_{M-\ell+1}$, which is greater than V^i_ℓ since he will be awarded the ℓth unit and he will pay a price above his valuation for this unit. Similarly, i cannot gain by understating his ℓ^{th} value since i may only lose the chance of purchasing the ℓth unit at a price below his valuation. This argument applies for all ℓ, and all vectors $\mathbf{V}^{-i}$, so i can never gain by mis-reporting his private information.

Vuong (1995), who used the revenue equivalence of Dutch and Vickrey auctions within the IPVP when potential bidders are risk neutral.

In order to simulate on a computer, pseudo-random numbers from the distribution $F_V(\cdot)$ are required. Without an explicit assumption concerning $F_V(\cdot)$, generating pseudo-random numbers is impossible. Thus, in addition to assuming that D_i follows the Poisson law with mean λ, Donald et al. also assumed that $F_V(v)$ followed the Weibull law having parameters α_1 and α_2, so

$$F(v; \alpha_1, \alpha_2) = [1 - \exp(-\alpha_1 v^{\alpha_2})] \quad \alpha_1 > 0, \ \alpha_2 > 0.$$

The theory of Donald et al. delivers the first moment of both the participation equation for the auction (the mean of a binomial random variable) and the winning price for the sale of unit m at the auction (the average winning price for unit m at a generalized Vickrey auction). Thus, a natural strategy for estimating the unknown parameters λ as well as α_1 and α_2, which we collect in $(\lambda, \alpha_1, \alpha_2)$ and denote by the unknown vector $\boldsymbol{\theta}$, would be to choose some estimate $\tilde{\boldsymbol{\theta}}$ that minimizes the distance between the observed data and the mean of the processes evaluated at $\tilde{\boldsymbol{\theta}}$. But how should the distance be chosen? Laffont et al. chose the sum of squared residuals, adjusted appropriately for pre-estimation error when the mean function of the winning bid is unknown and must be estimated using simulation methods. Donald et al. proposed a strategy based on the generalized method-of-moments (GMM).

Now, the mean of participation equation is

$$\mathcal{E}(N; r, \mathcal{N}, \lambda) = \mu_0(r, \mathcal{N}, \lambda) = \mathcal{N}\left(1 - \exp\{-\lambda[1 - F(r)]\}\right)$$

for some reserve price r: only those bidders who demand at least one unit whose valuation exceeds r show up. Under the Weibull assumption,

$$\mu_0(r, \mathcal{N}, \boldsymbol{\theta}) = \mathcal{N}\{1 - \exp[-\lambda \exp(-\alpha_1 r^{\alpha_2})]\}.$$

For a sample of T observations, in which there are up to $\hat{M}$ units, the population moment conditions are as follows:

$$\mathcal{E}(U_{0t}|r_t) = \mathcal{E}[N_t - \mu_0(r_t, \boldsymbol{\theta}^0)|r_t] = 0$$

$$\mathcal{E}(U_{mt}|\Omega_{mt}) = \mathcal{E}[P_m^t - \mu_m(\boldsymbol{z}_t, P_{m-1}^j, P_{m-2}^t, \ldots, \boldsymbol{\theta}^0)|\Omega_{mt}] = 0$$

$$\text{for} \quad m = 1, \ldots, M_t$$

where Ω_{mt} is the information set at sale m in the auction and includes $\boldsymbol{z}_t$, which equals $(r_t, M_t, n_t)^\top$ plus, at the very least, all winning prices for prior lots, the P_{m-k}^js. The U_{mt}s have the obvious interpretation of residuals. Here, $\boldsymbol{\theta}^0$ denotes the true, but unknown, value of the parameter vector $\boldsymbol{\theta}$ that Donald et al. sought to estimate. Donald et al. constructed instrument sets for each residual

$$\boldsymbol{X}_{0t} = r_t$$

$$\boldsymbol{X}_{1t} = (r_t, M_t, n_t)^\top = \boldsymbol{z}_t$$

$$\boldsymbol{X}_{2t} = (\boldsymbol{z}_t, P_1^t)^\top$$

$$\vdots$$

$$\boldsymbol{X}_{M_t t} = (\boldsymbol{z}_t, P_1^t, \ldots, P_{M_t - 1}^t)^\top,$$

so that

$$\mathcal{E}(U_{mt} | \boldsymbol{X}_{mt}) = 0$$

because $\boldsymbol{X}_{mt} \subset \Omega_{mt}$. Assuming that μ_m can be approximated arbitrarily well by driving up the number of simulations, so one can get the residuals as a function of data and parameters,

$$U_{0t}(\boldsymbol{\theta}) = N_t - \mu_0(r_t, \boldsymbol{\theta})$$

$$U_{mt}(\boldsymbol{\theta}) = P_m^t - \mu_m(\boldsymbol{z}_t, P_{m-1}^t, P_{m-2}^t, \ldots, \boldsymbol{\theta}).$$

Donald et al. formed the moment functions

$$\boldsymbol{g}_{0t}(\boldsymbol{\theta}) = \boldsymbol{X}_{0j} U_{0t}(\boldsymbol{\theta})$$

$$\boldsymbol{g}_{mt}(\boldsymbol{\theta}) = \begin{cases} \boldsymbol{X}_{mt} U_{mt}(\boldsymbol{\theta}) & \text{if } m \leq M_t \\ 0 & \text{otherwise.} \end{cases}$$

They introduced $\hat{M}$ to be $\max(M_1, \ldots, M_T)$ and then defined the average moment functions as

$$\bar{\boldsymbol{g}}_0(\boldsymbol{\theta}) = \frac{1}{T} \sum_{t=1}^J \boldsymbol{g}_{0t}(\boldsymbol{\theta})$$

$$\bar{\boldsymbol{g}}_m(\boldsymbol{\theta}) = \frac{1}{T} \sum_{t=1}^J \boldsymbol{g}_{mt}(\boldsymbol{\theta}) \quad \text{for} \quad m = 1, \ldots, \hat{M}.$$

Note that some of the terms in the latter will be zero if, for any auction t, there are not $\hat{M}$ units for sale. The standard way to define $\tilde{\boldsymbol{\theta}}$, the GMM estimator of $\boldsymbol{\theta}^0$ is as

$$\tilde{\boldsymbol{\theta}} = \underset{<\boldsymbol{\theta}>}{\operatorname{argmin}} \ \bar{\boldsymbol{g}}(\boldsymbol{\theta})^\top \mathbf{W} \bar{\boldsymbol{g}}(\boldsymbol{\theta})$$

where

$$\bar{\boldsymbol{g}}(\boldsymbol{\theta}) = [\bar{\boldsymbol{g}}_0(\boldsymbol{\theta})^\top, \bar{\boldsymbol{g}}_1(\boldsymbol{\theta})^\top, \dots, \bar{\boldsymbol{g}}_{\hat{T}}(\boldsymbol{\theta})^\top]^\top$$

and $\mathbf{W}$ is the weighting matrix. In its most general form, many moment conditions will exist, so $\mathbf{W}$ will be large. However, the sub-martingale structure of the equilibrium and the assumed independence across auctions simplifies matters considerably. In particular, the optimal weighting matrix will be the inverse of the variance-covariance matrix of $\sqrt{T}\bar{\boldsymbol{g}}(\boldsymbol{\theta})$. In the case of Donald et al., independence across auctions implies that

$$\mathcal{V}[\sqrt{T}\bar{\boldsymbol{g}}(\boldsymbol{\theta})] = \frac{1}{T}\sum_{t=1}^{T}\mathcal{E}[\boldsymbol{g}_j(\boldsymbol{\theta})\boldsymbol{g}_j(\boldsymbol{\theta})^\top]$$

$$= \frac{1}{T}\sum_{t=1}^{T}\mathbf{C}_j = \bar{\mathbf{C}}.$$

To compute the variances and covariances, Donald et al. did the following: First, they considered the covariances. Note that the structure above implies that

$$\boldsymbol{X}_{0t} \subset \boldsymbol{X}_{mt} \quad \text{for} \quad m = 1, \dots, M_t$$

and U_{0t} is known, given $\boldsymbol{X}_{mt}$ for $m = 1, \dots, M_t$. Thus,

$$\mathcal{E}[\bar{g}_{0t}(\boldsymbol{\theta}^0)\bar{g}_{mt\ell}(\boldsymbol{\theta}^0)] = 0.$$

For the other covariances, it is known that when m_1 is less than m_2,

$$\boldsymbol{X}_{m_1t} \subset \boldsymbol{X}_{m_2t} \quad \text{for} \quad m = 1, \dots, M_t$$

and U_{m_1t} is known, given $\boldsymbol{X}_{m_2t}$ for $m = 1, \dots, M_t$. Thus,

$$\mathcal{E}[g_{m_1tk}(\boldsymbol{\theta}^0)g_{m_2t\ell}(\boldsymbol{\theta}^0)] = 0,$$

so $\mathbf{W}$ is block diagonal with blocks given by

$$\mathbf{W}_0 = \mathcal{E}[\boldsymbol{g}_{0t}(\boldsymbol{\theta})\boldsymbol{g}_{0t}(\boldsymbol{\theta})^\top]^{-1}$$

$$\mathbf{W}_t = \mathcal{E}[\boldsymbol{g}_{mt}(\boldsymbol{\theta})\boldsymbol{g}_{tt}(\boldsymbol{\theta})^\top]^{-1}.$$

One can estimate these in the usual way by taking sample averages of the moment functions estimated with an initial consistent estimate of $\boldsymbol{\theta}^0$. Denote these by $\hat{\mathbf{W}}_m$, so

$$\tilde{\boldsymbol{\theta}} = \operatorname*{argmin}_{<\boldsymbol{\theta}>} \sum_{m=0}^{\hat{M}} \bar{\boldsymbol{g}}_m(\boldsymbol{\theta})^\top \hat{\mathbf{W}}_m \bar{\boldsymbol{g}}_m(\boldsymbol{\theta}).$$

One practical problem with using averages is that, for some auctions, only one observation may exist, so it is impossible to create a full-rank weight matrix. Also, in some cases, the optimal weighting matrix is ill-conditioned. In such cases, to avoid numerical problems, Donald et al. recommended substituting the identity matrix of the appropriate dimension.

Of course, $\mu_m(\cdot)$ is unknown in closed-form, but one can form an estimate of it by simulating the average winning bids at a generalized Vickrey auction to get $\hat{\mu}_m(\cdot)$ as was discussed earlier in the chapter. Note, too, that the simulation error is orthogonal to the instruments, so unlike in Laffont et al., Donald et al. do not need to adjust the objective function.

To undertake inference, two different options are available—first-order asymptotic methods and bootstrap resampling methods. Because Donald et al. had only 37 auctions, they chose to use bootstrap methods to calculate the standard errors of their parameter estimates.

5.6 Sequential, Clock Auctions: Nonrandom Demand

Brendstrup and Paarsch (forthcoming) considered a sequential, English auction at which M identical units were to be sold. As in Brendstrup (2003), they referred to the sale of a specific unit as a *stage* of the auction and assumed that all $\mathcal{N}(\geq 2)$ potential bidders have weakly positive marginal utility for all units of the good for sale. Thus, in the absence of a reserve price, each potential bidder demanded each of the M units. To admit full generality, Brendstrup and Paarsch allowed a potential bidder to be from one of J different classes where a potential bidder of class j draws his M independent valuations from the cumulative distribution function $F_j(v)$. They assumed that J was less than or equal to $\mathcal{N}$, but (to admit full generality) we shall make J and $\mathcal{N}$ the same.

Brendstrup and Paarsch also used the Milgrom–Weber clock model to describe the price at a multi-unit, sequential, English auction. Specifically, in the first stage, the clock is set initially at zero and then allowed to rise continuously, with bidders signaling their exit from this stage of the auction. When all but one of the bidders have dropped out, the remaining bidder is the winner and the price he pays is the last bid his last opponent was willing to pay. After the first stage of the auction, the price is reset to its reserve and the second unit is sold using the same clock mechanism. The auctioneer proceeds until all M units have been sold.

Rather than solving for the equilibrium of the entire M-stage sequential game of incomplete information, as Donald, Paarsch, and

Robert (forthcoming) did, following Brendstrup (2003), Brendstrup and Paarsch were content to focus on only the last stage of the game. They used the fact that, within the IPVP, it is a dominant strategy for each bidder (except the winner, of course), to bid his highest remaining valuation for the last unit on sale. In this stage of the auction, this strategy is unique, unlike the equilibrium bidding strategy for the entire auction which may not be. Moreover, this *last-unit* strategy is less informationally demanding than some other identification strategies proposed in the literature; e.g., Donald et al. needed to assume that bidders observe the dropout prices of their opponents (also known as *open exit*). The analysis of Brendstrup and Paarsch carries through when bidders do not observe the dropout prices of nonwinners other than the last active opponent of the winner (also known as *closed exit*).

Previous authors, such as Austin and Katzman (2002), have noted this last-unit result, but none of these authors derived the exact distribution of the winning bid in the last stage of the auction. What complicates matters is that, even if the potential bidders enter the auction symmetrically, by stage m of the auction, the distributions of remaining valuations will be asymmetric. Of course, when the potential bidders start out asymmetrically, these asymmetries are potentially magnified or diminished, depending on how the sequential auction has proceeded. Empirically, a strategy to disentangle these effects is needed. That was the contribution of Brendstrup and Paarsch (forthcoming).

To simplify notation, rank the valuations of a potential bidder, from highest to lowest. Thus, for potential bidder i who is of class j, denote the highest valuation by v_1^i and the lowest by v_M^i. Brendstrup and Paarsch assumed that v_1^i represented potential bidder i's marginal utility for the first unit won, v_2^i the marginal utility of the next unit won, and so forth. It is important to note that once a bidder's valuations are ranked, they become order statistics of the parent distribution F_j and are neither independent nor identically distributed. In fact, from appendix 2, we know that the marginal cumulative distribution function of the ℓth largest order statistic from a sample of M has the following form:

$$F_{(\ell:M)}^j(v_\ell) = \frac{M!}{(M-\ell)!(\ell-1)!} \int_0^{F_j(v_\ell)} u^{M-\ell}(1-u)^{\ell-1} \, du.$$

The above can be interpreted as the cumulative distribution function of the marginal utility of a class j bidder for the ℓth unit of the good when M are available.

Brendstrup and Paarsch assumed that a bidder will want to fulfill his most valuable opportunities first. Hence, the first unit he wins will correspond to the highest realization, the second to the second-highest realization, and so forth. Since each bidder values all units, a nonwinner of any stage realizes that he cannot win all units. Therefore, the lowest realizations of his valuations become irrelevant.

Determining the joint distribution of equilibrium winning bids at all stages of the auction game is computationally difficult, some might say impossible. But, within the IPVP, in the last stage of the auction, it is possible to use the standard dominance argument of English auctions to argue that the winning bid will be the second highest of the remaining valuations for this final unit.

As outlined in chapter 3, we know that the probability density function of the second-highest order statistic for $\mathcal{N}$ independent draws, each from a different type of distribution, has the following form:

$$g_{(2:\mathcal{N})}(y|\boldsymbol{F},\boldsymbol{w}) =$$

$$\frac{1}{(\mathcal{N}-2)!}\operatorname{Perm}\begin{pmatrix} F_{\mathbf{type}(1)}(y|w_1,M) & \cdots & F_{\mathbf{type}(\mathcal{N})}(y|w_{\mathcal{N}},M) \\ \vdots & \ddots & \vdots \\ F_{\mathbf{type}(1)}(y|w_1,M) & \cdots & F_{\mathbf{type}(\mathcal{N})}(y|w_{\mathcal{N}},M) \\ f_{\mathbf{type}(1)}(y|w_1,M) & \cdots & f_{\mathbf{type}(\mathcal{N})}(y|w_{\mathcal{N}},M) \\ [1-F_{\mathbf{type}(1)}(y|w_1,M)] & \cdots & [1-F_{\mathbf{type}(\mathcal{N})}(y|w_{\mathcal{N}},M)] \end{pmatrix}.$$

In this case, the generic element of the above matrix $F_{\mathbf{type}(i)}(y|w_i,M)$ depends not just on the parent class distribution from which bidder i's valuations were initially drawn $F_j(y)$, but also on total supply M as well as how many units that bidder has won in the earlier stages of the auction w_i.

To illustrate, suppose that bidder i is of class j and has won w_i units in the earlier stages of an auction for which M units were for sale. The cumulative distribution function of his highest remaining valuation will then be

$$F_{\mathbf{type}(i)}(y|w_i,M) =$$

$$\frac{M!}{(M-w_i-1)!w_i!}\int_0^{F_j(y)} u^{M-w_i-1}(1-u)^{w_i}\,du. \tag{5.5}$$

Of course, recovering the probability density function simply involves differentiating the above cumulative distribution function to get

$$f_{\mathbf{type}(i)}(y|w_i,M) = \frac{M!}{(M-w_i-1)!w_i!}F_j(y)^{M-w_i-1}[1-F_j(y)]^{w_i}f_j(y).$$

In the definition of $g_{(2:\mathcal{N})}$ above, $\boldsymbol{w}$ denotes an $(\mathcal{N} \times 1)$ vector summarizing the number of units won in the earlier stages of the auction by each bidder where $\sum_{i=1}^{\mathcal{N}} w_i$ equals $(M-1)$. Brendstrup and Paarsch assumed that $\boldsymbol{w}$ is observed by the researcher.

5.6.1 Nonparametric Identification

In this subsection, we show that the logic Brendstrup and Paarsch used to demonstrate nonparametric identification for single-object English auctions (section 8 of chapter 3) can be applied to the last unit sold at the multi-unit auction. However, one must be careful when comparing last-unit auctions as they will typically differ in the number of units won in earlier stages of the auctions by different classes of bidders. Brendstrup and Paarsch referred to the vector $\boldsymbol{w}$ that tabulates the number of units won by each bidder in the $(M-1)$ earlier stages of the auction as the *state* of the auction.[5] Note that when n is three and M is two, the states are

$$(1 \quad 0 \quad 0), (0 \quad 1 \quad 0), \text{ and } (0 \quad 0 \quad 1),$$

while when n is three and M is three, the states are

$$(1 \quad 1 \quad 0), (0 \quad 1 \quad 1), \text{ and } (1 \quad 0 \quad 1)$$

as well as

$$(2 \quad 0 \quad 0), (0 \quad 2 \quad 0), \text{ and } (0 \quad 0 \quad 2).$$

Obviously, the curse of dimensionality could plague an empirical worker as the total number of states can be potentially quite large relative to the total number of observations in a sample. Be that as it may, identification is done in terms of population quantities, and in the population all combinations of the $\boldsymbol{w}$s will be observed. Thus, Brendstrup and Paarsch demonstrated identification for one $\boldsymbol{w}$.

To begin, augment the notation of chapter 3. Let $G^0_{(2:\mathcal{N})}(y,i|\boldsymbol{w})$ denote the true population cumulative distribution function of the winning bid in the last stage of an auction won by bidder i when the state

---

[5] It is unnecessary to include M in the state vector as $(1+\sum_{i=1}^{\mathcal{N}} w_i)$ equals M. To wit, $\boldsymbol{w}$ is sufficient for M.

vector is $\boldsymbol{w}$. Now

$$G^0_{(2:\mathcal{N})}(y,1|\boldsymbol{w}) = [1 - F^0_{\mathsf{type}(1)}(y|w_1, M)] \prod_{i=2}^{n} F^0_{\mathsf{type}(i)}(y|w_i, M) +$$

$$\int_0^y \prod_{i=2}^{\mathcal{N}} F^0_{\mathsf{type}(i)}(u|w_i, M) \, dF^0_{\mathsf{type}(1)}(u|w_1, M)$$

$$G^0_{(2:\mathcal{N})}(y,2|\boldsymbol{w}) = [1 - F^0_{\mathsf{type}(2)}(y|w_2, M)] \prod_{i \neq 2} F^0_{\mathsf{type}(i)}(y|w_i, M) +$$

$$\int_0^y \prod_{i \neq 2} F^0_{\mathsf{type}(i)}(u|w_i, M) \, dF^0_{\mathsf{type}(2)}(u|w_2, M)$$

$$\vdots \qquad \qquad \vdots$$

$$G^0_{(2:\mathcal{N})}(y,\mathcal{N}|\boldsymbol{w}) = [1 - F^0_{\mathsf{type}(\mathcal{N})}(y|w_\mathcal{N}, M)] \prod_{i=1}^{\mathcal{N}-1} F^0_{\mathsf{type}(i)}(y|w_i, m) +$$

$$\int_0^y \prod_{i=1}^{\mathcal{N}-1} F^0_{\mathsf{type}(i)}(u|w_i, M) \, dF^0_{\mathsf{type}(\mathcal{N})}(u|w_\mathcal{N}, M)$$

which reduces to

$$\prod_{j \neq i} F^0_{\mathsf{type}(j)}(y|w_j, M) = \int_0^y [1 - F^0_{\mathsf{type}(i)}(y|w_i, M)]^{-1} \, dG^0_{(2:\mathcal{N})}(u, i|\boldsymbol{w})$$
$$i = 1, \ldots, \mathcal{N}.$$

Collecting the $F^0_{\mathsf{type}(i)}(y|w_i, M)$s in $\boldsymbol{F}^0_{\mathsf{type}}(y|\boldsymbol{w})$ and the $G^0_{(2:\mathcal{N})}(y,i|\boldsymbol{w})$s in $\boldsymbol{G}^0(y|\boldsymbol{w})$ and using results from chapter 3, we can write this as

$$\boldsymbol{F}^0_{\mathsf{type}}(y|\boldsymbol{w}) =$$
$$\exp\left\{ \mathbf{A}^{-1} \log\left[\mathrm{diag}\left(\int_0^y \exp\left\{ -\log[\iota_\mathcal{N} - \boldsymbol{F}^0_{\mathsf{type}}(u|\boldsymbol{w})] \right\} \, d\boldsymbol{G}^0(u|\boldsymbol{w})^\top \right) \right] \right\},$$

for which we know a unique solution exists. Now, from equation (5.5) we know that $F^0_{\mathsf{type}(i)}(y|w_i, M)$ has a strictly monotonic relationship with $F^0_j(y)$, so we can write

$$\boldsymbol{F}^0(y) = \boldsymbol{\phi}\big[\boldsymbol{F}^0_{\mathsf{type}}(y|\boldsymbol{w})\big]$$

where $\boldsymbol{\phi}(\cdot)$ is strictly monotonic in each element of its argument vector. Thus, there exists a one-to-one mapping, so nonparametric identification has been demonstrated.

5.6.2 Semi-Nonparametric Estimator

The SNP approach is numerically tractable in the presence of both states $\boldsymbol{w}_t$s and covariates $\boldsymbol{z}_t$s. Thus, given $\{(\boldsymbol{w}_t, \boldsymbol{z}_t, y_t)\}_{t=1}^T$, the SNP quasi-MLE $\{\hat{f}_{jT}\}_{j=1}^J$ is defined by

$$\{\hat{f}_{jT}\}_{j=1}^J = \underset{f_j \in \mathcal{F}_{jT}}{\operatorname{argmax}} \frac{1}{T} \sum_{t=1}^T \log g_{(2:\mathcal{N})}(u_t, i_t | \boldsymbol{F}, \boldsymbol{w}_t, \boldsymbol{z}_t)$$

where

$$\mathcal{F}_{jT} = \left\{ f_{jT} \in \mathcal{F}_j : \right.$$

$$f_{jT}(u | \boldsymbol{\delta}_j) = \left[\sum_{k=0}^{p_T} \delta_{jk} H_k(u) \right]^2 \exp(-u^2/2) + \varepsilon \exp(-u^2/2),$$

$$\left. u = (\log y - \boldsymbol{z} \boldsymbol{\gamma}_j), \ \boldsymbol{\gamma}_j \in \boldsymbol{R}^K, \ \boldsymbol{\delta}_j \in \boldsymbol{\Omega}_{jT} \right\}$$

and

$$\boldsymbol{\Omega}_{jT} = \left\{ \boldsymbol{\delta}_j = (\delta_{j0}, \ldots, \delta_{jp_T}) : \int_{-\infty}^{\infty} f_{jT}(u | \boldsymbol{z} \boldsymbol{\gamma}_j, \boldsymbol{\delta}_j) \, du = 1 \right\}$$

and $\{p_T\}$ is a non-decreasing sequence of integers, as before.

5.7 Practice Problems

The problems at the end of this chapter are designed to give you practice in estimating simple models of multi-unit, sequential, oral, ascending-price auctions using parametric and nonparametric methods.

1. Consider an environment in which $\mathcal{N}$ potential bidders have private valuations that are independent of one another. In this environment, each potential bidder gets M independent valuation draws from $F_V(\cdot)$. For potential bidder i, order these valuation draws, and represent them by the vector $\boldsymbol{V}^i$ which equals $(V_1^i, \ldots, V_M^i)$.

   a) Write a MATLAB procedure that will find the GVA allocations and prices when M goods are sold to n participating bidders.

   Suppose M is four and n is three. Assume that $\boldsymbol{V}^1$ equals $(5, 4, 2)$, while $\boldsymbol{V}^2$ equals $(6, 3, 1)$, and $\boldsymbol{V}^3$ equals $(4.5, 2.5, 0)$.

b) Use the program written to answer part a) to find the winning prices and the identities of the winners, assuming a reserve price r of zero.

c) Again, using the program from part a) as well as the data from part b), calculate the winning prices and the identity of the winners, assuming r is 2.6.

2. Consider a sequential, multi-unit, clock auction of two units of a good with three potential bidders in the absence of a reserve price. Suppose that the valuation of each potential bidder for each of the units is an independent draw from a distribution that is specific to that bidder.

   a) Derive the probability density function of the value for the highest-valued unit and the lowest-valued unit for each of the three bidders.

   Suppose that valuation draws for each potential bidder is from a different exponential distribution having hazard rate θ_i for potential bidder i.

   b) Derive the probability density function of the winning bid for the second unit sold.

   c) In the file `multi.dat`, which is located on the CD accompanying this book, you will find six columns of numbers. In the first is recorded an identification number, which ranges from 1 to 100, while in the second is recorded the dependent variable y_t, the winning bid for the last unit sold. In the next four are recorded for the tth auction the identity of the winner of the last unit i_t as well as the number of units won by each bidder in previous sales, w_{1t}, w_{2t}, and w_{3t}. Using the data from `multi.dat`, estimate the parameters $\boldsymbol{\theta}$ equal $(\theta_1, \theta_2, \theta_3)$ using the method of maximum likelihood.

Chapter 6

Directions for Further Research

$\mathcal{I}$N THIS chapter, we discuss some directions for future research. We first describe some research that is currently either under revision or underway, and then speculate on several fruitful directions in which researchers might go.[1] The most fruitful directions for further research will almost surely involve investigating the econometrics of multi-unit auctions under different formats. Perhaps the next-most fruitful directions for further research will involve investigating the econometrics of multi-object auctions under different formats. Of course, adapting the work we have outlined previously to different informational paradigms, such as the CVP and AVP, is also a fruitful direction, and some of this has already been done. For those just familiar with the methods described in this book, however, extending research to the CVP or the AVP will be more difficult than the other two directions suggested.

6.1 Simultaneous, Dependent, Sealed-Bid Auctions

One obvious direction in the case of multi-unit auctions is to consider simultaneous, dependent, sealed-bid auctions. In fact, Hortaçsu (2002a, b) has done just that. Within the IPVP, Hortaçsu investigated the sale of treasury bills in Turkey.

Chapman, McAdams, and Paarsch (2005) have investigated the implications of fixed bid increments in simultaneous, dependent sealed-bid auctions using data from Receiver General auctions conducted by the central bank of Canada (the Bank of Canada) in its role as fiscal agent for the federal government of Canada. One of the main features on which Chapman et al. focus is the fact that only a finite number of discrete (bid,quantity) pairs are permitted within this institutional environment.

---

[1] For work that is under revision, we are deliberately brief as both the content and the conclusions of that research are currently in flux.

6.2 Infinitely Lived Auction Games

Another direction is to consider repeated games, with a state variable. In Paarsch and Robert (1995), demand unfulfilled in this period evaporated, but in many models unfulfilled demand remains. Jofre-Bonet and Pesendorfer (2003) studied a dynamic, low-price, sealed-bid auction game at which the stage games are played repeatedly with an infinite horizon. In this model, Jofre-Bonet and Pesendorfer have investigated procurement auctions. The heterogeneities of the stage games and the heterogeneity of bidders in each game are captured by observable state variables. Jofre-Bonet and Pesendorfer focused on Markov-perfect equilibria in a stationary dynamic model, which allowed them to estimate the parameters of the underlying model interpreting a time-series $t = 1, 2, \ldots$ of auction data as a realization of the infinitely played dynamic game.

They applied their model to a data set concerning California highway procurement auctions. The bidders in this data set are construction firms engaged in bidding for highway procurement projects. Two types of bidders exist in their model—regular bidders, who are large construction firms which have won the largest dollar value projects and have submitted more than 80 bids, and fringe bidders, which are the remaining firms. Regular bidders stay in the dynamic game forever and care about the discounted payoff from the entire sequence of infinitely played dynamic auctions. Fringe bidders are myopic and only care about the current period payoff of a single first-price auction. The number of fringe bidders may vary with time.

Each stage game is a low-price, sealed-bid auction that is characterized by a vector of state variables. The state variables include the contract characteristics S_0^t which are assumed to be independent and identically distributed draws from an exogenous distribution $F_0(\cdot)$ which does not depend on t. The state variables S_i^t for bidder i at time t depend on the status of the uncompleted projects bidder i has won in previous auctions prior to date t.

Each bidder i learns his cost for the contract C_i^t after the contract characteristics are revealed. Conditional on the state variables, the cost is privately known, being independent and identically distributed across bidders. The cost of a regular bidder i is drawn from the continuous conditional distribution function $F\left(\cdot | s_0^t, s_i^t, \boldsymbol{s}_{-i}^t\right)$ having support on the closed interval $\left[\underline{c}\left(s_0^t, s_i^t, \boldsymbol{s}_{-i}^t\right), \bar{c}\left(s_0^t, s_i^t, \boldsymbol{s}_{-i}^t\right)\right]$ where $S_i^t \in \mathcal{S}_i$. Here, $\boldsymbol{s}_{-i}^t$ denotes the vector of other bidders' state variables. Now, let $\boldsymbol{s}_t$ denote $\left(s_i^t, \boldsymbol{s}_{-i}^t\right)$, $s_t \in \mathcal{S}$ and $\mathcal{S}$ equals $\times_{i=1}^{\mathcal{N}} \mathcal{S}_i$. For bidder i, the space of state vectors $\mathcal{S}_i$ is assumed to be a finite set. This finiteness assumption is key in the literature on the estimation of dynamic discrete-choice models and dynamic games to obtaining an asymptotic distribution for the estimator. Jofre-Bonet and Pesendorfer use stochastic dynamic programming to characterize the optimal, equilbrium strategy.

6.3 Multi-Object Auctions

Only a few researchers have considered the structural analysis of multi-object auctions. One example is Brendstrup and Paarsch (2005), who examined sequential, two-object clock auctions within the symmetric IPVP.

Brendstrup and Paarsch worked within the symmetric IPVP, assuming that each of the $\mathcal{N}$ potential bidders draws a pair of valuations, V_1 for object A and V_2 for object B, independently from the joint distribution $H_{12}(v_1, v_2)$ where $F_1(v_1)$ and $F_2(v_2)$ denote the marginal cumulative distribution functions of V_1 and V_2. For simplicity, they assumed that the two objects are substitutes. Thus, within their setting, cases where the utility of winning the second object depends on the outcome of the first auction are not admitted. As such, their model is that of Chakraborty (1999).

Brendstrup and Paarsch assumed that the two objects are sold sequentially at English auction under the Milgrom–Weber clock model, without a reserve price. Note that, within their model, regardless of the outcome at the first auction, it remains a dominant strategy to bid one's valuation at the second auction. This then implies that it is also a dominant strategy to bid up to one's valuation for the object on sale at the first auction. Thus, in their model, the order of sale is irrelevant.

Within this framework, an important policy decision faced by the auctioneer is whether to bundle the two objects and then to sell them as one. In fact, in the model described above, Chakraborty (1999) has derived a regularity condition concerning $H_{12}(v_1, v_2)$ that needs to be verified. As Chakraborty has mentioned, the regularity condition is a condition on the tails of the distributions. When the distributions of V_1 and V_2 are identical and the two random variables are independent, the distribution of their sum is more concentrated than either of the marginal distributions. A random draw from the convolution is more likely to yield a *central* value than would random draws from the marginal distributions. In an auction application, bundling—selling two objects together—will only be more profitable in expected-revenue terms when Chakraborty's regularity condition holds for a particular amount of competition. If this condition is met, then bundling is optimal, otherwise the two objects should be sold individually.

Brendstrup and Paarsch assumed that the econometrician observes the winning bids as well as the number of bidders. As we have seen, this is typical. The problem is that at English auctions researchers typically never observe each bidder's valuation for each object. Instead, most often, they just observe the winning bids at the auctions. Now, under the Milgrom–Weber clock model, the winning bid for object A is $V_1^{(2:n)}$, while that for object B is $V_2^{(2:n)}$. But $V_1^{(2:n)}$ may be the valuation of bidder i, while $V_2^{(2:n)}$ could be the valuation for bidder j. Only occasionally will one bidder win both objects. But even in such a circumstance, it is unclear whether one can obtain identification of the joint distribution $H_{12}(v_1, v_2)$. At English auctions, the winners are the bidders with the highest valuations, but they pay what their nearest opponents were willing to pay.

Brendstrup and Paarsch used the *copula* as a device to recover, semiparametrically, the joint distribution $H_{12}(v_1, v_2)$ using just information concerning the observed, winning-bid distributions.[2] Brendstrup and Paarsch applied their methods to data concerning sequential, English auctions of fish in Grenå, Denmark. In their application, bundling is not optimal; the observed practice of selling the objects individually is optimal under Chakraborty's regularity condition.

6.4 Summary

In this book, we have provided a brief introduction to the SEAD within the IPVP. While we recognize that the IPVP is a restrictive informational environment, we also hope that our presentation above as well as the solutions to the empirical exercises that follow provide the reader with enough structure to undertake her or his own research, either within the IPVP or within other informational environments. We look forward to reading about this research.

---

[2] The interested reader is directed to Nelsen (1999) for a detailed introduction to the theory of copulas.

Appendixes

A.1 Transformations of Random Variables

One of the most important features of auctions, when viewed through the lens of Harsanyi's noncooperative games of incomplete information, is that a bidder's equilibrium strategy is typically a function of his latent type—within the independent, private-values paradigm, his valuation. Thus, understanding how this dependence determines the distribution of the equilibrium bidding strategy is important.

A.1.1 Linear Transformations

The simplest, nontrivial transformation to analyze is a linear transformation. Suppose that V is a continuous random variable defined on the interval $[\underline{v}, \overline{v}]$, having cumulative distribution function $F_V(v)$ with corresponding probability density function $f_V(v)$, which equals $dF_V(v)/dv$. Consider B, a linear transformation of V,

$$B = \alpha + \beta V$$

where α and β are constants, with β being greater than zero, initially. Note that B is defined on the interval $[\alpha + \beta \underline{v}, \alpha + \beta \overline{v}]$. The cumulative distribution function of B, which is the probability of B being less than or equal to some value b, is

$$\begin{aligned}
F_B(b) &= \Pr(B \le b) \\
&= \Pr(\alpha + \beta V \le b) \\
&= \Pr\left[V \le \left(\frac{b - \alpha}{\beta}\right)\right] \\
&= F_V\left(\frac{b - \alpha}{\beta}\right).
\end{aligned}$$

Differentiating $F_B(b)$ with respect to b yields the probability density function of B; viz.,

$$
\begin{aligned}
f_B(b) &= \frac{dF_B(b)}{db} \\
&= \frac{d}{db} F_V\left[\frac{(b-\alpha)}{\beta}\right] \\
&= f_V\left[\frac{(b-\alpha)}{\beta}\right]\frac{d}{db}\left[\frac{(b-\alpha)}{\beta}\right] \\
&= f_V\left[\frac{(b-\alpha)}{\beta}\right]\frac{1}{\beta}.
\end{aligned}
$$

Consider now the case of β less than zero. Again, the cumulative distribution function is

$$
\begin{aligned}
F_B(b) &= \Pr(B \le b) \\
&= \Pr(\alpha + \beta V \le b) \\
&= \Pr\left[V \ge \left(\frac{b-\alpha}{\beta}\right)\right] \\
&= 1 - F_V\left(\frac{b-\alpha}{\beta}\right).
\end{aligned}
$$

Thus, the probability density function of B is

$$
\begin{aligned}
f_B(b) &= \frac{dF_B(b)}{db} \\
&= -\frac{d}{db} F_B\left[\frac{(b-\alpha)}{\beta}\right] \\
&= -f_V\left[\frac{(b-\alpha)}{\beta}\right]\frac{d}{db}\left[\frac{(b-\alpha)}{\beta}\right] \\
&= f_V\left[\frac{(b-\alpha)}{\beta}\right]\frac{1}{|\beta|}.
\end{aligned}
$$

To illustrate this method, consider the following example: Suppose that V is distributed uniformly on the interval $[0,1]$, so $f_V(v)$ is one on that interval, while B is defined by

$$
B = 2 - 4V.
$$

Note that the range of B is now $[-2,2]$ and, on that interval, the probability density function of B is

$$
f_B(b) = \frac{f_V[(2-b)/4]}{4} = \frac{1}{4}.
$$

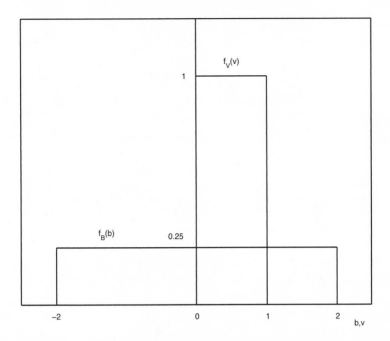

Figure A.1.1
Linear Transformation of a Uniform Random Variable

Thus, the lower bound of support of $f_V(v)$ has been shifted to the left by two units, while the upper bound of support of $f_V(v)$ has been shifted to the right by one unit. In order for the probability density function to integrate to one, it needs to be flattened out to stretch over four units, instead of one, as is depicted in figure A.1.1. Thus,

$$\int_{-2}^{2} f_B(b) \, db = \int_{-2}^{2} \frac{1}{4} \, db = b \bigg|_{-2}^{2} = \frac{2 - (-2)}{4} = \frac{4}{4} = 1.$$

A.1.2 Monotonic Nonlinear Transformations

The linear transformations considered above are special cases of more general transformations called *monotonic transformations*. A function S that equals $\sigma(V)$ is a monotonic function of V if the derivative of $\sigma(V)$ never changes sign. Thus,

$$\frac{d\sigma(v)}{dv} \geq 0 \text{ for all } v$$

231

or

$$\frac{d\sigma(v)}{dv} \leq 0 \text{ for all } v.$$

When $\sigma(V)$ is monotonic, there exists a unique function $\sigma^{-1}(\cdot)$ such that

$$\sigma^{-1}(S) = \sigma^{-1}[\sigma(V)] = V$$

where

$$\frac{d\sigma^{-1}(S)}{dS} = \left[\frac{d\sigma(V)}{dV}\right]^{-1} = \frac{dV}{dS}.$$

What is the probability density function of S when V is a continuous random variable defined on the interval $[\underline{v}, \overline{v}]$, having cumulative distribution function $F_V(v)$ with corresponding probability density function $f_V(v)$? Suppose, initially, that $\sigma'(V)$ is positive. Note that S is defined on the interval $[\sigma(\underline{v}), \sigma(\overline{v})]$. The cumulative distribution function of S, which is the probability of V being less than some value v, is

$$F_S(s) = \Pr(S \leq s)$$
$$= \Pr[\sigma(V) \leq s]$$
$$= \Pr[V \leq \sigma^{-1}(s)]$$
$$= F_V[\sigma^{-1}(s)].$$

Differentiating $F_S(s)$ or $F_V[\sigma^{-1}(s)]$ with respect to s yields the probability density function of S

$$f_S(s) = \frac{dF_S(s)}{ds}$$
$$= \frac{d}{ds}F_V[\sigma^{-1}(s)]$$
$$= f_V[\sigma^{-1}(s)]\frac{d\sigma^{-1}(s)}{ds}$$
$$= f_V[\sigma^{-1}(s)]\frac{dv}{ds}.$$

The above equation can be rewritten as

$$f_S(s)ds = f_V(v)dv$$

which has an interpretation in figure A.1.2. The area (mass) under the $f_S(s)$ curve between s_0 and $(s_0 + ds)$, denoted A, must equal the area (mass) under the $f_V(v)$ curve between v_0 and $(v_0 + dv)$, denoted B.

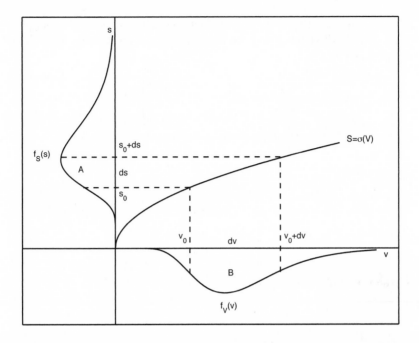

Figure A.1.2
Probability Density Function of a Monotonic Transformation

Consider now the case of $\sigma'(V)$ is less than zero. Again, the cumulative distribution function is

$$F_S(s) = \Pr(S \leq s)$$

$$= \Pr[\sigma(V) \leq s]$$

$$= \Pr[V \geq \sigma^{-1}(s)]$$

$$= 1 - F_V[\sigma^{-1}(s)],$$

so the probability density function of S is

$$f_S(s) = \frac{dF_S(s)}{ds}$$

$$= -\frac{d}{ds} F_V[\sigma^{-1}(s)]$$

$$= -f_V[\sigma^{-1}(s)] \frac{d\sigma^{-1}(s)}{ds}$$

$$= f_S[\sigma^{-1}(s)] \left| \frac{dv}{ds} \right|.$$

To illustrate this method, consider the following example: Suppose that the V is distributed log-normally, where the mean of $\log V$ is μ and its variance is σ^2. Thus,

$$f_V(v) = \frac{1}{v\sqrt{2\pi\sigma^2}} \exp\left[\frac{-(\log v - \mu)^2}{2\sigma^2}\right] \quad 0 < v < \infty.$$

Consider S, a monotonic function of V, defined by

$$S = \sigma(V) = \sqrt{V} \quad 0 < S.$$

Note that

$$\sigma^{-1}(S) = S^2 = V$$

and

$$\frac{dV}{dS} = 2S,$$

so the probability density function of S is

$$f_S(s) = f_V\left[\sigma^{-1}(s)\right]\frac{dv}{ds}$$
$$= f_V(2\log s)2s$$
$$= \frac{2}{s\sqrt{2\pi\sigma^2}} \exp\left[\frac{-(2\log s - \mu)^2}{2\sigma^2}\right] \quad 0 < s.$$

A.2 Order Statistics

At the heart of theoretical analyses of auctions are order statistics—the highest valuation, the second-highest valuation, the lowest cost, and so forth. For example, at a Vickrey auction the bidder with the highest valuation wins, but the price he pays is what his closest opponent bid. Within the IPVP, this is the second-highest valuation. At a low-bid, sealed-bid procurement auction, the firm with the least cost bids the least and, therefore, wins the auction. Thus, the distributions of maxima and minima as well as other order statistics are of interest.

A.2.1 Independent and Identically Distributed Case

To analyze order statistics, consider $\{V_i\}_{i=1}^{\mathcal{N}}$, a sequence of independent and identically distributed random variables having cumulative distribution function $F_V(v)$ and corresponding probability density function

$f_V(v)$. Order the sequence from smallest to largest, and introduce the notation $V_{(i:\mathcal{N})}$ where $(i:\mathcal{N})$ denotes the ith largest V in the sequence. Thus,

$$V_{(1:\mathcal{N})} > V_{(2:\mathcal{N})} > \ldots > V_{(\mathcal{N}-1:\mathcal{N})} > V_{(\mathcal{N}:\mathcal{N})}.$$

Denote the smallest member of the sequence by X and the largest by Z. Hence,

$$X = V_{(\mathcal{N}:\mathcal{N})} = \min(V_1, V_2, \ldots, V_{\mathcal{N}})$$

and

$$Z = V_{(1:\mathcal{N})} = \max(V_1, V_2, \ldots, V_{\mathcal{N}}).$$

Both X and Z (as well as all of the other order statistics) are functions of all of the V_is. Notice that the functions that define X and Z are continuous but not differentiable, so the methods we have considered hitherto do not apply.

The cumulative distribution function of Z is the probability of Z being less than some z. Thus,

$$F_Z(z) = \Pr(Z \le z).$$

Now the event $(Z \le z)$ requires $\left[(V_1 \le z) \cap (V_2 \le z) \cap \ldots \cap (V_{\mathcal{N}} \le z)\right]$. But each V_i is independent of the others, so functions of the V_is such as $(V_i \le z)$ will also be independent of one another. Thus,

$$F_Z(z) = \Pr\left[(V_1 \le z) \cap (V_2 \le z) \cap \ldots \cap (V_{\mathcal{N}} \le z)\right]$$

$$= \prod_{i=1}^{\mathcal{N}} \Pr[(V_i \le z)]$$

$$= F_V(z)^{\mathcal{N}},$$

so the probability density function of Z is

$$f_Z(z) = \frac{dF_Z(z)}{dz} = \mathcal{N} F_V(z)^{\mathcal{N}-1} f_V(z).$$

Consider now the smallest order statistic X. Note that the event $(X \ge x)$ requires $\left[(V_1 \ge x) \cap (V_2 \ge x) \cap \ldots \cap (V_{\mathcal{N}} \ge x)\right]$. Again, each V_i is independent of the others, so functions of the V_i such as $(X_i \ge x)$ will also be independent of one another. Thus,

$$\Pr\left[(V_1 \ge x) \cap (V_2 \ge x) \cap \ldots \cap (V_{\mathcal{N}} \ge x)\right] = \prod_{i=1}^{\mathcal{N}} \Pr[(V_i \ge x)]$$

$$= [1 - F_V(x)]^{\mathcal{N}}.$$

Now,

$$\Pr(X \geq x) = \left[1 - \Pr(X \leq x)\right] = \left[1 - F_X(x)\right],$$

so

$$F_X(x) = 1 - \left[1 - F_V(x)\right]^{\mathcal{N}}.$$

The probability density function of X is then

$$f_X(x) = \frac{dF_X(x)}{dx} = \mathcal{N}[1 - F_V(x)]^{\mathcal{N}-1} f_V(x).$$

What about other order statistics? Suppose one were interested in deriving the probability density function of the ith highest order statistic from a sample of $\mathcal{N}$ independent and identically distributed draws. Let Y denote $V_{(i:\mathcal{N})}$. For Y to be the ith order statistic and fall within the interval $[y, y + \Delta y)$, one must have $(\mathcal{N} - i)$ below y and $(i - 1)$ draws above $[y + \Delta y)$. The probability of this event is

$$\Pr\left\{Y \in [y, y + \Delta y)\right\} = \frac{\mathcal{N}!}{(\mathcal{N} - i)!(1 - 1)!(i - 1)!} F_V(y)^{\mathcal{N}-i}$$
$$\left[F_V(y + \Delta y) - F_V(y)\right]\left[1 - F_V(y + \Delta y)\right]^{i-1}.$$

Here, the expression

$$\frac{\mathcal{N}!}{(\mathcal{N} - i)!(1 - 1)!(i - 1)!}$$

is the multinomial combinatoric formula for the number of ways in $\mathcal{N}$ draws one can get $(\mathcal{N} - i)$ draws below y, $(i - 1)$ draws above $(y + \Delta y)$, and one between y and $(y + \Delta y)$. Now, finding $f_Y(y)$ simply involves taking the limit

$$\lim_{\Delta y \to 0} \frac{\Pr\left\{Y \in [y, y + \Delta y)\right\}}{\Delta y} = \lim_{\Delta y \to 0} \frac{\left[F_Y(y + \Delta y) - F_Y(y)\right]}{\Delta y},$$

so

$$f_Y(y) = \frac{\mathcal{N}!}{(\mathcal{N} - i)!(i - 1)!} F_V(y)^{\mathcal{N}-i}[1 - F_V(y)]^{i-1} f_V(y). \qquad \text{(A.2.1)}$$

Thus, for example, when Y is $V_{(2:\mathcal{N})}$, we have

$$f_Y(y) = \mathcal{N}(\mathcal{N} - 1)F_V(y)^{\mathcal{N}-2}[1 - F_V(y)]f_V(y).$$

One convenient way to summarize the relationship between $F_Y(y)$ and $F_V(v)$ is

$$F_Y(y) = \frac{\mathcal{N}!}{(\mathcal{N} - i)!(i - 1)!} \int_0^{F_V(y)} u^{\mathcal{N}-i}(1 - u)^{i-1} \, du. \qquad \text{(A.2.2)}$$

Notice that differentiating equation (A.2.2) with respect to y yields the probability density function defined by equation (A.2.1).

A.2.2 General Independent Case

To begin, consider a simple example of three independent draws, each from a different distribution—$F_1(v_1)$, $F_2(v_2)$, and $F_3(v_3)$, respectively. Focus on the second-highest order statistic Y, which equals $V_{(2:3)}$. Now, for Y to be the second-highest order statistic, one of the following six, mutually exclusive events must obtain: The draw from the first distribution is highest *and* the draw from the second is in the middle, and the draw from the third is lowest *or* the draw from the second is lowest, and the draw from the third is in the middle; *or* the draw is from the second distribution is highest *and* the draw from the first is in the middle, and the draw from the third is lowest *or* the draw from the first is lowest, and the draw from the third is in the middle; *or* the draw from the third distribution is highest *and* the draw from the first is in the middle, and the draw from the second is lowest *or* the draw from the first is lowest, and the draw from the second is in the middle. Thus, for any interval $[y, y + \Delta y)$, we can write this as

$$F_Y(y + \Delta y) - F_Y(y) = \Pr\{Y \in [y, y + \Delta y)\} =$$
$$\Pr(V_1 \geq y + \Delta y)\left[\Pr(V_2 \leq y + \Delta y) - \Pr(V_2 \leq y)\right]\Pr(V_3 \leq y)+$$
$$\Pr(V_1 \geq y + \Delta y)\left[\Pr(V_3 \leq y + \Delta y) - \Pr(V_3 \leq y)\right]\Pr(V_2 \leq y)+$$
$$\Pr(V_2 \geq y + \Delta y)\left[\Pr(V_1 \leq y + \Delta y) - \Pr(V_1 \leq y)\right]\Pr(V_3 \leq y)+$$
$$\Pr(V_2 \geq y + \Delta y)\left[\Pr(V_3 \leq y + \Delta y) - \Pr(V_3 \leq y)\right]\Pr(V_1 \leq y)+$$
$$\Pr(V_3 \geq y + \Delta y)\left[\Pr(V_1 \leq y + \Delta y) - \Pr(V_1 \leq y)\right]\Pr(V_2 \leq y)+$$
$$\Pr(V_3 \geq y + \Delta y)\left[\Pr(V_2 \leq y + \Delta y) - \Pr(V_2 \leq y)\right]\Pr(V_1 \leq y).$$

Also,

$$f_Y(y) = \lim_{\Delta y \to 0} \frac{[F_Y(y + \Delta y) - F_Y(y)]}{\Delta y},$$

so

$$f_Y(y) = S_1(y)f_2(y)F_3(y) + S_1(y)f_3(y)F_2(y)+$$
$$S_2(y)f_1(y)F_3(y) + S_2(y)f_3(y)F_1(y)+$$
$$S_3(y)f_1(y)F_2(y) + S_3(y)f_2(y)F_1(y).$$

As one can imagine, writing out all of these combinations can be tedious, so statisticians have invented a combinatorial operator for collecting them. It is referred to as the *permanent operator* and is often denoted by the symbol "Perm." The permanent is similar to the determinant, except that all the principal minors have a positive sign. An example for a (3×3) matrix is

$$\text{Perm} \begin{pmatrix} a & b & c \\ d & e & f \\ g & h & i \end{pmatrix} = a(ei + fh) + b(di + fg) + c(dh + eg).$$

Unlike the determinant, which in the transformation of random variables ensures that a probability density function integrates to one, the permanent is a counting device, like the permutation formula used above. It is especially useful when finding combinations from different types of distributions.

Hence, expanding along the third row of the matrix below,

$$f_Y(y|F_1, F_2, F_3) = \text{Perm} \begin{pmatrix} F_1(y) & F_2(y) & F_3(y) \\ f_1(y) & f_2(y) & f_3(y) \\ S_1(y) & S_2(y) & S_3(y) \end{pmatrix}$$

$$= S_1(y)f_2(y)F_3(y) + S_1(y)f_3(y)F_2(y) +$$
$$S_2(y)f_1(y)F_3(y) + S_2(y)f_3(y)F_1(y) +$$
$$S_3(y)f_1(y)F_2(y) + S_1(y)f_2(y)F_1(y)$$

which is the same as above.

What about the case involving the ith order statistic from a sample of size $\mathcal{N}$? Consider a sequence $\{V_i\}_{i=1}^{\mathcal{N}}$ of independently-distributed random variables having cumulative distribution functions $\{F_i(v)\}_{i=1}^{\mathcal{N}}$ and corresponding probability density functions $\{f_i(v)\}_{i=1}^{\mathcal{N}}$. Collect the F_is in the vector $\boldsymbol{F}$. Again, order the sequence from smallest to largest. In general, the probability density function of Y, which equals $V_{(i:\mathcal{N})}$ is

$$f_{(i:\mathcal{N})}(y|\boldsymbol{F}) = \frac{1}{(i-1)!(\mathcal{N}-i)!} \text{Perm} \begin{pmatrix} F_1(y) & \cdots & F_{\mathcal{N}}(y) \\ \vdots & \ddots & \vdots \\ F_1(y) & \cdots & F_{\mathcal{N}}(y) \\ f_1(y) & \cdots & f_{\mathcal{N}}(y) \\ [1-F_1(y)] & \cdots & [1-F_{\mathcal{N}}(y)] \\ \vdots & \ddots & \vdots \\ [1-F_1(y)] & \cdots & [1-F_{\mathcal{N}}(y)] \end{pmatrix}$$

where the matrix above, on the right-hand side of the equal sign, is $(\mathcal{N} \times \mathcal{N})$, with each column corresponding to a particular type, the first $(\mathcal{N} - i)$ rows being the cumulative distribution functions of the $\mathcal{N}$ different types, while the last $(i - 1)$ rows being the survivor functions

$[1 - F_i(y)]$ of the $\mathcal{N}$ different types, and the ith row being the probability density functions for the $\mathcal{N}$ types.

To see that the above equation collapses to the probability density function of the second-highest order statistic when the F_is are identical, consider the case of i equal two and recall that the probability density function of the second-highest order statistic from $\mathcal{N}$ independent and identically distributed draws from $F_V(v)$ is

$$f_{(2:\mathcal{N})}(y) = \mathcal{N}(\mathcal{N} - 1)F_V(y)^{\mathcal{N}-2}[1 - F_V(y)]f_V(y).$$

A.3 Simulation

Because the equilibrium strategies at auctions are often difficult to calculate, some researchers have proposed using simulation methods to approximate their expectations. In this appendix, we discuss the simple mechanics of simulation.

A.3.1 Distribution of Cumulative Distribution Functions

A very special transformation of a continuous random variable is the cumulative distribution function

$$F_V(v) = \Pr(V \leq v) = \int_{-\infty}^{v} f_V(u)\, du.$$

Note that $F_V(v)$ is an increasing, monotonic function of v because

$$\frac{dF_V(v)}{dv} = f_V(v) \geq 0.$$

Since $F_V(v)$ is a monotonic function of the random variable v, it is natural to ask what its distribution is. The methods discussed in section 2 of appendix 1 can be used to answer this question. In particular, letting U equal $F_V(V)$, one can find the probability density function of U by

$$f_U(u) = f_V(v)\frac{dv}{du}.$$

Because $F_V(v)$ is monotonic in v, we can invert $F_V(v)$ to get

$$v = F_V^{-1}(u)$$

where $F_V^{-1}(\cdot)$ is the inverse function of $F_V(v)$ having the property

$$v = F_V^{-1}\big[F_V(v)\big].$$

Now,

$$du = f_V(v)dv,$$

so

$$\frac{dv}{du} = \frac{1}{f_V(v)}.$$

Thus,

$$f_U(u) = f_V(v)\frac{1}{f_V(v)} = 1.$$

Although the random variable V is contained on the interval $(-\infty, \infty)$, the cumulative distribution function U is contained on the interval $[0, 1]$. Thus, the cumulative distribution function is a random variable having a probability density function equaling one everywhere on the interval $[0, 1]$: It is distributed uniformly on the unit interval.

This result has direct implications for the simulation method of approximating the probability density function for a random variable that is a function of another random variable. In particular, if we can devise a way of generating independent and identically distributed random variables from the uniform distribution on the interval $[0, 1]$, then using the inverse function $F_V^{-1}(\cdot)$, which exists for any continuous random variable, we can generate a wide variety of random variables. Thus, we have saved a lot of work: Instead of having to devise a method for each and every probability distribution, we only have to devise a method for the uniform, and then apply the inverse mapping. Also, in many cases, we can use uniform random variables to generate discrete random variables.

A.3.2 Generating Random Numbers

In the previous section, we demonstrated that the cumulative distribution function for any continuous random variable is distributed uniformly on the interval $[0, 1]$. Thus, if we could devise a way of generating uniform random numbers, then using the inverse function $F_V^{-1}(\cdot)$ we could generate random numbers according to any continuous law. For example, suppose we wanted Weibull random numbers given the parameter values θ_1 equal 10 and θ_2 equal 3.5, but all we had were uniform random numbers U, then we would use the transformation

$$F_V(V) = [1 - \exp(-\theta_1 V^{\theta_2})] = U$$

$$\exp(-\theta_1 V^{\theta_2}) = (1 - U)$$

$$-\theta_1 V^{\theta_2} = \log(1 - U)$$

$$\theta_1 V^{\theta_2} = -\log(1 - U)$$

$$V^{\theta_2} = \frac{-\log(1 - U)}{\theta_1}$$

$$V = \left[\frac{-\log(1 - U)}{\theta_1}\right]^{1/\theta_2}$$

$$V = \left[\frac{-\log(1 - U)}{10}\right]^{1/3.5}$$

to generate the Weibull Vs.

We could also use this method for some discrete random variables too. Suppose that V is distributed Bernoulli with parameter θ equal 0.6. Thus, if a U were generated that was greater than 0.4, then set V equal to one, otherwise set V to zero. Formally,

$$V = \begin{cases} 0 & \text{if } U \leq 0.4 \\ 1 & \text{if } U > 0.4. \end{cases}$$

The key to this approach is the uniform distribution. A variety of physical models for generating uniform numbers is available. For example, consider taking ℓ bingo balls and numbering them 0 to $(\ell - 1)$. Place the balls in an urn, and draw a ball at random. Divide the number on the ball by ℓ to obtain a uniform rational number on the interval $[0, (\ell - 1)/\ell]$. Note that as ℓ tends to infinity, the interval becomes packed with rational numbers and tends to $[0, 1]$. Of course, uncountably many of the irrational numbers, which make up the interval $[0, 1]$, are missing, but those irrational numbers are typically approximated by rational numbers on calculators and computers. Thus, their absence may be relatively unimportant. Now that we have some uniform Us, we can generate the Vs.

A.3.3 Pseudo-Random Numbers

The device described in the last section for generating random numbers from the uniform distribution built on a very concrete model of the data-generating process, the bingo urn. Often, however, it is inconvenient to use such devices. Moreover, such devices are not always foolproof; wear-and-tear can affect their properties. In addition, in experimental situations, researchers around the globe require random sequences that can be easily replicated, so that scientific findings can be reproduced. For the above reasons, numerical analysts have sought to devise methods of generating random numbers according to deterministic rules. Obviously, if something is generated according to a deterministic rule, it cannot be random. Thus, random numbers generated according to deterministic rules are often referred to as *pseudo-random numbers*. We shall examine a class of rules, which can be implemented on a computer and that can generate sequences of numbers that appear random by a variety of measures. Such rules (devices) are called *pseudo-random number generators* where the term "pseudo" is often suppressed.[1]

Congruential pseudo-random number generators are the most commonly used class of pseudo-random number generators, probably because of their simple structure. In particular, a random number u_i is generated by a congruential rule when

$$u_i = \frac{x_i}{\ell} \quad i = 1, 2, \ldots$$

where ℓ is an integer and where

$$x_i = \mathrm{mod}(\alpha + \beta x_{i-1}, \ell) \quad i = 1, 2, \ldots \text{ with } x_0 \text{ a known integer.}$$

Here, the function "mod" is the modulus function. The modulus is the remainder from dividing $(\alpha + \beta x_{i-1})$ by ℓ. Since x_i can take on the values $\{0, 1, 2, \ldots, \ell-1\}$, u_i will take on the rational values $\{0, 1/\ell, 2/\ell, \ldots, (\ell-1)/\ell\}$. If the x_is are distributed randomly on the the lattice of integers $\{0, 1, \ldots, \ell-1\}$, then the u_is will be distributed randomly on the lattice of rational numbers $\{0, 1/\ell, \ldots, (\ell-1)/\ell\}$. Moreover, the larger is ℓ, the closer will the u_i approximate the true uniform distribution. It turns out that, when the modulus function is implemented on a digital computer, the x_is appear to be distributed randomly on the lattice of points $\{0, 1, \ldots, \ell-1\}$. Note that congruential pseudo-random number generators depend on the choice of constants $(x_0, \ell, \alpha, \beta)$. What should they be?

Now, x_0 is the *seed*; it must be provided by the empirical worker. No rules for the choice of x_0 appear to exist.

What is ℓ? Typically, ℓ is the largest integer that can be represented on a computer, often referred to as *machine limit*. What determines how

---

[1] This section will only involve a small part of the work involving pseudo-random number generators. For more details, the interested reader should consider the work of Lewis and Orav (1989), which is cited in the bibliography.

large ℓ can be? The central processing units of computers come in many sizes. For example, many old personal computers were 16-bit machines. A bit is a bin where a number can be stored. Computers use binary arithmetic. What this means is that any number in base 10 is first converted into base 2 and stored in that form, before any computations are done. Thus, the number -1 would appear as the sequence

$$-000000000000001$$

on a 16-bit machine. Note that the first bit is used for the sign of the number. The number 2 would appear as

$$+000000000000010$$

while the number 3 would appear as

$$+000000000000011$$

and the number 9 would appear as

$$+000000000001001$$

The maximum number that can be presented on a 16-bit machine is $(2^{15} - 1)$ since at that point all of the bins, except the left most one which is used for the sign, are full

$$+111111111111111$$

Most modern computers are 32-bit machines, at least. Hence, on such machines ℓ would equal $(2^{31} - 1)$ or $2,147,483,647$.

The numbers α and β are referred to as the *increment* and the *multiplier*, respectively. No consensus appears to have emerged on the choice of α, and often α is set to zero. When α is zero, the generator falls within the class of *multiplicative congruential* pseudo-random number generators. Some consensus appears to have emerged concerning the choice of the multiplier β. In particular, β equals $397,204,094$ has been shown by Fishman and Moore (1982) to provide a reasonable combination of randomness and speed.

It should be noted that all congruential pseudo-random number generators have one failing: Eventually they will cycle. Thus, a limit exists to how many pseudo-random numbers can be generated by this rule.

A.4 Asymptotic Methods: Some Elementary Tools

In some empirical work, researchers assume that $F_V(v)$ belongs to a family of distributions indexed by the scalar parameter θ or a vector of parameters $\boldsymbol{\theta}$. This is often denoted by either $F_V(v; \theta)$ or $F_V(v; \boldsymbol{\theta})$, depending on the dimension of the parameter vector. The parameter(s) of the distribution function $F_V(v; \theta)$ of bidder valuations, embedded in θ (or the vector $\boldsymbol{\theta}$), are typically unobserved by the researcher and must be estimated from data. Perhaps the most important property of these estimates is parameter consistency; knowing the asymptotic distribution is also important. We shall review tools to investigate parameter consistency and asymptotic distribution, which are often referred to as *first-order asymptotic methods*. These are important tools for evaluating the large-sample properties of estimators.

A.4.1 Parameter Consistency: Laws of Large Numbers

Several definitions of parameter consistency exist. One notion is convergence in probability. An estimator $\hat{\theta}_T$ is a consistent estimator if it converges to the true value θ^0 in probability, as the sample gets very large; i.e.,

$$\lim_{T \to \infty} \Pr(|\hat{\theta}_T - \theta^0| \leq \varepsilon) = 1$$

for any ε greater than zero. Thus, consider any small distance ε from θ^0, the probability that $\hat{\theta}_T$ lies within the interval $[\theta^0 - \varepsilon, \theta^0 + \varepsilon]$ is arbitrarily close to one as the sample size T increases. In such cases, the *probability limit* or the "plim" of $\hat{\theta}_T$ is θ^0. This is often written as

$$\plim_{T \to \infty} \hat{\theta}_T = \theta^0 \quad \text{or} \quad \hat{\theta}_T \xrightarrow{\text{P}} \theta^0.$$

To illustrate our methods, we shall make use of the following example for the remainder of this section and in the next one too. Consider $\{V_t\}_{t=1}^T$ an independent and identically distributed sample of size T from an exponential distribution. For the parameter θ, the data-generating process is

$$f_V(v; \theta) = \theta \exp(-\theta v) \quad v > 0, \ \theta > 0$$

for which the kth raw population moment is

$$\mathcal{E}(V^k) = \mu_k(\theta) = \frac{k!}{\theta^k} \quad k = 1, 2, \dots \ .$$

Again, the true value of the parameter θ is denoted θ^0.

A *law of large numbers* allows one to conclude that the sample mean

$$\bar{V}_T = \frac{\sum_{t=1}^{T} V_t}{T}$$

converges to the population mean $\mu_1(\theta^0)$ with probability one as the sample size gets very large. We shall prove a law of large numbers as an example of convergence in probability using *Chebyshev's inequality*. Using the sample introduced above, note that $\mathcal{E}(\bar{V}_T)$ equals $\mathcal{E}(V)$ or $\mu_1(\theta^0)$ or $(1/\theta^0)$ in this example, while $\mathcal{V}(V)$ equals $[1/(\theta^0)^2]$ and $\mathcal{V}(\bar{V}_T)$ equals $\mathcal{V}(V)/T$. Both $\mathcal{E}(\bar{V}_T)$ and $\mathcal{V}(V)$ are finite when θ^0 is greater than zero. Chebyshev's inequality states that

$$\Pr\left[\,\left|\bar{V}_T - \mathcal{E}(V)\right| \geq d\sqrt{\mathcal{V}(\bar{V}_T)}\,\right] \leq \frac{1}{d^2} \quad d > 1.$$

In words, less than d^{-2} of the mass is contained outside of d standard deviations from the mean. For some ε larger than zero, consider

$$\Pr\left[\left|\bar{V}_T - (1/\theta^0)\right| \leq \varepsilon\right] = 1 - \Pr\left[\left|\bar{V}_T - (1/\theta^0)\right| \geq \varepsilon\sqrt{\mathcal{V}(\bar{V}_T)}/\sqrt{\mathcal{V}(\bar{V}_T)}\right]$$

$$\geq 1 - \frac{1}{\left[\varepsilon/\sqrt{\mathcal{V}(V)/T}\right]^2} = 1 - \frac{\mathcal{V}(V)}{T\varepsilon^2}.$$

Thus, for an arbitrary ε greater than zero,

$$\lim_{T\to\infty} \Pr\left[\left|\bar{V}_T - \mathcal{E}(V)\right| \leq \varepsilon\right] \geq \lim_{T\to\infty}\left[1 - \frac{\mathcal{V}(V)}{T\varepsilon^2}\right] = 1,$$

or

$$\operatorname*{plim}_{T\to\infty} \bar{V}_T = \mathcal{E}(V) = \mu_1(\theta^0).$$

Using this example, the kth raw sample moment is

$$M_k = \frac{\sum_{t=1}^{T} V_t^k}{T} \quad k = 1, 2, \ldots,$$

so, by a law of large numbers,

$$\operatorname*{plim}_{T\to\infty} M_k = \mu_k(\theta^0) \quad k = 1, 2, \ldots .$$

A.4.2 Asymptotic Normality: Central Limit Theorems

Frequently, the estimators that we shall encounter will be functions of the sample mean $\bar{V}_T$. Sometimes, we shall be able to find the exact distribution of the sample mean; e.g., when the estimators are linear in $\bar{V}_T$ and the samples are from the Bernoulli, Poisson, exponential, or normal laws. In other cases, typically when the estimators are nonlinear functions of $\bar{V}_T$, we may only be able to find the approximate distribution as the sample size gets very large, the asymptotic distribution. The idea behind asymptotic (or large-sample) theory can be formalized by the notion of *convergence in distribution.*

A sequence of random variables V_T is said to converge in distribution to V if for any bounded continuous function $g(\cdot)$ and for all v such that the cumulative distribution function of $g(V)$ is continuous at v:

$$\lim_{T \to \infty} \Pr[g(V_T) \leq v] = \Pr[g(V) \leq v].$$

This is often written as $V_T \overset{d}{\to} V$. The notation "$\overset{d}{\to}$" means *is approximately distributed* according to the term following it when the sample is large. If V is a constant μ, then $V_T \overset{d}{\to} V$ implies $V_T \overset{p}{\to} \mu$. When V_T is a suitably normalized function of the sample mean and V is a normal random variable, results concerning conditions under which $V_T \overset{d}{\to} V$ are called *central limit theorems*. V_T is said to be *asymptotically normal* in this case.

If the sample is from the Bernoulli law, then the deMoivre–Laplace central limit theorem allows one to conclude that an appropriately chosen transformation of $\bar{V}_T$ will be normally distributed, asymptotically

$$\frac{\sqrt{T}[\bar{V}_T - \mathcal{E}(V)]}{\sqrt{\mathcal{V}(V)}} \overset{d}{\to} \mathcal{N}(0,1).$$

The notation "$\mathcal{N}(0,1)$" means *normally distributed with mean zero and variance one.*

The Lindeberg–Levy central limit theorem is a more general central limit theorem than the deMoivre–Laplace central limit theorem. For any $\{V_t\}_{t=1}^{T}$, an independent and identically distributed sample of size T from $f_V(v; \theta)$ where the mean $\mathcal{E}(V)$ and variance $\mathcal{V}(V)$ are finite, this central limit theorem states that

$$\frac{\sqrt{T}[\bar{V}_T - \mathcal{E}(V)]}{\sqrt{\mathcal{V}(V)}} \overset{d}{\to} \mathcal{N}(0,1).$$

This is a major step forward since one can now consider the sample mean from *any* distribution satisfying the conditions (not just the Bernoulli

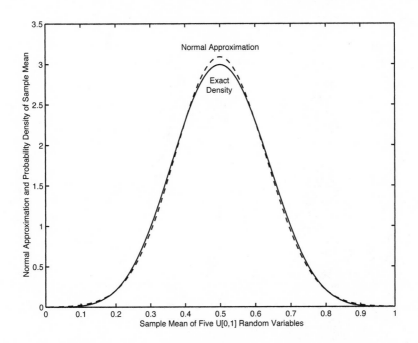

Figure A.4.1
Normal Approximation and Exact Probability Density Function:
Sample Mean of Five Uniform [0,1] Random Variables

law), and conclude that it is distributed normally, asymptotically. In our example above,

$$\sqrt{T}\big[M_k - \mu_k(\theta^0)\big] \overset{d}{\to} \mathcal{N}\big[0, \mathcal{V}(V^k)\big]$$

where

$$\mathcal{V}(V^k) = \frac{(2k)! - (k!)^2}{(\theta^0)^{2k}}$$

by the Lindeberg–Levy central limit theorem.

In figure A.4.1, we present the sample mean for five independent and identically distributed uniform random variables having support on the interval $[0, 1]$. Superimposed on this graph is the normal approximation to this distribution where the normal has mean $(1/2)$ and variance $(1/60)$. Notice how accurate this approximation is, even for a sample of size five. Much of this accuracy obtains from the symmetry of the probability density function for the uniform. In figure A.4.2, consider the sample mean for twenty-five independent and identically distributed exponential random variables having parameter θ^0 of one, a mean and

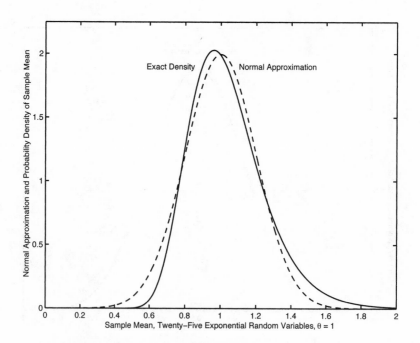

Figure A.4.2
Normal Approximation and Exact Probability Density Function:
Sample Mean of Twenty-Five Exponential Random Variables

variance of one. Note that each exponential is skewed to the right. Superimposed on this graph is the normal approximation to this distribution where the normal has mean one and variance $(1/25)$. This approximation is also quite accurate, but the distribution of the sample mean is still slightly skewed.

A.4.3 Continuous Mapping Theorem

Suppose that $g(V)$ is a continuous function of V with probability one, and that the V_T converges in distribution to V. Thus,

$$V_T \xrightarrow{\mathrm{d}} V.$$

The *continuous mapping theorem* allows one to find the limiting distribution of $g(V_T)$. In particular,

$$g(V_T) \xrightarrow{\mathrm{d}} g(V).$$

When V is a constant (e.g., μ), this implies that the operation of $g(\cdot)$ and calculating probability limits can be exchanged:

$$\operatorname*{plim}_{T\to\infty} g(V_T) = g\left(\operatorname*{plim}_{T\to\infty} V_T\right)$$
$$= g(\mu).$$

This is a very powerful result since we need only evaluate the function $g(V)$ at μ to calculate its probability limit.

In practice, we can analyze a random vector $\boldsymbol{V}_T$, which has a random scalar V_{1T}, which converges to a constant μ, and a subvector of $\boldsymbol{V}_{2T}$, which converges to a random vector $\boldsymbol{V}_2$. If

$$\operatorname*{plim}_{T\to\infty} \boldsymbol{V}_T = \operatorname*{plim}_{T\to\infty} \begin{pmatrix} V_{1T} \\ \boldsymbol{V}_{2T} \end{pmatrix} = \begin{pmatrix} \mu \\ \boldsymbol{V}_2 \end{pmatrix},$$

then the continuous mapping theorem states that

$$g(\boldsymbol{V}_T) \xrightarrow{\mathrm{d}} g(\mu, \boldsymbol{V}_2).$$

Several special cases of the continuous mapping theorem are often referred to as *Slutsky's theorem*:

Slutsky's Theorem: If $\boldsymbol{V}_{2T} \xrightarrow{\mathrm{d}} \boldsymbol{V}_2$ and $\operatorname{plim}_{T\to\infty} V_{1T} = \mu$, then

a) $\boldsymbol{V}_{2T} \pm V_{1T} \xrightarrow{\mathrm{d}} \boldsymbol{V}_2 \pm \mu$;

b) $\boldsymbol{V}_{2T} \times V_{1T} \xrightarrow{\mathrm{d}} \boldsymbol{V}_2 \times \mu$;

c) when $\mu \neq 0$,

$$\frac{\boldsymbol{V}_{2T}}{V_{1T}} \xrightarrow{\mathrm{d}} \frac{\boldsymbol{V}_2}{\mu}.$$

A.4.4 Delta Method

Suppose that $g(V_T)$ is a continuous and differentiable function of V_T, where the random variable converges in probability to μ, and that for some sequence of normalizing constants a_T,

$$a_T(V_T - \mu) \xrightarrow{\mathrm{d}} V.$$

When V_T is a sample mean, this usually follows from a law of large numbers and a central limit theorem and a_T equals $\sqrt{T}$. Slutsky's theorem allows one to conclude that

$$\operatorname*{plim}_{T\to\infty} g(V_T) = g(\mu).$$

In addition, one can take a first-order, Taylor-series expansion of $g(V_T)$ about μ to get

$$a_T[g(V_T) - g(\mu)] = g'(\mu)a_T(V_T - \mu) + o[a_T(V_T - \mu)]$$

where $o(v)$ indicates a term that is smaller in magnitude than v, in the sense that $[o(v)/v]$ tends to zero as v goes to zero. Slutsky's theorem then implies that

$$\plim_{T \to \infty} o[a_T(V_T - \mu)] = 0.$$

Another application of the Slutsky's theorem implies that

$$a_T[g(V_T) - g(\mu)] \xrightarrow{\text{d}} g'(\mu)V.$$

This is called the *delta method*. It is commonly used to show that smooth functions of sample averages are also asymptotically normally distributed. In particular, if V_T satisfies a central limit theorem, so

$$\sqrt{T}(V_T - \mu) \xrightarrow{\text{d}} \mathcal{N}[0, \mathcal{V}(V)],$$

then the delta method allows one to conclude that

$$\sqrt{T}[g(V_T) - g(\mu)] \xrightarrow{\text{d}} \mathcal{N}\left[0, g'(\mu)\mathcal{V}(V)g'(\mu)\right].$$

A.4.5 Extreme Value Theorems

Consider the following three different statistical experiments: In the first, a sequence of random variables $\{V_t\}_{t=1}^{T}$ is created by adding a sequence of independent and identically distributed lognormal random variables to the parameter θ, so

$$V_t = \theta + \exp(E_t) \quad E_t \sim \mathcal{N}(\mu, \sigma^2) \quad t = 1, \ldots, T.$$

Thus, the lower bound of support of V's distribution is θ. In the second experiment, the $\{V_t\}_{t=1}^{T}$ are from the Pareto law where the probability density function is

$$f_V(v) = \frac{\rho\theta^\rho}{v^{\rho+1}} \quad v \geq \theta; \; \theta, \; \rho > 0.$$

Again, the lower bound of support of V's distribution is θ. In the third experiment, the $\{V_t\}_{t=1}^{T}$ are from the Weibull law where the probability density function is

$$f_V(v) = \lambda\gamma(v - \theta)^{\gamma-1} \exp\left[-\lambda(v-\theta)^\gamma\right] \quad v \geq \theta; \; \lambda, \; \gamma > 0.$$

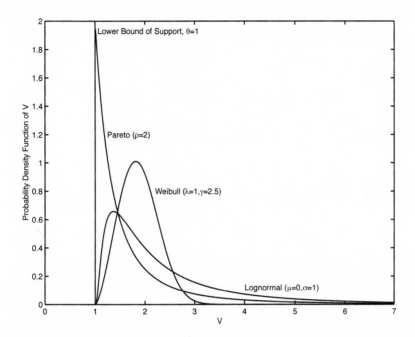

Figure A.4.3
Lognormal, Pareto, and Weibull
Probability Density Functions

Here, too, the lower bound of support of V's distribution is θ. In figure A.4.3, the above three probability density functions are graphed for particular parameter values: $(\theta, \rho, \lambda, \gamma)$ equal $(1, 2, 1, 2.5)$.

Note that the Pareto law has a strictly positive density at θ, while both the lognormal and the Weibull densities go to zero. It is trivial to show this in the Weibull case. In the lognormal case, consider what happens to the probability density function of a standard normal random variable $\phi[(e - \mu)/\sigma]$ as $e \to -\infty$, which must happen for V to attain θ; because it goes to zero, albeit only in the limit, so too must $f_V(\cdot)$.

Define X_T to be the $\min(V_1, V_2, \ldots, V_T)$. What is the behavior of this random variable's distribution as T varies? Well, for any T, we know that the exact small-sample cumulative distribution function of X_T is

$$\Pr(X_T \leq x) = F_{X_T}(x) = 1 - \Pr[(V_1 \geq x) \cap (V_2 \geq x) \cap \ldots \cap (V_T \geq x)]$$

$$= 1 - [1 - F_V(x)]^T.$$

Note, too, that for any positive δ, however small,

$$\Pr\left(X_T \in [\theta, \theta + \delta]\right) = F_{X_T}(\theta + \delta) = 1 - [1 - F_V(\theta + \delta)]^T,$$

so
$$\lim_{T \to \infty} \Pr(X_T \in [\theta, \theta + \delta]) = \lim_{T \to \infty} F_{X_T}(\theta + \delta)$$
$$= 1 - \lim_{T \to \infty} [1 - F_V(\theta + \delta)]^T$$
$$= 1 - 0$$
$$= 1.$$

Thus, as $T \to \infty$, the probability that X_T is within an arbitrary and small δ neighborhood of the lower bound θ is one. To wit, X_T converges in probability to θ. This result is similar to one derived when we demonstrated a law of large numbers by showing that the sample mean M_1 converges in probability to the population mean μ_1. Here, however, it is applied to an extreme order statistic, the sample minimum.

Knowing that the sample minimum converges to the lower bound of support of the distribution with probability one is typically not enough. In small samples, we often need to make probabilistic statements concerning X_T relative to θ. One way to proceed would involve using the exact distribution of X_T. However, this distribution depends on θ. What we would really like to do is examine the local behavior of X_T's distribution in the neighborhood of the lower bound θ as $T \to \infty$ to see if this distribution is independent of $F_V(\cdot)$ and thus θ; i.e., to see if a limit distribution exists. This is in the spirit of deriving a central limit theorem where we investigate the behavior of the distribution of the sample mean M_1 from an independently and identically distributed sample $\{V_t\}_{t=1}^T$ drawn from $F_V(v)$ in the neighborhood of $\mathcal{E}(V)$ (which equals μ_1) to see if that distribution is independent of $F_V(\cdot)$. But, as $T \to \infty$, the sample minimum X_T has a degenerate distribution at θ, so its distribution function is trivial. What to do?

In the analysis of a central limit theorem, because the limit distribution of M_1 is degenerate, we normalize M_1 by subtracting out its mean $\mathcal{E}(M_1)$, which equals μ_1, and then scale by dividing $(M_1 - \mu_1)$ by M_1's standard deviation, which equals $[\sqrt{\mathcal{V}(V)}/\sqrt{T}]$, to create a statistic

$$U_T = \frac{\sqrt{T}[M_1 - \mathcal{E}(M_1)]}{\sqrt{\mathcal{V}(V)}} = \frac{\sqrt{T}(M_1 - \mu_1)}{\sqrt{\mathcal{V}(V)}}$$

which has mean zero and variance one. We then show that

$$\lim_{T \to \infty} f_{U_T}(u) = \phi(u) = \frac{1}{\sqrt{2\pi}} \exp(-u^2/2),$$

the standard-normal, probability density function.

Thus, when examining the behavior of X_T, we want to do something similar. Since X_T converges to θ with probability one, let us subtract

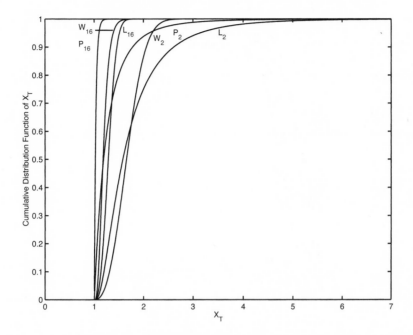

Figure A.4.4
Cumulative Distribution of X_T
Lognormal, Pareto, and Weibull Cases: $T = 2$ and $T = 16$

out a location parameter m_T and then multiply by a scaling parameter a_T to get a statistic

$$U_T = a_T(X_T - m_T).$$

Note that M_1 is an unbiased estimator of the location parameter μ_1, which is independent of T, and that the scale parameter decomposes into a constant $\sqrt{\mathcal{V}(V)}$ in the denominator and a term $\sqrt{T}$ as the lead term of the denominator. Unlike in the case of the sample mean, no natural decomposition seems obvious for U_T. Intuitively, subtracting θ from X_T might seem reasonable, but X_T is a biased estimator of θ. Moreover, it is unclear what the scaling factor should be. Nevertheless, if a limit distribution exists, then presumably some sort of scaling factor must apply.

Fortunately, from our perspective, statisticians have devoted considerable time and effort to investigating extreme order statistics. We shall borrow from this work. To begin, consider the random variable X_T. In figure A.4.4 are graphed the cumulative distribution functions of X_T when T is two and when T is sixteen for the lognormal (L), Pareto (P), and Weibull (W) cases considered in figure A.4.3; these are denoted

253

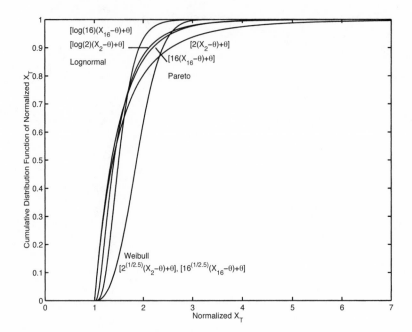

Figure A.4.5
Cumulative Distribution of Normalized X_T
Lognormal, Pareto, and Weibull Cases: $T = 2$ and $T = 16$

L_2, P_2, W_2, L_{16}, P_{16}, and W_{16} in this graph where the subscripts 2 and 16 denote the different values of T. Note that for most values of X_T, the cumulative distribution function labeled L_2 is further to the right than that labeled W_2 which is further to the right than that labeled P_2. Note, too, that the curve labeled P_{16} has shifted to the left relative to P_2 at a faster rate than the curve labeled W_{16} relative to W_2 which has shifted to the left faster than the curve labeled L_{16} relative to L_2. Thus, it appears that X_Ts from different statistical laws shift at different rates toward θ. Why?

Well, as mentioned above, under the Pareto law, V has a positive density at θ, while under the lognormal and Weibull laws it does not. Note, too, that, under the lognormal law, V's density in a neighborhood of θ goes to zero faster than it does under the Weibull law. Thus, under the Pareto law, X_T will pile up at the lower bound faster than under either the Weibull or the lognormal laws. In fact, the rate at which X_T tends to θ as T gets larger is the fastest under the Pareto law and slowest under the lognormal law. Under the lognormal law, X_T only gets to θ when the smallest E goes to $-\infty$, a very unlikely event, indeed. Under the Weibull law, this rate will depend on the parameter γ. The parameter γ determines how much mass is in the neighborhood of θ. If γ is one or smaller, then X_T will go to θ at a rate similar to that of the Pareto case, while when γ exceeds one it will go more slowly. As $\gamma \to \infty$, the Weibull rate will become as slow as the lognormal rate.

Figure A.4.5 depicts the cumulative distribution functions of X_T crudely normalized (first by subtracting out θ and then by multiplying by some function of T) when T is two and when T is sixteen, clearly not asymptotic cases. In the Pareto case, this means using a lead term of T in the definition of U_T instead of $\sqrt{T}$ as in the case of the sample mean, so

$$U_T = T(X_T - \theta).$$

In the lognormal case, a lead term of $\log(T)$ is used in the definition of U_T, so

$$U_T = \log(T)(X_T - \theta).$$

while in the Weibull case a lead term of $T^{1/\gamma}$ is used, so

$$U_T = T^{1/\gamma}(X_T - \theta).$$

Notice that the cumulative distribution functions of these transformed random variables are much closer.

Figure A.4.6 depicts the cumulative distribution functions of X_T, crudely normalized again, when T is thirty-two and when n is sixty-four, clearly not asymptotic cases either, but much closer to ∞ than in figure A.4.5. Notice in the Pareto case that the cumulative distribution functions for the different Ts are now virtually atop one another, while in the lognormal case they are quite close to one another too. As before, in the Weibull case, they appear coincident.

These results allow us to conclude tentatively that, when probability density functions are strictly positive at the boundaries of their support, extreme order statistics (either maxima or minima) appear to converge at rate T to the boundaries. When probability density functions equal zero at the boundaries of their support, extreme order statistics converge at rates slower than T, depending on how quickly the densities go to zero at the boundaries. Under some conditions, as in the lognormal case, this rate can be as slow as $\log(T)$, while in the Weibull case the rate will vary depending on the shape parameter γ of the distribution. In general, when γ exceeds one, the convergence rate for the Weibull is $T^{(1/\gamma)}$.

One curious fact is that the distributions of the crudely normalized X_T seem to *converge to a limit* much more quickly in the Weibull case than in either the lognormal or the Pareto case. In fact, in the Weibull case they appear coincident. Why?

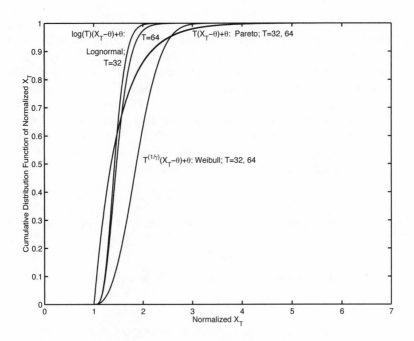

Figure A.4.6
Cumulative Distribution of Normalized X_T
Lognormal, Pareto, and Weibull Cases: $T = 32$ and $T = 64$

This has to do with the nature of the cumulative distribution function for the Weibull. Because we are interested in the local behavior of the distribution in the neighborhood of θ, it is easier to consider $S_{X_T}(x)$, the survivor function of X_T, instead of its cumulative distribution function. Note that the survivor function of X_T is

$$\Pr(X_T \geq x) = [1 - F_{X_T}(x)]$$
$$= S_{X_T}(x)$$
$$= S_V(x)^T$$
$$= \exp[-\lambda(x - \theta)^\gamma]^T$$
$$= \exp[-\lambda T(x - \theta)^\gamma].$$

Now, the mean of X_T is

$$\mathcal{E}(X_T) = \int_\theta^\infty S_{X_T}(x)\ dx = \theta + \int_0^\infty \exp(-\lambda T u^\gamma)\ du = \theta + \frac{\Gamma\left(1 + \frac{1}{\gamma}\right)}{(\lambda T)^{1/\gamma}}.$$

To get this to stabilize as $T \to \infty$, consider multiplying $(X_T - \theta)$ by $T^{(1/\gamma)}$. The mean of $T^{(1/\gamma)}(X_T - \theta)$ is then

$$\mathcal{E}\left[T^{(1/\gamma)}(X_T - \theta)\right] = \frac{\Gamma\left(1 + \frac{1}{\gamma}\right)}{\lambda^{1/\gamma}}$$

which is independent of T; the variance of $T^{(1/\gamma)}(X_T - \theta)$ is also independent of T in the Weibull case. It turns out that the minimum from a sample of T independent and identically distributed Weibull random variables follows a Weibull law. This result is analogous to the one where a sum of jointly normal random variables follows the Gaussian law.

What about the Pareto case? We can demonstrate that the minimum from a sample of T independent and identically distributed Pareto random variables has a Pareto law. To see this note that

$$\Pr(X_T \geq x) = S_{X_T} = S_V(x)^T = \left(\frac{\theta}{x}\right)^{\rho T}$$

which is just the survivor function for a Pareto random variable with parameters θ and ρT, instead of parameters θ and ρ. Why doesn't the normalized random variable $T(X_T - \theta)$ behave as nicely as the normalized Weibull one?

Well, the mean of X_T is

$$\mathcal{E}(X_T) = \int_\theta^\infty S_{X_T}(x)\, dx = \int_\theta^\infty \left(\frac{\theta}{x}\right)^{\rho T} dx = \frac{\rho T \theta}{\rho T - 1},$$

while its variance is

$$\mathcal{V}(X_T) = \mathcal{E}(X_T^2) - \left[\mathcal{E}(X_T)\right]^2 = \frac{\rho T \theta^2}{(\rho T - 1)^2 (\rho T - 2)}.$$

In this case, a location correction

$$m_T = \frac{\rho T \theta}{(\rho T - 1)}$$

and a scale correction

$$a_T = \sqrt{\frac{(\rho T - 1)^2 (\rho T - 2)}{\rho T \theta^2}}$$

are required to get U_T right. Just multiplying $(X_T - \theta)$ by T does not correct both the location and the scale term as multiplying by $T^{(1/\gamma)}$

does in the Weibull case. When T is small (for example, two), this really matters in comparison to when T is relatively large (for example, thirty-two or sixty-four).

What about the lognormal case? Now, E_t is within the location-scale family of distributions, so for any mean μ and variance σ^2 one can write

$$E_t = \mu + \sigma Z_t \quad Z_t \sim \mathcal{N}(0,1).$$

Thus, for an ordered sample of E_t, denoted $\{E_{(t:T)}\}_{t=1}^T$, where $E_{(1:T)}$ equals $\min(E_1, E_2, \ldots, E_T)$, we know that

$$E_{(1:T)} = \mu + \sigma Z_{(1:T)}$$

which implies that

$$\mathcal{E}[E_{(1:T)}] = \mu + \sigma \mathcal{E}[Z_{(1:T)}]$$

where

$$\mathcal{E}[Z_{(1:T)}] = \int_{-\infty}^{\infty} zT[1 - \Phi(z)]^{T-1}\phi(z) \ dz.$$

Note, too, that

$$\mathcal{V}[Z_{(1:T)}] = \mathcal{E}[Z_{(1:T)}^2] - \{\mathcal{E}[Z_{(1:T)}]\}^2$$

$$= \int_{-\infty}^{\infty} z^2 T[1 - \Phi(z)]^{T-1}\phi(z) \ dz - \{\mathcal{E}[Z_{(1:T)}]\}^2.$$

Now,

$$X_T = \theta + \exp[E_{(1:T)}] = \theta + \exp[\mu + \sigma Z_{(1:T)}],$$

so

$$\mathcal{E}(X_T) = \theta + \mathcal{E}\{\exp[E_{(1:T)}]\} \approx \theta + \exp\{\mu + \sigma\mathcal{E}[Z_{(1:T)}]\}$$

implying that a natural candidate for m_T is

$$m_T = \theta + \exp\{\mu + \sigma\mathcal{E}[Z_{(1:T)}]\}.$$

Using similar methods, one can derive a candidate a_T. It turns out that a_T is proportional to $\log T$.

It must seem obvious why X_T in the Weibull case is Weibull as $T \to \infty$, but what are the asymptotic distributions in the other cases? Well, the general answer is that they depend in a very elaborate way on the structure of the statistical experiments. Moreover, an asymptotic analysis of them is beyond this section, but can be found in a text by Galambos (1987).

Nevertheless, we now have enough intuition to state, without proof, two results concerning extreme order statistics. These two results are useful in our investigation of the maximum-likelihood estimator when derived for bid data from either Dutch or first-price, sealed-bid auctions within the independent private-values paradigm.

Result A.4.1: When the probability density function of a random variable is strictly positive at the boundary of support θ, then the sample extreme order statistic X_T converges at rate T to that boundary of support.

Result A.4.2: When the probability density function of a random variable is strictly positive at the boundary of support θ, then the normalized sample extreme order statistic $T(X_T - \theta)$ converges asymptotically to an exponentially distributed random variable.

A.5 Evaluating Estimators

Five steps exist in the analysis of any estimation problem. The first two steps involve proposing a strategy for estimating the parameter(s), and then implementing this strategy to obtain a rule, an estimator. We shall discuss the specifics of such strategies in sections that follow. Here, we simply imagine having derived an estimator. The next three steps in the analysis of any estimation problem involve evaluating the proposed rule—finding its mean, variance, and distribution. In order to undertake such an evaluation, we need to know how to describe the statistical properties of estimators.

In the remainder of this section, we shall use our example to illustrate this process. We know from a law of large numbers that

$$\plim_{T \to \infty} M_1 = \mu_1(\theta^0) = \frac{1}{\theta^0}.$$

This shows that M_1 should be close to $(1/\theta^0)$ if the sample size is relatively large. Intuitively, an estimator of θ^0 can then be defined by

$$\hat{\theta} = \frac{1}{M_1}.$$

This estimation strategy, formally known as the *method of moments*, will be discussed in detail in a later section.

We are interested in knowing whether $\hat{\theta}$ is a good estimator of θ^0. In other words, we need to investigate the statistical properties of the estimator $\hat{\theta}$. These properties include both the finite-sample as well as the large-sample properties.

A.5.1 Finite-Sample Properties

The finite-sample properties of $\hat{\theta}$ involve the mean and variance of the estimator.

A.5.1.1 Unbiasedness

$\hat{\theta}$ is an *unbiased* estimator of θ^0 if

$$\mathcal{E}(\hat{\theta}) = \theta^0.$$

An unbiased rule $\hat{\theta}$, on average, equals the true value of the parameter θ^0. This is a very desirable property for an estimator to have.

However, many estimators are biased, including $\hat{\theta}$, which equals $(1/M_1)$ in our example above. This is shown easily by appealing to *Jensen's inequality*.

Jensen's Inequality: Consider a convex function $g(V_T)$ of the random variable V_T where $\mathcal{E}(V_T)$ equals μ.

$$\mathcal{E}[g(V_T)] > g[\mathcal{E}(V_T)] = g(\mu).$$

We illustrate Jensen's inequality in figure A.5.1 where the random variable M takes on but two values, m_{low} and m_{high}. Now, the mean of M is between m_{low} and m_{high}, so the function $g(\cdot)$ evaluated at the mean of M is below the ray between $g(m_{\text{low}})$ and $g(m_{\text{high}})$.

Because $(1/M_1)$ is a strictly convex function of M_1, by Jensen's inequality,

$$\mathcal{E}(\hat{\theta}) > \frac{1}{\mathcal{E}(M_1)} = \frac{1}{\frac{1}{\theta^0}} = \theta^0.$$

However, Jensen's inequality provides no indication concerning the magnitude of the bias. To investigate this, consider a second-order, Taylor-series expansion of $\hat{\theta}$ about θ^0. Note that

$$g(M_1) = g\big[\mu_1(\theta^0)\big] + g'\big[\mu_1(\theta^0)\big]\big[M_1 - \mu_1(\theta^0)\big] +$$

$$g''\big[\mu_1(\theta^0)\big]\frac{\big[M_1 - \mu_1(\theta^0)\big]^2}{2} + R_3$$

where R_3 is a remainder that is assumed negligible so it can be ignored, then

$$\mathcal{E}(\hat{\theta}) = \mathcal{E}\big[g(M_1)\big]$$

$$\doteq g\big[\mu_1(\theta^0)\big] + g'\big[\mu_1(\theta^0)\big]\mathcal{E}\Big\{\big[M_1 - \mu_1(\theta^0)\big]\Big\} +$$

$$g''\big[\mu_1(\theta^0)\big]\mathcal{E}\left\{\frac{\big[M_1 - \mu_1(\theta^0)\big]^2}{2}\right\}.$$

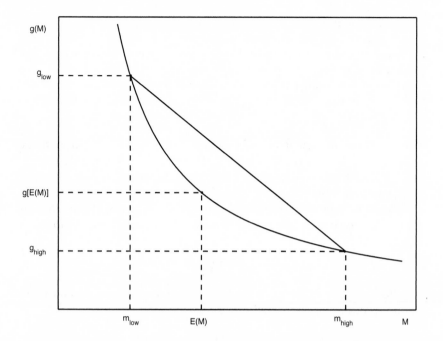

Figure A.5.1
An Example of Jensen's Inequality

Note that

$$\mathcal{E}\{[M_1 - \mu_1(\theta^0)]\} = 0 \quad \text{and} \quad \mathcal{E}\{[M_1 - \mu_1(\theta^0)]^2\} = \frac{\mathcal{V}(V)}{T} = \frac{1}{T(\theta^0)^2}.$$

Note, too, that

$$g[\mu_1(\theta^0)] = g(1/\theta^0) = \theta^0$$

and

$$g'(M_1) = \frac{-1}{M_1^2} \quad \text{and} \quad g''(M_1) = \frac{2}{M_1^3},$$

so

$$g'[\mu_1(\theta^0)] = g'(1/\theta^0) = -(\theta^0)^2 \quad \text{and} \quad g''[\mu_1(\theta^0)] = g''(1/\theta^0) = 2(\theta^0)^3.$$

Thus,

$$\mathcal{E}(\hat{\theta}) = \theta^0 + \frac{2(\theta^0)^3 \mathcal{V}(V)}{2T} = \theta^0 + \frac{2(\theta^0)^3}{2T(\theta^0)^2} = \frac{(T+1)\theta^0}{T},$$

so $\hat{\theta}$ is biased. Note, however, that when T is large this bias is relatively small. In fact, as $T \to \infty$, the bias in $\hat{\theta}$ goes away; $\hat{\theta}$ is an asymptotically unbiased estimator.

A.5.1.2 Variance

Consider $\hat{\theta}$ and $\tilde{\theta}$, two unbiased estimators of the parameter θ^0. The estimator $\hat{\theta}$ is said to be *more efficient* than the estimator $\tilde{\theta}$ if the variance of $\hat{\theta}$ is smaller than the variance of $\tilde{\theta}$; viz.,

$$\mathcal{V}(\hat{\theta}) < \mathcal{V}(\tilde{\theta}).$$

What this means is that more of the mass of $\hat{\theta}$ is clustered around the true value of θ^0 than is the case for $\tilde{\theta}$. Hence, $\hat{\theta}$ is more accurate than $\tilde{\theta}$.

Holding the bias of two estimators constant, equal, and zero (preferably), we prefer the estimator with the smallest variance.

Another way of looking at this notion is in terms of relative efficiency. The estimator $\hat{\theta}$ is relatively more efficient than the estimator $\tilde{\theta}$ if

$$\mathcal{RE}(\hat{\theta}, \tilde{\theta}) = \frac{\mathcal{V}(\hat{\theta})}{\mathcal{V}(\tilde{\theta})} < 1.$$

To illustrate efficiency, consider our example introduced above. In addition to the sample mean M_1, examine

$$\hat{M}_1 = \frac{V_1 + V_T}{2}.$$

Both M_1 and $\hat{M}_1$ are unbiased estimators of $\mu_1(\theta^0)$ since

$$\mathcal{E}(\hat{M}_1) = \frac{\mathcal{E}(V_1) + \mathcal{E}(V_T)}{2} = \frac{\mu_1(\theta^0) + \mu_1(\theta^0)}{2} = \mu_1(\theta^0).$$

The variance of $\hat{M}_1$ is

$$\mathcal{V}(\hat{M}_1) = \frac{1}{4}\left[\mathcal{V}(V_1) + \mathcal{V}(V_T) + 2\mathrm{cov}(V_1, V_T)\right]$$

$$= \frac{1}{4}\left[\mathcal{V}(V) + \mathcal{V}(V) + 2(0)\right] = \frac{1}{2}\mathcal{V}(V).$$

Thus, when T exceeds two, M_1 is more efficient than $\hat{M}_1$ because

$$\mathcal{V}(M_1) = \frac{1}{T}\mathcal{V}(V) < \frac{1}{2}\mathcal{V}(V) = \mathcal{V}(\hat{M}_1),$$

or, using the relative efficiency,

$$\mathcal{RE}(M_1, \hat{M}_1) = \frac{\mathcal{V}(M_1)}{\mathcal{V}(\hat{M}_1)} = \frac{2}{T} < 1.$$

A.5.1.3 Mean Squared-Error

If two estimators are biased estimators of θ^0, then one way in which to compare their performance is by the *mean squared-error* criterion. The mean squared-error of an estimator $\hat\theta$ is

$$\mathcal{MSE}(\hat\theta) = \mathcal{E}\big[(\hat\theta - \theta^0)^2\big],$$

which is the average squared-distance between $\hat\theta$ and θ^0.

Note that mean squared-error can be decomposed into the variance of $\hat\theta$ and the bias-squared of $\hat\theta$:

$$\mathcal{MSE}(\hat\theta) = \mathcal{E}\big\{[\hat\theta - \mathcal{E}(\hat\theta) + \mathcal{E}(\hat\theta) - \theta^0]^2\big\}$$

$$= \mathcal{E}\big\{[\hat\theta - \mathcal{E}(\hat\theta)]^2 - 2[\mathcal{E}(\hat\theta) - \theta^0][\hat\theta - \mathcal{E}(\hat\theta)] + [\mathcal{E}(\hat\theta) - \theta^0]^2\big\}$$

$$= \mathcal{E}\big\{[\hat\theta - \mathcal{E}(\hat\theta)]^2\big\} - 2[\mathcal{E}(\hat\theta) - \theta^0]\mathcal{E}\big\{[\hat\theta - \mathcal{E}(\hat\theta)]\big\} + [\mathcal{E}(\hat\theta) - \theta^0]^2$$

$$= \mathcal{V}(\hat\theta) + [\mathcal{BIAS}(\hat\theta)]^2.$$

since $\mathcal{E}[\hat\theta - \mathcal{E}(\hat\theta)]$ equals $[\mathcal{E}(\hat\theta) - \mathcal{E}(\hat\theta)]$ or zero.

To illustrate an application of the mean squared-error criterion, consider again our example. Introduce two biased estimators of $\mu_1(\theta^0)$:

$$\hat M_1 = \frac{1}{T-1}\sum_{t=1}^{T} V_t \quad\text{and}\quad \tilde M_1 = \frac{V_1 + V_T}{3}.$$

Both of these are biased estimators of $\mu_1(\theta^0)$ because

$$\mathcal{E}(\hat M_1) = \frac{T}{T-1}\mu_1(\theta^0) \quad\text{and}\quad \mathcal{E}(\tilde M_1) = \frac{2}{3}\mu_1(\theta^0).$$

Their biases are

$$\mathcal{BIAS}(\hat M_1) = \frac{1}{T-1}\mu_1(\theta^0) \quad\text{and}\quad \mathcal{BIAS}(\tilde M_1) = -\frac{1}{3}\mu_1(\theta^0).$$

Now, the mean squared-errors of $\hat M_1$ and $\tilde M_1$ are

$$\mathcal{MSE}(\hat M_1) = \mathcal{V}(\hat M_1) + \mathcal{BIAS}(\hat M_1)^2$$

$$= \left(\frac{T}{T-1}\right)^2 \mathcal{V}(V) + \frac{1}{(T-1)^2}\mu_1(\theta^0)^2$$

$$= \frac{T+1}{(T-1)^2(\theta^0)^2}$$

and

$$\mathcal{MSE}(\tilde{M}_1) = \mathcal{V}(\tilde{M}_1) + \mathcal{BIAS}(\tilde{M}_1)^2$$

$$= \frac{2}{9(\theta^0)^2} + \frac{1}{9(\theta^0)^2}$$

$$= \frac{1}{3(\theta^0)^2}.$$

Note that, if T is less than six, then $\mathcal{MSE}(\tilde{M}_1)$ is less than $\mathcal{MSE}(\hat{M}_1)$ and $\tilde{M}_1$ is preferred to $\hat{M}_1$ because the combined variability and bias, as measured by the mean squared-error, is the least. But if T exceeds six, then $\mathcal{MSE}(\hat{M}_1)$ is less than $\mathcal{MSE}(\tilde{M}_1)$ and $\hat{M}_1$ is preferred to $\tilde{M}_1$ since the combined variability and bias, as measured by the mean squared-error, is then the least.

A.5.2 Large-Sample Properties

The tools developed above can be used to show whether an estimator is consistent for the parameter value that is being estimated and, if so, what the approximate large-sample distribution of the estimator is.

A.5.2.1 Parameter Consistency

We know from a law of large numbers that

$$\plim_{T\to\infty} M_1 = \mu_1(\theta^0) = \frac{1}{\theta^0}.$$

Recall that $\hat{\theta}$ is $(1/M_1)$. For any real θ^0, it is always true that $(1/\theta^0)$ does not equal zero. Therefore, $(1/M_1)$ is always continuous at $\mu_1(\theta^0)$. Hence, we invoke the continuous mapping theorem to claim that

$$\plim_{T\to\infty} \hat{\theta} = \frac{1}{\plim_{T\to\infty} M_1} = \frac{1}{\mu_1(\theta^0)} = \theta^0.$$

In words, while $\hat{\theta}$ is a biased estimator of θ^0, it is a parameter-consistent estimator of θ^0. Another example is $\hat{M}_1$, which is a biased, but consistent, estimator of $\mu_1(\theta^0)$.

Usually, the sample mean is both an unbiased and a consistent estimator of the population mean. For example, M_1 is an unbiased and a consistent estimator of $\mu_1(\theta^0)$. $\tilde{M}_1$, on the other hand, is neither an unbiased nor a consistent estimator of $\mu_1(\theta^0)$. Consistent but biased estimators are commonly used in econometrics: The maximum-likelihood estimator and the generalized method-of-moments estimator, to be introduced in the next sections, are typically biased, but consistent estimators. Biased and inconsistent estimators, on the other hand, are rarely used in practice.

A notion related to convergence in probability is *convergence in mean squared-error*. An estimator $\hat{\theta}$ converges in mean squared-error to θ^0 if

$$\lim_{T \to \infty} \mathcal{MSE}(\hat{\theta}) = \lim_{T \to \infty} \mathcal{V}(\hat{\theta}) + \lim_{T \to \infty} [\mathcal{BIAS}(\hat{\theta})]^2 = 0.$$

If we can demonstrate that an estimator converges in mean squared-error, then we have demonstrated that it converges in probability, since convergence in mean squared-error implies convergence in probability.

For example, we have calculated the mean squared-error for $\hat{M}_1$, and

$$\lim_{T \to \infty} \mathcal{MSE}(\hat{M}_1) = \lim_{T \to \infty} \frac{T+1}{(T-1)^2(\theta^0)^2} = 0.$$

Hence, $\hat{M}_1$ is a consistent estimator of $\mu_1(\theta^0)$, even though it is a biased estimator.

On the other hand, the mean squared-error of $\tilde{M}_1$ is constant and does not decrease with the sample size T. Therefore, it is an *inconsistent* estimator; it is also a biased estimator. It is also possible for an estimator to be unbiased, but inconsistent. Consider

$$\check{M}_1 = \frac{V_1 + V_2}{2}.$$

A.5.2.2 Asymptotic Distribution

Many estimators that are functions of the sample mean are not only parameter consistent but are also approximately normally distributed in large samples. The delta method can be used to show that $\hat{\theta}$, which equals $(1/M_1)$, is asymptotically normally distributed.

We know from the Lindeberg–Levy central limit theorem that

$$\sqrt{T}[M_1 - \mu_1(\theta^0)] \xrightarrow{\mathrm{d}} \mathcal{N}[0, \mathcal{V}(V)].$$

The delta method can then be applied to $g(M_1)$, which equals $(1/M_1)$:

$$\sqrt{T}(\hat{\theta} - \theta^0) = \sqrt{T}\{g(M_1) - g[\mu_1(\theta^0)]\}$$

$$\xrightarrow{\mathrm{d}} g'[\mu_1(\theta^0)]\mathcal{N}[0, \mathcal{V}(V)] = \mathcal{N}[0, (\theta^0)^2].$$

In other words, $\hat{\theta}$ is approximately normally distributed with mean θ^0 and variance $(\theta^0)^2/T$. In this example, the exact distribution of $\hat{\theta}$ can also be derived. Note that

$$\hat{\theta} = \frac{T}{\sum_{t=1}^{T} V_t} = \frac{T}{S},$$

where S is $\sum_{t=1}^{T} V_t$, a sum of independent and identically distributed exponential random variables, so S is distributed gamma with parameters θ^0 and T. Thus,

$$f_S(s) = \frac{(\theta^0)^T}{\Gamma(T)} s^{T-1} \exp(-\theta^0 s).$$

Let R equal $\hat{\theta}$. Note that

$$f_R(r) = f_S(s) \left| \frac{ds}{dr} \right|, \quad \text{and} \quad \frac{dS}{dR} = \frac{-T}{R^2},$$

and since $S \in (0, \infty)$, it is also true that R, which equals $\hat{\theta} \in (0, \infty)$. Thus,

$$f_R(r) = \frac{(\theta^0)^T}{\Gamma(T)} \left(\frac{T}{r} \right)^{T-1} \exp(-\theta^0 T/r) \left| \frac{-T}{r^2} \right|$$

$$= \frac{(\theta^0 T)^T}{\Gamma(T)} \frac{1}{r^{T+1}} \exp(-\theta^0 T/r) \quad \text{for} \quad r > 0.$$

Parameter consistency and asymptotic normality state that when T is reasonably large this density looks like a normal density with mean θ^0 and variance $(\theta^0)^2/T$. We can actually calculate the exact mean and variance of $\hat{\theta}$ using this density; viz.,

$$\mathcal{E}(\hat{\theta}) = \frac{T}{T-1}\theta^0 \quad \text{and} \quad \mathcal{V}(\hat{\theta}) = \frac{T^2(\theta^0)^2}{(T-1)^2(T-2)}.$$

When T is large, these are very close to θ^0 and $[(\theta^0)^2/T]$. Therefore, the delta method approximation method appears fairly close to the actual variance as does the density; see figure A.5.2 for the exact and approximate distributions of $\hat{\theta}$ when θ^0 is one and T is twenty-five.

A.5.3 The Bootstrap

With the advent of cheap, fast, and powerful computing, alternative methods of estimation and inference have evolved. Perhaps the most

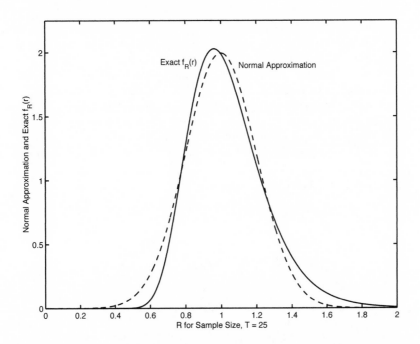

Figure A.5.2
Asymptotic and Exact Probability Density Function of R

influential idea in the latter two decades of the twentieth century is due to Efron (1982). It is called *the bootstrap*. We believe it is safe to say that this idea has revolutionized the practice of statistics. While a theoretical analysis of the bootstrap is well beyond the scope of a section of an appendix, outlining the elements of its mechanics is not. Moreover, under many conditions, that can be verified *ex ante*, one can implement the bootstrap on a computer without much mess or bother.

For a random sample of T observations $\{V_1, V_2, \ldots, V_T\}$, one way to view an estimator is a rule that maps the T values into a number. Because the T values can vary from sample to sample, so too will the estimate, hence the sampling variability in estimators. For a realized sample of T measurements $\{v_1, v_2, \ldots, v_T\}$, it is impossible to get any variation in the estimate since the v_ts do not change. However, if one thinks of $\{v_1, v_2, \ldots, v_T\}$ as an urn that represents well the cumulative distribution $F_V^0(v)$, then one can sample from $\{v_1, v_2, \ldots, v_T\}$ with replacement and thus create variability in an estimate, sampling variation, so to speak.

Treating $\{v_1, v_2, \ldots, v_T\}$ as an urn that represents $F_V^0(v)$ and then *resampling* from it is the essential idea behind the bootstrap. It was only made feasible with the advent of cheap and fast computation. Thus, the bootstrap is something between finite-sample and large-sample theory.

To motivate the bootstrap, we consider examples from three different classes of estimators, and contrast the methods used to investigate their stochastic behavior.

Some estimators are linear functions of the data. For example, consider $\{V_1, V_2, \ldots, V_T\}$, an independent and identically drawn sample of size T from the normal family of distributions having mean $\mathcal{E}(V)$ equal to μ^0 and variance $\mathcal{V}(V)$ equal to σ^2. In this case, the first raw sample moment M_1, which is also the sample mean, is often used as an estimator of μ^0 where M_1 is defined as

$$M_1 = \frac{\sum_{t=1}^{T} V_t}{T},$$

while an unbiased estimator of σ^2 is

$$S^2 = \frac{\sum_{t=1}^{T}(V_t - M_1)^2}{(T-1)}.$$

Recall that, on average, M_1 equals μ^0 since, with linearity,

$$\mathcal{E}(M_1) = \frac{\mathcal{E}\left(\sum_{t=1}^{T} V_t\right)}{T} = \frac{\sum_{t=1}^{T}\mathcal{E}(V_t)}{T} = \frac{T\mathcal{E}(V)}{T} = \mu^0.$$

Also, by independence,

$$\mathcal{V}(M_1) = \frac{\mathcal{V}\left(\sum_{t=1}^{T} V_t\right)}{T^2} = \frac{\sum_{t=1}^{T}\mathcal{V}(V_t)}{T^2} = \frac{T\mathcal{V}(V)}{T^2} = \frac{\sigma^2}{T}.$$

Finally, because M_1 is a linear combination of normal random variables, it too is distributed normally. Hence,

$$M_1 \sim \mathcal{N}(\mu^0, \sigma^2/T).$$

For $\{v_1, v_2, \ldots, v_T\}$, a realization of $\{V_1, V_2, \ldots, V_T\}$, an estimate of μ^0 is $\hat{m}_1$, which equals $\sum_{t=1}^{T} v_t/T$, and has a standard error $\hat{s}/\sqrt{T}$ where $\hat{s}^2$ equals $\sum_{t=1}^{T}(v_t - \hat{m}_1)^2/(T-1)$.

Next, consider $\{V_1, V_2, \ldots, V_T\}$, an independent and identically drawn sample of size T from the exponential distribution having parameter θ^0. In this case, the mean of V is

$$\mathcal{E}(V) = \mu_1(\theta^0) = \frac{1}{\theta^0},$$

while the variance of V is

$$\mathcal{V}(V) = \frac{1}{(\theta^0)^2}.$$

One estimator of θ^0 is

$$\hat{\theta} = \frac{T}{\sum_{t=1}^{T} V_t} = g(M_1)$$

where $g(M_1)$ is a continuous and differentiable function of M_1, which is defined by

$$M_1 = \frac{\sum_{t=1}^{T} V_t}{T}.$$

Notice that this estimator is a nonlinear function of the data. Such nonlinearities often make it difficult to find either the mean or the variance of $\hat{\theta}$, but by using the asymptotic methods developed above we know that

$$\sqrt{T}(\hat{\theta} - \theta^0) \xrightarrow{\mathrm{d}} \mathcal{N}\left[0, (\theta^0)^2\right].$$

For $\{v_1, v_2, \ldots, v_T\}$, a realization of $\{V_1, V_2, \ldots, V_T\}$, an estimate equal to $(T/\sum_{t=1}^{T} v_t)$, which has an estimated standard error $(\sqrt{T}/\sum_{t=1}^{T} v_t)$.

Finally, consider now the first example, but assume that contamination is potentially a problem. Contamination occurs when some observations are misrecorded or their recording is corrupted. It is well known that the sample mean *breaks down* when only one observation is contaminated. The sample median, on the other hand, is robust to contamination up to the point where just less than one-half of the sample is contaminated. What are the properties of the sample median

$$H_{0.5} = \mathrm{median}(V_1, V_2, \ldots, V_T)?$$

This estimator, like all order statistics, is not a differentiable function of the data, so the delta method cannot be used to investigate its asymptotic properties. However, later in appendix A.6.4, we shall examine other asymptotic methods that can be used to prove that the sample median is an asymptotically normal estimator of the population median $\xi_{0.5}$ having the following distribution:

$$\sqrt{T}(H_{0.5} - \xi_{0.5}) \xrightarrow{\mathrm{d}} \mathcal{N}\left[0, \frac{1}{4f_V^0\left(\xi_{0.5}\right)^2}\right]$$

where $f_V^0(\cdot)$ is the true probability density function of V. In the normal case, $\xi_{0.5}$ equals μ^0 and $f_V^0(\xi_{0.5})$ equals $1/\sqrt{2\pi\sigma^2}$, so

$$\sqrt{T}(H_{0.5} - \xi_{0.5}) \xrightarrow{\mathrm{d}} \mathcal{N}\left(0, \frac{\pi\sigma^2}{2}\right).$$

For $\{v_1, v_2, \ldots, v_T\}$, a realization of $\{V_1, V_2, \ldots, V_T\}$, an estimate of μ^0 is

$$\hat{h}_{0.5} = \text{median}(v_1, v_2, \ldots, v_T).$$

What is the standard error of $\hat{h}_{0.5}$? Clearly, it depends on an estimate of the probability density function $f_V^0(\cdot)$, perhaps evaluated at the sample median $\hat{h}_{0.5}$. The bootstrap is useful when evaluating estimators like the sample median $H_{0.5}$, especially when $f_V^0(\cdot)$ is unknown.

The bootstrap can also be useful to evaluate estimators like $\hat{\theta}$ when it may be suspect to assume that the remainder in a delta-method expansion is negligible. In fact, one interpretation of the bootstrap is that it takes into account all of the higher-order terms that are ignored when first-order asymptotic methods are undertaken.

In general, the bootstrap can be used to evaluate variability, estimate bias, and calculate tables of test statistics. Below, we shall discuss how to implement the *nonparametric* bootstrap standard error of an estimator $\hat{\theta}$ of θ^0 for $\{V_1, V_2, \ldots, V_T\}$, an independent and identically drawn sample of size T from some family of distributions $F_V^0(v)$.[2]

The mechanics we describe are often referred to as the *plug-in formula* for the nonparametric bootstrap standard error. Denote the data vector $\{V_1, V_2, \ldots, V_T\}$ by $\boldsymbol{V}$. Suppose one is interested in calculating the standard error of $\hat{\theta}(\boldsymbol{V})$. To calculate the nonparametric bootstrap standard error involves the following steps:

1. For $\boldsymbol{v}$, the sample realization of $\boldsymbol{V}$, calculate $\hat{\theta}(\boldsymbol{v})$, an estimate of θ^0.

2. From $\boldsymbol{v}$ take random samples of size T with replacement weighting each v_t equally by $(1/T)$. For the jth bootstrap sample $\boldsymbol{v}_j^*$, which equals $\{v_{1j}^*, v_{2j}^*, \ldots, v_{Tj}^*\}$ where $j = 1, \ldots, J$, calculate the estimator $\hat{\theta}(\boldsymbol{v}_j^*)$ to get $\hat{\theta}_j^*$.

3. To calculate the nonparametric bootstrap standard error of $\hat{\theta}$, use the following formula:

$$\text{se}_B(\hat{\theta}) = \sqrt{\frac{\sum_{j=1}^{J}(\hat{\theta}_j^* - \overline{\hat{\theta}^*})^2}{(J-1)}}$$

where

$$\overline{\hat{\theta}^*} = \frac{\sum_{j=1}^{J} \hat{\theta}_j^*}{J}.$$

---

[2] It should be noted that in the presence of contamination the sample median is robust, but the bootstrap variance estimate of the sample median need not be robust. In what follows, it shall be assumed that the bootstrap variance estimate of the sample median is robust to contamination.

To carry out the steps outlined above, one needs to be able to do the following:

1) calculate the estimator $\hat{\theta}(\boldsymbol{V})$;

2) sample randomly from $\boldsymbol{v}$.

Presumably, if one is interested in calculating the standard error of $\hat{\theta}$, an estimate of θ^0, then one knows the structure of $\hat{\theta}(\boldsymbol{V})$ and has implemented this on a computer, but how does one sample randomly from $\boldsymbol{v}$?

Central to the bootstrap is selecting randomly from $\boldsymbol{v}$ with replacement. To do this, one requires random numbers. In a previous appendix, we have discussed how to generate uniform pseudo-random numbers. But how can these uniform pseudo-random numbers be used to sample randomly with replacement from $\boldsymbol{v}$ using weights $(1/T)$?

Introduce an integer variable `itag` that marks which of the integers $1, 2, \ldots, \texttt{T}$ has been randomly chosen with replacement. How should `itag` be constructed? Consider generating a uniformly distributed random number from the interval $(0, 1)$. Suppose this number is 0.1539. Multiply 0.1539 by T. Suppose T is twenty-five. Now, if this result is assigned to a real variable, the number 25×0.1539 or 3.8475 will obtain. For any given uniform pseudo-random number $\texttt{u(j)}$, $\texttt{T} \times \texttt{u(j)}$ is randomly distributed on the interval $(0, 25)$. On the other hand, if 25×0.1539 is assigned to an integer, then the result will be truncated to be the integer 3. Thus, when any random number from $(0, 1)$ is multiplied by $\texttt{T}$ and then assigned to an integer, the least it can be is 0, while the most it can be is $(\texttt{T} - 1)$. Moreover, because of uniformity, each of the integers from the set $\{0, 1, \ldots, T - 1\}$ will have the same chance of being drawn. By adding 1 to `itag` one obtains integers sampled from the set $\{1, 2, \ldots, T\}$ with replacement and probability $(1/T)$.

A.6 Estimation Strategies

A number of different estimation strategies exist to recover estimates of $\boldsymbol{\theta}$ in $f_V(v; \boldsymbol{\theta})$ from a random sample $\{V_t\}_{t=1}^T$. Below, in the parametric case, we discuss two of the most common and important ones. Later, we shall review briefly nonparametric techniques.

A.6.1 Generalized Method of Moments

A commonly used strategy to estimate parameters is the *generalized method of moments*, GMM.

Appendixes

A.6.1.1 Definition

This method begins with a set of moment conditions

$$\boldsymbol{\mu}(V_t, \boldsymbol{\theta}) \equiv \begin{pmatrix} \mu_1(V_t, \boldsymbol{\theta}) \\ \mu_2(V_t, \boldsymbol{\theta}) \\ \vdots \\ \mu_K(V_t, \boldsymbol{\theta}) \end{pmatrix}$$

where $\boldsymbol{\mu}(V_t, \boldsymbol{\theta})$ is a set of continuously differentiable functions of V_t and the unknown $(p \times 1)$ parameter vector $\boldsymbol{\theta}$, such that their expectations equal zero uniquely at $\boldsymbol{\theta}$ equal $\boldsymbol{\theta}^0$. Thus,

$$\mathcal{E}\left[\boldsymbol{\mu}(V_t, \boldsymbol{\theta})\right] = \mathbf{0}_K \quad \text{if and only if} \quad \boldsymbol{\theta} = \boldsymbol{\theta}^0.$$

The population moment condition $\mathcal{E}[\boldsymbol{\mu}(V_t, \boldsymbol{\theta})]$ is unobserved, but can be approximated by its sample analogue:

$$\hat{\boldsymbol{\mu}}_T(\boldsymbol{\theta}) = \frac{1}{T} \sum_{t=1}^{T} \boldsymbol{\mu}(V_t, \boldsymbol{\theta}).$$

The GMM estimator is defined as the $\boldsymbol{\theta}$ that makes this sample average moment condition as close to zero as possible. The distance of $\hat{\boldsymbol{\mu}}_T(\boldsymbol{\theta})$ to zero is usually measured via a quadratic norm:

$$\hat{\boldsymbol{\theta}}_{\text{GMM}} = \arg\min_{\boldsymbol{\theta} \in \boldsymbol{\Theta}} \ \hat{\boldsymbol{\mu}}_T(\boldsymbol{\theta})^\top \mathbf{A}_T \hat{\boldsymbol{\mu}}_T(\boldsymbol{\theta})$$

where the $(K \times K)$ weighting matrix $\mathbf{A}_T \xrightarrow{\text{p}} \mathbf{A}$ as $T \to \infty$, and $\mathbf{A}$ is a $(K \times K)$ positive definite matrix. The parameter set $\boldsymbol{\Theta}$ is usually a subset of $\boldsymbol{R}^p$ where p does not exceed K.

When p equals K, the weighting matrix $\mathbf{A}_T$ is irrelevant and the model is *exactly identified*. In this case, $\hat{\boldsymbol{\theta}}_{\text{GMM}}$ can also be defined as the solution to a set of potentially nonlinear equations:

$$\hat{\boldsymbol{\mu}}_T(\hat{\boldsymbol{\theta}}_{\text{GMM}}) = \mathbf{0}_p.$$

In our example above, $\hat{\theta}$ equals $(1/M_1)$ can be considered a GMM estimator, where K and p equal one, and

$$\boldsymbol{\mu}(V_t, \theta) = V_t - \frac{1}{\theta}.$$

In this case, $\mathbf{A}_T$ is apparently irrelevant. In most applications, however, K exceeds p and the model is *overidentified*.

A.6.1.2 Parameter Consistency/Asymptotic Normality

GMM estimators are consistent under very general conditions. A set of sufficient conditions for $\operatorname{plim}_{T\to\infty} \hat{\boldsymbol{\theta}}_{\mathrm{GMM}}$ to equal $\boldsymbol{\theta}^0$ are:

1. $\operatorname{plim}_{T\to\infty} \boldsymbol{\mu}_T(\boldsymbol{\theta}) = \mathcal{E}[\boldsymbol{\mu}(V_t, \boldsymbol{\theta})]$ uniformly in $\boldsymbol{\theta} \in \boldsymbol{\Theta}$;
2. $\mathbf{A}\mathcal{E}[\boldsymbol{\mu}(V_t, \boldsymbol{\theta})] = \mathbf{0}_p$ if and only $\boldsymbol{\theta} = \boldsymbol{\theta}^0$.

These conditions are usually easy to verify in practice. In addition, GMM estimators are usually also asymptotically normally distributed. This can be shown using the tools developed above.

Assuming the solution to the optimization problem that defines the GMM estimator is in the interior of $\boldsymbol{\Theta}$, the first-order conditions are:

$$\frac{\partial \hat{\boldsymbol{\mu}}_T(\hat{\boldsymbol{\theta}}_{\mathrm{GMM}})^\top}{\partial \boldsymbol{\theta}} \mathbf{A}_T \hat{\boldsymbol{\mu}}_T(\hat{\boldsymbol{\theta}}_{\mathrm{GMM}}) = \mathbf{0}_p.$$

Expanding $\hat{\boldsymbol{\mu}}_T(\hat{\boldsymbol{\theta}}_{\mathrm{GMM}})$ about the truth $\boldsymbol{\theta}^0$ in a first-order, Taylor-series expansion yields:

$$\hat{\boldsymbol{\mu}}_T(\hat{\boldsymbol{\theta}}_{\mathrm{GMM}}) = \hat{\boldsymbol{\mu}}_T(\boldsymbol{\theta}_0) + \frac{\partial \hat{\boldsymbol{\mu}}_T(\boldsymbol{\theta}^*)}{\partial \boldsymbol{\theta}}(\hat{\boldsymbol{\theta}}_{\mathrm{GMM}} - \boldsymbol{\theta}^0)$$

where $\boldsymbol{\theta}^*$ is a mean value between $\boldsymbol{\theta}^0$ and $\hat{\boldsymbol{\theta}}_{\mathrm{GMM}}$. Substituting this into the second occurence of $\hat{\boldsymbol{\mu}}_T(\hat{\boldsymbol{\theta}}_{\mathrm{GMM}})$ one obtains

$$\sqrt{T}(\hat{\boldsymbol{\theta}}_{\mathrm{GMM}} - \boldsymbol{\theta}^0) = \left[\frac{\partial \hat{\boldsymbol{\mu}}_T(\hat{\boldsymbol{\theta}}_{\mathrm{GMM}})}{\partial \boldsymbol{\theta}} \mathbf{A}_T \frac{\partial \hat{\boldsymbol{\mu}}_T(\boldsymbol{\theta}^*)^\top}{\partial \boldsymbol{\theta}} \right]^{-1}$$
$$\frac{\partial \hat{\boldsymbol{\mu}}_T(\hat{\boldsymbol{\theta}}_{\mathrm{GMM}})^\top}{\partial \boldsymbol{\theta}} \mathbf{A}_T \sqrt{T} \hat{\boldsymbol{\mu}}_T(\boldsymbol{\theta}^0).$$

By a (uniform) law of large numbers, since $\boldsymbol{\theta}^* \xrightarrow{\mathrm{P}} \boldsymbol{\theta}^0$, we have

$$\frac{\partial \hat{\boldsymbol{\mu}}_T(\boldsymbol{\theta}^*)}{\partial \boldsymbol{\theta}} = \frac{1}{T}\sum_{t=1}^{T} \frac{\partial \boldsymbol{\mu}(V_t, \boldsymbol{\theta}^*)}{\partial \boldsymbol{\theta}} \xrightarrow{\mathrm{P}} \mathcal{E}\left[\frac{\partial \boldsymbol{\mu}(V_t, \boldsymbol{\theta}^0)}{\partial \boldsymbol{\theta}} \right] \equiv \mathbf{G}.$$

Similarly,

$$\frac{\partial \hat{\boldsymbol{\mu}}_T(\hat{\boldsymbol{\theta}}_{\mathrm{GMM}})}{\partial \boldsymbol{\theta}} = \frac{1}{T}\sum_{t=1}^{T} \frac{\partial \boldsymbol{\mu}(V_t, \hat{\boldsymbol{\theta}}_{\mathrm{GMM}})}{\partial \boldsymbol{\theta}} \xrightarrow{\mathrm{P}} \mathbf{G}.$$

An application of the continuous mapping theorem then implies that

$$\operatorname*{plim}_{T\to\infty} \left[\frac{\partial \hat{\boldsymbol{\mu}}_T(\hat{\boldsymbol{\theta}})^\top}{\partial \boldsymbol{\theta}} \mathbf{A}_T \frac{\partial \hat{\boldsymbol{\mu}}_T(\boldsymbol{\theta}^*)^\top}{\partial \boldsymbol{\theta}} \right]^{-1} \frac{\partial \hat{\boldsymbol{\mu}}_T(\hat{\boldsymbol{\theta}}_{\mathrm{GMM}})^\top}{\partial \boldsymbol{\theta}} \mathbf{A}_T$$
$$= (\mathbf{G}^\top \mathbf{A} \mathbf{G})^{-1} \mathbf{G}^\top \mathbf{A}.$$

When the variance of $\boldsymbol{\mu}(V_t, \boldsymbol{\theta}^0)$ is finite, one can apply the Lindeberg–Levy central limit theorem to conclude that

$$\sqrt{T}\hat{\boldsymbol{\mu}}_T(\boldsymbol{\theta}^0) \xrightarrow{\text{d}} \mathcal{N}\left\{\mathbf{0}_p, \mathcal{E}[\boldsymbol{\mu}(V_t, \boldsymbol{\theta}^0)\boldsymbol{\mu}(V_t, \boldsymbol{\theta}^0)^\top]\right\}.$$

Define the variance-covariance matrix above to be $\boldsymbol{\Sigma}$. An application of Slutsky's theorem then gives the asymptotic distribution of $\hat{\boldsymbol{\theta}}_{\text{GMM}}$:

$$\sqrt{T}(\hat{\boldsymbol{\theta}}_{\text{GMM}} - \boldsymbol{\theta}^0) \xrightarrow{\text{d}} -(\mathbf{G}^\top \mathbf{A} \mathbf{G})^{-1} \mathbf{G}^\top \mathbf{A} \times \mathcal{N}(\mathbf{0}_p, \boldsymbol{\Sigma})$$
$$= \mathcal{N}\left[\mathbf{0}_p, (\mathbf{G}^\top \mathbf{A} \mathbf{G})^{-1} \mathbf{G}^\top \mathbf{A} \boldsymbol{\Sigma} \mathbf{A}^\top \mathbf{G} (\mathbf{G}^\top \mathbf{A} \mathbf{G})^{-1}\right].$$

Each of the components in the variance-covariance matrix can be consistently estimated. $\mathbf{G}$ can be estimated by

$$\hat{\mathbf{G}} = \frac{1}{T} \sum_{t=1}^{T} \frac{\partial \boldsymbol{\mu}(V_t, \hat{\boldsymbol{\theta}}_{\text{GMM}})}{\partial \boldsymbol{\theta}}.$$

$\mathbf{A}$ can be estimated by $\mathbf{A}_T$, and $\boldsymbol{\Sigma}$ can be estimated by

$$\hat{\boldsymbol{\Sigma}}_T = \frac{1}{T} \sum_{t=1}^{T} \boldsymbol{\mu}(V_t, \hat{\boldsymbol{\theta}}_{\text{GMM}})\boldsymbol{\mu}(V_t, \hat{\boldsymbol{\theta}}_{\text{GMM}})^\top,$$

so

$$\hat{\boldsymbol{\theta}}_{\text{GMM}} \overset{\text{A}}{\sim} \mathcal{N}\left[\boldsymbol{\theta}^0, \frac{1}{T}(\hat{\mathbf{G}}^\top \mathbf{A}_T \hat{\mathbf{G}})^{-1}\hat{\mathbf{G}}^\top \mathbf{A}_T \hat{\boldsymbol{\Sigma}} \mathbf{A}_T^\top \hat{\mathbf{G}}(\hat{\mathbf{G}}^\top \mathbf{A}_T \hat{\mathbf{G}})^{-1}\right].$$

where the symbol "$\overset{\text{A}}{\sim}$" means *approximately distributed as*.

An efficient choice of $\mathbf{A}$ involves setting $\mathbf{A}$ to equal $\boldsymbol{\Sigma}^{-1}$, in which case,

$$\sqrt{T}(\hat{\boldsymbol{\theta}}_{\text{GMM}} - \boldsymbol{\theta}^0) \xrightarrow{\text{d}} \mathcal{N}[\mathbf{0}_p, (\mathbf{G}^\top \boldsymbol{\Sigma}^{-1} \mathbf{G})^{-1}].$$

When K equals p, so the model is exactly identified, $\mathbf{G}$ is invertible and it can also be written

$$(\mathbf{G}^\top \boldsymbol{\Sigma}^{-1} \mathbf{G})^{-1} = \mathbf{G}^{\top -1} \boldsymbol{\Sigma} \mathbf{G}^{-1}.$$

In our example, with

$$\boldsymbol{\mu}(V_t, \theta) = V_t - \frac{1}{\theta},$$

it is easy to see that

$$\mathbf{G} = -\frac{1}{\theta^2} \quad \text{and} \quad \boldsymbol{\Sigma} = \frac{1}{\theta^2}.$$

Therefore,

$$\sqrt{T}(\hat{\theta}_{\mathrm{GMM}} - \theta^0) \xrightarrow{\mathrm{d}} \mathcal{N}[0, (\theta^0)^2].$$

Note, too, in this example, $\mathbf{G}$ equals $-\boldsymbol{\Sigma}$. Usually, when this happens, $\hat{\theta}_{\mathrm{GMM}}$ will coincide with the efficient maximum-likelihood estimator, at least asymptotically. Indeed, as we shall see in the next section, this is the case here.

What happens if we make use of the second moment as well? In this case, where K is two, but p is one, and

$$\boldsymbol{\mu}\left(V_t, \theta\right) = \begin{pmatrix} V_t - 1/\theta \\ V_t^2 - 2/\theta^2 \end{pmatrix}.$$

Now,

$$\boldsymbol{\Sigma} = \begin{pmatrix} \frac{1}{\theta^2} & \frac{4}{\theta^3} \\ \\ \frac{4}{\theta^3} & \frac{20}{\theta^4} \end{pmatrix} \quad \text{and} \quad \mathbf{G} = \begin{pmatrix} \frac{1}{\theta^2} \\ \frac{4}{\theta^3} \end{pmatrix}.$$

When the efficient weighting matrix $\mathbf{A}$ equal $\boldsymbol{\Sigma}^{-1}$ is used, we can calculate the variance of the resulting GMM estimator:

$$(\mathbf{G}^\top \boldsymbol{\Sigma}^{-1} \mathbf{G})^{-1} = (\theta^0)^2$$

which coincides with the previous case when only the first moment is used. In this example, using higher moments does not improve the efficiency of the parameter estimator. As we shall see in the next section, the GMM estimator using the first moment coincides with the most efficient, maximum-likelihood, estimator.

However, except in special cases, which include the exponential and the normal distributions, using higher moments usually improves the efficiency of the estimator. The maximum-likelihood estimator can be considered a very special case of the GMM estimator where all the moments are used.

A.6.1.3 Testing Over-Identifying Restrictions

Frequently, we might be interested in knowing whether the parametric model used in estimation is correctly specified. For example, if we estimate the exponential model considered above using a set of field data, then we might be interested in knowing whether this assumed model is the *right* model. In other words, we would like to know whether the exponential distribution provides a close approximation to the true data-generating process.

Appendixes

J-statistics can be used to test overidentifying conditions using GMM estimators. Intuitively, if the model is true, then the objective function of the GMM estimator

$$\hat{\boldsymbol{\mu}}_T(\hat{\boldsymbol{\theta}}_{\text{GMM}})^\top \mathbf{A}_T \hat{\boldsymbol{\mu}}_T(\hat{\boldsymbol{\theta}}_{\text{GMM}})$$

should be close to zero. Formally, it can be shown that

$$J = T\hat{\boldsymbol{\mu}}_T(\hat{\boldsymbol{\theta}}_{\text{GMM}})^\top \mathbf{A}_T \hat{\boldsymbol{\mu}}_T(\hat{\boldsymbol{\theta}}_{\text{GMM}}) \xrightarrow{\text{d}} \chi^2(K-p)$$

when $\mathbf{A}_T$ is chosen optimally; i.e., $\mathbf{A}$ equal $\boldsymbol{\Sigma}^{-1}$. $(K-p)$ is the number of extra moment conditions used to define the estimator, usually the number of overidentifying restrictions. Obviously, when K equals p no such restriction exists.

To derive this result, apply the usual first-order, Taylor-series expansion

$$\sqrt{T}\hat{\boldsymbol{\mu}}_T(\hat{\boldsymbol{\theta}}_{\text{GMM}}) = \sqrt{T}\hat{\boldsymbol{\mu}}_T(\boldsymbol{\theta}^0) + \frac{\partial \hat{\boldsymbol{\mu}}_T(\boldsymbol{\theta}^*)}{\partial \boldsymbol{\theta}}\sqrt{T}\left(\hat{\boldsymbol{\theta}}_{\text{GMM}} - \boldsymbol{\theta}^0\right).$$

We already know that

$$\sqrt{T}(\hat{\boldsymbol{\theta}}_{\text{GMM}} - \boldsymbol{\theta}^0) = -\left[\frac{\partial \hat{\boldsymbol{\mu}}_T(\hat{\boldsymbol{\theta}})^\top}{\partial \boldsymbol{\theta}}\mathbf{A}_T \frac{\partial \hat{\boldsymbol{\mu}}_T(\boldsymbol{\theta}^*)^\top}{\partial \boldsymbol{\theta}}\right]^{-1}$$
$$\frac{\partial \hat{\boldsymbol{\mu}}_T(\hat{\boldsymbol{\theta}}_{\text{GMM}})^\top}{\partial \boldsymbol{\theta}}\mathbf{A}_T \sqrt{T}\hat{\boldsymbol{\mu}}_T(\boldsymbol{\theta}^0).$$

Therefore, we write $\sqrt{T}\hat{\boldsymbol{\mu}}_T(\hat{\boldsymbol{\theta}}_{\text{GMM}})$ as

$$\left\{\mathbf{I}_K - \frac{\partial \hat{\boldsymbol{\mu}}_T(\boldsymbol{\theta}^*)}{\partial \boldsymbol{\theta}}\left[\frac{\partial \hat{\boldsymbol{\mu}}_T(\hat{\boldsymbol{\theta}})^\top}{\partial \boldsymbol{\theta}}\mathbf{A}_T \frac{\partial \hat{\boldsymbol{\mu}}_T(\boldsymbol{\theta}^*)}{\partial \boldsymbol{\theta}}\right]^{-1}\frac{\partial \hat{\boldsymbol{\mu}}_T(\hat{\boldsymbol{\theta}}_{\text{GMM}})^\top}{\partial \boldsymbol{\theta}}\mathbf{A}_T\right\}\sqrt{T}\hat{\boldsymbol{\mu}}_T(\boldsymbol{\theta}^0).$$

The terms in the braces above converge in probability to

$$\mathbf{I}_K - \mathbf{G}\left(\mathbf{G}^\top \boldsymbol{\Sigma}^{-1}\mathbf{G}\right)^{-1}\mathbf{G}^\top \boldsymbol{\Sigma}^{-1}.$$

By Slutsky's theorem, we know that

$$\sqrt{T}\hat{\boldsymbol{\mu}}_T(\hat{\boldsymbol{\theta}}_{\text{GMM}}) \xrightarrow{\text{d}} \left[\mathbf{I}_K - \mathbf{G}\left(\mathbf{G}^\top \boldsymbol{\Sigma}^{-1}\mathbf{G}\right)^{-1}\mathbf{G}^\top \boldsymbol{\Sigma}^{-1}\right]\mathcal{N}(0, \boldsymbol{\Sigma}).$$

By the continuous mapping theorem,

$$J \xrightarrow{\text{d}} \mathcal{N}(0, \boldsymbol{\Sigma})^\top \mathbf{B}\mathcal{N}(0, \boldsymbol{\Sigma})$$

where $\mathbf{B}$ is equal to

$$\left[\mathbf{I}_K - \boldsymbol{\Sigma}^{-1}\mathbf{G}^\top \left(\mathbf{G}^\top\boldsymbol{\Sigma}^{-1}\mathbf{G}\right)^{-1}\mathbf{G}\right]\boldsymbol{\Sigma}^{-1}\left[\mathbf{I}_K - \mathbf{G}\left(\mathbf{G}^\top\boldsymbol{\Sigma}^{-1}\mathbf{G}\right)^{-1}\mathbf{G}^\top\boldsymbol{\Sigma}^{-1}\right].$$

We know from linear statistical analysis that if $\mathbf{G}\boldsymbol{\Sigma}$ is an idempotent matrix of rank $(K - p)$, then

$$J \xrightarrow{\mathrm{d}} \chi^2(K - p).$$

A.6.2 Method of Maximum Likelihood

Another popular estimation strategy is the method of maximum likelihood.

A.6.2.1 Definition

Consider an independent and identically distributed sample $\{V_t\}_{t=1}^T$ of size T from the probability density function $f_V(v; \boldsymbol{\theta}^0)$. When the true parameter value is $\boldsymbol{\theta}^0$, the joint density of the entire sample is

$$\prod_{t=1}^T f_V(V_t; \boldsymbol{\theta}^0).$$

Instead of conditioning on $\boldsymbol{\theta}^0$ and viewing the V_ts as varying, "fix" the V_ts and consider the *likelihood function* as a multivariate function of the unknown vector $\boldsymbol{\theta}$

$$\prod_{t=1}^T f_V(\boldsymbol{\theta}|V_t).$$

Now, maximizing the above likelihood function is computationally tedious, involving repeated applications of the chain rule. Also, it is a product, rather than a sum of random terms, so asymptotic analysis is difficult. Because a monotonic transformation of the likelihood function preserves the maximum, statisticians have chosen to investigate the maximum of the logarithm of the likelihood function

$$\mathcal{L}_T(\boldsymbol{\theta}) = \log\left[\prod_{t=1}^T f_V(\boldsymbol{\theta}|V_t)\right] = \sum_{t=1}^T \log\left[f_V(\boldsymbol{\theta}|V_t)\right].$$

Intuitively, the maximum-likelihood estimator (MLE) is the value of $\boldsymbol{\theta}$ that makes the observed data most likely. Specifically, the MLE is

$$\hat{\boldsymbol{\theta}}_{\mathrm{ML}} = \arg\min_{\boldsymbol{\theta}\in\boldsymbol{\Theta}} \mathcal{L}_T(\boldsymbol{\theta}).$$

A.6.2.2 Parameter Consistency/Asymptotic Normality

The MLE is generally parameter consistent. Given certain regularity conditions, it is usually also asymptotically normal.

Parameter consistency of the MLE can be proven using the general theory of extremum estimators. Under this theory, if

$$\operatorname*{plim}_{T\to\infty} \frac{1}{T}\mathcal{L}_T(\boldsymbol{\theta}) = \mathcal{L}_\infty(\boldsymbol{\theta})$$

uniformly in $\boldsymbol{\theta} \in \boldsymbol{\Theta}$ for some function $\mathcal{L}_\infty(\boldsymbol{\theta})$ and if $\boldsymbol{\theta}^0$ uniquely maximizes $\mathcal{L}_\infty(\boldsymbol{\theta})$, then

$$\operatorname*{plim}_{T\to\infty} \hat{\boldsymbol{\theta}}_{\mathrm{ML}} = \boldsymbol{\theta}^0.$$

Since $[\mathcal{L}_T(\boldsymbol{\theta})/T]$ is a sample average,

$$\frac{1}{T}\mathcal{L}_T(\boldsymbol{\theta}) = \frac{1}{T}\sum_{t=1}^{T}\log f(V_t;\boldsymbol{\theta}),$$

$\mathcal{L}_\infty(\boldsymbol{\theta})$ follows from a (uniform) law of large numbers:

$$\mathcal{L}_\infty(\boldsymbol{\theta}) = \mathcal{E}\left[\log f_V(V_t;\boldsymbol{\theta})\right].$$

That $\boldsymbol{\theta}^0$ maximizes $\mathcal{L}_\infty(\boldsymbol{\theta})$ follows from Jensen's inequality because $\log(\cdot)$ is a concave function. For any $\boldsymbol{\theta}$ not equal $\boldsymbol{\theta}^0$:

$$\mathcal{L}_\infty(\boldsymbol{\theta}) - \mathcal{L}_\infty(\boldsymbol{\theta}^0) = \mathcal{E}\left[\log \frac{f_V(V_t;\boldsymbol{\theta})}{f_V(V_t;\boldsymbol{\theta}^0)}\right]$$

$$< \log\left\{\mathcal{E}\left[\frac{f_V(V_t;\boldsymbol{\theta})}{f_V(V_t;\boldsymbol{\theta}^0)}\right]\right\} = \log\int f_V(V_t;\boldsymbol{\theta})\,dV_t \le 0.$$

In order for the model to be identified, $f_V(V_t;\boldsymbol{\theta})$ cannot equal $f_V(V_t;\boldsymbol{\theta}^0)$ for a set of V_t with positive probability under $\boldsymbol{\theta}^0$, so the first inequality is strict. The second inequality is strict when the supports of V_t under $\boldsymbol{\theta}$ and $\boldsymbol{\theta}^0$ are different.

Suppose $f_V(V_t;\boldsymbol{\theta})$ is twice continuously differentiable in $\boldsymbol{\theta}$ for all V_t. When $\hat{\boldsymbol{\theta}}_{\mathrm{ML}}$ is in the interior of $\boldsymbol{\Theta}$, it should satisfy the first-order condition:

$$\frac{1}{T}\frac{\partial \mathcal{L}_T(\hat{\boldsymbol{\theta}}_{\mathrm{ML}})}{\partial \boldsymbol{\theta}} = \mathbf{0}_p$$

where p is the dimension of $\boldsymbol{\theta}$. A first-order, Taylor-series expansion applied to this first-order condition implies:

$$\frac{1}{T}\frac{\partial \mathcal{L}_T(\boldsymbol{\theta}^0)}{\partial \boldsymbol{\theta}} + \frac{1}{T}\frac{\partial^2 \mathcal{L}_T(\boldsymbol{\theta}^*)}{\partial \boldsymbol{\theta}\partial \boldsymbol{\theta}^\top}\left(\hat{\boldsymbol{\theta}}_{\mathrm{ML}} - \boldsymbol{\theta}^0\right) = \mathbf{0}_p,$$

where $\boldsymbol{\theta}^*$ is a mean value between $\boldsymbol{\theta}^0$ and $\hat{\boldsymbol{\theta}}_{\mathrm{ML}}$. Therefore,

$$\sqrt{T}\left(\hat{\boldsymbol{\theta}}_{\mathrm{ML}} - \boldsymbol{\theta}^0\right) = -\left[\frac{1}{T}\frac{\partial^2 \mathcal{L}_T(\boldsymbol{\theta}^*)}{\partial\boldsymbol{\theta}\partial\boldsymbol{\theta}^{\top}}\right]^{-1}\frac{1}{\sqrt{T}}\frac{\partial \mathcal{L}_T(\boldsymbol{\theta}^0)}{\partial\boldsymbol{\theta}}.$$

The term inside the bracket is a sample average and its probability limit can be calculated using a (uniform) law of large numbers:

$$\operatorname*{plim}_{T\to\infty}\frac{1}{T}\frac{\partial^2 \mathcal{L}_T(\boldsymbol{\theta}^*)}{\partial\boldsymbol{\theta}\partial\boldsymbol{\theta}^{\top}} = \mathcal{E}\left[\frac{\partial^2 \log f_V(V_t;\boldsymbol{\theta}^0)}{\partial\boldsymbol{\theta}\partial\boldsymbol{\theta}^{\top}}\right].$$

Now, the term

$$\frac{1}{\sqrt{T}}\frac{\partial \mathcal{L}_T(\boldsymbol{\theta}^0)}{\partial\boldsymbol{\theta}}$$

has expectation zero under some regularity conditions, so

$$\mathcal{E}\left[\frac{1}{\sqrt{T}}\frac{\partial \mathcal{L}_T(\boldsymbol{\theta}^0)}{\partial\boldsymbol{\theta}}\right] = \sqrt{T}\mathcal{E}\left[\frac{\partial \log f_V(V_t;\boldsymbol{\theta}^0)}{\partial\boldsymbol{\theta}}\right]$$

$$= \sqrt{T}\int\frac{\partial f_V(V_t;\boldsymbol{\theta}^0)}{\partial\boldsymbol{\theta}}\,dV_t$$

and

$$\int\frac{\partial f_V(V_t;\boldsymbol{\theta}^0)}{\partial\boldsymbol{\theta}}\,dV_t = \frac{\partial}{\partial\boldsymbol{\theta}}\int f_V(V_t;\boldsymbol{\theta}^0)\,dV_t = 0.$$

Therefore, invoking a central limit theorem we obtain

$$\frac{1}{\sqrt{T}}\frac{\partial \mathcal{L}_T(\boldsymbol{\theta}^0)}{\partial\boldsymbol{\theta}}\xrightarrow{\mathrm{d}}\mathcal{N}\left\{0,\mathcal{E}\left[\frac{\partial \log f(V_t;\boldsymbol{\theta}^0)}{\partial\boldsymbol{\theta}}\right]\left[\frac{\partial \log f(V_t;\boldsymbol{\theta}^0)}{\partial\boldsymbol{\theta}}\right]^{\top}\right\}.$$

The so-called *information matrix* equality holds under the same regularity conditions that allow for the interchange of integration and differentiation:

$$\boldsymbol{\mathcal{I}} \equiv \mathcal{E}\left\{\left[\frac{\partial \log f(V_t;\boldsymbol{\theta}^0)}{\partial\boldsymbol{\theta}}\right]\left[\frac{\partial \log f(V_t;\boldsymbol{\theta}^0)}{\partial\boldsymbol{\theta}}\right]^{\top}\right\}$$

$$= -\mathcal{E}\left[\frac{\partial^2 \log f(V_t;\boldsymbol{\theta}^0)}{\partial\boldsymbol{\theta}\partial\boldsymbol{\theta}^{\top}}\right].$$

Slutsky's theorem can then be invoked to claim that

$$\sqrt{T}\left(\hat{\boldsymbol{\theta}}_{\mathrm{ML}} - \boldsymbol{\theta}^0\right)\xrightarrow{\mathrm{d}}\boldsymbol{\mathcal{I}}^{-1}\mathcal{N}\left(\mathbf{0}_p,\boldsymbol{\mathcal{I}}\right) = \mathcal{N}\left(\mathbf{0}_p,\boldsymbol{\mathcal{I}}^{-1}\right).$$

Appendixes

In our example, the logarithm of the likelihood function is

$$\mathcal{L}_T\left(\theta\right) = \log\left[\prod_{t=1}^{T}\theta\exp\left(-\theta V_t\right)\right] = T\log\theta - \theta\sum_{t=1}^{T}V_t.$$

whence

$$\hat{\theta}_{\mathrm{ML}} = \frac{T}{\sum_{t=1}^{T}V_t} = \frac{1}{M_1}.$$

This turns out to be the same as method-of-moments estimator derived using the first moment of V_t; we already know it is parameter consistent for θ^0. The information matrix in this example is

$$\mathcal{I} = \frac{\partial^2\left(\log\theta^0 - \theta^0 V_t\right)}{\partial\theta^2} = \frac{1}{(\theta^0)^2},$$

so

$$\sqrt{T}\left(\hat{\theta}_{\mathrm{ML}} - \theta^0\right) \xrightarrow{\mathrm{d}} \mathcal{N}\left[0,(\theta^0)^2\right].$$

This is the same as the asymptotic distribution for $\hat{\theta}_{\mathrm{ML}}$ found in the previous section. Under certain regularity conditions, it can be proven that the MLE is more efficient than any other estimators.

One of these regularity conditions requires the interchange of integration and differentiation. Such a condition is violated when the support depends on the unknown parameter θ and the probability density function is not smooth at the boundary. A violation of this sort occurs, for example, when V is uniformly distributed on the interval $[0,\theta]$, so its probability density function is

$$\frac{\mathbf{1}(0 \leq v \leq \theta)}{\theta}.$$

Note that the upper bound of support depends on the unknown parameter and the probability density function falls discretely from $(1/\theta)$ to zero at θ. We mention this condition here because the likelihood functions of data-generating processes for Dutch and first-price, sealed-bid auctions violate this regularity condition.

In the uniform-distribution example above, the logarithm of the likelihood function is not differentiable in θ with respect to the indicator part $\mathbf{1}(0 \leq v \leq \theta)$. If we ignore this part, then the integral of the derivative is not equal to the derivative of the integral.

A.6.3 Nonparametric Estimation

Unlike many theoretical approaches used in economics, auction theory makes very specific predictions about the relationship between the joint distribution of valuations and the joint distribution of bids. Thus, it is natural to investigate the distribution of bids, rather than just its moments. Nonparametric methods are the most flexible way in which to do this.

A.6.3.1 Histogram

For a realized sample of data $\{v_1, v_2, \ldots, v_T\}$, take the sample range and divide into J bins of equal width. Thus, the bin width w is

$$w = \frac{v_{\max} - v_{\min}}{J}.$$

Define the bins as follows:

$$\{[v_{\min}, v_{\min} + w), \; [v_{\min} + w, v_{\min} + 2w), \ldots,$$
$$[v_{\max} - 2w, v_{\max} - w), \; [v_{\max} - w, v_{\max}]\}.$$

For each bin, count how many of the observations fall within it. Denote the number of observations in bin j (the frequency) by f_j. Note that $\sum_{j=1}^{J} f_j = T$. Denote the midpoint of bin j by

$$b_j = \frac{v_{\min} + jw + v_{\min} + (j-1)w}{2} = v_{\min} + jw - 0.5w \quad j = 1, \ldots, J.$$

The *histogram* is a plot of bars at the bin midpoints (on the abscissa, the x-axis) with heights equal to the observed frequencies (on the ordinate, the y-axis)

$$\left\{ (b_j, f_j) \right\}_{j=1}^{J}.$$

An example of an histogram is presented in figure A.6.1. The histogram is the nonparametric maximum-likelihood estimate of the true probability density function $f_V^0(v)$.

The main choice variable in the construction of the histogram is the number of bins, and thus the bin width. If J is large (for example, consider the limit point where J is T, then many of the cells will have only a few members, and some may have no members. Thus, the histogram will provide an uninformative picture of the frequency distribution of the data. Similarly, if J is small (for example, consider the limit point where J equals one), then none of the dispersion in the data will be captured. A good rule of thumb is to permit no one bin to have more than twenty percent of the observations. Thus, continue to add bins until the maximum observed relative frequency in a cell is less than one-fifth of the sample.

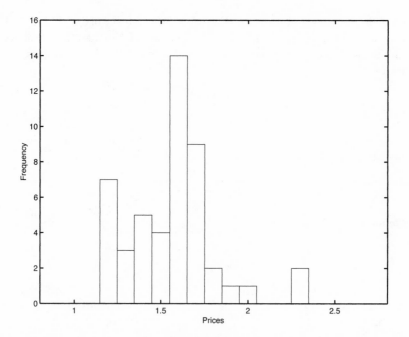

Figure A.6.1
Histogram

A.6.3.2 Kernel-Smoothed Density Functions

One problem with the histogram, or the relative histogram (the histogram with each of the frequencies scaled by T, so the mass under the relative histogram adds up to one), is that the function is kinky and nondifferentiable. In some applications, such as calculating the optimal reserve price at an auction, having a smooth and differentiable function is useful and important. Thus, researchers replace the relative histogram as an estimate of the true function $f_V^0(v)$ at point v by a smooth, differentiable version $\hat{f}_V(v)$.

A variety of ways exist to do this, but we shall consider only one here. Interested readers are referred to Silverman (1986) for other ways. From $\{V_t\}_{t=1}^T$, one can construct $\hat{f}_V(v)$, an estimate of $f_V^0(v)$ at v, using the following estimator:

$$\hat{f}_V(v) = \frac{1}{Th} \sum_{t=1}^{T} \kappa\left(\frac{V_t - v}{h}\right)$$

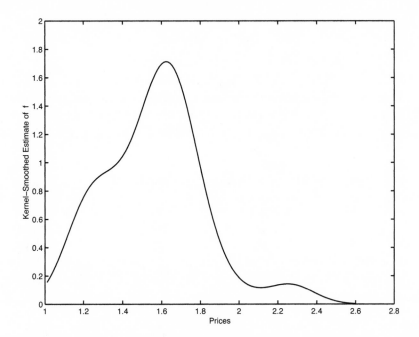

Figure A.6.2
Kernel-Smoothed Probability Density Function

where

$$\kappa\left(\frac{V_t - v}{h}\right) = \frac{1}{\sqrt{2\pi}} \exp\left[\frac{-(V_t - v)^2}{2h^2}\right]$$

is often referred to as the *kernel*, while the parameter h is a choice variable called the *bandwidth*. The bandwidth is a bit like the bin width for histograms in that if h is too small then the smoothed probability density function will wiggle a lot, while if h is too large then the estimate of the true function will be *oversmoothed*. Silverman (1986) has suggested h equal to $1.06\sigma T^{-1/5}$ as a rule of thumb for an *optimal* choice of h where σ is the standard deviation of V. In practice, researchers often use the sample standard deviation in lieu of σ. A kernel-smoothed probability density function with h equal $1.06\sigma T^{-1/5}$ using the data considered earlier is presented in figure A.6.2.

Consider now the case of two random variables (V_1, V_2) which we collect in the vector $\boldsymbol{V}$. We seek to estimate the joint probability density function $f_{\boldsymbol{V}}^0(\boldsymbol{v})$ from a sample of T observations $\{\boldsymbol{V}_t\}_{t=1}^T$. A standard estimator at the point v is

$$\hat{f}_V(v) = \frac{1}{Th_1 h_2} \sum_{t=1}^{T} \kappa\left(\frac{V_{1t} - v_1}{h_1}\right) \kappa\left(\frac{V_{2t} - v_2}{h_2}\right)$$

where the usual univariate kernel-density functions are used and where, potentially, different bandwidth parameters h_1 and h_2 can be used. Extensions to vectors of dimensions greater than two are similar, so are not discussed further here.

A.6.3.3 Empirical Distribution Function

Another description of the frequency of data is the empirical distribution function (EDF). Unlike the relative histogram, which describes the proportion of the data that lie in a particular bin, the EDF describes the proportion of the sample that lies below a particular value. Thus, $\tilde{F}_V(v)$, the EDF evaluated at v, is defined by the following formula:

$$\tilde{F}_V(v) = \frac{1}{T} \sum_{t=1}^{T} \mathbf{1}(V_t \leq v)$$

where

$$\mathbf{1}(V_t \leq v) = \begin{cases} 1 & \text{if } v_t \leq v; \\ 0 & \text{otherwise.} \end{cases}$$

The EDF for the data considered earlier is presented in figure A.6.3.

A probability density function is usually the derivative of the corresponding cumulative distribution function; however, the EDF is a non-smooth, step function of v that cannot be differentiated. To overcome this problem, one can approximate the indicator function using a smooth distribution function and a bandwidth parameter that goes to zero as the sample size increases:

$$K\left(\frac{V_t - v}{h}\right),$$

where h is the bandwidth parameter that decreases to zero as the sample size increase, and $K(\cdot)$ is a smooth distribution function. It can be thought of as the integral of a kernel density function $\kappa(\cdot)$. Clearly, as h approaches zero, $K[(V_t - v)/h]$ is approximately the indicator $\mathbf{1}(V_t \leq v)$. More generally, $K(\cdot)$ can be the integral of a higher-order kernel function and does not have to be strictly increasing. The modified empirical distribution function is then

$$\hat{F}_V(v) = \frac{1}{T} \sum_{t=1}^{T} K\left(\frac{V_t - v}{h}\right).$$

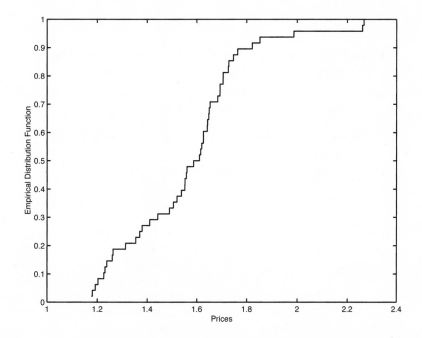

Figure A.6.3
Empirical Distribution Function

In fact, if we differentiate this smoothed empirical distribution function with respect to v, we shall obtain the kernel-density estimate itself; viz.,

$$\hat{f}_V(v) = \frac{1}{Th} \sum_{t=1}^{T} \kappa\left(\frac{V_t - v}{h}\right).$$

where $\kappa(\cdot)$ is the derivative of $K(\cdot)$.

A.6.4 Bandwidth Choice

The most important statistical issue with nonparametric estimation is the trade-off between bias and variance. The bandwidth parameter h is very similar to the bin size for the histogram. In fact, if $\kappa(\cdot)$ is chosen to be the uniform probability density function, then the kernel-density estimate is just the histogram itself. For standard parametric estimation, such as estimating the mean, when the sample size is T, the standard deviation of the sample mean is of the order of $1/\sqrt{T}$. When the bin size is h and the sample size is T, the number of observations falling into each bin is approximately of the order of Th. Therefore, the standard deviation of the kernel-density estimate is approximately of the order of $1/\sqrt{Th}$.

When the kernel-density function is symmetric around zero, it is not difficult to calculate that the order of bias, defined by

$$\mathcal{E}\left[\hat{f}_V(v) - f_V^0(v)\right],$$

is of the order of h^2. Therefore, the optimal choice of h should balance the magnitudes of the standard deviation and the bias (formally speaking, minimizing the mean squared-error), so

$$C_1/\sqrt{Th} \sim C_2 h^2$$

where C_1 and C_2 are constants that depend on the function being estimated and the kernel-density function being used. Therefore, the optimal bandwidth h is approximately of the order of $T^{-1/5}$. As mentioned above, when h is too large, the variance is small, but the bias is large relative to the optimal balance; *oversmoothing* occurs. When h is too small, the bias is small, but the variance is large; *undersmoothing* occurs.

The so-called *higher-order* kernel can help to reduce the bias even further. However, a discussion of higher-order kernels is beyond the scope of this section.

A.6.5 Asymptotic Distribution of Order Statistics

Consider $\{V_t\}_{t=1}^T$, an independent and identically distributed sample of T observations from $F_V^0(v)$. Order the sample so that

$$V_{\max} = V_{(1:T)} \geq V_{(2:T)} \geq \cdots V_{(T-1:T)} \geq V_{(T:T)} = V_{\min}.$$

Earlier, we investigated the exact small-sample distribution of the order statistics. In this section, we consider the asymptotic distribution of the ith order statistic. Let p equal (i/T). To begin, introduce some notation. Specifically, define ξ_p^0 according to

$$p = \int_{-\infty}^{\xi_p^0} f_V^0(v) \, dv = F_V^0(\xi_p^0).$$

Consider the empirical distribution function evaluated at ξ_p^0

$$\hat{F}_V(\xi_p^0) = \frac{1}{T}\sum_{t=1}^T \mathbf{1}(V_t \leq \xi_p^0).$$

286

Note that $\{\mathbf{1}(V_t \leq \xi_p^0)\}_{t=1}^T$ is a sequence of independent and identically distributed Bernoulli random variables, having mean p and variance $p(1-p)$. Now, by the deMoivre–Laplace central limit theorem, we know that

$$\sqrt{T}[\hat{F}_V(\xi_p^0) - p] \xrightarrow{\mathrm{d}} \mathcal{N}[0, p(1-p)].$$

Consider $\hat{\xi}_p$, an estimator of ξ_p^0, which is defined according to

$$\hat{\xi}_p = \hat{F}_V^{-1}(p).$$

What is the asymptotic distribution of $\hat{\xi}_p$? Because $\hat{F}_V(\cdot)$ has steps, it is neither a differentiable nor a continuous function of its arguments, so the conditions necessary to apply the continous mapping theorem and the delta method, as you know them, do not apply. What to do? Consider

$$\sqrt{T}[\hat{F}_V(\hat{\xi}_p) - F_V^0(\xi_p^0)] = \sqrt{T}(p - p) = 0.$$

Now,

$$
\begin{aligned}
0 &= \sqrt{T}[\hat{F}_V(\hat{\xi}_p) - F_V^0(\hat{\xi}_p)] + \sqrt{T}[F_V^0(\hat{\xi}_p) - F_V^0(\xi_p^0)] \\
&\doteq \sqrt{T}[\hat{F}_V(\hat{\xi}_p) - F_V^0(\hat{\xi}_p)] + \sqrt{T}[F_V^0(\xi_p^0) + f_V^0(\xi_p^0)(\hat{\xi}_p - \xi_p^0) - F_V^0(\xi_p^0)] \\
&= \sqrt{T}[\hat{F}_V(\hat{\xi}_p) - F_V^0(\hat{\xi}_p)] + \sqrt{T} f_V^0(\xi_p^0)(\hat{\xi}_p - \xi_p^0),
\end{aligned}
$$

so

$$\sqrt{T}(\hat{\xi}_p - \xi_p^0) = \frac{\sqrt{T}[\hat{F}_V(\hat{\xi}_p) - F_V^0(\hat{\xi}_p)]}{-f_V^0(\xi_p^0)}.$$

Researchers, such as van der Vaart (1998), have shown that the distribution of

$$\sqrt{T}[\hat{F}_V(\hat{\xi}_p) - F_V^0(\hat{\xi}_p)]$$

is the same, at least asymptotically, as

$$\sqrt{T}[\hat{F}_V(\xi_p^0) - p],$$

so

$$\sqrt{T}(\hat{\xi}_p - \xi_p^0) \xrightarrow{\mathrm{d}} \mathcal{N}\left[0, \frac{p(1-p)}{f_V^0(\xi_p^0)^2}\right].$$

A.6.6 Characteristic Functions: Deconvolution Methods

The distribution of a sum of independent random variables is often referred to as the *convolution*. Recovering the distributions of a sum's parts is often referred to as *deconvolution*. In some of the analysis in this book, we make use of deconvolution methods.

One deconvolution strategy makes use of the *characteristic function*. The characteristic function of a random variable V, having cumulative distribution function $F_V(v)$ and probability density function $f_V(v)$, is defined by

$$
\mathcal{C}_V(\tau) = \int_{-\infty}^{\infty} \exp(\mathbf{i}\tau v) f_V(v) \, dv
$$

$$
= \int_{-\infty}^{\infty} \cos(\tau v) f_V(v) \, dv + \mathbf{i} \int_{-\infty}^{\infty} \sin(\tau v) f_V(v) \, dv
$$

where $\mathbf{i}$ denotes the imaginary number $\sqrt{-1}$. In deterministic environments, the characteristic function is often referred to as the *Fourier transformation*. An advantage of the characteristic function, over say the moment-generating function, is that the characteristic always exists because the trigonometric functions are bounded. While the properties of characteristic functions are discussed in many textbooks—see, for example, Billingsley (1995)—one fact is worthy of special mention: A one-to-one relationship exists between any cumulative distribution function and its corresponding characteristic function. In particular, for any v_1 and v_2 that are points of continuity on the cumulative distribution function $F_V(v)$

$$
\Pr(v_1 \leq V \leq v_2) = \lim_{M \to \infty} \frac{1}{2\pi} \int_{-M}^{M} \frac{\exp(-\mathbf{i}\tau v_1) - \exp(-\mathbf{i}\tau v_2)}{\mathbf{i}\tau} \mathcal{C}_V(\tau) \, d\tau.
$$

In turn, this can be expressed as

$$
\frac{[F_V(v+h) - F_V(v)]}{h} =
$$

$$
\frac{1}{2\pi} \int_{-\infty}^{\infty} \frac{\exp(-\mathbf{i}\tau v) - \exp[-\mathbf{i}\tau(v+h)]}{\mathbf{i}\tau h} \mathcal{C}_V(\tau) \, d\tau.
$$

When h goes to zero, the probability density function $f_V(v)$ can be written as

$$
f_V(v) = \frac{1}{2\pi} \int_{-\infty}^{\infty} \exp(-\mathbf{i}\tau v) \mathcal{C}_V(\tau) \, d\tau.
$$

This is known as the *Fourier inversion formula*. Characteristic functions are particularly useful when analyzing the properties of sums (as well as products since the logarithm of a product is a sum) of independent random variables. Therefore, characteristic functions are used extensively in statistics to prove central limit theorems under general conditions.

To see how we shall use the characteristic function, let U and V be two independently-distributed random variables having probability density functions $f_U(u)$ and $f_V(v)$, respectively. The probability density function of their sum W equal $(U + V)$, is given by the convolution formula,

$$f_W(w) = \int_{-\infty}^{\infty} f_U(w - v) f_V(v) \ dv. \qquad (A.6.1)$$

Note that, under this definition, the kernel-density estimator, for example, can be considered as the convolution between empirical distribution function and the smoothed kernel-density function with a scale parameter decreasing to zero as the sample size increases.

Applying a formula like equation (A.6.1) to find the probability density functions of sums of more than two independent random variables can quickly become very involved. On the other hand, the characteristic functions of the sums of independent random variables are simply the product of the characteristic functions of the individual random variables. Thus, for example, the characteristic function of W is given by

$$C_W(\tau) = \mathcal{E}\left[\exp\left(\mathbf{i}\tau W\right)\right]$$

$$= \mathcal{E}\left[\exp\left[\mathbf{i}\tau\left(U + V\right)\right]\right]$$

$$= \mathcal{E}\left[\exp\left(\mathbf{i}\tau U\right)\right] \mathcal{E}\left[\exp\left(\mathbf{i}\tau V\right)\right]$$

$$= C_U(\tau) C_V(\tau).$$

Deconvolution refers to the analysis of recovering the cumulative distribution function of V using knowledge of the cumulative distribution functions of W and U. Methods of deconvolution have been used extensively in modern econometrics; see the models of panel data and measurement error discussed in Horowitz (1998), for example.

Suppose one knows the cumulative distribution functions $F_W(w)$ and $F_U(u)$ and is interested in recovering the cumulative distribution function $F_V(v)$. This can be done by the following steps: First, the characteristic functions of W and U can be calculated as

$$C_W(\tau) = \int_{-\infty}^{\infty} \exp(\mathbf{i}\tau w) f_W(w) \ dw$$

and

$$C_U(\tau) = \int_{-\infty}^{\infty} \exp(\mathbf{i}\tau u) f_U(u) \ du.$$

Next, $\mathcal{C}_V(\tau)$, the characteristic function of V, can be computed via

$$\mathcal{C}_V(\tau) = \frac{\mathcal{C}_W(\tau)}{\mathcal{C}_U(\tau)}.$$

Finally, the probability density function $f_V(v)$ can be recovered using the Fourier inversion formula, so

$$f_V(v) = \frac{1}{2\pi} \int_{-\infty}^{\infty} \exp(-\mathbf{i}\tau v) \frac{\mathcal{C}_W(\tau)}{\mathcal{C}_U(\tau)} \, d\tau.$$

Often, the characteristic functions of W and U are unknown, but, when they can be estimated from data, one can then estimate the characteristic function of V and, subsequently, estimate the probability density function of V.

A natural estimator of a characterisitic function is its empirical analogue. For example, for a sample of T observations concerning W, the empirical characteristic function is

$$\hat{\mathcal{C}}_W(\tau) = \frac{1}{T} \sum_{t=1}^{T} \exp(\mathbf{i}\tau w_t).$$

A similar estimator can be proposed for a sample of T observations concerning U. However, when applying the Fourier inversion formula to these empirical analogues, the resulting probability density function

$$\frac{1}{2\pi} \int_{-\infty}^{\infty} \exp(-\mathbf{i}\tau v) \frac{\hat{\mathcal{C}}_W(\tau)}{\hat{\mathcal{C}}_U(\tau)} \, d\tau$$

does not necessarily exist. Therefore, it is necessary to trim the tails of the empirical characteristic function when calculating an estimate of the probability density function; e.g.,

$$\hat{f}_V(v) = \frac{1}{2\pi} \int_{-M}^{M} \exp(-\mathbf{i}\tau v) \frac{\hat{\mathcal{C}}_W(\tau)}{\hat{\mathcal{C}}_U(\tau)} \, d\tau$$

where M increases to infinity as the sample size increases. Details of such trimming are discussed in Horowitz (1998). Trimming the tails of the characteristic functions is closely related to kernel-density smoothing.

A.7 Numerical Methods

In general, to implement the empirical methods described in this book will require considerable computation. In this appendix, we discuss some elementary, but important, numerical methods used in empirical work investigating auctions.

A.7.1 Finding the Zero of a Function

Often, the solution to an equation is defined only implicitly. For example, at a first-price, sealed-bid auction the equilibrium bid function, when the observed bid is s^* and the valuation consistent with it is v^*, then the following must hold:

$$g(v^*) = [s^* - \sigma(v^*)] = \left[s^* - v^* + \frac{\int_{\underline{v}}^{v^*} F_V(u)^{\mathcal{N}-1}\, du}{F_V(v^*)^{\mathcal{N}-1}} \right] = 0.$$

Often, no closed-form solution for $g(v)$ as a function of v need exist. If the $g(v)$ function is reasonably well-behaved (typically this means that $\sigma(v)$ is a monotonic function of v, which it is at an auction), then a number of methods exist to solve for $g(v)$ equal zero.

A.7.1.1 Bisection Method

Perhaps, the most commonly known and intuitively obvious method for finding a zero of a continuous, monotonic function is the method of *bisection*. This method, which high school students often learn, is easy to understand. To begin, let us introduce v_{low}^k and v_{up}^k which are the lower and upper values which bound v^*. Thus, $v^* \in [v_{\text{low}}^k, v_{\text{up}}^k]$. We need to use care in creating v_{low}^k and v_{up}^k.

Initially, set v_{low}^0 to equal $\underline{v}$ and v_{up}^0 to equal $\overline{v}$, the lower and upper bounds of support of $F_V(v)$ in the auction problem. In the auction problem considered above, we know that $g(\underline{v})$ is positive and $g(\overline{v})$ is negative. Now, create a new lower and upper bounds v_{low}^1, which equals v_{low}^0, and v_{up}^1, which equals $[(v_{\text{low}}^0 + v_{\text{up}}^0)/2]$. Evaluate $g(\cdot)$ at the new lower and upper bounds. Now, $g(v_{\text{low}}^1)$ is positive. If $g(v_{\text{up}}^1)$ is negative, then set v_{low}^2 to equal v_{low}^1 and let v_{up}^2 equal $[(v_{\text{low}}^1 + v_{\text{up}}^1)/2]$. On the other hand, if, say, $g(v_{\text{up}}^2)$ is positive, when $g(v_{\text{up}}^1)$ was negative, then set v_{low}^2 equal to the new v_{up}^2 and update v_{up}^2 to be $[(v_{\text{low}}^2 + v_{\text{up}}^1)/2]$. Continue to iterate until $|v_{\text{low}}^k - v_{\text{up}}^k|$ is less than some tolerance ε; e.g., ε equal to 10^{-3}.

A.7.1.2 Newton's Method

Another method, which is more sophisticated than the method of bisection, but which is used often in numerical optimization, is *Newton's method*. This method is relatively simple to implement, providing the derivative of the function can be reliably calculated.

k	v_k	$g(v_k)$	$g'(v_k)$	v_{k+1}
0	2.0000	0.6931	0.5000	0.6137
1	0.6137	−0.4882	1.6294	0.9133
2	0.9133	−0.0906	1.0949	0.9961
3	0.9961	−0.0039	1.0039	1.0000
4	1.0000	0.0000	1.0000	1.0000

Table A.1
Several Iterations of Newton's Method Applied to $\log(v) = 0$

Consider $g(v)$ any differentiable, monotonic function of v where $g(v^*)$ equal zero exists. From Taylor's theorem, one can write $g(v)$ as

$$g(v) = g(v_0) + g'(v_0)(v - v_0) + R_2$$

where v_0 is a starting point contained in $[\underline{v}, \overline{v}]$ and R_2 is a remainder term. If one ignores R_2, because it will be negligible near the solution, and imposes the solution $g(v)$ equal zero, then one can solve the above equation for v. In particular,

$$g(v_0) + g'(v_0)(v - v_0) = 0$$

$$g'(v_0)(v - v_0) = -g(v_0)$$

$$(v - v_0) = -[g'(v_0)]^{-1}g(v_0)$$

$$v = v_0 - [g'(v_0)]^{-1}g(v_0).$$

In general, the recursion relationship is

$$v_{k+1} = v_k - [g'(v_k)]^{-1}g(v_k) \qquad k = 0, 1, \dots .$$

If $g(v)$ is a well-behaved function (typically this means that $g(v)$ is monotonic in v), then the above recursion converges to v^*; i.e.,

$$\lim_{k \to \infty} v_k = v^*.$$

To see how this would work in practice, consider the function

$$g(v) = \log(v),$$

which one knows has solution $g(v^*)$ equals zero, when v^* equals one. In table A.1 is presented the iterative solution starting from v_0 equal two, while in figure A.7.1 is illustrated the path to the solution. As one can see, convergence is attained at one in four iterations. How many times one must iterate will depend on the function as well as the starting point. Sometimes, too, it can take several hundred iterations to attain convergence. Note that a poor starting point can cause Newton's method to "blow up." For example, let v_0 equal 100 in this example and see what happens.

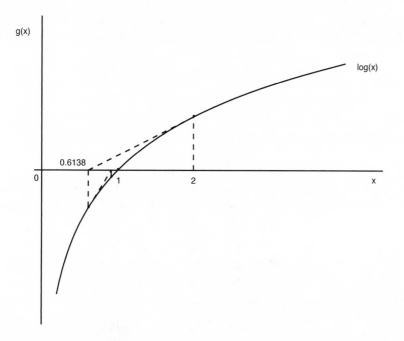

Figure A.7.1
Solving log(v) = 0 using Newton's Method

A.7.2 Unconstrained Optimization

In empirical work, researchers are often faced with the task of maximizing a function $f(\boldsymbol{\theta})$ with respect to the unknown parameter vector $\boldsymbol{\theta}$. In this book, the most common way in which this problem arises is in the context of the likelihood of observing a random sample of data. Suppose that for the tth observation the endogenous variable V has a conditional probability density function $f_{V|\boldsymbol{Z}}(v_t \mid \boldsymbol{z}_t, \boldsymbol{\theta})$ where $\boldsymbol{z}_t$ is a $(K \times 1)$ vector of covariates and $\boldsymbol{\theta}$ is a $(p \times 1)$ vector of unknown parameters. For a random sample of size T, the likelihood function is

$$f(\boldsymbol{\theta} \mid \boldsymbol{v}, \boldsymbol{Z}) = \prod_{t=1}^{T} f_{V|\boldsymbol{Z}}(\boldsymbol{\theta} \mid v_t, \boldsymbol{z}_t)$$

the logarithm of which is

$$\mathcal{L}(\boldsymbol{\theta}; \boldsymbol{v}, \boldsymbol{Z}) \equiv \sum_{t=1}^{T} \log f_{V|\boldsymbol{Z}}(\boldsymbol{\theta} \mid v_t, \boldsymbol{z}_t)$$

where $\boldsymbol{v}$ equals $(v_1, \ldots, v_T)^\top$ and $\mathbf{Z}$ equals $(\boldsymbol{z}_1, \ldots, \boldsymbol{z}_T)^\top$. Maximizing $\mathcal{L}(\boldsymbol{\theta})$ with respect to $\boldsymbol{\theta}$ is a well-defined optimization problem when $f(\boldsymbol{\theta})$ is concave in $\boldsymbol{\theta}$. Hereafter, we shall assume this property holds.

In maximizing $\mathcal{L}(\boldsymbol{\theta})$ with respect to $\boldsymbol{\theta}$, one wants to find a $\hat{\boldsymbol{\theta}}$ for which the gradient vector

$$\mathbf{g}(\hat{\boldsymbol{\theta}}) \equiv \frac{\partial \mathcal{L}(\hat{\boldsymbol{\theta}})}{\partial \boldsymbol{\theta}} = \mathbf{0}_p \qquad (A.7.1)$$

and for which the Hessian matrix

$$\mathbf{H}(\hat{\boldsymbol{\theta}}) \equiv \frac{\partial^2 \mathcal{L}(\hat{\boldsymbol{\theta}})}{\partial \boldsymbol{\theta} \partial \boldsymbol{\theta}^\top}$$

is negative definite. From a numerical standpoint, the easiest way to proceed is to linearize $\mathbf{g}(\boldsymbol{\theta})$ about some initial estimate $\boldsymbol{\theta}_0$

$$\mathbf{g}(\boldsymbol{\theta}) \approx \mathbf{g}(\boldsymbol{\theta}_0) + \mathbf{H}(\boldsymbol{\theta}_0)(\boldsymbol{\theta} - \boldsymbol{\theta}_0). \qquad (A.7.2)$$

Setting the right-hand side of equation (A.7.2) equal to the zero vector and solving for a new $\boldsymbol{\theta}$, which we shall denote $\boldsymbol{\theta}_1$, yields

$$\boldsymbol{\theta}_1 = \boldsymbol{\theta}_0 - \mathbf{H}(\boldsymbol{\theta}_0)^{-1}\mathbf{g}(\boldsymbol{\theta}_0).$$

When f is globally concave, the sequence

$$\boldsymbol{\theta}_{k+1} = \boldsymbol{\theta}_k - \mathbf{H}(\boldsymbol{\theta}_k)^{-1}\mathbf{g}(\boldsymbol{\theta}_k) \qquad k = 0, 1, \ldots$$

will typically converge to an equilibrium satisfying equation (A.7.1). Virtually all numerical routines adopt a strategy similar to (A.7.2), but very often use different approximations to $\mathbf{H}$, instead of the actual $\mathbf{H}$.

A.7.3 Constrained Optimization

One of the estimation problems that concerns us can be cast as a constrained optimization problem of the following form:

$$\max_{\boldsymbol{\theta}} \ f(\boldsymbol{\theta}) \quad \text{subject to} \quad \mathbf{c}(\boldsymbol{\theta}) \geq \mathbf{0}_K \qquad (A.7.3)$$

where $\boldsymbol{\theta}$ is $(p \times 1)$. When $f(\boldsymbol{\theta})$ is a quasi-concave function of $\boldsymbol{\theta}$, while the set of points defined by the constraint set is convex, applied mathematicians have characterized the optimum of $f(\boldsymbol{\theta})$. In addition, when $\mathbf{c}(\boldsymbol{\theta})$ is sufficiently smooth, then one can use the method of Lagrange, suitably modified, to find the optimum. Associated with equation (A.7.3) is the following Lagrangean:

$$\mathcal{J} = f(\boldsymbol{\theta}) + \boldsymbol{\lambda}^\top \mathbf{c}(\boldsymbol{\theta})$$

where $\boldsymbol{\lambda}$ is a $(K \times 1)$ vector of Lagrange multipliers. In our case, p is typically much smaller than K. In words, there are many more constraints than there are parameters to estimate. Also, in our case, the optimum typically obtains at the intersection of a subset of the constraints; the remaining constraints do not bind.

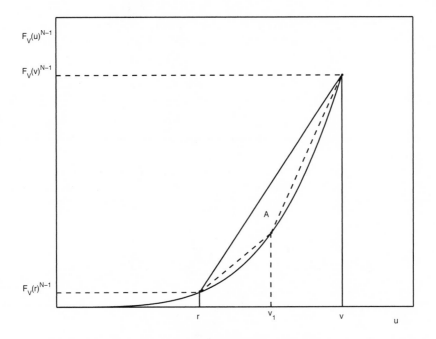

Figure A.7.2
Error in Trapezoidal Quadrature

A.7.4 Numerical Integration

When calculating the Bayes–Nash, equilibrium-bid function at either Dutch or first-price, sealed-bid auctions, one must calculate the integral

$$\Gamma(r, v) = \int_r^v F_V(u)^{\mathcal{N}-1} \, du.$$

How does one do this?

A.7.4.1 Newton–Cotes Formulae

One method, which students sometimes learn in college and which is one of the Newton–Cotes formulae, is called *trapezoidal quadrature*. This involves approximating $\Gamma(r, v)$ by an estimate, the area of a trapezoid,

$$\hat{G}_1(r, v) = (v - r)\frac{[F_V(v)^{\mathcal{N}-1} + F_V(r)^{\mathcal{N}-1}]}{2}.$$

This is depicted in figure A.7.2. Note that an error, which equals the area labeled A between the straight line and the curved line connecting $F_V(r)^{\mathcal{N}-1}$ and $F_V(v)^{\mathcal{N}-1}$ exist. This area is bounded from above by

$$\frac{(v-r)^3}{12} \frac{d^2 \left[F_V(v^*)^{\mathcal{N}-1}\right]}{dv^2}$$

where v^* is chosen to maximize the second derivative $d^2[F_V(v)^{\mathcal{N}-1}]/dv^2$ on the interval $[r,v]$. Notice that the error depends on $(v-r)$. If one were to break up the interval between r and v into K subintervals $[r,v_1]$, $[v_1,v_2]$, ..., $[v_{K-1},v_K]$ where $r = v_0 < v_1 < \ldots < v_K = v$, one could refine this estimate by using

$$\hat{G}_K(r,v) = \sum_{k=1}^{K} (v_k - v_{k-1}) \frac{[F_V(v_k)^{\mathcal{N}-1} + F_V(v_{k-1})^{\mathcal{N}-1}]}{2},$$

thus reducing the error. This too is illustrated in figure A.7.2 for the case of K equals two. When this is done the error is

$$\frac{\max[(v_k - v_{k-1})]^3}{12} \frac{d^2 \left[F_V(v^*)^{\mathcal{N}-1}\right]}{dv^2}.$$

Note too that

$$\lim_{K \to \infty} \hat{G}_K(r,v) = \Gamma(r,v).$$

Of course, for a fixed K, using a trapezoid to approximate the area is relatively inaccurate. For any three points v_{k-1}, v_k, and v_{k+1} one might approximate $F_V(u)^{\mathcal{N}-1}$ by a polynomial, a parabola, and then integrate it to find the area between v_{k-1} and v_{k+1}. This is known by numerical analysts as *Simpson's rule*. When K is even, and the points are evenly spaced h units apart, Simpson's rule is represented by the estimate

$$\tilde{G}_K(r,v) = \frac{h}{3} \left\{ F_V(r)^{\mathcal{N}-1} + \sum_{m=1}^{(K/2)-1} 2F_V(v_{2m})^{\mathcal{N}-1} + \right.$$
$$\left. \sum_{m=1}^{(K/2)} 4F_V(v_{2m-1})^{\mathcal{N}-1} + F_V(v)^{\mathcal{N}-1} \right\}.$$

The error associated with Simpson's rule is smaller than that associated with trapezoidal quadrature.

A.7.5 Approximation Methods

Often, a researcher is interested in approximating a function $f^0(v)$ using a simpler function $\hat{f}(v)$. When $f^0(v)$ has infinitely many derivatives (is C^∞), we know that $f^0(v)$ can be represented exactly by a Taylor-series expansion of the following form:

$$f^0(v) = f^0(v_0) + \sum_{j=1}^{\infty} \frac{d^{(j)} f^0(v_0)}{dv} \frac{(v - v_0)^j}{j!}.$$

The infinite order of this polynomial is troubling in practice: How does one represent ∞ on a digital computer? Also, in many instances the derivatives of $f^0(v)$ are unknown because $f^0(v)$ is unknown, and both need to be estimated. What to do?

Suppose one is willing to truncate $f^0(v)$ at some high order K, so

$$f^0(v) = f^0(v_0) + \sum_{j=1}^{K} \frac{d^{(j)} f^0(v_0)}{dv} \frac{(v - v_0)^j}{j!} + U(v_0).$$

Now, if the values of $f^0(v)$ are known at a finite set of $(K+1)$ points $(v_1, \ldots, v_{K+1})$, then one can estimate these derivatives according to the following linear system:

$$f^0(v_1) = y_1 = \alpha_0 + \alpha_1 v_1 + \ldots + \alpha_K v_1^K + U_1$$

$$f^0(v_2) = y_2 = \alpha_0 + \alpha_2 v_2 + \ldots + \alpha_K v_2^K + U_2$$

$$\vdots \quad = \quad \vdots$$

$$f^0(v_{K+1}) = y_{K+1} = \alpha_0 + \alpha_2 v_{K+1} + \ldots + \alpha_K v_{K+1}^K + U_{K+1}$$

or, in matrix notation,

$$\mathbf{y} = \mathbf{V}\boldsymbol{\alpha} + \mathbf{U}$$

so

$$\hat{\boldsymbol{\alpha}} = (\mathbf{V}^\top \mathbf{V})^{-1} \mathbf{V}^\top \mathbf{y}.$$

When K is quite large, solving for $\hat{\boldsymbol{\alpha}}$ is a delicate problem numerically as the matrix $(\mathbf{V}^\top \mathbf{V})$ is often ill-conditioned. This obtains because the column of v_k^js and the column of v_k^{j+1}s are almost colinear. What numerical analysts suggest is that one use an alternative basis, and replace the v_k^js by orthogonal polynomials; see Judd (1998).

A variety of different orthogonal bases exist. For example, when v is contained on $[-1, 1]$ Chebyshev polynomials are proposed, while when

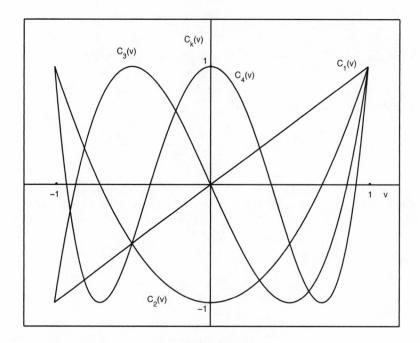

Figure A.7.3
Chebyshev Polynomials

v is contained $[0, \infty)$ Laguerre polynomials are proposed, and when v is contained $(-\infty, \infty)$ Hermite polynomials are proposed. In general, one approximates $f^0(v)$ by a polynomial

$$\hat{f}_K(v) = \sum_{k=0}^{K} \alpha_k P_k(v).$$

Typically, the polynomial terms $\{P_k(v)\}_{k=0}^{\infty}$ can be constructed recursively. For example, in the case of Chebyshev polynomials $C_0(v)$ is one while $C_1(v)$ is v. Subsequently,

$$C_{k+1} = 2vC_k(v) - C_{k-1}(v) \quad k = 1, 2, \ldots$$

Graphs of Chebyshev $C_k(v)$ polynomials for $k = 1, 2, 3, 4$ are presented in figure A.7.3.

In the case of Laguerre polynomials $L_0(v)$ is one while $L_1(v)$ is $(1 - v)$, and

$$L_{k+1} = \frac{1}{k+1}(2k + 1 - v)L_k(v) - \frac{k}{k+1}L_{k-1}(v) \quad k = 1, 2, \ldots$$

298

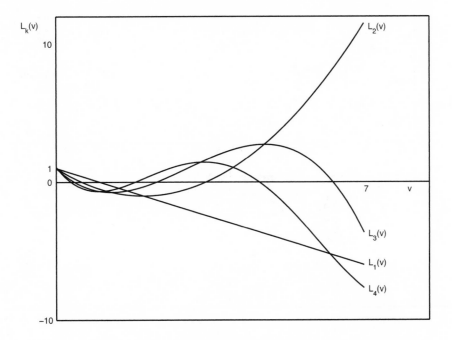

Figure A.7.4
Laguerre Polynomials

Graphs of Laguerre $L_k(v)$ polynomials for $k = 1, 2, 3, 4$ are presented in figure A.7.4.

In the case of Hermite polynomials $H_0(v)$ is one while $H_1(v)$ is $2v$, and

$$H_{k+1} = \frac{1}{k+1}(2k+1-v)H_k(v) - \frac{k}{k+1}H_{k-1}(v) \quad k = 1, 2, \ldots$$

Graphs of Hermite $H_k(v)$ polynomials for $k = 1, 2, 3, 4$ are presented in figure A.7.5.

In practice, the function $f^0(v)$ may be weakly positive at all points $[0, \infty)$; e.g., when $f^0(v)$ is the probability density function $f_V^0(v)$. In such cases, one might use the square of a sum of Laguerre polynomials $L_k(v)$ to approximate $f_V^0(v)$.; e.g.,

$$\hat{f}_V(v) = \left[\sum_{k=0}^{K} \alpha_k L_k(v) \right]^2.$$

In some cases, $f_{V|\mathbf{Z}}^0(v|\mathbf{z})$, the probability density function of V conditional on a vector of observed covariates $\mathbf{z}$ needs to be approximated.

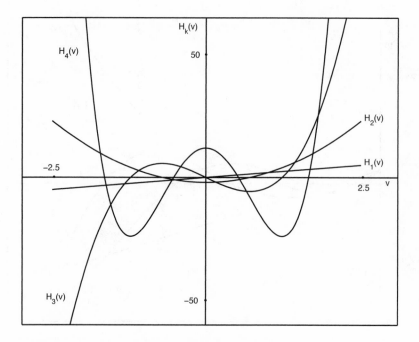

Figure A.7.5
Hermite Polynomials

In this circumstance, one might assume that

$$\log V = z^\top \gamma + U$$

and approximate the probability density function of U by a Hermite polynomial, so

$$\hat{f}_{U|Z}(u|z^\top \gamma) = \left[\sum_{k=0}^{K} \alpha_k H_k(u) \right]^2$$

where u is defined by

$$u = \log v - z^\top \gamma.$$

In these instances, one will use the observed data in conjunction with methods of optimization to choose both the α_ks, which we collect in the vector $\boldsymbol{\alpha}$, and the unknown vector $\boldsymbol{\gamma}$. In such cases, the criterion function will typically be the logarithm of the *quasi-likelihood function* and the estimation methods will often be referred to as *quasi-maximum-likelihood estimation* (QMLE). The term "quasi" is used because the likelihood function used involves a *false* model. However, as K tends to infinity, this model gets arbitrarily close to the true model.

A.8 A High-Level Programming Environment

Implementing the methods described in this book will typically require using either a programming language (such as C or FORTRAN), with or without the aid of a scientific subroutine library, or a high-level programming environment (such as GAUSS or MATLAB). We have chosen to use MATLAB to implement the solutions to those practice problems that involve computation because we believe that MATLAB represents a reasonable compromise between speed of computation and elegance in presentation; MATLAB is also easy to learn. Moreover, many scholars around the world have written books describing how to harness MATLAB's features in a variety of different fields, so supporting documentation is easily available. MATLAB also has excellent graphic capabilities. Also, because a researcher can incorporate user-developed code (written, for example, in C) using the **mex** option, MATLAB is extremely flexible. Most of all, however, MATLAB is a commonly used research tool among economists, so a novice user will be making an investment that has network externalities.

In this appendix, we do not attempt to replicate the work of others. Instead, we introduce an inexperienced user of MATLAB to its basics, so he or she can then get started implementing the methods described in this book.

A.8.1 Getting Started

In this section, we describe the essential features of MATLAB. Our discussion is divided into seven topics. For each topic, we include a description of the relevant MATLAB features and then provide illustrative examples related to the problems in this book as well as other helpful tips. The descriptions in this primer are based on MATLAB 7. Our version of MATLAB is also equipped with the Statistics and Optimization Toolboxes, both of which need to be installed prior to using the programs included on the CD that accompanies this book. In the discussion of topics that appear in subsequent sections of this appendix, we shall presume that the reader is familiar with the following introductory topics: 1) the MATLAB interface; 2) loading and cataloging data; 3) manipulating data; 4) basic matrix functions; 5) linear systems; 6) two-dimensional plotting; and 7) three-dimensional plotting.

Before we begin, three things must be made clear. First, MATLAB is not, unless equipped with a special Symbolic Math Toolbox, like Mathematica or Maple. Thus, users familiar with these other programs may, at first, find MATLAB awkward. However, time spent working with MATLAB will reveal quickly many of its advantages. Second, help concerning

301

Appendixes

MATLAB can be obtained simply by typing `help` at the prompt in the command window or by clicking on the `Help` drop-menu. Third, MATLAB is case-sensitive, so `SEAD` and `sead` can mean completely different things.

A.8.1.1 The Interface

On opening MATLAB, four distinct windows will appear. While each window serves a useful purpose, the command window and editor/debugger window are the most important; the others may be closed. The command window serves as the hub for running programs as well as an environment within which to perform quick calculations and function calls. For involved, lengthy calculations, we shall want to write an .m-file in the editor/debugger window, which can then be run (after saving) by typing the prefix of its filename at the ">>" prompt in the command window. For example, to run the program `foc.m`, we would simply type `foc` at the command prompt.

If we attempt to run the program `foc.m`, without first using the `set path` command, then the program may fail to execute properly. The `set path` command can be found under the file menu in the command window; its purpose is to direct MATLAB to the location (folder) where our files reside. For example, suppose the file `foc.m` is located in `c:/programs/`. Thus, we would direct MATLAB to this path by using the `set path` command, making certain that this path appears in the list of candidate pathways in the `set path` menu.

If we attempt to run the program `foc.m`, without first using the `clear all` command, then the program may fail to produce the correct output. The `clear all` command should be typed at the command prompt before running each program; `clear all` expunges, among other things, all existing variable definitions in the workspace.

Now that we have a basic understanding of the command and editor/debugger windows, we can describe how we might perform quick calculations at the command prompt or how we may write an .m-file in the editor/debugger window; examples of each follow.

A.8.1.2 Loading and Cataloging Data

When working some of the problems in this book, it will often be necessary to import data. The data files that appear on the CD are indexed by the .dat suffix. A variety of ways exist to load a data file; we include here one way that is particularly well-suited to the structure of the data used in this book.

Suppose the data file `vickrey.dat` lives in `c:/data/`. The first column in `.dat` files is always an observation identification number. In this particular data file, the second column is the winning bid, the third column is the number of potential bidders, and the fourth column is a covariate. Below is a listing of the first ten lines of this data file:

```
 1  54.5509  12  0.5995
 2   4.6631   9  0.7768
 3  60.7371  13  0.9762
 4   6.0791  11  0.9632
 5   3.2844  10  0.6577
 6   4.9756  12  0.8793
 7   5.5734   5  0.9355
 8   8.2835  14  0.3318
 9   2.7089  11  0.6024
10   7.2028  14  0.4922
```

We can load these data by opening a new `.m`-file in the editor/debugger window, call it `vickrey.m`, and typing the following code:

```
1  % Load the data.
2  load ('c:/data/vickrey.dat');
3  w = vickrey(:,2);
4  N = vickrey(:,3);
5  z = vickrey(:,4);
```

Note that the line numbers on the left are *not* part of the code, and are only included here to facilitate discussion of the code. Line 1 is a comment; all comments are identified by a lead percent sign in MATLAB. Line 2 tells MATLAB where to find the data file, and to load it into memory. In lines 3, 4, and 5 we catalogue the data by assigning a variable name (`w`, `N`, or `z`) to the corresponding column in the data file. For example, in line 4 we instruct MATLAB to assign the name `N` to the third column of data in `vickrey.dat`. Note the semicolon at the end of each line; its purpose is to prevent the data from physically appearing in the command window when we run this program, which is done by typing `vickrey` at the command prompt.

A.8.1.3 Manipulating Data

It is often necessary to manipulate matrices, specifically, matrices of data that have been loaded into MATLAB using the method outlined above. Frequently, for example, it is necessary to sort data in various

ways. Clearly, before we can perform a matrix sort, we must first create
the relevant data matrix. To demonstrate how to do this, consider
augmenting `vickrey.m` in the following way:

```
1  % Load the data.
2  load ('c:/data/vickrey.dat');
3  w = vickrey(:,2);
4  N = vickrey(:,3);
5  z = vickrey(:,4);
6  % Define the data matrix.
7  Data = [w N z];
8  data = Data(1:10,:);
```

Note that the line numbers on the left are *not* part of the code, and are
only included here to facilitate discussion of the code. Line 6 contains
another comment, while in line 7 we collect the vectors `w`, `N`, and `z` into
the matrix `Data`. In line 8, we create the matrix `data` (recall, MATLAB
is case-sensitive), which is nothing more than the first 10 rows of the
matrix `Data`.

If we run the program `vickrey.m` at this point, and then type `data`
at the $>>$ prompt, MATLAB will display the following output in the
command window:

```
data =
     54.5509   12   0.5995
      4.6631    9   0.7768
     60.7371   13   0.9762
      6.0791   11   0.9632
      3.2844   10   0.6577
      4.9756   12   0.8793
      5.5734    5   0.9355
      8.2835   14   0.3318
      2.7089   11   0.6024
      7.2028   14   0.4922
```

Now, suppose we want to sort `data` in ascending order by the elements
in the first column `w`. It is tempting to try

```
>> sort(data)
```

However, this would be a mistake because the `sort` command will simply
rank *each* column, completely ignoring the fact that each row is an
observation. The (incorrect) result looks like this:

```
ans =
       2.7089    5   0.3318
       3.2844    9   0.4922
       4.6631   10   0.5995
       4.9756   11   0.6024
       5.5734   11   0.6577
       6.0791   12   0.7768
       7.2028   12   0.8793
       8.2835   13   0.9355
      54.5509   14   0.9632
      60.7371   14   0.9763
```

To sort the data correctly, we should use, instead, the command

```
>> sortrows(data,1)
```

which instructs MATLAB to sort the matrix `data` in ascending order by column 1, while making certain that each row remains unchanged. The (correct) result looks like this:

```
ans =
       2.7089   11   0.6024
       3.2844   10   0.6577
       4.6631    9   0.7768
       4.9756   12   0.8793
       5.5734    5   0.9355
       6.0791   11   0.9632
       7.2028   14   0.4922
       8.2835   14   0.3318
      54.5509   12   0.5995
      60.7371   13   0.9762
```

A somewhat more challenging, yet necessary, task involves extracting all rows with, say, 11 potential bidders. To do this, consider augmenting the code in `vickrey.m` in the following way:

```
1  % Load the data.
2  load ('c:/data/vickrey.dat');
3  w = vickrey(:,2);
4  N = vickrey(:,3);
5  z = vickrey(:,4);
6  % Define the data matrix.
7  Data = [w N z];
```

305

```
 8  data = Data(1:10,:);
 9  % Extract the rows where N = 11.
10  dataN = data(find(data(:,2) == 11),:)
```

In line 10, we instruct MATLAB to find the row numbers where N equals 11, and then extract those rows, in this case two of them, to the matrix dataN. If we save these changes to vickrey.m and run it again, then the following output will appear in the command window:

```
dataN =
      6.0791   11   0.9632
      2.7089   11   0.6024
```

From this example, it should be clear how MATLAB sorts matrices, how it can extract rows (or columns) and assign them to a new matrix, how a colon is used to reference rows and columns of a matrix, how the find command works, and when we would use an "==" sign instead of an "=" sign.

A.8.1.4 Basic Matrix Functions

MATLAB, as its name (an acronym for *matrix laboratory*) suggests, is particularly well-suited to calculations concerning vectors and matrices as well as arrays. While numerous matrix functions exist in MATLAB, we consider here only those relevant to the problems in this book.

To begin, consider some basic matrix operations. Suppose, for example, we would like to add the matrix D to the vector d. Obviously, this is not a well-defined mathematical operation, so MATLAB would immediately realize this and return a conformability error. However, if we typed

```
>> D + 2
```

or

```
>> d - pi
```

where 2 and pi are scalars, MATLAB would simply add 2 to each element of D and subtract 3.14159... from each element of d, and no conformability error would appear. A similar set of rules applies when multiplying a matrix or a vector by a constant.

Now suppose that we would like to multiply two (column) vectors c and d, element by element. This is used frequently when forming the logarithm of the likelihood function or when plotting functions. If we type

```
>> c*d
```

then we shall get a conformability error. If we type

```
>> c'*d
```

then we shall get the inner product of c and d, which is not what we want either. The correct way to produce the desired output is to type

```
>> c.*d
```

which will produce a (column) vector, each element of which is the product of the corresponding values in the vectors c and d. Note that this command requires that c and d have the same dimension, so

```
>> c'.*d
```

will fail. A similar set of rules applies to dividing two vectors, element by element, in which case the ./ command is used. A similar set of rules also applies when multiplying or dividing matrices, element by element. From this example, it should be clear that MATLAB interprets an apostrophe as a transpose, that the asterisk is the multiplication operator, that the forward slash is the division operator, and that both operators should be preceded by a period if we want to perform element-by-element calculations.

A.8.1.5 Linear Systems

A common problem particularly relevant to many econometric techniques involves solving a system of K linear equations in K unknowns. Often, this is written as

$$\mathbf{Ax} = \mathbf{b},$$

which, of course, has the solution

$$\mathbf{x} = \mathbf{A}^{-1}\mathbf{b},$$

when $\mathbf{A}$, $\mathbf{x}$, and $\mathbf{b}$ are conformable and $\mathbf{A}$ is nonsingular.

To demonstrate some of MATLAB's matrix functions, suppose we have a simple (2×2) linear system to solve. One way to solve this problem would be to type the following at the $>>$ prompt:

```
>> A = [1 1;1 2]
>> b = [2 3]'
>> x = inv(A)*b
```

At the end of each line, hit < enter >. The solution is $(1,1)^\top$. From this example, it should be clear that `inv` is the matrix inversion function and that rows of a matrix are entered within square brackets, separated by semicolons. Note, too, that MATLAB has a number of other methods for inverting a matrix.

Suppose now that the linear system given above is actually the system of necessay first-order conditions that results from minimizing the quadratic form

$$\frac{\mathbf{x}^\top \mathbf{A} \mathbf{x}}{2} - \mathbf{b}^\top \mathbf{x} + \mathbf{c}.$$

How can we make sure that $(1,1)^\top$ is a minimum? One way to accomplish this would be to verify that the matrix $\mathbf{A}$ (the Hessian matrix) is positive definite. Thus, we may type

```
>> eig(A)
```

The result is the vector of eigenvalues $(0.382, 2.618)^\top$. Since both eigenvalues are positive, we know that we have, indeed, isolated a minimum. Note that, instead of performing the calculations in the command window, we could have collected these calculations in an .m-file called, say, `foc.m`. If we had done so, then here is what we would have written

```
1  % Enter the matrix A.
2  A = [1 1;1 2];
3  % Enter the vector b.
4  b = [2 3]';
5  % Solve the linear system.
6  x = inv(A)*b
7  % Check that the solution is a minimum.
8  eig(A)
```

Note that the line numbers on the left are *not* part of the code, and are only included here to facilitate discussion of the code. Suppose we saved this file to `c:/programs/foc.m`. We could run this program, assuming the path is set correctly, and obtain the same output as above. From this example, it should be clear that writing an .m-file is a convenient way to proceed when the program is large or when it needs to be reproduced; it should also be clear that working directly from the command prompt is useful for quick, small-scale calculations; finally, it should be clear how the **eig** function works.

A.8.1.6 Two-Dimensional Plotting

Another of MATLAB's advantages is its graphical capabilities. However, because it is not symbolic software (unless equipped with the Symbolic Math Toolbox), its graphing functions are a bit different from what one might expect. For example, if we type

```
>> plot f(x) = x*log(x)
```

MATLAB will have no clue what to do. In fact, typing

```
>> f(x) = x*log(x)
```

will confuse MATLAB too, even if x has been defined. Why? MATLAB will not understand what is meant by f(x), as it will not know to treat x as the argument of a function. (We shall, however, devote considerable time later to defining and using functions in MATLAB.) Moreover, even if x has been defined (as a vector of points), the multiplication on the right-hand side will fail, citing a conformability error. How then to proceed?

The first difficulty is avoided by writing the function more plainly, while the second difficulty is avoided by using the .* command instead of the plain multiplication operator. The correct command would look this

```
>> fx = x.*log(x)
```

Still, however, simply typing this command will not produce a plot of the desired function. Two items remain. First, we need to have a *domain* for the function and, second, we need to call MATLAB's plotting function. Domain appears in italics above because we cannot reproduce on a computer the entire half-open real line, but rather only a truncated vector of (discrete) points in the function's domain. The function values at each of these points, collected in the vector fx, are constructed using the code on the line above. Enter now MATLAB's plotting function, which connects these points on the function using piecewise linear splines. Bringing all these pieces together will result in the following three-line sequence of commands required to plot this function on the closed interval [0.01,5]:

```
>> x = 0.01:0.001:5;
>> fx = x.*log(x);
>> plot(x,fx)
```

The command on the first line instructs MATLAB to create a (row) vector of domain values from 0.01 to 5 in increments of 0.001. (Note that, instead, we could manually enter a vector of domain points or use the `linspace` command, to be discussed later.) In the second line, we instruct MATLAB to calculate the function values at the domain points specified in the first line. In the third line, we instruct MATLAB to invoke its plotting command. Note that the argument is listed first in the plotting command. Also, if we wanted to save this figure for future use, then we could write an .m-file using these same commands. From this example, it should be clear that three basic steps are necessary to construct a plot in MATLAB.

When creating figures in MATLAB, a number of other, useful, cosmetic effects are available. Often in this book, we shall need to plot more than one function in a single figure. For example, suppose we type the following:

```
>> x = 0.01:0.001:5;
>> fx1 = x.*log(x);
>> fx2 = log(x);
>> plot(x,fx1,x,fx2,':'), axis([0 5 -4 8])
```

Here, we plot both functions in the same figure using, again, the `plot` command. Note the colon used in the plotting command; it tells MATLAB to plot the second of the two function as a dotted line. A number of other plotting options are available; these can be accessed by typing `help plot` at the command prompt. The `axis` command simply specifies the horizontal and vertical span of the figure. The figure may be *labeled* and *titled* using the `xlabel`, `ylabel`, and `title` commands. In addition, a small set of TEX characters can also be incorporated in figures. For example, if we wanted to put the letter α at the coordinate $(1.0, 2.0)$ in the figure, we could include the following:

```
>> text(1.0.2.0,'\alpha')
```

A.8.1.7 Three-Dimensional Plotting

A number of the problems that appear in this book require that we create a three-dimensional (3-D) figure. While plotting in three dimensions is mostly an intuitive extension of the two-dimensional (2-D) case, there are some noteworthy differences. Suppose, for example, that we type the following:

```
>> [x,y] = meshgrid(-1:0.05:1,-1:0.05:1);
```

```
>> fxy = sin(exp(x + tan(y)));
>> plot3(x,y,fxy), axis([-1 1 -1 1 -1 1])
```

The function we seek to plot is written in the second line. In the first line, again, we have a discrete subset of the domain; the `meshgrid` command makes this easy. The 3-D analogue of the `plot` function is `plot3`. Note that the `plot3` command could be replaced, in this instance, with the `mesh` or `surf` command and a similar figure would obtain. Note how the `axis` command, as used here, is an intuitive extension of the 2-D case.

Sometimes, it will be necessary to create a figure that includes level curves of the relevant surface; we ask you to do so for a 3-D figure of the logarithm of the likelihood function in chapter 4, problem 3. There are a number of ways to accomplish this. The `contour3` command will plot the level curves on the surface itself in 3-D space. The `contour` command will produce 2-D level curves of a 3-D surface. It is, in fact, possible to create a single figure where the level curves appear both on the 3-D surface and on the corresponding 2-D plane; this is an example of a so-called *2.5-D graph*. Much like the 2-D case, a 3-D figure may be labeled and titled using the `xlabel`, `ylabel`, `zlabel`, and `title` commands.

A.8.2 Statistics Toolbox

In this section, we introduce the statistics toolbox, an add-on to the MATLAB programming environment. While the `Statistics Toolbox` does not solve all problems involving maximum-likelihood estimation, this toolbox does contain some very useful functions. A number of these functions are described and demonstrated below. We break our discussion into the following five topics: 1) descriptive statistics; 2) pseudo-random number generators; 3) probability density functions; 4) cumulative distribution functions; and 5) bootstrapping.

A.8.2.1 Descriptive Statistics

Many of the problems in this book involve data sets that we may want to summarize. For example, having loaded the data from `vickrey.dat`, the first ten lines are again

```
1   54.5509   12   0.5995
2    4.6631    9   0.7768
3   60.7371   13   0.9762
4    6.0791   11   0.9632
```

311

```
 5    3.2844   10   0.6577
 6    4.9756   12   0.8793
 7    5.5734    5   0.9355
 8    8.2835   14   0.3318
 9    2.7089   11   0.6024
10    7.2028   14   0.4922
```

Suppose we open the file `vickrey.m`, which currently contains the following code:

```
1   % Load the data.
2   load ('c:/haley/data/vickrey.dat');
3   w = vickrey(:,2);
4   N = vickrey(:,3);
5   z = vickrey(:,4);
6   % Define the data matrix.
7   Data = [w N z];
8   data = Data(1:10,:);
9   % Extract the rows where N = 11.
10  dataN = data(find(data(:,2) == 11),:)
```

To augment this program so that it computes the minimum, maximum, mean, median, and variance of each of the three variables in the matrix Data would involve the following:

```
1   % Load the data.
2   load ('c:/haley/data/vickrey.dat');
3   w = vickrey(:,2);
4   N = vickrey(:,3);
5   z = vickrey(:,4);
6   % Define the data matrix.
7   Data = [w N z];
8   data = Data(1:10,:);
9   % Extract the rows where N = 11.
10  dataN = data(find(data(:,2) == 11),:)
11  minima = min(Data)
12  maxima = max(Data)
13  means = mean(Data)
14  medians = median(Data)
15  variances = var(Data)
```

Each of the descriptive-statistic functions operates on the columns of the matrix Data. Thus, the output of each of the commands will be a (3×1) row vector.

A.8.2.2 Pseudo-Random Number Generators

In a number of problems, it is necessary to create a variety of pseudo-random numbers. MATLAB has a number of ways to perform this task. We begin with an important first step — seeding the pseudo-random number generator.

Often, it is desirable to replicate exactly the results from a *random* experiment. Thus, most .m-files that involve pseudo-random number generation should begin by setting the *seed*. Suppose we open a new .m-file, called `prnums.m` which, for now, includes the following code:

```
1  % Seed the uniform, pseudo-random number generator.
2  rand('state',123457);
```

The number 123457 is the seed, commonly referred to as the *state* in newer versions of MATLAB.

It is well known that cumulative distribution functions are distributed $U(0, 1)$, which means that random numbers for any continuous random variable can be created by piping a uniform sample through the inverse of the relevant cumulative distribution function, provided it exists in closed-form. The statistics toolbox includes inverse functions for a wide variety of frequently used probability laws. To continue our example, suppose we want to create a (100×3) matrix E of exponential random variables with hazard rate 1 and a (100×1) vector of normal random variables n with mean 2 and standard deviation 4. Here is how we augment the code in `prnums.m` to perform these computations:

```
1  % Seed the uniform, pseudo-random number generator.
2  rand('state',123457);
3  U = rand(100,4);
4  E = expinv(U(:,1:3),1);
5  n = norminv(U(:,4),2,4);
```

Note that MATLAB has other ways to create pseudo-random draws for a large number of frequently used probability laws. However, setting the seed properly can sometimes be tricky in these other approaches so, for the purposes of this appendix, we prefer our approach.

A.8.2.3 Probability Density Functions

In a number of problems, it will be necessary to compute a large number of function evaluations using the probability density function of various laws. MATLAB has a way to make these computations very easy. In particular, suppose we have a vector of values x at which we wish to compute the normal probability density values. Suppose, too, that the mean and the standard deviation of the relevant normal law are 2 and 4. To accomplish this task, we would type the following code:

```
>> x = linspace(0,6,25);
>> pdfx = normpdf(x,2,4)
```

Note that the `linspace` command is just a quick way to create, in this case 25, points on the interval $[0, 6]$.

Similarly, suppose we wanted to compute the values of the log-normal probability density function at the points in the vector y. Suppose, too, that the mean and the standard deviation of the relevant log-normal law are 1 and 3. To accomplish these tasks, we would type the following code:

```
>> y = linspace(0,6,25);
>> pdfy = lognpdf(y,1,3)
```

Finally, MATLAB has similar `pdf`-style functions for a number of other frequently used probability laws.

A.8.2.4 Cumulative Distribution Functions

In a number of problems, it will be necessary to compute a large number of function evaluations using the cumulative distribution function for various probability laws. MATLAB has a way to make these computations very easy too. In particular, suppose we have a vector of values x at which we wish to compute the cumulative distribution values. Suppose, too, that the mean and the standard deviation of the relevant normal law are 2 and 4. To accomplish this task, we would type the following code:

```
>> x = linspace(0,6,25);
>> cdfx = normcdf(x,2,4)
```

Similarly, as above, suppose we wanted to compute the cumulative distribution values at the points in the vector y. Suppose, too, that the mean and the standard deviation of the relevant log-normal law are 1 and 3. To accomplish this task, we would type the following code:

```
>> y = linspace(0,6,25);
>> cdfy = logncdf(y,1,3)
```

Finally, MATLAB has similar `cdf`-style functions for a number of other frequently-used probability laws.

A.8.2.5 Bootstrapping

The bootstrap is a common econometric technique, one necessary in a number of problems in this book. The statistics toolbox includes a bootstrapping function called `bootstrp`. Note, too, the misspelling is not a typographical error. While in many respects this function is useful, in others it is restrictive. We shall illustrate the restrictions and how to circumvent them later.

The key feature of the bootstrap is resampling, with replacement, from a realized sample. Usually, it will be of interest to compute various moments, such as the mean, for each bootstrap sample. We can instruct MATLAB to draw a specific number of bootstrap samples; we can further instruct MATLAB to compute various moments of each of these samples. Suppose, for example, that we have in hand a (100×1) sample w, which we wish to bootstrap 100 times, each time using a sample size of 100. Suppose, too, that we want MATLAB to compute the mean of each of these samples during the resampling process. To produce these results, we would type the following code:

```
>> w = linspace(1,100,100);
>> bootw = bootstrp(100,'mean',w);
```

Note again the use of the `linspace` command. The second line of code instructs MATLAB to draw 100 bootstrap samples from w, computing the mean for each, which are then recorded in the vector bootw. Similarly, if we wanted instead to compute the median for each bootstrap sample, we would type

```
>> w = linspace(1,100,100);
>> bootw = bootstrp(100,'median',w);
```

Finally, note that the `bootstrp` function does not allow us to compute deciles or quartiles for each bootstrap sample. Because of this inflexibility, we have written our own bootstrapping function, which will be one of the examples of a *user-defined function*.

A.8.3 User-Defined Functions

Sometimes, we may encounter a circumstance in which none of the built-in functions in MATLAB will perform the calculations we need. One example of such a shortcoming is MATLAB's `bootstrp` function, which is not flexible enough to perform the analysis required in some of the problems found in chapter 1. Fortunately, MATLAB can easily accommodate user-defined functions. The purpose of this section is to introduce the methodology for constructing generic, user-defined MATLAB functions. Our presentation will be organized into the following three topics: 1) a generic MATLAB function; 2) writing a user-defined function—bootstrap.m; and 3) writing another user-defined function—steepdscnt.m.

A.8.3.1 A Generic Function

Many of the .m-files we have presented in this appendix have been problem-specific; i.e., they were written to solve the immediate problem. Frequently, however, it is advantageous to rewrite such programs so that they may be applied generally. Almost every built-in MATLAB function has been designed so that it can be used in a variety of different circumstances without our changing the code itself. To cement the distinction, we could easily write a program that applied Newton's method to a *specific* objective function or we could write a generic MATLAB function that performed Newton's method on *any* function we specify.

A.8.3.2 Writing a User-Defined Function

Perhaps the best way to learn the process of *generalizing* code is to consider some examples. Chapter 1 contains a problem where we must draw bootstrap samples, computing the lower quartile for each sample. The built-in bootstrp function does not allow for this specific calculation, so we must, instead, write our own bootstrap function, which we call bootstrap.[3] The following fits our needs:

```
1  function bootsamps = bootstrap(boots,sample)

2  % BOOTSAMPS = BOOTSTRAP(BOOTS,SAMPLE)
3  % User-specified inputs:
4  %    BOOTS -- number of bootstrap samples
5  %    SAMPLE -- the samples to be bootstrapped
6  % User-requested output:
7  %    BOOTSAMPS -- the matrix of bootstrap samples

8  % Determine the sample size.
```

---

[3] For the sake of clarity and space, the version of bootstrap that appears here is a somewhat shortened version of the one contained on the CD which accompanies this book.

```
 9  T = length(sample);

10  % Makes sure the sample is a row vector.
11  [i,j] = size(sample);
12  if j < i
13      sample = sample';
14  end

15  % Create a sampling mechanism.
16  U = unidrnd(T,boots,T);

17  % Using U, construct the bootstrap samples.
18  for i = 1:boots
19      bootsamps(i,:)  = sample(U(i,:));
20  end

21  % Rows of BOOTSAMPS are the (size T) bootstrap samples.
```

Note that the line numbers on the left are *not* part of the code, and are only included here to facilitate discussion of the code. A fully documented version of this code can be found on the CD that accompanies this book. When writing a user-defined function, it is important to define the function in the first (uncommented) line of the program; in line 1 we do so. The function's name is `bootstrap`. The commented lines that appear below the function definition (lines 2–7) are the `help`; in them we describe each of the inputs and outputs of our function. Note, too, that if we type `help bootstrap` at the command prompt (assuming, again, that the path is set correctly), it is lines 2–7 that will appear.

In the next lines, 8 and 9, we determine the length of the incoming sample, which we shall soon be drawing bootstrap samples (of the same size) from. In lines 10–14, we include a conformability check, which is necessary in case the user enters the sample as a column vector rather than a row vector. In lines 15 and 16, we create a matrix of discrete uniform random numbers on the interval [1,T]; the dimensions of this matrix equal the number of user-requested bootstrap samples by the size of each of these samples; viz., T. In lines 17–20, we instruct MATLAB to construct each of the bootstrap samples using the sampling mechanism embedded in the matrix U. The matrix that results from this process, called `bootsamps`, contains a bootstrap sample in each row, which we note on line 21 in a comment. Our function allows us access to the actual bootstrap samples, something the built-in MATLAB function `bootstrp` does not.

A.8.3.3 Another User-Defined Function

It is often necessary to optimize a function numerically. Some of the built-in MATLAB functions for performing these calculations will be discussed below in the optimization section. Here, we demonstrate how to write a user-defined function that finds a minimum using the method of steepest descent. The goal is to provide another example of a user-defined function that is closely related to the optimization tools needed in many of the problems found in this book.

The method of steepest descent is perhaps the simplest of the so-called *first-order methods*. To implement the method of steepest descent, we need to supply the objective function and its gradient function to the algorithm. The algorithm then searches for a minimum by taking a sequence of steps (iterations) in the direction of steepest descent, which is mathematically equivalent to searching along the direction given by the negative of the gradient. The question of how far to search in the steepest-descent direction is given by the step-length, which in the version of steepest descent presented here, is fixed at 0.001; a better coding of this algorithm would include a line-search subroutine for selecting the step-length, but we leave this aside and focus instead on the coding lesson.

```
1   function [x,fval,gval] = steepdscnt(fun,dfun,x,itmax)

2   % [X,FVAL,GVAL] = steepdscnt(FUN,DFUN,X,ITMAX)
3   % This function searches for minimum of function FUN
4   % starting from X using the method of steepest descent.
5   % User-specified inputs:
6   %    FUN -- objective function
7   %    DFUN -- gradient of the objective function
8   %    X -- initial guess for X
9   %    ITMAX -- maximum number of iterations
10  % User-requested output:
11  %    X -- solutions
12  %    FVAL -- function value at the solution
13  %    GVAL -- gradient value at the solution

14  % Make sure that X will be conformable.
15  [i,j] = size(x);
16  if i < j
17      x = x';
18  end

19  % Initialize iteration counter and set step-length.
20  it = 0;
21  step = 0.001;

22  % Start the iteration loop.
```

```
23   while it <= itmax
24       % Evaluate the gradient function at the current X.
25       gval = feval(dfun,x);
26       % Make sure that GVAL will be conformable.
27       [i,j] = size(x);
28       if i < j
29          gval = gval';
30       end
31       % Take a descent step.
32       x = x - step*gval;
33       % Advance the iteration counter.
34       it = it + 1;
35   end;

36   % Compute the function value at X.
37   fval = feval(fun,x);
```

Note that the line numbers on the left are *not* part of the code, and are only included here to facilitate discussion of the code. Again, when writing a user-defined function it is important to define the function in the first (uncommented) line of the program; in line 1 we do so. The function's names is **steepdscnt**. The commented lines that appear below the function definition (lines 2–13) are the **help**; in them we describe each of the inputs and outputs of our function. Note, again, that if we type **help steepdscnt** at the command prompt (assuming, again, that the path is set correctly), it is lines 2–13 that will appear.

In the next lines, 14–18, we determine the size of the incoming initial guess vector, and adjust it so that it conforms to the rest of the code, if necessary. In lines 19–21, we initialize the iteration counter and set the length of the descent step. In lines 22–35, we create the main iteration loop. We enter this loop with the initial guess vector, compute the gradient vector at that point, pass the gradient vector through a conformability check, take a descent step, advance the iteration counter, and then repeat until the user-specified number of iterations **itmax** is exhausted. In lines 36 and 37, we compute the value of the objective function at the resulting value of **x**.

To demonstrate our implementation of this algorithm, we used it to solve the maximum-likelihood estimation problem in chapter 1, problem 3, part c. Using starting values of $(1, 1, 1, 1)^\top$ and the default step-length, 0.001, successful convergence obtained in 839 iterations to an infinity-norm, gradient-tolerance of 0.0001.

Note that the code to implement the method of steepest descent is extremely basic. We could easily add a stopping tolerance for the gradient, a verbosity parameter, various warning messages, an adaptive step-length subroutine, and so on. Nevertheless, it should be clear that MATLAB offers a great deal of flexibility in constructing user-defined functions, and that it is relatively straightforward to write user-defined functions when necessary.

A.8.4 Optimization Toolbox

A large number of the problems that appear in this book must be solved using optimization techniques. Some of these problems involve minimization (of, say, the sum of squared errors), while other problems involve maximization (of, say, the logarithm of the likelihood function). The optimization toolbox contains a number of functions that are very useful when solving such problems. In this section, we introduce some of these functions. We recommend that the user open the relevant MATLAB files from the CD that accompanies this book when reading the examples given below. Our discussion is divided into the following five specific topics: 1) driver files and objective functions; 2) gradient vectors and Hessian matrices; 3) unconstrained optimization; 4) constrained optimization; and 5) algorithm options — `optimset`.

A.8.4.1 Driver Files and Objective Functions

The most frequently encountered optimization problems in this book involve estimation by the method of maximum likelihood. The objective in these problems is, of course, to maximize the logarithm of the likelihood function by choosing parameter estimates, conditional on the available data.

MATLAB's structure requires that the logarithm of the likelihood function be defined in its own .m-file. Usually, problems involving maximum-likelihood estimation have associated with them three separate files: a driver .mi-file, such as `prog13c.m`; a function file where the logarithm of the likelihood function is defined, such as `fun13c.m`; and a data file, such as `logser.dat`. The naming convention that appears in the previous sentence illustrates our method of cataloging these files. In fact, these particular files, which can be found on the CD that accompanies this book, are for chapter 1, problem 3, part c.

The so-called *driver* file is where we declare the optimization algorithm to be used, where we input the initial guess for the maximum-likelihood estimate, and where we specify any options associated with the optimization routine. The so-called *function* file is where the logarithm of the likelihood function is defined, the name of this function file will be the handle MATLAB uses to access the correct logarithm of the likelihood function when running the driver file. The so-called *data* file, all of which appear with a .dat suffix, contains all the data relevant to the estimation.

A.8.4.2 Gradient Vectors and Hessian Matrices

When optimizing a function, it is generally recommended, whenever possible, to use the actual (analytic) gradient vector and Hessian matrix. MATLAB will default to using numerical first- and second-partial derivatives if we do not specify a gradient vector or Hessian matrix. MATLAB can easily incorporate a user-defined gradient vector and Hessian matrix into its built-in optimization routines. In the next subsection, some examples will make clear how this is done.

A.8.4.3 Unconstrained Optimization

In MATLAB, the main function we shall use to calculate the maximum-likelihood estimates is the built-in `fminunc` function. A specific example of these calculations can be found in the trio of files prog13c.m, fun13c.m, and logser.dat.[4] We begin with the main features of the driver file prog13c.m:

```
1   % Set some options and write out the function call.
2   options = optimset('GradObj','on','Hessian','on', ...
3   'TolFun',1e-10);
4   [gamma,fval,flag,output,grad,hessian] = ...
5   fminunc('fun13c',[1 1 1 1 ]', options)
```

Note that the line numbers at left are *not* part of the code, and are only included here to facilitate discussion of the code. In line 2, we set some options of the optimization routine `fminunc`; these will be discussed in more detail later on. Note that this line ends with ... which is the way to notify MATLAB that the text of the line is too long for one line and will be continued on the next line, 3. In line 4, we write out the function call. The items that appear on the left-hand side of the equal sign are the output variables, which include the minimizing argument, the function value at the minimizing argument, a flag indicating whether the algorithm converged successfully, a summary of the optimization process (e.g., iteration count, algorithm used, and so on), the value of

---

[4] Again, these are somewhat modified versions of those that appear on the CD which accompanies this book.

the gradient vector at the minimizing argument, and the value of the Hessian matrix at the minimizing argument.

On the right-hand side of the equal sign, in line 5, appears the name of the optimization routine and its inputs, in parentheses. The first input is the name of the .m-file where the logarithm of the likelihood function is defined; note that it appears between apostrophes. The second input is the (4×1) initial guess vector, which is followed by `options`, which funnels all the options set on line 2 into the optimization routine.

It is particularly important to note that all of MATLAB's optimization routines are actually minimization routines. Thus, whenever we want to maximize a function, we must do so using a minimization routine. Fortunately, we can easily convert any maximization problem into a minimization problem by simply multiplying the objective function by negative one; this conversion must also be applied to the gradient vector and the Hessian matrix, if they are supplied by the user.

The first (uncommented) line in the file defining the logarithm of the likelihood function, `fun13c.m`, is

```
function [L,g,H] = fun13c(gamma)
```

The items that appear on the left-hand side of the equal sign, which are specified later in the file `fun13c.m`, correspond to the logarithm of the likelihood function (L), the gradient vector (g), and the Hessian matrix (H). The item on the right-hand side of the equal sign is the function name, and the parentheses enclose the argument we are optimizing over, here `gamma`. By including L, g, and H in the brackets at left, we are instructing MATLAB to recognize L, g, and H as functions of `gamma`.

Suppose, by way of contrast, that we have the actual gradient vector, but not the actual Hessian matrix. In this case, we would write the following code instead:

```
function [L,g] = fun13c(gamma)
```

MATLAB would proceed by computing a numerical approximation to the Hessian matrix using a method such as Davidon–Fletcher–Powell (DFP) or Broyden–Fletcher–Goldfarb–Shanno (BFGS).

Suppose, again by way of contrast, that neither the actual gradient vector nor the actual Hessian matrix are available. In this case, MATLAB would proceed by computing numerical first derivatives and an appropriate approximation to the Hessian matrix in order to perform the analysis. In this case, the first line of the code would read

```
function L = fun13c(gamma)
```

From this example, it should be clear what structure MATLAB requires of function calls, how to interpret input for and output from the built-in MATLAB function `fminunc`, how to write a user-defined gradient vector and Hessian matrix function in the objective function file, and how MATLAB would proceed if we do not input the actual gradient vector or Hessian matrix.

A.8.4.4 Constrained Optimization

In some problems, it will be necessary to use MATLAB's built-in constrained optimization function `fmincon`. Structuring a function call using `fmincon` is, in principle, no different from calling the unconstrained optimizer `fminunc`, except that a separate constraint function .m-file must be written for any nonlinear constraints. In addition, the input list of `fmincon` differs considerably from the input list of `fminunc`. The source of this difference is the way `fmincon` treats different types of constraints. In fact, `fmincon` has unique input placeholders for linear inequality constraints, linear equality constraints, lower bounds on the arguments, upper bounds on the arguments, and nonlinear constraints. How to structure the `fmincon` function call in the presence of only some of the constraint types will be demonstrated below.

One problem, in particular, that requires the `fmincon` function is the constrained maximum-likelihood estimation problem found in chapter 4, problem 3, part h). The solution to this problem requires four files: prog43h.m, fun43h.m, cfun43h.m, and nlp.dat. The estimation is governed by the driver file `prog43h.m`; the logarithm of the likelihood function is defined in `fun43h.m`; the constraints on the logarithm of the likelihood function are defined in `cfun43h.m`; and the relevant data are contained in `nlp.dat`.

The optimization call in `prog43h.m` is as follows:

```
1   % Initial guess for the parameters.
2   guess = [1 1]';
3   % Call the constrained optimization routine.
4   theta = fmincon('fun43h',guess,[],[],[],[],[],[], ...
5   'cfun43h',options)
```

Note that the line numbers at left are *not* part of the code, and are only included here to facilitate discussion of the code. Unlike the example of unconstrained optimization above, here we input the initial guess for the parameters on line 2, which we then insert into the `fmincon` as `guess`. Note the []s that appear in the `fmincon` function call; their purpose is to instruct MATLAB that we are not placing constraints of the type that correspond to these placeholders in the input list. The last two inputs are the nonlinear constraints and the options we have set; we shall discuss the latter in the next subsection.

The first (uncommented) line in `cfun43h` is

```
function [c,ceq] = cfun43h(theta);
```

Note that MATLAB requires that the constraint function return two outputs, one for nonlinear inequality constraints (`c`) and another for nonlinear equality constraints (`ceq`). In this particular problem, we do not have any equality constraints. Thus, we simply set `ceq = []` in the body of the code in `cfun43h.m`.

Note that it is necessary to take special care when solving a constrained maximization problem (as we are doing here) using a constrained minimization routine. In particular, the inequality constraints must be modified (in sign and inequality direction), so that the minimization routine solves the desired maximization problem.

A.8.4.5 Algorithm Options: `optimset`

Many of the optimization programs on the CD that accompanies this book include user-specified options. These are set using the `optimset` command. This feature allows the user to adjust various features of the optimization routine such as stopping tolerance, algorithm used, display of run-time information about the optimization process, and so on. The `optimset` command is the main way to set function options for both `fminunc` and `fmincon`. By typing `help optimset` at the command prompt, we can view a complete listing of the available function options.

As an example, consider again the core lines of code in `prog13c.m`

```
1  % Set some options and write out the function call.
2  options = optimset('GradObj','on','Hessian','on', ...
3  'TolFun',1e-10);
4  [gamma,fval,flag,output,grad,hessian] = ...
5  fminunc('fun13c',[1 1 1 1 ]', options)
```

Note that the line numbers at left are *not* part of the code, and are only included here to facilitate discussion of the code. While there is a long list of options that we can adjust using `optimset`, we only change three in this particular program. The first, `GradObj`, is paired with the right-adjacent string, which, here, says `on`. Setting this options to `on` is how we tell MATLAB to use the actual gradient. A similar rule applies to the incorporation of the actual Hessian. The third option, `TolFun`, allows us to set a stopping tolerance on the function values, here equal to `1e-10`.

It is unnecessary to specify any options. In fact, if the following lines were used instead:

```
1   % Set some options and write out the function call.
2   [gamma,fval,flag,output,grad,hessian] = ...
3   fminunc('fun13c',[1 1 1 1 ]')
```

then MATLAB would proceed using the default option values embedded in the `fminunc` function. Note that, in this instance, the gradient vector and Hessian matrix would be computed numerically by the optimization routine.

Two additional options, which we use with some frequency in the programs that appear on the CD that accompanies this book, are set as follows:

```
1   options = optimset('display','iter');
2   options = optimset('LargeScale','off');
```

Note that the line numbers at left are *not* part of the code, and are only included here to facilitate discussion of the code. Line 1 contains the verbosity option; setting it to **iter** instructs MATLAB to display run-time information (in the command window) about the optimization process such as the current iterate value, the current gradient value, and so on. The option on line 2 instructs MATLAB to use the medium-scale algorithm instead of the large-scale algorithm; the former uses a quasi-Newton method with a line-search subroutine, while the latter uses a quasi-Newton method with a trust-region (dogleg) subroutine. Note that the large-scale method requires that we supply the actual gradient vector.

References

Amemiya, Takeshi. *Advanced Econometrics*. Cambridge, Massachusetts: Harvard University Press, 1985.

Andersen, Erling B. "Asymptotic Properties of Conditional Maximum-Likelihood Estimators," *Journal of the Royal Statistical Society*, Series B, 32 (1970), 283–301.

Athey, Susan and Philip A. Haile. "Identification of Standard Auction Models," *Econometrica*, 70 (2002), 2107–2140.

Athey, Susan and Philip A. Haile. "Nonparametric Approaches to Auctions," in *Handbook of Econometrics*, Volume 6, edited by James J. Heckman and Edward Leamer. Amsterdam: Elsevier, 2005.

Austin, Adrian M. and Brett Katzman. "Testing a Model of Multi-Unit Bidder Demands using Tobacco Auction Data," typescript. Coral Gables: Department of Economics, University of Miami, 2002.

Ausubel, Lawrence M. "An Efficient Ascending-Bid Auction for Multiple Objects," *American Economic Review*, 94 (2004), 1452–1475.

Ausubel, Lawrence M. and Peter Cramton. "Demand Reduction and Inefficiency in Multi-Unit Auctions," typescript. College Park: Department of Economics, University of Maryland, 2002.

Avery, Christopher. "Strategic Jump Bidding in English Auctions," *Review of Economic Studies*, 65 (1998), 185–210.

Bajari, Patrick. *The First Price Auction with Asymmetric Bidders: Theory and Applications*. Ph.D. dissertation, Department of Economics, University of Minnesota, 1997.

Bajari, Patrick. "Comparing Competition and Collusion: A Numerical Approach," *Economic Theory*, 18 (2001), 187–205.

Bickel, Peter J. and David A. Freedman. "Some Asymptotic Theory for the Bootstrap," *The Annals of Statistics*, 9 (1981), 1196–1217.

References

Bierens, Herman J. "Kernel Estimators of Regression Functions" in *Advances in Economic Theory*, edited by Truman F. Bewley. Cambridge, England: Cambridge University Press, 1987.

Billingsley, Patrick. *Probability and Measure*, Third Edition. New York: John Wiley & Sons, 1995.

Black, Jane and David de Meza. "Systematic Price Differences between Successive Auctions are No Anomaly," *Journal of Economics & Management Strategy*, 1 (1992), 607–628.

Boyce, William E. and Richard C. DiPrima. *Elementary Differential Equations*, Third Edition. New York: John Wiley & Sons, 1977.

Brendstrup, Bjarne. "Non-Parametric Estimation of Sequential English Auctions," typescript. Aarhus: Department of Economics, University of Aarhus, 2003.

Brendstrup, Bjarne and Harry J. Paarsch. "Nonparametric Estimation of Dutch and First-Price, Sealed-Bid Auction Models with Asymmetric Bidders," typescript. Iowa City: Department of Economics, University of Iowa, 2003.

Brendstrup, Bjarne and Harry J. Paarsch. "Nonparametric Estimation in Models Multi-Unit, Sequential Dutch Auctions with Asymmetric Bidders," typescript. Iowa City: Department of Economics, University of Iowa, 2004.

Brendstrup, Bjarne and Harry J. Paarsch. "Semiparametric Estimation in Models of Multi-Object, Sequential, English Auctions," typescript. Iowa City: Department of Economics, University of Iowa, 2005.

Brendstrup, Bjarne and Harry J. Paarsch. "Identification and Estimation in Sequential, Asymmetric, English Auctions," *Journal of Econometrics*, (forthcoming).

Campo, Sandra, Emmanuel Guerre, Isabelle Perrigne, and Quang H. Vuong. "Semiparametric Estimation of First-Price Auctions with Risk Averse Bidders," typescript. Los Angeles: Department of Economics, University of Southern California, 2000.

Capen, Edward C., Robert V. Clapp, and William M. Campbell. "Competitive Bidding in High-Risk Situations," *Journal of Petroleum Technology*, 23 (1971), 641–653.

Cassady, Ralph Jr. *Auctions and Auctioneering*. Berkeley: University of California Press, 1967.

Chakraborty, Indranil. "Bundling Decisions for Selling Multiple Objects," *Economic Theory*, 13 (1999), 723–733.

Chapman, James T.E., Harry J. Paarsch, and David McAdams. "Sequential, Multi-Unit, Sealed-Bid, Discriminatory-Price Auctions," typescript. Iowa City: Department of Economics, University of Iowa, 2005.

Chernozhukov, Victor and Han Hong. "Likelihood Estimation and Inference in a Class of Nonregular Econometric Models," *Econometrica*, 72 (2004), 1445–1480.

Clarke, Edward H. "Multipart Pricing of Public Goods," *Public Choice*, 2 (1971), 19–33.

Davidson, Russell and James G. MacKinnon. *Econometric Theory and Methods*. New York: Oxford University Press, 2004.

Donald, Stephen G. and Harry J. Paarsch. "Piecewise Pseudo-Maximum Likelihood Estimation in Empirical Models of Auctions," *International Economic Review*, 34 (1993), 121–148.

Donald, Stephen G. and Harry J. Paarsch. "Identification, Estimation, and Testing in Parametric Empirical Models of Auctions within the Independent Private Values Paradigm," *Econometric Theory*, 12 (1996), 517–567.

Donald, Stephen G. and Harry J. Paarsch. "Superconsistent Estimation and Inference in Structural Econometric Models Using Extreme Order Statistics," *Journal of Econometrics*, 109 (2002), 305–340.

Donald, Stephen G., Harry J. Paarsch, and Jacques Robert. "An Empirical Model of the Multi-Unit, Sequential, Clock Auction," *Journal of Applied Econometrics*, (forthcoming).

Eastwood, Brian J. and A. Ronald Gallant. "Adaptive Rules for Semi-nonparametric Estimators that Achieve Asymptotic Normality," *Econometric Theory*, 7 (1991), 307–340.

Efron, Bradley. *The Jackknife, the Bootstrap, and Other Resampling Plans*. Philadelphia: SIAM, 1982.

Eso, Péter and Lucy White. "Precautionary Bidding in Auctions," *Econometrica*, 72 (2004), 77–92.

Fenton, Victor M. and A. Ronald Gallant. "Convergence Rates of SNP Density Estimators," *Econometrica*, 64 (1996), 719–727.

References

Fishman, George S. and Louis R. Moore. "A Statistical Evaluation of Multiplicative Congruential Random Number Generators with Modulus $2^{31} - 1$," *American Statistical Association Journal*, 77 (1982), 129–136.

Flinn, Christopher J. and James J. Heckman. "New Methods for Analyzing Structural Models of Labor Force Dynamics," *Journal of Econometrics*, 18 (1982), 115–168.

Friedman, Milton. *A Program of Monetary Stability*. New York: Fordham University Press, 1959.

Galambos, Janos. *The Asymptotic Theory of Extreme Order Statistics*, Second Edition. Malabar, Florida: Robert E. Krieger Publishing Company, 1987.

Gallant, A. Ronald and Douglas W. Nychka. "Semi-Nonparametric Maximum Likelihood Estimation," *Econometrica*, 55 (1987), 363–390.

Gibbons, Robert. *Game Theory for Applied Economists*. Princeton: Princeton University Press, 1992.

Gourieroux, Christian and Alain Monfort. "Simulation Based Inference in Models with Heterogeneity," *Annales d'Economie et de Statistique*, 20/21 (1991), 69–107.

Groves, Theodore. "Incentives in Teams," *Econometrica*, 41 (1973), 617–631.

Guerre, Emmanuel, Isabelle Perrigne, and Quang H. Vuong. "Optimal Nonparametric Estimation of First Price Auctions," *Econometrica*, 68 (2000), 525–574.

Haile, Philip A. and Elie Tamer. "Inference with an Incomplete Model of English Auctions," *Journal of Political Economy*, 111 (2003), 1–51.

Han, Aaron K. "Non-parametric Analysis of a Generalized Regression Model — The Maximum Rank Correlation Estimator," *Journal of Econometrics*, 35 (1987), 303–316.

Hanselman, Duane C., and Bruce L. Littlefield. *Mastering* MATLAB® 7. Upper Saddle River, New Jersey: Prentice Hall, 2004.

Hansen, Bruce E. "Inference when a Nuisance Parameter is Not Identified under the Null Hypothesis," *Econometrica*, 64 (1996), 413–430.

Hansen, Lars Peter. "Large Sample Properties of Generalized Method of Moments Estimators," *Econometrica* 50 (1982), 1029–1054.

References

Harsanyi, John C. "Games of Incomplete Information Played by 'Bayesian' Players, Parts I–III," *Management Science*, 14 (1967/68), 159–182, 320–334, and 486–502.

Hoadley, Bruce. "Asymptotic Properties of Maximum Likelihood Estimators for the Independent Not Identically Distributed Case," *Annals of Mathematical Statistics*, 42 (1971), 1977–1991.

Hong, Han. *Econometric Models of Asymmetric Ascending Auctions*. Ph.D. dissertation, Department of Economics, Stanford University, 1998.

Hong, Han and Matthew Shum. "Rates of Information Aggregation in Common Value Auctions," *Journal of Economic Theory*, 116 (2004), 1–40.

Horowitz, Joel L. *Semiparametric Methods in Econometrics*. New York: Springer–Verlag, 1998.

Horowitz, Joel L. "The Bootstrap in Econometrics" in *Handbook of Econometrics*, Volume 5, edited by James J. Heckman and Edward E. Leamer. Amsterdam: Elsevier, 2001.

Horowitz, Joel L. and Charles F. Manski. "Identification and Robustness with Contaminated and Corrupted Data," *Econometrica*, 63 (1995), 281–302.

Hortaçsu, Ali. "Mechanism Choice and Strategic Bidding in Divisible Good Auctions: An Empirical Analysis of the Turkish Treasury Auction Market," typescript. Chicago: Department of Economics, University of Chicago, 2002a.

Hortaçsu, Ali. "Bidding Behavior in Divisible Good Auctions: Theory and Evidence from the Turkish Treasury Auction Market," typescript. Chicago: Department of Economics, University of Chicago, 2002b.

Ichimura, Hidehiko. "Semiparametric Least Square (SLS) and Weighted SLS Estimation of Single-Index Models," *Journal of Econometrics*, 58 (1993), 71–120.

Jofre-Bonet, Mireia and Martin Pesendorfer. "Estimation of a Dynamic Auction Game," *Econometrica*, 71 (2003), 1443–1489.

Judd, Kenneth L. *Numerical Methods in Economics*. Cambridge, Massachusetts: MIT Press, 1998.

Katzman Brett. "A Two Stage Sequential Auction with Multi-Unit Demands," *Journal of Economic Theory*, 86 (1999), 77–99.

331

References

Krasnokutskaya, Elena. "Identification and Estimation in Highway Procurement Contracts under Unobserved Auction Heterogeneity," typescript. Philadelphia: Department of Economics, University of Pennsylvania, 2004.

Krishna, Vijay. *Auction Theory*. San Diego: Academic Press, 2002.

Laffont, Jean-Jacques, Patrick Loisel, and Jacques Robert. "Repeated Descending-Price Auctions I: Theory," typescript. Toulouse: Institut d'Economie Industrielle, 1994.

Laffont, Jean-Jacques, Hervé Ossard, and Quang H. Vuong. "Econometrics of First-Price Auctions," *Econometrica*, 63 (1995), 953–980.

Laffont, Jean-Jacques and Quang H. Vuong. "Structural Analysis of Auction Data," *American Economic Review*, 86 (1996), 414–420.

Lebrun, Bernard. "First Price Auctions in the Asymmetric N Bidder Case," *International Economic Review*, 40 (1999), 125–142.

LeCam, Lucien. "On Some Asymptotic Properties of Maximum Likelihood Estimates and Related Bayes Estimates," *University of California Publications in Statistics*, 1 (1953), 277–330.

Lehmann, Erich L. *Theory of Point Estimation*. New York: John Wiley & Sons, 1983.

Lerman, Steven R. and Charles F. Manski. "On the Use of Simulated Frequencies to Approximate Choice Probabilities" in *Structural Analysis of Discrete Data with Econometric Applications*, edited by Charles F. Manski and Daniel L. McFadden. Cambridge, Massachusetts: MIT Press, 1981.

Lewis, Peter A.W. and E. John Orav. *Simulation Methodology for Statisticians, Operations Analysts, and Engineers*, Volume 1. Pacific Grove, California: Wadsworth, 1989.

Li, Tong. "Econometrics of First-Price Auctions with Entry and Binding Reservation Prices," *Journal of Econometrics*, 126 (2005), 173–200.

Li, Tong and Isabelle Perrigne. "Timber Sale Auctions with Random Reserve Prices," *Review of Economics and Statistics*, 85 (2003), 189–200.

Li, Tong and Quang H. Vuong. "Using All Bids in Parametric Estimation of First-Price Auction," *Economics Letters*, 55 (1997), 321–325.

Li, Tong, Isabelle Perrigne, and Quang H. Vuong. "Conditionally Independent Private Information in OCS Wildcat Auctions," *Journal of Econometrics*, 98 (2000), 129–161.

Li, Tong, Isabelle Perrigne, and Quang H. Vuong. "Semiparametric Estimation of the Optimal Reserve Price in First-Price Auctions," *Journal of Business and Economic Statistics*, 21 (2003), 53–64.

Lu, Jingfeng. "Stochastic Private Values in Auctions: Identification and Estimation," typescript. Los Angeles: Department of Economics, University of Southern California, 2004.

Lucking-Reiley, David. "Vickrey Auctions in Practice: From Nineteenth-Century Philately to Twenty-First-Century E-Commerce," *Journal of Economic Perspectives*, 14 (2000), 183–192.

Maddala, G.S. *Limited-Dependent and Qualitative Variables in Econometrics*. Cambridge, England: Cambridge University Press, 1983.

Mangasarian, Olvi L. *Nonlinear Programming*. New York: McGraw-Hill, 1969.

Manski, Charles F. and Elie Tamer. "Inference on Regressions with Interval Data on a Regressor or Outcome," *Econometrica*, 70 (2002), 519–546.

Maskin, Eric S. and John G. Riley. "Optimal Auctions with Risk Averse Buyers," *Econometrica*, 52 (1984), 1473–1518.

Maskin, Eric S. and John G. Riley. "Auction Theory with Private Values," *American Economic Review*, 75 (1985), 150–155.

Maskin, Eric S. and John G. Riley. "Asymmetric Auctions," *Review of Economic Studies*, 67 (2000), 413–438.

McAdams, David. "Identification and Testable Restrictions in Private Value Multi-Unit Auctions," typescript. Cambridge, Massachusetts: Sloan School of Management, MIT, 2005.

McAfee, R. Preston and John McMillan. "Auctions and Bidding," *Journal of Economic Literature*, 25 (1987), 699–738.

McAfee, R. Preston and Daniel Vincent. "The Declining Price Anomaly," *Journal of Economic Theory*, 60 (1993), 191–212.

McFadden, Daniel L. "A Method of Simulated Moments for Estimation of Discrete Response Models without Numerical Integration," *Econometrica*, 57 (1989), 995–1026.

Meilijson, Isaac. "Estimation of the Lifetime Distribution of the Parts from the Autopsy Statistics of the Machine," *Journal of Applied Probability*, 18 (1981), 829–838.

Milgrom, Paul R. *Putting Auction Theory to Work*. Cambridge, England: Cambridge University Press, 2004.

References

Milgrom, Paul R. and Robert Weber J. "A Theory of Auctions and Competitive Bidding," *Econometrica*, 50 (1982), 1089–1122.

Myerson, Roger B. "Optimal Auction Design," *Mathematics of Operations Research*, 6 (1981), 58–73.

Myerson, Roger B. *Game Theory: Analysis of Conflict*. Cambridge, Massachusetts: Harvard University Press, 1991.

Myerson, Roger B. and Mark A. Satterthwaite. "Efficient Mechanisms for Bilateral Trading," *Journal of Economic Theory*, 29 (1983), 265–281.

Nelsen, Roger B. *An Introduction to Copulas*. New York: Springer–Verlag, 1999.

Newey, Whitney K. and Daniel L. McFadden. "Large Sample Estimation and Hypothesis Testing" in *Handbook of Econometrics*, Volume 4, edited by Robert F. Engle and Daniel L. McFadden. Amsterdam: Elsevier, 1994.

Paarsch, Harry J. "Empirical Models of Auctions within the Independent Private Values Paradigm and an Application to British Columbian Timber Sales," Discussion Paper #89–14. Vancouver: Department of Economics, University of British Columbia, 1989.

Paarsch, Harry J. "Empirical Models of Auctions and an Application to British Columbian Timber Sales," Discussion Paper #91–19. Vancouver: Department of Economics, University of British Columbia, 1991.

Paarsch, Harry J. "Deciding between the Common and Private Value Paradigms in Empirical Models of Auctions," *Journal of Econometrics*, 51 (1992), 191–215.

Paarsch, Harry J. "A Comparison of Estimators for Empirical Models of Auctions," *Annales d'Economie et de Statistique*, 34 (1994), 143–157.

Paarsch, Harry J. "Deriving an Estimate of the Optimal Reserve Price: An Application to British Columbian Timber Sales," *Journal of Econometrics*, 78 (1997), 333–357.

Paarsch Harry J. and Jacques Robert. "Sequential, Oral, Ascending-Price, Open-Exit Auctions with Multi-Unit Demand and an Application to the Sale of Siberian Timber Export Permits," typescript. London, Canada: Department of Economics, University of Western Ontario, 1995.

References

Paarsch Harry J. and Jacques Robert. "Testing Equilibrium Behaviour at First-Price, Sealed-Bid Auctions with Discrete Bid Increments" typescript. Iowa City: Department of Economics, University of Iowa, 2003.

Pakes, Ariel and David Pollard. "Simulation and the Asymptotics of Optimization Estimators," *Econometrica*, 57 (1989), 1027–1057.

Perrigne, Isabelle and Quang H. Vuong "Structural Econometrics of First-Price Auctions: A Survey of Methods," *Canadian Journal of Agricultural Economics*, 47 (1999), 203–223.

Pesendorfer, Wolfgang and Jeroen M. Swinkels. "The Loser's Curse and Information Aggregation in Common Value Auctions," *Econometrica*, 65 (1997), 1247–1282.

Pesendorfer, Wolfgang and Jeroen M. Swinkels. "Efficiency and Information Aggregation in Auctions," *American Economic Review*, 90 (2000), 499–525.

Powell, James L., James H. Stock, and Thomas M. Stoker. "Semiparametric Estimation of Index Coefficients," *Econometrica*, 57 (1989), 1403–1430.

Prakasa Rao, B.L.S. *Identifiability in Stochastic Models: Characterization of Probability Distributions*. San Diego: Academic Press, 1992.

Reiss, Peter C. and Frank A. Wolak. "Structural Econometric Modeling: Rationales and Examples for Industrial Organization" in *Handbook of Econometrics*, Volume 6, edited by James J. Heckman and Edward Leamer. Amsterdam: Elsevier, 2005.

Reiss, R.-D. *Approximate Distributions of Order Statistics: with Applications to Nonparametric Statistics*. New York: Springer–Verlag, 1989.

Riley, John G. and William F. Samuelson. "Optimal Auctions," *American Economic Review*, 71 (1981), 381–392.

Rothkopf, Michael H., Thomas J. Teisberg, and Edward P. Kahn. "Why are Vickrey Auctions Rare?," *Journal of Political Economy*, 98 (1990), 94–109.

Sherman, Robert P. "The Limiting Distribution of the Maximum Rank Correlation Estimator," *Econometrica*, 61 (1993), 123–137.

Silverman, Bernard W. *Density Estimation for Statistics and Data Analysis*. London: Chapman and Hall, 1986.

References

Thaler, Richard H. "Anomalies: The Winner's Curse," *Journal of Economic Perspectives*, 2 (1988), 191–202.

van der Vaart, A.W. *Asymptotic Statistics*. Cambridge, England: Cambridge University Press, 1998.

Varian, Hal. *Intermediate Microeconomics: A Modern Approach*, Fifth Edition. New York: Norton, 1999.

Vickrey, William S. "Counterspeculation, Auctions, and Competitive Sealed Tenders," *Journal of Finance*, 16 (1961), 8–37.

Vuong, Quang H. "Misspecification and Conditional Maximum Likelihood Estimation," Social Science Working Paper 503. Pasadena, California: Division of the Humanities and Social Sciences, California Institute of Technology, 1983.

Wald, Abraham. "Note on the Consistency of the Maximum Likelihood Estimate," *Annals of Mathematical Statistics*, 20 (1949), 595–601.

Weber, Robert J. "Multiple-Object Auctions" in *Auctions, Bidding, and Contracting: Uses and Theory*, edited by Richard Engelbrecht-Wiggans, Martin Shubik, and Richard M. Stark. New York: New York University Press, 1983.

White, Halbert. "Maximum Likelihood Estimation of Misspecified Models," *Econometrica*, 50 (1982), 1–25.

Wilson, Robert B. "A Bidding Model of Perfect Competition," *Review of Economic Studies*, 44 (1977), 511–518.

Wilson, Robert B. "Auctions of Shares," *Quarterly Journal of Economics*, 93 (1979), 675–689.

Wilson, Robert B. "Strategic Analysis of Auctions" in *Handbook of Game Theory with Economic Applications, Volume 1*, edited by Robert J. Aumann and Sergiu Hart. Amsterdam: Elsevier, 1992.

Solutions

1.1 Logarithmic Series

a) Following the hint, a Maclaurin-series expansion of $\log(1+x)$, which is a Taylor-series expansion about zero, yields

$$\log(1 + x) = x - \frac{x^2}{2!} + \frac{2x^3}{3!} - \frac{6x^4}{4!} + \ldots$$

$$= x - \frac{x^2}{2} + \frac{x^3}{3} - \frac{x^4}{4} + \ldots$$

Now, replace x with $-\theta^0$, so

$$\log(1 - \theta^0) = -\theta^0 - \frac{(-\theta^0)^2}{2} + \frac{(-\theta^0)^3}{3} - \frac{(-\theta^0)^4}{4} + \ldots$$

$$= -\sum_{n=1}^{\infty} \frac{(\theta^0)^n}{n}.$$

Thus,

$$\sum_{n=1}^{\infty} f_N(n; \theta^0) = \frac{\log(1 - \theta^0)}{\log(1 - \theta^0)} = 1.$$

b) Recall the definition of expected value

$$\mathcal{E}(N) = \sum_{n=1}^{\infty} n f_N(n; \theta^0).$$

Applying this yields

$$\mathcal{E}(N) = -\sum_{n=1}^{\infty} \frac{n(\theta^0)^n}{n \log(1 - \theta^0)}$$

$$= \frac{-1}{\log(1 - \theta^0)} \sum_{n=1}^{\infty} (\theta^0)^n$$

$$= \frac{-\theta^0}{(1 - \theta^0) \log(1 - \theta^0)},$$

where the last equality obtains by the property of an infinite geometric series given in the hint. Note that the restrictions on θ^0 (viz., $0 < \theta^0 < 1$) are sufficient to guarantee the convergence of the sum.

c) Recall the definition of variance

$$\mathcal{V}(N) = \mathcal{E}(N^2) - [\mathcal{E}(N)]^2.$$

Note that the second expression on the right-hand side of the equal sign can be determined easily using the result from part b). Now, the kth raw moment is

$$\mathcal{E}(N^k) = \sum_{n=1}^{\infty} n^k f_N(n; \theta^0),$$

so

$$\mathcal{E}(N^2) = -\sum_{n=1}^{\infty} \frac{n^2 (\theta^0)^n}{n \log(1 - \theta^0)}$$

$$= \frac{-1}{\log(1 - \theta^0)} \sum_{n=1}^{\infty} n(\theta^0)^n.$$

To compute the sum in this expression, note that

$$\sum_{n=1}^{\infty} n(\theta^0)^n = \theta^0 \sum_{n=1}^{\infty} n(\theta^0)^{n-1}$$

$$= \theta^0 \sum_{n=1}^{\infty} \frac{d(\theta^0)^n}{d\theta^0}$$

$$= \theta^0 \frac{d}{d\theta^0} \left[\sum_{n=1}^{\infty} (\theta^0)^n \right]$$

$$= \frac{\theta^0}{(1 - \theta^0)^2}.$$

The third step obtains because the sum of the derivatives equals the derivative of the sum. The last step obtains by, again, exploiting the property of the geometric series given in the hint to part b), and then taking the derivative of this result. Thus,

$$\mathcal{V}(N) = \frac{-\theta^0}{(1 - \theta^0)^2 \log(1 - \theta^0)} - \left[\frac{-\theta^0}{(1 - \theta^0) \log(1 - \theta^0)} \right]^2$$

$$= \frac{-\theta^0}{(1-\theta^0)^2 \log(1-\theta^0)} - \frac{(-\theta^0)^2}{(1-\theta^0)^2 [\log(1-\theta^0)]^2}$$

$$= \frac{-\theta^0 \log(1-\theta^0) - (-\theta^0)^2}{(1-\theta^0)^2 [\log(1-\theta^0)]^2}$$

$$= \frac{-\theta^0 [\log(1-\theta^0) + \theta^0]}{(1-\theta^0)^2 [\log(1-\theta^0)]^2}.$$

This expression is positive because the numerator is the product of two negative numbers; $\log(1-\theta^0)$ is negative for all feasible θ^0, while $|\log(1-\theta^0)|$ is greater than θ^0. The denominator is clearly positive, being the product of two squared terms.

d) The method-of-moments estimator of the parameter θ^0 is defined by

$$\hat{\theta}_{\mathrm{MM}} = \left\{ \theta : \bar{N}_T + \frac{\theta}{(1-\theta) \log(1-\theta)} = 0 \right\}.$$

In words, find the value of θ such that the sample mean $\bar{N}_T$ matches the population mean $\mathcal{E}(N)$ or $\mu(\theta)$.

e) In figure 1.1.e, we present a plot of the condition and its zero point, assuming a value for $\bar{N}_T$ that is greater than one. You can find the MATLAB code for this figure on the CD that accompanies this book; see the file `prog1le.m`. To demonstrate that the function has a unique solution, verify that it satisfies the assumptions of the intermediate value theorem and that it is monotonic in θ. Let

$$g(\theta) = \bar{N}_T + \frac{\theta}{(1-\theta) \log(1-\theta)}.$$

We first use the intermediate value theorem to show that the condition has at least one zero point. Now, $\bar{N}_t$ is almost surely greater than one because the lower bound on N is one. Recall, too, that $g(\cdot)$ is a continuous function. Thus, there exist θ_L and θ_H such that $g(\theta_L)$ and $g(\theta_H)$ have different signs. This can be verified by noting

$$\lim_{\theta \to 0} \bar{N}_T + \frac{\theta}{(1-\theta) \log(1-\theta)} = \bar{N}_T - 1 > 0$$

$$\lim_{\theta \to 1} \bar{N}_T + \frac{\theta}{(1-\theta) \log(1-\theta)} = \bar{N}_T - \infty < 0.$$

To show that this solution is unique, recall that when a function is monotonic, its derivative always has the same sign. Here, the relevant derivative is

$$g'(\theta) = \frac{\log(1-\theta) + \theta}{[\log(1-\theta)]^2 (1-\theta)^2},$$

339

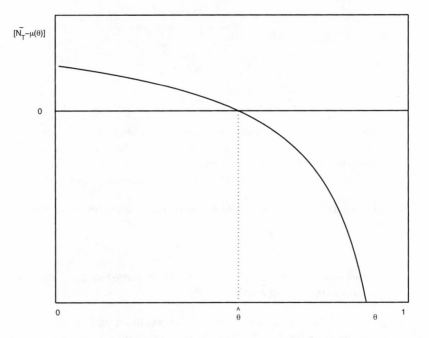

Figure 1.1.e
Graph of the Moment Condition

which is negative for all θ between zero and one because $\log(1-\theta)$, which is negative, is greater in absolute value than θ, while the denominator of $g'(\theta)$ is positive. Thus, only one zero exists, so we have established the existence and uniqueness of $\hat{\theta}_{\text{MM}}$.

f) Newton's method is based on Taylor's theorem, which states

$$g(\theta) = g(\theta_0) + g'(\theta_0)(\theta - \theta_0) + R_2$$

where R_2 is the second-order remainder term. To obtain Newton's method, ignore R_2 (set it to zero) because in the neighborhood of a solution it will be negligible, and then set $g(\theta)$ to zero. Thus,

$$g(\theta_0) + g'(\theta_0)(\theta - \theta_0) = 0.$$

Solving for θ delivers the following recursion, which is often referred to as *Newton's method*:

$$\theta_{k+1} = \theta_k - \frac{g(\theta_k)}{g'(\theta_k)} \quad k = 0, 1, \ldots$$

g) First, define the likelihood function

$$f(\theta; N_1, \ldots, N_T) = \prod_{t=1}^{T} \frac{-\theta^{N_t}}{N_t \log(1-\theta)}.$$

The logarithm of the likelihood function is

$$\mathcal{L}(\theta; N_1, \ldots, N_T) = \log \theta \sum_{t=1}^{T} N_t - \sum_{t=1}^{T} \log N_t - T \log[-\log(1-\theta)].$$

To find the maximum-likelihood estimator $\hat{\theta}_{\mathrm{ML}}$, differentiate the logarithm of the likelihood function with respect to θ, set this derivative equal to zero, and then solve for $\hat{\theta}_{\mathrm{ML}}$. The necessary, first-order condition is

$$\frac{d\mathcal{L}(\hat{\theta}_{\mathrm{ML}}; N_1, \ldots, N_T)}{d\theta} = \sum_{t=1}^{T} \frac{N_t}{\hat{\theta}_{\mathrm{ML}}} + \frac{T}{(1-\hat{\theta}_{\mathrm{ML}}) \log(1-\hat{\theta}_{\mathrm{ML}})} = 0,$$

which yields

$$g(\hat{\theta}_{\mathrm{ML}}) = \bar{N}_T + \frac{\hat{\theta}_{\mathrm{ML}}}{(1-\hat{\theta}_{\mathrm{ML}}) \log(1-\hat{\theta}_{\mathrm{ML}})} = 0.$$

Note that this is the same condition that defined the method-of-moments estimator.

h) Since, in this case, $\hat{\theta}_{\mathrm{MM}}$ and $\hat{\theta}_{\mathrm{ML}}$ are the same, it suffices to show that one of them is parameter consistent for θ^0. Note that, by the law of large numbers, the $\mathrm{plim}_{T\to\infty} \bar{N}_T$ is $\mathcal{E}(N)$ or $\mu(\theta^0)$. Also, $\hat{\theta}_{\mathrm{MM}}$ is $\mu^{-1}(\bar{N}_T)$ where $\mu^{-1}(\cdot)$ is a continuous function. Thus, by the continuous mapping theorem, often referred to as *Slutsky's theorem*,

$$\mathrm{plim}_{T\to\infty} \hat{\theta}_{\mathrm{MM}} = \mathrm{plim}_{T\to\infty} \mu^{-1}(\bar{N}_T) = \mu^{-1}(\mathrm{plim}_{T\to\infty} \bar{N}_T) = \mu^{-1}[\mu(\theta^0)] = \theta^0.$$

i) One candidate variance approximation would be the inverse of *Fisher's information matrix*, which is the negative of the expected value of the Hessian, the second derivative of the logarithm of the likelihood function. Hence,

$$\mathcal{V}(\hat{\theta}_{\mathrm{MM}}) = \mathcal{V}(\hat{\theta}_{\mathrm{ML}}) = \left\{ -\mathcal{E} \left[\frac{d^2 \log L(\theta^0; N_1, \ldots, N_T)}{d\theta^2} \right] \right\}^{-1}.$$

Solutions

In this case,

$$\mathcal{V}(\hat{\theta}_{\mathrm{MM}}) = \mathcal{V}(\hat{\theta}_{\mathrm{ML}})$$

$$= \frac{-\theta^0(1-\theta^0)^2\left[\log(1-\theta^0)\right]^2}{T\left[\log(1-\theta^0)+\theta^0\right]}.$$

Note that the variance depends on the value of unknown parameter θ^0, but it is typically evaluated at the maximum-likelihood estimate $\hat{\theta}_{\mathrm{ML}}$ for the purposes of implementation.

j) By the Lindeberg–Levy central limit theorem, we know that the sample mean $\bar{N}_T$ has the following asymptotic distribution:

$$\sqrt{T}\left[\bar{N}_T - \mu(\theta^0)\right] \overset{\mathrm{d}}{\to} \mathcal{N}\left[0, \mathcal{V}(N)\right].$$

Now, by the delta method, when higher-order terms are ignored as they will be neglible when T is large, we know that

$$\sqrt{T}(\hat{\theta}_{\mathrm{MM}} - \theta^0) = \sqrt{T}\frac{d\mu^{-1}(\theta^0)}{d\bar{N}_T}\left[\bar{N}_T - \mu(\theta^0)\right],$$

so the asymptotic distribution of these two estimators is

$$\hat{\theta}_{\mathrm{ML}} = \hat{\theta}_{\mathrm{MM}} \overset{\mathrm{d}}{\to} \mathcal{N}[\theta^0, \mathcal{V}(\hat{\theta}_{\mathrm{MM}})]$$

where the variance is estimated by the result from part i).

k) You can find the MATLAB code for this part on the CD that accompanies this book; see the file prog11k.m. The program returns $\hat{\theta}_{\mathrm{ML}}$ equal to 0.5188.

l) We know that

$$\frac{\hat{\theta}_{\mathrm{ML}} - \theta^0}{\sqrt{\mathcal{V}(\hat{\theta}_{\mathrm{ML}})}} \overset{\mathrm{d}}{\to} \mathcal{N}(0,1)$$

under the null hypothesis. The calculated, standard normal variable Z for this test is 1.081; at size 0.05, the critical value for this test statistic is 1.96. Thus, we fail to reject the null hypothesis.

m) In this case, under the null hypothesis, the relevant asymptotic distribution is different. In particular, by an application of the delta method,

$$h(\hat{\theta}_{\mathrm{ML}}) \overset{\mathrm{d}}{\to} \mathcal{N}[h(\theta^0), h'(\theta^0)\mathcal{V}(\hat{\theta}_{\mathrm{ML}})h'(\theta^0)]$$

where
$$h(\theta^0) = \log \theta^0$$

and
$$h'(\theta^0) = \frac{1}{\theta^0}.$$

Hence,
$$h(\hat{\theta}_{\mathrm{ML}}) \xrightarrow{\mathrm{d}} \mathcal{N}[\log(\theta^0), (\theta^0)^{-2}\mathcal{V}(\hat{\theta}_{\mathrm{ML}})].$$

With the estimate of $\hat{\theta}_{\mathrm{ML}}$ in hand,
$$\hat{h}(\hat{\theta}_{\mathrm{ML}}) = \log(0.5188) = -0.6562$$

and
$$\mathcal{V}[\hat{h}(\hat{\theta}_{\mathrm{ML}})] = \frac{(0.0174)^2}{(0.5188)^2} = 0.0011.$$

Thus,
$$\frac{h(\hat{\theta}_{\mathrm{ML}}) - h(\theta^0)}{\sqrt{\mathcal{V}[\hat{h}(\hat{\theta}_{\mathrm{ML}})]}} \xrightarrow{\mathrm{d}} \mathcal{N}(0,1).$$

The calculated, standard normal variable is 1.32; at size 0.10, the critical value for this test statistic is 1.645. Thus, we fail to reject the null hypothesis. Note, however, that the test statistics have different calculated values, so if we had used the same size for both tests we could have gotten different conclusions. The moral of the story is that it matters where one takes the asymptotic expansion.

n) First, treat $\hat{\theta}_{\mathrm{ML}}$ as the truth; i.e., proceed as if
$$\theta^0 = 0.5188.$$

Now, Fisher's χ^2 *goodness-of-fit* test uses the following statistic:
$$\chi^2 = \sum_{n=1}^{9} \frac{[O_n - E_n]^2}{E_n}$$

where O_n denotes the observed frequency for outcome n, and E_n denotes the average frequency $1000 \times f_N(n; \theta^0)$; viz., the product of the total number of observations and the "true" population frequency of outcome n. Here, we have used the maximum-likelihood estimate $\hat{\theta}_{\mathrm{ML}}$ in place of θ^0. Making the appropriate substitutions and computing this sum yields a test statistic value equal to 7.383. At size 0.05, the critical value of this test statistic can be found in a χ^2 table where the appropriate degrees of freedom here are eight, so $\chi^2_{0.05}(8)$ is 2.733. Thus, we reject the null hypothesis that the empirical frequency is consistent with the logarithmic-series distribution. You can find the MATLAB code for this part on the CD that accompanies this book; see the file `prog11n.m`.

1.2 Log-Normal Estimation

a) Given the assumption of a log-normal random variable and given an independent and identically distributed sample $\{V_t\}_{t=1}^T$, the likelihood function is

$$f(\theta_1, \theta_2; V_1, \ldots, V_T) = \prod_{t=1}^T \frac{1}{V_t} \frac{1}{\sqrt{2\pi\theta_2}} \exp\left[\frac{-(\log V_t - \theta_1)^2}{2\theta_2}\right].$$

The logarithm of the likelihood function is then

$$\mathcal{L}(\theta_1, \theta_2; V_1, \ldots, V_T) = \sum_{t=1}^T \log\left\{\frac{1}{V_t}\frac{1}{\sqrt{2\pi\theta_2}}\exp\left[\frac{-(\log V_t - \theta_1)^2}{2\theta_2}\right]\right\}.$$

Expanding this expression, using some basic properties of the logarithmic function, yields

$$\mathcal{L}(\theta_1, \theta_2; V_1, \ldots, V_T) = -\sum_{t=1}^T \log V_t + T \log\left(\frac{1}{\sqrt{2\pi}}\right) +$$

$$T \log\left(\frac{1}{\sqrt{\theta_2}}\right) - \frac{1}{2\theta_2}\sum_{t=1}^T (\log V_t - \theta_1)^2.$$

To find the *score vector* (also known as the *gradient vector*), simply differentiate $\mathcal{L}(\theta_1, \theta_2; V_1, \ldots, V_T)$ with respect to θ_1 and θ_2. Thus,

$$\begin{pmatrix} \frac{\partial \mathcal{L}(\theta_1, \theta_2; V_1, \ldots, V_T)}{\partial \theta_1} \\ \frac{\partial \mathcal{L}(\theta_1, \theta_2; V_1, \ldots, V_T)}{\partial \theta_2} \end{pmatrix} = \begin{pmatrix} \sum_{t=1}^T \frac{(\log V_t - \theta_1)}{\theta_2} \\ \frac{-T}{2\theta_2} + \frac{1}{2\theta_2^2}\sum_{t=1}^T (\log V_t - \theta_1)^2 \end{pmatrix} = g(\theta).$$

To solve for the maximum-likelihood estimators $\hat{\theta}_1^{\mathrm{ML}}$ and $\hat{\theta}_2^{\mathrm{ML}}$, set the score vector $g(\theta)$ equal to $\mathbf{0_2}$ and solve. Performing this algebra yields

$$\hat{\theta}_1^{\mathrm{ML}} = \frac{1}{T}\sum_{t=1}^T \log V_t$$

$$\hat{\theta}_2^{\mathrm{ML}} = \frac{1}{T}\sum_{t=1}^T \left(\log V_t - \hat{\theta}_1^{\mathrm{ML}}\right)^2.$$

b) The expectations of the maximum-likelihood estimators are

$$\mathcal{E}(\hat{\theta}_1^{\mathrm{ML}}) = \frac{T\theta_1^0}{T} = \theta_1^0$$

$$\mathcal{E}(\hat{\theta}_2^{\mathrm{ML}}) = \frac{(T-1)\theta_2^0}{T}.$$

In words, when $\log V$ is distributed normally, the sample mean $\hat{\theta}_1^{\mathrm{ML}}$ is an unbiased estimator of the population mean, but the maximum-likelihood estimator of the variance $\hat{\theta}_2^{\mathrm{ML}}$ is a biased estimator of the population variance. Because $\hat{\theta}_1^{\mathrm{ML}}$ is an estimator that is linear in independent $\log V_t$s, it is easy to show that its variance is

$$\mathcal{V}(\hat{\theta}_1^{\mathrm{ML}}) = \frac{\theta_2^0}{T},$$

which implies that

$$\hat{\theta}_1^{\mathrm{ML}} \sim \mathcal{N}(\theta_1^0, \theta_2^0/T).$$

c) To find the method-of-moments estimators $\hat{\theta}_1^{\mathrm{MM}}$ and $\hat{\theta}_2^{\mathrm{MM}}$, set the sample moments equal to their population counterparts, and then solve for the estimators. To begin, recall that, for any natural number k,

$$\mathcal{E}(V^k) = \exp\left(k\theta_1^0 + \frac{k^2}{2}\theta_2^0\right).$$

Use this relation to obtain the following two moment conditions:

$$M_1 \equiv \frac{1}{T}\sum_{t=1}^{T} V_t = \exp(\hat{\theta}_1^{\mathrm{MM}} + \hat{\theta}_2^{\mathrm{MM}}/2)$$

$$M_2 \equiv \frac{1}{T}\sum_{t=1}^{T} V_t^2 = \exp(2\hat{\theta}_1^{\mathrm{MM}} + 2\hat{\theta}_2^{\mathrm{MM}}).$$

Some algebra yields

$$\hat{\theta}_1^{\mathrm{MM}} = 2\log M_1 - \frac{1}{2}\log M_2$$

$$\hat{\theta}_2^{\mathrm{MM}} = \log M_2 - 2\log M_1.$$

Even though both M_1 and M_2 are unbiased estimators of $\mathcal{E}(V)$ and $\mathcal{E}(V^2)$, because $\hat{\theta}_1^{\mathrm{MM}}$ and $\hat{\theta}_2^{\mathrm{MM}}$ are nonlinear functions of these two statistics, both are biased estimators. This can be seen by applying the expectation operator to each. Note that

$$\mathcal{E}(\log M_1) < \log[\mathcal{E}(M_1)]$$

by Jensen's inequality.

d) Because both moment-condition equations have continuous inverses, it follows from the continuous mapping theorem that $\hat{\theta}_1^{\mathrm{MM}}$ and $\hat{\theta}_2^{\mathrm{MM}}$ are parameter consistent estimators of θ_1^0 and θ_2^0. This is simply an application of Slutsky's theorem. Specifically, by the law of large numbers,

$$\operatorname*{plim}_{T\to\infty} M_1 = \exp(\theta_1^0 + \theta_2^0/2)$$
$$\operatorname*{plim}_{T\to\infty} M_2 = \exp(2\theta_1^0 + 2\theta_2^0),$$

so, by Slutsky's theorem,

$$\operatorname*{plim}_{T\to\infty} \hat{\theta}_1^{\mathrm{MM}} = 2\theta_1^0 + \theta_2^0 - \theta_1^0 - \theta_2^0 = \theta_1^0$$
$$\operatorname*{plim}_{T\to\infty} \hat{\theta}_2^{\mathrm{MM}} = 2\theta_1^0 + 2\theta_2^0 - 2\theta_1^0 - \theta_2^0 = \theta_2^0,$$

establishing the parameter consistency of both method-of-moments estimators.

e) By the Lindeberg–Levy central limit theorem,

$$\sqrt{T}\left[M_1 - \mu_1\left(\theta_1^0, \theta_2^0\right)\right] \overset{\mathrm{d}}{\to} \mathcal{N}\left[0, \mathcal{V}(V)\right].$$

When θ_2^0 is one,

$$\mathcal{V}(V) = \exp(2\theta_1^0 + 2) - \left[\exp(\theta_1^0 + 0.5)\right]^2.$$

Now, we can apply the delta method to calculate the asymptotic distribution of $\hat{\theta}_1^{\mathrm{MM}}$. Note that $\hat{\theta}_1^{\mathrm{MM}}$ is a continuous and differentiable function of M_1 since

$$\hat{\theta}_1^{\mathrm{MM}} = \log M_1 - \frac{1}{2}$$

when θ_2^0 is one. Differentiating the expression on the right-hand side of the equal sign with respect to M_1 yields

$$\frac{1}{M_1}.$$

Thus, we can conclude that

$$\hat{\theta}_1^{\mathrm{MM}} \overset{\mathrm{d}}{\to} \mathcal{N}(\theta_1^0, \sigma^2),$$

where

$$\sigma^2 = \frac{\mathcal{V}(V)}{T\left[\exp(\theta_1^0 + 0.5)\right]^2}.$$

Since the MLE of θ_1^0 attains the Cramér-Rao lower bound, the variance of $\hat{\theta}_1^{\mathrm{ML}}$ is smaller than the variance of $\hat{\theta}_1^{\mathrm{MM}}$. To demonstrate this, note that

$$\frac{\mathcal{V}(V)}{T\left[\exp(\theta_1^0 + 0.5)\right]^2} > \frac{(\theta_2^0)^2}{T}$$

$$\mathcal{V}(V) > \left[\exp(\theta_1^0 + 0.5)\right]^2$$

$$\mathcal{E}(V^2) - \left[\mathcal{E}(V)\right]^2 > \left[\mathcal{E}(V)\right]^2$$

$$\mathcal{E}(V^2) > 2\left[\mathcal{E}(V)\right]^2$$

$$\exp(2\theta_1^0 + 2) > 2\exp(2\theta_1^0 + 1)$$

$$\exp(2\theta_1^0)\exp(2) > 2\exp(2\theta_1^0)\exp(1)$$

$$\exp(2) > 2\exp(1)$$

$$7.3891 > 5.4366.$$

1.3 Logarithmic Series with Covariates

a) By direct substitution, the likelihood function is

$$f(\boldsymbol{\gamma}; n_1, \ldots, n_T, \boldsymbol{z}_1, \ldots, \boldsymbol{z}_T) = \prod_{t=1}^{T} \frac{-\left[\frac{\exp(\boldsymbol{z}_t^\top \boldsymbol{\gamma})}{1 + \exp(\boldsymbol{z}_t^\top \boldsymbol{\gamma})}\right]^{n_t}}{n_t \log\left[\frac{1}{1 + \exp(\boldsymbol{z}_t^\top \boldsymbol{\gamma})}\right]}.$$

Note that n_t is a scalar and that $\boldsymbol{z}_t$ is a K-vector. Collect all of the $(n_1, \ldots, n_T)$ in $\boldsymbol{n}$ and and all of the $(\boldsymbol{z}_1, \ldots, \boldsymbol{z}_T)$ in $\mathbf{Z}$. The logarithm of the likelihood function is

$$\mathcal{L}(\boldsymbol{\gamma}; \boldsymbol{n}, \mathbf{Z}) = \sum_{t=1}^{T} \log\left\{\left[\frac{\exp(\boldsymbol{z}_t^\top \boldsymbol{\gamma})}{1 + \exp(\boldsymbol{z}_t^\top \boldsymbol{\gamma})}\right]^{n_t}\right\} - \sum_{t=1}^{T} \log n_t -$$

$$\sum_{t=1}^{T} \log\left\{-\log\left[\frac{1}{1 + \exp(\boldsymbol{z}_t^\top \boldsymbol{\gamma})}\right]\right\}.$$

This can be written compactly as

$$\mathcal{L}(\boldsymbol{\gamma};\boldsymbol{n},\mathbf{Z}) = \sum_{t=1}^{T} n_t \log\left\{\left[\frac{\exp(\boldsymbol{z}_t^\top\boldsymbol{\gamma})}{1+\exp(\boldsymbol{z}_t^\top\boldsymbol{\gamma})}\right]\right\} - \sum_{t=1}^{T}\log n_t - $$

$$\sum_{t=1}^{T}\log\left\{\log\left[1+\exp(\boldsymbol{z}_t^\top\boldsymbol{\gamma})\right]\right\}.$$

Denote by θ_t the logistic term $\exp(\boldsymbol{z}_t^\top\boldsymbol{\gamma})/[1+\exp(\boldsymbol{z}_t^\top\boldsymbol{\gamma})]$. Now,

$$\log\theta_t = \boldsymbol{z}_t^\top\boldsymbol{\gamma} - \log\left[1+\exp(\boldsymbol{z}_t^\top\boldsymbol{\gamma})\right],$$

so

$$\frac{\partial\log\theta_t}{\partial\gamma_k} = \frac{\frac{\partial\theta_t}{\partial\gamma_k}}{\theta_t}$$

$$= z_{kt} - \frac{1}{\left[1+\exp(\boldsymbol{z}_t^\top\boldsymbol{\gamma})\right]}\exp(\boldsymbol{z}_t^\top\boldsymbol{\gamma})z_{kt}$$

$$= (1-\theta_t)z_{kt}.$$

Thus,

$$\frac{\partial\theta_t}{\partial\gamma_k} = \theta_t(1-\theta_t)z_{kt}.$$

Using this result, one can show that

$$\frac{\partial\mathcal{L}(\boldsymbol{\gamma};\boldsymbol{n},\mathbf{Z})}{\partial\gamma_k} = \sum_{t=1}^{T} n_t(1-\theta_t)z_{kt} + \sum_{t=1}^{T}\frac{\theta_t z_{kt}}{\log(1-\theta_t)}$$

$$= \sum_{t=1}^{T} g_{tk}(\boldsymbol{\gamma})$$

$$= g_k(\boldsymbol{\gamma}),$$

so the gradient vector $\mathbf{g}(\boldsymbol{\gamma})$ collects $[g_1(\boldsymbol{\gamma}), g_2(\boldsymbol{\gamma}), \ldots, g_K(\boldsymbol{\gamma})]^\top$. Now, the matrix of second partial derivatives, the Hessian, can be calculated by brute force to have the following representative (k,ℓ)-element:

$$\frac{\partial^2\mathcal{L}(\boldsymbol{\gamma};\boldsymbol{n},\mathbf{Z})}{\partial\gamma_k\partial\gamma_\ell} = -\sum_{t=1}^{T} n_t\theta_t(1-\theta_t)z_{kt}z_{\ell t}$$

$$+ \sum_{t=1}^{T}\frac{\theta_t(1-\theta_t)\log(1-\theta_t)+\theta_t^2}{\left[\log(1-\theta_t)\right]^2}z_{kt}z_{\ell t}.$$

Alternatively, one can form an approximation to this matrix, often referred to as the *outer-product of the gradient* approximation. This has the following representative (k, ℓ)-element:

$$\mathbf{H}(\boldsymbol{\gamma}) = [h_{k,\ell}(\boldsymbol{\gamma})] = - \left[\sum_{t=1}^{T} g_{tk}(\boldsymbol{\gamma}) g_{t\ell}(\boldsymbol{\gamma}) \right].$$

b) The recursion to solve for $\hat{\boldsymbol{\gamma}}$ is a general version of Newton's method:

$$\boldsymbol{\gamma}_{k+1} = \boldsymbol{\gamma}_k - \mathbf{H}(\boldsymbol{\gamma}_k)^{-1} \mathbf{g}(\boldsymbol{\gamma}_k) \quad k = 0, 1, \ldots$$

c) You can find the MATLAB code for this part on the CD that accompanies this book; see the files `fun13c.m` and `prog13c.m`. The estimates should equal $(-0.3482, 0.0341, 0.4128, 0.3721)^\top$.

d) To perform this test, compute the logarithm of the likelihood function under the parameter values stated by the null hypothesis and then compare this to the logarithm of the unconstrained likelihood function. Note that the large-sample distribution of -2 times the difference in the logarithms of the likelihood functions follows a χ^2 distribution where the degrees of freedom equals the number of restrictions under the null. In this case, the following calculated test statistic obtains:

$$-2(-920.73 + 918.14) = 5.18.$$

At size 0.05, the χ^2 critical value with three degrees of freedom is 7.815, so we fail to reject the null hypothesis.

1.4 Practice with the Bootstrap

a) You can find the MATLAB code for this part on the CD that accompanies this book; see the files `prog14a.m` and `bootstrap.m`. A description of the results of this experiment can be found in the code.

b) You can find the MATLAB code for this part on the CD that accompanies this book; see the files `prog14b.m` and `bootstrap.m`. A description of the results of this experiment can be found in the code.

1.5 Approximating Functions

a) In figure 1.5.a, we present a plot of the function. You can find the MATLAB code for this figure on the CD that accompanies this book; see the files `prog15a.m` and `fun15.m`.

b) In figure 1.5.b, we present a plot of the function and its Chebyshev approximations. The solid line is the actual function, while the dotted lines are different approximations. You can find the MATLAB code for this figure on the CD that accompanies this book; see the files `prog15b.m` and `fun15.m`. To make the figure easier to interpret, we plot only the polynomials of first, fourth, and seventh order.

c) In figure 1.5.c, we present a plot of the function and its least-squares approximation for polynomials of first, fourth, and seventh order. You can find the MATLAB code for this figure on the CD that accompanies this book; see the files `prog15c.m` and `fun15.m`.

1.6 Approximating Integrals

a) In figure 1.6.a, we present a plot of the function and the trapezoid. You can find the MATLAB code for this figure on the CD that accompanies this book; see the file `prog16a.m`. Computing the area of the trapezoid yields 0.6839. Note that this estimate is larger than the actual area, which is not surprising when one considers figure 1.6.a. The absolute error is equal to 0.0518; the relative error is 0.0758.

b) You can find the MATLAB code for this program on the CD that accompanies this book; see the file `prog16b.m`. In this case, the approximation improves; the estimate of the integral is 0.6326 and the absolute error is 0.0005; the relative error is 0.0009.

c) To begin, let h equal $[(b-a)/K]$, where K is the number of trapezoids. The error is then given by

$$-\frac{(b-a)h^2}{12}f''(\xi),$$

where $\xi \in [a,b]$. In particular, the point ξ is the location where $f''(\cdot)$ is largest on $[0,1]$. In terms of this particular problem, the error formula reduces to

$$-\frac{1}{12K^2}\exp(-\xi) = -\frac{1}{12K^2}\exp(-0) = -\frac{1}{12K^2}.$$

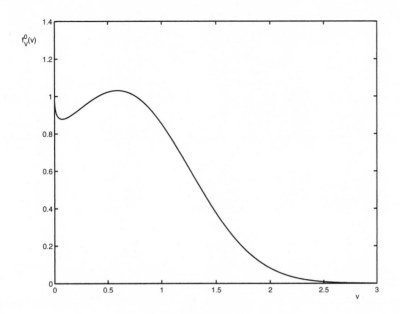

Figure 1.5.a
Graph of the Function

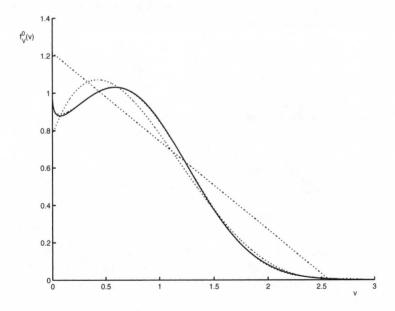

Figure 1.5.b
Graph of the Generalized Chebyshev Polynomials

351

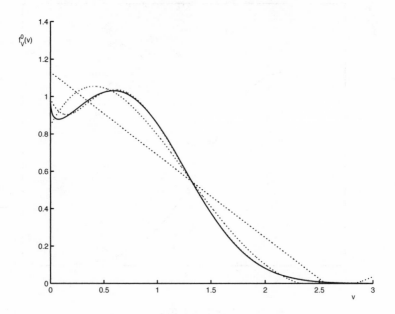

Figure 1.5.c
Graph of the Least-Squares Approximation

d) Now,

$$\mathcal{E}[\exp(-U)] = \int_0^1 \exp(-u) f_U(u) \, du = \int_0^1 \exp(-u) \, du = \Gamma(0,1),$$

which is the integral we seek to estimate, while

$$\mathcal{V}[\exp(-U)] = \mathcal{E}[\exp(-2U)] - \{\mathcal{E}[\exp(-U)]\}^2$$
$$= \int_0^1 \exp(-2u) \, du - \{\mathcal{E}[\exp(-U)]\}^2$$

is the variance of that integral.

e) Now, an unbiased estimator of $\mathcal{E}[\exp(-U)]$ is the sample average of K independent and identically distributed exponentiated uniform draws $\{\exp(-U_k)\}_{k=1}^K$; viz.,

$$G_K(0,1) = \frac{1}{K} \sum_{k=1}^K \exp(-U_k)$$

352

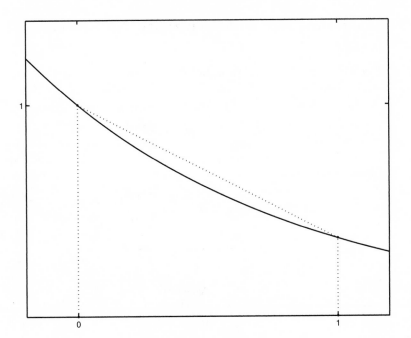

Figure 1.6.a
Trapezoidal Quadrature

where

$$\mathcal{E}[G_K(0,1)] = \frac{1}{K} \sum_{k=1}^{K} \mathcal{E}[\exp(-U_k)] = \mathcal{E}[\exp(-U)] = \Gamma(0,1),$$

while

$$\mathcal{V}[G_K(0,1)] = \frac{\mathcal{V}[\exp(-U)]}{K}.$$

Also, by the Lindeberg–Levy central limit theorem,

$$\sqrt{K}[G_K(0,1) - \Gamma(0,1)] \xrightarrow{\mathrm{d}} \mathcal{N}\{0, \mathcal{V}[\exp(-U)]\},$$

where an unbiased estimator of $\mathcal{V}[\exp(-U)]$ is

$$\frac{1}{(K-1)} \sum_{k=1}^{K} [\exp(-U_k) - G_K(0,1)]^2.$$

You can find the MATLAB code for this program on the CD that accompanies this book; see the file `prog16e.m`.

f) Recall that the absolute error from part a) is 0.0518. In order to obtain a root mean-squared error of, say, 0.05, K must be about fifteen; see the file `prog16e.m` as well.

2.1 Uniform Case: Risk Neutrality, No Reserve

a) The Bayes–Nash, equilibrium-bid function given by equation (2.5) in this book is

$$\sigma(v) = v - \frac{\int_{\underline{v}}^{v} F_V(u)^{(\mathcal{N}-1)} \, du}{F_V(v)^{(\mathcal{N}-1)}}.$$

Here, $F_V(v)$ is (v/θ), while $\underline{v}$ is zero and $\bar{v}$ is θ. Substituting this information yields

$$\sigma(v) = v - \frac{\int_0^v (u/\theta)^{(\mathcal{N}-1)} \, du}{(v/\theta)^{(\mathcal{N}-1)}}$$

$$= v - \frac{\int_0^v u^{(\mathcal{N}-1)} \, du}{v^{(\mathcal{N}-1)}}$$

$$= v - \frac{v^{\mathcal{N}}}{\mathcal{N} v^{(\mathcal{N}-1)}}$$

$$= \frac{v(\mathcal{N}-1)}{\mathcal{N}}.$$

b) The probability density function of Y, the second-highest order statistic, is given by

$$f_Y(y) = \mathcal{N}(\mathcal{N}-1) F_V(y)^{(\mathcal{N}-2)} [1 - F_V(y)] f_V(y).$$

Making the necessary substitutions yields

$$f_Y(y) = \frac{\mathcal{N}(\mathcal{N}-1)}{\theta} \left(\frac{y}{\theta}\right)^{(\mathcal{N}-2)} \left(\frac{\theta - y}{\theta}\right)$$

$$= \frac{\mathcal{N}(\mathcal{N}-1)}{\theta^{\mathcal{N}}} y^{(\mathcal{N}-2)} (\theta - y).$$

c) To find the cumulative distribution function for Y, compute the following integral:

$$\int_0^y f_Y(u) \, du = \int_0^y \frac{\mathcal{N}(\mathcal{N}-1)}{\theta^{\mathcal{N}}} u^{(\mathcal{N}-2)} (\theta - u) \, du.$$

Completing the integration yields

$$F_Y(y) = \frac{\mathcal{N}(\mathcal{N}-1)}{\theta^{\mathcal{N}}} \left[\frac{\theta y^{(\mathcal{N}-1)}}{\mathcal{N}-1} - \frac{y^{\mathcal{N}}}{\mathcal{N}} \right]$$

$$= \frac{\mathcal{N} \theta y^{(\mathcal{N}-1)} - (\mathcal{N}-1) y^{\mathcal{N}}}{\theta^{\mathcal{N}}}.$$

d) Use the standard definition of the expected value, and integrate.

$$\mathcal{E}(Y) = \int_0^\theta y \frac{\mathcal{N}(\mathcal{N}-1)}{\theta^\mathcal{N}} y^{(\mathcal{N}-2)}(\theta-y)\,dy$$
$$= \frac{\mathcal{N}(\mathcal{N}-1)}{\theta^\mathcal{N}}\left[\frac{\theta^{(\mathcal{N}+1)}}{\mathcal{N}} - \frac{\theta^{(\mathcal{N}+1)}}{\mathcal{N}+1}\right]$$
$$= \frac{\theta(\mathcal{N}-1)}{\mathcal{N}+1}.$$

e) Recall that $\mathcal{V}(Y)$ equals $\mathcal{E}(Y^2) - [\mathcal{E}(Y)]^2$, where

$$\mathcal{E}(Y^2) = \int_0^\theta y^2 \frac{\mathcal{N}(\mathcal{N}-1)}{\theta^\mathcal{N}} y^{(\mathcal{N}-2)}(\theta-y)\,dy$$
$$= \frac{\mathcal{N}(\mathcal{N}-1)\theta^2}{(\mathcal{N}+1)(\mathcal{N}+2)}.$$

Thus, with the result from part d),

$$\mathcal{V}(Y) = \frac{2\theta^2(\mathcal{N}-1)}{(\mathcal{N}+1)^2(\mathcal{N}+2)}.$$

f) The cumulative distribution function of the first order statistic Z is

$$F_Z(z) = [F_V(z)]^\mathcal{N}$$
$$= \left(\frac{z}{\theta}\right)^\mathcal{N}.$$

g) The probability density function of Z is

$$f_Z(z) = \frac{dF_Z(z)}{dz}$$
$$= \mathcal{N} F_V(z)^{(\mathcal{N}-1)} f_V(z)$$
$$= \frac{\mathcal{N} z^{(\mathcal{N}-1)}}{\theta^\mathcal{N}}.$$

h) Use the standard definition of the expected value, and integrate.

$$\mathcal{E}(Z) = \int_0^\theta z \frac{\mathcal{N} z^{(\mathcal{N}-1)}}{\theta^\mathcal{N}}\,dz$$
$$= \frac{\mathcal{N}\theta}{\mathcal{N}+1}.$$

355

i) Recall that $\mathcal{V}(Z)$ equals $\mathcal{E}(Z^2) - [\mathcal{E}(Z)]^2$, where

$$\mathcal{E}(Z^2) = \int_0^\theta z^2 \frac{\mathcal{N} z^{(\mathcal{N}-1)}}{\theta^{\mathcal{N}}}\, dz$$
$$= \frac{\mathcal{N}\theta^2}{\mathcal{N}+2}.$$

Thus, with the result from part h),

$$\mathcal{V}(Z) = \frac{\mathcal{N}\theta^2}{(\mathcal{N}+1)^2(\mathcal{N}+2)}.$$

j) From part a),
$$W = \frac{Z(\mathcal{N}-1)}{\mathcal{N}}.$$

Since the distribution of Z is known, we need only apply the method of transformations to find the probability density function of W. To accomplish this, first solve this equation for Z; i.e.,

$$Z = \frac{W\mathcal{N}}{(\mathcal{N}-1)}.$$

Next, differentiate this function with respect to W to get the Jacobian of the transformation.

$$\frac{dZ}{dW} = \frac{\mathcal{N}}{(\mathcal{N}-1)}.$$

This then implies that

$$f_W(w) = f_Z(z)\frac{dz}{dw}$$
$$= \frac{\mathcal{N}}{\theta^{\mathcal{N}}}\left[\frac{w\mathcal{N}}{(\mathcal{N}-1)}\right]^{(\mathcal{N}-1)} \frac{\mathcal{N}}{(\mathcal{N}-1)}$$
$$= \mathcal{N}\left(\frac{\mathcal{N}}{\mathcal{N}-1}\right)^{\mathcal{N}} \frac{w^{(\mathcal{N}-1)}}{\theta^{\mathcal{N}}},$$

which has support on

$$0 \le w \le \frac{(\mathcal{N}-1)\theta}{\mathcal{N}}.$$

k) Use the standard definition of the expected value, and integrate.

$$\mathcal{E}(W) = \int_0^{\frac{(\mathcal{N}-1)\theta}{\mathcal{N}}} w\mathcal{N} \left(\frac{\mathcal{N}}{\mathcal{N}-1}\right)^{\mathcal{N}} \frac{w^{(\mathcal{N}-1)}}{\theta^{\mathcal{N}}} \, dw$$
$$= \frac{\theta(\mathcal{N}-1)}{\mathcal{N}+1}.$$

l) Recall that $\mathcal{V}(W)$ equals $\mathcal{E}(W^2) - [\mathcal{E}(W)]^2$, where

$$\mathcal{E}(W^2) = \int_0^{\frac{(\mathcal{N}-1)\theta}{\mathcal{N}}} w^2\mathcal{N} \left(\frac{\mathcal{N}}{\mathcal{N}-1}\right)^{\mathcal{N}} \frac{w^{(\mathcal{N}-1)}}{\theta^{\mathcal{N}}} \, dw$$
$$= \frac{[\theta(\mathcal{N}-1)]^2}{\mathcal{N}(\mathcal{N}+2)}.$$

Thus, with the result from part k),

$$\mathcal{V}(W) = \frac{\theta^2(\mathcal{N}-1)^2}{\mathcal{N}(\mathcal{N}+1)^2(\mathcal{N}+2)}.$$

m) Under risk neutrality, both English and first-price, sealed-bid auctions, on average, garner the same revenue to the seller; i.e., both auction formats have the same expected value for W:

$$\frac{\theta(\mathcal{N}-1)}{\mathcal{N}+1}.$$

One might think that it is sufficient just to compare the variances of the revenues under the two formats, but the distributions are highly skewed. Thus, to find the auction format that a risk-averse seller would prefer, one must decide which distribution dominates the other in the sense of second-order stochastic dominance. For two cumulative distribution functions, *first-order stochastic dominance* is defined as follows:

$F_V(v)$ stochastically dominates $F_Y(y)$ in the first-order sense if

$$F_V(y) \geq F_Y(y) \ \forall \ y.$$

For two cumulative distribution functions, *second-order stochastic dominance* is defined as follows:

$F_W(w)$ stochastically dominates $F_Y(y)$ in the second-order sense if

$$\int_0^y [F_W(u) - F_Y(u)] \, du > 0 \ \forall \ y.$$

Routine and tedious integration allows one to demonstrate that $F_W(\cdot)$ dominates $F_Y(\cdot)$ in the second-order sense, so a risk-averse seller would prefer the first-price, sealed-bid to the English auction.

2.2 Uniform Case: Risk Neutrality, Positive Reserve

a) With a binding reserve price r, the Bayes–Nash, equilibrium-bid function at a first-price, sealed-bid auction is

$$\sigma(v) = v - \frac{\int_r^v F_V(u)^{(\mathcal{N}-1)} \, du}{F_V(v)^{(\mathcal{N}-1)}},$$

so

$$\sigma(v) = v - \frac{\int_r^v \left(\frac{u}{\theta}\right)^{(\mathcal{N}-1)} \, du}{\left(\frac{v}{\theta}\right)^{(\mathcal{N}-1)}}$$

$$= v - \frac{\left.\frac{u^{\mathcal{N}}}{\mathcal{N}}\right|_r^v}{v^{(\mathcal{N}-1)}}$$

$$= v - \frac{v^{\mathcal{N}} - r^{\mathcal{N}}}{\mathcal{N} v^{(\mathcal{N}-1)}}$$

$$= \frac{v(\mathcal{N}-1)}{\mathcal{N}} + \frac{r^{\mathcal{N}}}{\mathcal{N} v^{(\mathcal{N}-1)}}.$$

b) In the presence of a binding reserve price, the number of participants N follows a binomial distribution, which depends on r and $\mathcal{N}$ as well as $F_V(v)$. In particular,

$$f_N(n) = \binom{\mathcal{N}}{n} F_V(r)^{(\mathcal{N}-n)} [1 - F_V(r)]^n \quad n = 0, 1, \dots, \mathcal{N}.$$

Under the uniform distribution given in practice problem 1 of this chapter,

$$f_N(n) = \binom{\mathcal{N}}{n} \left(\frac{r}{\theta}\right)^{(\mathcal{N}-n)} \left(\frac{\theta - r}{\theta}\right)^n.$$

c) The optimal reserve price is given by the following equation:

$$\rho^* = v_0 + \frac{[1 - F_V(\rho^*)]}{f_V(\rho^*)}.$$

Under the uniform distribution,

$$\rho^* = v_0 + \theta \left(\frac{\theta - \rho^*}{\theta}\right) = v_0 + \theta - \rho^*,$$

so ρ^* equals $[(v_0 + \theta)/2]$.

2.3 Uniform Case: Risk Aversion, No Reserve

a) The dominant-strategy, equilibrium-bid function at an English auction is for a participant to bid his valuation. Thus,

$$B_i = \beta(V_i) = V_i.$$

b) At a first-price, sealed-bid auction, risk aversion matters. When preferences are within the von Neumann–Morgenstern family and, in particular, the HARA family, the following is the expected utility to bidder 1 from bidding s_1:

$$\eta(v_1 - s_1)^{1/\eta} \Pr(\text{win}|s_1).$$

We focus on bidder 1 without loss of generality because *ex ante* the bidders are symmetric. Now, what is

$$\Pr(\text{win}|s_1)?$$

Bidder 1 wins when all of his opponents bid less than s_1. Suppose that all of his opponents are using an increasing strategy $\tilde{\sigma}(v)$. Thus,

$$\Pr(\text{win}|s_1) = \Pr\left[(S_2 < s_1) \cap (S_3 < s_1) \cap \ldots \cap (S_\mathcal{N} < s_1)\right]$$

$$= \prod_{i=2}^{\mathcal{N}} \Pr(S_i < s_1) \quad \text{(independence)}$$

$$= \prod_{i=2}^{\mathcal{N}} \Pr\left[V_i < \tilde{\sigma}^{-1}(s_1)\right] \quad \text{(monotonicity)}$$

$$= F_V\left[\tilde{\sigma}^{-1}(s_1)\right]^{(\mathcal{N}-1)} \quad \text{(identical distribution)}.$$

Thus, under HARA preferences, the objective is to choose s_1 so as to maximize

$$\eta(v_1 - s_1)^{1/\eta} F_V\left[\tilde{\sigma}^{-1}(s_1)\right]^{(\mathcal{N}-1)}.$$

The first part of this expression is the utility from winning the auction with a bid s_1, while the second part is the probability that bid s_1 will, in fact, win the auction. The necessary, first-order condition for this maximization problem implies

$$F_V\left[\tilde{\sigma}^{-1}(s_1)\right] = -\eta(v_1 - s_1)(\mathcal{N} - 1)\frac{dF_V[\tilde{\sigma}^{-1}(s_1)]}{d\tilde{\sigma}^{-1}(s_1)}\frac{d\tilde{\sigma}^{-1}(s_1)}{ds_1},$$

Solutions

which is equivalent to

$$F_V\left[\tilde{\sigma}^{-1}(s_1)\right] = -\eta(v_1 - s_1)(\mathcal{N} - 1)f_V\left[\tilde{\sigma}^{-1}(s_1)\right]\frac{d\tilde{\sigma}^{-1}(s_1)}{ds_1}.$$

At a Bayes–Nash equilibrium, $\tilde{\sigma}^{-1}(s)$ equals v, so

$$\sigma'(v) = \frac{-\eta\left[v - \sigma(v)\right](\mathcal{N} - 1)f_V(v)}{F_V(v)}$$

because

$$\frac{d\sigma^{-1}(s)}{ds} = \frac{1}{\frac{d\sigma(v)}{dv}} = \frac{1}{\sigma'(v)}.$$

Now, expand this expression to get

$$\sigma'(v) - \sigma(v)\frac{\eta(\mathcal{N} - 1)f_V(v)}{F_V(v)} = -\frac{v\eta(\mathcal{N} - 1)f_V(v)}{F_V(v)}.$$

Imposing a boundary condition that a bidder having the lowest valuation $\underline{v}$ bids that valuation, one can solve this linear, first-order differential equation using standard techniques to get the following Bayes–Nash, equilibrium-bid function:

$$\sigma(v;\eta,\mathcal{N}) = v - \frac{\int_{\underline{v}}^v F_V(u)^{\eta(\mathcal{N}-1)}\,du}{F_V(v)^{\eta(\mathcal{N}-1)}} = \frac{v\eta(\mathcal{N} - 1)}{\eta(\mathcal{N} - 1) + 1}.$$

c) The winning bid W at a first-price, sealed-bid auction is simply the Bayes–Nash, equilibrium-bid function evaluated at the highest valuation Z. Under uniform valuations, with HARA risk aversion,

$$W = \frac{Z\eta(\mathcal{N} - 1)}{\eta(\mathcal{N} - 1) + 1}.$$

Since the distribution of Z is known, we need only apply the method of transformations to find the probability density function of W. To accomplish this, first solve this equation for Z

$$Z = \frac{W[\eta(\mathcal{N} - 1) + 1]}{\eta(\mathcal{N} - 1)}.$$

Next, differentiate this function with respect to W

$$\frac{dZ}{dW} = \frac{\eta(\mathcal{N} - 1) + 1}{\eta(\mathcal{N} - 1)}.$$

360

Making the necessary substitution, following the method of transformations, yields

$$f_W(w) = \frac{\mathcal{N}}{\theta^{\mathcal{N}}} \left\{ \frac{w[\eta(\mathcal{N}-1)+1]}{\eta(\mathcal{N}-1)} \right\}^{(\mathcal{N}-1)} \left[\frac{\eta(\mathcal{N}-1)+1}{\eta(\mathcal{N}-1)} \right]$$

$$= \frac{\mathcal{N}w^{(\mathcal{N}-1)}}{\theta^{\mathcal{N}}} \left[\frac{\eta(\mathcal{N}-1)+1}{\eta(\mathcal{N}-1)} \right]^{\mathcal{N}},$$

which has support on

$$0 \leq w \leq \frac{\theta\eta(\mathcal{N}-1)}{\eta(\mathcal{N}-1)+1}.$$

d) Use the standard definition of the expected value, and integrate.

$$\mathcal{E}(W) = \int_0^{\frac{\theta\eta(\mathcal{N}-1)}{\eta(\mathcal{N}-1)+1}} w \frac{\mathcal{N}w^{(\mathcal{N}-1)}}{\theta^{\mathcal{N}}} \left[\frac{\eta(\mathcal{N}-1)+1}{\eta(\mathcal{N}-1)} \right]^{\mathcal{N}} dw$$

$$= \left[\frac{\eta(\mathcal{N}-1)+1}{\eta(\mathcal{N}-1)} \right]^{\mathcal{N}} \frac{\mathcal{N}}{\theta^{\mathcal{N}}} \int_0^{\frac{\theta\eta(\mathcal{N}-1)}{\eta(\mathcal{N}-1)+1}} w^{\mathcal{N}} \, dw$$

$$= \left[\frac{\eta(\mathcal{N}-1)+1}{\eta(\mathcal{N}-1)} \right]^{\mathcal{N}} \frac{\mathcal{N}}{\theta^{\mathcal{N}}} \frac{1}{\mathcal{N}+1} \left[\frac{\theta\eta(\mathcal{N}-1)}{\eta(\mathcal{N}-1)+1} \right]^{(\mathcal{N}+1)}$$

$$= \frac{\theta\mathcal{N}}{\mathcal{N}+1} \left[\frac{\eta(\mathcal{N}-1)}{\eta(\mathcal{N}-1)+1} \right].$$

e) Recall that $\mathcal{V}(W)$ equals $\mathcal{E}(W^2) - [\mathcal{E}(W)]^2$, where

$$\mathcal{E}(W^2) = \int_0^{\frac{\theta\eta(\mathcal{N}-1)}{\eta(\mathcal{N}-1)+1}} w^2 \frac{\mathcal{N}w^{(\mathcal{N}-1)}}{\theta^{\mathcal{N}}} \left[\frac{\eta(\mathcal{N}-1)+1}{\eta(\mathcal{N}-1)} \right]^{\mathcal{N}} dw$$

$$= \left[\frac{\eta(\mathcal{N}-1)+1}{\eta(\mathcal{N}-1)} \right]^{\mathcal{N}} \frac{\mathcal{N}}{\theta^{\mathcal{N}}} \int_0^{\frac{\theta\eta(\mathcal{N}-1)}{\eta(\mathcal{N}-1)+1}} w^{(\mathcal{N}+1)} \, dw$$

$$= \left[\frac{\eta(\mathcal{N}-1)+1}{\eta(\mathcal{N}-1)} \right]^{\mathcal{N}} \frac{\mathcal{N}}{\theta^{\mathcal{N}}} \frac{1}{\mathcal{N}+2} \left[\frac{\theta\eta(\mathcal{N}-1)}{\eta(\mathcal{N}-1)+1} \right]^{(\mathcal{N}+2)}$$

$$= \frac{\theta^2\mathcal{N}}{\mathcal{N}+2} \left[\frac{\eta(\mathcal{N}-1)}{\eta(\mathcal{N}-1)+1} \right]^2.$$

Now, use this in conjunction with the result from part d) to obtain

$$\mathcal{V}(W) = \frac{\theta^2\mathcal{N}}{\mathcal{N}+2} \left[\frac{\eta(\mathcal{N}-1)}{\eta(\mathcal{N}-1)+1} \right]^2 - \left\{ \frac{\theta\mathcal{N}}{\mathcal{N}+1} \left[\frac{\eta(\mathcal{N}-1)}{\eta(\mathcal{N}-1)+1} \right] \right\}^2$$

$$= \frac{\theta^2\mathcal{N}}{\mathcal{N}+2} \left[\frac{\eta(\mathcal{N}-1)}{\eta(\mathcal{N}-1)+1} \right]^2 - \frac{\theta^2\mathcal{N}^2}{(\mathcal{N}+1)^2} \left[\frac{\eta(\mathcal{N}-1)}{\eta(\mathcal{N}-1)+1} \right]^2$$

$$= \theta^2\mathcal{N} \left[\frac{\eta(\mathcal{N}-1)}{\eta(\mathcal{N}-1)+1} \right]^2 \left[\frac{1}{\mathcal{N}+2} - \frac{\mathcal{N}}{(\mathcal{N}+1)^2} \right].$$

f) A seller who is risk-neutral will prefer the auction format that delivers the highest expected revenue. Thus, the seller would compare the expected revenues at the English auction $\mathcal{E}_E$ with the expected revenues at the first-price, sealed-bid auction $\mathcal{E}_F$, and select the format with the highest expected revenue. In particular,

$$\mathcal{E}_E = \frac{\theta(\mathcal{N}-1)}{\mathcal{N}+1};$$

$$\begin{aligned}\mathcal{E}_F &= \frac{\theta\mathcal{N}}{\mathcal{N}+1}\left[\frac{\eta(\mathcal{N}-1)}{\eta(\mathcal{N}-1)+1}\right] \\ &= \frac{\theta(\mathcal{N}-1)}{\mathcal{N}+1}\left[\frac{\eta\mathcal{N}}{\eta(\mathcal{N}-1)+1}\right].\end{aligned}$$

Note that these two expressions are equivalent when η equals one. In that case, the seller will be indifferent between the two auction formats. When η is greater than one, the seller will prefer the first-price, sealed-bid auction; i.e.,

$$\begin{aligned}\mathcal{E}_E &< \mathcal{E}_F \\ \frac{\theta(\mathcal{N}-1)}{\mathcal{N}+1} &< \frac{\theta(\mathcal{N}-1)}{\mathcal{N}+1}\left[\frac{\eta\mathcal{N}}{\eta(\mathcal{N}-1)+1}\right] \\ 1 &< \frac{\eta\mathcal{N}}{\eta(\mathcal{N}-1)+1} \\ \eta\mathcal{N}-\eta+1 &< \eta\mathcal{N} \\ 1 &< \eta.\end{aligned}$$

2.4 Procurement with Independent, Private Costs

a) Here, the bid function will depend on costs, as opposed to valuations. Without loss of generality, focus on bidder 1. Suppose that the opponents of bidder 1 are using a common, increasing, differentiable, bid function $\hat{\sigma}(c)$. Now, the probability that bidder 1 wins given strategy s_1 is

$$\begin{aligned}\Pr(\text{win}|s_1) &= \Pr\left[(S_2 > s_1)\cap\ldots\cap(S_\mathcal{N} > s_1)\right] \\ &= \prod_{i=2}^{\mathcal{N}}\Pr(S_i > s_1)\quad\text{(independence)}\end{aligned}$$

$$= \prod_{i=2}^{\mathcal{N}} \Pr\left[\hat{\sigma}(C_i) > s_1\right]^{(\mathcal{N}-1)}$$

$$= \prod_{i=2}^{\mathcal{N}} \Pr\left[C_i > \hat{\sigma}^{-1}(s_1)\right]^{(\mathcal{N}-1)} \quad \text{(monotonicity)}$$

$$= \left\{1 - F_C\left[\hat{\sigma}^{-1}(s_1)\right]\right\}^{(\mathcal{N}-1)} \quad \text{(identical distribution)}.$$

The objective is to maximize expected profit which, for bidder 1, equals

$$(s_1 - c_1)\left\{1 - F_C\left[\hat{\sigma}^{-1}(s_1)\right]\right\}^{(\mathcal{N}-1)}.$$

The first part of this expression is the payoff to winning the auction with a bid s_1, while the second part is the probability that bid s_1 will, in fact, win the auction. To find the Bayes–Nash, equilibrium-bid function, first maximize this expression with respect to s_1. The necessary, first-order condition for this maximization problem implies

$$1 - F_C[\hat{\sigma}^{-1}(s_1)] = (s_1 - c_1)(\mathcal{N} - 1)\frac{dF_C[\hat{\sigma}^{-1}(s_1)]}{d\hat{\sigma}^{-1}(s_1)}\frac{d\hat{\sigma}^{-1}(s_1)}{ds_1},$$

which is equivalent to

$$1 - F_C[\hat{\sigma}^{-1}(s_1)] = (s_1 - c_1)(\mathcal{N} - 1)f_C[\hat{\sigma}^{-1}(s_1)]\frac{d\hat{\sigma}^{-1}(s_1)}{ds_1}.$$

Now, at a Bayes–Nash equilibrium $\hat{\sigma}^{-1}(s)$ equals c. Rearranging this expression, we get

$$\sigma'(c) = \frac{[\sigma(c) - c](\mathcal{N} - 1)f_C(c)}{[1 - F_C(c)]},$$

which makes use of the fact that

$$\frac{d\sigma^{-1}(s)}{ds} = \frac{1}{\frac{d\sigma(c)}{dc}} = \frac{1}{\sigma'(c)}.$$

Now, expand this expression and rearrange to get the following linear differential equation:

$$\sigma'(c) - \sigma(c)\frac{(\mathcal{N} - 1)f_C(c)}{[1 - F_C(c)]} = -c\frac{(\mathcal{N} - 1)f_C(c)}{[1 - F_C(c)]}.$$

The Bayes–Nash, equilibrium-bid function is

$$\sigma(c) = c + \frac{\int_c^\infty [1 - F_C(u)]^{(\mathcal{N}-1)}\, du}{[1 - F_C(c)]^{(\mathcal{N}-1)}}.$$

b) When the distribution of costs is from the exponential family, the
bid function is

$$\sigma(c) = c + \frac{\int_c^\infty [1 - 1 + \exp(-\lambda u)]^{(\mathcal{N}-1)}\ du}{[1 - 1 + \exp(-\lambda c)]^{(\mathcal{N}-1)}},$$

which simplifies to

$$\sigma(c) = c + \frac{1}{\lambda(\mathcal{N} - 1)}.$$

c) When the distribution of costs is from the Pareto family, the bid
function is

$$\sigma(c) = c + \frac{\int_c^\infty [1 - 1 + (\theta_0/u)^{\theta_1}]^{(\mathcal{N}-1)}\ du}{[1 - 1 + (\theta_0/c)^{\theta_1}]^{(\mathcal{N}-1)}}$$

$$= c + \frac{\int_c^\infty [(\theta_0/u)^{\theta_1}]^{(\mathcal{N}-1)}\ du}{[(\theta_0/c)^{\theta_1}]^{(\mathcal{N}-1)}}.$$

Performing the integration

$$\int_c^\infty [(\theta_0/u)^{\theta_1}]^{(\mathcal{N}-1)}\ du = \frac{\theta_0^{\theta_1(\mathcal{N}-1)}}{[\theta_1(\mathcal{N}-1) - 1]c^{[\theta_1(\mathcal{N}-1)-1]}},$$

plus a little bit of algebra yields

$$\sigma(c) = c\frac{\theta_1(\mathcal{N} - 1)}{\theta_1(\mathcal{N} - 1) - 1}.$$

d) When the distribution of costs is from the Weibull family, the bid
function is

$$\sigma(c) = c + \frac{\int_c^\infty \left[1 - 1 + \exp\left(-\theta_2 u^{\theta_3}\right)\right]^{(\mathcal{N}-1)}\ du}{[1 - 1 + \exp\left(-\theta_2 c^{\theta_3}\right)]^{(\mathcal{N}-1)}}$$

$$= c + \frac{\int_c^\infty \exp\left[-(\mathcal{N} - 1)\theta_2 u^{\theta_3}\right]\ du}{\exp\left[-(\mathcal{N} - 1)\theta_2 c^{\theta_3}\right]}.$$

Note that the integral does not exist in closed form. To implement
this model will require using numerical integration; see part g).

e) When it exists, the integral of the survivor function is the expected
value of the random variable. The survivor function to the power

$(\mathcal{N}-1)$ is the survivor function for the smallest of $(\mathcal{N}-1)$ independent and identically distributed draws. Thus, within the symmetric independent-costs paradigm, when evaluating the bid function at the lower bound, one is finding the integral of the survivor function for the smallest of $(\mathcal{N}-1)$ draws; i.e., the expected value of the smallest order statistic of the $(\mathcal{N}-1)$ opponents.

f) The bidder is assumed to maximize the expected utility of profit, assuming HARA utility function. The bidder's objective function is then

$$\max_{<s>} \ \eta(s-c)^{1/\eta} \left\{ 1 - F_C \left[\tilde{\sigma}^{-1}(s) \right] \right\}^{(\mathcal{N}-1)}.$$

The analysis proceeds as was demonstrated in part a), the single exception being that η must be carried through the algebra. A differential equation like that found in part a) also arises. Completing these steps carefully will result in the following expression for the Bayes–Nash, equilibrium-bid function:

$$\sigma(c) = c + \frac{\int_c^\infty [1 - F_C(u)]^{\eta(\mathcal{N}-1)} \, du}{[1 - F_C(c)]^{\eta(\mathcal{N}-1)}}.$$

For the exponential case, the equilibrium-bid function is

$$c + \frac{1}{\lambda \eta (\mathcal{N}-1)}.$$

For the Pareto case, the equilibrium-bid function is

$$c \frac{\theta_1 \eta (\mathcal{N}-1)}{\theta_1 \eta (\mathcal{N}-1) - 1}.$$

For the Weibull case, the equilibrium-bid function is

$$c + \frac{\int_c^\infty \left[\exp(-\theta_2 u^{\theta_3}) \right]^{\eta(\mathcal{N}-1)} \, du}{\left[\exp(-\theta_2 c^{\theta_3}) \right]^{\eta(\mathcal{N}-1)}}.$$

Note that the Weibull case again requires a numerical approximation to the integral.

g) As mentioned in part d), the integral in the bid function does not exist in closed form. Thus, we require an alternative strategy for computing the integral. One such candidate is trapezoidal quadrature. The idea is to approximate the area under the integrand with a sequence of adjacent trapezoids, the sum of the areas of which will

Solutions

provide an approximation to the actual area under the integrand. Let $f(u)$ denote the integrand, then

$$\int_c^t f(u)\,du \approx \frac{h}{2}\left[f(c) + 2\sum_{k=1}^{K-1} f(u_k) + f(t)\right]$$

is the composite trapezoidal rule, where $(K-1)$ is the number of trapezoids, and h is the width of each of trapezoid. One problem with this approach is that t is ∞ in this application, and it is impossible to represent ∞ on a computer. Thus, we introduce a change of variables. Thus, we let

$$B = \frac{C}{1+C},$$

so the Jacobian of this transformation is

$$\frac{dB}{dC} = \frac{1}{(1+C)^2}.$$

Under this transformation, the domain of B is $[0,1]$. In figure 2.4.g, we present an example using three trapezoids, where the parameter vector $(\theta_2, \theta_3, \mathcal{N})^\top$ equals $(2,3,5)^\top$, and where the integration is computed on the interval $[0, 0.9]$. You can find the MATLAB code for this figure on the CD that accompanies this book; see the file prog24g.m.

h) In this case, you are to play the role of a government that seeks to back out the underlying costs of the bidders based on their submitted bids, knowledge of the distribution of the costs, and under the hypothesis of Bayes–Nash equilibrium behavior. To apply Newton's method to this problem, we simply set the bid function up as root-finding problem; i.e.,

$$g(c) \equiv \sigma(c) - c - \frac{\int_c^\infty [1 - F_C(u)]^{(\mathcal{N}-1)}\,du}{[1 - F_C(c)]^{(\mathcal{N}-1)}} = 0.$$

The recursion has the following structure:

$$c_{k+1} = c_k - \frac{g(c_k)}{g'(c_k)} \quad k = 0, 1, \ldots$$

Note that, under some distributions, this will be straightforward because the integral vanishes. In other cases, such as Weibull-distributed costs, the integral will need to be approximated numerically at each iteration of Newton's method.

366

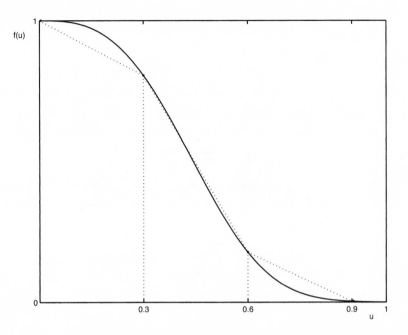

Figure 2.4.g
Graph of the Composite Trapezoidal Rule

i) Under the exponential assumption,

$$S = C + \frac{1}{\lambda(\mathcal{N} - 1)}.$$

Now, since we know the distribution of the random variable C, we can derive the distribution of bids using the method of transformations. Note first that

$$f_C(c) = \lambda \exp(-\lambda c) \quad c \geq 0.$$

Now, compute the inverse function

$$C = S - \frac{1}{\lambda(\mathcal{N} - 1)}.$$

Next, compute the derivative of the inverse function

$$\frac{dC}{dS} = 1.$$

Now, use these pieces to obtain the desired probability density function

$$f_S(s) = \lambda \exp\left(-\lambda s + \frac{1}{\mathcal{N}-1}\right) \quad s \geq \frac{1}{\lambda(\mathcal{N}-1)}.$$

j) Under the Pareto assumption,

$$S = C\frac{\theta_1(\mathcal{N}-1)}{\theta_1(\mathcal{N}-1)-1}.$$

Now, since we know the distribution of the random variable C, we can derive the distribution of bids using the method of transformations. Note first that

$$f_C(c) = \frac{\theta_1\theta_0^{\theta_1}}{c^{\theta_1+1}} \quad \theta_0 < c, \ 0 < \theta_1.$$

Now, compute the inverse function

$$C = S\frac{\theta_1(\mathcal{N}-1)-1}{\theta_1(\mathcal{N}-1)}.$$

Next, compute the derivative of the inverse function

$$\frac{dC}{dS} = \frac{\theta_1(\mathcal{N}-1)-1}{\theta_1(\mathcal{N}-1)}.$$

Now, use these pieces to obtain the desired probability density function

$$f_S(s) = \frac{\theta_1(\mathcal{N}-1)-1}{\theta_1(\mathcal{N}-1)} \frac{\theta_1\theta_0^{\theta_1}}{\left[s\frac{\theta_1(\mathcal{N}-1)-1}{\theta_1(\mathcal{N}-1)}\right]^{\theta_1+1}}$$

$$= \frac{\theta_1}{s^{\theta_1+1}}\left[\frac{\theta_1(\mathcal{N}-1)\theta_0}{\theta_1(\mathcal{N}-1)-1}\right]^{\theta_1}$$

where the support is

$$\frac{\theta_0\theta_1(\mathcal{N}-1)}{\theta_1(\mathcal{N}-1)-1} < s < \infty.$$

k) Under the Weibull assumption,

$$S = C + \frac{\int_C^\infty [\exp(-\theta_2 u^{\theta_3})]^{(\mathcal{N}-1)}\, du}{[\exp(-\theta_2 C^{\theta_3})]^{(\mathcal{N}-1)}}.$$

Now, since we know the distribution of the random variable C, we can derive the distribution of bids using the method of transformations. Note first that

$$f_C(c) = \theta_2\theta_3 c^{\theta_3-1}\exp(-\theta_2 c^{\theta_3}).$$

Now, to compute the Jacobian of the transformation, again use the fact that

$$\frac{dC}{dS} = \frac{1}{\frac{dS}{dC}},$$

so the derivative of the inverse function is

$$\frac{dC}{dS} = \frac{1}{1 + \frac{d}{dC}\left\{ \frac{\int_C^\infty \exp\left[-(\mathcal{N}-1)\theta_2 u^{\theta_3}\right]\, du}{\exp\left[-(\mathcal{N}-1)\theta_2 C^{\theta_3}\right]} \right\}}.$$

Collecting terms yields

$$\frac{1}{(\mathcal{N}-1)\theta_2\theta_3 C^{\theta_3-1}\exp[(\mathcal{N}-1)\theta_2 C^{\theta_3}]\int_C^\infty \exp\left[-(\mathcal{N}-1)\theta_2 u^{\theta_3}\right]\, du}.$$

Now, use these pieces to obtain the desired probability density function

$$f_S(s) = \frac{\exp[-\theta_2\mathcal{N} c^{\theta_3-1}]}{(\mathcal{N}-1)\int_c^\infty \exp[-\theta_2 u^{\theta_3}(\mathcal{N}-1)]\, du}$$

where c is obtained by solving

$$s = c + \frac{\int_c^\infty [\exp(-\theta_2 u^{\theta_3})]^{(\mathcal{N}-1)}\, du}{[\exp(-\theta_2 c^{\theta_3})]^{(\mathcal{N}-1)}}.$$

The lower bound of support of S is

$$\frac{\Gamma\left(1+\frac{1}{\theta_3}\right)}{[\theta_2(\mathcal{N}-1)]^{1/\theta_3}}.$$

1) The distribution of the winning bid can be derived by finding the cumulative distribution function of a bid, and then finding the distribution of the lowest order statistic of $\mathcal{N}$ independent bids from the same distribution. For the exponential case, the cumulative distribution function of a bid S is

$$F_S(s) = 1 - \exp\left(-\lambda s + \frac{1}{\mathcal{N}-1}\right).$$

The probability density function of the winning bid W (the lowest order statistic of bids) is then

$$f_W(w) = \mathcal{N}[1 - F_S(w)]^{(\mathcal{N}-1)} f_S(w)$$

$$= \mathcal{N}\left[\exp\left(-\lambda w + \frac{1}{\mathcal{N}-1}\right)\right]^{(\mathcal{N}-1)} \lambda \exp\left(-\lambda w + \frac{1}{\mathcal{N}-1}\right)$$

$$= \lambda \mathcal{N}\left[\exp\left(-\lambda w + \frac{1}{\mathcal{N}-1}\right)\right]^{\mathcal{N}}$$

$$= \lambda \mathcal{N} \exp\left(-\lambda \mathcal{N} w + \frac{\mathcal{N}}{\mathcal{N}-1}\right).$$

m) The distribution of the winning bid can be derived by finding the cumulative distribution function of a bid, and then finding the distribution of the lowest order statistic of $\mathcal{N}$ independent bids from the same distribution. For the Pareto case, the cumulative distribution function of a bid S is

$$F_S(s) = 1 - \left\{\frac{\theta_0\theta_1(\mathcal{N}-1)}{s[\theta_1(\mathcal{N}-1)-1]}\right\}^{\theta_1}.$$

The distribution of the winning bid (the lowest order statistic) is

$$f_W(w) = \mathcal{N}[1 - F_S(w)]^{(\mathcal{N}-1)} f_S(w)$$

$$= \mathcal{N}\left(\frac{\theta_0\theta_1(\mathcal{N}-1)}{w[\theta_1(\mathcal{N}-1)-1]}\right)^{\theta_1(\mathcal{N}-1)} \frac{\theta_1\theta_0^{\theta_1}}{w^{\theta_1+1}}\left[\frac{\theta_1(\mathcal{N}-1)}{\theta_1(\mathcal{N}-1)-1}\right]^{\theta_1}$$

$$= \frac{\theta_1\mathcal{N}}{w}\left(\frac{\theta_0\theta_1(\mathcal{N}-1)}{w[\theta_1(\mathcal{N}-1)-1]}\right)^{\theta_1\mathcal{N}}.$$

n) Follow the method from part m) to obtain the desired probability density function

$$f_W(w) = \frac{\mathcal{N}\exp[-\theta_2 z^{\theta_3}(2\mathcal{N}-1)]}{(\mathcal{N}-1)\int_z^\infty \exp[-\theta_2(\mathcal{N}-1)u^{\theta_3}]\,du}$$

where z is obtained by solving

$$w = z + \frac{\int_z^\infty [\exp(-\theta_2 u^{\theta_3})]^{(\mathcal{N}-1)}\,du}{[\exp(-\theta_2 z^{\theta_3})]^{(\mathcal{N}-1)}}.$$

2.5 All-Pay Auction

a) Here, the expected profit of bidder 1 is

$$v_1 \Pr(\text{win}|s_1) - s_1$$

where, for a monotonically, increasing strategy $\hat{\sigma}(v)$,

$$
\begin{aligned}
\Pr(\text{win}|s_1) &= \Pr\left[(S_2 < s_1) \cap \ldots \cap (S_{\mathcal{N}} < s_1)\right] \\
&= \prod_{i=2}^{\mathcal{N}} \Pr(S_i < s_1) \quad \text{(independence)} \\
&= \prod_{i=2}^{\mathcal{N}} \Pr\left[\hat{\sigma}(V_i) < s_1\right]^{(\mathcal{N}-1)} \\
&= \prod_{i=2}^{\mathcal{N}} \Pr\left[V_i < \hat{\sigma}^{-1}(s_1)\right]^{(\mathcal{N}-1)} \quad \text{(monotonicity)} \\
&= \left\{F_V\left[\hat{\sigma}^{-1}(s_1)\right]\right\}^{(\mathcal{N}-1)} \quad \text{(identical distribution).}
\end{aligned}
$$

Thus, the expected profit function for bidder 1 is

$$v_1 F_V\left[\hat{\sigma}^{-1}(s_1)\right]^{(\mathcal{N}-1)} - s_1.$$

The first part of this expression is the expected payoff to winning the auction with a bid s_1, while the second part is the cost of bidding s_1. This is incurred regardless of whether bidder 1 wins the auction.

b) To find the Bayes–Nash, equilibrium-bid function, first maximize this expression with respect to s_1. The necessary, first-order condition for this maximization problem implies

$$v_1(\mathcal{N}-1)F_V[\hat{\sigma}^{-1}(s_1)]^{\mathcal{N}-2} f_V[\hat{\sigma}^{-1}(s_1)]\frac{d\hat{\sigma}^{-1}(s_1)}{ds_1} - 1 = 0.$$

c) Now, at a Bayes–Nash equilibrium, $\hat{\sigma}^{-1}(s)$ equals v. Rearranging this expression, we get the following differential equation:

$$\sigma'(v) = v(\mathcal{N}-1)F_v(v)^{\mathcal{N}-2} f_V(v),$$

which makes use of the fact that

$$\frac{d\sigma^{-1}(s)}{ds} = \frac{1}{\frac{d\sigma(v)}{dv}} = \frac{1}{\sigma'(v)}.$$

The relevant boundary condition is $\sigma(0)$ is zero: when the object has no value, the bidder bids zero. To solve this differential equation, one should use *integration-by-parts*. To this end, let r equal $[F_V(v)]^{\mathcal{N}-1}$ and s equal v, so

$$\int_0^{\hat{v}} v(\mathcal{N}-1)F_v(v)^{\mathcal{N}-2}f_V(v)\ dv = \int_0^{\hat{v}} s\ dr$$

$$= rs\Big|_0^{\hat{v}} - \int_0^{\hat{v}} r\ ds.$$

The Bayes–Nash, equilibrium-bid function is

$$\sigma(v) = vF_v(v)^{\mathcal{N}-1} - \int_0^v F_V(u)^{\mathcal{N}-1}\ du.$$

When V is distributed uniformly on the $[0,1]$ interval, $F_V(v)$ is v, so

$$\sigma(v) = v^{\mathcal{N}} - \int_0^v u^{\mathcal{N}-1}\ du$$

$$= v^{\mathcal{N}} - \frac{v^{\mathcal{N}}}{\mathcal{N}}$$

$$= \frac{(\mathcal{N}-1)}{\mathcal{N}}v^{\mathcal{N}}.$$

d) At an all-pay auction, each of the $\mathcal{N}$ bidders pays his bid. The expected payment for a representative bidder is

$$\mathcal{E}\left[\sigma(V)\right] = \int_0^1 \sigma(v)f_V(v)\ dv$$

$$= \frac{(\mathcal{N}-1)}{\mathcal{N}}\int_0^1 v^{\mathcal{N}}\ dv$$

$$= \frac{(\mathcal{N}-1)}{\mathcal{N}}\frac{1}{(\mathcal{N}+1)}.$$

As there are $\mathcal{N}$ bidders, the total revenue that a seller can expect is $[(\mathcal{N}-1)/(\mathcal{N}+1)]$.

On the other hand, from an earlier exercise, we know that at a first-price, sealed-bid auction, the Bayes–Nash, equilibrium-bid function is

$$\sigma_F(v) = \frac{\mathcal{N}-1}{\mathcal{N}} v.$$

Now, under this format, the bidder with the highest valuation Z, which equals $\max(V_1, \ldots, V_{\mathcal{N}})$, wins the auction and pays his bid. Thus,

$$W_F = \frac{\mathcal{N}-1}{\mathcal{N}} Z,$$

so the seller's expected revenue is

$$\mathcal{E}(W_F) = \frac{\mathcal{N}-1}{\mathcal{N}} \int_0^1 z f_Z(z)\, dz$$

$$= \frac{\mathcal{N}-1}{\mathcal{N}} \int_0^1 \mathcal{N} z^{\mathcal{N}}\, dz$$

$$= \frac{\mathcal{N}-1}{\mathcal{N}} \frac{\mathcal{N}}{\mathcal{N}+1}$$

$$= \frac{\mathcal{N}-1}{\mathcal{N}+1}.$$

3.1 Test Scores within the Location-Scale Family

a) To begin, let

$$V_{(1:\mathcal{N}_t)} > V_{(2:\mathcal{N}_t)} > \ldots > V_{(\mathcal{N}_t:\mathcal{N}_t)}.$$

Now, Y_t is $V_{(1:\mathcal{N}_t)}$. Recall that the cumulative distribution function of the highest order statistic is

$$F_Y(y|\mathcal{N}_t) = F_V(y)^{\mathcal{N}_t}.$$

Applying this result in the normal case yields

$$F_Y(y|\mathcal{N}_t) = \Phi\left(\frac{y-\mu}{\sigma}\right)^{\mathcal{N}_t}.$$

To get the probability density function of the highest order statistic, differentiate the cumulative distribution function with respect to y; i.e.,

$$f_Y(y|\mathcal{N}_t) = \frac{\mathcal{N}_t}{\sigma} \Phi\left(\frac{y-\mu}{\sigma}\right)^{\mathcal{N}_t - 1} \phi\left(\frac{y-\mu}{\sigma}\right).$$

b) Using the hint,

$$V_{(i:\mathcal{N}_t)} = \mu + \sigma Z_{(i:\mathcal{N})}$$

where $Z_{(i:\mathcal{N}_t)}$ is the ith largest order statistic for a sample of size $\mathcal{N}_t$ from an independent and identically distributed, standard-normal random variable, we know then, for the highest order statistic, the following must be true:

$$\mathcal{E}(Y_t|\mathcal{N}_t) = \mu + \sigma \mathcal{E}\left[Z_{(1:\mathcal{N}_t)}\right]$$

$$= \mu + \sigma \int_{-\infty}^{\infty} z\mathcal{N}_t\Phi(z)^{\mathcal{N}_t-1}\phi(z)\ dz.$$

Note that the integral above must be computed numerically.

c) The gathered data contain only the highest test scores $\{y_t\}_{t=1}^{T}$ and the class size $\{\mathcal{N}_t\}_{t=1}^{T}$. Thus, the probability density function relevant to the derivation of the likelihood function is that of the highest order statistic. The likelihood function is

$$\prod_{t=1}^{T} \frac{\mathcal{N}_t}{\sigma}\Phi\left(\frac{y_t-\mu}{\sigma}\right)^{\mathcal{N}_t-1}\phi\left(\frac{y_t-\mu}{\sigma}\right).$$

Thus, the logarithm of the likelihood function is

$$\mathcal{L}(\mu,\sigma;\boldsymbol{y},\mathcal{N}) = \sum_{t=1}^{T}\log\mathcal{N}_t + \sum_{t=1}^{T}(\mathcal{N}_t-1)\log\left[\Phi\left(\frac{y_t-\mu}{\sigma}\right)\right] + $$
$$\sum_{t=1}^{T}\log\left[\phi\left(\frac{y_t-\mu}{\sigma}\right)\right] - T\log\sigma.$$

d) The regression is constructed by exploiting the location-scale property mentioned in part b). In particular, the regression equation is

$$Y_t = \mathcal{E}[Y_t|\mathcal{N}_t] + U_t$$
$$= \mu + \sigma\mathcal{E}[Z_{(1:\mathcal{N}_t)}] + U_t$$

where $\mathcal{E}(U_t|\mathcal{N}_t)$ is zero, while the variance of U_t depends on $\mathcal{N}_t$.

e) You can find the MATLAB code for this program on the CD that accompanies this book; see the file `prog31e.m`. Note, you will need the data file `testscor.dat` and the function file `fun31e.m`. Here, $(98.9203, 15.7873)^\top$ is the maximum-likelihood estimate of $(\mu, \sigma)^\top$.

f) You can find the MATLAB code for this program on the CD that accompanies this book; see the file `prog31f.m`. In this program, we use a change of variables to map the real line to the $(0, 1)$ interval. The results are written to the file `testscorf.dat` for use in part g).

g) Recall from part d) that the relevant regression equation is

$$Y_t = \mu + \sigma \mathcal{E}[Z_{(1:\mathcal{N}_t)}] + U_t.$$

where $\mathcal{E}(U_t|\mathcal{N}_t)$ has mean zero, but a variance that depends on $\mathcal{N}_t$. Note too that the expected values computed in part f) are necessary to perform the estimation. You can find the MATLAB code for this program on the CD that accompanies this book; see the file `prog31g.m`. Here, $(74.9841, 27.9348)^\top$ is the least-squares estimate of the vector $(\mu, \sigma)^\top$, while the robust standard errors are $(29.2682, 14.9108)^\top$.

3.2 Vickrey Auctions and the Location-Scale Family

a) To begin, let

$$V_{(1:\mathcal{N}_t)} > V_{(2:\mathcal{N}_t)} > \ldots > V_{(\mathcal{N}_t:\mathcal{N}_t)}.$$

Now, W_t is $V_{(2:\mathcal{N}_t)}$. Recall that the cumulative distribution function of the second-highest order statistic is given by

$$F_W(w|\mathcal{N}_t) = \mathcal{N}_t(\mathcal{N}_t - 1) \int_0^{F_V(w)} u^{\mathcal{N}_t - 2}(1 - u) \, du$$

$$= \mathcal{N}_t F_V(w)^{\mathcal{N}_t - 1} - (\mathcal{N}_t - 1) F_V(w)^{\mathcal{N}_t}.$$

Applying this result here yields

$$F_W(w|\mathcal{N}_t) = \mathcal{N}\Phi\left(\frac{\log w - \mu}{\sigma}\right)^{\mathcal{N}_t - 1} - (\mathcal{N}_t - 1)\Phi\left(\frac{\log w - \mu}{\sigma}\right)^{\mathcal{N}_t}.$$

To get the probability density of the second-highest order statistic, differentiate the cumulative distribution function with respect to w, so

$$f_W(w|\mathcal{N}_t) = \frac{\mathcal{N}_t(\mathcal{N}_t - 1)}{w\sigma}\Phi\left(\frac{\log w - \mu}{\sigma}\right)^{\mathcal{N}_t - 2}$$

$$\left[1 - \Phi\left(\frac{\log w - \mu}{\sigma}\right)\right]\phi\left(\frac{\log w - \mu}{\sigma}\right).$$

375

b) Using the hint,
$$\log V_{(i:\mathcal{N}_t)} = \mu + \sigma Z_{(i:\mathcal{N}_t)}$$

where $Z_{(i:\mathcal{N}_t)}$ is the ith largest order statistic from a sample of $\mathcal{N}_t$ independent and identically distributed standard normal random variables, we know then, for the second-highest order statistic, the following must be true:

$$\mathcal{E}[\log(W_t)|\mathcal{N}_t]$$
$$= \mu + \sigma\mathcal{E}\left[Z_{(2:\mathcal{N}_t)}\right]$$
$$= \mu + \sigma \int_{-\infty}^{\infty} z\mathcal{N}_t(\mathcal{N}_t - 1)\Phi(z)^{\mathcal{N}_t-2}[1 - \Phi(z)]\phi(z) \ dz.$$

Note that the integral above must be computed numerically.

c) The gathered data contain only the winning bid $\{w_t\}_{t=1}^T$ and the number of bidders $\{\mathcal{N}_t\}_{t=1}^T$. Thus, the probability density function relevant to the derivation of the likelihood function is that of the second-highest order statistic. The likelihood function is

$$\prod_{t=1}^T \frac{\mathcal{N}_t(\mathcal{N}_t - 1)}{w_t\sigma}\Phi\left(\frac{\log w_t - \mu}{\sigma}\right)^{\mathcal{N}_t-2}$$
$$\left[1 - \Phi\left(\frac{\log w_t - \mu}{\sigma}\right)\right]\phi\left(\frac{\log w_t - \mu}{\sigma}\right).$$

Thus, the logarithm of the likelihood function is

$$\mathcal{L}(\mu, \sigma; \boldsymbol{w}, \boldsymbol{\mathcal{N}}) = \sum_{t=1}^T \log[\mathcal{N}_t(\mathcal{N}_t - 1)]+$$
$$\sum_{t=1}^T (\mathcal{N}_t - 2)\log\left[\Phi\left(\frac{\log w_t - \mu}{\sigma}\right)\right]+$$
$$\sum_{t=1}^T \log\left[1 - \Phi\left(\frac{\log w_t - \mu}{\sigma}\right)\right]+$$
$$\sum_{t=1}^T \log\left[\phi\left(\frac{\log w_t - \mu}{\sigma}\right)\right]-$$
$$\sum_{t=1}^T \log w_t - T\log(\sigma).$$

d) The regression is constructed by exploiting the location-scale property mentioned in part b). In particular, the regression equation is

$$\log(W_t) = \mathcal{E}[\log(W_t)|Z_{(2:\mathcal{N}_t)}] + U_t$$
$$= \mu + \sigma\mathcal{E}[Z_{(2:\mathcal{N}_t)}] + U_t$$

where $\mathcal{E}(U_t|\mathcal{N}_t)$ is zero, but the variance of U_t depends on $\mathcal{N}_t$.

e) You can find the MATLAB code for this program on the CD that accompanies this book; see the file `prog32e.m`. Note, you will also need the data file `vickrey.dat` and the function file `fun32e.m`. The estimate of $(\hat{\gamma}_0^{\mathrm{ML}}, \hat{\gamma}_1^{\mathrm{ML}}, \hat{\sigma}^{\mathrm{ML}})^\top$ is $(0.0700, -0.1342, 2.0388)^\top$.

f) You can find the MATLAB code for this program on the CD that accompanies this book; see the file `prog32f.m`. In this program, we use a change of variables to map the real line to the $(0,1)$ interval. The results are written to the file `vickreyf.dat` for use in part g).

g) Recall from part d) that the relevant regression equation is

$$\log(W_t) = \gamma_0 + \gamma_1 z_t + \sigma\mathcal{E}[Z_{(2:\mathcal{N})}] + U_t.$$

where $\mathcal{E}(U_t|\mathcal{N}_t, z_t)$ is zero, but the variance of U_t depends on $\mathcal{N}_t$. Note, the expected values computed in part f) are necessary to perform the estimation. You can find the MATLAB code for this program on the CD that accompanies this book; see the file `prog32g.m`. The least-squares estimate of $(\hat{\gamma}_0^{\mathrm{LS}}, \hat{\gamma}_1^{\mathrm{LS}}, \hat{\sigma}^{\mathrm{LS}})^\top$ equals $(-0.3818, -0.1513, 2.5233)^\top$, while the robust standard errors are $(0.4873, 0.3184, 0.4638)^\top$.

3.3 ML Estimation of Vickrey Auctions

a) Since there exists a potentially binding reserve price, we must incorporate this fact into the likelihood function. The idea is to divide the probability density function of the second-highest order statistic by the survivor function evaluated at the reserve price r. Thus,

$$f_{W_t}(w) = \frac{\mathcal{N}_t(\mathcal{N}_t - 1)F_V(w)^{\mathcal{N}_t - 2}[1 - F_V(w)]f_V(w)}{[1 - F_V(r)^{\mathcal{N}_t}]},$$

which implies that the likelihood function is

$$\prod_{t=1}^{T} \frac{\mathcal{N}_t(\mathcal{N}_t - 1)F_V(w)^{\mathcal{N}_t-2}[1 - F_V(w)]f_V(w)}{[1 - F_V(r)^{\mathcal{N}_t}]},$$

and that the logarithm of the likelihood function is

$$\sum_{t=1}^{T} \log[\mathcal{N}_t(\mathcal{N}_t - 1)] + \sum_{t=1}^{T}(\mathcal{N}_t - 2)\log[F_V(w_t)] + \sum_{t=1}^{T}\log[1 - F_V(w_t)]$$

$$+ \sum_{t=1}^{T}\log[f_V(w_t)] - \sum_{t=1}^{T}\log[1 - F_V(r)^{\mathcal{N}_t}].$$

b) As in part a), it will be necessary to account for the presence of a potentially binding reserve price. Here, the relevant probability density function is

$$g\left[\boldsymbol{b}_{(n)}, n\right] = n! \prod_{i=1}^{n} \frac{f_V\left[b_{(i:n)}\right]}{[1 - F_V(r)]}.$$

Thus, the relevant likelihood function is

$$\prod_{t=1}^{T} n_t! \prod_{i=1}^{n_t} \frac{f_V\left[b_{(i:n_t)}\right]}{[1 - F_V(r)]},$$

for which the following contribution to the logarithm of the likelihood function applies:

$$\log(n_t!) + \sum_{i=1}^{n_t} \log\{f_V\left[b_{(i:n_t)}\right]\} - n_t \log[1 - F_V(r)].$$

Note that n_t denotes the number of bidders that actually participated in auction t. This number is obtained (for each auction t) by simply summing the number of observed bids.

c) You can find the MATLAB code for this program on the CD that accompanies this book; see the files **fun33c.m** and **prog33c.m**. Note $(\hat{\theta}_1^{\text{ML}}, \hat{\theta}_2^{\text{ML}})^{\top}$ is $(0.9088, 2.0145)^{\top}$.

d) You can find the MATLAB code for this program on the CD that accompanies this book; see the files **fun33d.m** and **prog33d.m**. Note $(\hat{\theta}_1^{\text{ML}}, \hat{\theta}_2^{\text{ML}})^{\top}$ is $(0.9177, 2.1138)^{\top}$.

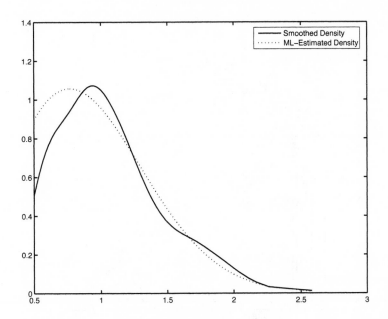

Figure 3.3.e
Parametric and Nonparametric Estimates of $f_V^o(v)$:
All Bids

e) You can find the MATLAB code for this program on the CD that accompanies this book; see the files **prog33e.m**. The results appear in figure 3.3.e.

f) You can find the MATLAB code for this program on the CD that accompanies this book; see the files **prog33f.m**. The results appear in figure 3.3.f.

g) Use the likelihood-ratio test of the hypothesis that θ_2 equals one against the alternative that θ_2 is greater than one. You can find the MATLAB code for this program on the CD that accompanies this book; see the file **prog33g.m**. The test statistic for the specification in part c) is 5.1725, while the test statistic for the specification in part d) is 6.6991. Thus, we find evidence that both specifications are consistent with Myerson's (1981) regular case.

h) Use the likelihood-ratio test to test the hypothesis that θ_{11} equals zero. You can find the MATLAB code for this program on the CD that accompanies this book; see the files **fun33h.m** and **prog33h.m**. Note $(\hat{\theta}_{10}^{ML}, \hat{\theta}_{11}^{ML}, \hat{\theta}_2^{ML})^\top$ is $(-0.1230, 0.0062, 2.0138)^\top$. Also, the

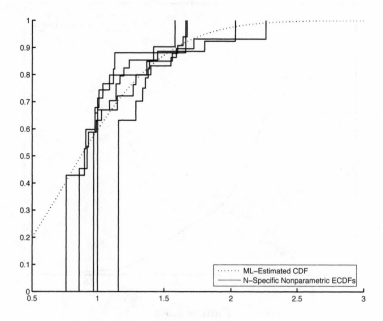

Figure 3.3.f
Parametric and Nonparametric Estimates of $F_V^o(v)$:
Winning Bids

likelihood-ratio statistic is 0.0763, which implies that one fails to reject at, say, size 0.05.

i) Use the likelihood-ratio test to test the hypothesis that θ_{11} equals zero. You can find the MATLAB code for this program on the CD that accompanies this book; see the files fun33i.m and prog33i.m. Note $(\hat{\theta}_{10}^{\text{ML}}, \hat{\theta}_{11}^{\text{ML}}, \hat{\theta}_2^{\text{ML}})^\top$ is $(-0.0619, -0.0055, 2.1154)^\top$. Also, the likelihood-ratio statistic is 0.0658, which implies that one fails to reject at, say, size 0.05.

j) You can find the MATLAB code for this program on the CD that accompanies this book; see the files fun33j.m and prog33j.m. To characterize the asymptotic distribution, begin by defining

$$g(\hat{\rho}, \theta_1, \theta_2) = \hat{\rho} - v_0 - \frac{1}{\hat{h}_V(\hat{\theta}_1, \hat{\theta}_2)} = 0$$

where $\hat{h}_V(\cdot)$ denotes the hazard function. For simplicity, let $\boldsymbol{\theta}^0$ denote (θ_1^0, θ_2^0). Now, using a first-order, Taylor-series expansion, write

$$(\hat{\rho} - \rho^0) = \frac{-\nabla_{\boldsymbol{\theta}} g(\rho^0, \boldsymbol{\theta}^0)}{g_\rho(\rho^0, \boldsymbol{\theta}^0)} (\hat{\boldsymbol{\theta}} - \boldsymbol{\theta}^0)$$

where $g_\rho(\cdot)$ denotes the derivative of $g(\cdot)$ with respect to ρ. Thus,

$$\sqrt{T}(\hat{\rho} - \rho^0) \xrightarrow{\mathrm{d}} \mathcal{N}\left[0, \mathbf{a}^\top \mathcal{I}^{-1}(\boldsymbol{\theta}^0) \mathbf{a}\right]$$

where

$$\mathbf{a} = \frac{-\nabla_{\boldsymbol{\theta}} g(\rho^0, \boldsymbol{\theta}^0)}{g_\rho(\rho^0, \boldsymbol{\theta}^0)}$$

and where $\mathcal{I}^{-1}$ denotes the inverse of Fisher's information matrix. Now, $\hat{\rho}^*$ is 0.7309, with a standard error of 0.0413, so the corresponding standard-normal test statistic is 5.5877, implying that one can reject the hypothesis that an r of 0.50 is optimal.

k) You can find the MATLAB code for this program on the CD that accompanies this book; see the files `fun33k.m` and `prog33k.m`. Now, $\hat{\rho}^*$ is 1.3055, with a standard error of 0.0413, so the corresponding standard-normal test statistic is 19.4914, implying that one can reject the hypothesis that an r of 0.50 is optimal.

3.4 Nonparametric Estimation of English Auctions

a) You can find the MATLAB code for this program on the CD that accompanies this book; see the file `prog34a.m`. The results appear in figure 3.4.a.

b) You can find the MATLAB code for this program on the CD that accompanies this book; see the files `fun34b.m`, `dksdensity.m`, and `prog34b.m`. The results appear in figure 3.4.b.

c) You can find the MATLAB code for this program on the CD that accompanies this book; see the files `fun34c.m` and `prog34c.m`. The maximum-likelihood estimate of θ is 2.0716. The results appear in figure 3.4.c.

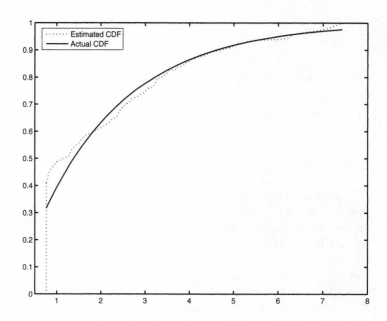

Figure 3.4.a
Nonparametric Estimate of $F_V^o(v)$

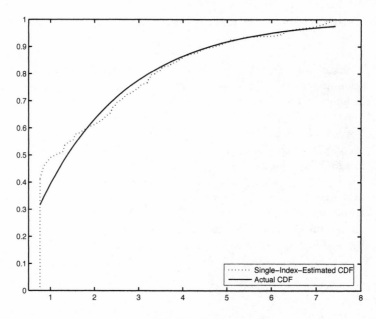

Figure 3.4.b
Density-Weighted Derivative Estimate of $F_{V|Z}^o(v|z)$

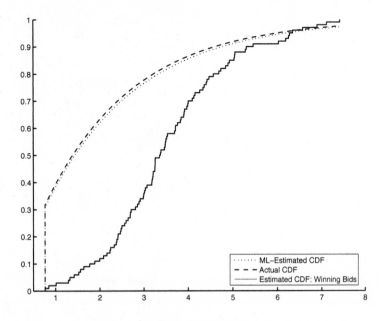

Figure 3.4.c
Estimates of $F_V^0(v)$ and $F_W(v)$

3.5 English Auctions: Incomplete Data and Inference

a) You can find the MATLAB code for this program on the CD that
accompanies this book; see the files `fun35a.m` and `prog35a.m`. The
results appear in figure 3.5.a.

b) You can find the MATLAB code for this program on the CD that
accompanies this book; see the file `prog35b.m`. The estimated lower
bound on the optimal reserve price is 3.1031; the estimated upper
bound on the optimal reserve price is 8.0080.

c) You can find the MATLAB code for this program on the CD that
accompanies this book; see the files `fun35c.m` and `prog35c.m`. The
maximum-likelihood estimate of $\hat{\boldsymbol{\theta}}$ is $(0.0415, 1.8647)^{\top}$.

d) You can find the MATLAB code for this program on the CD that
accompanies this book; see the files `fun35d.m` and `prog35d.m`. The
maximum-likelihood estimate of the optimal reserve price equals
5.1383, which falls within the bounds derived in part b).

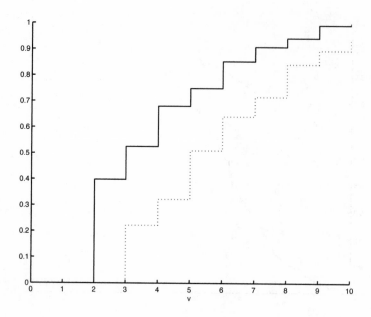

Figure 3.5.a
Haile and Tamer Bounds

4.1 Uniform Case: First-Price, Sealed-Bid Auctions

a) Recall that the probability density function of a uniform random variable is

$$f_V(v; \theta^0) = \begin{cases} \frac{1}{\theta^0} & v \in [0, \theta^0] \\ 0 & \text{otherwise.} \end{cases}$$

To find the cumulative distribution function of V requires solving the following integral:

$$F_V(v; \theta^0) = \frac{1}{\theta^0} \int_0^v du.$$

Performing the integration yields

$$F_V(v; \theta^0) = \begin{cases} 0 & v \in (-\infty, 0) \\ \frac{v}{\theta^0} & v \in [0, \theta^0] \\ 1 & v \in (\theta^0, \infty). \end{cases}$$

b) Finding the expected value of V requires solving the following integral:

$$\mathcal{E}(V) = \int_0^{\theta^0} \frac{v}{\theta^0} \, dv = \frac{\theta^0}{2}.$$

c) Recall that the variance of a random variable can be computed by

$$\mathcal{V}(V) = \mathcal{E}(V^2) - [\mathcal{E}(V)]^2.$$

Thus, we need only compute the second raw moment

$$\mathcal{E}(V^2) = \int_0^{\theta^0} \frac{v^2}{\theta^0}\, dv = \frac{(\theta^0)^2}{3}.$$

Using this result, in conjunction with the result from part b), yields

$$\mathcal{V}(V) = \frac{(\theta^0)^2}{3} - \frac{(\theta^0)^2}{4} = \frac{(\theta^0)^2}{12}.$$

d) Compute the expectation by

$$\mathcal{E}(M_1) = \mathcal{E}\left(\sum_{t=1}^{T} \frac{V_t}{T}\right) = \frac{1}{T}\sum_{t=1}^{T}\mathcal{E}(V_t) = \frac{1}{T}\frac{T\theta^0}{2} = \frac{\theta^0}{2}.$$

e) Compute the variance by

$$\mathcal{V}(M_1) = \mathcal{V}\left(\sum_{t=1}^{T} \frac{V_t}{T}\right) = \frac{1}{T^2}\sum_{t=1}^{T}\mathcal{V}(V_t) = \frac{1}{T^2}\frac{T(\theta^0)^2}{12} = \frac{(\theta^0)^2}{12T}.$$

f) The method-of-moments estimator is derived by solving the following root-finding problem:

$$\frac{1}{T}\sum_{t=1}^{T} V_t - \frac{\hat{\theta}_{MM}}{2} = 0.$$

Performing the calculation yields

$$\hat{\theta}_{MM} = \frac{2}{T}\sum_{t=1}^{T} V_t = 2M_1.$$

g) Compute the expectation by

$$\mathcal{E}(\hat{\theta}_{MM}) = \mathcal{E}\left(\sum_{t=1}^{T} \frac{2V_t}{T}\right) = \frac{2}{T}\sum_{t=1}^{T}\mathcal{E}(V_t) = \frac{2}{T}\frac{T\theta^0}{2} = \theta^0.$$

h) Compute the variance by

$$\mathcal{V}(\hat{\theta}_{\mathrm{MM}}) = \mathcal{V}\left(\sum_{t=1}^{T} \frac{2V_t}{T}\right) = \frac{4}{T^2}\sum_{t=1}^{T}\mathcal{V}(V_t) = \frac{4}{T^2}\frac{T(\theta^0)^2}{12} = \frac{(\theta^0)^2}{3T}.$$

i) By the Lindeberg–Levy central limit theorem,

$$\frac{[M_1 - \mathcal{E}(M_1)]}{\sqrt{\mathcal{V}(M_1)}} \xrightarrow{\mathrm{d}} \mathcal{N}(0,1),$$

so

$$\sqrt{T}(\hat{\theta}_{\mathrm{MM}} - \theta^0) \xrightarrow{\mathrm{d}} \mathcal{N}[0, 4\mathcal{V}(V)].$$

j) The method of maximum likelihood, as is typically implemented, cannot be applied here because the support of the random variable V depends on the parameter to be estimated, θ^0.

k) The cumulative distribution function of the highest order statistic is

$$F_Z(z) = F_V(z)^T.$$

Making the necessary substitutions yields

$$F_Z(z) = \left(\frac{z}{\theta^0}\right)^T.$$

l) The probability density function is obtained by differentiating the cumulative distribution function with respect to z, so

$$f_Z(z) = \frac{T}{\theta^0}\left(\frac{z}{\theta^0}\right)^{T-1}.$$

m) Compute the expectation by

$$\mathcal{E}(Z) = \int_0^{\theta^0} T\left(\frac{z}{\theta^0}\right)^T dz$$
$$= \frac{(\theta^0)^{T+1}}{T+1}\frac{T}{(\theta^0)^T}$$
$$= \frac{\theta^0 T}{T+1}.$$

n) Recall that the variance of a random variable can be computed by

$$\mathcal{V}(Z) = \mathcal{E}(Z^2) - [\mathcal{E}(Z)]^2.$$

Thus, we need only compute the second raw moment

$$\mathcal{E}(Z^2) = \int_0^{\theta^0} zT \left(\frac{z}{\theta^0}\right)^T dz$$

$$= \frac{(\theta^0)^{T+2}}{T+2} \frac{T}{(\theta^0)^T}$$

$$= \frac{(\theta^0)^2 T}{T+2}.$$

Using this result, in conjunction with the result from part m), yields

$$\mathcal{V}(Z) = \frac{(\theta^0)^2 T}{T+2} - \left(\frac{\theta^0 T}{T+1}\right)^2 = \frac{T(\theta^0)^2}{(T+2)(T+1)^2}.$$

o) Recall that Z equals $\max(V_1, V_2, \ldots, V_T)$. Thus,

$$\Pr(Z > z) = 1 - \Pr(Z \le z)$$
$$= 1 - \Pr[(V_1 \le z) \cap (V_2 \le z) \cap \ldots \cap (V_T \le z)]$$
$$= 1 - [F_V(z)]^T.$$

Note too that for any δ greater than zero, however small,

$$\Pr(Z \in [\theta^0, \theta^0 + \delta]) = F_V(\theta^0 + \delta) = 1 - [F_V(\theta^0 + \delta)]^T,$$

so

$$\lim_{T\to\infty} \Pr(Z \in [\theta^0, \theta^0 + \delta]) = 1 - \lim_{T\to\infty} [F_V(\theta^0 + \delta)]^T = 1.$$

Thus, the probability that Z is within an arbitrary and small δ-neighborhood of the upper bound θ^0 is one. To wit, Z converges in probability to θ^0.

p) By result A.4.2, the asymptotic distribution is

$$T(Z - \theta^0) \xrightarrow{d} \mathcal{E}(\cdot),$$

where $\mathcal{E}(\cdot)$ denotes an exponential random variable.

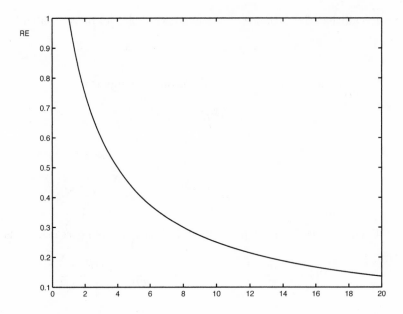

Figure 4.1.t
Graph of the Relative Efficiency Function

q) This estimator controls for the fact that Z is a biased estimator of the upper bound of support θ^0.

r) Compute the expectation by

$$\mathcal{E}(\hat{\theta}_{\mathrm{ML}}) = \frac{T+1}{T}\mathcal{E}(Z) = \frac{T+1}{T}\frac{\theta^0 T}{T+1} = \theta^0.$$

Thus, the bias-adjusted, maximum-likelihood estimator $\hat{\theta}_{\mathrm{ML}}$ is an unbiased estimator of θ^0.

s) Since $\hat{\theta}_{\mathrm{ML}}$ is unbiased, the mean-squared error equals the variance of the maximum-likelihood estimator. Thus,

$$\begin{aligned}
\mathcal{MSE}(\hat{\theta}_{\mathrm{ML}}) &= \frac{(T+1)^2}{T^2}\mathcal{V}(Z) \\
&= \frac{(T+1)^2}{T^2}\frac{T(\theta^0)^2}{(T+2)(T+1)^2} \\
&= \frac{(\theta^0)^2}{T(T+2)}.
\end{aligned}$$

t) In figure 4.1.t, we present a graph of the relative efficiency function. You can find the MATLAB code for this figure on the CD that accompanies this book; see the file `prog41t.m`.

4.2 Pareto Case: Low-Price, Sealed-Bid Auctions

a) To find the cumulative distribution function of C requires solving the following integral:

$$F_C(c; \theta^0) = \int_{\theta^0}^{c} \frac{3(\theta^0)^3}{u^4} \, du.$$

Performing the integration yields

$$F_C(c; \theta^0) = 1 - \left(\frac{\theta^0}{c}\right)^3 \quad c \geq \theta^0.$$

b) Finding the expected value of C requires solving the following integral:

$$\int_{\theta^0}^{\infty} c \frac{3(\theta^0)^3}{c^4} \, dc.$$

Performing the integration yields

$$\mathcal{E}(C) = \frac{3\theta^0}{2}.$$

c) Recall that the variance of a random variable can be computed as

$$\mathcal{V}(C) = \mathcal{E}(C^2) - [\mathcal{E}(C)]^2.$$

Thus, we need only compute the second raw moment

$$\mathcal{E}(C^2) = \int_{\theta^0}^{\infty} c^2 \frac{3(\theta^0)^3}{c^4} \, dc.$$

Performing the integration yields

$$\mathcal{E}(C^2) = 3(\theta^0)^2.$$

Using this result, in conjunction with the result from part b), yields

$$\mathcal{V}(C) = 3(\theta^0)^2 - \frac{9(\theta^0)^2}{4} = \frac{3(\theta^0)^2}{4}.$$

d) Compute the expectation by

$$\mathcal{E}(M_1) = \mathcal{E}\left(\sum_{t=1}^{T}\frac{C_t}{T}\right) = \frac{1}{T}\sum_{t=1}^{T}\mathcal{E}(C_t) = \frac{1}{T}\frac{T3\theta^0}{2} = \frac{3\theta^0}{2}.$$

e) Compute the variance by

$$\mathcal{V}(M_1) = \mathcal{V}\left(\sum_{t=1}^{T}\frac{C_t}{T}\right) = \frac{1}{T^2}\sum_{t=1}^{T}\mathcal{V}(C_t) = \frac{1}{T^2}\frac{T3(\theta^0)^2}{4} = \frac{3(\theta^0)^2}{4T}.$$

f) The method-of-moments estimator is derived by solving the following root-finding problem:

$$\frac{1}{T}\sum_{t=1}^{T}C_t - \frac{3\hat{\theta}_{\mathrm{ML}}}{2} = 0.$$

Performing the calculation yields

$$\hat{\theta}_{\mathrm{MM}} = \frac{2}{3T}\sum_{t=1}^{T}C_t = \frac{2M_1}{3}.$$

g) Compute the expectation by

$$\mathcal{E}(\hat{\theta}_{\mathrm{MM}}) = \mathcal{E}\left(\frac{2}{3T}\sum_{t=1}^{T}C_t\right) = \frac{2}{3T}\sum_{t=1}^{T}\mathcal{E}(C_t) = \frac{2}{3T}\frac{T3\theta^0}{2} = \theta^0.$$

h) Compute the variance by

$$\mathcal{V}(\hat{\theta}_{\mathrm{MM}}) = \mathcal{V}\left(\frac{2}{3T}\sum_{t=1}^{T}C_t\right)$$
$$= \frac{4}{9T^2}\sum_{t=1}^{T}\mathcal{V}(C_t)$$
$$= \frac{4}{9T^2}\frac{T3(\theta^0)^2}{4}$$
$$= \frac{(\theta^0)^2}{3T}.$$

i) By the Lindeberg–Levy central limit theorem,

$$\frac{M_1 - \mathcal{E}(M_1)}{\sqrt{\mathcal{V}(M_1)}} \xrightarrow{\text{d}} \mathcal{N}(0, 1),$$

so

$$\sqrt{T}(\hat{\theta}_{\text{MM}} - \theta^0) \xrightarrow{\text{d}} \mathcal{N}\left[0, \frac{4}{9}\mathcal{V}(C)\right].$$

j) The method of maximum likelihood, as is typically implemented, cannot be applied here because the support of the random variable C depends on the parameter to be estimated, θ^0.

k) The cumulative distribution function of the lowest order statistic is

$$F_X(x) = 1 - [1 - F_C(x)]^T.$$

Making the necessary substitutions yields

$$F_X(x) = 1 - \left(\frac{\theta^0}{x}\right)^{3T}.$$

l) To find the probability density function of the random variable X, differentiate the cumulative distribution function with respect to x, so

$$f_X(x) = \frac{3T(\theta^0)^{3T}}{x^{3T+1}}.$$

m) Compute the expectation by

$$\mathcal{E}(X) = \int_{\theta^0}^{\infty} x \frac{3T(\theta^0)^{3T}}{x^{3T+1}} \, dx.$$

Performing the integration yields

$$\mathcal{E}(X) = \frac{3T\theta^0}{3T - 1}.$$

n) Recall that the variance of a random variable can be computed by

$$\mathcal{V}(X) = \mathcal{E}(X^2) - [\mathcal{E}(X)]^2.$$

Thus, we need only compute the second raw moment

$$\mathcal{E}(X^2) = \int_{\theta^0}^{\infty} x^2 \frac{3T(\theta^0)^{3T}}{x^{3T+1}} \, dx.$$

Performing the integration yields

$$\mathcal{E}(X^2) = \frac{3T(\theta^0)^2}{3T-2}.$$

Using this result, in conjunction with the result from part m), yields

$$\mathcal{V}(X) = \frac{3T(\theta^0)^2}{(3T-2)(3T-1)^2}.$$

o) Recall that X equals $\min(C_1, C_2, \ldots, C_T)$. Thus,

$$\Pr(X \leq x) = 1 - \Pr[(C_1 \geq x) \cap (C_2 \geq x) \cap \ldots \cap (C_T \geq x)]$$
$$= 1 - [1 - F_C(x)]^T.$$

Note too that for any δ greater than zero, however small,

$$\Pr(X \in [\theta^0, \theta^0 + \delta]) = F_X(\theta^0 + \delta) = 1 - [1 - F_C(\theta^0 + \delta)]^T,$$

so

$$\lim_{T \to \infty} \Pr(X \in [\theta^0, \theta^0 + \delta]) = 1 - \lim_{T \to \infty} [1 - F_C(\theta^0 + \delta)]^T = 1.$$

Thus, the probability that X is within an arbitrary and small δ-neighborhood of the upper bound θ^0 is one. To wit, X converges in probability to θ^0.

p) By result A.4.2, the asymptotic distribution is

$$T(X - \theta^0) \xrightarrow{d} \mathcal{E}(\cdot),$$

where $\mathcal{E}(\cdot)$ denotes an exponential random variable.

q) This estimator controls for the fact that X is a biased estimator of the lower bound of support θ^0.

r) Compute the expectation as

$$\mathcal{E}(\hat{\theta}_{\mathrm{ML}}) = \frac{(3T-1)}{3T}\mathcal{E}(X) = \frac{(3T-1)}{3T}\frac{3T\theta^0}{(3T-1)} = \theta^0.$$

Thus, the bias-adjusted, maximum-likelihood estimator $\hat{\theta}_{\mathrm{ML}}$ is an unbiased estimator of θ^0.

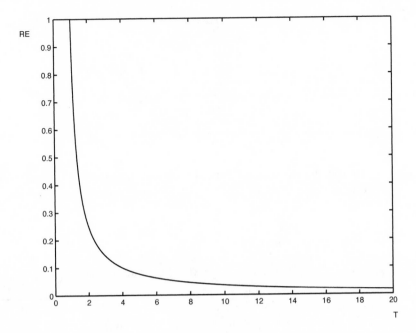

Figure 4.2.t
Graph of the Relative Efficiency Function

s) Since $\hat{\theta}_{\mathrm{ML}}$ is unbiased, the mean-squared error is equal to the variance of the maximum-likelihood estimator. Thus,

$$
\begin{aligned}
\mathcal{MSE}(\hat{\theta}_{\mathrm{ML}}) &= \frac{(3T-1)^2}{9T^2}\mathcal{V}(X) \\
&= \frac{(3T-1)^2}{9T^2}\frac{3T(\theta^0)^2}{(3T-2)(3T-1)^2} \\
&= \frac{(\theta^0)^2}{3T(3T-2)}.
\end{aligned}
$$

t) In figure 4.2.t, we present a plot of the relative efficiency function. You can find the MATLAB code for this figure on the CD that accompanies this book; see the file `prog42t.m`.

4.3 Government Procurement

a) From the solution to problem 4, part a), in chapter 2, the Bayes–Nash, equilibrium-bid function is

$$\sigma(c) = c + \frac{\int_c^\infty [1 - F_C(u)]^{(\mathcal{N}-1)}\, du}{[1 - F_C(c)]^{(\mathcal{N}-1)}}.$$

b) When the distribution of unobserved heterogeneity is from the Pareto family,

$$\sigma(c) = c\frac{\theta_1^0(\mathcal{N}-1)}{\theta_1^0(\mathcal{N}-1) - 1},$$

which is proportional to c.

c) The distribution of the winning bid can be found by finding the cumulative distribution function for the distribution of bids, and then finding the distribution of that distribution's lowest order statistic. For the Pareto case, the cumulative distribution function is

$$F_S(s) = 1 - \left\{ \frac{\theta_0^0\theta_1^0(\mathcal{N}-1)}{s[\theta_1^0(\mathcal{N}-1) - 1]} \right\}^{\theta_1^0}.$$

The probability density function of the winning bid, the lowest order statistic, is determined by

$$f_W(w) = \mathcal{N}[1 - F_S(w)]^{(\mathcal{N}-1)} f_S(w)$$

$$= \mathcal{N} \left\{ \frac{\theta_0^0\theta_1^0(\mathcal{N}-1)}{w[\theta_1^0(\mathcal{N}-1) - 1]} \right\}^{\theta_1^0(\mathcal{N}-1)} \frac{\theta_1^0(\theta_0^0)^{\theta_1^0}}{w^{\theta_1^0+1}} \left[\frac{\theta_1^0(\mathcal{N}-1)}{\theta_1^0(\mathcal{N}-1) - 1} \right]^{\theta_1^0}$$

$$= \frac{\theta_1^0\mathcal{N}}{w} \left\{ \frac{\theta_0^0\theta_1^0(\mathcal{N}-1)}{w[\theta_1^0(\mathcal{N}-1) - 1]} \right\}^{\theta_1^0\mathcal{N}}.$$

Now,

$$0 < \theta_0^0 \le c,$$

and

$$c = w\frac{\theta_1^0(\mathcal{N}-1) - 1}{\theta_1^0(\mathcal{N}-1)},$$

which implies that

$$0 < \frac{\theta_0^0\theta_1^0(\mathcal{N}-1)}{\theta_1^0(\mathcal{N}-1) - 1} = \underline{s}(\boldsymbol{\theta}^0, \mathcal{N}) \le w.$$

d) The likelihood function is

$$
\prod_{t=1}^{T} \frac{\theta_1 \mathcal{N}_t}{w_t} \left\{ \frac{\theta_0 \theta_1 (\mathcal{N}_t - 1)}{w_t [\theta_1 (\mathcal{N}_t - 1) - 1]} \right\}^{\theta_1 \mathcal{N}_t} \mathbf{1} \left\{ w_t \in [\underline{s}(\boldsymbol{\theta}, \mathcal{N}_t), \infty) \right\}.
$$

Maximizing this likelihood function is equivalent to maximizing

$$
\begin{aligned}
\mathcal{L}(\theta_0, \theta_1; \boldsymbol{w}, \mathcal{N}) &= \sum_{t=1}^{T} \log \left(\frac{\theta_1 \mathcal{N}_t}{w_t} \left\{ \frac{\theta_0 \theta_1 (\mathcal{N}_t - 1)}{w_t [\theta_1 (\mathcal{N}_t - 1) - 1]} \right\}^{\theta_1 \mathcal{N}_t} \right) \\
&= \sum_{t=1}^{T} \log(\theta_1 \mathcal{N}_t) + \sum_{t=1}^{T} \theta_1 \mathcal{N}_t \log[\theta_0 \theta_1 (\mathcal{N}_t - 1)] - \\
&\quad \sum_{t=1}^{T} \theta_1 \mathcal{N}_t \log\{ w_t [\theta_1 (\mathcal{N}_t - 1) - 1] \} - \\
&\quad \sum_{t=1}^{T} \log w_t
\end{aligned}
$$

subject to $\quad \underline{s}(\boldsymbol{\theta}, \mathcal{N}_t) \le w_t \quad t = 1, \ldots, T.$

Maximizing the logarithm of the likelihood function without addressing the constraints will typically lead to an estimate which is inconsistent with the unobserved data. Because the support of the probability density function depends on unknown parameters, the standard way of defining the maximum-likelihood estimator does not apply.

e) The objective here is to formulate a constrained optimization problem, which defines the maximum-likelihood estimator, using the objective function derived in part d),

$$
\mathcal{L}(\theta_0, \theta_1; w_1, \ldots, w_T, \mathcal{N}_1, \ldots, \mathcal{N}_T),
$$

along with T equal 144 constraints, each of which has the following form:

$$
\underline{s}(\boldsymbol{\theta}, \mathcal{N}_t) = \frac{\theta_0 \theta_1 (\mathcal{N}_t - 1)}{\theta_1 (\mathcal{N}_t - 1) - 1} \le w_t.
$$

The idea is to maximize the likelihood function in the usual way, except constraining the parameters so that the smallest of the bids submitted at an auction with $\mathcal{N}_t$ potential bidders is observed.

f) In figure 4.3.f, we present a plot of the important constraints; in this problem, 144 constraints exist, but only twelve (those corresponding

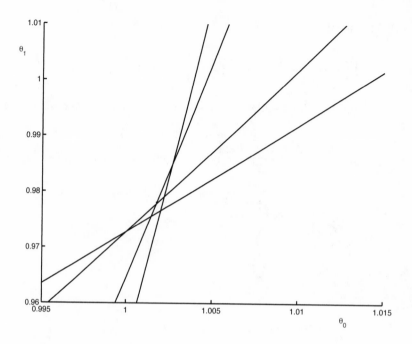

Figure 4.3.f
Graph of the Constraint Functions

to the smallest w_ts for a given $\mathcal{N}$) are relevant. In fact, only four constraints are potentially binding at the maximum of the constrained likelihood function, which is why only four appear in the figure. You can find the MATLAB code for this figure on the CD that accompanies this book; see the file `prog43f.m`.

g) In figure 4.3.g, we present a plot of a nonparametric estimate of the cumulative distribution function $F_C^0(c)$. Note that we have superimposed on this solution the GMM-estimated Pareto cumulative distribution function from part i). You can find the MATLAB code for this figure on the CD that accompanies this book; see the file `prog43g.m`.

h) In figure 4.3.h, we present a plot of the feasible parameter set as demarked by the relevant constraints and the level sets of the likelihood function. You can find the MATLAB code for the maximum-likelihood program on the CD that accompanies this book; see the files `prog43h.m`, `fun43h.m`, `fig43h.m`, and `cfun43h.m`. The estimated vector $(\hat{\theta}_0^{\mathrm{ML}}, \hat{\theta}_1^{\mathrm{ML}})^{\top}$ equals $(1.0018, 0.9777)^{\top}$.

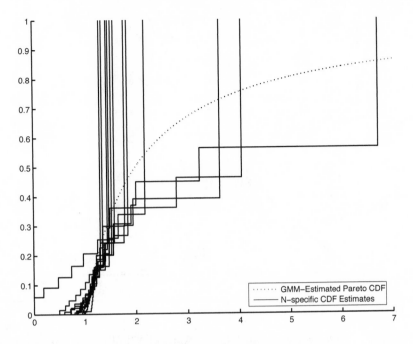

Figure 4.3.g
Nonparametric Estimates of $F_C^o(c)$

i) We begin by calculating the first two raw moments of W_t, conditional on $\mathcal{N}_t$. Now,

$$\mathcal{E}(W|\mathcal{N}) = \mu_1(\theta_0, \theta_1|\mathcal{N})$$

$$= \int_{\frac{\theta_0\theta_1(\mathcal{N}-1)}{\theta_1(\mathcal{N}-1)-1}}^{\infty} \theta_1\mathcal{N} \left\{ \frac{\theta_0\theta_1(\mathcal{N}-1)}{w[\theta_1(\mathcal{N}-1)-1]} \right\}^{\theta_1\mathcal{N}} dw.$$

Performing the integration yields

$$\mathcal{E}(W|\mathcal{N}) = \mu_1(\boldsymbol{\theta}|\mathcal{N})$$

$$= \frac{\theta_0(\theta_1)^2\mathcal{N}(\mathcal{N}-1)}{(\theta_1\mathcal{N}-1)[\theta_1(\mathcal{N}-1)-1]}.$$

Also,

$$\mathcal{E}(W^2|\mathcal{N}) = \mu_2(\theta_0, \theta_1, \mathcal{N})$$

$$= \int_{\frac{\theta_0\theta_1(\mathcal{N}-1)}{\theta_1(\mathcal{N}-1)-1}}^{\infty} w\theta_1\mathcal{N} \left\{ \frac{\theta_0\theta_1(\mathcal{N}-1)}{w[\theta_1(\mathcal{N}-1)-1]} \right\}^{\theta_1\mathcal{N}}.$$

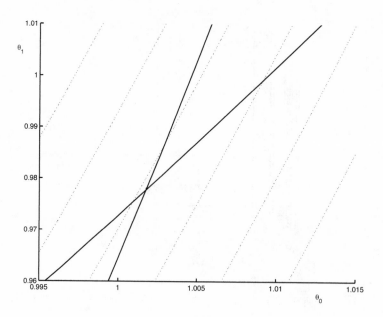

Figure 4.3.h
Graph of Constraints and Level Sets of Likelihood Function

Performing the integration yields

$$\mathcal{E}(W^2|\mathcal{N}) = \mu_2(\boldsymbol{\theta}|\mathcal{N}) = \frac{(\theta_0)^2(\theta_1)^3\mathcal{N}(\mathcal{N}-1)^2}{(\theta_1\mathcal{N}-2)[\theta_1(\mathcal{N}-1)-1]^2}.$$

We can write these two conditional moments as

$$U_{1t} = [W_t - \mu_1(\boldsymbol{\theta}|\mathcal{N}_t)]$$

$$U_{2t} = \left[W_t^2 - \mu_2(\boldsymbol{\theta}|\mathcal{N}_t)\right]$$

for $t = 1, \ldots, T$. Now, the following four population moment restrictions must hold:

$$\mathcal{E}(U_{1t}|\mathcal{N}_t) = 0$$

$$\mathcal{E}(U_{2t}|\mathcal{N}_t) = 0$$

$$\mathrm{cov}(U_{1t}, \mathcal{N}_t) = 0$$

$$\mathrm{cov}(U_{2t}, \mathcal{N}_t) = 0,$$

so both the constant and the covariate $\mathcal{N}_t$ are orthogonal to U_{1t} and U_{2t}. The sample analogues to the left-hand side of these four population equations are:

$$U(\boldsymbol{\theta}) = \begin{pmatrix} \frac{1}{T}\sum_{t=1}^{T}\left[W_t - \mu_1(\boldsymbol{\theta}|\mathcal{N}_t)\right] \\ \frac{1}{T}\sum_{t=1}^{T}\left[W_t^2 - \mu_2(\boldsymbol{\theta}|\mathcal{N}_t)\right] \\ \frac{1}{T}\sum_{t=1}^{T}\left[W_t - \mu_1(\boldsymbol{\theta}|\mathcal{N}_t)\right]\mathcal{N}_t \\ \frac{1}{T}\sum_{t=1}^{T}\left[W_t^2 - \mu_2(\boldsymbol{\theta}|\mathcal{N}_t)\right]\mathcal{N}_t \end{pmatrix}.$$

We chose the identity matrix $\mathbf{I}_4$ as the weighting matrix. In this case, the GMME of $\boldsymbol{\theta}^0$ was defined by

$$\hat{\boldsymbol{\theta}}_{\mathrm{GMM}} = \underset{\boldsymbol{\theta}}{\mathrm{argmin}}\ U(\boldsymbol{\theta})^{\top}\mathbf{I}_4 U(\boldsymbol{\theta}).$$

You can find the MATLAB code for this program on the CD that accompanies this book; see the files `fun43i.m` and `prog43i.m`. The generalized method-of-moments estimate of $(\hat{\theta}_0^{\mathrm{GMM}}, \hat{\theta}_1^{\mathrm{GMM}})^{\top}$ equals $(1.0082, 1.0151)^{\top}$.

j) You can find the MATLAB code for this program on the CD that accompanies this book; see files `fun43j.m` and `prog43j.m`. The estimate of $(\hat{\theta}_0^{\mathrm{EGMM}}, \hat{\theta}_1^{\mathrm{EGMM}})^{\top}$ equals $(1.0087, 0.9405)^{\top}$.

k) You can find the MATLAB code for the maximum-likelihood program on the CD that accompanies this book; see files `prog43k.m`, `fun43k.m`, and `cfun43k`. If we include the covariate z_t, then the estimate of $(\hat{\gamma}_0^{\mathrm{ML}}, \hat{\gamma}_1^{\mathrm{ML}}, \hat{\theta}_1^{\mathrm{ML}})^{\top}$ equals $(0.0019, 0.0005, 0.9791)^{\top}$.

4.4 Solving Asymmetric Auctions

a) We include here a brief summary of how to implement Bajari's first method in the case of independent costs. Within this method, the first-order conditions are used in tandem with the fact that, at the lower bound of support, the bid functions will both equal $\underline{s}$. Bajari then imposes the condition that the inverse-bid functions belong to the set of functions

$$\mathcal{F} \equiv \{f \mid f \in C^1[\underline{c}, \bar{c}];\ f : [\underline{c}, \bar{c}] \to [\underline{c}, \bar{c}];\ f(s) < s\ \forall\ s < \bar{c}\}.$$

The first condition necessary for membership in $\mathcal{F}$ is that the candidate function be a member of the set of functions that has one continuous derivative on $[\underline{c}, \bar{c}]$. The second condition requires that s be a bijection and, hence, monotone. The third conditions requires that the inverse-bid functions lie everywhere (except at $\bar{c}$) below the 45-degree line. The objective, then, is to make a guess for $\underline{s}$,

399

call it s_{guess}, solve the system of differential equations produced by the first-order conditions using that guess, and then determine whether the resulting solutions belong to $\mathcal{F}$. Bajari has proven that, if the resulting solution is not in $\mathcal{F}$, then the solution diverges. This means that $s_{\text{guess}} \in [\underline{c}, \bar{c}]$; a new guess can then be generated using this information. Similarly, if the system does converge, then $s_{\text{guess}} \in [\underline{s}, \bar{c}]$, which can likewise be used to create a new guess. This continues until $\underline{s}$ has been bracketed by a sufficiently narrow interval. You can find the MATLAB code for this program on the CD that accompanies this book; see the files `fun44a.m`, `prog44a.m`, and `verify44.m`. The estimated bid functions appear in figure 4.4.a. Below is a schematic of the code:

Step 1: Define $[s_{\text{low}}, s_{\text{high}}]$ to be the interval that contains $\underline{s}$. Initially, this will be $[\underline{c}, \bar{c}]$.

Step 2: Set s_{guess} to be the midpoint of $[s_{\text{low}}, s_{\text{high}}]$.

Step 3: Solve the system and determine if the resulting inverse bid functions belong to $\mathcal{F}$.

Step 4: If the system does not converge (i.e., the solutions are not in $\mathcal{F}$), re-define $[s_{\text{low}}, s_{\text{high}}]$ to be $[s_{\text{guess}}, s_{\text{high}}]$ and then create a new s_{guess} that is the midpoint of this new interval.

Step 5: If the system does converge (i.e., the solutions are in $\mathcal{F}$), re-define $[s_{\text{low}}, s_{\text{high}}]$ to be $[s_{\text{low}}, s_{\text{guess}}]$ and then create a new s_{guess} that is the midpoint of this new interval.

Step 6: Determine if the new interval is within tolerance; i.e., of length less than `itol` (in the notation used our MATLAB code). If so, end, if not, return to **Step 2** and repeat.

b) You can find the MATLAB code for this program on the CD that accompanies this book; see the file `prog44b.m`; the results of this program appear in figure 4.4.b. Inefficient procurement occurs when the low-cost bidder loses the auction. For example, if bidder 2's cost draw c_2 falls in $[c^*, c_1]$ (see figure 4.4.b), the low-cost bidder (in this example, bidder 2) will submit a higher bid than bidder 1, despite the latter's higher cost.

c) You can find the MATLAB code for this program on the CD that accompanies this book; see the file `prog44c.m`. The incidence of inefficiency is approximately eleven percent.

d) You can find the MATLAB code for this program on the CD that accompanies this book; see the files `fun44d.m`, `prog44d.m`, and `verify44.m`. The estimated bid functions appear in figure 4.4.d.

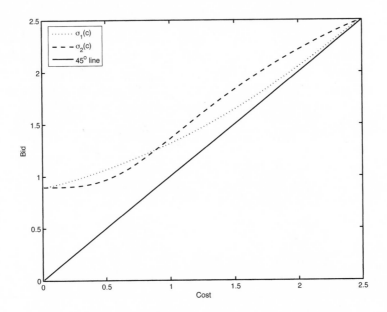

Figure 4.4.a
Estimated Bid Functions

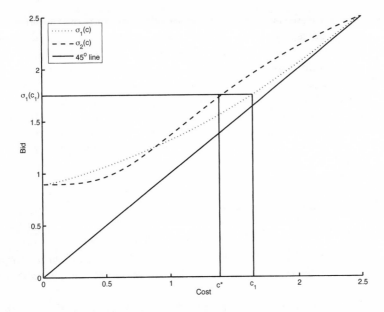

Figure 4.4.b
Evidence of Inefficiency

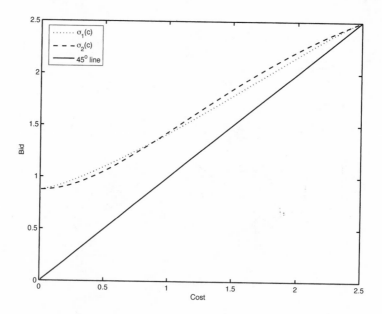

Figure 4.4.d
Estimated Bid Functions

e) You can find the MATLAB code for this program on the CD that accompanies this book; see the file `prog44e.m`. The incidence of inefficiency is approximately zero percent, thus the different cost structure for bidder 2 has reduced the incidence of inefficient procurement. Comparing figures 4.4.a and 4.4.d reveal that the bid functions are more similar in part d) than in part a). This fact makes it more difficult for inefficient procurement to occur because, for any given draw by bidder 1, the interval where bidder 2's cost draw must fall to induce an inefficient outcome is smaller in part d) than in part a).

5.1 Generalized Vickrey Auctions

a) You can find the MATLAB code for this program on the CD that accompanies this book; see the files `orderstats.m` and `prog51a.m`.

b) You can find the MATLAB code for this program on the CD that accompanies this book; see the file `prog51b.m`. The order of winners is $(2, 1, 3, 1)^\top$ and the corresponding prices paid are $(2.5, 2.5, 3, 3)^\top$.

c) You can find the MATLAB code for this program on the CD that accompanies this book; see the file `prog51c.m`. The order of winners is $(2, 1, 3, 1)^\top$ and the corresponding prices paid are $(2.6, 2.6, 3, 3)^\top$. Note how the reserve price influences the prices, but that the order of winners remains unchanged.

5.2 Multi-Unit, Sequential, Clock Auctions

a) Denote the bidder-specific cumulative distribution functions by $F_1(v)$, $F_2(v)$, and $F_3(v)$. Now, the cumulative distribution function of the highest valuation of two draws for bidder i is

$$F_{(1:2)}^i(y) = [F_i(y)]^2 \quad i = 1, 2, 3.$$

The corresponding probablity density function is

$$f_{(1:2)}^i(y) = 2F_i(y)f_i(y) \quad i = 1, 2, 3.$$

If bidder i has won the first unit for sale, then the cumulative distribution function of his second-highest valuation is

$$F_{(2:2)}^i(y) = 2F_i(y) - [F_i(y)]^2,$$

so the corresponding probability density function is

$$f_{(2:2)}^i(y) = 2[1 - F_i(y)]f_i(y).$$

On the other hand, the cumulative distribution functions of the valuations for the second unit by bidders j and k, who did not win the first unit for sale, are as before; viz.,

$$F_{(1:2)}^j(y) = [F_j(y)]^2 \quad \text{and} \quad F_{(1:2)}^k(y) = [F_k(y)]^2,$$

so their corresponding probability density functions are

$$f_{(1:2)}^j(y) = 2F_j(y)f_j(y) \quad \text{and} \quad f_{(1:2)}^k(y) = 2F_k(y)f_k(y).$$

When bidder i has won the first unit, the probability density function of the winning bid for the second unit, under the clock model, should bidder j win, is the second-highest valuation of three independent draws each from a different distribution, with j having the highest valuation. To wit, when i and j are different,

$$g_{(2:3)}(y, j \mid i \text{ won unit 1}) = F_{(2:2)}^i(y)S_{(1:2)}^j(y)f_{(1:2)}^k(y) +$$

$$F_{(1:2)}^k(y)S_{(1:2)}^j(y)f_{(2:2)}^i(y),$$

while when j wins both units

$$g_{(2:3)}\left(y,j\mid j \text{ won unit } 1\right) = F^i_{(1:2)}(y)S^j_{(2:2)}(y)f^k_{(1:2)}(y)+$$
$$F^k_{(1:2)}(y)S^j_{(2:2)}(y)f^i_{(1:2)}(y).$$

b) Assuming bidder i has won the first unit, one can find the solution to this problem by substituting the bidder-specific exponential probability density functions and bidder-specific exponential cumulative distribution functions into the expressions above. To wit, without loss of generality, letting bidder i have exponential hazard rate θ_i, then

$$F^i_{(2:2)}(y) = 2[1 - \exp(-\theta_i y)] - [1 - \exp(-\theta_i y)]^2,$$

and

$$f^i_{(2:2)}(y) = 2\theta_i \exp(-2\theta_i y),$$

while for bidders j and k one has

$$F^j_{(1:2)}(y) = [1 - \exp(-\theta_j y)]^2$$
$$F^k_{(1:2)}(y) = [1 - \exp(-\theta_k y)]^2$$

and

$$f^j_{(1:2)}(y) = 2[1 - \exp(-\theta_j y)]\theta_j \exp(-\theta_j y)$$
$$f^k_{(1:2)}(y) = 2[1 - \exp(-\theta_k y)]\theta_k \exp(-\theta_k y).$$

c) To calculate the contributions to the likelihood function, consider the following example in which bidder 3 has won the first unit, while bidder 1 has won the second unit. In this case, the following cumulative distribution and probability density functions would enter the contribution to the likelihood function:

$$F^1_{(1:2)}(y) = [1 - \exp(-\theta_1 y)]^2$$
$$F^2_{(1:2)}(y) = [1 - \exp(-\theta_2 y)]^2$$
$$F^3_{(2:2)}(y) = 2[1 - \exp(-\theta_3 y)] - [1 - \exp(-\theta_3 y)]^2$$
$$f^1_{(1:2)}(y) = 2[1 - \exp(-\theta_1 y)]\theta_1 \exp(-\theta_1 y)$$
$$f^2_{(1:2)}(y) = 2[1 - \exp(-\theta_2 y)]\theta_2 \exp(-\theta_2 y)$$
$$f^3_{(2:2)}(y) = 2\theta_3 \exp(-2\theta_3 y).$$

The contribution to the likelihood function would, in fact, be

$$g_{(2:3)}\left[y, 1 | \boldsymbol{\theta}, (3 \text{ won unit } 1)\right] = F^3_{(2:2)}(y) S^1_{(1:2)}(y) f^2_{(1:2)}(y) +$$
$$F^2_{(1:2)}(y) S^1_{(1:2)}(y) f^3_{(2:2)}(y)$$

where $\boldsymbol{\theta}$ collects the $(\theta_1, \theta_2, \theta_3)$. The logarithm of the likelihood function is then

$$\mathcal{L}(\boldsymbol{\theta}) = \sum_{t=1}^{T} \sum_{i=1}^{3} \sum_{j=1}^{3} D^{ij}_t \log\{g_{(2:3)}\left[y_t, i_t | \boldsymbol{\theta}, (j_t \text{ won unit } 1)\right]\}$$

where

$$D^{ij}_t = \begin{cases} 1 & \text{if } j \text{ won unit 1 and } i \text{ won 2 at auction } t; \\ 0 & \text{otherwise.} \end{cases}$$

You can find the MATLAB code for this program on the CD that accompanies this book; see the files `fun52c.m` and `prog52c.m`. The maximum-likelihood estimate $\hat{\boldsymbol{\theta}}$ is $(1.1182, 1.1796, 1.4398)^\top$.

Name Index

Subject Index